Treasures

A Reading/Language Arts Program

Mc Graw Hill **Macmillan/McGraw-Hill**

Contributors

Time Magazine, Accelerated Reader

 RFB&D
learning through listening

 **Accelerated Reader**

Students with print disabilities may be eligible to obtain an accessible, audio version of the pupil edition of this textbook. Please call Recording for the Blind & Dyslexic at 1-800-221-4792 for complete information.

A

The *McGraw·Hill* Companies

Macmillan/McGraw-Hill

Published by Macmillan/McGraw-Hill, of McGraw-Hill Education, a division of The McGraw-Hill Companies, Inc., Two Penn Plaza, New York, New York 10121.

Printed in the United States of America

1 2 3 4 5 6 7 8 9 071/055 13 12 11 10 09

A Reading/Language Arts Program

Program Authors

Dr. Diane August
Senior Research Scientist, Center for
  Applied Linguistics
Washington, D.C.

Dr. Donald R. Bear
University of Nevada, Reno
Reno, Nevada

Dr. Janice A. Dole
University of Utah
Salt Lake City, Utah

Dr. Jana Echevarria
California State University, Long Beach
Long Beach, California

Dr. Douglas Fisher
San Diego State University
San Diego, California

Dr. David J. Francis
University of Houston
Houston, Texas

Dr. Vicki L. Gibson
Educational Consultant, Gibson Hasbrouck
  and Associates, Massachusetts

Dr. Jan E. Hasbrouck
Educational Consultant – J.H. Consulting
Los Angeles, California

Dr. Scott G. Paris
Center for Research and Practice,
National Institute of Education
Singapore

Dr. Timothy Shanahan
University of Illinois at Chicago
Chicago, Illinois

Dr. Josefina V. Tinajero
University of Texas at El Paso
El Paso, Texas

Mc Graw Hill **Macmillan/McGraw-Hill**

Program Authors

Dr. Diane August

Center for Applied Linguistics, Washington, D.C.

- Principal Investigator, Developing Literacy in Second-Language Learners: Report of the National Literacy Panel on Language-Minority Children and Youth
- Member of the New Standards Literacy Project, Grades 4–5

Dr. Donald R. Bear

University of Nevada, Reno

- Author of *Words Their Way* and *Words Their Way with English Learners*
- Director, E.L. Cord Foundation Center for Learning and Literacy

Dr. Janice A. Dole

University of Utah

- Investigator, IES Study on Reading Interventions
- National Academy of Sciences, Committee Member: Teacher Preparation Programs, 2005–2007

Dr. Jana Echevarria

California State University, Long Beach

- Author of *Making Content Comprehensible for English Learners: The SIOP Model*
- Principal Researcher, Center for Research on the Educational Achievement and Teaching of English Language Learners

Dr. Douglas Fisher

San Diego State University

- Co-Director, Center for the Advancement of Reading, California State University
- Author of *Language Arts Workshop: Purposeful Reading and Writing Instruction* and *Reading for Information in Elementary School*

Dr. David J. Francis

University of Houston

- Director of the Center for Research on Educational Achievement and Teaching of English Language Learners (CREATE)
- Director, Texas Institute for Measurement, Evaluation, and Statistics

Dr. Vicki Gibson

Educational Consultant Gibson Hasbrouck and Associates, Massachusetts

- Author of *Differentiated Instruction: Grouping for Success*

Dr. Jan E. Hasbrouck

Educational Consultant JH Consulting, Los Angeles

- Developed Oral Reading Fluency Norms for Grades 1–8
- Author of *The Reading Coach: A How-to Manual for Success*

Dr. Scott G. Paris

Center for Research and Practice, National Institute of Education, Singapore

- Principal Investigator, CIERA, 1997–2004

Dr. Timothy Shanahan

University of Illinois at Chicago

- Member, National Reading Panel
- President, International Reading Association, 2006
- Chair, National Literacy Panel and National Early Literacy Panel

Dr. Josefina V. Tinajero

University of Texas at El Paso

- Past President, NABE and TABE
- Co-Editor of *Teaching All the Children: Strategies for Developing Literacy in an Urban Setting* and *Literacy Assessment of Second Language Learners*

Consulting and Contributing Authors

Dr. Adria F. Klein
Professor Emeritus,
California State University,
San Bernardino

• President, California
Reading Association, 1995
• Co-Author of *Interactive
Writing* and *Interactive
Editing*

Dolores B. Malcolm
St. Louis Public Schools
St. Louis, MO

• Past President, International
Reading Association
• Member, IRA Urban
Diversity Initiatives
Commission
• Member, RIF Advisory
Board

Dr. Doris Walker-Dalhouse
Minnesota State University,
Moorhead

• Author of articles on
multicultural literature and
reading instruction in urban
schools
• Co-Chair of the Ethnicity, Race,
and Multilingualism Committee,
NRC

Dinah Zike
Educational Consultant

• Dinah-Might Activities, Inc.
San Antonio, TX

Program Consultants

Kathy R. Bumgardner
Language Arts Instructional
Specialist
Gaston County Schools, NC

Elizabeth Jimenez
CEO, GEMAS Consulting
Pomona, CA

Dr. Sharon F. O'Neal
Associate Professor
College of Education
Texas State University
San Marcos, TX

Program Reviewers

Mable Alfred
Reading/Language Arts Administrator
Chicago Public Schools, IL

Suzie Bean
Teacher, Kindergarten
Mary W. French Academy
Decatur, IL

Linda Burch
Teacher, Kindergarten
Public School 184
Brooklyn, NY

Robert J. Dandorph
Principal
John F. Kennedy Elementary School
North Bergen, NJ

Suzanne Delacruz
Principal, Washington Elementary
Evanston, IL

Carol Dockery
Teacher, Grade 3
Mulberry Elementary
Milford, OH

Karryl Ellis
Teacher, Grade 1
Durfee School, Decatur, IL

Christina Fong
Teacher, Grade 3
William Moore Elementary School
Las Vegas, NV

Lenore Furman
Teacher, Kindergarten
Abington Avenue School
Newark, NJ

Sister Miriam Kaeser
Assistant Superintendent
Archdiocese of Cincinnati
Cincinnati, OH

LaVonne Lee
Principal, Rozet Elementary School
Gillette, WY

SuEllen Mackey
Teacher, Grade 5
Washington Elementary School
Decatur, IL

Jan Mayes
Curriculum Coordinator
Kent School District
Kent, WA

Bonnie Nelson
Teacher, Grade 1
Solano School, Phoenix, AZ

Cyndi Nichols
Teacher, Grade K/1
North Ridge Elementary School
Commack, NY

Sharron Norman
Curriculum Director
Lansing School District
Lansing, MI

Renee Ottinger
Literacy Leader, Grades K–5
Coronado Hills Elementary School
Denver, CO

Michael Pragman
Principal, Woodland Elementary School
Lee's Summit, MO

Carol Rose
Teacher, Grade 2
Churchill Elementary School
Muskegon, MI

Laura R. Schmidt-Watson
Director of Academic Services
Parma City School District, OH

Dianne L. Skoy
Literacy Coordinator, Grades K–5
Minneapolis Public Schools
Minneapolis, MN

Charles Staszewski
ESL Teacher, Grades 3–5
John H. William School, No. 5
Rochester, NY

Patricia Synan
New York City Department
of Education

Stephanie Yearian
Teacher, Grade 2
W. J. Zahnow Elementary
Waterloo, IL

Unit 1   The Big Question

How can our actions help others?

Enduring Understanding and Essential Questions

In this unit, students will listen, read, and write about how their actions can help others. As they progress through the unit, they will also develop and apply key comprehension skills that good readers use as they read.

Big Idea	Enduring Understanding	Essential Questions
Theme: Take Action	Our actions can cause good things to happen.	How can our actions help others?

Comprehension	Enduring Understanding	Essential Questions
Character and Setting Weeks 1, 2	Good readers think about the roles, functions, and relationships of characters in a story, as well as where the story is set.	What conflicts did the main character in this story have, and how were they affected by the setting and story events?
Main Idea and Details Weeks 3, 5	Good readers think about what the sentences in a passage have in common to determine the main idea and maintain meaning.	What do all of the important details in this selection have in common?
Cause and Effect Week 4	Good readers look for cause-and-effect relationships to determine how one event in a story gives rise to another.	What cause-and-effect relationships did you find in this story?

Theme: Take Action

Planning the Unit

Unit Planner **16B**

Unit Resources **16D**

Assessment Resources **16F**

Unit Opener **16H**

> Research and Inquiry Instruction and Cross-Curricular Projects

Using the Student Book

The Summer of the Swans **16J**

Lost City: The Discovery of Machu Picchu **40A**

TIME "Gecko Glue, Cockroach Scouts, and Spider Silk
Bridges" **66A**

The Magic Gourd **78A**

Interrupted Journey **102A**

TEST PREP Test Strategy: Think and Search **124**

Wrapping Up the Unit

Writing Workshop **127A**

 **Personal Narrative**

Computer Literacy **127I**

Unit Closer **127K**

Unit Assessment

> Diagnose and Prescribe **127M**

Glossary **127O**

Additional Lessons and Teacher Resources

Additional Lessons **T1**

Classroom Library Lessons **T11**

Theme Bibliography **T17**

Word Lists **T20**

Scope and Sequence **T26**

Index **T34**

Main Selections

Unit Assessment

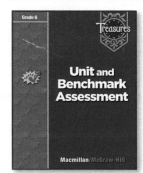

Theme: **Take Action**

pages 16J–39V   pages 40A–65V

WEEK 1 | WEEK 2

ORAL LANGUAGE

- **Listening, Speaking, Viewing**

WORD STUDY

- **Vocabulary**

- **Phonics/Decoding**

READING

- **Comprehension**

- **Fluency**

- **Leveled Readers/ELL Readers**

LANGUAGE ARTS

- **Writing**
- **Grammar**
- **Spelling**

WEEK 1

Theme Rescue Teams

Build Background

Vocabulary
intersection, engulf, abruptly, conscious, anxiety, cascade, procedure, souvenir

Dictionary: Multiple-Meaning Words

Phonics
Short Vowels

Comprehension
Strategy: Analyze Story Structure
Skill: Character, Setting, Plot

Fluency
Repeated Reading: Intonation/Pausing

APPROACHING
The Lost Cave

ON LEVEL
Rachel's Choice

BEYOND
Surprises in the Desert

ENGLISH LANGUAGE LEARNERS
The Rescue Team

Writing Personal Narrative

Grammar Sentence Types and Fragments

Spelling Short Vowel Words

WEEK 2

Theme A Lost City

Build Background

Vocabulary
foretold, withstood, remote, interpreter, undergrowth, venomous, escort, vegetation

Word Parts: Compound Words

Phonics
Long Vowels

Comprehension
Strategy: Analyze Story Structure
Skill: Character, Setting, Plot

Fluency
Repeated Reading: Intonation/Pausing

APPROACHING
I Discover Pompeii: or How I Spent My Summer Vacation

ON LEVEL
Queen Pu-abi's Royal Tomb

BEYOND
The Ancient Secret of Cliff Canyon

ENGLISH LANGUAGE LEARNERS
A Great Discovery

Writing Friendly Letter

Grammar Subjects and Predicates

Spelling Long Vowel Words

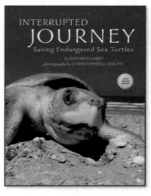

pages 66A–77V

pages 78A–101V

pages 102A–123V

Review and Assess

WEEK 3

Theme Science for All

Build Background

Vocabulary
altered, erode, absorb, concentrated, innovations

Context Clues: Definitions

Phonics
ei or *ie*

Comprehension
Strategy: Make Inferences and Analyze
Skill: Main Idea and Details

Fluency
Repeated Reading: Punctuation

APPROACHING
Technology and Nature: Water

ON LEVEL
From Dragonflies to Helicopters: Learning from Nature

BEYOND
Plants: An Amazing Resource

ENGLISH LANGUAGE LEARNERS
Learning to Fly from Nature

Writing Expository

Grammar Sentence Combining

Spelling *ei* or *ie* Words

WEEK 4

Theme Sharing Traditions

Build Background

Vocabulary
chameleon, rummaged, scrounging, pathetic, undetected, generosity, ricocheting, famine

Context Clues: Restatement

Phonics
r-Controlled Vowels

Comprehension
Strategy: Make Inferences and Analyze
Skill: Cause and Effect

Fluency
Repeated Reading: Punctuation

APPROACHING
The Art of Origami

ON LEVEL
Arts of the Navajo

BEYOND
The Tradition of Dance

ENGLISH LANGUAGE LEARNERS
Navajo Indian Art

Writing Poem

Grammar Clauses and Complex Sentences

Spelling *r*-Controlled Vowel Words

WEEK 5

Theme Protecting Wildlife

Build Background

Vocabulary
vital, analyzing, speculated, embedded, sedated, dehydrated, propelled, conserve

Analogies: Antonyms

Phonics
Compound Words

Comprehension
Strategy: Make Inferences and Analyze
Skill: Main Idea and Details

Fluency
Repeated Reading: Tempo/Pacing

APPROACHING
Saving Right Whales

ON LEVEL
Saving Peregrine Falcons

BEYOND
Saving Alligators

ENGLISH LANGUAGE LEARNERS
The King of Birds

Writing Diary

Grammar Run-on Sentences

Spelling Compound Words

WEEK 6

Test Strategy
Think and Search

Writing Workshop
Personal Narrative

Unit 1 Assessment, 7–24

Comprehension
Character, Setting, Plot; Main Idea and Details; Cause and Effect

Vocabulary Strategies
Dictionary: Multiple-Meaning Words; Word Parts: Compound Words; Context Clues: Definitions, Restatement; Analogy: Antonyms

Text Features/ Study Skills/ Literary Elements
Photos and Captions; Textbook; Media Center; Time Line; Alliteration and Imagery

Grammar
Sentences

Writing
Personal Narrative

Fluency Assessment

Diagnose and Prescribe
Interpret Assessment Results

Unit 1 Planner

Take Action **16C**

Unit 1 Resources

Literature

Read-Aloud Anthology
Includes plays for
Readers Theater

Student Edition

Leveled Readers

ELL Leveled Readers

**Classroom Library
Tradebooks**

Teaching Support

Teacher's Edition

Transparencies

ELL Teacher's Guide

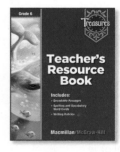

Teacher's Resource Book

**Dinah Zike
Foldables™**

Vocabulary Cards

Class Management Tools

**Small Group
How-To Guide**

**Weekly
Contracts**

**Rotation
Chart**

16D

Student Practice

| Approaching Level | On Level | Beyond Level | English Language Learners |

Leveled Practice

Spelling Practice Book   **Grammar Practice Book**

Home-School Connection
- Take-Home Stories
- Homework Activities

Literacy Workstation Activities

Technology

 AUDIO CD
- Listening Library
- Fluency Solutions

 CD-ROM
- Vocabulary PuzzleMaker
- Handwriting
- Instructional Navigator Interactive Lesson Planner
- Student Navigator
- Accelerated Reader Quizzes

www.macmillanmh.com
- Author/Illustrator Information
- Research and Inquiry Activities
- Vocabulary and Spelling Activities
- Oral Language Activities
- Computer Literacy
- Leveled Reader Database

Professional Development

READING, YES!
- Videos
- Online Course

TREASURES FOR TEACHERS
- Videos

READING Triumphs
AN INTERVENTION PROGRAM

Also Available

Treasure Chest
FOR ENGLISH LANGUAGE LEARNERS

Also Available

Screening, Diagnostic, and Placement Assessments

Screening

Use the Oral Reading Fluency passages on pages 52–63 in our **Screening, Diagnostic, Placement Assessment** book for screening.

Diagnostic Tools for Instructional Placement

For an individually administered Diagnostic, use the Informal Reading Inventory passages on pages 120–127 in our **Screening, Diagnostic, Placement Assessment** book.

For a group-administered Placement Test, see pages 243–253 in our **Screening, Diagnostic, Placement Assessment** book.

Use the results from these assessments to determine the instructional levels of your students for differentiated instruction grouping.

Monitoring Progress

Ongoing Informal Assessments

- Daily Quick Check Observations
- Weekly Comprehension Check
- Weekly Fluency Practice Passages

Formal Assessments

- **Weekly Assessment** includes

    On Level Assessments

    Approaching Level Assessments

- **Fluency Assessment**
- **Running Records**
- **Unit and Benchmark Assessment**
- **ELL Practice and Assessment**

    Weekly Tests

    Unit Progress Test

Managing and Reporting

 Assessment Online

 Instructional Navigator Interactive Lesson Planner
- All Teacher Edition Pages
- Electronic Lesson Planner
- Student Blackline Masters

 Assessment Tool

National Test Correlation

GRADE 6 UNIT 1 ASSESSED SKILLS	NAEP	TerraNova/ CAT6	ITBS	SAT10
COMPREHENSION STRATEGIES AND SKILLS				
• Strategies: Analyze story structure, summarize	◆	◆	◆	◆
• Skills: Character and setting, plot, mood, tone, main idea and details, cause and effect	◆	◆	◆	◆
VOCABULARY STRATEGIES				
• Dictionary		◆	◆	◆
• Word parts		◆	◆	◆
• Context clues	◆	◆	◆	◆
• Antonyms		◆	◆	◆
TEXT FEATURES AND STUDY SKILLS				
• Photos and captions	◆	◆	◆	◆
• Social Studies textbook	◆	◆	◆	◆
• Using the library/media center	◆	◆	◆	◆
• Time lines	◆	◆	◆	◆
GRAMMAR, MECHANICS, USAGE				
• Sentence types and fragments		◆	◆	◆
• Subjects and predicates		◆	◆	◆
• Conjunctions and compound sentences		◆	◆	◆
• Clauses and complex sentences		◆	◆	◆
• Run-on sentences		◆	◆	◆
• End punctuation		◆	◆	◆
• Using proper punctuation while writing a letter		◆	◆	◆
WRITING				
• Personal Narrative	◆			

KEY

NAEP	National Assessment of Educational Progress	**ITBS**	Iowa Tests of Basic Skills
TerraNova/ CAT6	TerraNova, the Second Edition	**SAT10**	Stanford Achievement Test

Theme Project

Build Background Write this theme statement on the board: *Our actions can create change.* Ask students:

- Talk about how actions create change. Who can you name who has changed the world?
- What kinds of actions did these people take to create change?
- Are we all responsible for our actions? Why or why not?

Research and Inquiry
Self-Selected Theme Project

Step 1 **State the Problem and Identify Needed Information** Have students create a KWL chart and write their own questions to research. Remind them to narrow their focus if they have too many questions. The questions may be about a person who took action or suggested a way of taking action. Encourage students to develop and revise questions before, during, and after reading.

Step 2 **Strategies for Finding Information** Have students list primary and secondary sources of information to help them answer their questions. Tell students to use primary sources such as photographs, letters, and autobiographies, and secondary sources such as newspapers, films, television, and the Internet. Have them rank their list of sources in order of priority.

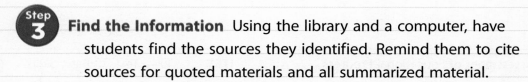

RESEARCH STRATEGIES

Evaluate Sources

To determine if a source is accurate and reliable, check:
- publication date
- author's background and experience
- author's purpose and perspective
- if coverage is reliable and timely

Step 3 **Find the Information** Using the library and a computer, have students find the sources they identified. Remind them to cite sources for quoted materials and all summarized material.

Step 4 **Organize the Information** Tell students to view or read their sources, take notes, and cite their sources. Tell them to compare what they view or read with what they already know. If the information is contradictory, have them check several different sources and decide which information seems most reliable.

Evaluate and Process the Product See the Unit Closer on pages 127K–127L for **Step 5** and **Step 6**.

Cross-Curricular Projects

Media

CRITICAL VIEWING

Media can be used to persuade others to take action. By choosing events and explaining them, the media helps shape people's opinions about important issues.

- Have students research how two forms of media treat the same topic. You may wish to assign a topic.

- Have students compare how the topic is treated in any two media such as newspaper and television. Ask them to think about the points of view that are presented in each form of media.

- For their final presentation, have students write a summary that presents the perspectives on the topic they chose. Ask them to evaluate which form of media was more effective and what elements or techniques made it more effective.

Media and Art

WRITE ABOUT ART

Art can create different moods, such as joy or sadness.

- Have students research two examples of visual media—a photograph and a painting or a sculpture and an illustration, for example. Encourage students to find two works that portray the same subject or theme.

- Have students compare and contrast the artworks, and think about what makes one more effective than another.

- Have students write an essay that identifies the two artists, describes the artworks, and compares them.

CHARACTER BUILDING—CARING

- When the class is finished comparing visual media, discuss how people can be caring. Some ways are being kind and helping people in need.
- Ask students to give specific examples of people who showed they cared.
- Before students hear each other's essays, encourage them to be caring when giving feedback.

 For technology **research** and **presentation** strategies see the Computer Literacy Lessons on pages 127I–127J.

Weekly Literature

Weekly Theme: Rescue Teams

Week At A Glance

Whole Group

VOCABULARY
abruptly, anxiety, conscious, intersection, engulf, procedure, souvenir, cascade

Strategy: Use a Dictionary/ Multiple-Meaning Words

COMPREHENSION
Strategy: Analyze Story Structure
Skill: Character, Setting, Plot

WRITING
Personal Narrative

Social Studies Link

Individual Society and Culture
Cooperation Among Individuals and Groups

Small Group Options

Differentiated Instruction for Tested Skills

Tested Skills for the Week

THE SUMMER OF THE SWANS
by Betsy Byars • illustrated by John Rowe

Main Selection
Genre Realistic Fiction

Sam's Summer Search
by Kristi McGee

Vocabulary/ Comprehension

Boston Globe, December 9
Storm Surprises Maine Students
By Brian MacQuarrie

Social Studies Link
Genre Newspaper Article

INTERACTIVE
Read-Aloud
ANTHOLOGY with PLAYS

Macmillan/McGraw-Hill

Read-Aloud Anthology
• Listening Comprehension
• Readers Theater

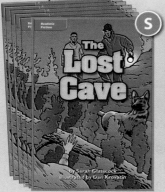 ## Leveled Readers

GR Levels S–Y

Genre Realistic Fiction

- **Same Theme**
- **Same Vocabulary**
- **Same Comprehension Skills**

 **S**

The Lost Cave
by Sarah Glasscock
illustrated by Dan Krovatin

Approaching Level

 **V**

RACHEL'S CHOICE
by Sarah Glasscock
illustrated by Dan Krovatin

On Level

 **Y**

Surprises in the Desert
by Sofía Cruz
illustrated by Dan Krovatin

Beyond Level

The Rescue Team
by Sarah Glasscock
illustrated by Dan Krovatin

English Language Leveled Reader

On Level Reader sheltered for English Language Learner

ELL Teacher's Guide also available

**Also Available
LEVELED READER PROGRAM**

CLASSROOM LIBRARY

Genre Expository Nonfiction

COME BACK, SALMON

Approaching

A DROP OF WATER
WALTER WICK

On Level

Interrupted Journey

Beyond

Trade books to apply Comprehension Skills

INTERVENTION ANTHOLOGY

- Phonics and Decoding
- Comprehension
- Vocabulary

Also available, *Reading Triumphs* Intervention Program

 READING Triumphs

LEVELED PRACTICE

Practice Book A

Practice Book O

Practice Book B

ELL Practice and Assessment

Approaching | **On Level** | **Beyond** | **ELL**

Grade 6
Treasures
Home-School Connection

🏠 **HOME-SCHOOL CONNECTION**

- Family letters in English and Spanish
- Take-Home Stories

Technology

 ONLINE INSTRUCTION
www.macmillanmh.com

 **AUDIO CD**
- Listening Library
- Fluency Solutions

 CD-ROM
- Vocabulary PuzzleMaker

Suggested Lesson Plan

CD ROM
Instructional Navigator
Interactive Lesson Planner

The Summer of the Swans, 20–32

Leveled Readers

Integrated **ELL** Support Every Day

Whole Group

ORAL LANGUAGE
- **Listening**
- **Speaking**
- **Viewing**

WORD STUDY
- **Vocabulary**
- **Phonics/Decoding**

READING
- **Develop Comprehension**

- **Fluency**

LANGUAGE ARTS
- **Writing**

- **Grammar**

- **Spelling**

ASSESSMENT
- **Informal/Formal**

Turn the page for
Small Group Lesson Plan

16L

Day 1

Listening/Speaking/Viewing

? Focus Question What do you think it would be like to be part of a rescue team?

Build Background, 16

Read Aloud: "Dangerous Rescues are Part of the Job for Coast Guard," 17

Vocabulary
abruptly, anxiety, conscious, intersection, engulf, procedure, souvenir, cascade, 18

Practice Book A-O-B, 1

Strategy: Dictionary/Multiple-Meaning Words, 19

Read "Sam's Summer Search," 18–19

Student Book

Comprehension, 19A–19B
Strategy: Story Structure
Skill: Character, Setting, Plot

Practice Book A-O-B, 2

Fluency Partner Reading, 16R
Model Fluency, 17

Writing
Daily Writing Prompt: Write a paragraph explaining how you could work together with friends to help the environment.

Personal Narrative, 38–39B

Grammar Daily Language Activities, 39I
Sentence Types and Fragments, 39I
Grammar Practice Book, 1

Spelling Pretest, 39G
Spelling Practice Book, 1–2

Quick Check Vocabulary, 18
Comprehension, 19B

Differentiated Instruction 39M–39V

Day 2

Listening/Speaking

? Focus Question What does Sara learn about herself as she searches for Charlie?

Vocabulary
Review Vocabulary Words, 20
Phonics/Decoding
Decode Words with Short Vowels, 39E

Practice Book A-O-B, 7

Read *The Summer of the Swans,* 20–33

Student Book

Comprehension, 20–33
Strategy: Story Structure
Skill: Character, Setting, Plot

Practice Book A-O-B, 3

Fluency Partner Reading, 16R
Read with Expression, 30

Writing
Daily Writing Prompt: Write a paragraph explaining why you think teamwork is important to firefighters.

Personal Narrative, 38–39B

Grammar Daily Language Activities, 39I
Sentence Types and Fragments, 39I
Grammar Practice Book, 2

Spelling Short Vowels, 39G
Spelling Practice Book, 3

Quick Check Comprehension, 29, 33
Phonics, 39E

Differentiated Instruction 39M–39V

Skills/Strategies

Vocabulary	Comprehension	Writing
Vocabulary Words	**Strategy:** Analyze Story Structure	Personal Narrative
Dictionary/Multiple Meaning Words	**Skill:** Character, Setting, Plot	

Turn the Page for Small Group Options

Day 3

Listening/Speaking

❓ Focus Question How do friends help in the two situations?

Summarize, 35

Vocabulary

Review Words in Context, 39C

Strategy: Dictionary/Multiple-Meaning Words, 39D

Practice Book A-O-B, 6

Phonics

Decode Multisyllabic Words, 39E

Read *The Summer of the Swans*, 20–33

Student Book

Comprehension

Comprehension Check, 35

Maintain Skill: Character, Setting, Plot, 35B

Fluency Partner Reading, 16R
Repeated Reading, 35A
Practice Book A-O-B, 4

Writing

Daily Writing Prompt: How would you and your friends work together to find a person who had become lost in the woods?

Writer's Craft: A Good Paragraph, 39A
Personal Narrative, 38–39B

Grammar Daily Language Activities, 39I
End Punctuation and Capitalization, 39J
Grammar Practice Book, 3

Spelling Short Vowels, 39H
Spelling Practice Book, 4

Quick Check Fluency, 35A

Differentiated Instruction 39M–39V

Day 4

Listening/Speaking/Viewing

❓ Focus Question How were the rescue team in this article and the rescue effort in *The Summer of the Swans* the same? In what ways were they different?

Media Literacy: Finding a Lost Pet, 33

Expand Vocabulary: Rescue Teams, 39F

Vocabulary

Content Vocabulary: *terrain, canvas, turbulence, descending*, 36
Multiple-Meaning Words, 39F
Apply Vocabulary to Writing, 39F

Read "Storm Surprises Maine Students," 36–37

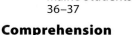
Student Book

Comprehension

Informational Nonfiction, 36

Text Feature: Photographs with Captions, 36

Practice Book A-O-B, 5

Fluency Partner Reading, 16R

Writing

Daily Writing Prompt: Write a letter to the leader of a community group explaining how you could help raise money for charity.

Writing Trait: Ideas and Content, 39B
Personal Narrative, 38–39B

Grammar Daily Language Activities, 39I
Sentence Types and Fragments, 39J
Grammar Practice Book, 4

Spelling Short Vowels, 39H
Spelling Practice Book, 5

Quick Check Vocabulary, 39D

Differentiated Instruction 39M–39V

Day 5

Review and Assess

Listening/Speaking/Viewing

❓ Focus Question If you were to conduct a search, which character's efforts would you want to follow? Explain your answer.

Speaking and Listening Strategies, 39A

Vocabulary

Spiral Review of Vocabulary Words, 39F

Read Self-Selected Reading, 16R

Student Book

Comprehension

Connect and Compare, 37

Fluency Partner Reading, 16R
Practice, 35A

Writing

Daily Writing Prompt: Write a short summary of a book or movie in which people work together to accomplish something important.

Personal Narrative, 38–39B

Grammar Daily Language Activities, 39I
Sentence Types and Fragments, 39J
Grammar Practice Book, 5–6

Spelling Posttest, 39H
Spelling Practice Book, 6

Weekly Assessment, 5–12

Differentiated Instruction 39M–39V

Differentiated Instruction

What do I do in small groups?

Teacher-Led Small Groups

Literacy Workstations

Independent Activities

Skills Focus → Use your **Quick Check** observations to guide additional instruction and practice.

Phonics
Short Vowels

Vocabulary
Words: abruptly, anxiety, cascade, conscious, engulf, intersection, procedure, souvenir

Strategy: Dictionary/Multiple-Meaning Words

Comprehension
Strategy: Analyze Story Structure

Skill: Character, Setting, and Plot

Fluency

Suggested Lesson Plan

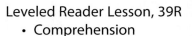

Instructional Navigator
Interactive Lesson Planner

	Day 1	**Day 2**

Approaching Level
• **Additional Instruction/Practice**
• **Tier 2 Instruction**
	Fluency, 39N
	Vocabulary, 39N
	Comprehension, 39O
		Phonics, 39M
		Vocabulary, 39O
		Leveled Reader Lesson, 39P
		  • Vocabulary
		  • Comprehension

On Level
• **Practice**
	Vocabulary, 39Q
	Leveled Reader Lesson, 39R
	  • Comprehension
	ELL Leveled Reader, 39U–39V
		Leveled Reader Lesson, 39R
		  • Comprehension
		  • Vocabulary

Beyond Level
• **Extend**
	Vocabulary, 39S
	Leveled Reader Lesson, 39T
	  • Comprehension
		Leveled Reader Lesson, 39T
		  • Comprehension
		  • Vocabulary

For intensive intervention see **READING Triumphs**

Small Group Options

Apply *tested* skills and strategies while reading appropriate leveled books.

Leveled Reader Library

Levels S–Y

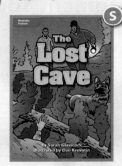
S The Lost Cave
by Sarah Glasscock
illustrated by Dan Krovatin

Approaching

V RACHEL'S CHOICE
by Sarah Glasscock
illustrated by Dan Krovatin

On Level

Y Surprises in the Desert
by Sofia Cruz
illustrated by Dan Krovatin

Beyond

The Rescue Team
by Sarah Glasscock
illustrated by Dan Krovatin

ELL

Additional Leveled Reader Resources

 LOG ON

Leveled Reader Database
Go to **www.macmillanmh.com**

Search by

- Comprehension Skill
- Content Area
- Genre
- Text Feature
- Guided Reading Level
- Reading Recovery Level
- Lexile Score
- Benchmark Level

Subscription also available

Day 3

Phonics, 39M
Fluency, 39N
Vocabulary, 39O
Leveled Reader Lesson, 39P
- Comprehension

Fluency, 39Q
Vocabulary, 39Q
Leveled Reader Lesson, 39R
- Comprehension

Fluency, 39S
Vocabulary, 39S
Leveled Reader Lesson, 39T
- Comprehension

Day 4

Phonics, 39M
Leveled Reader Lesson, 39P
- Comprehension
ELL Time Order Words, 39P

Text Feature, 39Q
Leveled Reader Lesson, 39R
- Comprehension

Text Feature, 39S
Leveled Reader Lesson, 39T
- Comprehension
ELL Personal Experience, 39S

Day 5

Fluency, 39N
Leveled Reader Lesson, 39P
- Make Connections
  Across Texts

Fluency, 39Q
Leveled Reader Lesson, 39R
- Make Connections
  Across Texts

Fluency, 39S
Self-Selected Reading, 39T

Managing the Class

What do I do with the rest of my class?

Teacher-Led Small Groups

Literacy Workstations

Independent Activities

Class Management Tools

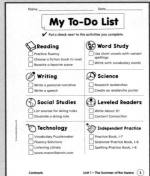

My To-Do List
✔ Put a check next to the activities you complete.

☐ **Reading**
☐ Practice fluency
☐ Choose a fiction book to read
☐ Rewrite a favorite scene

☐ **Word Study**
☐ Use short vowels with variant spellings
☐ Write with vocabulary words

☐ **Writing**
☐ Write a personal narrative
☐ Write a speech

☐ **Science**
☐ Research avalanches
☐ Create an avalanche poster

☐ **Social Studies**
☐ List sources for skiing rules
☐ Illustrate a skiing rule

☐ **Leveled Readers**
☐ Write About It!
☐ Content Connection

☐ **Technology**
☐ Vocabulary Puzzlemaker
☐ Fluency Solutions
☐ Listening Library
☐ www.macmillanmh.com

☐ **Independent Practice**
☐ Practice Book, 1–7
☐ Grammar Practice Book, 1–6
☐ Spelling Practice Book, 1–6

Contracts   Unit 1 • The Summer of the Swans

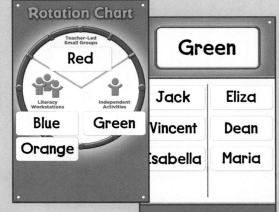

Rotation Chart

Teacher-Led Small Groups

Red

Literacy Workstations   Independent Activities

Blue   Green

Orange

Green

Jack	Eliza
Vincent	Dean
Isabella	Maria

Includes:
• How-To Guides   • Rotation Chart   • Weekly Contracts

FOLDABLES™

Hands-on activities to reinforce weekly skills.

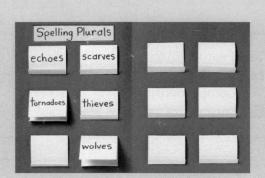

Spelling Plurals

echoes | scarves
tornadoes | thieves
wolves

Matchbook Foldable

Word	Synonym	Antonym	Prefix or Suffix
normal	typical	unusual	normally

Folded Foldable

Independent Activities

Leveled Readers

For Repeated Readings and Literacy Activities

| Approaching | On Level | ELL | Beyond |

LEVELED PRACTICE

Skills: Vocabulary (p. 1), Comprehension: Character, Setting, Plot (p. 2), Graphic Organizer (p. 3), Fluency (p. 4), Text Feature: Photo and Captions (p. 5), Vocabulary Strategy: Multiple-Meaning Words (p. 6), Phonics (p. 7)

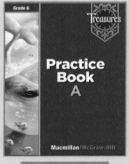

| Approaching | On Level | Beyond | ELL |

Technology

 ONLINE INSTRUCTION www.macmillanmh.com

- Meet the Author/Illustrator
- Computer Literacy Lessons
- Research and Inquiry Activities

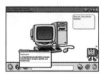

- Oral Language Activities
- Vocabulary and Spelling Activities
- Leveled Reader Database

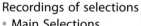 **LISTENING LIBRARY**
Recordings of selections
- Main Selections
- Leveled Readers
- ELL Readers
- Intervention Anthology

 FLUENCY SOLUTIONS
Recorded passages for modeling and practicing fluency

VOCABULARY PUZZLEMAKER
Activities providing multiple exposures to vocabulary, spelling, and high-frequency words including crossword puzzles, word searches, and word jumbles

Turn the page for Literacy Workstations.

Managing the Class

Literacy Activities
Collaborative Learning Activities

 Reading

Objectives
- Time reading to practice fluency.
- Read passage fluently with expression.
- Select literature daily for reading enjoyment.

 **Word Study**

Objectives
- Build words with short vowel variant spellings and use them in sentences.
- Use vocabulary words in a story.

 **Reading** — Fluency — *20 Minutes*

- Choose a paragraph from the fluency passage on page 4 of your Practice Book.
- Take turns reading the sentences aloud with a partner, making sure to pause and stop as the punctuation indicates.

Extension
- Read each sentence twice. Pause longer at the commas the first time and not as long the second time.
- Discuss which rhythm sounded best for each sentence and why.
- Time Your Reading: Listen to the Audio CD.

Things you need:
- Practice Book
- Audio Disc

Fluency Solutions
Listening Library

1

 Word Study — Short Vowels with Variant Spellings — *20 Minutes*

- Combine word segments in each column to make words that have short vowel sounds with variant spellings.
- Use each word in a sentence.

fr	aid
s	iend
t	ea
thr	ough

Extension
Work with a partner to make a crossword puzzle that uses words that have short vowel sounds with variant spellings.

Things you need:
- paper
- pencil

For additional vocabulary and spelling games, go to www.macmillanmh.com

1

 Reading — Independent Reading — *20 Minutes*

- Choose a fiction book to read on your own.
- Pick a favorite character and act out a scene.
- Perform your interpretation for friends.

Extension
- Work with a partner to rewrite your favorite scene as a script.
- Describe the setting and then write dialogue. Read your script aloud. Discuss which revisions need to be made to the dialogue.

Things you need:
- book
- paper and pencil

For more books about rescue teams, go to the Author/Illustrator section at www.macmillanmh.com

2

 Word Study — Vocabulary Words — *20 Minutes*

- Write a short, short story about riding in a bus or car.
- Use the vocabulary words *intersection*, *abruptly*, *anxiety*. What time of year is it? What's the weather like? Where are you going? Why? What happens?

Extension
- Look up the word *souvenir* in a dictionary.
- What is the origin of the word?
- Make an illustrated card that shows this information.

Things you need:
- dictionary
- paper and pencil

For additional vocabulary and spelling games, go to www.macmillanmh.com

 Vocabulary PuzzleMaker

2

Literacy Workstations

WORKSTATION FLIP CHART — Reading — Grade 6 — Macmillan/McGraw-Hill

WORKSTATION FLIP CHART — Word Study — Grade 6 — Macmillan/McGraw-Hill

WORKSTATION FLIP CHART — Writing — Grade 6 — Macmillan/McGraw-Hill

WORKSTATION FLIP CHART — Science/Social Studies — Grade 6 — Macmillan/McGraw-Hill

✏️ Writing

Objectives
- Write a personal narrative and create a safety advisory poster.
- Write a persuasive speech about an environmental issue in your community.

🔍 Content Literacy

Objectives
- Use an encyclopedia to research a topic and create a diagram.
- Evaluate research sources and create an illustrated list of safety tips.

✏️ Writing — RESCUE TEAMS
20 Minutes

- Have you ever heard about or been involved in a rescue?
- What was the emergency? What was the final outcome?
- Write a personal narrative describing the events.

Extension
- Work with a partner to design a poster advising people about several ways to prevent forest fires.
- Use gripping images and exciting headlines to make viewers remember your message.

Things you need:
- paper and pencil
- poster board
- paints

1

🔬 Science — Avalanches
20 Minutes

- Look in an encyclopedia to find information about avalanches.
- Take notes on what happens before, during, and after an avalanche.
- Use your notes to draw a diagram of what happens when an avalanche occurs.

Extension
- Create a poster using the diagram of your avalanche.
- Include a paragraph describing what happens before, during, and after an avalanche.
- Explain your poster to the class.

Things you need:
- reference materials
- paper and pencil
- paints
- poster board

LOG ON — Internet Research and Inquiry Activity
Students can find more facts at www.macmillanmh.com

1

✏️ Writing — Rescuing a Community
20 Minutes

- Team with a partner to write a speech explaining what needs rescuing in your community: Your parks? Your lakes? Your schools? Your roads?
- Tell what needs to be done. Use words that create vivid images.

Extension
- Take turns reading aloud the speech to your partner. Vary the tempo and volume of your voice.
- Use gestures to emphasize certain points.
- Remember to look at your audience as you speak.

Things you need:
- paper
- pencil

2

🌎 Social Studies — Safety When Skiing
20 Minutes

- Use different sources to research safety tips for going skiing. Then pretend you are a member of the National Ski Patrol.
- Make a safety list of tips for people about to ski.

Extension
- Draw an illustration to make your safety list clearer, more interesting, or more fun to read.
- Then paste the list and illustration on heavy paper to display.

Things you need:
- reference materials
- paper and pencil
- colored markers
- paste
- poster board

LOG ON — Internet Research and Inquiry Activity
Students can find more facts at www.macmillanmh.com

2

ORAL LANGUAGE
- Build Background
- Read Aloud
- Expand Vocabulary

✓ VOCABULARY
- Teach Words in Context
- Multiple-Meaning Words

COMPREHENSION
- **Strategy:** Analyze Story Structure
- ✓ **Skill:** Character, Setting, Plot

SMALL GROUP OPTIONS
- Differentiated Instruction, pp. 39M–39V

Oral Language

Build Background

ACCESS PRIOR KNOWLEDGE

Share information to help students think about this week's theme.

The Red Cross develops courses for rescue teams, such as lifeguarding and first aid. It also provides disaster services to victims of earthquakes, floods, fires, and storms.

TALK ABOUT RESCUE TEAMS

Discuss the weekly theme.

Invite students to describe the qualities of people who rescue others.

 FOCUS QUESTION Ask a volunteer to read aloud "Talk About It" on **Student Book** page 17 and describe the photo.

What is happening in the photo?

RESCUE TEAMS

16

ENGLISH LANGUAGE LEARNERS

 Access for All

Beginning Name and Repeat Point to the photo and say, *These are firemen. They are putting out a fire. They help people when there is a fire.* Help students point to, name, and describe things in the picture.

Intermediate Build Background Draw on students' experiences by developing a word web for *rescue teams*. Include other rescue teams, rescue vehicles, and disaster situations. Supply and explain vocabulary as needed. Draw pictures to convey meaning.

Advanced Elaborate Do the Intermediate task. Encourage students to make sentences from the word web. Model how to respond using more complex sentences. Easy: *The lifeguards rescued the girl.* Expand: *The lifeguards rescued the girl when she swam out too far.*

Talk About It

What do you think it would be like to be part of a rescue team?

LOG ON Find out more about rescue teams at **www.macmillanmh.com**

17

Picture Prompt

Look at the picture. Write about what you see. You can write a story, a description, or use any other type of writing you like.

 Technology

For an extended lesson plan and Web site activities for **oral language development,** go to **www.macmillanmh.com**

Read Aloud

Read "Dangerous Rescues Are Part of Job for Coast Guard"

GENRE: Informational Nonfiction
Review features of informational nonfiction:

- presents information and facts about a topic

- has a main idea and supporting details

Read Aloud pages 9–13

LISTENING FOR A PURPOSE

Ask students to listen carefully for words that can have more than one meaning as you read "Dangerous Rescues Are Part of Job for Coast Guard" in the **Read-Aloud Anthology.** Choose from among the teaching suggestions.

Fluency Ask students to listen carefully as you read aloud. Tell students to listen to your phrasing, expression, and tone of voice.

RESPOND TO THE ARTICLE

Reread the article with students and discuss the multiple-meaning words *approach, commercial,* and *patrol.* Ask volunteers to come up with a sentence for each meaning identified for the words.

Expand Vocabulary

Help students brainstorm words related to rescue teams. Create a list of the words and phrases that students associate with rescue teams and encourage students to add to it throughout the week.

Vocabulary

TEACH WORDS IN CONTEXT

Use the following routine.

Routine

Define: If you do something **abruptly**,[2] you do it quickly and unexpectedly.

Example: My brother abruptly shut the door.

Ask: What is a synonym for *abruptly*?

SYNONYM

- **Anxiety**[6] causes a person to feel nervous and afraid. Jacob felt anxiety about his final exam. What kinds of things might cause anxiety? EXPLANATION

- You are **conscious**[7] if you are aware of what is going on around you. Indie was conscious of her mother coming in. What is an antonym of *conscious*? ANTONYM

- An **intersection**[3] is where two or more roads or streets meet. I often turn right at the intersection of Main Street and Fulton Avenue. Which intersection is closest to your house? EXAMPLE

- To **engulf**[5] something is to swallow it up or surround it. The floodwaters look like they will engulf the town. When do you feel joy engulf you? EXAMPLE

Access for All

- A **procedure**[4] is a standard way of doing things. The judge followed the procedure for giving a verdict. Tell about a procedure that you have followed. DESCRIPTION

- A **souvenir**[1] is a memento, something that serves as a reminder. I bought a T-shirt as a souvenir of our vacation. What is another kind of souvenir? EXAMPLE

Vocabulary

abruptly	engulf
anxiety	procedure
conscious	souvenir
intersection	cascade

STRATEGY SKILL

Dictionary

Multiple-meaning Words have more than one definition.

conscious *adj.* knowing or realizing

conscious *adj.* awake

Sam's Summer Search

by Kristi McGee

Sam **abruptly** stopped swinging. He jumped off the swing without even slowing down. He yelled, "Mommmm, where's Champ?" He realized he hadn't seen his new puppy for over an hour.

Sam looked around the yard, behind the bushes, and under the picnic table. No Champ! His mother heard the **anxiety** and fear build in his voice as he called her a second time. "Mom, I can't find Champ!" She was **conscious** of the mounting fear in her son.

She came outside quickly. "Let's look around the yard first. I'm sure he has just gone to take a nap."

18

- A **cascade**[8] refers to something falling or rushing like a waterfall. A cascade of rain fell down the back of her slicker. What besides water could form a cascade? PRIOR KNOWLEDGE

Quick Check — Do students understand word meanings?

During **Small Group Instruction**

If No → Approaching Level
Vocabulary, p. 39N

If Yes → On Level Options,
pp. 39Q–39R

Beyond Level Options,
pp. 39S–39T

ELL   Access for All

Reinforce Vocabulary
Ask, *Do you raise your hand when you ask a question in class? This is the procedure for asking a question. A procedure is the way you do something.* Discuss other classroom *procedures.*

"Champ! Champ! Come here, boy!" shouted Sam and his mother over and over. But still no Champ. They did get other responses, though. José, the next-door neighbor, immediately agreed to help Sam and his mom search for the lost dog. Then Sam's friend Tasha joined in the search, along with her older brother, Jamal.

The group decided to split up to look for Champ. They scoured the neighborhood from the main **intersection** of the big streets to the smallest alley. Still no Champ. Sam felt sadness and fear **engulf** him. He was sure that his best friend was gone forever. He was overwhelmed by the thought it was his fault.

After an hour, Tasha suggested they go home and make posters with pictures of Champ. It was the **procedure**, or way of doing things, animal rescue had suggested when she had lost her cat. She explained, "Somebody called the next day. He found Boots in his backyard. Posters really work!"

Vocabulary and Comprehension

REWARD!
Lost Puppy
His name is Champ.
Please call Sam: 555-2610

Sam agreed. When they got home, Sam made a poster with a picture of Champ. It was a **souvenir** photograph from doggie kindergarten that Sam received to remind him of Champ's progress. Then Sam heard a noise and opened his bedroom door. He was greeted with a **cascade** of wet kisses. Champ had been locked in the bedroom this whole time! Sam's mom was right. Champ had been napping. Sam had never been so happy in his entire life!

Reread for **Comprehension**

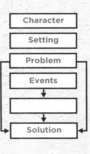

Story Structure

Character, Setting, Plot
A Story Map helps you figure out the characters, setting, and plot of a story. These are important parts of the story structure. The plot is often based on a problem that a character has. As the character tries to find a solution, the setting may have an influence on whether he or she is successful.

Use the Story Map as you reread "Sam's Summer Search."

Character
Setting
Problem
Events
Solution

19

Vocabulary

STRATEGY
USE A DICTIONARY

Multiple-Meaning Words Remind students that when they look up words in the dictionary, they will see that many words have more than one definition. They will need to determine which meaning is being used by looking at the context of the word.

Point to the word *conscious* on **Student Book** page 18. Have a volunteer read the definitions of the word from a dictionary, and discuss which meaning of the word is intended in the story. (knowing or aware)

Read "Sam's Summer Search"

As you read "Sam's Summer Search" with students, ask them to identify context clues that reveal the meanings of the highlighted words. Tell students they will read these words again in *The Summer of the Swans.*

On Level Practice Book O, page 1

Use the vocabulary words below to complete the sentences.

| intersection | engulf | abruptly | conscious |
| anxiety | cascade | procedure | souvenir |

1. Marian often had the best ideas, but her ___anxiety___ about public speaking kept her from running for class president.
2. I would have liked to take a ___souvenir___ from the archaeological site, but it was strictly forbidden.
3. Though the task was not difficult, I had to be careful to follow the ___procedure___ exactly.
4. We were startled when the author ___abruptly___ closed her book and left.
5. The actor was extremely well trained—always ___conscious___ of the audience's reaction to his performance.
6. The papers fell in a ___cascade___ from the top of the shelf.
7. I was taught to look both ways when crossing an ___intersection___
8. The huge wave was about to ___engulf___ the tiny islands in the sea.

Choose two of the vocabulary words in the box above and write a sentence for each. Possible responses provided.
9. I sat by the bank of the river and watched the water as it fell in a cascade over the falls.
10. The play ended so abruptly Noah could not tell if it was actually finished or if it was just another intermission.

⭐ **Approaching Practice Book A,** page 1
◆ **Beyond Practice Book B,** page 1

Reread for Comprehension

STRATEGY
ANALYZE STORY STRUCTURE

Story structure is the way an author organizes a story. A fictional narrative includes a setting, characters, and a plot. The events of a plot are usually told in chronological sequence, but they may also include a flashback to earlier events.

SKILL
CHARACTER, SETTING, PLOT

Explain to students that every fictional narrative has **characters,** the people or animals that appear in the story. The narrative occurs at a certain time and place, the **setting.** The series of events that take place in the story is called the **plot.** To find the plot, readers identify the problem the main character faces and then analyze the steps he or she takes to solve it. These steps may include a flashback to an earlier event.

Objectives

- Analyze story structure
- Use academic language: *character, setting, plot*
- Identify the characters, setting, and plot in a story

Materials

- Comprehension Transparencies 1a, 1b
- Graphic Organizer Transparency 1
- Leveled Practice Books, p. 2

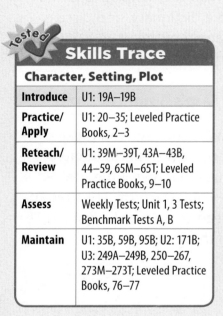

Skills Trace

Character, Setting, Plot

Introduce	U1: 19A–19B
Practice/ Apply	U1: 20–35; Leveled Practice Books, 2–3
Reteach/ Review	U1: 39M–39T, 43A–43B, 44–59, 65M–65T; Leveled Practice Books, 9–10
Assess	Weekly Tests; Unit 1, 3 Tests; Benchmark Tests A, B
Maintain	U1: 35B, 59B, 95B; U2: 171B; U3: 249A–249B, 250–267, 273M–273T; Leveled Practice Books, 76–77

ELL / Access for All

Clarify Explain what the word *structure* means. Draw the framework of a house and ask, *What's this?* (a house) Outline the structure of the house as you say, *A house has this structure. Stories have structure, too.* Write the words *characters, setting,* and *plot* and review the meanings of the words.

Transparency 1a

Transparency 1b

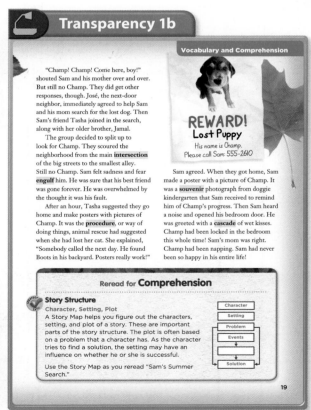

Student Book pages 18–19 available on Comprehension Transparencies 1a and 1b

MODEL

Read aloud the first few paragraphs of "Sam's Summer Search" from **Student Book** page 18.

Think Aloud From the title, I know that this story takes place in the summer. Sam is playing on a swing set in his backyard. He jumped off the swing without even slowing down, so that must mean Sam is excited or upset about something. It turns out that Sam's puppy is missing. This is the problem the main character faces. I will continue to read to see how Sam solves his problem.

GUIDED PRACTICE

Display the Story Map on **Transparency 1.** Ask students to identify the first two characters they read about. What is the setting at the beginning of this story? How is the setting important to the story? Call for volunteers to find clues in the passage, and describe what Sam's yard looks like. Begin to fill in the items on the Story Map.

Ask students if Sam has a problem. If so, what is it? What might a possible solution be? What other characters appear in the story? What are some of the other settings? How might the setting influence the conflict and solution? What is the solution to Sam's problem?

APPLY

Work with students to complete the Story Map. Ask them to explain why Champ had been missing all day.

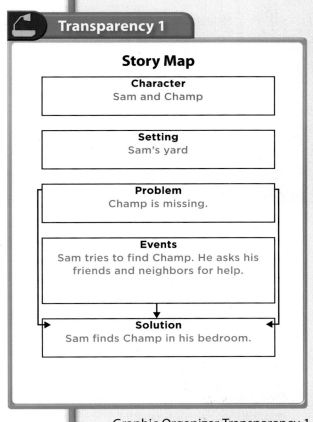

Transparency 1

Story Map

Character
Sam and Champ

Setting
Sam's yard

Problem
Champ is missing.

Events
Sam tries to find Champ. He asks his friends and neighbors for help.

Solution
Sam finds Champ in his bedroom.

Graphic Organizer Transparency 1

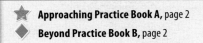

On Level Practice Book O, page 2

Read the passage and answer the questions.

It was dark when I woke up. I was so cold. At first, I didn't know where I was. I started to panic. I couldn't move my arms or legs. What was happening to me? Then I remembered. I had been skiing. I had heard a really loud noise, like a freight train. When I had looked behind me, all I had seen was a wall of snow coming my way—fast!

"I must be buried in that snow," I said to myself. Talk about panic! Now I had a good reason. To make myself feel better, I thought about all the TV shows I had watched about people being rescued. I drifted in and out of consciousness.

Meanwhile, I learned later, the rescue teams were gathering, just like on TV! Several skiers were missing after the avalanche. Luckily, I had been skiing on a marked path. The rescue teams would know where to look for me. After what seemed like forever, I heard voices. I tried to scream, but the snow covering me blocked any noise. At last, I felt something touch my legs. A dog was digging me out. I had been rescued! **Possible responses provided.**

1. What do you know about the narrator? The narrator has survived an avalanche. He or she was rescued by a search team that used a dog. The narrator was very frightened but has a sense of humor about the event.

2. Where is the story set? It is set in the mountains during ski season.

3. How does the setting affect the story? Without the setting of ski season and the mountains, there would be no story. The plot has an avalanche, which occurs only in this kind of setting.

4. What is the main conflict in the story? The conflict involves a human against nature. The narrator is trapped in the snow by an avalanche.

⭐ **Approaching Practice Book A,** page 2

◆ **Beyond Practice Book B,** page 2

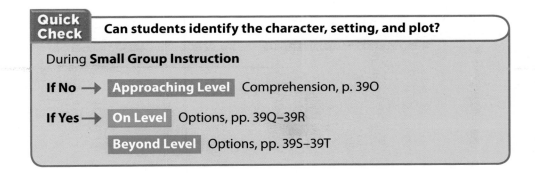

Quick Check **Can students identify the character, setting, and plot?**

During **Small Group Instruction**

If No → **Approaching Level** Comprehension, p. 39O

If Yes → **On Level** Options, pp. 39Q–39R

Beyond Level Options, pp. 39S–39T

Read

MAIN SELECTION
* *The Summer of the Swans*
* **Skill:** Character, Setting, Plot

PAIRED SELECTION
* "Storm Surprises Maine Students"
* **Text Feature:** Photo and Caption

SMALL GROUP OPTIONS
* Differentiated Instruction, pp. 39M–39V

Comprehension

GENRE: REALISTIC FICTION

Have a student read the definition of Realistic Fiction on **Student Book** page 20. Students should look for events that could happen in real life.

STRATEGY
ANALYZE STORY STRUCTURE

To **analyze story structure** a good reader identifies the main characters, the setting, and how the events, or plot, in the story are organized.

SKILL
CHARACTER, SETTING, AND PLOT

Every fictional story has **characters,** or the people or animals who appear in the story. The story occurs at a certain time and place, the **setting.** The order of events that occur in the story is called the **plot.**

Comprehension

Genre
Realistic Fiction is an invented story that could have happened in real life.

Story Structure
Character, Setting, Plot
As you read, use your Story Map.

| Character |
| Setting |
| Problem |
| Events |
| |
| Solution |

Read to Find Out
What does Sara learn about herself as she searches for Charlie?

20

Vocabulary

Vocabulary Words Review the tested vocabulary words: **intersection, engulf, abruptly, conscious, anxiety, cascade, procedure,** and **souvenir.**

Story Word Students might find this word difficult. Pronounce the word and present the meaning as necessary.

knickknacks (p. 28): small objects used for decoration

THE SUMMER OF THE
SWANS

by Betsy Byars • illustrated by John Rowe

Sara and Joe must find Sara's little brother Charlie, a ten-year-old who suffered a brain injury as a small child and doesn't speak. Charlie leaves home during the night to find some swans he's seen on a nearby lake. After becoming lost in the woods near his home, Charlie doesn't know where to turn. In the morning Sara and her classmate Joe join the town's all-out search for the lost boy. But after frantically looking for hours, Sara and Joe have found only a slipper belonging to Charlie.

21

Read Together

If your students need support to read the Main Selection, use the prompts to guide comprehension and model how to complete the graphic organizer.

Read Independently

If your students can read the Main Selection independently, have them read and complete the graphic organizer. Remind students to set and modify purposes when reading and use purposes to set or adjust their reading rate.

If your students need an alternate selection, choose the **Leveled Readers** that match their instructional level.

Technology

Story available on **Listening Library Audio CD**

Preview and Predict

Ask students to read the title, preview the illustrations, and note questions and predictions about what may happen in the story. Have students write about their predictions and what they want to know about the story.

Set Purposes

FOCUS QUESTION Discuss the "Read to Find Out" question with students and how to look for the answer as they read.

Point out the Story Map in the Student Book and on **Leveled Practice Book** page 3. Explain that students will fill it in as they read.

Read *The Summer of the Swans*

Use the questions and Think Alouds for additional instruction to support the comprehension strategy and skill.

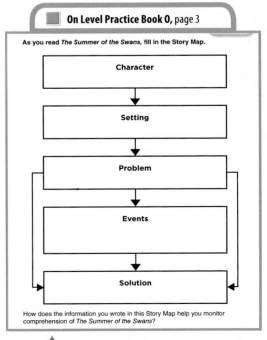

On Level Practice Book O, page 3

As you read *The Summer of the Swans*, fill in the Story Map.

Character

Setting

Problem

Events

Solution

How does the information you wrote in this Story Map help you monitor comprehension of *The Summer of the Swans*?

⭐ **Approaching Practice Book A,** page 3

◆ **Beyond Practice Book B,** page 3

Develop Comprehension

1 STRATEGY
ANALYZE STORY STRUCTURE

Teacher Think Aloud Having read the introduction, I know that the characters, Sara and Joe, are looking for Sara's little brother Charlie. As I begin to read the story, I will look for the steps they are taking to find him, and I will think about how they are feeling as the search continues. Paying attention to the structure of the story will help me understand it better.

2 SETTING

Describe the setting. (The story is set in a coal-mining area, where a huge bank of earth has been formed by machines and the leaves are covered with dirt.) Record this information in your Story Map.

Characters
Sara, Joe, Charlie

↓

Setting
A mining area with a steep bank and trees

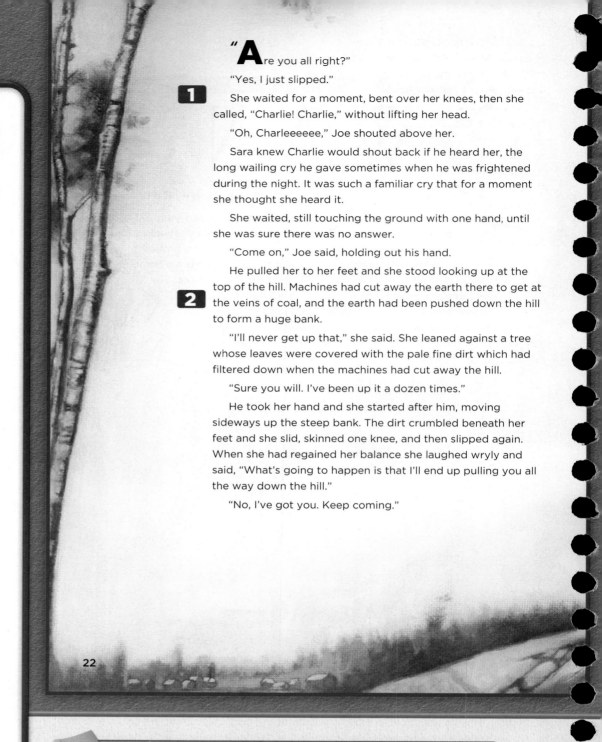

"**A**re you all right?"

"Yes, I just slipped."

1 She waited for a moment, bent over her knees, then she called, "Charlie! Charlie," without lifting her head.

"Oh, Charleeeeee," Joe shouted above her.

Sara knew Charlie would shout back if he heard her, the long wailing cry he gave sometimes when he was frightened during the night. It was such a familiar cry that for a moment she thought she heard it.

She waited, still touching the ground with one hand, until she was sure there was no answer.

"Come on," Joe said, holding out his hand.

He pulled her to her feet and she stood looking up at the top of the hill. Machines had cut away the earth there to get at **2** the veins of coal, and the earth had been pushed down the hill to form a huge bank.

"I'll never get up that," she said. She leaned against a tree whose leaves were covered with the pale fine dirt which had filtered down when the machines had cut away the hill.

"Sure you will. I've been up it a dozen times."

He took her hand and she started after him, moving sideways up the steep bank. The dirt crumbled beneath her feet and she slid, skinned one knee, and then slipped again. When she had regained her balance she laughed wryly and said, "What's going to happen is that I'll end up pulling you all the way down the hill."

"No, I've got you. Keep coming."

22

Comprehension

Literary Element: *Mood*

Explain Authors choose their words and details carefully to communicate a feeling or atmosphere to their readers. For example, words like *sunny* and *sparkling* convey a happy feeling. This feeling is called the mood of a selection.

Discuss What kind of mood does the story have at the beginning? What does the writer hope the reader will feel? (The writer hopes the reader will feel anxiety about Charlie's whereabouts and doubts about Sara's ability to get up the hill.) What words does she use to help convey the mood? (*wailing, frightened, wryly*)

Apply Ask students to predict how changing certain words would change the mood of the story. Then have them choose a new mood for the story. Have them list words that would fit the mood.

She started again, putting one foot carefully above the other, picking her way over the stones. When she paused, he said, "Keep coming. We're almost there."

"I think it's a trick, like at the dentist's when he says, 'I'm almost through drilling.' Then he drills for another hour and says, 'Now, I'm really almost through drilling,' and he keeps on and then says, 'There's just one more spot and then I'll be practically really through.' "

"We must go to the same dentist."

"I don't think I can make it. There's no skin at all left on the sides of my legs."

"Well, we're really almost practically there now, in the words of your dentist."

She fell across the top of the dirt bank on her stomach, rested for a moment, and then turned and looked down the valley.

Character
Describe Sara's emotions at this point. Support your answer.

23

Develop Comprehension

3 **CHARACTER**

Describe Sara's emotions at this point. Support your answer. (Answers will vary but may include that Sara is concerned about Charlie. She calls his name and waits in vain for his answer. She also seems to be feeling stressed and uncertain at the prospect of climbing up the hill. Her mention of the dentist's drill indicates that she's feeling tense and anxious.)

RESEARCH
Why It Matters

Students who understand the structure of a story understand how the story is organized from beginning to end. Understanding how a story is organized helps students draw inferences from the story and understand causal relationships—how one event leads to or causes another event.

Janice A. Dole

 For more information, go to Teacher Resources at **www.macmillanmh.com**

Comprehension

Monitor and Clarify: *Self-Correct*

Explain Point out there are different techniques students can use if they do not understand a text. One is to ask themselves questions such as *Why?, What if?* and *How?* and then look for answers.

Discuss What other questions can you ask to clarify your understanding of a story? (Answers will vary but might include *Where?* or *Who?*) Why is it important to look for evidence in the text to support the answers to your questions? (It will help you make sure your understanding of the text is correct.)

Apply Ask students to brainstorm questions they might ask themselves about this story, for example: *How did Sara feel when she and Joe had almost reached the top of the hill?* Record students' responses on a group chart. Encourage students to ask themselves questions as they read to clarify their understanding.

Develop Comprehension

4 SETTING

How does the setting change when Sara and Joe reach the top of the hill? Does this change the mood? (At the top of the hill Sara and Joe can see the whole valley below them, including houses, roads, and stores. However, the mood still seems to be threatening as Sara imagines the trees crowding out and closing over the houses.)

5 CHARACTER, PLOT

How are the characters connected? (Sara and her friend Joe are searching for Sara's little brother Charlie.) What is their problem? (Charlie is missing.) What actions are the characters taking to solve the problem? (Sara and Joe are calling for Charlie and searching the woods.) Fill in the Story Map.

Characters
Sara, Joe, Charlie

↓

Setting
A mining area with a steep bank and trees

↓

Problem
Charlie is missing.

↓

Events
Sara and Joe are searching for Charlie.

She could not speak for a moment. There lay the whole valley in a way she had never imagined it, a tiny finger of civilization set in a sweeping expanse of dark forest. The black treetops seemed to crowd against the yards, the houses, the roads, giving the impression that at any moment the trees would close over the houses like waves and leave nothing but an unbroken line of black-green leaves waving in the sunlight.

Up the valley she could see the **intersection** where they shopped, the drugstore, the gas station where her mother had once won a set of twenty-four stemmed glasses which Aunt Willie would not allow them to use, the grocery store, the lot where the yellow school buses were parked for the summer. She could look over the valley and see another hill where white cows were all grouped together by a fence and beyond that another hill and then another.

She looked back at the valley and she saw the lake and for the first time since she had stood up on the hill she remembered Charlie.

5 Raising her hand to her mouth, she called, "Charlie! Charlie! Charlie!" There was a faint echo that seemed to waver in her ears.

"Charlie, oh, Charlie!" Her voice was so loud it seemed to ram into the valley.

Sara waited. She looked down at the forest, and everything was so quiet it seemed to her that the whole valley, the whole world was waiting with her.

"Charlie, hey, Charlie!" Joe shouted.

"Charleeeeee!" She made the sound of it last a long time. "Can you hear meeeeee?"

With her eyes she followed the trail she knew he must have taken—the house, the Akers' vacant lot, the old pasture, the forest. The forest that seemed powerful enough to **engulf** a whole valley, she thought with a sinking feeling, could certainly swallow up a young boy.

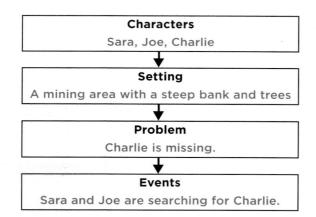

24

"Charlie! Charlie! Charlie!" There was a waver in the last syllable that betrayed how near she was to tears. She looked down at the Indian slipper she was still holding.

"Charlie, oh, Charlie." She waited. There was not a sound anywhere. "Charlie, where are you?"

"Hey, Charlie!" Joe shouted.

They waited in the same dense silence. A cloud passed in front of the sun and a breeze began to blow through the trees. Then there was silence again.

"Charlie, Charlie, Charlie, Charlie, Charlie."

She paused, listened, then bent **abruptly** and put Charlie's slipper to her eyes. She waited for the hot tears that had come so often this summer, the tears that had seemed so close only a moment before. Now her eyes remained dry. **6**

25

Develop Comprehension

6 **GENRE: REALISTIC FICTION**

Does Sara seem like a real person? What makes you think so? (Yes. Sara feels frightened; she was nervous about getting up the hill; she is worried about her brother and near tears. She acts the way a real person might act in an upsetting situation.) Do the events of the plot so far seem believable? Explain your answer. (Yes. People do get lost in the woods and search parties are often organized to look for them.)

Comprehension

Literary Device: *Flashback*

Explain Sometimes authors do not present a story's events in time order. Authors might take the reader back in time to a past event that influences a current situation in the story. This is called a *flashback*.

Discuss What kind of flashback might the author of this story include to help you better understand the characters and what they experience in the story?

Apply Tell students to look for a flashback on the next spread that helps explain why one of the characters feels the way he does.

Vocabulary

Read the sentence that contains the word **abruptly**. What word or phrase is the opposite of *abruptly*? (slowly, gradually, little by little, step by step)

Develop Comprehension

7 SELF-CORRECT

What kinds of questions could you ask yourself to help you understand Sara's relationship with her little brother? (Answers will vary, but could include *Has Charlie ever been lost before? Is Sara responsible for looking after Charlie?*)

8 MOOD

How does the author capture Sara's mood of desperation? (The author uses vivid words and phrases to describe Sara's actions and convey her anxiety. Sara's whole body is motionless. She stiffens. She twists the slipper. Finally she sinks to the ground.)

Vocabulary

What other words might the author have used instead of **anxiety**? (fear, worry, nervousness)

7

I have cried over myself a hundred times this summer, she thought, I have wept over my big feet and my skinny legs and my nose, I have even cried over my stupid shoes, and now when I have a true sadness there are no tears left.

She held the felt side of the slipper against her eyes like a blindfold and stood there, feeling the hot sun on her head and the wind wrapping around her legs, **conscious** of the height and the valley sweeping down from her feet.

"Listen, just because you can't hear him doesn't mean anything. He could be—"

"Wait a minute." She lowered the slipper and looked down the valley. A sudden wind blew dust into her face and she lifted her hand to shield her eyes.

"I thought I heard something. Charlie! Answer me right this minute."

She waited with the slipper held against her, one hand to her eyes, her whole body motionless, concentrating on her brother. Then she stiffened. She thought again she had heard something—Charlie's long high wail. Charlie could sound sadder than anyone when he cried.

8   In her **anxiety** she took the slipper and twisted it again and again as if she were wringing water out. She called, then stopped abruptly and listened. She looked at Joe and he shook his head slowly.

She looked away. A bird rose from the trees below and flew toward the hills in the distance. She waited until she could see it no longer and then slowly, still listening for the call that didn't come, she sank to the ground and sat with her head bent over her knees.

Beside her, Joe scuffed his foot in the dust and sent a **cascade** of rocks and dirt down the bank. When the sound of it faded, he began to call, "Charlie, hey, Charlie," again and again.

26

Comprehension

Literary Devices and Techniques

Explain Authors express their ideas through the use of figurative language (such as simile, metaphor, hyperbole, idioms, imagery), satire, characterization, narration, dialogue, dialect, tone, mood, and sound techniques and devices such as alliteration and sensory words and details.

Discuss What are some literary devices and techniques the author has used in the story so far? (mood, dialogue, flashback, sensory details) Do you think these techniques are used successfully? (Answers will vary.)

Apply Have students find examples in the text of literary devices and techniques that the author has used. Ask them to list their examples. As they read pages 27–28, have them discuss how and why the author shifts the narrative point of view.

Charlie awoke, but he lay for a moment without opening his eyes. He did not remember where he was, but he had a certain dread of seeing it.

There were great parts of his life that were lost to Charlie, blank spaces that he could never fill in. He would find himself in a strange place and not know how he had got there. Like the time Sara had been hit in the nose with a baseball at the ice cream shop, and the blood and the sight of Sara kneeling on the ground in helpless pain had frightened him so much that he had turned and run without direction, in a frenzy, dashing headlong up the street, blind to cars and people. **9**

By chance Mr. Weicek had seen him, put him in the car, and driven him home, and Aunt Willie had put him to bed, but later he remembered none of this. He had only awakened in bed and looked at the crumpled bit of ice-cream cone still clenched in his hand and wondered about it.

His whole life had been built on a strict routine, and as long as this routine was kept up, he felt safe and well. The same foods, the same bed, the same furniture in the same place, the same seat on the school bus, the same class **procedure** were all important to him. But always there could be the unexpected, the dreadful surprise that would topple his carefully constructed life in an instant. **11**

27

ELL

Access for All

Explain Help students understand the flashback on page 27. Explain that a flashback is something that happened earlier in someone's life. In this case, Charlie is having a flashback about something that happened at an ice cream shop. Have students read paragraphs two and three and retell what happened. Discuss why Charlie is thinking of that incident now.

Develop Comprehension

9 **STRATEGY**
ANALYZE STORY STRUCTURE

Teacher Think Aloud The author is using a flashback here as part of the story structure. A flashback tells about an event that happened before the story started. How does the author use the flashback to reveal more information about Charlie's character?

Encourage students to apply the strategy in a Think Aloud.

Student Think Aloud The flashback explains how Charlie reacts when something unexpected happens. If it disturbs his routine, he often cannot remember something that happened, such as Sara's accident. This helps me understand how Charlie got lost in the first place.

10 **CHARACTER**

Tested

Anyone can become frightened of being lost. Why is it especially terrifying for Charlie? (Charlie needs to follow a strict routine in order to feel safe. He needs to be surrounded by familiar people and places. Being in a strange place with no one he knows to help him is the most terrifying thing that can happen to him.)

11 **WRITER'S CRAFT: A GOOD PARAGRAPH**

Which sentence states the main idea of this paragraph? (the first sentence) How do the other sentences support that sentence? (They provide more details about why a strict routine was important for Charlie.)

The Summer of the Swans **27**

Develop Comprehension

12 **SUMMARIZE**

Summarize the main events of the story so far. Remember to look for gaps or contradictions in your summaries. (Sara and Joe are searching the woods for Charlie. Sara gets more desperate when they keep calling his name and get no response. Charlie wakes up and realizes he isn't at home. He hears someone calling his name.)

The first thing he became aware of was the twigs pressing into his face, and he put his hand under his cheek. Still he did not open his eyes. Pictures began to drift into his mind; he saw Aunt Willie's box which was filled with old jewelry and buttons and knickknacks, and he found that he could remember every item in that box—the string of white beads without a clasp, the old earrings, the tiny book with **souvenir** fold-out pictures of New York, the plastic decorations from cakes, the turtle made of sea shells. Every item was so real that he opened his eyes and was surprised to see, instead of the glittering contents of the box, the dull and unfamiliar forest.

He raised his head and immediately felt the aching of his body. Slowly he sat up and looked down at his hands. His fingernails were black with earth, two of them broken below the quick, and he got up slowly and sat on the log behind him and inspected his fingers more closely.

Then he sat up straight. His hands dropped to his lap. His head cocked to the side like a bird listening. Slowly he straightened until he was standing. At his side his fingers twitched at the empty air as if to grasp something. He took a step forward, still with his head to the side. He remained absolutely still.

12 Then he began to cry out in a hoarse excited voice, again and again, screaming now, because he had just heard someone far away calling his name.

28

Comprehension

Figurative Language: *Simile*

Explain Authors draw word pictures to help readers visualize the events of a story. To do this authors sometimes compare two things that are not usually thought of as similar. A simile uses the word *like* or *as* to compare two essentially unlike things.

Discuss On page 28 the author writes that Charlie's head cocked to the side "like a bird listening." How does this simile help you to picture the scene in your mind as you read? What idea is the author expressing? Do you like this simile? Does it affect the mood of the story? Why or why not?

Apply Ask students to think of similes they might use to describe their own everyday activities. Start them with a few examples: *The cold made my voice sound like sandpaper; My neighbors are as busy as bees in a hive.*

At the top of the hill Sara got slowly to her feet and stood looking down at the forest. She pushed the hair back from her forehead and moistened her lips. The wind dried them as she waited.

Joe started to say something but she reached out one hand and took his arm to stop him. Scarcely daring to believe her ears, she stepped closer to the edge of the bank. Now she heard it unmistakably—the sharp repeated cry—and she knew it was Charlie.

"Charlie!" she shouted with all her might.

29

Develop Comprehension

 PLOT, CHARACTER

What words would you choose to describe Sara and Charlie? How have the events in the plot affected both of these characters? (Answers will vary, but may include that Sara seems like a responsible, sensitive young woman who is very nervous because she is afraid something has happened to her brother. Charlie is also sensitive, because he cannot cope with any changes to his routine. Becoming lost in the woods has made him confused.)

Have students respond to the selection by confirming or revising their predictions and purposes. Encourage students to revise or write additional questions they have about the selection. Remind them that asking questions will help them understand the story better.

Quick Check　Can students look ahead to events in the plot by analyzing the characters? If not, see the **Extra Support** on this page.

Extra Support

Plot and Character

Ask students how they think Sara feels while she's looking for Charlie. Does the story give them clues? Have them reread pages 22–26 as you help them point to sentences that describe, or hint at, Sara's emotions. Then ask: *How do you think Sara feels now that she knows Charlie is nearby? What clues can you find on this page?*

Stop here if you wish to read this selection over two days.

Develop Comprehension

 14 CHARACTER

How have Sara's emotions changed from the beginning of the story to when she hears Charlie? (At first Sara was worried and depressed. She felt that she could not climb the hill and probably would not find her brother. When she continued to call his name but saw no sign of him, she became even more frightened and was almost defeated. Now she no longer thinks about her skinned knees and legs, and feels she could crush the whole hill if she wanted to.)

She paused and listened, and his cries were louder and she knew he was not far away after all, just down the slope, in the direction of the ravine.

"It's Charlie, it's Charlie!"

14 A wild joy overtook her and she jumped up and down on the bare earth and she felt that she could crush the whole hill just by jumping if she wanted.

She sat and scooted down the bank, sending earth and pebbles in a cascade before her. She landed on the soft ground, ran a few steps, lost her balance, caught hold of the first tree trunk she could find, and swung around till she stopped.

She let out another whoop of pure joy, turned and ran down the hill in great strides, the puce tennis shoes slapping the ground like rubber paddles, the wind in her face, her hands grabbing one tree trunk after another for support. She felt like a wild creature who had traveled through the forest this way for a lifetime. Nothing could stop her now.

At the edge of the ravine she paused and stood gasping for breath. Her heart was beating so fast it pounded in her ears, and her throat was dry. She leaned against a tree, resting her cheek against the rough bark.

 Character
How have Sara's emotions changed from the beginning of the story to when she hears Charlie?

30

Fluency

Read with Expression

Explain An author frequently provides hints for the reader about what dialogue should sound like. When you read aloud with expression, you should use the author's textual clues to change the tone and inflection of your voice.

Discuss What kind of voice does Sara use when she calls Charlie? (a loud voice) How do you know? (The passage says that she shouted with all her might.)

Apply Ask students to read aloud this sentence from the story: *"Charlie!" she shouted with all her might.* Have the class look through the rest of the story to see if there are any other hints for reading dialogue with expression.

She thought for a minute she was going to faint, a thing she had never done before, not even when she broke her nose. She hadn't even believed people really did faint until this minute when she clung to the tree because her legs were as useless as rubber bands. **15**

There was a ringing in her ears and another sound, a wailing siren-like cry that was painfully familiar.

"Charlie?"

Charlie's crying, like the sound of a cricket, seemed everywhere and nowhere.

31

Develop Comprehension

15 **STRATEGY**
USE A DICTIONARY

Tested

Look at the word *faint* in the first line on page 31. It is a **multiple-meaning word.** What does it mean here? What other meanings do you know for *faint*? (It means "lose consciousness briefly" in the story. Other meanings include "feeble," "weak and dizzy," and "with little courage.")

Cross–Curricular Connection

CHANGES IN TEMPERATURE

Often when people get lost in the woods the worry is that they will get hypothermia if the temperature drops too low at night. Discuss with students why the temperature drops at night and how changes in temperatures affect the body.

• Create a KWL chart with students and have them generate questions about temperature and its effects on the human body.

• Once students generate questions have them work with a partner or in small groups to choose a particular question to research.

Students can write a summary of their findings using a question-and-answer format. Remind them to note the sources that they used.

Develop Comprehension

16 MOOD

How has the mood of the story changed from the beginning of the story to now? How has the author used descriptive words to change the mood? (The mood has changed from anxious to joyful as Sara finds Charlie. The author uses phrases like "wonder and joy and disbelief.")

17 STRATEGY
ANALYZE STORY STRUCTURE

How has the story's solution affected the main characters? Explain.

Student Think Aloud Charlie is overjoyed to see Sara—someone he knows and loves. But I think that Sara is the most affected character. Now that she has found Charlie, she realizes how much he means to her, and how important she is to him.

Fill in the last box in the Story Map.

Characters
Sara, Joe, Charlie

↓

Setting
A mining area with a steep bank and trees

↓

Problem
Charlie is missing.

↓

Events
Sara and Joe are searching for Charlie. Charlie wakes up and hears someone calling him.

↓

Solution
Sara hears Charlie's cries and finds him.

She walked along the edge of the ravine, circling the large boulders and trees. Then she looked down into the ravine where the shadows lay, and she felt as if something had turned over inside her because she saw Charlie.

He was standing in his torn pajamas, face turned upward, hands raised, shouting with all his might. His eyes were shut tight. His face was streaked with dirt and tears. His pajama jacket hung in shreds about his scratched chest.

16 He opened his eyes and as he saw Sara a strange expression came over his face, an expression of wonder and joy and disbelief, and Sara knew that if she lived to be a hundred no one would ever look at her quite that way again.

She paused, looked down at him, and then, sliding on the seat of her pants, went down the bank and took him in her arms.

"Oh, Charlie."

His arms gripped her like steel.

"Oh, Charlie."

She could feel his fingers digging into her back as he clutched her shirt. "It's all right now, Charlie, I'm here and we're going home." His face was buried in her shirt and she patted his head, said again, "It's all right now. Everything's fine."

17 She held him against her for a moment and now the hot tears were in her eyes and on her cheeks and she didn't even notice.

32

33

Develop Comprehension

RETURN TO PREDICTIONS AND PURPOSES

Review students' predictions and purposes. Were they correct? Did students find out what Sara learned about herself? (Sara learns how important she and Charlie are to each other.)

REVIEW READING STRATEGIES

Discuss how analyzing the characters, setting, plot, and mood helped students to appreciate this story.

PERSONAL RESPONSE

Ask students to write about a time when they thought someone or something was lost and they realized how important that person or thing was to them.

Quick Check   **Can students analyze character, setting, and plot?**

During **Small Group Instruction**

If No → **Approaching Level**   Leveled Reader Lesson, p. 39P

If Yes → **On Level**   Options, pp. 39Q–39R

Beyond Level   Options, pp. 39S–39T

Media Literacy

Using the Media to Locate a Missing Pet

Explain   In *The Summer of the Swans*, a young boy named Charlie is missing. Today many people use the media to find a missing person or pet.

Discuss   Talk about the different kinds of media that the townspeople might have used to help find Charlie. For example, they might have created signs with Charlie's name and picture, posted his photograph on an Internet Web site, or given information about him to a local radio program. Ask students to describe the strengths and weaknesses of each medium when used to locate a missing person.

Apply   Have students apply what they know to come up with a media plan for finding a lost pet.

Author

Have students read the biography of the author.

DISCUSS

Ask students:

- What can you tell about Betsy Byars after reading her biography?

- Why does the author think of her works as "scrapbooks"? Why do you think she chose to describe them this way?

WRITE ABOUT IT

Remind students that the day Charlie got lost was the longest of Sara's life. Explore why that seemed like the longest day to Sara, and discuss other reasons a particular day might seem long to someone. Then have each student write about the day that seemed to be the longest of his or her life.

Author's Purpose

Remind students that an author may have more than one purpose for writing. Discuss how Byars both informs her audience about people with disabilities through her portrayal of Charlie and entertains them by creating a suspenseful story about the search for a missing person. Determining the author's purpose can help readers better evaluate their material.

Technology

Tell students they can find more information about Betsy Byars at www.macmillanmh.com

MEET THE AUTHOR

Betsy Byars's first book was rejected eleven times! But she kept reading (a book a day) and writing, and now she has many published books. *The Summer of the Swans* won the Newbery Medal, a distinguished honor. All of Byars's stories come from her life. She calls them scrapbooks because they bring back memories from her past. When Betsy is not reading or writing, she is flying in her plane, parked at the end of her airstrip outside her front door!

LOG ON Find out more about Betsy Byars at www.macmillanmh.com

Other books by Betsy Byars: *The Midnight Fox* and *The 18th Emergency*

Author's Purpose

Authors write to inform, persuade, entertain, or explain. In describing the longest day in Sara's life, Byars both entertains and informs. Give examples.

34

Author's Craft
Character Development

Betsy Byars shows how Sara's experiences lead to character development. Explain to students that:

- **Character development** is the growth of a character's personality and complexity as a result of something that occurs in the story.

Discuss how Sara's experiences help her develop, and how her development adds interest to the story. Have students find and discuss other instances of character development in the text and how they contribute depth to the story.

Use the vocabulary words below to complete the sentences.

intersection	engulf	abruptly	conscious
anxiety	cascade	procedure	souvenir

1. Marian often had the best ideas, but her _____ about public speaking kept her from running for class president.

2. I would have liked to take a _____ from the archaeological site, but it was strictly forbidden.

3. Though the task was not difficult, I had to be careful to follow the

   _____ exactly.

4. We were startled when the author _____ closed her book and left.

5. The actor was extremely well trained—always _____ of the audience's reaction to his performance.

6. The papers fell in a _____ from the top of the shelf.

7. I was taught to look both ways when crossing an _____.

8. The huge wave was about to _____ the tiny islands in the sea.

Choose two of the vocabulary words in the box above and write a sentence for each.

9. _____

   _____

10. _____

   _____

   _____

Use the vocabulary words below to complete the sentences.

intersection	engulf	abruptly	conscious
anxiety	cascade	procedure	souvenir

1. Marian often had the best ideas, but her _____ about public speaking kept her from running for class president.

2. I would have liked to take a _____ from the archaeological site, but it was strictly forbidden.

3. Though the task was not difficult, I had to be careful to follow the _____ exactly.

4. We were startled when the author _____ closed her book and left.

5. The actor was extremely well trained—always _____ of the audience's reaction to his performance.

6. The papers fell in a _____ from the top of the shelf.

7. I was taught to look both ways when crossing an _____.

8. The huge wave was about to _____ the tiny islands in the sea.

Choose two of the vocabulary words in the box above and write a sentence for each.

9. _____

_____

10. _____

_____

_____

Comprehension Check

Comprehension Check

Summarize

Use your Story Map to summarize *The Summer of the Swans*. Tell about the different emotions that Sara feels while searching for Charlie.

Character
Setting
Problem
Events
Solution

Think and Compare

1. Reread page 32, paragraph 3. How do you think Charlie's reaction to seeing Sara changes how Sara feels about herself? **Story Structure: Character, Setting, Plot**

2. Why does Sara feel **anxiety** when she looks at the forest? Use evidence from the text to support your answer. **Analyze**

3. Reread the flashback section on page 27. If you saw the world like Charlie does, how would you handle being lost? **Evaluate**

4. The setting of the story presents many obstacles for Sara to overcome. If you were to plan a search for Charlie, what would you need in order to overcome these obstacles? **Synthesize**

5. Read "Sam's Summer Search" on pages 18–19. How do friends help in the two situations? **Reading/Writing Across Texts**

35

Strategies for Answering Questions

Author and Me

Model the Author and Me strategy with questions 1 and 5.

The answer to this question is not directly stated in the text, but there may be clues. Connect these text clues with what you know to answer the question.

Question 1: Think Aloud First I'll think about how Sara felt at the beginning of the summer. She says that she has cried over herself a hundred times. Charlie's reaction to Sara will make her realize how important she is to him. That will make her feel better about herself.

Question 5: Think Aloud I have to think about the two different stories. Sam is anxious that Champ is missing, and Sara is anxious that Charlie is missing. The friends in both stories help by searching.

SUMMARIZE

Have students reread and then summarize *The Summer of the Swans* in their own words. Remind students to use the Story Map they completed to help them organize their summaries.

THINK AND COMPARE

Sample answers are given.

1. **Character, Setting, Plot:** Sara feels bad about herself at the beginning of the story. Sara will feel better about herself after finding Charlie because in Charlie's eyes she is perfect. USE AUTHOR AND ME

2. **Analyze:** Sara feels anxious when she looks at the forest because it is enormous. She fears that Charlie could be lost in the forest forever.

3. **Text to Self:** Students may say that they would panic and run away.

4. **Text to World:** Students may say that they would need a large group to search for Charlie, a map of the area, and medical supplies.

FOCUS QUESTION

5. **Text to Text:** Students may say that in both situations friends help Sara and Sam by looking for Charlie and Champ. USE AUTHOR AND ME

Objectives
- Read accurately with good prosody
- Rate: 117–137 WCPM

Materials
- Fluency Transparency 1
- Fluency Solutions Audio CD
- Leveled Practice Books, p. 4

ELL — Access for All

Build Comprehension
Discuss what is happening in the passage to make sure students understand it. Echo-read the passage with students before they read chorally. You may also have students read along with the recording on the Audio CD.

On Level Practice Book O, page 4

As I read, I will pay attention to pauses and stops.

	Lucky sidestepped impatiently once the saddle was
7	cinched tightly. Using the wooden fence as a ladder, Rachel
17	swung into the saddle. She twitched the reins, and Lucky
27	trotted across the pasture. The grass was so tall that it swept
39	Rachel's boots as she rode.
44	Rachel couldn't believe how quickly the summer had
52	passed. School would be starting in another week. Soon,
61	instead of taking afternoon rides in the California hills, she'd
71	be learning French and algebra. Rachel remembered the
79	beginning of the last school year. Just walking by the
89	geometry classroom had filled her with **anxiety.** It was easy
99	now to laugh about how worried she'd been.
107	Luckily, her friend Abra had been in the same geometry
117	class. She'd helped Rachel really understand lines and angles.
126	Yesterday Abra had confessed that she was nervous about
135	taking biology. Rachel hoped she could return the favor and
145	help Abra in biology.
149	Lucky stopped abruptly. Her head rose as she smelled the air.
160	Rachel had learned to pay attention to Lucky's sudden stops.
170	If she didn't, she'd be sure to miss something important. 180

Comprehension Check

1. How did Abra help Rachel in geometry class? **Character, Setting, Plot** Abra helped Rachel understand geometry.
2. What clues indicate that Rachel and Abra might make a good team? **Character, Setting, Plot** Last year Abra helped Rachel understand geometry. This year Rachel will probably help Abra with biology. They work well together.

	Words Read	–	Number of Errors	=	Words Correct Score
First Read		–		=	
Second Read		–		=	

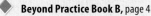
⭐ **Approaching Practice Book A,** page 4
◆ **Beyond Practice Book B,** page 4

35A

Fluency
Repeated Reading: *Intonation/Pausing*

EXPLAIN/MODEL Tell students that part of reading with good prosody, or good expression, is grouping words in meaningful phrases. Explain that the text on **Transparency 1** has been marked with slashes to indicate pauses and stops. A single slash indicates a pause, usually between phrases. A double slash indicates a stop, usually between sentences. Ask students to listen carefully to your intonation and pauses as you read.

Transparency 1

She held the felt side of the slipper against her eyes like a blindfold and stood there,/ feeling the hot sun on her head and the wind wrapping around her legs,/ conscious of the height and the valley sweeping down from her feet.//

"Listen,/ just because you can't hear him doesn't mean anything.// He could be—"//

"Wait a minute."// She lowered the slipper and looked down the valley.// A sudden wind blew dust into her face and she lifted her hand to shield her eyes.//

Fluency Transparency 1 from *The Summer of the Swans*, page 26

Think Aloud As I read, I paid attention to the slash marks. I paused at a single slash between phrases, and I came to a full stop when I saw a double slash at the end of a sentence.

PRACTICE/APPLY Have the class read the entire passage chorally twice. Ask students to copy your intonation and pauses. Then have partners read the passage to each other. For additional practice have students use **Leveled Practice Book** page 4 or Fluency Solutions Audio CD.

Quick Check — Can students read accurately with good prosody?

During **Small Group Instruction**

If No → **Approaching Level** Fluency, p. 39N

If Yes → **On Level** Options, pp. 39Q–39R

Beyond Level Options, pp. 39S–39T

Comprehension

MAINTAIN SKILL
CHARACTER, SETTING, PLOT

EXPLAIN/MODEL

Review with students that:

- Story structure is the way the story events are organized into a **plot.** The plot occurs in a certain time and place, or **setting.** The plot includes a problem or conflict that the **characters** have to solve. Identifying the main problem and how the characters solve it helps the reader better understand the story structure.

- A **flashback** is a return to an event that took place before the story events. The characters and setting in a flashback may be different from those of the main plot.

PRACTICE/APPLY

Divide the class into four groups. Have each discuss the story structure of *The Summer of the Swans* and then answer one of these questions:

- Why would an author include a flashback in a story?

- Suppose the main characters were adults, not children. How might the plot be different?

- What is the one event that drives the plot of *The Summer of the Swans*?

- How does the setting influence the conflict and the climax?

Have each group cite one example of a flashback in the story and compare their answers.

For comprehension practice use Graphic Organizers on pages 40–64 in the **Teacher's Resource Book.**

Objective
- Analyze story structure

Skills Trace

Character, Setting, Plot	
Introduce	U1: 19A–19B
Practice/ Apply	U1: 20–35; Leveled Practice Books, 2–3
Reteach/ Review	U1: 39M–39T, 43A–43B, 44–59, 65M–65T; Leveled Practice Books, 9–10
Assess	Weekly Tests; Unit 1, 3 Tests; Benchmark Tests A, B
Maintain	U1: 35B, 59B, 95B; U2: 171B; U3: 249A–249B, 250–267, 273M–273T; Leveled Practice Books, 76–77

Informational Text:
Social Studies

GENRE: NEWSPAPER ARTICLE

Have students read the bookmark on **Student Book** page 36. Explain that a newspaper article:

- has a headline that states the main idea of the story

- gives information that tells who was involved, what happened, and where it took place

- often will include a photograph and caption

Text Feature: Photographs with Captions

EXPLAIN Point out that photographs and captions can provide information that illustrates, explains, or embellishes the text in a newspaper article.

- A photo and caption can illustrate a text by providing a picture of the people, places, things, or events described.

- A photo and caption can explain a text by helping a reader understand what the text says.

- A photo and caption can embellish a text by adding new information.

APPLY Have students identify the photo and its caption. Discuss how the photo and caption add information that may not be included in the text.

Social Studies

Genre

Newspaper Articles tell about current events and ask who, what, when, where, how, and why.

Text Feature

Photographs with Captions provide further visual information about the subject.

Content Vocabulary

terrain   turbulence

canvass   descending

Caleb and Lisa Bryant, wearing snowshoes, headed up Route 113 in Stow, Maine, yesterday, in search of eight missing high school students and two teachers. **1**

Storm Surprises Maine Students

By Brian MacQuarrie

SOUTH PARIS, Maine—For eight students in the Wilderness Leadership class at Oxford Hills High School, a three-day weekend hike in the White Mountain National Forest sounded like a fun, challenging course requirement.

But when a storm dumped up to 3 feet of snow on western Maine, a rugged learning experience turned into a crash course in winter survival.

**After anxious night,
all found cold, tired**

Reported missing from their scheduled rendezvous in Gilead at 5:30 P.M. Sunday, the eight students and two teachers were not found until 11 A.M. yesterday [Monday], after a pilot spotted the group moving single-file in rugged snow-blanketed **terrain**. The discovery

36

Content Vocabulary

Discuss the meaning and spelling of the four content vocabulary words on **Student Book** page 36: *terrain, canvass, turbulence, descending.*

- **Terrain** means *land*. On what kind of terrain is our school built?

- To **canvass** is to examine carefully. The search party decided to canvass the park area first.

- **Turbulence** is an unstable weather condition. What happens when an airplane flies into turbulence?

- **Descending** is going down. In what direction are you going when you are descending a staircase?

Boston Globe, December 9

followed an unsuccessful ground search by volunteers on snowshoes.

After the group was reported missing Sunday, volunteers hiked 3 miles into the woods to look for the students. The five-hour effort turned up nothing, and the decision was made to wait until yesterday morning to also **canvass** the area by air.

A Maine Warden Service pilot lifted off and spotted the group close to their intended trail at about 11 A.M. Heavy **turbulence** prevented him from **descending** toward the hikers but the group clearly recognized the plane as part of a search team.

"They waved at the plane. They laid down, spread out, and waved," said Mark Latti, a spokesman for the Maine Warden Service. "The pilot then guided a [search] party in to their location."

Connect and Compare

1. Look at the picture and read the caption. What clues do they give you about the subject of the article? **Reading a Caption**

2. What can these hikers do differently next time to be safer? **Analyze**

3. How was the rescue team in this article and the rescue effort in *The Summer of the Swans* the same? In what ways were they different? **Reading/Writing Across Texts**

Social Studies Activity

Research how police officers or firefighters rescue people in trouble. Then write a news article about a police or fire rescue team. Read your article to the class as if you were a TV reporter broadcasting live from the scene.

 Find out more about rescue teams at **www.macmillanmh.com**

37

Social Studies Activity

Have volunteers present their news articles to the class. Encourage students to present their articles as though they were a TV reporter. You may wish to have students rehearse their presentations and keep within a time limit. Discuss with students the kind of information that is important to include in a news article.

 Technology

Students can find more facts about rescue teams at **www.macmillanmh.com**

Read "Storm Surprises Maine Students"

As students read, remind them to apply what they have learned about photos and captions.

1 TEXT FEATURE: PHOTOGRAPHS WITH CAPTIONS

Tested

Who is in the photograph? What are they doing? (Two rescuers are hunting for the missing students.) Does this photo and caption illustrate, explain, or embellish? Explain your answer.

2 GENRE

Newspaper articles tell *who, what, when, where,* and *how.* Write a summary of the information in this article using *who, what, when, where,* and *how.*

Connect and Compare

Tested

SUGGESTED ANSWERS

1. The photo shows who is involved and what the weather is like. The caption tells that the people are searching for missing students and teachers. **PHOTOS AND CAPTIONS**

2. Hikers might check weather reports ahead of time. **ANALYZE**

3. **FOCUS QUESTION** In both stories, people are trying to rescue children. In *The Summer of the Swans,* two of the rescuers are children themselves. In the article, they are all professionals and adults. **READING/ WRITING ACROSS TEXTS**

WRITING
- Personal Narrative
- **Writer's Craft:** A Good Paragraph

WORD STUDY

- Words in Context
- Multiple-Meaning Words
- **Phonics:** Words with Short Vowels
- Vocabulary Building

SPELLING

- Words with Short Vowels

GRAMMAR

- Sentence Types and Fragments

SMALL GROUP OPTIONS
- Differentiated Instruction, pp. 39M–39V

Writing

A Good Paragraph

READ THE STUDENT MODEL

Read the bookmark about the building blocks of a good paragraph. Explain that good writers include a topic sentence that tells the paragraph's main idea. They also include details that help support the topic.

Have students turn to the second paragraph on page 27. Point out the topic sentence and supporting details.

Now have students read Kayla's **personal narrative** and the callouts. Tell students they will write a narrative about a time they achieved a goal. As they write, they will learn to craft a good paragraph.

Writer's Craft

A Good Paragraph

A **good paragraph** includes a topic sentence that tells the reader what the subject of the paragraph will be. Supporting details add information about the topic.

Write About Working with Others

Save Our Parks

by Kayla J.

My topic sentence tells about a problem in my neighborhood.

Our local parks were in bad shape. It was spring, and they needed to be cleaned up and to have new flowers planted. No one was doing anything, so I called the parks department. That's when I learned there was no money to take care of our parks. I talked to my friends, and then we decided to do something about it.

"Do you want to help fix up the park down the street on Saturday?" I asked over and over again. I called at least twenty adults and students in the neighborhood that week. Most people were happy to help.

I used different types of supporting details to make my story interesting.

Saturday morning came, and all my neighbors were at the park ready to work! They were waiting for me to give them directions. I asked, "Will you clean those leaves?" to the people who had rakes. I told others where to plant the flowers.

It was a fantastic day! The park became a true neighborhood place after we worked together.

38

Features of a Personal Narrative

In a personal narrative, the writer shares with readers an experience in his or her own life. The writer usually tells not only what happened but also how he or she felt about it.

- A personal narrative tells a story from the writer's life. It often describes the writer's feelings about the event.

- It tells events in chronological, or time, order.

- It is written in the first person, using words such as *I, me,* and *my.*

- It contains paragraphs with clear topic sentences and supporting details that provide relevant elaboration. The last paragraph ends with a strong concluding sentence.

Your Turn

Write a few paragraphs about a time you worked with others to achieve a goal. Perhaps you worked together to complete a school project or to play a game. Be sure to use a topic sentence and supporting details to organize your writing. Use the Writer's Checklist to evaluate your narrative.

Writer's Checklist

✓ **Ideas and Content:** Did I express the importance of cooperation in my narrative?

✓ **Organization:** Did I form **good paragraphs** by beginning each with a topic sentence and then giving details to back it up?

✓ **Voice:** What about my writing makes it obviously mine? What can I add to make it more interesting?

✓ **Word Choice:** Did I use vivid adjectives and verbs?

✓ **Sentence Fluency:** Did I use a variety of sentence types?

✓ **Conventions:** Did I punctuate each sentence correctly? Did I check my spelling?

39

Transparency 1: **Idea Web**
Transparency 2: **Draft**
Transparency 3: **Revision**

Transparency 1

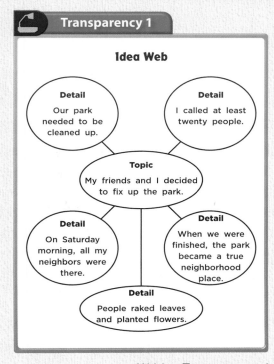

Idea Web

Detail
Our park needed to be cleaned up.

Detail
I called at least twenty people.

Topic
My friends and I decided to fix up the park.

Detail
On Saturday morning, all my neighbors were there.

Detail
When we were finished, the park became a true neighborhood place.

Detail
People raked leaves and planted flowers.

Writing Transparency 1

PREWRITE

Discuss the writing prompt on page 39. Have students list possible topics in their writer's notebooks. Urge students to think about who their readers will be. Tell students to choose the topic they think will interest their readers.

Display **Transparency 1**. Discuss how Kayla began to plan her narrative by writing her chosen topic in the center of the web and including details around it. Have students use an idea web to plan their own stories. Ask them to discuss their ideas with a classmate. See page 39B for **Using a Graphic Organizer to Plan Writing**.

DRAFT

Display **Transparency 2**. Discuss how Kayla used her ideas from her web to create her draft. Before students begin writing, present the lesson **A Good Paragraph** on page 39A. Then have students use their webs to write their stories. Remind them to formulate a topic sentence and include details that give more information.

REVISE

Display **Transparency 3**. Discuss how Kayla's opening fails to grab the attention of readers. Discuss other strategies for improving the draft. Then discuss the revisions. Students can revise their drafts or place them in portfolios to work on later.

If students choose to revise, have them work in pairs to evaluate their drafts using the Writer's Checklist on page 39. Have them **proofread** their writing. For **Publishing Options** see page 39A.

For lessons on **Ideas, Sentence Types and Fragments,** and **Short Vowels** see page 39B and **5 Day Spelling** and **5 Day Grammar** on pages 39G–39J.

Writer's Craft

A Good Paragraph

Publishing Options

Allow students to present their stories orally if they wish. See Speaking and Listening tips below. Tell students to use their best cursive to write their narratives. (See **Teacher's Resource Book** pages 168–173 for cursive models and practice.) Publish students' narratives in a class anthology that includes space after each story for classmate comments.

Speaking and Listening

SPEAKING STRATEGIES

- Use rehearsal techniques to plan and practice your presentation beforehand. Be sure your presentation will fit your time slot.

- Use effective volume, tone, and gestures to keep the audience's attention.

- Analyze your purpose, the audience, and the occasion when planning your presentation.

LISTENING STRATEGIES

- Focus your attention on the speaker and listen.

- Ask for explanation after the presentation to clarify meaning.

- After the presentation, offer personal opinions based on what you heard.

4- and 6-Point Scoring Rubrics

Use the rubrics on pages 127G–127H to score published writing.

Writing Process

For a complete lesson, see Unit Writing pages 127A–127H.

39A

EXPLAIN/MODEL

A good paragraph has a main idea. Writers usually state the main idea in a topic sentence. The topic sentence is frequently the first sentence in the paragraph, although sometimes it is the last. The rest of the sentences in a good paragraph provide details that support or expand on the main idea. They give examples of it, help explain it, or elaborate on it. Display **Transparency 4**.

Think Aloud I know that the details in a good paragraph support the main idea. What is the main idea of the details listed here? They all tell about a winter coat drive. I can write a single sentence that pulls all these details together to tell about the main idea. This is like an umbrella sentence; it covers all the other sentences. This will be my paragraph's topic sentence.

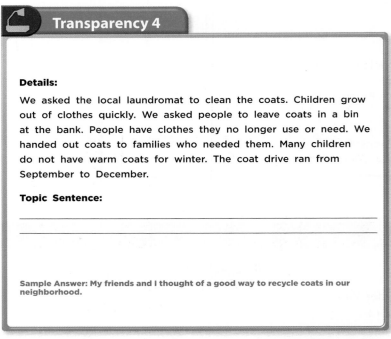

Transparency 4

Details:

We asked the local laundromat to clean the coats. Children grow out of clothes quickly. We asked people to leave coats in a bin at the bank. People have clothes they no longer use or need. We handed out coats to families who needed them. Many children do not have warm coats for winter. The coat drive ran from September to December.

Topic Sentence:

_____

_____

Sample Answer: My friends and I thought of a good way to recycle coats in our neighborhood.

Writing Transparency 4

PRACTICE/APPLY

Help students formulate a topic sentence based on the details listed. Then have students work with partners to write a paragraph that begins with the topic sentence and includes all the details in a logical order. Encourage students to add other details, to choose more colorful words, and to combine sentences as needed. Also challenge student pairs to identify the topic sentence and supporting details in a paragraph from a story they have read recently.

As students write their narratives, remind them to use topic sentences and supporting details to build good paragraphs.

Writer's Toolbox

Writing Trait: Ideas and Content

Explain/Model A personal narrative, like any other story, needs a plot, or story line. A good writer draws on his or her memories of an event or experience to create an engaging narrative. Point out details in the narrative, such as what Kayla thought and said, that make her story come alive.

Practice/Apply As students write, encourage them to include their own ideas, observations, or memories. Tell students that details describing what they thought or felt about what happened will make their stories vivid and appealing.

Using a Graphic Organizer to Plan Writing

Explain/Model A graphic organizer, such as an idea web, can be useful in planning writing. Display **Transparency 1** and discuss how Kayla used an idea web to identify the main idea and details in her narrative.

Practice/Apply Have students use an idea web to plan their narratives. Then have students critique each other's idea webs, suggesting a narrower topic or identifying details that do not support the topic.

Technology

Remind students that they can use the cut-and-paste feature to move words, sentences, or even whole paragraphs. Suggest that students print their work and proofread it. Have them also proofread it on the screen using the spell-check function. Then have them tell which way works best.

Sentence Types and Fragments

Explain/Model Point out that a sentence fragment is a group of words that does not express a complete thought. Give examples of sentence fragments and ask students to correct them. Then introduce the four types of sentences. A declarative sentence is a statement. An imperative sentence gives a command. An interrogative sentence asks a question. An exclamatory sentence expresses excitement.

Practice/Apply Have students identify examples of different sentence types on page 38. Remind students to make sure that the sentences in their narratives are complete. For a complete lesson on sentence types and fragments, see pages 39I–39J.

Mechanics Explain that every sentence begins with a capital letter and ends with a punctuation mark. A statement ends with a period; a question ends with a question mark. An exclamation ends with an exclamation point, and a command ends with either a period or an exclamation point. Have students correct end punctuation as they proofread.

Spelling Words with Short Vowels

Point out the word *bad* in the first sentence on page 38. The letter *a* in *bad* has the short vowel sound /a/. In some words, different vowels may represent this short vowel sound. Remind students to pay attention when they spell words with short vowel sounds. Students can use a print or online dictionary to check spelling in their drafts. For a complete lesson on short vowels, see pages 39G–39H.

Objectives

- Apply knowledge of word meanings and context clues
- Use a dictionary for multiple-meaning words

Materials

- Vocabulary Transparency 1
- Vocabulary Strategy Transparency 2
- Leveled Practice Books, p. 6

Vocabulary

2 **intersection** (p. 24) place where two lines or streets meet or cross

4 **engulf** (p. 24) to swallow up or completely surround

8 **abruptly** (p. 25) suddenly, without warning

6 **conscious** (p. 26) knowing or realizing; aware

3 **anxiety** (p. 26) feeling uneasy or worried

7 **cascade** (p. 26) a small, steep waterfall; anything resembling this

5 **procedure** (p. 27) a particular way of doing something

1 **souvenir** (p. 28) an object that is kept as a reminder of something

ELL

Use Vocabulary Have students use the words in sentence frames. For example: *I feel a lot of anxiety when _____ because _____.*

Review
Vocabulary

Words in Context

EXPLAIN/MODEL

Review the meanings of the vocabulary words. Display **Transparency 1.** Model how to use word meanings and context clues to fill in the missing word in the first sentence.

Think Aloud In the first sentence, I can tell that the missing word is a noun. Only two of the words listed at the top are nouns, and only one of those words seems to make sense here. So, I think the missing word is *intersection*. If Elm Street crosses Oak Street, then I think that an intersection is the place where two streets cross each other.

Transparency 1

conscious intersection anxiety abruptly engulf

At the (1) <u>intersection</u> where Elm Street crossed Oak Street, Sara saw the empty lot where school buses were parked.

The forest seemed big enough to (2) <u>engulf</u> the smaller valley.

Before anyone saw what she was doing, Sara (3) <u>abruptly</u> picked up Charlie's shoe.

From such a height, Sara was (4) <u>conscious</u> of the valley far below.

Sara was twisting the shoe in her hand because of the (5) <u>anxiety</u> she felt about her missing brother.

Vocabulary Transparency 1

PRACTICE/APPLY

Have students use context clues to find the missing words for sentences 2–5 on their papers. Ask students to work with a partner to create sentences with context clues for *cascade, souvenir,* and *procedure.*

Word Spotting Encourage students to use a small notebook to record vocabulary words that they see or hear outside of class. They should note where they heard or saw the word (such as a conversation, the nightly news, or a headline) and how the word was used. At least once a unit, students should discuss their findings in small groups.

STRATEGY
DICTIONARY: MULTIPLE-MEANING WORDS

EXPLAIN/MODEL Tell students that using a dictionary can help them figure out the definition of multiple-meaning words. Explain that:

- Multiple-meaning words have more than one definition.

- If after using context clues the specific definition of a multiple-meaning word is still unclear, good readers use the dictionary to determine the word's meaning.

Read this sentence on **Student Book** page 22: *She leaned against a tree whose leaves were covered with the pale fine dirt which had filtered down when the machines had cut away the hill.* Then model how to figure out the meaning of *filtered* by trying out each meaning on the transparency.

Transparency 2

> #### Multiple-Meaning Words
>
> **filter** *verb.* **1.** to pass a liquid or air through a filter in order to clean out any dirt or other matter: *The water was filtered through sand.* **2.** To take out or separate by filter: *The dirt was filtered from the water.* **3.** To go through very slowly: *The smell of popcorn filtered through the movie theater.*

Vocabulary Strategy Transparency 2

PRACTICE/APPLY

Discuss the different meanings of the word *filtered*. Then have partners create and compare sentences using the different dictionary meanings for the word *conscious*.

> **Quick Check** **Can students identify the correct vocabulary words?**
> **Can students choose the correct meaning of a word?**

During **Small Group Instruction**

If No → **Approaching Level** Vocabulary, pp. 39N–39O

If Yes → **On Level** Options, pp. 39Q–39R

Beyond Level Options, pp. 39S–39T

■ **On Level Practice Book O,** page 6

Multiple-meaning words have more than one definition. When you come across a multiple-meaning word, you need to determine which meaning is being used by looking at its context. These words will have various entries in the dictionary.

Consider the multiple meanings of the word *conscious*.

> **conscious** (kon shəs) *adj.*
> 1. having an awareness of one's self and one's surroundings; *The patient remained conscious after her surgery.*
> 2. fully aware of something; *I was not conscious that time was passing quickly.*
> 3. intentionally meant; *Marianne made a conscious effort not to tease her little brother.*

Each word below has more than one meaning. Use a dictionary to identify two different meanings for each word. Write two sentences—one for each meaning of the word. Possible responses provided.

1. kind
   a. My aunt is gentle and kind to animals.
   b. What kind of food do you want for dinner?

2. produce
   a. What sort of machinery does that factory produce?
   b. The produce at the farmer's market looked delicious.

3. proceeds
   a. I hope he proceeds with caution.
   b. The proceeds raised will be donated to charity.

4. park
   a. The park flowers bloom in spring.
   b. Park the car next to the curb.

★ **Approaching Practice Book A,** page 6
◆ **Beyond Practice Book B,** page 6

Word Study

Objective

- Decode words with short vowels

Materials

- Leveled Practice Books, p. 7
- Teacher's Resource Book, p. 5

ELL · Access for All

Pronunciation Pronouncing the short *u* sound is difficult for many students. Have students say the sound in isolation and in words. Next, say two words and have students identify the word that contains the short *u* sound; for example, *human* and *trouble*. (*trouble*)

Phonics

Decode Words with Short Vowels

EXPLAIN/MODEL When a one-syllable word has a CVC (consonant-vowel-consonant) or CVCC (consonant-vowel-consonant-consonant) pattern, as in *fan* or *track*, the vowel sound is usually short. The short vowel sound /a/, as in *past*, is usually spelled *a*. Sometimes it is spelled *ai*, as in *plaid*. The /e/ sound, as in *fence*, is usually spelled *e*. Sometimes it is spelled *ea* or *ue*, as in *head* and *guest*. The /i/ sound, as in *wing*, is usually spelled *i*. Sometimes it is spelled *y*, as in *myth*. The /o/ sound, as in *slop*, is usually spelled *o*. The /u/ sound, as in *stunt*, is usually spelled *u*. Sometimes it is spelled *ou*, as in *tough*. Write the word *strict* on the board.

Think Aloud This one-syllable word follows the CVCC pattern. I know that a word with this pattern usually has a short vowel sound, so the vowel sound must be /i/. I know how to pronounce the consonant blends at the beginning and end of the word. When I put them all together, I get /strikt/. That is a word I have heard before. I can check my pronunciation in a dictionary.

 PRACTICE/APPLY Write *rough, flock, thread, quest, brink, fund, dense, clash, prank, cleanse, clutch*. Ask volunteers to read each word and identify the short vowel sound and the letters that stand for it. Students can check their work by using a dictionary.

Decode Multisyllabic Words Explain that prefixes are word parts added at the beginning of a root word. Write *un-* and *non-* on the board. These prefixes mean "not." Write *unjust* on the board. Point to and read the prefix *un-* and the root word *just*. Draw a line between them. Read them together. Tell students that *unjust* means "not just" or "not fair." Display *nonstop, unlink, nonstick, unsnap, unlatch*. Work with students to identify the prefix and root word in *nonstop*. Have them decode the remaining words. For more practice, see the decodable passages on page 5 of the **Teacher's Resource Book**.

On Level Practice Book O, page 7

Short vowel sounds are often spelled using just the vowel itself. For example, the letter *u* stands for the /u/ sound in *bug, cut,* and *nun*. The letter *i* stands for the /i/ sound in *big, kick,* and *lid*. Sometimes short vowel sounds have different spellings. For example, the /u/ sound is spelled by the *ou* in *trouble* and the /u/ in *shove*. The short /e/ sound can be spelled by the *ea* in *thread*.

Read the word in the left column. Then circle the words on the right that make the same short vowel sound using a different spelling.

rug bone (done) through (shove) over (double) (money) though

din (rhythm) encyclopedia (pretty) very (myth) women

let fiend (friend) (said) laid haystack (says) (thread) (head)

Choose five of the words above that have the short vowel sound in them. Write a sentence for each word you chose. Underline the word you chose in each sentence. Possible responses provided.

1. My <u>friend</u> can sometimes be a fiend.

2. I love to play <u>Double</u> Dutch when I jump rope.

3. I think my mother is very <u>pretty</u>.

4. I like to stand on my <u>head</u>.

5. My brother <u>said</u> the slide was too high.

 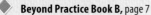
★ **Approaching Practice Book A,** page 7
◆ **Beyond Practice Book B,** page 7

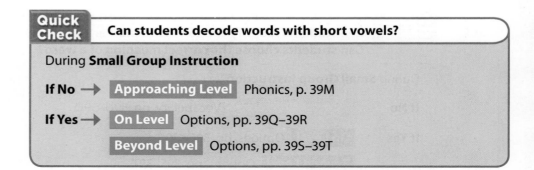

Quick Check **Can students decode words with short vowels?**

During **Small Group Instruction**

If No → **Approaching Level** Phonics, p. 39M

If Yes → **On Level** Options, pp. 39Q–39R

Beyond Level Options, pp. 39S–39T

Vocabulary Building

Oral Language

Expand Vocabulary Ask students to brainstorm aloud other words that they might use if they were writing a story about a rescue team. Write some of these words on the board, and call for volunteers to create sentences that they would like to have in the story.

Apply Vocabulary

Write a Journal Entry Ask students to think about how Sara felt about her day looking for Charlie. What thoughts and feelings would she write in her journal that night? Have students write a journal entry that Sara might have written. Encourage them to use vocabulary words and details from the story.

Vocabulary Building

Multiple-Meaning Words There are several multiple-meaning words in *The Summer of the Swans* including *conscious, cascade,* and *bank*. What other multiple-meaning words can students find in the story? Have them make a list and then use two of their words in sentences that demonstrate different meanings of each word. Remind students to use the dictionary to check spelling and pronunciation.

Vocabulary Review

Vocabulary Game Divide the class into eight teams, one for each vocabulary word for the lesson. Shuffle and distribute the Vocabulary Cards, one to each team. Call out a definition. The team that holds the card that matches the definition should stand. Each student on the team must then correctly use that word in a sentence.

Technology

Vocabulary PuzzleMaker

For additional vocabulary and spelling games go to
www.macmillanmh.com

Spelling Words

gram	swan	dwell
clash	prod	fund
dense	shrunk	text
dread	**scuff**	rank
prank	**clutch**	brink
strict	threat	mock
drill		plaid

Review stuff, batch, sense

Challenge guest, cleanse

Dictation Sentences

1. A raisin weighs about one **gram**.
2. The colors <u>clash</u>.
3. The fog was <u>dense</u>.
4. Do you **dread** giving a speech?
5. Sarah played a <u>prank</u> on Julio.
6. His father was **strict** but kind.
7. When is the fire **drill**?
8. A black <u>swan</u> floated on the pond.
9. Do not <u>prod</u> Jimmy for information.
10. I had <u>shrunk</u> my wool skirt.
11. My new shoe has a **scuff**.
12. **Clutch** your bag tightly in the city.
13. Beetles are a <u>threat</u> to trees.
14. Min's relatives <u>dwell</u> in the city.
15. Give to the relief <u>fund</u>.
16. Reread the <u>text</u> to find the answer.
17. What <u>rank</u> is higher than major?
18. She is on the <u>brink</u> of tears.
19. Some birds <u>mock</u> other birds.
20. The drummers wore <u>plaid</u> kilts.

Review/Challenge Words

1. <u>Stuff</u> the tent in the bag.
2. Tomi baked a <u>batch</u> of cookies.
3. Shaheed has good common <u>sense</u>.
4. The <u>guest</u> left early.
5. <u>Cleanse</u> the wound daily.

Note: Words in **bold** type are from *The Summer of the Swans.*

Display the Spelling Words throughout the week.

Words with Short Vowels

Day 1 Pretest

ASSESS PRIOR KNOWLEDGE

Use the Dictation Sentences. Say the underlined word, read the sentence and repeat the word. Have students write the words on **Spelling Practice Book** page 1, and then correct their own papers. For a modified list, use the first 17 Spelling Words and the Review Words. For a more challenging list, use Spelling Words 3–20 and the Challenge Words.

Have students cut apart the Spelling Word Cards BLM on **Teacher's Resource Book** page 66 and figure out a way to sort them. Have them save the cards for use throughout the week.

For **Leveled Word Lists,** go to **www.macmillanmh.com**

Day 2 Word Sorts

TEACHER AND STUDENT SORTS

Write *gram, dwell, strict, mock,* and *shrunk* on the board as column headings. Underline *a, e, i, o, u.* Point out that each word has a short vowel sound spelled with a single vowel letter followed by one or more consonant letters.

- Use the cards on the Spelling Word Cards BLM. Draw a card, say the word and ask students to identify the vowel sound and match it to the key word.

- Shuffle the remaining cards and have each student draw a card, say the word, and tell where it goes on the sort. Then write the word in that column.

- Invite students to sort their word cards using the same key words.

Spelling Practice Book, pages 1–2

Fold back the paper along the dotted line. Write the words in the blanks as they are read aloud. When you finish the test, unfold the paper. Use the list at the right to correct any spelling mistakes.

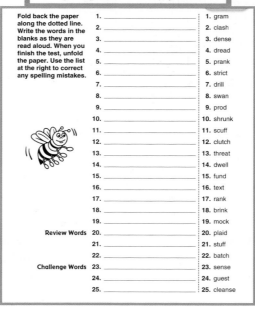

1. _____	1. gram
2. _____	2. clash
3. _____	3. dense
4. _____	4. dread
5. _____	5. prank
6. _____	6. strict
7. _____	7. drill
8. _____	8. swan
9. _____	9. prod
10. _____	10. shrunk
11. _____	11. scuff
12. _____	12. clutch
13. _____	13. threat
14. _____	14. dwell
15. _____	15. fund
16. _____	16. text
17. _____	17. rank
18. _____	18. brink
19. _____	19. mock
Review Words 20. _____	20. plaid
21. _____	21. stuff
22. _____	22. batch
Challenge Words 23. _____	23. sense
24. _____	24. guest
25. _____	25. cleanse

Spelling Practice Book, page 3

gram	prank	prod	threat	rank
clash	strict	shrunk	dwell	brink
dense	drill	scuff	fund	mock
dread	swan	clutch	text	plaid

Write the spelling words with each of the spelling patterns.

Short a spelled:

a
1. gram
2. clash
3. prank
4. rank

ai
5. plaid

Short e spelled:

e
6. dense
7. dwell
8. text

ea
9. dread
10. threat

Short i spelled:

i
11. strict
12. drill
13. brink

Short o spelled:

a
14. swan

o
15. prod
16. mock

Short u spelled:

u
17. shrunk
18. scuff
19. clutch
20. fund

Day 3 Word Meanings

WORD CLUES

Display the word clues below. Have students write the clues and the Spelling Words in their word study notebook.

1. short *a* word that means "a trick" *(prank)*

2. short *e* word that means "thick" *(dense)*

3. short *i* word that means "edge" *(brink)*

4. short *o* word that means "to imitate" *(mock)*

5. short *u* word that means "hold tightly" *(clutch)*

Challenge students to come up with clues for other spelling words, including Review and Challenge words.

Day 4 Review and Proofread

SPELLING REVIEW

Review short vowel sounds. Write *stuff, batch,* and *sense* on the board. Have students identify the letters that spell the short vowel sounds.

Write these sentences on the board. Have students proofread, circle each misspelled word, and write the word correctly.

1. I shruk my plad shirt. *(shrunk; plaid)*

2. I dred driving in dinse traffic. *(dread; dense)*

PARTNER SORT

Have students sort this week's words with a partner. Direct them to write the words in their word study notebook under the following headings: **short a, short e, short i, short o, short u.**

Day 5 Assess and Reteach

POSTTEST

Use the Dictation Sentences on page 39G for the Posttest.

If students have difficulty with any words in the lesson, have them place them on a list called "Spelling Words I Want to Remember" in their word study notebook. Suggest that they write a context sentence for each word. Students should refer to their word lists during later writing activities.

WORD STUDY NOTEBOOK

Challenge students to search for other words with letters that spell short vowels in their reading for the week and write them in their word study notebook under the heading "Other Words with Short Vowels."

Spelling Practice Book, page 4

gram	prank	prod	threat	rank
clash	strict	shrunk	dwell	brink
dense	drill	scuff	fund	mock
dread	swan	clutch	text	plaid

Definitions
Write the spelling word that matches each definition.
1. a unit of measurement ____gram____
2. the edge or verge ____brink____
3. to brood ____dwell____
4. status ____rank____
5. words on a page ____text____
6. a joke or a trick ____prank____

Sentence Completion
Fill in the blank with the appropriate spelling word.
7. All the students in the sixth grade participated in a ____mock____ rescue mission.
8. Our team wore ____plaid____ shirts with khaki pants.
9. We used a ____drill____ to make a wooden raft.
10. We floated over the pond where we saw the ____swan____ yesterday.
11. The ____threat____ of drowning in such shallow water was unlikely.
12. The underbrush was so ____dense____ it was hard to walk through it.

Spelling Practice Book, page 5

Proofreading Activity
There are five spelling mistakes in this story. Circle the misspelled words. Write the words correctly on the lines below.

At midnight, I awoke to find the rain outside dripping in through my bedroom window. I put on my plade bathrobe and walked outside to see if I could stop it. I was surprised to see that the land around my house was covered in dence fog. As I was trying to prodd the window closed, I thought of the thret of being stranded in my house alone for days. This scared me so much that I forgot about the window and ran back into my house, full of dred.

1. ____plaid____
2. ____dense____
3. ____prod____
4. ____threat____
5. ____dread____

Writing Activity
Scary experiences can be fun to read about or write about. Do you like to read about such adventures? Write about a scary adventure. Use five spelling words in your writing.

Students' writing should reflect the topic and include five spelling words.

Spelling Practice Book, page 6

Look at the words in each set below. One word in each set is spelled correctly. Use a pencil to fill in the circle next to the correct word. Before you begin, look at the sample set of words. Sample A has been done for you. Do Sample B by yourself. When you are sure you know what to do, you may go on with the rest of the page.

Sample A:
Ⓐ lump
Ⓑ lumpe
Ⓒ lumpp
Ⓓ luump

Sample B:
Ⓔ tacke
Ⓕ taak
Ⓖ tack
Ⓗ takk

1. Ⓐ gram
Ⓑ gramm
Ⓒ grame
Ⓓ gremm

2. Ⓔ clashe
Ⓕ claash
Ⓖ clash
Ⓗ clahsh

3. Ⓐ denss
Ⓑ dens
Ⓒ dehns
Ⓓ dense

4. Ⓔ dred
Ⓕ dread
Ⓖ dreade
Ⓗ drede

5. Ⓐ prank
Ⓑ pranke
Ⓒ prenk
Ⓓ praank

6. Ⓔ stricte
Ⓕ strockt
Ⓖ strekt
Ⓗ strict

7. Ⓐ dril
Ⓑ drill
Ⓒ drile
Ⓓ drihl

8. Ⓔ swan
Ⓕ swon
Ⓖ swahn
Ⓗ swane

9. Ⓐ prode
Ⓑ prod
Ⓒ prodd
Ⓓ prode

10. Ⓔ shrunke
Ⓕ shruhnk
Ⓖ shrenk
Ⓗ shrunk

11. Ⓐ scuf
Ⓑ scufe
Ⓒ scuff
Ⓓ scof

12. Ⓔ clutch
Ⓕ cluch
Ⓖ cluche
Ⓗ clutche

13. Ⓐ thret
Ⓑ thrat
Ⓒ threate
Ⓓ threat

14. Ⓔ dwel
Ⓕ dwele
Ⓖ dwell
Ⓗ dwal

15. Ⓐ fund
Ⓑ funde
Ⓒ fundd
Ⓓ fuund

16. Ⓔ texte
Ⓕ texet
Ⓖ text
Ⓗ tixt

17. Ⓐ rank
Ⓑ ranke
Ⓒ renke
Ⓓ renk

18. Ⓔ brink
Ⓕ brinke
Ⓖ briink
Ⓗ brinkk

19. Ⓐ moock
Ⓑ mocke
Ⓒ mock
Ⓓ moke

20. Ⓔ plad
Ⓕ plaid
Ⓖ pladd
Ⓗ plade

Sentence Types and Fragments

Daily Language Activities

Use these activites to introduce each day's lesson. Write the day's activities on the board or use **Transparency 1.**

DAY 1

my cat sleeped at my feet last night. She kept me warm? (1: My; 2.: slept; 3: warm.)

DAY 2

when do we get to go to the ice cream shop! Want to go? (1: When; 2: shop? 3: Do you want)

DAY 3

What a wonderful day it has been? can you believe we made it home! (1: been! *or* been. 2: Can 3: home?)

DAY 4

mrs. moore wants us to turn in our stories today. did you finish yours! (1. Mrs. Moore; 2. Did; 3. yours?)

DAY 5

After lunch and recess. We had math class? (1: recess, 2: we 3: class.)

ELL · Access for All

Generate Sentences
Write on the board the word *weekend*. Co-construct sentences for each of the four sentence types using the word *weekend* in each one. Then have students choose another word and repeat the activity in pairs.

Day 1 · Introduce the Concept

INTRODUCE SENTENCE TYPES AND FRAGMENTS

Present the following:

- A **sentence** is a group of words that expresses a complete thought.

- Every sentence should begin with a **capital letter** and end with an **end punctuation mark.**

- A **sentence fragment** is a group of words that does not express a complete thought yet is punctuated like a sentence.

Example:

like dogs. I have (I like dogs. I have no socks on.)

Day 2 · Teach the Concept

REVIEW SENTENCE TYPES AND FRAGMENTS

Review what components are required for complete sentences.

Example:

i can't keep (I can't keep the book.)

INTRODUCE SENTENCE TYPES

Present the following:

- A **declarative sentence** is a statement.

- An **imperative sentence** gives a command.

- An **interrogative sentence** asks a question.

- An **exclamatory sentence** expresses excitement.

 See Grammar Transparency 1 for modeling and guided practice.

 See Grammar Transparency 2 for modeling and guided practice.

Grammar Practice Book, page 1

- A **sentence** is a group of words that expresses a complete thought. Every sentence begins with a capital letter.
- A **sentence fragment** does not express a complete thought.
- A **declarative sentence** makes a statement. It ends with a period.
- An **interrogative sentence** asks a question. It ends with a question mark.

Read each sentence or phrase below. Write *S* beside it if it is a sentence. Write *F* if it is a fragment. Then add words to the fragments so that they express complete thoughts. Possible answers are given.

1. Toni and Beth went hiking in the woods yesterday.
   S

2. Lost their way.
   F; The two girls lost their way.

3. Forgot flashlights and water.
   F; They forgot flashlights and water.

4. Why did their parents allow them to go?
   S

5. Luckily for the girls.
   F; Luckily for the girls, they found some campers who helped them.

Put the correct punctuation mark at the end of each sentence.

6. Name several safety tips for hiking and climbing.
7. Wearing proper clothing and footwear are basic tips.
8. Why is it important to carry water?
9. Penny wants to know more about camping.
10. Why must climbers sign up before beginning their climb?

Grammar Practice Book, page 2

- An **imperative sentence** gives a command or makes a request. It ends with a period.
- An **exclamatory sentence** expresses strong feeling. It ends with an exclamation point.

Read each sentence. Write whether it is *declarative, interrogative, imperative,* or *exclamatory.*

1. What a wonderful camping trip that was!
   exclamatory

2. Think about what Peter said about staying safe on a hike.
   imperative

3. How many times have you climbed in the Shawangunk Mountains?
   interrogative

4. Don't delay getting down the mountain before sunset.
   imperative

5. Richard couldn't decide whether or not to go.
   declarative

6. I'm so excited to be on this hike!
   exclamatory

Revise the first four sentences. Change them to either interrogative or declarative sentences. Possible answers are given.

7. Wasn't that a wonderful camping trip?
8. What did you think about what Peter said about staying safe on a hike?
9. I have climbed in the Shawangunk Mountains three times.
10. My friends don't delay getting down the mountain before sunset.

Day 3 — Review and Practice

REVIEW SENTENCE TYPES AND FRAGMENTS

Review sentence fragments with students.

MECHANICS & USAGE: END PUNCTUATION AND CAPITALIZATION

- Every sentence begins with a capital letter.
- A statement ends with a period.
- A command ends with a period or exclamation point.
- A question ends with a question mark.
- An exclamation ends with an exclamation point.

Day 4 — Review and Proofread

REVIEW SENTENCE TYPES

Ask students to identify the characteristics of each of the types of sentences.

PROOFREAD

Have students correct the fragments in the items below. Invite volunteers to write their corrections on the board.

1. Three hours after the movie. (Three hours after the movie we went home.)

2. Turkey dinner and family fun. (On Thanksgiving we had a turkey dinner and family fun.)

Day 5 — Assess and Reteach

ASSESS

Use the Daily Language Activity and page 5 of the **Grammar Practice Book** for assessment.

RETEACH

Write the following sentences on the board. Have students label each as *Dec., Imp., Int.,* or *Exc.*

1. I went to the lake to see some swans. (Dec.)

2. Can you help me find Charlie? (Int.)

3. Please wish us good luck. (Imp.)

4. I can't believe we found Charlie! (Exc.)

Use page 6 of the **Grammar Practice Book** for additional reteaching.

 See Grammar Transparency 3 for modeling and guided practice.

 See Grammar Transparency 4 for modeling and guided practice.

 See Grammar Transparency 5 for modeling and guided practice.

Grammar Practice Book, page 3

- Capitalize the first word of every sentence.
- End each sentence with the correct punctuation mark—a period, a question mark, or an exclamation point.

Correct the capitalization or punctuation of each sentence. Then identify the sentence type in the space provided.

1. Talk to Tiana about food to bring on the trip?
   .; imperative
2. what a beautiful sight Mohonk Mountain is!
   W; exclamatory
3. Why must he always complain about his aching back!
   ?; interrogative
4. the Shawangunk Mountains are in New York state.
   T; declarative
5. Bring your cell phone on the trip tomorrow?
   .; imperative
6. hiking is great exercise.
   H; declarative
7. How long will we be gone.
   ?; interrogative
8. Don't expect to be home before 8:00 P.M.!
   .; imperative
9. go to sleep early the night before the hike!
   G; exclamatory
10. We will be leaving at 5:00 A.M.?
    .; declarative

Grammar Practice Book, page 4

- Begin a new sentence with a capital letter.
- **Declarative sentences** and **imperative sentences** end with a period.
- **Interrogative sentences** end with a question mark.
- **Exclamatory sentences** end with an exclamation point.

Rewrite the passage, correcting all capitalization and punctuation mistakes.

i am so happy that rescue teams are on alert at all times to come to the aid of stranded or lost hikers i recently attended one of the classes teams hold to help campers think ahead about unexpected situations what if someone in my group became ill or injured what kind of weather conditions might I expect do I have the skills necessary to safely complete the trip I plan to make these questions never occurred to me

I am so happy that rescue teams are on alert at all times to come to the aid of stranded or lost hikers. I recently attended one of the classes teams hold to help campers think ahead about unexpected situations. What if someone in my group became ill or injured? What kind of weather conditions might I expect? Do I have the skills necessary to safely complete the trip I plan to make? These questions never occurred to me!

Grammar Practice Book, pages 5–6

Add to the beginning of each group of words so that it forms a sentence. The information in parentheses will tell you what type of sentence it should be. Be sure to begin each sentence with a capital letter and end it with the correct punctuation mark. **Possible answers are given.**

1. each hiker from the nature group (declarative)
   I met each hiker from the nature group.
2. know the location of the nearest ranger station (interrogative)
   Do you know the location of the nearest ranger station?
3. embarrassing to the group (exclamatory)
   Having Dave's little brother tag along was embarrassing to the group!
4. extra food and clothing (imperative)
   Pack extra food and clothing.
5. good idea to have an extra map (declarative)
   It is always a good idea to have an extra map.
6. a mother bear (exclamatory)
   A mother bear is right behind you!
7. with her buddy Tasha, (declarative)
   With her buddy Tasha, Susan hiked up the mountain.
8. know they were such good friends (interrogative)
   Did you know they were such good friends?
9. can check your supplies (imperative)
   Arrive early so that Mrs. Perez and Ms. Green can check your supplies.
10. never shows up late (declarative)
    Susan never shows up late.

End-of-Week Assessments

Administer the Test

 ### Weekly Reading Assessment,
Passages and questions, pages 5–12

ASSESSED SKILLS

- Character, Setting, Plot
- Vocabulary Words
- Dictionary: Multiple-Meaning Words
- Short Vowels
- Sentence Types and Fragments

  Assessment Tool

Administer the **Weekly Assessment** online or on CD-ROM.

Weekly Assessment, 5–12

 ## Fluency

Assess fluency for one group of students per week. Use the Oral Fluency Record Sheet to track the number of words read correctly. Fluency goal for all students:
117–137 words correct per minute (WCPM).

Approaching Level	Weeks 1, 3, 5
On Level	Weeks 2, 4
Beyond Level	Week 6

Fluency Assessment

 ## Alternative Assessments

- **Leveled Weekly Assessment** for Approaching Level, pages 13–20
- **ELL Assessment,** pages 32–33

ELL Practice and Assessment, 32–33

Diagnose		Prescribe
	IF...	**THEN...**
VOCABULARY WORDS **VOCABULARY STRATEGY** Dictionary: Multiple-Meaning Words Items 1, 2, 3, 4	0–2 items correct . . .	Reteach skills using the **Additional Lessons** page T4 Reteach skills: Log on to **www.macmillanmh.com** Vocabulary PuzzleMaker Evaluate for Intervention.
COMPREHENSION **Skill:** Character, Setting, Plot Items 5, 6, 7, 8	0–2 items correct . . .	Reteach skills using the **Additional Lessons** page T1 Evaluate for Intervention.
GRAMMAR Sentence Types and Fragments Items 9, 10, 11	0–1 items correct . . .	Reteach skills: **Grammar Practice Book** page 6
SPELLING Short Vowels Items 12, 13, 14	0–1 items correct . . .	Reteach skills: Log on to **www.macmillanmh.com**
FLUENCY	109–116 WCPM 0–108 WCPM	Fluency Solutions Evaluate for Intervention.

READING
Triumphs
AN INTERVENTION PROGRAM

Also Available

To place students in the Intervention Program, use the **Diagnostic Assessment** in the Intervention Teacher's Edition.

The Summer of the Swans

Objective	Decode one-syllable and multisyllabic words that include short vowels in both familiar and unfamiliar text
Materials	• **Student Book** "Sam's Summer Search"

SHORT VOWELS

Model/Guided Practice

■ Write the letters *j, u, m, p* on the board. Segment the sounds: /j//u//m//p/. Then blend the sounds: /jump/. *Say the word with me:* jump. *In* jump, *the letter* u *represents the short* u *sound. In some words, other vowels may represent this short vowel sound.*

■ Repeat the process with *touch. When I say* touch, *I hear the short* u *sound. So I know the letters* ou *represents the short* u *sound in this word.*

■ Ask students to give other examples of words with the short *u* sound.

■ Extend the review to include words with other short vowel sounds: /a/ (*tap, plaid*), /e/ (*den, spread*), /i/ (*mix, gym*), and /o/ (*cost, caught, dawn*).

MULTISYLLABIC WORDS WITH SHORT VOWELS

■ Write the letters *d, e, d, i, c, a, t, e* on the board. Segment the sounds. Then blend the sounds: /ded/ /i/ /kāt/, /ded i kāt/. *Say the word with me:* dedicate. *In* dedicate *the first letter* e *represents a short vowel sound.*

■ Have students work in pairs to practice decoding longer words with short vowel sounds. Provide students with a list of the following words. *Say each word. Draw a line to show where syllables begin and end. Say the syllables that have short vowel sounds. Then sound out the whole word.*

alphabetical	definition	practice
distribute	unsatisfactory	illustrate
vocabulary	habitat	negative
contest	activity	description

■ Check each pair for their progress and accuracy. Provide constructive feedback.

WORD HUNT: SHORT VOWELS IN CONTEXT

■ Review these different spellings of short vowel sounds: *a, ai* (/a/), *e, ue, ea* (/e/), *i, y* (/i/), *o,* (/o/), *u, ou* (/u/).

■ Have students look through "Sam's Summer Search" to find at least two words for each short vowel sound. Then have students explain which letters make the short vowel sound in each word. Have students sort the words according to sound.

Additional Resources

For each skill below, additional lessons are provided. You can use these lessons on consecutive days after teaching the lessons presented during the week.
• Character, Setting, Plot, T1
• Dictionary: Multiple-Meaning Words, T4
• Text Feature: Photographs and Captions, T9

Constructive Feedback

Isolate the error sound and repeat with students. If students say /ā/ instead of /a/ as in *tap*, for instance, point to the letter *a* and say:

Look at the word *tap*. Only a consonant follows the vowel. There is no final *e*. Without a final *e*, the vowel is short.

Repeat as needed with other short vowels.

Decodable Text

To help students build speed and accuracy when reading multisyllabic words, use the additional decodable text on page 5 of the **Teacher's Resource Book**.

Skills Focus ▶ Fluency

Objective Read with increasing prosody and accuracy at a rate of 117–127 WCPM
Materials • index cards • **Approaching Practice Book A,** p. 4

MODEL EXPRESSIVE READING

Model reading the Fluency passage on **Approaching Practice Book A** page 4. Tell students to pay close attention to your pauses and intonation as you read. Then read one sentence at a time and have students echo-read the sentence back, copying your pauses and intonation. Listen carefully to their reading, monitoring for accuracy. Repeat as needed.

REPEATED READING

Have students continue practicing reading the passage aloud as you circulate and provide constructive feedback. During independent reading time, have students work with a partner. Have one student read aloud, and the other repeat each sentence. Students should continue practicing the passage throughout the week.

TIMED READING

At the end of the week, tell students they will do a timed reading of the passage that they have been practicing. Have each student

- place the passage from **Approaching Practice Book A** page 4 facedown
- begin reading the passage aloud when you say "Go"
- stop reading the passage when you say "Stop"

As students read, note any miscues. Stop them after one minute. Help students record and graph the number of words they read correctly.

Skills Focus ▶ Vocabulary

Objective Apply vocabulary word meanings
Materials • Vocabulary Cards • Transparencies 1a and 1b

VOCABULARY WORDS

Display the **Vocabulary Cards** for *intersection, engulf, abruptly, conscious, anxiety, cascade, procedure,* and *souvenir.* Help students locate and read these words in "Sam's Summer Search" on **Transparencies 1a** and **1b**. Review the meaning of each word using the Glossary in the **Student Book**. Have students circle context clues for each vocabulary word on the transparency. Challenge partners to name a synonym or antonym for at least two of the words.

Constructive Feedback

Remind students to pay attention to commas, periods, and other punctuation as they read. Model how punctuation affects pacing and the rise and fall in pitch in several sentences from the passage. Then read the sentences again and have students echo-read, mimicking your pauses and intonation.

⭐ **Approaching Practice Book A,** page 4

As I read, I will pay attention to pauses and stops.

Anderson tried extremely hard to be patient as his father,
10 Walter, double-checked the equipment. He stared out the
18 window at the tips of the pine trees that seemed to scratch
30 the blue sky. It was only October, but already the morning
41 air in Maine had turned crisp and cool. He shivered and
52 yawned **abruptly**, and the sudden movement made his ears pop.
62 Walter gave his son a stern warning look. When Anderson
72 opened his mouth to protest, Walter shook his head. He
82 continued to lay out King's equipment: a working harness,
91 leashes, and a vest that would protect the German shepherd.
101 Then Walter examined his own equipment: hard hat,
109 compass, flashlight with extra batteries, and radios.
116 Anderson knew how important it was for his father to be
127 prepared. The phone might ring at any time. Walter would
137 grab his gear, and he and King would hurry out the door.
149 Someone had to be found or rescued. 156

Comprehension Check

1. Who are the main characters in this story and where is it set? **Character, Setting, Plot** Walter and his son Anderson are the main characters. The story is set in Maine.
2. Why must Walter always be prepared? **Character, Setting, Plot** He works as a rescuer and he never knows when his services will be needed.

	Words Read	–	Number of Errors	=	Words Correct Score
First Read		–		=	
Second Read		–		=	

Small Group

Vocabulary

Review this week's words *(abruptly, anxiety, conscious, intersection, engulf, procedure, souvenir, cascade)*. Brainstorm memory aids for difficult words.

Student Book or Transparencies 1a and 1b

Skills Focus → Vocabulary

Objective   Use a dictionary to understand multiple-meaning words
Materials   • dictionary

DICTIONARY: MULTIPLE-MEANING WORDS

Work with students to break each vocabulary word into syllables. Have them identify any short vowel sounds in each word. Next, have students look up the words in a dictionary and make note of the words that have more than one meaning. Ask students to note pronunciations and parts of speech. As a group, brainstorm other multiple-meaning words students know and create silly sentences containing different meanings of the same word.

Skills Focus → Comprehension

Objective   Analyze character, setting, and plot
Materials   • **Student Book** "Sam's Summer Search"   • **Transparencies 1a and 1b**

STRATEGY
ANALYZE STORY STRUCTURE

Review with students that analyzing story structure is recognizing how a story is organized.

SKILL
CHARACTER, SETTING, PLOT

Explain/Model

- The characters are the people whom the story is about.

- The setting is the time and place in which the story's events occur.

- The plot is the series of events that happen in the story.

Display **Transparencies 1a** and **1b**. Reread the first two paragraphs of "Sam's Summer Search." Model analyzing what readers learn about the characters and plot of the story from these paragraphs.

Think Aloud Already I can tell a lot about this story. From the title and the first two paragraphs, I know that Sam is the main character, and his mother is also a character. They are both worried. I know the plot will be about his search for his missing dog, Champ.

Practice/Apply

Reread the rest of "Sam's Summer Search" with students. Have students underline key phrases that describe Sam. Discuss events in the story and its setting.

Leveled Reader Lesson

Objective Read to apply strategies and skills

Materials
- **Leveled Reader** *The Lost Cave*
- **Student Book** *The Summer of the Swans* • chart paper

Leveled Reader

PREVIEW AND PREDICT

Have the students read the title and preview the first chapter. Ask them to make predictions and note questions about the characters and the plot.

VOCABULARY WORDS

Before reading, review the vocabulary words as necessary. As you read together, discuss how each word is used in context.

STRATEGY
ANALYZE STORY STRUCTURE

Remind students to pay attention to the setting and the characters. Point out that the characters' actions in the setting will affect the plot. Invite students to create a Story Map on chart paper.

SKILL
CHARACTER, SETTING AND PLOT

Remind students that recognizing how the story is organized can help them understand the plot. Begin reading the story aloud.

Think Aloud In the first chapter, I learn that Anderson is the son of Walter, a dog handler who conducts search-and-rescue missions. Anderson thinks he knows a lot about search and rescue. I think Anderson's belief in his own abilities is going to be an important part of the story. I need to remember this information.

READ AND RESPOND

Students should read orally to the end of Chapter 2. Have them discuss Anderson's actions and encourage students to voice their personal responses. Students should read the rest of the book independently and complete the Story Map.

MAKE CONNECTIONS ACROSS TEXTS

Have the group summarize and discuss *The Summer of the Swans* and *The Lost Cave*. Invite students to compare and contrast the main characters and plots.

- Which character would you rather have as a friend, Sara or Anderson?
- If the characters switched places, how do you think Anderson would have dealt with the hunt for Charlie?

ELL
Access for All

Time-Order Words Explain that when writing stories, authors often use time words, such as *first, then, next,* and *finally,* to help the reader understand when each action happens in the story. Write the words *first, then, next,* and *finally* on the board. Then co-construct a story, using each of the words.

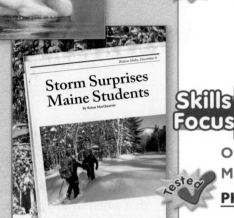

Student Book

Storm Surprises Maine Students

Student Book

Skills Focus ▶ Vocabulary

Tested ✓

Objective	Apply vocabulary words and determine the appropriate meaning of a multiple-meaning word
Materials	• **Vocabulary Cards** • **Student Book** *The Summer of the Swans*

VOCABULARY WORDS

Hold up a **Vocabulary Card**. If a volunteer gives the correct definition, he or she gets a point. If the definition is incorrect, use the same vocabulary card until someone provides the correct definition.

Tested ✓

DICTIONARY: MULTIPLE-MEANING WORDS

Ask students to look in the dictionary for vocabulary and other unfamiliar words from *The Summer of the Swans* that might have more than one meaning. Have them check pronunciations and parts of speech.

Skills Focus ▶ Text Features

Tested ✓

Objective	Use photos and create captions for text
Materials	• **Student Book** "Storm Surprises Maine Students" • magazines or newspapers

PHOTOGRAPHS WITH CAPTIONS

Discuss the importance of captions and photos in a newspaper article such as "Storm Surprises Maine Students." Then have students look through magazines or newspapers to point out the most effective photos and captions. Ask if they would change any captions.

Skills Focus ▶ Fluency

On Level Practice Book O, page 4

As I read, I will pay attention to pauses and stops.

	Lucky sidestepped impatiently once the saddle was
7	cinched tightly. Using the wooden fence as a ladder, Rachel
17	swung into the saddle. She twitched the reins, and Lucky
27	trotted across the pasture. The grass was so tall that it swept
39	Rachel's boots as she rode.
44	Rachel couldn't believe how quickly the summer had
52	passed. School would be starting in another week. Soon,
61	instead of taking afternoon rides in the California hills, she'd
71	be learning French and algebra. Rachel remembered the
79	beginning of the last school year. Just walking by the
89	geometry classroom had filled her with **anxiety.** It was easy
99	now to laugh about how worried she'd been.
107	Luckily, her friend Abra had been in the same geometry
117	class. She'd helped Rachel really understand lines and angles.
126	Yesterday Abra had confessed that she was nervous about
135	taking biology. Rachel hoped she could return the favor and
145	help Abra in biology.
149	Lucky stopped abruptly. Her head rose as she smelled the air.
160	Rachel had learned to pay attention to Lucky's sudden stops.
170	If she didn't, she'd be sure to miss something important. 180

Comprehension Check

1. How did Abra help Rachel in geometry class? **Character, Setting, Plot** Abra helped Rachel understand geometry.
2. What clues indicate that Rachel and Abra might make a good team? **Character, Setting, Plot** Last year Abra helped Rachel understand geometry. This year Rachel will probably help Abra with biology. They work well together.

	Words Read	−	Number of Errors	=	Words Correct Score
First Read		−		=	
Second Read		−		=	

Objective	Read accurately with good prosody at a rate of 117–137 WCPM
Materials	• **On Level Practice Book O,** p. 4

REPEATED READING

Model reading the Fluency passage on page 4 of **On Level Practice Book O**. Work with students to begin marking up the passage to indicate proper phrasing. Remind them that one slash means "pause" and should come after commas, dashes, and other places where they would naturally pause when reading or speaking. Two slashes mean "stop" and should come after end marks or semicolons. Have students practice reading the passage to each other. Circulate and provide feedback.

Timed Reading At the end of the week, have students do a timed reading to check how many words they read correctly in one minute.

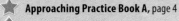

★ **Approaching Practice Book A,** page 4

◆ **Beyond Practice Book B,** page 4

Leveled Reader Lesson

Objective Read to apply strategies and skills
Materials • **Leveled Reader** *Rachel's Choice* • chart paper

PREVIEW AND PREDICT

Show the cover and read the title of the book. Ask what Rachel's choice might be.

STRATEGY
ANALYZE STORY STRUCTURE

Remind students that analyzing story structure is recognizing how a story is organized.

SKILL
CHARACTER , SETTING, AND PLOT

Review with students that characters are the people in a story. The setting is the story's time and place. The plot is made up of the events that happen in the story. Explain that students can fill in information about the characters, setting, and plot in a Story Map on chart paper.

READ AND RESPOND

Read the first chapter. Pause to discuss Rachel's personality. At the end of the first chapter, help students fill in the Story Map.

Have the group finish reading the story. Have students tell how the characters' actions and reactions changed the events of the story. Did their opinion of Rachel change at all as they read?

- How would you describe Rachel's personality?
- How does her personality affect her actions?

VOCABULARY WORDS

Discuss the vocabulary words as they are used in the story. Reteach meanings as necessary. Have students use the vocabulary words to discuss the story.

MAKE CONNECTIONS ACROSS TEXTS

Invite students to summarize and draw connections between *Rachel's Choice* and *The Summer of the Swans*.

- How do the characters react to a missing person or pet?
- Which story did you find more exciting? Why?

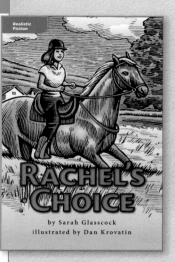

Leveled Reader

RACHEL'S CHOICE
by Sarah Glasscock
illustrated by Dan Krovatin

ELL
Leveled Reader
Go to pages
39U–39V.

Small Group

Student Book

 Beyond Practice Book B, page 4

As I read, I will pay attention to pauses and stops.

	Last summer, the Lopez family had spent its vacation in
10	Florida. Daniel remembered swimming in the Atlantic
17	Ocean, where the water had been the perfect temperature.
26	This year, he was stuck in a desert in the middle of nowhere.
39	What were they going to do all day long besides watch
50	jackrabbits leap through the grass or stare up at the turkey
61	vultures circling in the sky? The birds, with their hunched
71	red heads and black bodies, gave him the creeps. As a matter
83	of fact, the entire Chihuahuan Desert gave Daniel the creeps.
93	When Suzanne asked him to search for more firewood
102	along the trail, Daniel trudged down the path toward the
112	creek bed. A few trees grew along the banks of a small
124	stream of water, which flowed lazily over the rocks. Daniel
134	thought he heard a rustling sound behind the trees. He turned
145	so quickly that he lost his balance and fell over backward.
156	That's great, Daniel thought, whatever's making that sound—
164	a mountain lion or maybe a bear—can attack me. He
175	reached for a rock to use as a weapon. As the rustling grew
188	louder, Daniel's **anxiety** increased. 192

Comprehension Check

1. How do you know that Daniel has an active imagination? **Character, Setting, Plot** Daniel imagines that he will be attacked even though such an event is unlikely.
2. Why does Daniel think his vacation will be unenjoyable? **Plot** Last year Daniel played in the ocean. This year he is in the desert where he thinks there is nothing to do.

	Words Read	–	Number of Errors	=	Words Correct Score
First Read		–		=	
Second Read		–		=	

Skills Focus ▶ Vocabulary

Objective Generate questions and answers using content vocabulary words
Materials • **Student Book** "Storm Surprises Maine Students"

EXTEND VOCABULARY

Help students review the content vocabulary words *terrain, canvass, turbulence,* and *descending* as they are used in "Storm Surprises Maine Students." Have the group collaborate on questions for the content words that provide context clues to their meanings. For example: *Which word describes the motion of a plane that is preparing to land?* (*descending*)

Skills Focus ▶ Text Features

Objective Use photos and create captions for text
Materials • **Student Book** "Storm Surprises Maine Students" • magazines

PHOTOGRAPHS WITH CAPTIONS

Ask students: *How do the photos and captions in "Storm Surprises Maine Students" help add information to the text? What other photos or captions might be effective?*

Have students use photos from a magazine to create one example of a photo and caption that adds information to a text.

Skills Focus ▶ Fluency

Objective Read accurately and with good prosody at a rate of 127–137 WCPM
Materials • **Beyond Practice Book B,** p. 4

REPEATED READING

Model reading the Fluency passage on page 4 of **Beyond Practice Book B**. Then work with students to begin marking up the passage for proper phrasing. Remind them that one slash means "pause" and should come after commas, dashes, and other places where they would naturally pause when reading or speaking. Two slashes mean "stop" and should come after end marks or semicolons. Partners can finish marking the passage on their own and then practice reading it together.

During independent reading time, partners can take turns reading the passage they have marked. Remind students to wait until their partner gets to the next punctuation mark before they correct a mistake. You may wish to have students do a timed reading at the end of the week.

Leveled Reader Lesson

Objective   Read to apply strategies and skills
Materials   • **Leveled Reader** *Surprises in the Desert*

PREVIEW AND PREDICT

Have students preview *Surprises in the Desert*, predict what it is about, and set a purpose for reading.

 VOCABULARY WORDS

Have students pay attention to vocabulary words as they come up. Review definitions as needed.

SKILL

CHARACTER, SETTING, AND PLOT

Ask a volunteer to explain the meaning of the terms *character, setting*, and *plot*. Have students discuss why these elements are important in a story. Tell students that they will read *Surprises in the Desert* together and will discuss information about the characters, setting, and plot.

READ AND RESPOND

Have students read Chapters 1 and 2. Discuss who the characters are and what they are like, the setting, and the main plot events and how they affect the characters.

After students finish reading the story, have them share personal responses.

■ Would you recomment this book to a friend? Why or why not?
■ How did the setting influence the characters?
■ Were the main plot events difficult to follow?

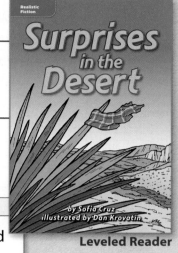

Leveled Reader

Skills Focus ▶ **Self-Selected Reading**

Objective   Read independently to analyze character, setting, and plot
Materials   • Leveled Readers or trade books at students' reading level

READ TO ANALYZE CHARACTER, SETTING, AND PLOT

Invite students to select a fiction book to read independently. For a list of theme-related titles, see the Theme Bibliography on pages T17–T18. As students read, have them take notes about the characters, setting, and plot. Have each student write short paragraphs about each main character. How might the plot change if the characters were different?

Academic Language

Throughout the week the English language learners will need help in building their understanding of the academic language used in daily instruction and assessment instruments. The following strategies will help increase their language proficiency and comprehension of content and instructional words.

Technology

For additional language support and oral vocabulary development, go to **www.macmillanmh.com**

Strategies to Reinforce Academic Language

- **Use Context** Academic language (see chart below) should be explained in the context of the task during Whole Group. Use gestures, expressions, and visuals to support meaning.

- **Use Visuals** Use charts, transparencies, and graphic organizers to explain key labels to help students understand classroom language.

- **Model** Demonstrate the task using academic language in order for students to understand instruction.

Academic Language Used in Whole Group Instruction

Content/Theme Words	Skill/Strategy Words	Writing/Grammar Words
rescue (p. 16)	analyze (p. 19A)	narrative (p. 38)
disaster (p. 16)	character (p. 19A)	organization (p. 39)
terrain (p. 36)	setting (p. 19A)	punctuation (p. 39B)
canvass (p. 36)	plot (p. 19A)	declarative (p. 39I)
turbulence (p. 36)	structure (p. 19A)	imperative (p. 39I)
descending (p. 36)	caption (p. 36)	interrogative (p. 39I)
	article (p. 36)	audience (p. 39A)

Leveled Reader Library

ELL Leveled Reader Lesson

Realistic Fiction

The Rescue Team

by Sarah Glasscock
illustrated by Dan Krovatin

Before Reading

DEVELOP ORAL LANGUAGE

LOG ON

Build Background Lead a discussion with students to prepare them for reading. Say: *Suppose a group of you gets lost when you go hiking. How will you be saved or rescued?* Brainstorm possible rescue scenarios as you guide students toward the story plot.

Tested ✓

Review Vocabulary Write the vocabulary and story support words on the board. Model using them. Say: *When something happens abruptly, it happens all of a sudden.* Point out the word *compass* as an example of a multiple-meaning word.

PREVIEW AND PREDICT

Point to the cover illustration and read the title aloud. Ask: *Who are the characters in this story? What does the word* rescue *tell you?* Have students predict what might happen in the story.

Tested ✓

Set a Purpose for Reading Show the Story Map. Remind students they have used it before. Tell them to do a similar map with details about the characters, setting, and plot.

During Reading

Choose from among the differentiated strategies to support students' reading at all levels of language acquisition.

Beginning	**Intermediate**	**Advanced**
Shared Reading Do a shared reading, pausing to go over key events. Ask questions to help students identify the main characters, problems, complications, and time and place of events. After reading, pair students to complete the map.	**Read Together** Read chapter 2 and review what has happened. Prompt students to describe the characters, their concerns, and interactions. Record responses on a story map. Review and record key events as they take place.	**Independent Reading** Have students read the story. Ask them to stop at the end of each chapter to record story details. Ask them how they felt as they realized the characters might be in danger. Have students complete the map and write a summary.

After Reading

Remind students to use the vocabulary and story words in their whole group activities.

Objective

- **To apply vocabulary and comprehension skills**

Materials

- **ELL Leveled Reader**

5-Day Planner

DAY 1	• Academic Language • Oral Language and Vocabulary Review
DAY 2	• Academic Language • ELL Leveled Reader
DAY 3	• Academic Language • ELL Leveled Reader
DAY 4	• Academic Language • ELL Leveled Reader
DAY 5	• Academic Language • ELL Leveled Reader Literacy Activities

Grade 6 • ELL TEACHER'S GUIDE

Treasures

English Language Learners

Macmillan/McGraw-Hill

ELL Teacher's Guide for students who need additional instruction

Weekly Literature

Week At A Glance

Whole Group

Tested ✓

VOCABULARY
remote, escort, interpreter, vegetation, undergrowth, venomous, withstood, foretold

Tested ✓

Strategy: Use Word Parts/ Compound Words

COMPREHENSION
Strategy: Analyze Story Structure

Tested ✓

Skill: Character, Setting, Plot

WRITING
Personal Narrative

Social Studies

Social Studies Link

History

Small Group Options

Differentiated Instruction for Tested Skills

Tested ✓ Tested Skills for the Week

Main Selection
Genre Historical Fiction

Vocabulary/ Comprehension

Social Studies
Social Studies Link
Genre Nonfiction: Textbook

Read-Aloud Anthology
• Listening Comprehension
• Readers Theater

40A

Leveled Readers

GR Levels S–Y

Genre Realistic Fiction

- **Same Theme**
- **Same Vocabulary**
- **Same Comprehension Skills**

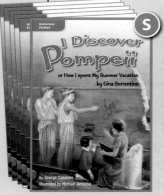 **S**

 **V**

 **Y**

Approaching Level

On Level

Beyond Level

On Level Reader sheltered for English Language Learner

ELL Teacher's Guide also available

English Language Leveled Reader

Also Available
LEVELED READER PROGRAM

CLASSROOM LIBRARY

Genre Expository Nonfiction

Approaching   **On Level**   **Beyond**

Trade books to apply Comprehension Skills

INTERVENTION ANTHOLOGY

- Phonics and Decoding
- Comprehension
- Vocabulary

Also available, *Reading Triumphs*
Intervention Program

LEVELED PRACTICE

Approaching   **On Level**   **Beyond**   **ELL**

HOME-SCHOOL CONNECTION

- Family letters in English and Spanish
- Take-Home Stories

Technology

ONLINE INSTRUCTION
www.macmillanmh.com

AUDIO CD
- Listening Library
- Fluency Solutions

CD-ROM
- Vocabulary PuzzleMaker

Lost City: The Discovery of Machu Picchu, 44–57

Leveled Readers

Integrated ELL Support Every Day

Whole Group

ORAL LANGUAGE
- Listening
- Speaking
- Viewing

WORD STUDY
- Vocabulary
- Phonics/Decoding

READING
- Develop Comprehension

- Fluency

LANGUAGE ARTS
- Writing

- Grammar

- Spelling

ASSESSMENT
- Informal/Formal

Turn the page for
Small Group Lesson Plan

Day 1

Listening/Speaking/Viewing

❓ Focus Question If you could uncover a lost city, what do you think it would be like?

Build Background, 40

Read Aloud: "The Search for Lost Cities," 41

Vocabulary

remote, escort, interpreter, vegetation, undergrowth, venomous, withstood, foretold, 43

Practice Book A-O-B, 8

Strategy: Word Parts/ Compound Words, 42

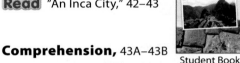

Read "An Inca City," 42–43

Student Book

Comprehension, 43A–43B
Strategy: Story Structure
Skill: Character, Setting, Plot
Practice Book A-O-B, 9

Fluency Partner Reading, 40I
Model Fluency, 41

Writing

Daily Writing Prompt: Write a story about a made-up lost city.

Personal Narrative, 64–65B

Grammar Daily Language Activities, 65I
Subjects and Predicates, 65I
Grammar Practice Book, 7

Spelling Pretest, 65G
Spelling Practice Book, 7–8

Quick Check Vocabulary, 42
Comprehension, 43B

Differentiated Instruction 65M–65V

Day 2

Listening/Speaking

❓ Focus Question Why did Hiram Bingham embark on such a risky adventure?

Vocabulary

Review Vocabulary Words, 44

Phonics/Decoding

Decode Words with Long Vowels, 65E

Practice Book A-O-B, 14

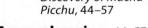

Read Lost City: The Discovery of Machu Picchu, 44–57

Student Book

Comprehension, 44–57
Strategy: Story Structure
Skill: Character, Setting, Plot
Practice Book A-O-B, 10

Fluency Partner Reading, 40I

Writing

Daily Writing Prompt: Write about the lost city of Troy.

Personal Narrative, 64–65B

Grammar Daily Language Activities, 65I
Subjects and Predicates, 65I
Grammar Practice Book, 8

Spelling Long Vowels, 65G
Spelling Practice Book, 9

Quick Check Comprehension, 51, 57
Phonics, 65E

Differentiated Instruction 65M–65V

Skills/Strategies

Vocabulary
Vocabulary Words
Word Parts/
  Compound Words

Comprehension
Strategy: Analyze
  Story Structure
Skill: Character,
  Setting, Plot

Writing
Personal Narrative

Turn the Page for
Small Group Options

Day 3

Listening/Speaking

❓ **Focus Question** Pretend that Maria has written you a similar letter detailing her trip to Machu Picchu. Write her back and tell her about *Lost City*. Talk about a character or an event that she might find interesting.

Summarize, 59

Vocabulary

Review Words in Context, 65C
Strategy: Word Parts, 65D
Practice Book A-O-B, 13

Phonics

Decode Multisyllabic Words, 65E

Read *Lost City: The Discovery of Machu Picchu*, 44–57

Student Book

Comprehension

Comprehension Check, 59
Maintain Skill: Setting, 59B

Fluency Partner Reading, 40I
Repeated Reading, 59A
Practice Book A-O-B, 11

✏ Writing

Daily Writing Prompt: Write a paragraph about why you would be interested in exploring a lost city.

Writer's Craft: Topic Sentence and Details, 65A
Personal Narrative, 64–65B

Grammar Daily Language Activities, 65I
Using Proper Punctuation While Writing a Letter, 65J
Grammar Practice Book, 9

Spelling Long Vowels, 65H
Spelling Practice Book, 10

Quick Check Fluency, 59A

Differentiated Instruction 65M–65V

Day 4

Listening/Speaking/Viewing

❓ **Focus Question** Compare "Empire in the Andes" with *Lost City*. Give examples of two details in *Lost City* that are explained further here.

Media Literacy: Photographs, 56

Expand Vocabulary: A Lost City, 65F

Vocabulary

Content Vocabulary: *maize, quipo, terracing, aqueducts, legacy*, 60
Compound Words, 65F
Apply Vocabulary to Writing, 65F

Read "Empire in the Andes," 60–63

Student Book

Comprehension

Informational Nonfiction, 60
Text Feature: Textbook, 60

Practice Book A-O-B, 12

Fluency Partner Reading, 40I

✏ Writing

Daily Writing Prompt: Write a paragraph stating your hypothesis about how a city becomes lost.

Writing Trait: Word Choice, 65B
Personal Narrative, 64–65B

Grammar Daily Language Activities, 65I
Subjects and Predicates, 65J
Grammar Practice Book, 10

Spelling Long Vowels, 65H
Spelling Practice Book, 11

Quick Check Vocabulary, 65D

Differentiated Instruction 65M–65V

Day 5
Review and Assess

Listening/Speaking/Viewing

❓ **Focus Question** Why do people search for lost things from the past?

Speaking and Listening Strategies, 65A

Vocabulary

Spiral Review of Vocabulary Words, 65F

Read Self-Selected Reading, 40I

Student Book

Comprehension

Connect and Compare, 61

Fluency Partner Reading, 40I
Practice, 59A

✏ Writing

Daily Writing Prompt: Which items in your city do you think would be of interest to future historians?

Personal Narrative, 64–65B

Grammar Daily Language Activities, 65I
Subjects and Predicates, 65J
Grammar Practice Book, 11–12

Spelling Posttest, 65H
Spelling Practice Book, 12

Weekly Assessment, 21–28

Differentiated Instruction 65M–65V

Differentiated Instruction

What do I do in small groups?

Teacher-Led Small Groups

Literacy Workstations

Independent Activities

Focus on Skills

 Skills Focus → Use your **Quick Check** observations to guide additional instruction and practice.

Phonics
Long Vowels

 Vocabulary
Words: escort, foretold, interpreter, remote, undergrowth, vegetation, venomous, withstood
 Strategy: Word Parts: Compound Words

Comprehension
 Strategy: Analyze Story Structure
Skill: Character, Setting, and Plot

Fluency

Suggested Lesson Plan

 Instructional Navigator
Interactive Lesson Planner

	Day 1	Day 2
Approaching Level • **Additional Instruction/Practice** • **Tier 2 Instruction**	Fluency, 65N Vocabulary, 65N Comprehension, 65O	Phonics, 65M Vocabulary, 65O Leveled Reader Lesson, 65P • Vocabulary • Comprehension
On Level • **Practice**	Vocabulary, 65Q Leveled Reader Lesson, 65R • Comprehension **ELL** Leveled Reader, 65U–65V 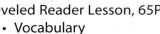	Leveled Reader Lesson, 65R • Comprehension • Vocabulary
Beyond Level • **Extend**	Vocabulary, 65S Leveled Reader Lesson, 65T • Comprehension	Leveled Reader Lesson, 65T • Comprehension • Vocabulary

For intensive intervention see **READING Triumphs**

Small Group Options

Focus on Leveled Readers

Apply skills and strategies while reading appropriate leveled books.

Levels S–Y

  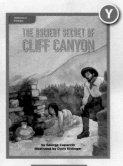

Ⓢ Ⓥ Ⓨ

Approaching — **On Level** — **Beyond**

ELL

Additional Leveled Reader Resources

LOG ON

Leveled Reader Database
Go to **www.macmillanmh.com**

Search by

- Comprehension Skill
- Content Area
- Genre
- Text Feature

- Guided Reading Level
- Reading Recovery Level
- Lexile Score
- Benchmark Level

Subscription also available

Day 3

Phonics, 65M
Fluency, 65N
Vocabulary, 65O
Leveled Reader Lesson, 65P
  • Comprehension

Fluency, 65Q
Vocabulary, 65Q
Leveled Reader Lesson, 65R
  • Comprehension

Fluency, 65S
Vocabulary, 65S
Leveled Reader Lesson, 65T
  • Comprehension

Day 4

Phonics, 65M
Leveled Reader Lesson, 65P
  • Comprehension
ELL Predict, 65P

Text Feature, 65Q
Leveled Reader Lesson, 65R
  • Comprehension

Text Feature, 65S
Leveled Reader Lesson, 65T
  • Comprehension
ELL Character, Setting, and Plot, 65T

Day 5

Fluency, 65N
Leveled Reader Lesson, 65P
  • Make Connections
    Across Texts

Fluency, 65Q
Leveled Reader Lesson, 65R
  • Make Connections
    Across Texts

Fluency, 65S
Self-Selected Reading, 65T

Managing the Class

What do I do with the rest of my class?

Teacher-Led Small Groups

Literacy Workstations

Independent Activities

Class Management Tools

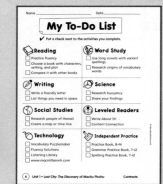

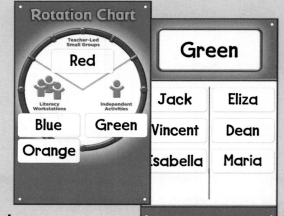

Includes:
• How-To Guides • Rotation Chart • Weekly Contracts

FOLDABLES™

Hands-on activities to reinforce weekly skills

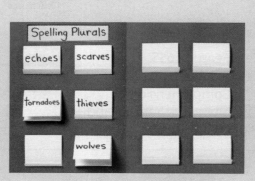

Matchbook Foldable

Word	Synonym	Antonym	Prefix or Suffix
normal	typical	unusual	normally

Folded Foldable

Independent Activities

Leveled Readers

For Repeated Readings and Literacy Activities

Write a Letter

Think about the story from Jason's point of view. What experiences do you think he and his mother had before they were rescued? Write a letter from Jason's point of view that describes one of their experiences.

Research and Give a Report

The story takes place in Maine. Research Maine. Tell about industries, vacation spots, and land forms found there. Then give an oral report about Maine and why people would want to live there.

Approaching

Write a Newspaper Article

Write a newspaper article about the events in the story. Remember that a newspaper article tells who, what, when, where, and how. Be sure to create a headline for your article.

California Plants

Rachel was looking forward to studying biology. Several plants are mentioned in the text. Choose a plant found in California. Then research the plant and report your findings to the class.

On Level

Write a Newspaper Article

Write a newspaper article about the events in the story. Remember that a newspaper article tells who, what, when, where, and how. Be sure to create a headline for your article.

California Plants

Rachel was looking forward to studying biology. Several plants are mentioned in the text. Choose a plant found in California. Then research the plant and report your findings to the class.

ELL

Write a Speech

Suppose Buzz and Leo asked Daniel and Carmen to give a talk to other kids. The topic would be "Don't Get Lost in the Chihuahuan Desert—But If You Do, Don't Do What We Did." Write a speech from Daniel and Carmen's point of view. Be informative and entertaining.

Research the Desert

Research one of the following American deserts: the Chihuahuan, Sonoran, Mojave, or Great Basin. Create a guidebook that gives an overview of the desert and spotlights at least five plants and animals you might encounter there.

Beyond

LEVELED PRACTICE

Skills: Vocabulary (p. 8), Comprehension: Character, Setting, Plot (p. 9), Graphic Organizer (p. 10), Fluency (p. 11), Text Feature: Textbook (p. 12), Vocabulary Strategy: Compound Words (p. 13), Phonics (p. 14)

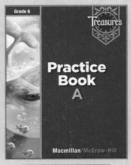

Grade 6 · Treasures

Practice Book A

Macmillan/McGraw-Hill

Approaching

Grade 6 · Treasures

Practice Book O

Macmillan/McGraw-Hill

On Level

Grade 6 · Treasures

Practice Book B

Macmillan/McGraw-Hill

Beyond

Grade 6 · Treasures

ELL Practice and Assessment

Macmillan/McGraw-Hill

ELL

Technology

 LOG ON

ONLINE INSTRUCTION www.macmillanmh.com

- Meet the Author/Illustrator
- Computer Literacy Lessons
- Research and Inquiry Activities

  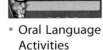

- Oral Language Activities
- Vocabulary and Spelling Activities
- Leveled Reader Database

 LISTENING LIBRARY

Recordings of selections
- Main Selections
- Leveled Readers
- ELL Readers
- Intervention Anthology

 FLUENCY SOLUTIONS

Recorded passages for modeling and practicing fluency

VOCABULARY PUZZLEMAKER

Activities providing multiple exposures to vocabulary, spelling, and high-frequency words including crossword puzzles, word searches, and word jumbles

Turn the page for Literacy Workstations.

Literacy Activities

Collaborative Learning Activities

Reading

Objectives

- Practice fluency with Readers Theater.
- Read a story and create a schematic story element chart.
- Read daily as a leisure activity.

Word Study

Objectives

- Build words with long vowel variant spellings and use them in sentences.
- Look up origins of vocabulary words.

Reading — Fluency

20 Minutes

- Choose a paragraph from the fluency passage on page 11 of your Practice Book.
- Have your partner read a sentence. Then echo, or repeat, the sentence your partner reads.
- Make sure you pronounce proper nouns correctly and pause where the punctuation indicates.
- Look up the pronunciation of any difficult proper nouns.

Extension

Readers' Theater: Practice fluency with the play *Taming the Plastic Monster*.

> **Things you need:**
> - Practice Book
> - *Taming the Plastic Monster*, page 142, Read-Aloud Anthology

Fluency Solutions
Listening Library

3

Word Study — Long Vowels with Variant Spellings

20 Minutes

- Combine word segments in each of the columns below to make words that have long vowel sounds with variant spellings.
- Use the words in sentences.

th	aint
qu	eme
l	oax
c	eague

Extension

- Use these words and others like them to create a word-search puzzle.
- Give your puzzle to a friend to solve.

> **Things you need:**
> - paper
> - pencil

For additional vocabulary and spelling games, go to www.macmillanmh.com

3

Reading — Independent Reading

20 Minutes

- Choose a book to read that contains characters, a setting, and a plot.
- Fill in a character, setting, and plot chart for your story.

Extension

- In your response journal compare the story you read to other stories that you think are similar. Are the themes the same? Are the characters alike?

Schematic Story Element Chart

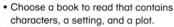

Character	Plot	Setting

> **Things you need:**
> - book
> - paper and pencil
> - response journal

For more books about lost cities, go to the Author/Illustrator section at www.macmillanmh.com

4

Word Study — Vocabulary Words

20 Minutes

- Look up the origin of one of these vocabulary words: *interpreter, venomous, undergrowth, remote, vegetation, escort*.
- Write a paragraph that explains the history of the word.

Extension

- Use the vocabulary words to create a word jumble.
- Exchange jumbles with a classmate.

> **Things you need:**
> - dictionary
> - paper and pencil

For additional vocabulary and spelling games, go to www.macmillanmh.com

Vocabulary PuzzleMaker

4

Literacy Workstations

Writing

Objectives

- Write a friendly letter about a lost community in outer space and fill out an envelope properly.
- Compile a list and distinguish between wants and needs.

Writing — Lost Cities
20 Minutes

- ⏱ Pretend you are in an abandoned city on an unknown planet.
- Write a friendly letter to someone back home on planet Earth.

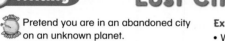

Extension

- Write the address of the Earth person who will receive your letter.
- Don't forget your return address—whatever it is!

Things you need:
- paper
- pencil

3

Writing — Lost in Space
20 Minutes

- You are moving to a new planet. List in one column all the things you will need in your new home in space.
- List in a second column all the things you would like to have in your new home.

Extension

- Draw a color diagram of your new home.
- Label the major items.
- Include its most unusual features.

Things you need:
- paper and pencil
- colored markers

4

Content Literacy

Objectives

- Research the elements of buoyancy and present findings orally.
- Use an encyclopedia to research indigenous people and design a visual for an encyclopedia entry on the topic.

Science — BUOYANCY
20 Minutes

- What gives objects buoyancy?
- Use reference books or the Internet to discover why objects float.
- Write a summary of your findings.

Extension

- Get a basin of water and different objects.
- Place each object in the water, and explain to your classmates what happens.

Things you need:
- reference books
- paper and pencil
- basin of water
- objects

LOG ON Internet Research and Inquiry Activity
Students can find more facts at www.macmillanmh.com

3

Social Studies — The First
20 Minutes

- The first people who inhabit an area are called *indigenous* people.
- Use an encyclopedia or the Internet to find information about the indigenous people of Hawaii.
- Write a short paragraph based on your research.

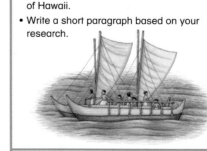

Extension

- Create a map, time line, or other visual to illustrate your paragraph.
- Does your visual make the information clearer?

Things you need:
- reference materials
- paper and pencil
- colored markers

LOG ON Internet Research and Inquiry Activity
Students can find more facts at www.macmillanmh.com

4

40

Prepare

ORAL LANGUAGE
- Build Background
- Read Aloud
- Expand Vocabulary

VOCABULARY
- Teach Words in Context
- Compound Words

COMPREHENSION
- **Strategy:** Analyze Story Structure
- **Skill:** Character, Setting, Plot

SMALL GROUP OPTIONS
- Differentiated Instruction, pp. 65M–65V

Oral Language

Build Background

ACCESS PRIOR KNOWLEDGE

Share information to help students think about this week's theme.

One of the best-known lost cities is Chichén Itzá, located in Mexico. It was the center of Mayan economic and political life from about 445 B.C. to about 1204 A.D.

TALK ABOUT A LOST CITY

Discuss the weekly theme.

Why do you think archaeologists search for lost cities? What do you think they hope to learn?

FOCUS QUESTION Ask a volunteer to read "Talk About It" on **Student Book** page 41 and describe the photo.

What clues in the photograph indicate this might be a lost city?

40

ENGLISH LANGUAGE LEARNERS
Access for All

Beginning Name and Repeat Point to the photo and say, *This is a city. The city is old.* Have students repeat after you. Help them point to, name, and describe things in the picture.

Intermediate Activate Prior Knowledge Have students describe the photo. Explain that a *lost city* means that people used to live there at one time, but then they all left. People forgot it existed. Then someone rediscovered it. Have students discuss "lost cities" they know about.

Advanced Elaborate Complete the Intermediate task. Help students use complex sentences. Model extending their sentences. Then ask: *Why do you think a city becomes "lost"?*

Talk About It

If you could uncover a lost city, what would it be like?

 Find out more about lost cities at **www.macmillanmh.com**

A LOST CITY

41

Picture Prompt

Look at the picture. Write about what you see. You can write a poem, a story, a description, or use any other type of writing you like.

Technology

For an extended lesson plan and Web site activities for **oral language development,** go to **www.macmillanmh.com**

Read Aloud
Read "The Search for Lost Cities"

GENRE: Informational Nonfiction Review features of informational nonfiction:

Read Aloud pages 14–18

- presents facts and ideas about a specific topic
- is about a real person, place, or thing

LISTENING FOR A PURPOSE

Ask students to listen carefully for the reasons cities become "lost." They should be prepared to name one of the lost cities described in the article in the **Read-Aloud Anthology.** Choose from among the teaching suggestions.

Fluency Ask students to listen carefully as you read aloud. Tell students to listen to your phrasing, expression, and tone of voice.

RESPOND TO THE SELECTION

Reread the selection. Ask: If your town were to be discovered two thousand years from now, what things do you think would be most interesting to the archaeologists in the future?

Expand Vocabulary

Have students identify synonyms for the word *lost.* Ask them to think of other words they heard in "The Search for Lost Cities" that relate to this week's theme. Have students write the words in their word study notebooks.

Vocabulary

TEACH WORDS IN CONTEXT

Use the following routine.

Routine

Define: When something is **remote**, it is secluded, or out of the way.
Example: We took a vacation on a remote beach.
Ask: How is being remote different from being close by? COMPARE AND CONTRAST

- An **escort** will provide you with company or protection. The police often serve as an escort for ambulances. When might you need an escort? EXPLANATION

- An **interpreter** translates conversations between people who speak different languages. When I visited France, I used an interpreter. What kind of companies might need an interpreter? EXPLANATION

- **Vegetation** describes the plant life in an area. Arizona's vegetation includes cactus and over 3,000 other species of plants. What kind of vegetation grows in your area? EXAMPLE

- **Undergrowth** is the plant life that covers a forest floor. The undergrowth made our hike through the woods a challenge. Tell what undergrowth would look like. DESCRIPTION

- If something is **venomous**, it can inflict a poisonous wound. Watch out for venomous snakes in the jungle! What is a synonym for *venomous*? SYNONYM

- If something is **withstood**, it is endured or survived. The parachute jumper withstood the impact of landing. Give an example of something that is withstood. EXAMPLE

Access for All

- When an event is **foretold**, a person has been warned of its coming. The newspaper foretold the baseball team's defeat. What is a synonym of *foretold*? SYNONYM

Quick Check
Do students understand word meanings?

During **Small Group Instruction**

If No → **Approaching Level**
Vocabulary, p. 65N

If Yes → **On Level**
Options, pp. 65Q–65R

Beyond Level
Options, pp. 65S–65T

Vocabulary

remote	undergrowth
escort	venomous
interpreter	withstood
vegetation	foretold

Word Parts

STRATEGY SKILL

Compound Words are made up of two or more words. The meanings of the individual words provide clues to the compound word's meaning.

undergrowth = *under* + *growth* = small trees and bushes that grow under large trees

AN INCA CITY
by Miguel Rojas

Dear Li,

I'm sorry I didn't write sooner. I was away for the last month. I went to Peru with my mom and dad. My mom's company sent her there on business. It was great! We flew into Cusco. One weekend we took a train to visit Machu Picchu.

"What is Machu Picchu?" you ask. Well, it is a **remote**—and I mean secluded—Inca city. Actually, it is the remains of that city. Machu Picchu is on top of a mountain peak that overlooks the Urubamba River. It is more than 7,000 feet above sea level!

Greetings from Machu Picchu

42

ELL
Access for All

Reinforce Vocabulary To explain *withstood*, write the following sentences on the board and discuss them: *The building was not destroyed by the tornado. It withstood the force of the tornado.* Point out that *withstood* is the past tense form of *withstand*.

How did we get up that high? We could have hiked the Inca Trail for four days. Instead we decided to ride the train. It runs right along the river. It takes only a few hours. Our **escort** was a man from the area who is descended from the Inca. Not only did he provide information about the area, he also worked as our **interpreter**. Some of the people of Peru speak Quechua, which of course we don't understand.

As we rode the train, our escort pointed out unfamiliar **vegetation** that grows in the rain forest. The **undergrowth**, the plants that grow near the floor of the rain forest, was so thick I could hardly imagine trying to get through it back in 1911. That was when Hiram Bingham, the man who searched for the ruins, started his expedition. We also learned about the animals that inhabit the region. There are some **venomous** snakes that live there.

One bite can kill a person. It must have been quite a journey that Bingham took!

His trip was well worth it, in my opinion. Machu Picchu was so big and beautiful! The stones have **withstood** the test of time. They have been there since the 1400s. There were terraces cut into the sides of the mountain, and green was everywhere. To top it all off, we were in the clouds!

We saw where the people lived, where they worshipped, and where they farmed. The history is fascinating!

The travel brochure **foretold** we would have an amazing adventure, and it certainly didn't lie!

Yours truly,
Maria

Reread for **Comprehension**

Story Structure
Character, Setting, Plot
By analyzing the structure of a story readers can see how the characters, setting, and events are depicted and how they develop.

Use a Character, Setting, Plot Chart to help you note particular people, places, and events as you reread "An Inca City."

Character	Setting	Plot

43

On Level Practice Book O, page 8

Use the clues to complete the crossword.

remote	withstood	venomous	vegetation
undergrowth	interpreter	escort	foretold

Across
4. low vegetation on the floor of a forest
5. a person who accompanies another to give protection
7. secluded
8. resisted the effect of

Down
1. poisonous
2. plants
3. person who translates
6. predicted

⭐ **Approaching Practice Book A,** page 8
◆ **Beyond Practice Book B,** page 8

Vocabulary

STRATEGY
USE WORD PARTS

Compound Words Explain that students can use three basic strategies to help them understand an unfamiliar word.

- First, they can look up the word in a dictionary, if one is handy.

- Second, they can look for context clues, though sometimes they will not find any helpful clues (and may even be misled).

- Third, they can look closely at the word and see if they recognize any parts of the word. This strategy will often help with compound words, for example.

Explain that compound words are words that consist of two or more words joined together as one word, two words, or a hyphenated word. When students do not know the meaning of a compound word, they should think about the meaning of the individual words within the compound.

Point to the word *undergrowth* on **Student Book** page 43. Discuss the two parts of the compound word and how they can help you understand its meaning. (growth that is under something)

Read *"An Inca City"*

As you read "An Inca City," ask students to use context clues and word parts to determine the meaning of each highlighted word. Tell students they will read these words again in *Lost City*.

Reread for Comprehension

STRATEGY
ANALYZE STORY STRUCTURE

Story structure refers to the way a story or narrative is organized. Many stories are organized in chronological sequence, so that the events are told in the order in which they happened. Sometimes a story might be told with two different chronological sequences. Analyzing the way an author organizes a story helps readers understand the characters, setting, and plot.

 Access for All

SKILL
CHARACTER, SETTING, PLOT

 Tested

The main elements in a story are **character, setting,** and **plot.** Characters are the people or animals who appear in a story. Setting is the time and place in which a story happens. Plot is the action of a story. To recognize the plot, identify the problem or conflict the main character faces. Find the turning point or climax of the story, or the point at which the main character begins to find a way to solve the problem. Then identify the events in the story that lead to a solution and resolution of the problem.

Transparency 2a

Transparency 2b

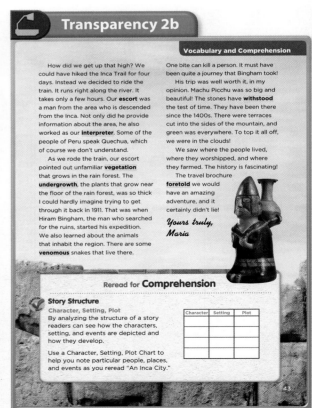

Student Book pages 42–43 available on Comprehension Transparencies 2a and 2b

MODEL

Reread aloud the first two paragraphs of "An Inca City" on **Student Book** page 42.

Think Aloud This letter was written by a kid who went to Peru. She and her family visited an Inca city called Machu Picchu. I want to see what this girl is like, and what happened on her trip.

GUIDED PRACTICE

The setting of a story is where and when it takes place. Good readers try to analyze how the setting can have an effect on both the characters and the plot. Sometimes the date and location are stated outright, but other times the setting is implied. Settings can also change from one location to another within a story.

Begin the Character, Setting, Plot chart with the setting (Cusco) and the first event in the plot. (Maria's family takes a trip to Peru.)

APPLY

Reread the rest of the selection, and have students complete the graphic organizer.

 Transparency 2

Character, Setting, Plot Chart

Character	Setting	Plot
Maria and her parents	Cusco	Maria's family take trip to Peru
Maria, her parents, the escort	train	take train to Machu Picchu
Maria, her parents, the escort	Machu Picchu	see ruins

Graphic Organizer Transparency 2

On Level Practice Book O, page 9

Read the passage. Then answer the questions.

"How does a whole city get lost?" Todd asked his mother.

"It isn't actually lost," she explained. "It's more like people forgot it was there."

Todd was very excited. He and his mother were on their way to visit Machu Picchu. It was the first time Todd and his mother would be going to Peru.

The tour guide explained that Machu Picchu, or at least what was left of it, was discovered by a man named Hiram Bingham. Todd listened intently as the tour guide described the dangers Bingham and his crew faced while trying to reach the city—a city they were not sure even existed!

"At least we don't have to cut our way through the forest to get there," Todd said. His mother agreed.

When the tour guide finished, both Todd and his mother settled into their train seats to take in the view of the rain forest.

Todd tried to imagine the way Bingham had felt as he climbed the mountain. Todd could hardly wait to see the actual city. It was going to be one of the best times of his life, he was sure. When he finally arrived, he was not disappointed.

1. What happens in the story? A boy and his mother travel to visit Machu Picchu.

2. Who is the main character of the story? Todd

3. Where is the story set? On a train going to Machu Picchu, Peru

4. How does Todd feel about seeing Machu Picchu? He is excited to see the city.

5. What does Todd learn on the way? He learns about Hiram Bingham's discovery of Machu Picchu's ruins.

Quick Check **Can students identify the character, setting, and plot?**

During **Small Group Instruction**

If No → **Approaching Level** Comprehension, p. 65O

If Yes → **On Level** Options, pp. 65Q–65R

Beyond Level Options, pp. 65S–65T

 Approaching Practice Book A, page 9

 **Beyond Practice Book B,** page 9

Read

MAIN SELECTION
- *Lost City: The Discovery of Machu Picchu*
- **Skill:** Character, Setting, Plot

PAIRED SELECTION
- "Empire in the Andes"
- **Text Feature:** Textbook

SMALL GROUP OPTIONS
- Differentiated Instruction, pp. 65M–65V

Comprehension

GENRE: HISTORICAL FICTION

Have a student read the definition of Historical Fiction on **Student Book** page 44. Students should decide which people and events are historically accurate and which may not be.

STRATEGY
ANALYZE STORY STRUCTURE

Story structure is the way a story or narrative is organized. Analyzing the way an author organized a story helps readers understand the characters, setting, and plot.

SKILL
CHARACTER, PLOT, AND SETTING

The main elements in a story are **character, setting,** and **plot.** Characters are the people or animals in a story. Setting is the time and place in which a story takes place. The story's events make up its plot.

Comprehension

Genre
Historical Fiction is set in a real time and place in the past. It may include real people and incidents that actually happened along with fictional characters and events.

Story Structure
Character, Setting, Plot
As you read, use your Character, Setting, Plot Chart.

Character	Setting	Plot

Read to Find Out
Why did Hiram Bingham embark on such a risky adventure?

44

Vocabulary

Vocabulary Words Review the tested vocabulary words: **foretold, withstood, remote, interpreter, undergrowth, venomous, escort,** and **vegetation.**

Story Words Students might find these words difficult. Pronounce the words and present the meanings as necessary.

granite (p. 50): a very hard rock used especially for buildings and monuments

fer-de-lance (p. 53): a large, venomous snake found in Central and South America

Quechua (p. 53): an indigenous person of central Peru

Lost City
The Discovery of
Machu Picchu
written and illustrated
by Ted Lewin

In his first journey to South America, Yale professor Hiram Bingham longed to explore the hidden lands that lay beyond the snowcapped peaks of the Andes. Legend had it that the lost city of the Inca, Vilcapampa, lay there. Bingham was determined to discover it. So in 1910 the Yale Peruvian Expedition was organized. Finally, in July 1911, Bingham and his fellow adventurers arrived in Cusco, the first capital city of the Inca. What lay ahead for them was far from what they had expected. And more amazing. Our story begins high in the mountains of Peru . . . .

45

Read Together

If your students need support to read the Main Selection, use the prompts to guide comprehension and model how to complete the graphic organizer.

Read Independently

If your students can read the Main Selection independently, have them read and complete the graphic organizer. Remind students to set and modify purposes when reading and use purposes to set or adjust their reading rate.

If your students need an alternate selection, choose the **Leveled Readers** that match their instructional level.

Technology

Story available on **Listening Library Audio CD**

Preview and Predict

Ask students to read the title, preview the illustrations, and note questions and predictions about what may happen in the story. When and where might this story be taking place?

Set Purposes

FOCUS QUESTION Discuss the "Read to Find Out" and advise students how to find the answer as they read.

Point out the Character, Setting, Plot Chart in the Student Book and on **Leveled Practice Book** page 10. Explain that students will use the chart to keep track of events in the story.

Read *Lost City: The Discovery of Machu Picchu*

Use the questions and Think Alouds for additional instruction to support the comprehension strategy and skill.

On Level Practice Book O, page 10

As you read *Lost City*, fill in the Character, Setting, Plot Chart.

Character	Setting	Plot

How does the information you wrote in this Character, Setting, Plot Chart help you analyze the story structure of *Lost City*?

★ **Approaching Practice Book A,** page 10

◆ **Beyond Practice Book B,** page 10

Develop Comprehension

1 STRATEGY
ANALYZE STORY STRUCTURE

Teacher Think Aloud Sometimes authors give readers a hint of what is to come later in the story. This makes the story more mysterious and makes me want to read on to learn more. Based on the information about Bingham on the previous page, I think that the boy's dream hints at, or foreshadows, the arrival of an explorer. The rest of this page is about Bingham too, so I think he might be the "tall stranger" in the boy's dream. I am not sure what the black box is but I will read on to find out.

2 CHARACTER, SETTING, PLOT

Reread the first two paragraphs on page 46. Let's list the character, setting, and plot in the first row of the Character, Setting, Plot Chart.

Character	Setting	Plot
a boy	in the mountains of Peru	The boy dreams about a tall stranger.

The boy looked out at the cloud-covered peaks all around him. Already his papa was working in the terraced fields. But last night he had dreamed of a tall stranger carrying a small black box. He could not get the dream out of his mind.

Suddenly, the clouds burned off and the mountains were bathed in glorious light. The dream **foretold** of something wonderful, he was sure.

Sixty miles south, in Cusco, Hiram Bingham gazed thoughtfully at the old Incan stone wall. He had come to Peru in search of Vilcapampa, the lost city of the Inca. But right here was the most beautiful stonework he had ever seen—huge stones cut so perfectly that not even a razor blade could be slipped between them.

The Inca had no iron tools to carve them, no wheel or draft animals to move them. The wall had **withstood** time and earthquakes. How had the Inca built them!

It was a mystery.

He walked through the cobbled streets of the old capital. The Spanish had come to this city, conquered the Inca, taken their gold, and built churches over their temples. Suddenly, he stopped. Before him was the famous Temple of the Sun. He placed his hands on the sun-warmed stones so beautifully carved, as if they had grown together.

46

Comprehension

Literary Device: *Foreshadowing*

Explain Sometimes authors use a technique called foreshadowing to provide clues about what might happen next in a story.

Discuss What clues from the boy's dream help you to predict what will happen in the story? Do you think including details from a dream is a good way to foreshadow events in a story? Why or why not? (Students' answers will vary. Some of them may believe that giving the details of a dream is a convenient way to hint at the future.)

Apply Ask students to imagine and describe a dream that foreshadows a fictitious event they would like to have happen.

4

47

Develop Comprehension

3 **STRATEGY**
USE WORD PARTS

Tested

A **compound word** is made up of two words that join to form a new word. Together they often provide hints at the meaning of the new word. What two words make up *earthquake*? What does this word mean? (The words *earth* and *quake* come together to describe the earth shaking.)

4 **USE ILLUSTRATIONS**

How does the illustration on page 47 reflect the events in the story? (The artist shows the moment when Bingham places his hands on the Temple of the Sun. The scale and detail of the buildings reflect the author's description of the ancient city: "the most beautiful stonework he had ever seen," "huge stones," "stones so beautifully carved.")

Develop Comprehension

5 **MAKE INFERENCES**

What do you think the author means when he describes the city as "lost"? (Students should base their responses on the idea that, when a city is abandoned, it becomes "lost," or forgotten, because people eventually forget that it ever existed.)

6 **STRATEGY**
ANALYZE STORY STRUCTURE

Teacher Think Aloud When Bingham arrives in Ollantaytambo, he goes to a cantina and sits for hours asking people questions. I think his actions reveal more information about his character. Tell me what Bingham's actions reveal to you about his character, and why the sudden changes in setting in this part of the story may be important to the plot.

Encourage students to apply the strategy in a Think Aloud.

Student Think Aloud The fact that Bingham sat for hours in the cantina and asked everyone who came in whether they knew of the lost city of Vilcapampa tells me that he is very determined. Even though no one in Ollantaytambo had heard of the lost city, Bingham and his team kept traveling north. This may be a turning point in the plot. The fact that the village of Ollantaytambo was built on the ruins of an ancient city may mean that there are other ancient ruins nearby.

48

---

5 Hidden in the mountains, the lost city would be built of stones like these. Would it hold gold and fabulous riches like the Spanish had found in Cusco?

More than ever he was determined to find that city.

The next day Bingham began his search. He would look for ruins—that might be the key.

He and his party, accompanied by military **escort** Sergeant Carrasco, left by mule train for the sacred valley of the Urubamba River.

6 They came to the sleepy old village of Ollantaytambo, long ago an important city. Its ancient stone terraces stepped up into the clouds.

"Are there any ruins nearby?" Bingham asked. He went door to door. He sat for hours in the cantina. "Are there any ruins near here?" he asked anyone who came in. "Do you know of the lost city of Vilcapampa?" No one knew of it.

7 Traveling north, the adventurers came upon a **remote** and wild canyon. Granite cliffs rose thousands of feet above the roaring rapids of the Urubamba River. In the distance were snowcapped mountains over three miles high. Bingham's determination to find the lost city grew with each turn of the increasingly wild trail.

48

Comprehension

Monitor and Clarify: *Adjust Reading Rate*

Explain Tell students that they may want to try adjusting their reading rate if they are having trouble making sense of information.

Discuss *When is it useful to read more slowly?* (Answers will vary. Students may say that they read more slowly when a text is filled with informational details or scientific facts. This may improve their understanding.) *Why is it helpful to be aware of your reading rate?* (Students can slow down if they are confused.)

Apply Ask students to practice adjusting their reading rate as they continue reading. Have them describe any differences they notice between reading quickly and reading more slowly. Encourage students to adjust their reading rate or determine other appropriate fix-up strategies when reading independently. They should consider their purpose for reading, the type of text and its characteristics, and the difficulty level of the text.

Develop Comprehension

7 SETTING

Where has Bingham traveled since leaving Cusco? What details about each setting does the author provide on page 48? Add each change of setting to your chart. (Bingham travels from Cusco to Ollantaytambo, then heads north into a remote canyon near the Urubamba River. The river has roaring rapids, and in the distance Bingham can see snowcapped mountains.)

Character	Setting	Plot
a boy	in the mountains of Peru	The boy dreams about a tall stranger.
Bingham, Carrasco	Cusco, Ollantay-tambo, Urubamba River Valley	Bingham is in Peru searching for Vilcapampa.

49

STRATEGIES FOR EXTRA SUPPORT

Question 7 SETTING
Help students recognize important descriptive words and explain them using the illustrations when possible: *wild canyon, granite cliffs, roaring rapids, snowcapped mountains, wild trail.* Ask: *Why are these details about the setting important for you to know?*

Vocabulary

What synonyms might the author have used for **remote**? (isolated, lonely, secluded, out-of-the-way)

Develop Comprehension

8 **ADJUST READING RATE**

Good readers recognize that when they read complex text, such as the kind they might find in a social studies or science text, they often need to read more slowly. Why would adjusting your reading rate also be a good idea when you are reading historical fiction? (Answers should include that historical fiction can contain facts and other details that can be easily missed.) Use this strategy as you continue to read the selection.

9 **FORESHADOWING**

Who do you think the stranger with the black box might turn out to be? (Bingham) What evidence can you find in the text to support your answer? (Bingham has his camera with him.)

10 **SETTING AND PLOT**

How does the dangerous setting contribute to the story's suspense? (It gives the reader an idea of Bingham's determination to achieve his goal, despite the risks involved. It also makes the reader wonder whether or not he'll find the city, and if he'll be injured in the process.) What problems might arise because of the setting? (Answers will vary.)

8
9

Meanwhile, high on one of these granite ridges, the boy tried to help his papa on the terraces. But he couldn't shake the dream from his mind. Who was this stranger with the black box? When would he come? What was in the black box? Anxiously, he searched the mountains for a sign.

Far below in the valley, Bingham's party camped on a sandy beach alongside the thundering rapids of the Urubamba. Days had gone by. He was tired and discouraged. No one knew of any ruins.

But now the travelers aroused the curiosity of a local farmer named Arteaga.

"Are there ruins nearby?" Bingham asked when Arteaga ventured into camp.

This time, through the **interpreter**, the farmer said, "Yes. There are very good ruins on top of the mountain called Machu Picchu."

The farmer pointed straight up.

"Can you take us there?" Bingham asked.

10 "No," said Arteaga. "It is a very hard climb and there are many snakes." Bingham offered him coins. Arteaga nodded—he would show them the way.

Arteaga led them down the river trail. Suddenly, he plunged into the jungle. Bingham and the sergeant followed Arteaga **11** through dense **undergrowth** down to the very edge of the river to a flimsy bridge made of slim logs. What was he getting himself into!

Sergeant Carrasco and Arteaga took off their shoes and crossed easily, gripping with their bare feet. Bingham was terrified—he crept **12** across the bridge on hands and knees. One slip and he would be dashed to pieces in the roaring torrent below.

Setting and Plot
How does the dangerous setting contribute to the story's suspense?

50

STRATEGIES FOR EXTRA SUPPORT

Question 10 SETTING AND PLOT
Explain that stories have a sense of adventure when they make you feel excited and frightened at the same time. Point out to students words on page 50 that cause excitement and fear: *very hard climb, many snakes, plunged into the jungle, flimsy bridge.* Discuss how Bingham becomes more and more afraid. How does the setting create a sense of adventure?

Develop Comprehension

11 GENRE: HISTORICAL FICTION

Which parts of the story do you think are real? Which do you think are made up? Why? (The dialogue is probably made up, but the places where Bingham stopped and the way he conducted the expedition are likely real.)

12 CHARACTER

 Based on what you have read so far, what words would you use to describe Bingham? (Answers will vary. Students may consider Bingham brave, resourceful, or ambitious. Bingham puts himself in danger but forges on despite his fears and setbacks. He is determined to be the first to find the lost city.)

 Have students respond to the selection by confirming or revising their predictions and purposes. Encourage students to revise or write additional questions they have about the selection. Remind them that asking questions will help them understand the story better.

 Can students analyze character, setting, and plot? If not, see the Extra Support on this page.

51

Extra Support

Character, Setting, and Plot

If students have difficulty, have them reread the text on pages 48 and 50. Help students identify details in the text and illustrations that give them information about the setting. Ask: *Why is Bingham terrified as he climbs to the top of Machu Picchu? How does the setting influence the way his character feels?* Point out that despite the danger of snakes and a flimsy bridge, Bingham is determined to find his lost city.

Stop here if you wish to read this selection over two days.

Develop Comprehension

13 SUMMARIZE

Review what has happened up to this point in the story. (First, a Peruvian boy has a dream about a tall stranger. Then an explorer named Bingham comes to Peru to find a lost city of the Inca. He travels through the countryside looking for people who can tell him about the lost city. He meets Arteaga, who agrees to guide Bingham and his party to the ruins. Together they cross a dangerous river and climb through a jungle. At the top of a mountain, they meet the boy.) Compare your summary with a partner's. If there are differences, go back and skim and scan to find the appropriate section. Then carefully reread that section and correct your summary based on evidence in the text.

52

Cultural Perspectives

INCA FOODS

The Inca built their diet around three main foods: corn (*sara*), potatoes *(chuno)*, and the seeds of a leafy plant called quinoa. Quinoa seeds have been called a "supergrain" because they are very high in protein, iron, calcium, and many other vitamins and minerals.

Activity Have students use the Internet to research the diet of the Inca and recipes. Have students plan an Inca meal in which the main ingredients are corn and potatoes (and, if available, quinoa). Ask students to compare their diet to the Incan diet. Encourage students to try some of the Incan dishes at home and report on the experience.

13

They climbed the bank into dense jungle. Now the slopes were slippery and the heat terrible. Arteaga had warned them of the fer-de-lance, a very **venomous** snake. Bingham's eyes searched the jungle.

Up and up they climbed. The wide river was now but a silver thread, far below. Arteaga could think of nothing but the fer-de-lance; Sergeant Carrasco thought about his good, sturdy shoes; Bingham thought of nothing but the lost city. They cut their way through tangled thickets. Up and up they climbed.

Had an hour passed? Two? Three? Now they crept on all fours. They slipped and slid. In some places, they held on by their fingertips.

Finally, thirsty and exhausted, they broke through the jungle into sunlight. Above them stood a little Quechua boy beside a stone hut. What could he be doing at the top of this mountain?

"*Ama llulla, ama quella, ama su'a*" (Don't lie, don't be lazy, don't steal), the boy called out in the traditional Quechua greeting.

It was the tall stranger from his dream. Carrying the black box!

The boy's whole family crowded around to greet the exhausted travelers, then brought gourds of cool water and boiled sweet potatoes.

Bingham, still gasping for breath, asked, "Where are the ruins?" **14**

The boy said, "*Amuy, amuy!*" (Come, come!)

Bingham and the sergeant left Arteaga behind and followed at the boy's urging. "*Amuy, amuy!*" he kept saying.

At first they saw only stone terraces like the ones they had seen at Ollantaytambo. They looked as if they had been recently cleared of jungle and the **vegetation** burned off in order to plant crops. **15**

But there were no ruins. Just more jungle beyond. Bingham had climbed this mountain and found—no lost city.

53

Cross-Curricular Connection

ANDEAN MUSIC

People living in the Andes mountains still play many of the same instruments that their ancestors played. The Inca played recorder-like flutes made from llama bones. (Today these flutes are made from wood.) One of the most popular instruments which is still used today is the *panpipe*. A panpipe is made by tying together hollow reeds of different sizes. Each size reed produces a different note—the shorter the reed, the higher the pitch.

Research and Inquiry Have students research panpipes. For fun, you might provide students with glass beverage bottles, each filled with different amounts of water. Allow the classroom "orchestra" to improvise tunes on their bottle-pipes.

Develop Comprehension

14 **CHARACTER, SETTING, PLOT**

Who are the characters at this point in the story, and where are they? Fill in the chart. As they climb, what do each character's thoughts reveal about him? (Arteaga, Carrasco, Bingham and the boy are climbing a hill in dense jungle. Arteaga thinks of the fer-de-lance and Carrasco is glad he has strong boots. They are both more concerned with the reality of the moment. Bingham thinks only of the lost city.)

Character	Setting	Plot
a boy	in the mountains of Peru	The boy dreams about a tall stranger.
Bingham, Carrasco	Cusco, Ollantay-tambo, Urubamba River Valley	Bingham is in Peru searching for Vilcapampa.
Arteaga, Carrasco, Bingham, the boy	the jungle and mountains of Peru	The explorers climb through jungle in search of ruins.

15 **MAKE PREDICTIONS**

Do you think Bingham will find the city? Why or why not? (Students should predict that Bingham will find the ruins based on the story's introduction and clues in the text.)

Vocabulary

What simpler word could the author have used instead of **vegetation**? (plants) The word *vegetation* is derived from the Latin word *vegetare*, which means *to grow*. Can you think of a common English word derived from *vegetare*? (vegetable)

Develop Comprehension

16 **MAKE INFERENCES**

At the top of the staircase, Bingham finds a small vegetable garden. What does this information reveal about the lost city? (Answers may vary, but students should note that the presence of a small vegetable garden indicates that, while the city may be "lost" to most people, the people who live in its vicinity still go there.)

54

"*Amuy, amuy!*" Still, the boy beckoned him into the jungle beyond. Weary and discouraged, Bingham followed. At first all he saw were bamboo thickets and more tangled vines. Then he looked closer. Through the vines, he saw—stones. Inca stones. Then walls, beautiful stone walls! They were covered with mosses. And trees.

"*Jaway, jaway!*" (See, see!) the boy whispered, pointing ahead to a curved stone wall. Bingham pushed his way to it and placed his hands on the fine granite stones. A sun temple. More beautiful even than the one in Cusco.

They came to a grand stone staircase. Where could this lead? What else was here?

"*Jaway, jaway,*" the boy called.

At the top of the staircase was a clearing. A small vegetable garden, and then . . . a temple built of enormous stones. Grander than any Bingham had ever seen. It stole his breath away. **16**

Something was going on here, he could sense it. Something just beyond his eyes. What was it?

He followed the boy to another temple. As magnificent. This one had three windows. But now he looked across the countryside. He looked past the thickets, past the vines. He began to see the outlines of stone streets and stone cottages. He began to see the outlines of a city!

"Here, boy," he said as he opened the black box that he had been carrying, extended the bellows and focused his camera.

17

18

 Character and Plot
Why does Bingham decide to stop and take the picture?

55

STRATEGIES FOR EXTRA SUPPORT

Question 18 CHARACTER AND PLOT
Ask, *What was Bingham's reason for going to Peru? Did he find what he was looking for?* Reread page 55 and ask students to look for clues that identify this as an important moment for Bingham. Say, *Bingham is very happy to find the lost city. This is exactly what he was looking for and he has been through many dangerous situations on his journey.* Ask: *Why does Bingham take the picture?*

Develop Comprehension

17 STRATEGY
ANALYZE STORY STRUCTURE

What happens at this point in the story? Why is this moment important?

Student Think Aloud This is the moment we have been waiting for. The story is built around the question: Will Bingham find the lost city? Here we learn that he has achieved his goal. I will fill in the last row of the chart.

Character	Setting	Plot
a boy	in the mountains of Peru	The boy dreams about a tall stranger.
Bingham, Carrasco	Cusco, Ollantay-tambo, Urubamba River Valley	Bingham is in Peru searching for Vilcapampa.
Arteaga, Carrasco, Bingham, the boy	the jungle and mountains of Peru	The explorers climb through jungle in search of ruins.
Bingham, the boy	Machu Picchu	Bingham finds the lost city.

18 CHARACTER AND PLOT

Why does Bingham decide to stop and take the picture? (He wants to record this historic moment, and the photograph will prove he found the "lost" city.)

Develop Comprehension

19 DRAW CONCLUSIONS

How do you think Bingham feels about the boy? What evidence in the text shows this? (Bingham is grateful that the boy led him to the city. The evidence is that he wants the first picture to be of the boy.)

19 The first picture would be of the boy. The boy who had led him to Vilcapampa, lost city of the Incas.

But about this Bingham was wrong. When the vines were removed and the tales told, he had discovered not Vilcapampa, but a place even more amazing.

He had stumbled on Machu Picchu, a city lost in time, a city lost in the clouds.

56

Media Literacy

Recording Discoveries

Explain At the end of *Lost City,* Bingham uses photographs to record a historic and emotional moment.

Discuss What kind of emotions can photos provoke? How can they contribute information about something? What other kinds of visual media are there? How do visual media shape how we think about other cultures? How do we make decisions about important issues, such as elections?

Apply Ask students to come up with a set of criteria to compare visual media and the effectiveness of each medium. Have them summarize their findings.

57

Develop Comprehension

RETURN TO PREDICTIONS AND PURPOSES

Review students' predictions and purposes. Were students correct about Bingham's discovery? (Students should confirm that Bingham finds the lost city.)

REVIEW READING STRATEGIES

How did analyzing character, setting, and plot help you enjoy this story?

PERSONAL RESPONSE

Think about how Bingham figured out that he had actually found the Lost City of Machu Picchu, and not Vilcapampa. How did he figure this out? Many inventions and discoveries have happened accidentally. Write about a time you tried to solve a problem or create something, only to create something else or solve another problem.

Comprehension

Plot: *Conflict, Climax, and Resolution*

Explain The plot of a story has five main parts. The background, or exposition, introduces the characters and the situation. The conflict is a problem that causes the events in the story to happen. Complication, or rising action, is what happens as the main character tries to overcome the conflict. The climax is the turning point in the plot which resolves the conflict. It is usually the most exciting moment in a story. The falling action is the resolution of the conflict and the events that come after it.

Discuss What was the conflict that caused the events in Lost City to happen? (Bingham is looking for Vilcapampa.)

Apply Tell students to identify the climax and the resolution of the story in writing. Ask them to support their answers with evidence from the text. Also have them identify all five main parts of a story they have read independently.

Quick Check Can students analyze character, setting, and plot?

During **Small Group Instruction**

| If No → | **Approaching Level** Leveled Reader Lesson, p. 65P |

| If Yes → | **On Level** Options, pp. 65Q–65R |
| | **Beyond Level** Options, pp. 65S–65T |

Author and Illustrator

TRAVELING WITH TED LEWIN

Have students read the biography of the author/illustrator.

DISCUSS

Ask students:

- What experiences did Ted Lewin have growing up that may have led him to write about Hiram Bingham? Are the two men similar in any way?

- Why might Ted Lewin have chosen to illustrate the story himself? What information do the illustrations provide that the text does not?

WRITE ABOUT IT

Discuss how the discovery of the lost city of Machu Picchu provided a glimpse into another time and culture. Ask students what would be the most fascinating thing about discovering a lost city. Then have students write about the most interesting thing they have ever discovered.

Author's Purpose

Check that the three things students have described accurately reflect details from the story. For example, students may describe the amazing stonework of the Inca, the poisonous fer-de-lance snake, and Bingham's unexpected discovery of Machu Picchu. Make sure students understand that this selection is historical fiction based on true events.

LOG ON   Technology

Tell students they can find out more about Ted Lewin at www.macmillanmh.com

Traveling with Ted Lewin

Ted Lewin grew up with a lion, an iguana, a chimpanzee, … oh, and a mom, a dad, a sister, and two brothers. He always wanted to be an illustrator and paid for art school by being a professional wrestler. Today he and his wife, Betsy, also an artist, travel the world finding stories. In Machu Picchu, Ted took thousands of pictures, which he used to sketch his illustrations. After that, the painting went very fast. Ted says it was more fun than anything he has ever done before.

Other books illustrated by Ted Lewin:
Peppe the Lamplighter and *Elephant Quest*

PEPPE THE LAMPLIGHTER

ELEPHANT QUEST

Author's Purpose
Ted Lewin's account of the discovery of Machu Picchu is both entertaining and informative. Describe three things that you enjoyed learning from this selection.

LOG ON Find out more about Ted Lewin at **www.macmillanmh.com**

58

Author's Craft
Suspense

Ted Lewin uses suspense in *Lost City* to create a sense of excitement and expectation.

Review with students:

- An author uses suspense, or the building of tension, to hint at what is to come. For example:

  "Something was going on here, he could sense it. Something just beyond his eyes." (p. 55)

- Discuss how suspense creates tension, excitement, and expectation.

Have students identify other passages that help create suspense in the text. How do the selections make them feel as they read?

Comprehension Check

Summarize

Use your Character, Setting, Plot Chart to help you summarize *Lost City: The Discovery of Machu Picchu*. How does Professor Bingham find the lost city?

Character	Setting	Plot

Think and Compare

1. Before he realizes what he has really discovered, what is Professor Bingham searching for? Use evidence from the text to support your answer. **Story Structure: Character, Setting, Plot**

2. Why is the boy's dream at the beginning of the story so important? **Analyze**

3. Think about a time when you discovered something that surprised you. What was it? Where did you find it? Why was it important to you? **Synthesize**

4. Why do you think it would be important to uncover something like these **remote** ruins? Explain your answer. **Evaluate**

5. Read Maria's letter to Li on pages 42–43. Pretend that Maria has written you a similar letter detailing her trip to Machu Picchu. Write her back and tell her about *Lost City*. Talk about a character or an event that she might find interesting. **Reading/Writing Across Texts**

59

Strategies for Answering Questions

On My Own

Model the On My Own strategy with questions 3 and 4.

The answer is not in the selection. Students have to use critical thinking skills to go beyond the text.

Question 3: Think Aloud The story tells how Bingham discovered Machu Picchu. Once I discovered something that surprised me, and it was pretty important to me too. I remember being very excited and eager to tell everyone I knew. I'll write about that.

Question 4: Think Aloud This question asks me what I think, so I know the answer will be my opinion. When I think about it, I realize that ruins are cool because they show you a piece of the past.

Comprehension Check

SUMMARIZE

Have students summarize the events of *Lost City: The Discovery of Machu Picchu* in their own words. Remind students to use the Character, Setting, Plot Chart they completed to help them organize their summaries.

THINK AND COMPARE

Sample answers are given.

1. **Plot:** Professor Hiram Bingham was searching for Vilcapampa, the lost city of the Inca, before realizing that he had discovered the lost city of Machu Picchu.

2. **Analyze:** Answers will vary. Students may say that the dream is important because it tells the boy that it is important to recognize Hiram Bingham and to lead him to the lost city.

3. **Text to Self:** Answers will vary. Students should include details about the excitement of discovery. USE ON MY OWN

4. **Text to World:** Answers will vary. Students should point out that these objects can teach us more about ancient cultures. Knowing about these ancient cultures may in turn teach us more about our own civilization. USE ON MY OWN

FOCUS QUESTION

5. **Text to Text:** Answers will vary. Students will give a brief summary of *Lost City* and explain its significance to Maria.

Objectives

- Read accurately with good prosody, including correct pronunciation and intonation
- Rate: 117–137 WCPM

Materials

- Fluency Transparency 2
- Fluency Solutions Audio CD
- Leveled Practice Books, p. 11

ELL   Access for All

Echo-Read Check that students understand expressions such as *stepped up into the clouds, door to door,* and *for hours.* Have students echo-read the dialogue with you first. You may want students to echo-read and not switch roles.

On Level Practice Book O, page 11

As I read, I will pay attention to the pronunciation of city names, pauses, and intonation.

	Abdullah (Ahb-DUL-lah) loosened his black-and-white
4	head covering. Another grueling day of work was under way.
14	His job was to help remove dirt from ancient tombs, or
25	graves. Abdullah looked around the excavation site and tried
34	to count all of the exposed graves. But he soon gave up.
46	"There are too many of them," he thought. "Besides, if
56	Sheik Hamoudi (Shayk hah-MOOD-ee) catches me counting
61	graves instead of working, he will send me away." Abdullah
71	threw himself into removing dirt, but while he worked,
80	he secretly dreamed of discovering a hidden treasure.
88	Sheik Hamoudi was the foreman on the site. He had
98	worked for the Englishman for a long time. For the past
109	week, the Sheik had been the boss while the Englishman and
120	his wife were away in Baghdad. He treated his workers fairly,
131	and yet he frightened Abdullah when he yelled. Abdullah had
141	grown up in the south of Iraq and had never been more than
154	a few miles from his village. 160

Comprehension Check

1. What words would you use to describe Abdullah? **Character, Setting, Plot** Abdullah is a hard worker. He does not have much experience at his job and is easily frightened.
2. What does Abdullah dream of finding? **Character, Setting, Plot** Abdullah dreams of discovering hidden treasure.

	Words Read	–	Number of Errors	=	Words Correct Score
First Read		–		=	
Second Read		–		=	

 ★ **Approaching Practice Book A,** page 11

◆ **Beyond Practice Book B,** page 11

59A

Fluency
Repeated Reading: *Intonation/Pausing*

EXPLAIN/MODEL Explain that you will model reading accurately and with good prosody, or the proper phrasing, intonation, and stress. Read the passage on **Transparency 2.** Then reread it one sentence at a time. Have students repeat each sentence after you. Have students pay attention to the pronunciation of names.

Transparency 2

They came to the sleepy old village of Ollantaytambo, long ago an important city. Its ancient stone terraces stepped up into the clouds.

"Are there any ruins nearby?" Bingham asked. He went door to door. He sat for hours in the cantina. "Are there any ruins near here?" he asked anyone who came in. "Do you know of the lost city of Vilcapampa?" No one knew of it.

Fluency Transparency 2 from *Lost City,* page 48

Think Aloud As I read each sentence, I will be careful to pronounce the names of people and places correctly. I will also be careful to read with the correct intonation and phrasing, pausing at commas and coming to a full stop at periods. Notice how my voice rises at a question mark.

PRACTICE/APPLY Divide students into two sections. One section will read each sentence, and the other will echo-read it. Sections may then switch roles. Have students list any words they could not pronounce or understand. Have students practice fluency using **Leveled Practice Books** page 11 or Fluency Solutions Audio CD.

Quick Check
Can students read accurately with good prosody, including correct pronunciation and intonation?

During **Small Group Instruction**

If No → **Approaching Level** Fluency, p. 65N

If Yes → **On Level** Options, pp. 65Q–65R

Beyond Level Options, pp. 65S–65T

Comprehension

MAINTAIN SKILL
SETTING

EXPLAIN/MODEL

Review with students:

- The **setting** of a story is when and where the story takes place. Stories may take place in the present, in the past, or in the future.

- The setting can have an important effect on the characters and the plot.

PRACTICE/APPLY

Discuss the story structure of *Lost City*. Ask students:

- Where and when does the story take place? How does the setting influence the story?

- Compare the setting of *Lost City* to your own town. How are they alike or different?

Divide students into groups. Ask students to imagine a mysterious setting of their own. Have a representative from each group tell how the characters in their setting would differ from those in *Lost City*.

For comprehension practice use Graphic Organizers on pages 40–64 in the **Teacher's Resource Book.**

Objective

- Review story structure and analyze plot

Skills Trace

Character, Setting, Plot	
Introduce	U1: 19A–19B
Practice/ Apply	U1:20–35; Leveled Practice Books, 2–3
Reteach/ Review	U1: 39M–39T, 43A–43B, 44–59, 65T; Leveled Practice Books, 9–10
Assess	Weekly Tests; Unit 1, 3 Tests; Benchmark Tests A, B
Maintain	U1: 35B, 59B, 95B; U2: 171B; U3: 249A–249B, 250–267, 273M–273T; Leveled Practice Books, 76–77

Informational Text: Social Studies

GENRE: TEXTBOOK

Have students read the bookmark on **Student Book** page 60. Explain that a social studies textbook:

- focuses on facts about a place and time in history

- may use original sources and documents as well as expository text

- organizes material in sequential order

Text Features: Captions, Labels, Key Words, and Changes in Print

EXPLAIN Point out that textbooks use a variety of labeling strategies to help readers follow complicated material.

- **Captions** explain what is happening in photographs or illustrations.

- **Labels** identify parts of illustrations or diagrams.

- **Key words** are often written in boldface type.

- **Changes in print** may divide sections of text. They show where an original or primary source begins and ends.

APPLY Using a textbook, have students identify captions, labels, key words, and changes in print. Discuss why these text features help clarify complicated material.

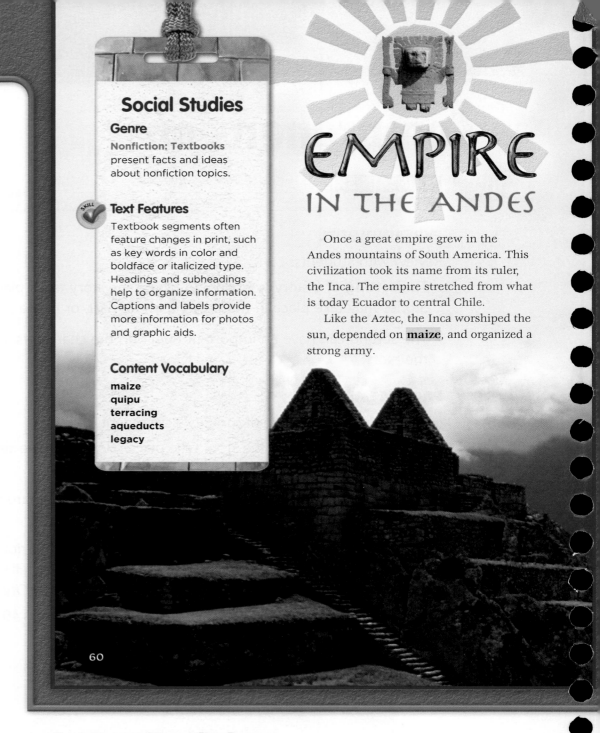

Social Studies

Genre

Nonfiction: Textbooks present facts and ideas about nonfiction topics.

Text Features

Textbook segments often feature changes in print, such as key words in color and boldface or italicized type. Headings and subheadings help to organize information. Captions and labels provide more information for photos and graphic aids.

Content Vocabulary

maize
quipu
terracing
aqueducts
legacy

EMPIRE IN THE ANDES

Once a great empire grew in the Andes mountains of South America. This civilization took its name from its ruler, the Inca. The empire stretched from what is today Ecuador to central Chile.

Like the Aztec, the Inca worshiped the sun, depended on **maize**, and organized a strong army.

60

Content Vocabulary

Review the spelling and meaning of each content vocabulary word on **Student Book** page 60: *maize, terracing, aqueducts, legacy, quipu.*

- What the Indians called **maize**, we call corn. Where can you find maize today?

- A **quipu** was an Incan way of recording information using colorful threads on a cord. What do we use today instead of a quipu?

- **Terracing** is arranging land on a hillside in horizontal layers. Why might terracing allow you to plant more crops?

- **Aqueducts** were aboveground pipe systems for moving water. How would these help farmers?

- Your **legacy** is what you leave behind for others to learn from. What legacy did your ancestors leave for you?

FROM VILLAGE TO EMPIRE

The Inca Empire began around 1200 in Cuzco (KOOS koh), a small village in a fertile mountain valley in what is today Peru. A drought reduced their farmland, so the Inca took over their neighbors' land. During the 1300s, the Inca ruled most of the valley.

In 1438, a ruler called Pachakuti (pah chah KOO tee) Inca extended the Inca borders west to the Pacific Ocean and south to Lake Titicaca high in the central Andes. **1**

SWEAT OF THE SUN

The Inca worked rich gold mines. They called the metal "sweat of the sun" and used it to decorate temples to their sun god. The sun god's temple in Cuzco had a huge sculpture of him decorated with precious stones. There was even a golden "garden" with flowers and birds made of gold.

THE INCA CAPITAL

Cuzco served as the center of government, religion, and trade. The temples and government buildings at the center of Cuzco were constructed of stone blocks. These blocks still fit together so well that it is impossible to put a knife between them. They can also withstand earthquakes.

Beyond the main plaza were the palaces of the emperor and wealthy nobles. The nobles wore special headbands and earrings. One of the Spanish soldiers who visited the city was impressed by Inca wealth and skill. He wrote the following description in the 1500s:

The interior of the temple [of the Sun] was . . . a mine of gold. On the western wall was . . . [the sun god] . . . engraved on a massive plate of gold of enormous [size], thickly powdered with emeralds and special stones . . . The morning sun fell directly upon it at its rising, lighting up the whole apartment.

The ruins of Machu Picchu, an ancient city of the Inca Empire, high in the Andes

61

Informational Text

Read "Empire in the Andes"

Access for All As you read, remind students to apply what they have learned about reading a social studies textbook. Have them identify clues to the meanings of the highlighted words.

1 **TEXT FEATURES: CAPTIONS, LABELS, KEY WORDS, CHANGES IN PRINT**

Tested

How do the subheadings *From Village to Empire, Sweat of the Sun,* and *The Inca Capital* work as labeling strategies to help you organize the information in the article? (Answers may vary, but should include that subheadings are labeling strategies that help you organize complicated material. They are useful when looking for answers to questions, or to identify the main ideas in a selection.)

2 **ADJUST READING RATE**

Why might you want to slow down as you read a social studies textbook? (Some of the concepts, names, and facts may be difficult to understand; you may be tested on what you read.)

ELL

Access for All

Understand Academic Vocabulary Briefly summarize the article. Show how to use the title and headings to predict what the text will be about. Discuss the information in the captions. As you read, pause at times and restate with students what they have learned.

For the vocabulary, use the photos when possible. Explain that *maize* is Spanish for corn. For *aqueducts*, draw bridges to illustrate their meaning. For *legacy*, explain that it can be a gift or idea that people leave after they die: *Martin Luther King left a legacy of equal rights for all.*

Informational Text

3 **TEXT FEATURES: CAPTIONS, LABELS, KEY WORDS, CHANGES IN PRINT**

How do the headings in this article help you as a reader? (They divide the information into manageable pieces; They give the main idea of each section.)

4 **DRAW CONCLUSIONS**

Why might information on the Inca be included in a social studies textbook? (Studying their legacy helps us understand our past.) What can you conclude about the accomplishments of the Inca compared to other ancient cultures that you have studied? (Answers will vary.)

5 **WRITER'S CRAFT: TOPIC SENTENCE AND DETAILS**

Which sentence in this paragraph is the topic sentence? (the first sentence) How can you tell? (It states the main idea of the paragraph. The other sentences provide details about that idea.)

Peruvian quipu for counting and recording facts and events; of Inca workmanship.

TECHNOLOGY: SPEAKING WITH THREAD

The Inca used a special cord called a **quipu** (KEE poo). A quipu was about two feet long and had many threads of different colors hanging from it. For example, white threads stood for silver, yellow stood for gold, and red stood for war. By tying knots in the strings in a particular order, the Inca could send messages and keep records of battles, items traded, and births and deaths in a village.

PUTTING IT TOGETHER

Inca farmers began **terracing** and using fertilizer to increase the crops their land produced. In addition to many roads, Inca engineers built large **aqueducts**.

The Inca Empire controlled much of western South America until it was conquered by the Spanish in 1532. However, the Inca **legacy** remains. Millions of people still speak the Inca language, and many of the songs and poems of the Inca are still recited today.

3 ## A LOST CITY

The Inca built a vast network of highways over 19,000 miles in length. One road climbed into the Andes and ended at the city called Machu Picchu (MAHCH oo PEEK choo). This town was forgotten until an American explorer named Hiram Bingham came across it in 1911.

No one is sure why Machu Picchu was built or why it was abandoned. Machu Picchu is just one of many Inca mysteries. Although Spanish conquerors destroyed many Inca treasures in the 1500s, those remaining can give us a sense of the brilliant culture created by **4** the "Children of the Sun."

62

On Level Practice Book O, page 12

Social studies includes information about government, economics, geography, and history. Here are some special features that might help you use a social studies textbook.

a. **Table of Contents**—lists the book's units and chapters and their page numbers

b. **Headings and Subheadings**—identifies the contents of the page, section, or paragraph

c. **Glossary**—defines specific terms used in the text

d. **Index**—alphabetical list of subjects in the book with their page numbers

e. **Captions for Photographs**—often provide information about the subject

Answer the questions by writing the letter of the correct feature.

1. Where would you look for the beginning page number for Chapter 3? a

2. Where would you look if you wanted to find information on Julius Caesar? d

3. Where would you look to find out what the word *triumvirate* means? c

4. Where would you look to find out what the article on page 156 concerns? b or a

5. Where would you look to locate information on ancient Rome? a or d

6. Where would you find information about a photograph of The Grand Canyon? e

7. Where could you look to find the date of the beginning of World War I? d

8. Where would you find the definition of *treaty*? c

9. Where would you find further information about a specific topic? d or c

10. Where would you find the page number of the beginning of a chapter on Japan? a

---

 Approaching Practice Book A, page 12

Beyond Practice Book B, page 12

The Inca built terraces on hillsides to hold rainwater for crops.

A stone wall (right) from Machu Picchu

Connect and Compare

1. How do the subheadings, photos, and captions help you understand the text better? **Reading Text Features**

2. How do we know the Inca were brilliant engineers? **Analyze**

3. Compare "Empire in the Andes" with *Lost City*. Give examples of two details in *Lost City* that are explained further here. **Reading/ Writing Across Texts**

Social Studies Activity

If you were with Hiram Bingham in Machu Picchu in 1911, what would you include in a journal entry? Include some facts you have read about Machu Picchu.

 Find out more about Machu Picchu at **www.macmillanmh.com**

63

Informational Text

Connect and Compare

SUGGESTED ANSWERS

1. Subheadings help to organize the information in the text. Photos and captions help you to visualize information. **READING TEXT FEATURES**

2. The Inca used terracing, built aqueducts and a network of highways. **ANALYZE**

FOCUS QUESTION

3. Answers could include that no one is sure why *Machu Picchu* was built or why it was abandoned and that the Inca Empire was conquered by the Spanish in 1532. **READING/ WRITING ACROSS TEXTS**

Social Studies Activity

To help students get started, ask them to imagine what it must have been like to see something no one had seen for centuries. Then have them write a journal entry that explains their feelings on that special day.

 Technology

Internet Research and Inquiry Activity
Students can find more facts about Machu Picchu at **www.macmillanmh.com**

Research and Inquiry

Theme: A Lost City

Ask students to work in teams to research one of the topics below.

- The Lost Continent of Atlantis
- Pueblo Grande de Nevada
- The Ruins of Subashi
- The Remains of Herakleion

Have students write questions about what they want to know before they begin their research. Tell them to use library or online resources to find out what they can about their city's significance, loss, and rediscovery—if any. Have them work together to write a short report to share with the class. Remind them to include a page listing the sources they used.

Connect
Language Arts

WRITING
- Personal Narrative
- **Writer's Craft:** Topic Sentence and Details

WORD STUDY
- Words in Context
- Compound Words
- **Phonics:** Long Vowels
- Vocabulary Building

SPELLING
- Words with Long Vowels

GRAMMAR
- Subjects and Predicates

SMALL GROUP OPTIONS
- Differentiated Instruction, pp. 64M–64V

Writing

Topic Sentence and Details

READ THE STUDENT MODEL

Read the bookmark and explain that a strong topic sentence makes the main idea clear. Including only important details keeps the reader's focus on the main idea.

Have students find the topic sentence on page 62 under "Technology." Note that it is the first sentence.

Have the class read Jennifer's **friendly letter** and the callouts. Tell students they will write a letter to a friend or relative about an interesting place. They will learn how to use a strong topic sentence and important details.

Write a Friendly Letter

Writer's Craft

Topic Sentence and Details

Even when writing a letter, you should include a strong topic sentence and important details. Delete **unimportant details** that do not relate to your topic or improve your writing.

October 16, 2008

Dear Aunt Becky,

> My topic sentence is about my visit to a science center.

How are you? Yesterday, Mom, Dad, my friend Nicole, and I went to COSI, Columbus's Center of Science and Industry.

COSI is enormous! We went to the planetarium and saw a show about our universe. We sat on benches around the edges of the room and leaned our heads back to look up at the stars.

> I remembered to make my letter interesting by including only the specific details about my special day.

My favorite part of the center was the Gadgets section. It had places where people can take things apart and put them back together again to see how they work. I actually lifted myself up off the floor with a pulley.

Do you remember how I told you that I wanted to be a scientist when I grow up? Well after visiting the Gadgets exhibit, I think I want to be an engineer.

Before we left, we got the calendar of events. I want to be sure to go back to see the dinosaur exhibit next month.

Love,
Jennifer

64

Features of a Friendly Letter

In a friendly letter, the writer often shares a personal experience and his or her thoughts and feelings about it with a friend or relative. The writer uses informal, or everyday, language to tell what he or she did and felt. However, a friendly letter includes certain conventions of letter writing:

- A friendly letter is usually addressed to a friend or a relative, has the date, and is written in conversational language.

- It begins with a capitalized salutation.

- It includes details of the writer's actions and feelings in its body.

- It ends with an indented, capitalized closing and signature.

Your Turn

Write a letter to a friend or a relative. In your letter, describe an interesting place you visited. You might describe a visit to a local historical site or a trip to a local museum. Use details to capture the feeling of the place. Remember to use complete sentences and proper punctuation. Use the Writer's Checklist to review your letter.

Columbus's Center of Science and Industry Gadget Display

Writer's Checklist

☑ **Ideas and Content:** Did I delete **unimportant details** about the place I chose?

☑ **Organization:** What kind of order did I use? Why does it work well for this letter?

☑ **Voice:** Does the letter express my feelings about the place? Which words clearly express my opinions?

☑ **Word Choice:** Which words bring the description to life? Which words could be more vivid?

☑ **Sentence Fluency:** Did I write in complete sentences?

☑ **Conventions:** Did I punctuate the letter properly, using commas where needed? Did I capitalize the greeting and the first word in the closing? Did I check my spelling?

65

Transparency 5: **Main Idea and Details Chart**
Transparency 6: **Draft**
Transparency 7: **Revision**

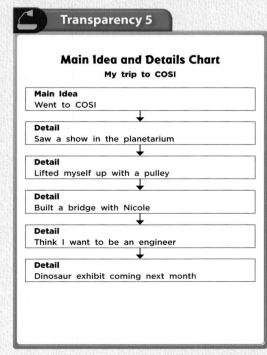

Main Idea and Details Chart
My trip to COSI

Main Idea
Went to COSI

↓

Detail
Saw a show in the planetarium

↓

Detail
Lifted myself up with a pulley

↓

Detail
Built a bridge with Nicole

↓

Detail
Think I want to be an engineer

↓

Detail
Dinosaur exhibit coming next month

Writing Transparency 5

PREWRITE

Ask students to read the writing prompt on page 65. In small groups, have students list interesting places they have visited. Tell students to choose a place they especially enjoyed visiting or self-select another topic.

Display **Transparency 5**. Discuss how Jennifer included information in a main idea and details chart to plan her friendly letter about her visit to COSI. Have students use a chart to plan their letter. Have them discuss their ideas with a classmate. See page 65B for **Identify Purpose and Audience**.

DRAFT

Display **Transparency 6**. Discuss how Jennifer used her chart to draft her letter. Before students begin writing, present the lesson on **Topic Sentence/ Important and Unimportant Details** on page 65A. Then have students use their charts to write their letters. Remind them to include a strong topic sentence and only important details.

REVISE

Display **Transparency 7.** Call on a volunteer to read Jennifer's topic sentence aloud. Talk about how it could be strengthened. Then point out the other revisions. Students can revise their drafts or place them in writing portfolios to work on later.

If students choose to revise, have them work with partners, using the Writer's Checklist on page 65. Have students **proofread** their writing. For **Publishing Options** see page 65A.

For lessons on **Word Choice, Subjects and Predicates**, and **Long Vowels** see page 65B and **5 Day Spelling** and **5 Day Grammar** on pages 65G–65J.

Publishing Options

Suggest that students mail their letters to the friend or relative to whom they have written, or ask students to read their letters aloud. See Speaking and Listening tips below. Encourage students to use their best cursive handwriting in their letters. (See **Teacher's Resource Book** pages 168–173 for cursive models and practice.) Publish students' letters in a bulletin board display that features a map locating the places students have visited.

Speaking and Listening

SPEAKING STRATEGIES

- Practice your presentation.
- Speak clearly with appropriate pacing and grammar. Adjust your volume and inflection to suit your purpose and to help the audience.
- Look at the audience.

LISTENING STRATEGIES

- Look at the speaker.
- Sit quietly and listen carefully to draw conclusions.
- Discuss the information in the friendly letters in order to get to know the writer and each other. Offer personal opinions.

4- and 6-Point Scoring Rubrics

Use the rubrics on pages 127G–127H to score published writing.

Writing Process

For a complete lesson, see Unit Writing pages 127A–127H.

Topic Sentence/Important and Unimportant Details

EXPLAIN/MODEL

Writers use topic sentences in friendly letters as in other forms of personal narrative. A strong topic sentence at the opening of a letter tells the recipient what the letter is about. To hold the recipient's interest, the letter writer should include only important details about the subject. Details that do not relate to the subject are distracting and should be deleted. Display **Transparency 8**.

Think Aloud It's easy to find the topic sentence in this letter. It's right in the first paragraph. It reads: *The best part was our trip to Fort Raleigh in North Carolina.* The topic sentence tells me that this letter is going to be about Caleb's visit to Fort Raleigh.

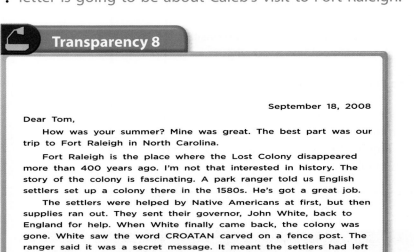

Transparency 8

September 18, 2008

Dear Tom,

How was your summer? Mine was great. The best part was our trip to Fort Raleigh in North Carolina.

Fort Raleigh is the place where the Lost Colony disappeared more than 400 years ago. I'm not that interested in history. The story of the colony is fascinating. A park ranger told us English settlers set up a colony there in the 1580s. He's got a great job.

The settlers were helped by Native Americans at first, but then supplies ran out. They sent their governor, John White, back to England for help. When White finally came back, the colony was gone. White saw the word CROATAN carved on a fence post. The ranger said it was a secret message. It meant the settlers had left for a place called Croatan. But the Lost Colony was never found.

That's a history mystery, don't you think?

Yours truly,
Caleb

Writing Transparency 8

PRACTICE/APPLY

With students' help, identify details in Caleb's letter. Circle the details on the transparency. Then have students work in small groups to categorize the details as important or unimportant. Emphasize that important details relate to the topic, but unimportant details do not. Ask the groups which details they would delete. Draw a line through them on the transparency.

As students write their letters, remind them to include a strong topic sentence and details that relate to the topic. Suggest that student pairs search each other's letters for unimportant details.

Writer's Toolbox

Writing Trait: Word Choice

Explain/Model Friendly letters usually have a casual tone. Writers use the everyday language in friendly letters that they use in conversations with friends and family. Help students identify examples in Jennifer's letter on page 64 that are typical of friendly conversation. Point out the word *Well* in the fourth paragraph and the question that opens the paragraph.

Practice/Apply As students draft their letters, encourage them to choose words and phrases they might use in spoken conversation with friends and family. Have students check each other's letters for words and phrases that seem too formal.

Identifying Purpose and Audience

Explain/Model Tell students that one purpose of a friendly letter is to entertain the reader. The letter's audience is usually a friend or relative. Have students identify the specific purpose and audience of Jennifer's letter on page 64. Ask them to speculate about how Jennifer's letter might have been different if she had been writing to a younger relative or friend.

Practice/Apply Remind students to keep their purpose in mind as they write their letters. Encourage them also to consider the age, gender, social position, and cultural traditions of the recipient as they write.

Technology

Remind students that as they draft they do not need to worry about spelling errors. They can use the delete and insert features later to fix any words that are incorrect.

Subjects and Predicates

Explain/Model Point out that a complete sentence has a subject and a predicate. The subject tells what or whom the sentence is about. The predicate tells what the subject does or is. Direct students to look at the second sentence in the letter on page 64. The subject is *Mom, Dad, my friend Nicole, and I*. The predicate is *went*. Tell students that the subject and its verb must agree in number. A singular subject has a singular verb: *Jennifer visits the COSI*. A compound subject has a plural verb: *Jennifer and Nicole visit the COSI*.

Practice/Apply Have students identify the subject and predicate of each sentence in the letter on page 64. Remind them to make sure that the sentences in their letters contain subjects and predicates and that the subjects and verbs agree. For a complete lesson on subjects and predicates, see pages 65I–65J.

Mechanics Explain that every sentence begins with a capital letter and ends with a period, question mark, or exclamation point. The opening and closing of a letter also begin with capital letters. Each is usually followed by a comma. A comma is also used in the date.

Spelling Words with Long Vowels

Point out the word *leaned* in the letter on page 64. Tell students that the long vowel sound /ē/ in *leaned* is spelled with two vowels coming together: *ea*. Long vowel sounds are also spelled with a vowel followed by a consonant and a silent *e*, as in the word *take*. Students can use a print or online dictionary to check spelling in their drafts. For a complete lesson on long vowels, see pages 65G–65H.

Objective

- Apply knowledge of word meanings and compound words

Materials

- Vocabulary Transparency 3
- Vocabulary Strategy Transparency 4
- Leveled Practice Books, p. 13

Vocabulary

2 **remote** (p. 48) secluded; far removed in place, time, or relation

5 **escort** (p. 48) a person or group of persons accompanying another to give protection or show courtesy

3 **interpreter** (p. 50) a person who translates orally for people speaking different languages

8 **vegetation** (p. 53) plant life or cover

4 **undergrowth** (p. 50) low growth on the floor of a forest, including seedlings, saplings, shrubs, and herbs

6 **venomous** (p. 53) having or producing venom

7 **withstood** (p. 46) stood against

1 **foretold** (p. 46) told of an event before it happened

ELL   Access for All

Vocabulary Remind students of Bingham's character in the story. Co-construct sentences about him using the words *escort, remote,* and *interpreter.*

Review
Vocabulary
 ### Words in Context

EXPLAIN/MODEL Review the meanings of the vocabulary words. Display **Transparency 3.** Model how to use word meanings and context clues to fill in the missing words in the first two sentences.

Think Aloud In the first sentence, I think the word is *undergrowth.* The clues *thick* and *beneath tall trees* make me think that the word means "the vegetation that grows underneath trees."

 ### Transparency 3

remote   interpreter   undergrowth   withstood

Once they reached the jungle, the party had to make its way through the thick (1) undergrowth beneath the tall trees.

Because they did not speak the same language, Bingham's party depended on an (2) interpreter to help them communicate with the local farmer.

It was many miles before the adventurers reached the (3) remote canyon so far from any village.

The explorers were surprised to find that the stone wall had (4) withstood both time and earthquakes.

Vocabulary Transparency 3

  PRACTICE/APPLY Have students use context clues to find the missing words for sentences 2–4. Ask students to work with a partner to check their answers and to explain the context clues they used to find the missing words. Then have them create context sentences for *escort, vegetation, venomous,* and *foretold.*

Word Relationships Have students answer each question using a vocabulary word and explain to partners why they chose the answer.

- Which word goes with *translator*? (*interpreter*)

- Which word goes with *poisonous*? (*venomous*)

- Which word means "a person who accompanies someone else"? (*escort*)

65C

STRATEGY
USE WORD PARTS: COMPOUND WORDS

EXPLAIN/MODEL Tell students:

- Using word parts to find the definition of a compound word is one strategy to determine its meaning.

- A compound word is made up of two words. The two words often provide hints for the meaning of the compound word.

Read the following sentence in **Student Book** page 50 and model how to use the word parts to determine the meaning of *undergrowth*: *Bingham and the sergeant followed Arteaga through dense undergrowth down to the very edge of the river to a flimsy bridge made of slim logs.*

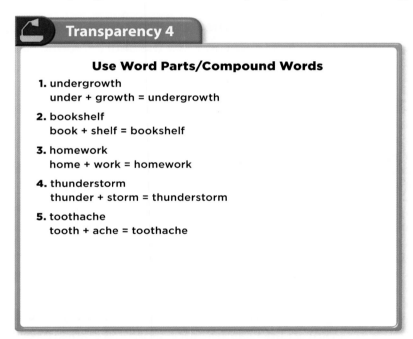

Transparency 4

Use Word Parts/Compound Words

1. undergrowth
   under + growth = undergrowth

2. bookshelf
   book + shelf = bookshelf

3. homework
   home + work = homework

4. thunderstorm
   thunder + storm = thunderstorm

5. toothache
   tooth + ache = toothache

Vocabulary Strategy Transparency 4

PRACTICE/APPLY

 Discuss the two words that make up *undergrowth*. Work with students to show them how the meanings of the two word parts help them understand the meaning of the compound word. Help students analyze the remaining compound words on the transparency.

Quick Check Can students identify the correct vocabulary words? Can students use word parts to understand compound words?

During **Small Group Instruction**

If No → **Approaching Level** Vocabulary, pp. 65N–65O

If Yes → **On Level** Options, pp. 65Q–65R

Beyond Level Options, pp. 65S–65T

ELL | **Access for All**

Compound Words Check students' understanding of the compound words on the transparency. Have students use each compound word in a sentence illustrating its meaning.

On Level Practice Book O, page 13

Compound words are words that consist of two or more words joined together. They can be hyphenated, closed, or open. If you are not sure how to write a compound word, look it up in the dictionary.

sister-in-law   everybody   roller skate

You can use the separate parts of compound words to determine their meaning.

under + growth = undergrowth

Low plants on the floor of a forest.

Possible responses provided.

A. Identify the separate words that make up each compound word. Explain how they create the meaning of the word.

1. foretold _Fore means something that happens ahead of or before something else. Told means said. Foretold means said something before it happened._

2. snowcapped _Snow means frozen precipitation. Capped means topped. Snowcapped means something has snow on top._

3. stonework _Stone means rock. Work means labor or effort. Stonework means a product made of stone._

4. staircase _Stair means one of a set of steps. Case means a set of something. Staircase means a set of steps._

Write a sentence using a compound word. You may use one listed, or you may choose one on your own.

5. _Students should use compound words in their sentences._

 Approaching Practice Book A, page 13

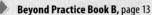 **Beyond Practice Book B,** page 13

Objective
- Decode words with long vowels

Materials
- Leveled Practice Books, p. 14
- Teacher's Resource Book, p. 6

ELL

Access for All

Vowel Patterns Write these vowel groups on the board: *ee, ea, ai, aa.* Explain that each of the letter groups can make a long vowel sound. Give examples of each. Then have students think of words that contain the vowels.

On Level Practice Book O, page 14

A common way to spell a **long vowel** sound is to use the pattern: vowel-consonant-silent e. Some examples: *gate, hide, eve, lone, mute.* There are also other ways to form long vowel sounds. The letter *y* can stand for the long *i* sound, as in *fly.* Two vowels together are called a diphthong and can stand for one sound. For example, the *ea* in *mean* stands for the long *e* sound. Other diphthongs that stand for long vowel sounds include *ee, ai,* and *oa.*

Look at each item. Fill in the missing vowel(s) to spell the sound. Then write the complete word in the space.

Vowels and Diphthongs

a	e	i	o	u	y	ee	ea	ai	oa

1. st_ea_m   long e   steam
2. f_i_n_e_   long i   fine
3. f_ai_nt   long a   faint
4. h_u_g_e_   long u   huge
5. c_y_cle   long i   cycle
6. l_oa_n   long o   loan
7. n_ai_l   long a   nail
8. r_ea_d   long e   read
9. enc_y_clopedia   long i   encyclopedia
10. d_o_m_e_   long o   dome

★ **Approaching Practice Book A,** page 14

◆ **Beyond Practice Book B,** page 14

Phonics
Decode Words with Long Vowels

Access for All

EXPLAIN/MODEL In words that follow the VC*e* (vowel-consonant-*e*) pattern, the vowel sound is usually long, as in *gaze, theme, like, tone,* and *fuse.* The final *e* is silent. Sometimes a vowel digraph (a pair of vowels) stands for a long vowel sound. For example, the digraphs *oa, ow,* and *oe* can stand for /ō/, as in *coax, mow,* and *foe.* The digraphs *ee* and *ea* can stand for /ē/, as in *tree* and *league.*

The vowel *i* may stand for /ī/ when it is followed by two consonants, such as *nd* in *grind* and *ld* in *wild.* Sometimes /ī/ is spelled with the letters *igh* or the letter *y,* as in *high, rhyme,* and *nylon.* Write the word *bleach* on the board.

Think Aloud When I see this word, I recognize the vowel digraph *ea.* I know *ea* can have the short *e* sound, as in *weather,* or the long *e* sound, as in *leap.* When I try the short *e* sound, I get /blech/. That doesn't make sense. When I try the long *e* sound, I get /blēch/. *Bleach* is a word I know, so the *ea* stands for the long *e* sound in this word.

Cooperative Learning

PRACTICE/APPLY Write these words on the board: *meanwhile, sunshine, sightsee, whitewash, rattlesnake, bathrobe, roommate, humidifier.* Have students say each of these words aloud to partners and identify the letters that stand for the long vowel sounds.

Decode Multisyllabic Words Explain that word parts such as *-ing* and *-ed* are endings added at the end of a root word; *-ing* shows an action that is happening in the present; *-ed* shows an action happening in the past. Write the endings and *floated* on the board. Point to and say the root word *float* and then the ending *ed.* Draw a line between them. Read the word. Tell students that *ed* means the action, *float,* was done in the past. Display *heaping, sighed, towing, peaked.* Together with students decode *heaping.* Then have them decode the remaining words. For more practice, see the decodable passages on page 6 of the **Teacher's Resource Book**.

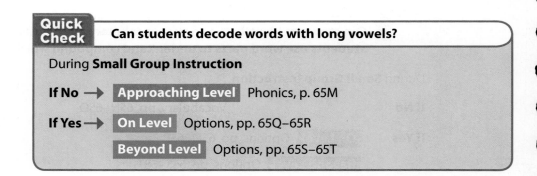

Quick Check **Can students decode words with long vowels?**

During **Small Group Instruction**

If No → **Approaching Level** Phonics, p. 65M

If Yes → **On Level** Options, pp. 65Q–65R

Beyond Level Options, pp. 65S–65T

Vocabulary Building

Oral Language

Expand Vocabulary Ask students to envision a lost city. Have volunteers describe the mental pictures they see. Write some of their descriptive words on the board, and challenge the class to use these words in other sentences.

Spiral Review

Vocabulary Game Divide the class into two teams and provide each player with a buzzer, whistle, or other noisemaker. Read a word from a Vocabulary Card. The player who makes a noise first must define the word correctly and use it in a sentence. If the player is correct, his or her team gets to keep the Vocabulary Card. Otherwise, the other team gets a chance to win it by defining the word and using it in a sentence. Undefined words are put at the bottom of the pile of active cards. The team that earns the most cards wins.

Apply Vocabulary

Write an Adventure Story Ask students to imagine some exciting things that might happen to an explorer looking for a lost city. Discuss their ideas, and have classmates embellish them. Ask students to write two paragraphs of an adventure story based on these ideas. Encourage them to use some of the vocabulary words from the story. Tell them to include a title that is interesting and reflects the topic.

Vocabulary Building

Compound Words Write these words from the story: *undergrowth, stonework, something,* and *earthquakes.* Ask students to draw a vertical line in each word, dividing it into its two parts. Then ask students to think of other compound words they know. Challenge the class to create sentences that contain both a vocabulary word and a compound word.

Technology

Vocabulary PuzzleMaker

LOG ON

For additional vocabulary and spelling games go to
www.macmillanmh.com

5 Day Spelling

Words with Long Vowels

Spelling Words

slope	tile	coax
acute	fuse	bleak
remote	bleach	cue
bathe	loan	pave
gaze	tote	meek
rhyme	foal	shrine
keen	foe	

Review grasp, dread, shrunk

Challenge trait, capsule

Dictation Sentences

1. Rocks rolled down the **slope**.
2. The pain was acute.
3. Antarctica is a **remote** continent.
4. Karen is going to **bathe** the baby.
5. Ludovic's gaze was suspicious.
6. Do the words *toe* and *foe* rhyme?
7. Sven has a keen mind.
8. Every tile is broken.
9. We blew a fuse in the kitchen.
10. Bleach is poisonous.
11. Would you loan me money?
12. People tote groceries in bags.
13. The foal galloped.
14. Are you a friend or foe?
15. Ana had to coax her brother.
16. The prognosis is bleak.
17. That is my cue to go on stage.
18. City workers will pave the street.
19. A meek person is timid.
20. Thousands of fans visit the shrine.

Review/Challenge Words

1. Grasp the handle tightly.
2. I dread taking math tests.
3. Have you shrunk the sheets?
4. Height is a dominant trait.
5. I took the capsule.

Note: Words in **bold** type are from *Lost City*.

Display the Spelling Words throughout the week.

Day 1 Pretest

ASSESS PRIOR KNOWLEDGE

Use the Dictation Sentences. Say the underlined word, read the sentence and repeat the word. Have students write the words on **Spelling Practice Book** page 7 and then correct their own papers. For a modified list, use the first 17 Spelling Words and the Review Words. For a more challenging list, use Spelling Words 3–20 and the Challenge Words.

Have students cut apart the Spelling Word Cards BLM on **Teacher's Resource Book** page 67 and figure out a way to sort them. Have them save the cards for use throughout the week.

For **Leveled Word Lists,** go to **www.macmillanmh.com**

Day 2 Word Sorts

TEACHER AND STUDENT SORTS

- Attach the column headings **CVCe** and **CVV** to a bulletin board. Explain each spelling pattern. Tell students they will sort their Spelling Words according to these spelling patterns.

- Draw a card, say the word, and ask students to listen for the vowel sound. For example, *keen* has the long *e* sound, spelled with two vowels together. Place *keen* in the **CVV** column on the board.

- Discuss that *rhyme* is different because the long *i* sound is spelled with the consonant letter *y*.

- After sorting, help students check and correct their sort as needed.

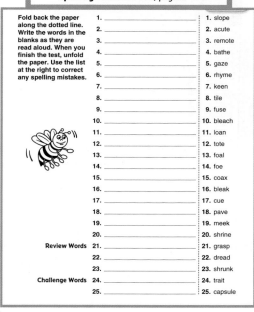

Spelling Practice Book, pages 7–8

Fold back the paper along the dotted line. Write the words in the blanks as they are read aloud. When you finish the test, unfold the paper. Use the list at the right to correct any spelling mistakes.

1. _____	1. slope
2. _____	2. acute
3. _____	3. remote
4. _____	4. bathe
5. _____	5. gaze
6. _____	6. rhyme
7. _____	7. keen
8. _____	8. tile
9. _____	9. fuse
10. _____	10. bleach
11. _____	11. loan
12. _____	12. tote
13. _____	13. foal
14. _____	14. foe
15. _____	15. coax
16. _____	16. bleak
17. _____	17. cue
18. _____	18. pave
19. _____	19. meek
20. _____	20. shrine
Review Words 21. _____	21. grasp
22. _____	22. dread
23. _____	23. shrunk
Challenge Words 24. _____	24. trait
25. _____	25. capsule

Spelling Practice Book, page 9

slope	gaze	fuse	foal	cue
acute	rhyme	bleach	foe	pave
remote	keen	loan	coax	meek
bathe	tile	tote	bleak	shrine

Write the spelling words with each of the spelling patterns below.

Long a spelled:

a_e
1. bathe
2. gaze
3. pave

Long e spelled:

ee
4. keen
5. meek

ea
6. bleach
7. bleak

Long i spelled:

y
8. rhyme

i_e
9. tile
10. shrine

Long o spelled:

o_e
11. slope
12. remote
13. tote

oa
14. loan
15. foal
16. coax

oe
17. foe

Long u spelled:

u_e
18. acute
19. fuse

ue
20. cue

Day 3 Word Meanings

WORD CONNECTIONS

Review sorting words by long vowel sounds. Ask students to copy the words below into their word study notebook, completing the group by adding a Spelling Word. Have them use the column headings from Day 2. Read each group of words below.

1. watch, stare, _____ (gaze)

2. mild, calm, _____ (meek)

3. far away, distant, _____ (remote)

4. enemy, opponent, _____ (foe)

5. lamb, calf, _____ (foal)

Invite students to select five words to draw and label.

Day 4 Review and Proofread

SPIRAL REVIEW

Review words with short vowels. Write *grasp*, *dread*, and *shrunk*. Have students identify the letters that spell short vowels.

PROOFREAD AND WRITE

Write a paragraph on the board, including misspelled words. Have students proofread and underline words that are misspelled, and then write the word correctly.

REVIEW AND SORT

Have students use their spelling sort from last week to review the spelling pattern CVC. Ask students to add new short vowel words to this word sort in their Word Study notebook.

Day 5 Assess and Reteach

POSTTEST

Use the Dictation Sentences on page 65G for the Posttest.

If students have difficulty with any words in the lesson, have them place them on a list called "Spelling Words I Want to Remember" in their word study notebook.

WORD STUDY NOTEBOOK

Challenge students to search for other words with letters that spell long vowels in their reading for the week and write them in their word study notebook under the heading "Other Words with Long Vowels."

Spelling Practice Book, page 10

slope	gaze	fuse	foal	cue
acute	rhyme	bleach	foe	pave
remote	keen	loan	coax	meek
bathe	tile	tote	bleak	shrine

Synonyms

A synonym is a word that means the same as another word. Write the spelling word that matches each synonym.

1. carry _____ tote
2. stare _____ gaze
3. enthusiastic _____ keen
4. signal _____ cue
5. distant _____ remote
6. colt _____ foal

Antonyms

An antonym is a word that means the opposite of another word. Write the spelling word that matches each antonym.

7. friend _____ foe
8. separate _____ fuse
9. strong _____ meek
10. rise _____ slope
11. mild _____ acute
12. lively _____ bleak

Spelling Practice Book, page 11

There are five spelling mistakes in this paragraph. Circle the misspelled words. Write the words correctly on the lines below.

When Randy is left to take care of his little brother, they play at being explorers. Randy takes his horse, his brother takes his (folc), and together they (paive) the way into a forgotten city. When they reach the (tyle) floor of the bathroom, the room becomes an ancient (shryn) Playtime makes it much easier for Randy to (coks) his brother to sleep.

1. _____ foal
2. _____ pave
3. _____ tile
4. _____ shrine
5. _____ coax

Writing Activity

Have you ever played at being an explorer? What did you do and where did you go on your explorer's expedition? Write a letter to a friend describing such an adventure as if it were real. Use five spelling words.

Students' writing should reflect the topic and include five spelling words.

Spelling Practice Book, page 12

Look at the words in each set below. One word in each set is spelled correctly. Use a pencil to fill in the circle next to the correct word. Before you begin, look at the sample set of words. Sample A has been done for you. Do Sample B by yourself. When you are sure you know what to do, you may go on with the rest of the page.

Sample A:
- Ⓐ doom
- Ⓑ dume
- Ⓒ duum
- Ⓓ doome

Sample B:
- Ⓔ taik
- Ⓕ taak
- Ⓖ take
- Ⓗ tehk

1.
- Ⓐ slopp
- Ⓑ slope
- Ⓒ sloop
- Ⓓ slohp

2.
- Ⓔ acoot
- Ⓕ acut
- Ⓖ acyute
- Ⓗ acute

3.
- Ⓐ remote
- Ⓑ reemote
- Ⓒ reemot
- Ⓓ remot

4.
- Ⓔ bayth
- Ⓕ bethe
- Ⓖ bathe
- Ⓗ beth

5.
- Ⓐ gaze
- Ⓑ gass
- Ⓒ geze
- Ⓓ gez

6.
- Ⓔ rime
- Ⓕ rhyme
- Ⓖ rhime
- Ⓗ ryme

7.
- Ⓐ kene
- Ⓑ keen
- Ⓒ ken
- Ⓓ kein

8.
- Ⓔ tile
- Ⓕ til
- Ⓖ tihl
- Ⓗ tale

9.
- Ⓐ foose
- Ⓑ fus
- Ⓒ fuse
- Ⓓ fyuse

10.
- Ⓔ bleech
- Ⓕ bleach
- Ⓖ bleche
- Ⓗ blech

11.
- Ⓐ lon
- Ⓑ lone
- Ⓒ loan
- Ⓓ lohn

12.
- Ⓔ tote
- Ⓕ tott
- Ⓖ toat
- Ⓗ toht

13.
- Ⓐ foal
- Ⓑ fole
- Ⓒ fohl
- Ⓓ foll

14.
- Ⓔ fo
- Ⓕ fow
- Ⓖ foh
- Ⓗ foe

15.
- Ⓐ coxe
- Ⓑ coax
- Ⓒ cohx
- Ⓓ cokes

16.
- Ⓔ bleek
- Ⓕ bleke
- Ⓖ blek
- Ⓗ bleak

17.
- Ⓐ cyu
- Ⓑ cue
- Ⓒ coo
- Ⓓ cu

18.
- Ⓔ pav
- Ⓕ paive
- Ⓖ pave
- Ⓗ paiv

19.
- Ⓐ meak
- Ⓑ meke
- Ⓒ mek
- Ⓓ meek

20.
- Ⓔ shrin
- Ⓕ shrine
- Ⓖ shrihn
- Ⓗ shriin

5 Day Grammar

Subjects and Predicates

Daily Language Activities

Use these activites to introduce each day's lesson. Write the day's activities on the board or use **Transparency 2.**

DAY 1
off to South America. We went?
(1. Off; 2. South America; we 3. went.)

DAY 2
We we're looking for the lost sity.
(1. We; 2. were; 3. city)

DAY 3
our party passed through remot villages? (1. Our; 2. remote; 3. villages.)

DAY 4
dear Julius
Will you come to my party?
best regards,
Kim (1. Dear; 2. Julius,; 3. Best)

DAY 5
Dear Amanda
how do you like your new home. I miss you terribly.
Kira (1. Amanda,; 2. How; 3. home?)

ELL
Access for All

Clarify Subjects
Write on the board: *They climbed the bank into dense jungle. Bingham's eyes searched the jungle.* Discuss the sentences. Have students identify the verb and the subject in each sentence. Continue with other sentences.

Day 1 — Introduce the Concept

INTRODUCE SUBJECTS

Present the following:

- A sentence is a group of words that expresses a complete thought.

- A subject of a sentence is what or who the sentence is about.

- A subject often performs the action of a sentence.

- A subject is usually a noun or a pronoun.

Example:

Peru is near the equator. (subject: Peru)

Amaya will go to the game. (subject: Amaya)

 See Grammar Transparency 6 for modeling and guided practice.

Grammar Practice Book, page 7

- The **complete subject** includes all the words that tell what or whom the sentence is about.
- The **simple subject** is the main word or words in the complete subject.
- You can sometimes correct a sentence fragment by adding a subject.

Read each sentence. Write the complete subject on the line provided below each example. Put parentheses ( ) around the simple subject. (In some sentences, the complete subject and the simple subject may be the same.)

1. The ruins of many ancient cities are located in Mexico.
   The (ruins) of many ancient cities
2. The Mexican people live and work near ancient archaeological sites.
   The Mexican (people)
3. My cousin Isabel is studying to become an archaeologist.
   My cousin (Isabel)
4. The large capital of Mexico is her home.
   The large (capital) of Mexico
5. Isabel hopes to travel to Tulum sometime soon with her classmates.
   (Isabel)
6. The entire class will be guided on the trip by a well-known scientist.
   The entire (class)
7. The students are looking forward to seeing some real artifacts.
   The (students)
8. The department's leading professor has arranged the trip.
   The department's leading (professor)

Day 2 — Teach the Concept

REVIEW SUBJECTS

Discuss with students how to recognize subjects in a sentence. How does a subject differ from other parts of the sentence?

INTRODUCE PREDICATES

Present the following:

- A predicate is the part of the sentence that describes the action or the state of being.

- The simple predicate is a verb.

- A complete predicate is the verb and any words that modify it.

Example:

Bingham might be getting close to the lost city. (simple predicate: might be; complete predicate: might be getting close to the lost city)

 See Grammar Transparency 7 for modeling and guided practice.

Grammar Practice Book, page 8

- The **complete predicate** includes all the words that tell what the subject does or is.
- The **simple predicate** is the main word or words in the complete predicate.
- You can sometimes correct a sentence fragment by adding a predicate.

Read each sentence. Write the complete predicate on the space provided below each example. Put parentheses around the simple predicate. (In some sentences, the complete predicate and the simple predicate may be the same.)

1. Isabel learns languages as part of her schoolwork in archaeology.
   (learns) languages as part of her schoolwork in archaeology
2. She and her classmates practice their English with each other.
   (practice) their English with each other
3. Sometimes at home Isabel speaks English or French.
   (speaks) English or French
4. She even knows a little Chinese!
   (knows) a little Chinese!
5. The dean of the language department at Isabel's university approves.
   (approves)
6. Chinese is a difficult language to learn.
   (is) a difficult language to learn
7. She works hard to master the characters.
   (works) hard to master the characters
8. Late into the night, Isabel is often studying.
   (is) often studying

Day 3 Review and Practice

REVIEW SUBJECTS AND PREDICATES

Present the Daily Language Activity for Day 3. Have students identify the subjects, simple predicates, and complete predicates for each sentence.

MECHANICS & USAGE: USING PROPER PUNCTUATION WHILE WRITING A LETTER

- Every sentence begins with a capital letter.

- The opening and closing of a letter begin with capital letters.

- The opening and closing are generally followed by commas.

See Grammar Transparency 8 for modeling and guided practice.

Grammar Practice Book, page 9

- Begin the greeting and closing of a letter with a capital letter.
- Use a comma after the greeting and closing of a friendly letter.
- Use a comma between the names of a city and a state.
- Use a comma between the day and year in a date.

Proofread this friendly letter for errors in commas and capitalization. Add commas as necessary. Cross out the letters that should be capitalized.

> 1723 Carolyn Lane
> Orlando, FL 32819
> June 1, 2006
>
> dear Lupe,
>
> Let me tell you about my fabulous trip to Mexico! I took an archaeological tour with my family through the Yucatan Peninsula. We learned about the great Maya civilization and saw the ruins of many of their cities. The Maya had a calendar and written language. They also studied the planets and stars.
>
> Our trip began on May 5, 2006 and we did not get home until Memorial Day! The weather in Mexico was perfect for hiking the ruins, and the beaches of Cancun were fantastic. I learned how to snorkel, and Danny saw a barracuda! Coming home to Orlando, Florida, may seem a lot less exciting, but it's good to be back.
>
> Your friend,
> Marisa

Day 4 Review and Proofread

REVIEW SUBJECTS AND PREDICATES

Write the sentences on the board and have students identify each simple subject and simple predicate.

PROOFREAD

Have students identify and correct the punctuation and capitalization errors in the following letter.

dear Cristo.
How are you. We really miss you a lot? When will you be home next! with love:
Nola (Dear; a lot.; next? love,)

See Grammar Transparency 9 for modeling and guided practice.

Grammar Practice Book, page 10

- Begin the greeting and closing of a letter with a capital letter.
- Use a comma after the greeting and closing of a friendly letter.
- Use a comma between the names of a city and a state.
- Use a comma between the day and year in a date.

Proofread the letter Ivelise wrote to her cousin Isabel. Add commas as necessary. Cross out incorrect punctuation and the letters that should be capitalized. Use correct punctuation.

> 1800 Fortune Avenue
> Tampa, FL 33624
> December 11, 2006
>
> dear Isabel
>
> I received your letter last week, but I've been quite busy. Do you remember I told you about my history class? Well, we are learning about ancient cities like the ones you have been visiting.
>
> My homework load is heavy, but I am enjoying learning about the South American cities? Are the Maya people like the ancient Inca people I am learning about? I wish you were here so you could help me with this essay I have to write?
>
> Write soon and tell me about your trip to the Yucatan. My mom says we may be coming to Mexico City to visit soon. I can't wait to show you my photos.
>
> Your cousin,
> Ivelise

Day 5 Assess and Reteach

ASSESS

Use the Daily Language Activity and page 11 of the **Grammar Practice Book** for assessment.

RETEACH

List five nouns and five verbs on the board. Then, have students take turns making up sentences. Remind students that they will have to change the forms of the verbs to agree with the nouns. After students have used all of the words in the list, challenge them to identify the subjects and complete predicates in each sentence.

Use Grammar Practice Book page 12 for additional reteaching.

See Grammar Transparency 10 for modeling and guided practice.

Grammar Practice Book, pages 11–12

Decide which word or group of words is the sentence part named in parentheses. Circle the letter of your answer.

1. My cousin Lupe enjoyed her visit to Key West, Florida. (simple subject)
   a. enjoyed her visit
   b. enjoyed
   c. My cousin Lupe
   d. Lupe

2. She visited many of the historic sites for which the city is famous. (complete predicate)
   a. She visited
   b. visited many of the historic sites for which the city is famous
   c. for which the city is famous
   d. many of the historic sites

3. Lupe gradually felt more at home in the city. (simple predicate)
   a. felt
   b. gradually felt more at home
   c. at home in the city
   d. Lupe gradually

4. An exhausting day of travel can make anyone feel tired. (complete subject)
   a. day of travel
   b. An exhausting day of travel
   c. anyone
   d. can make anyone feel tired

5. A nice cup of tea usually makes Lupe feel a lot better. (simple subject)
   a. A nice cup of tea
   b. a lot better
   c. makes Lupe feel
   d. cup

Administer the Test

 ### Weekly Reading Assessment,
Passages and questions, pages 21–28

ASSESSED SKILLS

- Character, Setting, Plot
- Vocabulary Words
- Word Parts: Compound Words
- Long Vowels
- Subjects and Predicates

  **Assessment Tool**

Macmillan/McGraw-Hill

Administer the **Weekly Assessment** online or on CD-ROM.

Weekly Assessment, 21–28

 ### Fluency

Assess fluency for one group of students per week. Use the Oral Fluency Record Sheet to track the number of words read correctly. Fluency goal for all students:
117–137 words correct per minute (WCPM).

Approaching Level	Weeks 1, 3, 5
On Level	Weeks 2, 4
Beyond Level	Week 6

Fluency Assessment

 ### Alternative Assessments

- **ELL Assessment,** pages 36–37

ELL Practice and Assessment, 36–37

Diagnose		Prescribe
	IF...	**THEN...**
VOCABULARY WORDS **VOCABULARY STRATEGY** Word Parts: Compound Words Items 1, 2, 3, 4	0–2 items correct . . .	Reteach skills using the **Additional Lessons** page T5 **LOG ON** Reteach skills: Go to **www.macmillanmh.com** **CD ROM** Vocabulary PuzzleMaker Evaluate for Intervention.
COMPREHENSION **Skill:** Character, Setting, Plot Items 5, 6, 7, 8	0–2 items correct . . .	Reteach skills using the **Additional Lessons** page T1 Evaluate for Intervention.
GRAMMAR Sentence Types and Fragments Items 9, 10, 11	0–1 items correct . . .	Reteach skills: **Grammar Practice Book** page 12
SPELLING Long Vowels Items 12, 13, 14	0–1 items correct . . .	**LOG ON** Reteach skills: Go to **www.macmillanmh.com**
FLUENCY	109–116 WCPM 0–108 WCPM	**AUDIO CD** Fluency Solutions Evaluate for Intervention.

READING
Triumphs
AN INTERVENTION PROGRAM

Also Available

To place students in the Intervention Program, use the **Diagnostic Assessment** in the Intervention Teacher's Edition.

Lost City: The Discovery of Machu Picchu   **65L**

Skills Focus ▶ **Phonics**

Objective	Decode one-syllable and multisyllabic words that include long vowels in both familiar and unfamiliar text
Materials	• **Student Book** "An Inca City"

LONG VOWELS

Model/Guided Practice

■ Write the letters *t, a, p* on the board. Segment the sounds: /t//a//p/. Then blend the sounds: /tap/. *Say the word with me:* tap. Write the letter *e* after *tap. The* e *at the end is silent, but it changes the sound of the vowel* a. *The new word is* tape. *Say it with me:* /tāp/. *When a vowel is followed by a consonant and a silent* e, *it is often pronounced with a long vowel sound.*

■ Write the word *coach. When I say* coach, *I hear the long* o *sound:* /kōch/. *When two vowels are together, they may make the long vowel sound of the first vowel in the pair.*

■ Write the word *rhyme.* Say the word. *When I say* rhyme, *I hear the long* i *sound. Sometimes the letter* y *is pronounced with the long* i *sound.*

■ Write the word *main* on the board. *Now you say the word. What long vowel sound do you hear? What letters make this sound?*

■ Ask students to give other examples of words with long vowels.

MULTISYLLABIC WORDS WITH LONG VOWELS

■ Write the letters *c, o, m, p, l, e, t, e* on the board. Segment the sounds. Then blend the sounds: /kum plēt/. *Say the word with me:* complete. *In* complete, *the final* e *is silent, so the* e *before the consonant* t *has a long vowel sound.*

■ Have students work with partners to decode longer words with long vowel sounds. Write the following words on the board, or provide students with copies of the list. *Choose a word with your partner. Say the word. Draw a line to show where syllables begin and end. Then draw a line under the syllable or syllables with long vowels.*

decorate	feature	exceedingly	document
combine	compete	enrage	vacant
attain	telescope	distribute	interface

■ Check each pair for accuracy. Provide constructive feedback.

WORD SORT: LONG VOWELS IN CONTEXT

■ Have students search through "An Inca City" for words with long vowel sounds. Have them list the words and underline the letters in each that make the long vowel sound.

■ Have students work with a partner to sort the words according to sound.

Additional Resources

For each skill below, additional lessons are provided. You can use these lessons on consecutive days after teaching the lessons presented during the week.
• Character, Setting, Plot, T1
• Word Parts: Compound Words, T5
• Text Features, T9

Constructive Feedback

Isolate the error sound and repeat with students. If students say /a/ instead of /ā/ in *tame*, for instance, point to the letters *a* and *e* and say:

Look at the CVCe pattern in the word. The final *e* is silent, but it makes the *a* stand for the long *a* sound. Say it with me: /ā/. Let's sound out the word again: /tām/, *tame*

Repeat as needed with other sounds/spellings of long vowels.

Decodable Text

To help students build speed and accuracy when reading multisyllabic words, use additional decodable text on page 6 of the **Teacher's Resource Book.**

Skills Focus ▶ Fluency

Objective	Read with increasing prosody and accuracy at a rate of 117–127 WCPM
Materials	• **Approaching Practice Book A,** p. 11

MODEL EXPRESSIVE READING

Model reading the Fluency passage on **Approaching Practice Book A** page 11. Tell students to pay close attention and listen to your pauses and intonation as you read. Then read one sentence at a time and have students echo-read the sentence back, copying your pauses and intonation. Listen carefully to their reading, monitoring for accuracy. You may want to have individual students echo-read.

REPEATED READING

Have students continue practicing reading the passage aloud as you circulate and provide constructive feedback. During independent reading time, have students work with a partner. Have one student read aloud, and the other repeat each sentence. Students should continue practicing the passage throughout the week.

TIMED READING

At the end of the week, tell students that they will do a timed reading of the passage that they have been practicing. With each student:

- Place the passage from **Approaching Practice Book A** page 11 facedown.
- When you say "Go," the student begins reading the passage aloud.
- When you say "Stop," the student stops reading the passage.

Stop each student after one minute. Review their miscues and help them graph their scores.

Skills Focus ▶ Vocabulary

Objective	Apply vocabulary word meanings
Materials	• **Vocabulary Cards** • **Transparencies 2a and 2b**

VOCABULARY WORDS

Divide the group into teams. Display the **Vocabulary Cards** for *foretold, withstood, remote, interpreter, undergrowth, venomous, escort, vegetation*. Hold up one card. Have each team try to locate the vocabulary word in "An Inca City" on **Transparencies 2a and 2b** and read it aloud in its sentence. Review the meaning of each word. Have teams write and share sentences containing two vocabulary words each.

Constructive Feedback

Students may have difficulty pronouncing the proper nouns included in the passage. List them on the board, say each one, and have students repeat your pronunciation. Then have the class choral read the proper nouns aloud. Correct any errors in pronunciation, including which syllable is stressed.

★ **Approaching Practice Book A,** page 11

As I read, I will pay attention to the pronunciation of city names, pauses, and intonation.

	Imagine finding a city frozen in time. That's exactly what
10	you'd find if you went to Pompeii. This ancient city was
21	once under the rule of the Roman Empire. It sits at the foot
34	of Mount Vesuvius, an active volcano in southern Italy. No
44	one has lived in Pompeii for nearly two thousand years. On a
56	bright summer afternoon in A.D. 79 the volcano erupted. It
66	caused one of history's worst natural disasters. Most of the
76	people living there fled the city as soon as they felt the first
89	shock wave and saw the sky darken. But a few thousand
100	people stayed behind. By the following day, the city of
110	Pompeii lay covered in tons of rock and ash. Death came
121	swiftly for those who had not escaped. The volcanic debris
131	killed them, but it also sealed their final moments. Today, we
142	can see how these people lived thanks to the volcano. 152

Comprehension Check

1. What was the cause of Pompeii's disaster? What was the effect? **Cause and Effect** A volcano caused the disaster and left Pompeii buried and preserved for almost 2,000 years.
2. Why do you think no one has lived in Pompeii for nearly 2,000 years? **Make Inferences** No one has lived in Pompeii probably because it is near an active volcano.

	Words Read	−	Number of Errors	=	Words Correct Score
First Read		−		=	
Second Read		−		=	

Vocabulary

Review last week's words *(abruptly, anxiety, conscious, intersection, engulf, procedure, souvenir, cascade)* and this week's words *(remote, escort, interpreter, vegetation, undergrowth, venomous, withstood, foretold)*. Have students write a story using the words.

Student Book, or Transparencies 2a and 2b

RESEARCH
Why It Matters

Teach students how to take apart and how to add to words. Students write the key words from the vocabulary lesson in their word study notebooks, and then take words apart and add syllables to words. Vocabularies are enriched as they add and take words apart.

Dr. Donald Bear

LOG ON For more information, go to Teacher Resources at www.macmillanmh.com

---

Skills Focus

Vocabulary

Objective	Use word parts to understand the meaning of compound words
Materials	• **Student Book** *Lost City: The Discovery of Machu Picchu*

WORD PARTS: COMPOUND WORDS

Suggest that students say each vocabulary word slowly in order to hear the syllables clearly. Work with students to break the word into syllables. Have the group identify any compound words. Then have students identify, break apart, and define at least three other compound words in *Lost City*.

Skills Focus

Comprehension

Objective	Identify character, setting, and plot
Materials	• **Student Book** "An Inca City" • **Transparencies 2a and 2b**

STRATEGY
ANALYZE STORY STRUCTURE

Review with students that analyzing story structure, or how a story is organized, is key to understanding the story's plot.

SKILL
CHARACTER, SETTING, PLOT

Explain/Model

- The characters are the people or animals in a story.
- The setting is the story's time and place.
- The plot is the series of events that happen in the story.

Display **Transparencies 2a** and **2b**. Reread the first paragraph of "An Inca City." Model analyzing what readers learn about the characters, setting, and plot from this paragraph.

Think Aloud From the title and the first paragraph, I know the main character traveled with her parents to Peru and visited the historic Inca city, Machu Picchu. I know the plot will be about the visit.

Practice/Apply

Reread the rest of "An Inca City" with students. Have students underline details about the characters, setting, and events that make up the plot.

Leveled Reader Lesson

Leveled Reader Library

Objective Read to apply strategies and skills

Materials
- **Leveled Reader** *I Discover Pompeii, or How I Spent My Summer*
- **Student Book** *Lost City: The Discovery of Machu Picchu* • chart paper

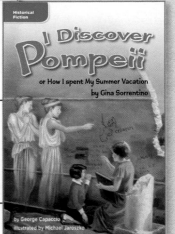

Leveled Reader

PREVIEW AND PREDICT

Have students read the title and preview the first chapter. Have students make predictions about the characters and the plot and write down any questions they have about the story.

VOCABULARY WORDS

Before reading, review the vocabulary words as necessary. Remind students to notice how the vocabulary words are used in the story.

STRATEGY
ANALYZE STORY STRUCTURE

Tell students that recognizing how the story is organized can help them understand the plot. Read pages 3–5 aloud and model analyzing story structure.

Think Aloud In the first chapter, I learn that Gina's parents are archaeologists headed for the ancient city of Pompeii. Gina's parents seem enthusiastic about this project, but Gina admits in her journal that she's not really that interested. From these details I can tell that character, setting, and plot will be closely linked in this story.

SKILL
CHARACTER, SETTING AND PLOT

As they read, remind students to pay attention to the setting and the characters. The characters' actions in the setting will affect the plot. Begin a Character, Setting, and Plot Chart on chart paper.

READ AND RESPOND

Students should read orally to the end of Chapter 2. Ask: *What effect is the setting having on Gina?* Then have them read and discuss relevant plot developments of each chapter and complete the chart.

MAKE CONNECTIONS ACROSS TEXTS

Invite students to compare *Lost City* and *I Discover Pompeii, or How I Spent My Summer Vacation.*

- If you could spend an hour working with either Hiram Bingham or Giuseppe Fiorelli, which one would you pick? Why?

- If Gina Sorrentino's parents went to Machu Picchu, do you think she would want to go along? Explain.

ELL Access for All

Predict Discuss what it means to predict. Explain that before we read a story, we often predict, or guess what will happen. Use these sentence frames to have students make predictions about what may happen next. Have them take turns reading their predictions aloud. 1. When I heard the loud crash, _____. 2. As the bear approached our tent, _____.

Student Book

Student Book

Skills Focus ▶ Vocabulary

Tested ✓

Objective Apply vocabulary words and define compound words

Materials • **Vocabulary Cards** • **Student Book** *Lost City: The Discovery of Machu Picchu*

VOCABULARY WORDS

Give each student a Vocabulary Card. Ask a volunteer to read a definition of his or her word from the Glossary or a dictionary. The first student in the class to guess the correct word gets a point. Have each student take a turn reading the definition for his or her word.

WORD PARTS: COMPOUND WORDS

Tested ✓

Review that compound words are made up of two or more words. To determine the definition, students must think about the meaning of each word and figure out what the words might mean when combined. For instance, *under* and *growth* combine to form *undergrowth*. Have students suggest a definition for *undergrowth* based on its parts. Ask students to identify and define other compound words in *Lost City*.

Skills Focus ▶ Text Features

Objective Use a textbook and its text features

Materials • Student Book "Empire in the Andes" • science or social studies textbook

Tested ✓

TEXTBOOK FEATURES

Discuss the purpose and importance of headings, labels, captions, and other textbook features in a textbook article like "Empire in the Andes."

Skills Focus ▶ Fluency

Objective Read accurately with good prosody at a rate of 117–137 WCPM

Materials • **On Level Practice Book O,** p. 11

REPEATED READING

Work with students to begin marking up the Fluency passage on page 11 of **On Level Practice Book O** for proper phrasing. Remind students that one slash means "pause" and should come after commas, dashes, and other places where they would normally pause when reading or speaking. Tell them that two slashes mean "stop" and should come after end marks or semicolons.

Model reading the passage before and after students mark the slashes. Have students practice reading the Fluency passage during independent reading time throughout the week. Circulate and provide feedback.

Timed Reading Have students read the passage and record their rate.

■ **On Level Practice Book O,** page 11

As I read, I will pay attention to the pronunciation of city names, pauses, and intonation.

	Abdullah (Ahb-DUL-lah) loosened his black-and-white
4	head covering. Another grueling day of work was under way.
14	His job was to help remove dirt from ancient tombs, or
25	graves. Abdullah looked around the excavation site and tried
34	to count all of the exposed graves. But he soon gave up.
46	"There are too many of them," he thought. "Besides, if
56	Sheik Hamoudi (Shayk hah-MOOD-ee) catches me counting
61	graves instead of working, he will send me away." Abdullah
71	threw himself into removing dirt, but while he worked,
80	he secretly dreamed of discovering a hidden treasure.
88	Sheik Hamoudi was the foreman on the site. He had
98	worked for the Englishman for a long time. For the past
109	week, the Sheik had been the boss while the Englishman and
120	his wife were away in Baghdad. He treated his workers fairly,
131	and yet he frightened Abdullah when he yelled. Abdullah had
141	grown up in the south of Iraq and had never been more than
154	a few miles from his village. 160

Comprehension Check

1. What words would you use to describe Abdullah? **Character, Setting, Plot** Abdullah is a hard worker. He does not have much experience at his job and is easily frightened.
2. What does Abdullah dream of finding? **Character, Setting, Plot** Abdullah dreams of discovering hidden treasure.

	Words Read	–	Number of Errors	=	Words Correct Score
First Read		–		=	
Second Read		–		=	

Leveled Reader Lesson

Objective   Read to apply strategies and skills
Materials   • **Leveled Reader** *Queen Pu-abi's Royal Tomb* • chart paper

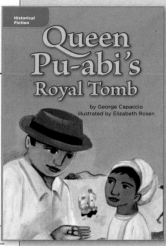

Leveled Reader

PREVIEW AND PREDICT

Show the cover and read the title of the book. Ask students to preview and make predictions about the story and to share any questions they have.

- Where do you think this story will take place?
- What do you think the story will be about?

STRATEGY
ANALYZE STORY STRUCTURE

Remind students that analyzing how a story is organized can help them see how characters and plot events develop.

SKILL
CHARACTER , SETTING, AND PLOT

Read aloud through page 5. Discuss Abdullah's feelings and actions:

- What are some of Abdullah's character traits?
- How do his actions affect events in the story?

Begin a Character, Setting, Plot chart on chart paper.

READ AND RESPOND

After students finish reading the story, have them share personal responses.

- Would you recommend this book to a friend? Why or why not?
- What ancient "secrets" have you heard about?

VOCABULARY WORDS

Discuss the vocabulary words as they are used in the story. Reteach meanings as necessary.

MAKE CONNECTIONS ACROSS TEXTS

Invite students to summarize and draw connections between *Lost City* and *Queen Pu-abi's Royal Tomb*.

- What subject do the stories have in common?
- How do boys help both Charles Leonard Woolley and Hiram Bingham?

ELL
Leveled Reader
Go to pages
65U–65V.

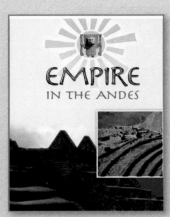

Student Book

Beyond Practice Book B, page 11

As I read, I will pay attention to the pronunciation of names, pauses, and intonation.

	Ouray (oo-RAY) veered off the trail and scrambled down the steep
11	side of the cliff. There wasn't much **vegetation** in his way, only a
24	scattering of pinyon pines and cactus. Soon the boy was sitting on a
37	sandstone ledge and looking down into a deep pool of icy, blue water.
50	An underground spring gushed through the rocks and kept the water cold
62	even on the hottest days. In the summer, Ouray loved imagining he was
75	a red-tailed hawk about to seize his prey. He would leap off the ledge
89	with his arms outstretched and swoop headfirst into the cool water
100	beneath him.
102	But now it was still early in the spring, and Ouray had something else
116	on his mind besides swimming. He untangled a long line of leather
128	strands that were knotted together and then weighted one end with a
140	round piece of lead. Next Ouray attached a small barbed bone and
152	concealed it under a few shiny feathers. He was ready.
162	Ouray threw out his fishing line and heard it hit the surface of the
176	pond with a perfect plunk. There was nothing left for him to do but
190	dangle his legs over the side of the sandstone ledge and wait for a big, fat
206	trout to strike. 209

Comprehension Check

1. How do you know that Ouray likes to daydream **Character, Setting, Plot** Ouray often imagines himself as a hawk, about to seize his prey.
2. What clues tell you that this story takes place in the Southwest? **Setting** The story describes pinyon pines, cactus, and sandstone, which indicates a Southwest setting.

	Words Read	–	Number of Errors	=	Words Correct Score
First Read		–		=	
Second Read		–		=	

Skills Focus ▶ Vocabulary

Objective Apply content vocabulary words
Materials • **Student Book** "Empire in the Andes"

EXTEND VOCABULARY

Review how the content vocabulary words are used in "Empire in the Andes." Have students create short riddles using the sound or spelling of each content vocabulary word and its definition. Examples: *What kind of corn sounds like a kind of puzzle?* (maize/maze); *What kind of leg lasts for a long time?* (a legacy) Students can then take turns asking each other riddles.

Skills Focus ▶ Text Features

Objective Use a textbook and its text features
Materials • **Student Book** Lost City

TEXTBOOK FEATURES

Point out that there are many kinds of **textbook features**. Some are headings and subheadings, captions, labels, changes in print, and key words. Have students identify various textbook features in "Empire in the Andes" and explain whether the features highlight important points in the text, help explain the text, illustrate the text, or elaborate on the text.

Skills Focus ▶ Fluency

Objective Read accurately with good prosody at a rate of 127–137 WCPM
Materials • **Beyond Practice Book B,** p. 11

REPEATED READING

Work with students to begin marking up the Fluency passage on page 11 of **Beyond Practice Book B** for proper phrasing. Remind them that one slash means "pause" and should come after commas, dashes, and other places where they would naturally pause when reading or speaking. Two slashes mean "stop" and should come after end marks or semicolons. Partners can finish marking the passage on their own. Model reading the passage for students.

During independent reading time, partners can take turns reading the passage they have marked. Remind students to wait until their partner gets to the next punctuation mark before they correct a mistake. Listen carefully to their reading, monitoring for accuracy.

Leveled Reader Library

Leveled Reader Lesson

Objective Read to apply strategies and skills

Materials • **Leveled Reader** *The Ancient Secret of Cliff Canyon*

PREVIEW AND PREDICT

Have students preview *The Ancient Secret of Cliff Canyon*, predict what it is about, and set a purpose for reading. *What questions do you have?*

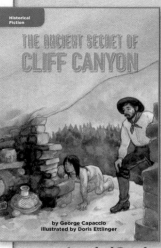

Leveled Reader

STRATEGY

ANALYZE STORY STRUCTURE

Review with students that by analyzing the structure of a story, readers can see how the characters and plot develop.

SKILL

CHARACTER, SETTING, AND PLOT

Ask a volunteer to explain the meaning of the terms *character, setting,* and *plot*. Have students discuss these elements in *The Ancient Secret of Cliff Canyon*, and insert information in a Character, Setting, and Plot Chart.

READ AND RESPOND

Students should identify the characters, setting, and main plot events, and complete filling in their Character, Setting, and Plot Chart. After students finish reading the story, have them share personal responses.

VOCABULARY WORDS

Have students form two teams. Give teams five minutes to write a brief story using all the vocabulary words. Have teams read their stories to the rest of the class. Ask the class to choose the most creative story.

Skills Focus

Self-Selected Reading

Objective Read independently to analyze character, setting, and plot

Materials • Leveled Readers or trade books at students' reading level

READ TO ANALYZE CHARACTER, SETTING, AND PLOT

Invite students to select a fiction book to read independently. For a list of theme-related titles, see pages T17–T18. As students read, have them take notes about the main characters, the setting, and the plot.

Afterward, partners should create a dialogue between the main characters in their books. The dialogue should include at least five detailed lines about each character's personality traits, a description of the setting, and the main plot event. Have pairs share their dialogues.

ELL **Access for All**

Character, Setting, and Plot Ask, *What are the characters in a story?* (the people in the story) *What is the setting?* (where the story takes place) *What is plot?* (the action in the story) Have students work in pairs to brainstorm examples of characters, setting, and plot for a story they might write.

Academic Language

Throughout the week, the English Language Learners in your class will need help in building their understanding of the academic language used in daily instruction and assessment instruments. The following strategies will help to increase their language proficiency and comprehension of content and instructional words.

LOG ON Technology

Oral Language For oral vocabulary development, go to
www. macmillanmh.com

Strategies to Reinforce Academic Language

- **Use Context** Academic Language used by the teacher (see chart below) should be explained in the context of the task during Whole Group. You may use gestures, expressions and visuals to support meaning.

- **Use Visuals** Use charts, transparencies, and graphic organizers to explain key labels to help students understand classroom language.

- **Model** Demonstrate the task using academic language in order for students to understand instruction.

Academic Language Used in Whole Group Instruction

Content/Theme Words	Skill/Strategy Words	Writing/Grammar Words
maize (p. 60)	headings (p. 62)	conventions (p. 64)
terracing (p. 60)	subheadings (p. 62)	subject (p. 65I)
aqueducts (p. 60)	boldface (p. 60)	predicate (p. 65I)
legacy (p. 60)	labels (p. 60)	letter (p. 64)
quipu (p. 60)	research (p. 53)	nonfiction (p. 60)
ruins (p. 48)	key words (p. 60)	reading rate (p. 48)

ELL Leveled Reader Lesson

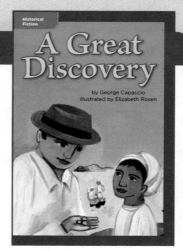

Historical Fiction

A Great Discovery

by George Capaccio
illustrated by Elizabeth Rosen

Before Reading

ORAL LANGUAGE

LOG ON

Build Background Point to the Middle East on a map. *What civilizations lived in this area in ancient times?* Explain that archaeologists have studied ruins of cities and kingdoms that existed there thousands of years ago. *Why do we study ruins? What famous ruins do you know?*

Review Vocabulary Write the vocabulary and story support words on the board and discuss their meaning. Model using them in sentences. *Guards* escort *workers at the ruins. An* archaeologist *is in charge of the excavation.*

PREVIEW AND PREDICT

Point to the cover illustration and read the title aloud. *What do you think this story will be about? Explain. Who do you think the characters are? What will be the plot and setting?*

Set a Purpose for Reading Show the Character, Setting, and Plot Chart and remind students they have used this chart before. Ask them to create a similar chart as they analyze the characters, setting, and plot of this story.

During Reading

Choose from among the differentiated strategies to support students' reading at all levels of language acquisition.

Beginning	Intermediate	Advanced
Shared Reading Do a shared reading of the story. Model how to analyze the characters, plot and setting. *Who is Abdullah? Where does he work?* Use the information to fill in the chart. Check students' comprehension and use vocabulary and support words.	**Read Together** Read through Chapter 1. Help students analyze the characters, setting, and plot up to this point. Record responses on the chart. Resume reading the story, taking turns with students. Have them continue to analyze the story elements.	**Independent Reading** Have students read the story. After reading each day, ask them to analyze the characters, setting, and plot and to write their ideas on their charts. Challenge students to write a paragraph that compares how Mr. Woolley and Sheik Hamoudi feel about Abdullah.

After Reading

Remind students to use the vocabulary and story words in their whole group activities.

Objective

- **To apply vocabulary & comprehension skills.**

Materials

- **ELL Leveled Reader** *A Great Discovery*
- **map of the Middle East**

5-Day Planner

DAY 1	• Academic Language • Oral Language and Vocabulary Review for the ELL Leveled Reader
DAY 2	• Academic Language • ELL Leveled Reader
DAY 3	• Academic Language • ELL Leveled Reader
DAY 4	• Academic Language • ELL Leveled Reader Comprehension Check
DAY 5	• Academic Language • ELL Leveled Reader Literacy Activities

Grade 6 • ELL TEACHER'S GUIDE

English Language Learners

Treasures

Macmillan/McGraw-Hill

ELL Teacher's Guide for students who need additional instruction.

Weekly Literature

Weekly Theme: Adapting to Survive

Week At A Glance

Whole Group

VOCABULARY
altered, erode, absorb, concentrated, innovations

Strategy: Use Context Clues/Definitions

COMPREHENSION
Strategy: Make Inferences and Analyze
Skill: Main Idea and Details

TEST STRATEGY
Right There

WRITING
Expository Writing

Science Link

Life Science
The Kingdoms of Life

Small Group Options

Differentiated Instruction for Tested Skills

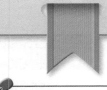
Tested Skills for the Week

Real World Reading

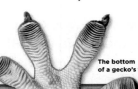

Comprehension

Genre
A Nonfiction Article in a newspaper or magazine presents facts and information.

Make Inferences and Analyze
Main Idea and Details
The main idea is the most important point an author makes. Details give more information about the main idea.

Gecko Glue, Cockroach Scouts, And Spider Silk Bridges

How can lizards, cockroaches, and spiders help make life better for humans?

How do product makers come up with big **innovations?** For some of their best new ideas, methods, and devices, scientists and researchers turn to designs found in nature for inspiration.

WHAT MAKES GECKOS STICK?
They run across ceilings. They zip up and down walls. What kind of crazy glue keeps geckos from tumbling down? Researchers at the University of California, Berkeley, and Lewis and Clark College in Portland, Oregon, have solved the mystery.

Scientists say that what makes geckos stick isn't tacky glue or suction, it's geometry. "We've solved the puzzle of how geckos use millions of tiny foot hairs to adhere to even smooth surfaces, such as polished glass," says scientist Kellar Autumn.

Gecko feet are covered with millions of tiny hairs called setae (SEE-tee), which split into hundreds of even tinier branches. Each gecko foot has as many as one billion of these split ends. Researchers

The bottom of a gecko's foot

70

Science Link
Main Selection
Genre Nonfiction Article

Real World Reading

Vocabulary
altered
erode
absorb
concentrated
innovations

How LONG Will We LIVE?

In 1900 the average American lived to be 47 years old. By the end of the twentieth century, the average life span was 76 years. The U.S. government predicts that by the year 2100, 5 million Americans will be 100 or more years old. Many of today's kids will live to see the year 2100. Some may be around to ring in 2140!

FOREVER YOUNG
In the future, scientists may be able to more easily replace body parts that don't work well with new ones.

Cynthia Kenyon, a scientist who studies aging, believes it may be possible for humans to live twice as long and still look and feel half their age. Kenyon has proved that this is possible for tiny creatures called round worms. She **altered** some chemicals inside their bodies. This change allowed worms to live four times as long as they normally would. The change also turns back the effects of aging. The worms look as young as when they were babies!

No matter what the future may hold for us, one thing seems certain: we will have longer, healthier lives to look forward to!

Vocabulary/ Comprehension

Answer Questions

Test Strategy
Right There
You can put your finger on the answer. Look for key words in the question. Then find those key words in the selection.

SLEEP IS GOOD FOR YOUR BRAIN

Tired of puzzling over a problem? Sleep on it! Research by a group of German scientists shows that getting enough sleep makes people better problem solvers. They found that people who sleep for at least eight hours each night are better at solving problems and thinking creatively. For their research study, the scientists divided 106 people into groups. The group that got eight hours of sleep was more than twice as likely to find a shortcut for solving a math problem than the group that had stayed awake all night.

Skimping on sleep has become a bad habit for many American kids. According to a survey by the National Sleep Foundation, 51% of kids ages 10 to 18 go to bed at 10 P.M. or later on school nights. The foundation reported that nearly 60% of 7- to 12-year-olds admitted that they felt tired during the day.

This is important information for parents and big kids. Getting enough sleep can improve a kid's performance at school.

Test Strategy
Right There

Treasures
INTERACTIVE
Read-Aloud
ANTHOLOGY with PLAYS
Macmillan/McGraw-Hill

Read-Aloud Anthology
• Listening Comprehension
• Readers Theater

Resources for Differentiated Instruction

Leveled Readers

GR Levels S–Y

Genre Informational Nonfiction

- Same Theme
- Same Vocabulary
- Same Comprehension Skills

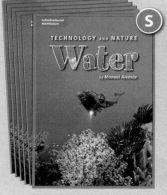

Approaching Level

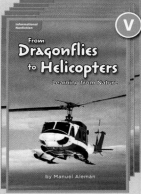

On Level

Beyond Level

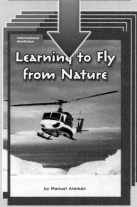

On Level Reader sheltered for English Language Learner

ELL Teacher's Guide also available

English Language Leveled Reader

Also Available LEVELED READER PROGRAM

CLASSROOM LIBRARY

Genre Expository Nonfiction

Approaching   **On Level**   **Beyond**

Trade books to apply Comprehension Skills

INTERVENTION ANTHOLOGY

- Phonics and Decoding
- Comprehension
- Vocabulary

Also available, *Reading Triumphs* Intervention Program

LEVELED PRACTICE

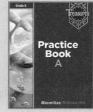   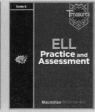

Approaching   **On Level**   **Beyond**   **ELL**

HOME-SCHOOL CONNECTION

- Family letters in English and Spanish
- Take-Home Stories

Technology

ONLINE INSTRUCTION
www.macmillanmh.com

 AUDIO CD
- Listening Library
- Fluency Solutions

 CD-ROM
- Vocabulary PuzzleMaker

Suggested Lesson Plan

 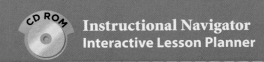 CD ROM **Instructional Navigator** Interactive Lesson Planner

Gecko Glue, Cockroach Scouts, and Spider Silk Bridges, 70–73

Leveled Readers

Whole Group

ORAL LANGUAGE
- **Listening**
- **Speaking**
- **Viewing**

WORD STUDY
- **Vocabulary**
- **Phonics/Decoding**

READING
- **Develop Comprehension**
- **Fluency**

LANGUAGE ARTS
- **Writing**
- **Grammar**
- **Spelling**

ASSESSMENT
- **Informal/Formal**

Turn the page for
Small Group Lesson Plan

66C

Day 1

Listening/Speaking/Viewing
- **❓ Focus Question** What is the role of science in people's daily lives?
- Build Background, 66
- Read Aloud: "Becky Schroeder," 67

Vocabulary
- *altered, erode, absorb, concentrated, innovations*, 68
- Practice Book A-O-B, 15
- **Strategy:** Context Clues/ Definitions, 69

Read "How Long Will We Live?," 68–69

 Student Book

Comprehension, 69A–69B
- **Strategy:** Make Inferences and Analyze
- **Skill:** Main Idea and Details
- Practice Book A-O-B, 16

Fluency Partner Reading, 66I
Model Fluency, 67

Writing
- Daily Writing Prompt: Describe reasons why it is important to preserve nature.
- Informational Essay, 77A–77B

Grammar Daily Language Activities, 77I
- Sentence Combining, 77I
- Grammar Practice Book, 13

Spelling Pretest, 77G
- Spelling Practice Book, 13–14

Quick Check Vocabulary, 68
Comprehension, 69B

Differentiated Instruction 77M–77V

Day 2

Listening/Speaking
- **❓ Focus Question** How can lizards, cockroaches, and spiders help make life better for humans?

Vocabulary
- Review Vocabulary Words, 70

Phonics/Decoding
- Words with *ei* and *ie*, 77E
- Practice Book A-O-B, 21

Read *Gecko Glue, Cockroach Scouts, and Spider Silk Bridges*, 70–73

 Student Book

Comprehension, 70–73
- **Strategy:** Make Inferences and Analyze
- **Skill:** Main Idea and Details
- Practice Book A-O-B, 17

Fluency Partner Reading, 66I

Writing
- Daily Writing Prompt: Write a paragraph about an animal you would be excited to study.
- Informational Essay, 77A–77B

Grammar Daily Language Activities, 77I
- Sentence Combining, 77I
- Grammar Practice Book, 14

Spelling *ei* or *ie*, 77G
- Spelling Practice Book, 15

Quick Check Comprehension, 73
Phonics, 77E

Differentiated Instruction 77M–77V

Skills/Strategies

Vocabulary
Vocabulary Words
Context Clues/
Definitions

Comprehension
Strategy: Make
Inferences and
Analyze
Skill: Main Idea and
Details

Writing
Informational

**Turn the Page for
Small Group
Options**

Day 3

Listening/Speaking

❓ **Focus Question** How are the scientific innovations described in "How Long Will We Live?" different from those in *Gecko Glue, Cockroach Scouts,* and *Spider Silk Bridges*?

Summarize, 73

Vocabulary

Review Words in Context, 77C
Strategy: Context Clues/Definitions, 77D
Practice Book A-O-B, 20

Phonics

Decode Multisyllabic Words, 77E

Read *Gecko Glue, Cockroach Scouts, and Spider Silk Bridges,* 70–73

Student Book

Comprehension

Comprehension Check, 73
Maintain Skill: Main Idea and Details, 73A

Fluency Partner Reading, 66I
Repeated Reading, 73A
Practice Book A-O-B, 18

✎ Writing

Daily Writing Prompt: Create a list of steps of a process you have used to reach a goal.

Informational Essay, 77A–77B

Grammar Daily Language Activities, 77I
Sentence Combining, 77J
Grammar Practice Book, 15

Spelling *ei* or *ie*, 77H
Spelling Practice Book, 16

 Vocabulary, 77D

Differentiated Instruction 77M–77V

Day 4

Listening/Speaking/Viewing

❓ **Focus Question** Why do you think so many kids skimp on sleep?

Expand Vocabulary: Science for All, 77F

Vocabulary

Suffixes, 77F
Apply Vocabulary to Writing, 77F

Read "Sleep Is Good for the Brain," 74
Test Strategy: Right There

Student Book

Research and Study Skills

Using the Library and Media Center, 73B
Practice Book A-O-B, 19

Fluency Partner Reading, 66I

✎ Writing

Daily Writing Prompt: Envision an undiscovered creature and create a poem that captures this image.

Informational Essay, 77A–77B

Grammar Daily Language Activities, 77I
Sentence Combining, 77J
Grammar Practice Book, 16

Spelling *ei* or *ie*, 77H
Spelling Practice Book, 17

 Vocabulary, 77D

Differentiated Instruction 77M–77V

Day 5
Review and Assess

Listening/Speaking/Viewing

❓ **Focus Question** How has scientific exploration benefitted our society?

Speaking and Listening Strategies, 77A

Vocabulary

Spiral Review of Vocabulary Words, 77F

Read Self-Selected Reading, 66I

Student Book

Comprehension

Strategy: Make Inferences and Analyze
Skill: Main Ideas and Details

Fluency Partner Reading, 66I
Practice, 73A

✎ Writing

Daily Writing Prompt: In a few sentences, describe how spiders make you feel.

Informational Essay, 77A–77B

Grammar Daily Language Activities, 77I
Sentence Combining, 77J
Grammar Practice Book, 17–18

Spelling Posttest, 77H
Spelling Practice Book, 18

Weekly Assessment, 29–36

Differentiated Instruction 77M–77V

Differentiated Instruction

What do I do in small groups?

Teacher-Led Small Groups

Literacy Workstations

Independent Activities

Focus on Skills

 Skills Focus ▶ Use your **Quick Check** observations to guide additional instruction and practice.

Phonics
Words with *ei* and *ie*

 Vocabulary
Words: absorb, altered, concentrated, erode, innovations
 Strategy: Context Clues: Definition

Comprehension
 Strategy: Make Inferences and Analyze
Skill: Main Idea and Details

 Fluency

Suggested Lesson Plan

 Instructional Navigator
Interactive Lesson Planner

	Day 1	**Day 2**
Approaching Level • **Additional Instruction/Practice** • **Tier 2 Instruction**	Fluency, 77N Vocabulary, 77N Comprehension, 77O **ELL** Context Clues, 77O	Phonics, 77M Vocabulary, 77O Leveled Reader Lesson, 77P • Vocabulary • Comprehension
On Level • **Practice**	Vocabulary, 77Q Leveled Reader Lesson, 77R • Comprehension **ELL** Leveled Reader, 77U–77V	Leveled Reader Lesson, 77R • Comprehension • Vocabulary
Beyond Level • **Extend**	Vocabulary, 77S Leveled Reader Lesson, 77T • Comprehension	Leveled Reader Lesson, 77T • Comprehension • Vocabulary

For intensive intervention see **READING Triumphs**

Small Group Options

Apply skills and strategies while reading appropriate leveled books.

Levels S–Y

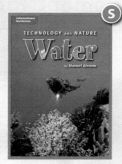 (S) **Approaching**

 (V) **On Level**

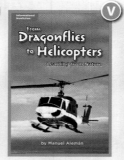 (Y) **Beyond**

ELL

Additional Leveled Reader Resources

LOG ON

Leveled Reader Database

Go to **www.macmillanmh.com**

Search by

- Comprehension Skill
- Content Area
- Genre
- Text Feature

- Guided Reading Level
- Reading Recovery Level
- Lexile Score
- Benchmark Level

Subscription also available

Day 3

Phonics, 77M
Fluency, 77N
Vocabulary, 77O
Leveled Reader Lesson, 77P
- Comprehension

Fluency, 77Q
Vocabulary, 77Q
Leveled Reader Lesson, 77R
- Comprehension

Fluency, 77S
Vocabulary, 77S
Leveled Reader Lesson, 77T
- Comprehension

Day 4

Phonics, 77M
Leveled Reader Lesson, 77P
- Comprehension

Study Skill, 77Q
Leveled Reader Lesson, 77R
- Comprehension

Study Skill, 77S
Leveled Reader Lesson, 77T
- Comprehension
ELL Questions and Answers, 77T

Day 5

Fluency, 77N
Leveled Reader Lesson, 77P
- Make Connections
  Across Texts

Fluency, 77Q
Leveled Reader Lesson, 77R
- Make Connections
  Across Texts

Fluency, 77S
Self-Selected Reading, 77T

Managing the Class

What do I do with the rest of my class?

Teacher-Led Small Groups

Literacy Workstations

Independent Activities

Class Management Tools

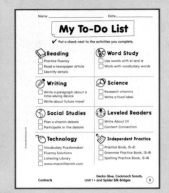

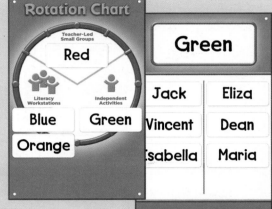

Rotation Chart

Includes:
- How-To Guides
- Rotation Chart
- Weekly Contracts

FOLDABLES™

Hands-on activities to reinforce weekly skills

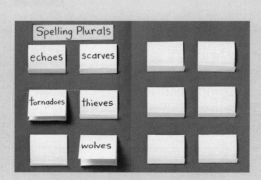

Matchbook Foldable

Word	Synonym	Antonym	Prefix or Suffix
normal	typical	unusual	normally

Folded Foldable

Independent Activities

Leveled Readers
For Repeated Readings and Literacy Activities

Approaching

On Level

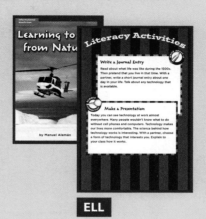
ELL

Beyond

LEVELED PRACTICE

Skills: Vocabulary (p. 15), Comprehension: Main Idea and Details (p. 16), Graphic Organizers (p. 17), Fluency (p. 18), Study Skill: Media Center (p. 19), Vocabulary Strategy: Definitions (p. 20), Phonics (p. 21)

Approaching

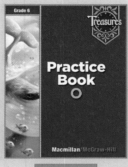
On Level

Beyond

ELL

Technology

 ONLINE INSTRUCTION www.macmillanmh.com

- Meet the Author/Illustrator
- Computer Literacy Lessons
- Research and Inquiry Activities

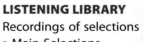

- Oral Language Activities
- Vocabulary and Spelling Activities
- Leveled Reader Database

 LISTENING LIBRARY
Recordings of selections
- Main Selections
- Leveled Readers
- ELL Readers
- Intervention Anthology

 FLUENCY SOLUTIONS
Recorded passages for modeling and practicing fluency

VOCABULARY PUZZLEMAKER
Activities providing multiple exposures to vocabulary, spelling, and high-frequency words including crossword puzzles, word searches, and word jumbles

Turn the page for Literacy Workstations.

Managing the Class

Literacy Activities
Collaborative Learning Activities

 **Reading**

Objectives

- Time reading to practice fluency.
- Read passage fluently with expression.
- Identify main idea and supporting details.
- Read daily for enjoyment.

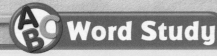 **Word Study**

Objectives

- Identify words with long vowels spelled *ei* or *ie* and use them in sentences.
- Create word jumbles using vocabulary words.

 Reading — Fluency — 20 Minutes

- Choose a paragraph from the fluency passage on page 18 of your Practice Book.
- Review difficult vocabulary words before you echo-read with your partner. Then echo-read the passage, using appropriate intonation as you read.

Extension

- Discuss how you raised and lowered your voices to suit each statement, question or command.
- Time Your Reading: Listen to the Audio CD.

Things you need:
- Practice Book

Fluency Solutions
Listening Library — 5

Word Study — ei and ie — 20 Minutes

- Circle the letters that make the long vowel sound in each of the following words.

| eight | yield | receive |
| neighbor | weigh | seize |

- Identify the long vowel sound. Then use each word in a sentence.

Weight

Extension

- Make a list of words with *ei* and *ie*.
- Leave blank spaces where the vowels *ei* or *ie* go.
- Give your list to a partner. Can he or she fill in the blanks correctly?

Things you need:
- paper
- pencil

 For additional vocabulary and spelling games, go to www.macmillanmh.com — 5

Reading — Independent Reading — 20 Minutes

- Read the first paragraph of a newspaper or magazine article.
- On a sheet of paper, list the main idea.
- Read the remainder of the article and list the supporting details.
- Use what you have learned about rereading to help you understand the article.

Extension

- Choose one supporting detail and illustrate it.
- Write a caption for your illustration.

Things you need:
- newspaper or magazine
- paper and pencil
- colored markers

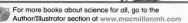 For more books about science for all, go to the Author/Illustrator section at www.macmillanmh.com — 6

Word Study — Vocabulary Words — 20 Minutes

- Write a definition of each of the following words on the back of a card:

| erode | altered | absorb |
| concentrated | innovations | |

- On the front of the card create a word jumble for the definition on the back of the card.

Extension

- Hand out cards to your classmates and see if they can solve the word jumbles.
- If they need help, tell them to look at the definition on the back of the card.

Things you need:
- index cards
- pencil or pen

 For additional vocabulary and spelling games, go to www.macmillanmh.com — Vocabulary PuzzleMaker — 6

Literacy Workstations

Writing

Objectives

- Make an outline with main idea and details and write an expository paragraph.
- Write an expository piece and design an accompanying illustration.

Content Literacy

Objectives

- Use reference books to research vitamins and write a summary of what you discover.
- Argue for or against a topic in front of an audience.

Writing — Science for All   20 Minutes

- Write a paragraph on how a time-saving device in your home or school helps you each day.
- Include a topic sentence and supporting details.

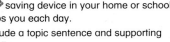

Extension
Research information about the time-saving device. Who invented it? When was it sold to the public?

Things you need:
- reference books
- paper and pencil

Science — Vitamins   20 Minutes

- Long ago, people neither knew about nor understood the importance of vitamins.
- Use reference books to research information about a vitamin or mineral.
- Write a summary of what you discover.

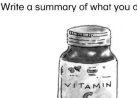 

Extension
- Use your notes to write a label for a package of food that contains this vitamin or mineral.
- Make the food and vitamin sound irresistible to a buyer.
- Read your label to a partner or the class.

Things you need:
- reference books
- paper and pencil

LOG ON Internet Research and Inquiry Activity
Students can find more facts at www.macmillanmh.com

5

Writing — The Ideal Commute   20 Minutes

- Imagine yourself twenty years from now. There are many new inventions in the world.
- What is your favorite way to travel from your home to your job?
- Describe your vehicle of the future.

Extension
- Draw an illustration of your vehicle or commute.
- Create a mood that shows how you feel about this futuristic world.
- Include a caption.

Things you need:
- paper and pencil
- colored markers

Social Studies — Vitamin Debate   20 Minutes

- Should school cafeterias offer vitamin pills with lunch? Why or why not?
- Separate into groups of three or four, research vitamins, and plan a debate on the topic. One team will argue for giving out vitamin pills with lunch and the other team will argue against this practice.

Extension
- Schedule the debate for the entire class to hear.
- Encourage a general discussion about the points covered in the debate.
- Remind everyone to listen carefully and not interrupt.

Things you need:
- reference materials
- paper and pencil

LOG ON Internet Research and Inquiry Activity
Students can find more facts at www.macmillanmh.com

6

ORAL LANGUAGE
- Build Background
- Read Aloud
- Expand Vocabulary

 VOCABULARY
- Teach Words in Context
- Definitions

COMPREHENSION
- **Strategy:** Make Inferences and Analyze
- **Skill:** Identify Main Idea and Details

SMALL GROUP OPTIONS
- Differentiated Instruction, pp. 77M–77V

Oral Language

Build Background

ACCESS PRIOR KNOWLEDGE

Share the following information:

The word *science* is derived from a French word meaning "to know."

TALK ABOUT SCIENCE FOR ALL

Discuss the weekly theme.

Why do you think a person would decide to be a scientist?

 FOCUS QUESTION Ask a volunteer to read "Talk About It" on **Student Book** page 66. Ask:

What are the children doing in the picture?

Have you ever observed something? What did you want to learn?

Talk About It
What is the role of science in people's daily lives?

 Find out more about scientists at **www.macmillanmh.com**

66

ENGLISH LANGUAGE LEARNERS

Access for All

Beginning Name and Repeat Point to and name items in the photo. Have students repeat. Ask questions such as *What do you see? What are they looking at?* Allow students to say what they can. Then model the answers. Have students repeat.

Intermediate Activate Prior Knowledge Discuss the kinds of activities students have done in science class. Provide language as needed. For Spanish-speaking students, point out the cognates *science/ciencia*. Ask: *What would you like to study as a scientist?*

Advanced Elaborate Complete the task in the Intermediate column. Restate what students say in more complex sentences: *You say you'd like to study space because you are interested in learning more about black holes.*

SCIENCE FOR ALL

67

Read Aloud
Read "Becky Schroeder"

GENRE: Nonfiction Article
Review features of a nonfiction article:

Read Aloud
pages 19–22

- presents facts and information about real people, things, or events

- sometimes includes the author's opinions

LISTENING FOR A PURPOSE

Ask students to listen carefully for the reasons Becky Schroeder decided to invent the Glow-Sheet. They should be prepared to identify and discuss these reasons. Choose from among the teaching suggestions found in the **Read-Aloud Anthology.**

Fluency Ask students to listen carefully to your phrasing and expression as you read aloud.

RESPOND TO THE STORY

Ask students to write a description of a product they would like to invent to help them in their daily lives.

Expand Vocabulary

Ask students to choose a word from "Becky Schroeder" that relates to the theme, Science for All. Have students make a word web using the words they chose.

Technology

For an extended lesson plan and Web site activities for **oral language development,** go to **www.macmillanmh.com**

Picture Prompt

Look at the picture. Write about what you see. You can write a poem, a story, or a description, or use any other type of writing you like.

Vocabulary

TEACH WORDS IN CONTEXT

Use the following routine.

Routine

Define: Something is **altered** when it is changed.
Example: The scientist altered her dinner plans when she decided to work late.
Ask: Name an antonym for *altered*.
ANTONYM

- To **erode** is to wear away. Hurricane winds can erode beaches. What natural forces might erode a mountain? EXAMPLE

- To **absorb** means to take in, or soak up. He used a sponge to absorb the water he spilled. What might you use to absorb water from your hair? EXAMPLE

- A substance becomes **concentrated** when it accumulates and is not weakened by mixing with something else. The bodies of the poisoned fish contained concentrated mercury. How might a swimmer feel if chlorine became too concentrated in a swimming pool? EXPLANATION

- **Innovations** are inventions or new ideas. We can probably expect many more computer innovations in the next few years. What scientific innovations would you like to see? EXAMPLE

Access for All

Real World Reading

Vocabulary

altered
erode
absorb
concentrated
innovations

How LONG Will We LIVE?

In 1900 the average American lived to be 47 years old. By the end of the twentieth century, the average life span was 76 years. The U.S. government predicts that by the year 2100, 5 million Americans will be 100 or more years old. Many of today's kids will live to see the year 2100. Some may be around to ring in 2140!

FOREVER YOUNG

In the future, scientists may be able to more easily replace body parts that don't work well with new ones.

Cynthia Kenyon, a scientist who studies aging, believes it may be possible for humans to live twice as long and still look and feel half their age. Kenyon has proved that this is possible for tiny creatures called round worms. She **altered** some chemicals inside their bodies. This change allowed worms to live four times as long as they normally would. The change also turns back the effects of aging. The worms look as young as when they were babies!

No matter what the future may hold for us, one thing seems certain: we will have longer, healthier lives to look forward to!

68

Quick Check **Do students understand word meanings?**

During **Small Group Instruction**

If No → **Approaching Level** Vocabulary, p. 77N

If Yes → **On Level** Options, pp. 77Q–77R

Beyond Level Options, pp. 77S–77T

ELL   **Access for All**

Demonstrate Vocabulary Demonstrate the word *absorb* by using a sponge or paper towel and a glass of water. Discuss and list objects that can and can't *absorb* water using the sentence frame ___ *can/can't absorb water.* On the board, write the word *erode* and say, Erode *means to slowly destroy something.* Draw on the board how waves can erode a beach.

Where did all that SALT come from?

Have you ever wondered why the ocean is salty? The short answer to that question is because sodium and chloride, the two ingredients in salt, flow into it.

Want a little more information? Here's the full answer: Rivers **erode,** or wear away, rocks containing sodium and carry it out to sea. Undersea volcanoes spit up chloride. Sea creatures **absorb** many of the other minerals found in the ocean, such as calcium and sulfur. They do not soak up sodium or chloride, however, so the salt gets **concentrated**. It stays in the sea water and accumulates.

Indian Ocean

TIME FOR KIDS.

Household Inventions Time Line

Here are a few of history's most amazing **innovations**, or inventions. Many seem almost magical, while others are tools to make life a little easier or more fun.

Dorothea Lange with camera

Alexander Graham Bell, inventor of the telephone

ca. 3800-3600 B.C.	Wheel
ca. A.D. 100	Paper
1870	Chewing gum
1876	Telephone
1885	Bicycle
1888	Hand-held camera
1891	Zipper
1893	Movies
1904	Ice-cream cone
1927	Television
1938	Ballpoint pen
1945	Microwave oven
1963	Home video recorder
1972	Compact disc
1983	Cell phones
1991	World Wide Web
1995	DVDs

LOG ON Find out more about inventions at www.macmillanmh.com

69

Vocabulary

Tested

STRATEGY
USE CONTEXT CLUES

Definitions Tell students that when they see an unfamiliar word, they should check for a **definition** in the same sentence or paragraph. The definition will tell them what the unfamiliar word means.

Point to the word *innovations* in "Household Inventions Time Line." Ask what definition the author provided. (invention)

Read "Where did all that SALT come from?"

As you read "Where did all that SALT come from?" with students, ask them to identify clues that reveal the meanings of the highlighted words in the selections on pages 68–69. Tell students they will read these words again in *Gecko Glue, Cockroach Scouts, and Spider Silk Bridges*.

On Level Practice Book O, page 15

A. Write the vocabulary word that matches each clue.

| altered | erode | absorb | concentrated | innovations |

1. This is what happens to ice when it melts. It means "changed."
   __altered__

2. This is another word for inventions or changes. __innovations__

3. Things that are really packed together are called this. You can buy orange juice in this form. __concentrated__

4. Water and wind wear away at rocks and soil over time to do this.
   __erode__

5. A sponge or a paper towel can do this with liquid. __absorb__

B. Write a sentence of your own using vocabulary words from the list above. Possible responses provided.

6. Paint can erode and fall off in flakes.

7. Julian likes to absorb as much information about spiders as he can find.

8. Ulrike's handwriting is so concentrated that it is sometimes hard to read.

9. Nicole's innovations helped her company become a leader.

10. Sandy's mother altered the prom gown so it fit her perfectly.

⭐ **Approaching Practice Book A,** page 15

◆ **Beyond Practice Book B,** page 15

Objectives

Students will:
- Make inferences and analyze
- Use academic language: *main idea, details*
- Identify the main idea and details in an article

Materials

- Comprehension Transparency 3
- Leveled Practice Books, p. 16

Skills Trace

Main Idea and Details

Introduce	U1: 69A–69B
Practice/ Apply	U1: 70–73; Leveled Practice Books, 16–17
Reteach/ Review	U1: 77M–77T, 105A–105B, 106–119, 123M–123T; Leveled Practice Books, 30–31
Assess	Weekly Tests; Unit 1 Tests; Benchmark Tests A, B
Maintain	U1: 73A, 119B; U2: 185A; U3: 309A

ELL — Access for All

Main Idea and Details
Have students tell you the difference between a detail and the main idea to make sure they understand the concepts. Have students explain what the word *infer* means. Point out how the title can often give you clues to the main idea.

Reread for
Comprehension

STRATEGY
MAKE INFERENCES AND ANALYZE

Authors do not always tell readers everything that takes place in a story. Sometimes they provide details that help readers to figure things out. Good readers must call upon their own understanding of the clues in the text and then think about their own experiences. This will help them identify the main idea and details in a text.

SKILL
MAIN IDEA AND DETAILS

The main idea is the most important point an author makes about a topic. The main idea is often stated in a sentence at the beginning of a paragraph or section of text. The rest of the sentences give details and other information that help support the main idea. Sometimes, though, the main idea is stated elsewhere—or not stated at all. Good readers should be able to infer the main idea from the other information given by the author.

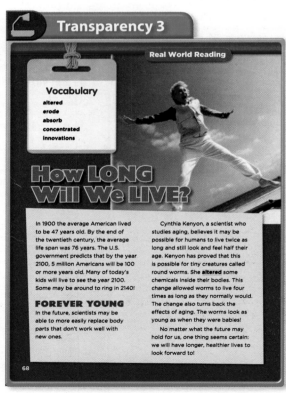

Student Book page 68 available on Comprehension Transparency 3

MODEL

Reread "How Long Will We Live?" from **Student Book** page 68.

Think Aloud The first sentence of the first paragraph is about how long the average American lived in 1900. I don't think that's the main idea, because the second sentence is about how long the average life span was at the end of the twentieth century. The author did not state the main idea, so I'll have to infer it by analyzing the text. All the sentences are about life span, which has been getting longer and longer from 1900 on. I think that's the main idea: Since 1900, the average American's life span has been getting longer.

GUIDED PRACTICE

Display **Transparency 3.** Ask students to:

- Identify the details in the first paragraph that support the main idea that since 1900 the average American's lifespan has been getting longer. Have a volunteer come up and circle a detail on the transparency. (Every sentence provides a detail.)

- Help students find the main idea in the third paragraph. Have them work through the procedure that was modeled in the Think Aloud.

APPLY

Point out that sometimes the main idea of an article is explicitly stated in the final paragraph. Read aloud the last paragraph. Have students find the main idea of the entire selection and identify two details that support the main idea.

Quick Check **Can students identify the main idea and details in the selection?**

During **Small Group Instruction**

If No → **Approaching Level** Comprehension, p. 77O

If Yes → **On Level** Options, pp. 77Q–77R

Beyond Level Options, pp. 77S–77T

On Level Practice Book O, page 16

Read the passages. Then list the main idea and three supporting details for each one. Possible responses provided.

Science is all around us. Due to scientific research, we are able to communicate through the Internet and cell phones. Every time we bake something, we are participating in a scientific process. Our baked goods are new substances formed from a variety of single substances. Look around you. Many of the objects surrounding you, such as plastic or metal products, are the results of much scientific research and study.

Main Idea: Science is all around us.

Supporting Details: We are able to communicate through the Internet and cell phones. Baking is an example of a scientific process. Many of the objects around us were discovered or developed by scientists.

Medicine helps us improve the quality of our lives. If you have a headache, you can take medicine to ease the pain. If you have an infection, a doctor can give you medicine to heal it. Without medicine, your infection could be deadly. In addition, doctors and researchers help people fight diseases with the help of vaccinations and antibiotics. Measles, tuberculosis, and polio are not nearly as threatening as they were 100 years ago because of medicine.

Main Idea: Medicine helps us improve the quality of our lives.

Supporting Details: If you have a headache, medicine can help ease the pain. If you have an infection, a doctor can give you medicine to heal it. In addition, doctors and researchers help people fight diseases with the use of vaccinations and antibiotics.

★ **Approaching Practice Book A,** page 16

◆ **Beyond Practice Book B,** page 16

Read

MAIN SELECTION
- *Gecko Glue, Cockroach Scouts, and Spider Silk Bridges*
- **Skill:** Main Idea and Details

TEST PREP
- *Sleep Is Good for Your Brain*
- **Test Strategy:** Right There

SMALL GROUP OPTIONS
- Differentiated Instruction, pp. 77M–77V

Comprehension

GENRE: NONFICTION ARTICLE

Have a student read the definition of a nonfiction article on **Student Book** page 70. Students should look for facts and information.

STRATEGY
MAKE INFERENCES AND ANALYZE

Remind students that an author does not always include everything in the text. A good reader must use whatever details are offered and **make inferences** about the main idea of the text.

SKILL
MAIN IDEA AND DETAILS

The **main idea** of a selection is what the story or article is about. Sometimes readers must make an inference to figure out the main idea. Details are statements that support the main idea.

Comprehension

Genre

A Nonfiction Article in a newspaper or magazine presents facts and information.

Make Inferences and Analyze

Main Idea and Details
The main idea is the most important point an author makes. Details give more information about the main idea.

Gecko Glue, Cockroach Scouts, And Spider Silk Bridges

How can lizards, cockroaches, and spiders help make life better for humans?

How do product makers come up with big **innovations?** For some of their best new ideas, methods, and devices, scientists and researchers turn to designs found in nature for inspiration.

🌿 WHAT MAKES GECKOS STICK?
They run across ceilings. They zip up and down walls. What kind of crazy glue keeps geckos from tumbling down? Researchers at the University of California, Berkeley, and Lewis and Clark College in Portland, Oregon, have solved the mystery.

Scientists say that what makes geckos stick isn't tacky glue or suction, it's geometry. "We've solved the puzzle of how geckos use millions of tiny foot hairs to adhere to even smooth surfaces, such as polished glass," says scientist Kellar Autumn.

Gecko feet are covered with millions of tiny hairs called setae (SEE-tee), which split into hundreds of even tinier branches. Each gecko foot has as many as one billion of these split ends. Researchers

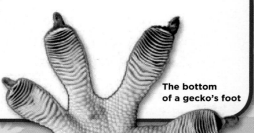

The bottom of a gecko's foot

70

Vocabulary

Vocabulary Words Review the tested vocabulary words: **altered, erode, absorb, concentrated, innovations**

Selection Words Students may find these words difficult. Pronounce the words and present the meanings as necessary.

setae (p. 70): tiny hairs

durable (p. 71): tough, sturdy, and strong

bacteria (p. 73): common microscopic organisms

found that the angle the toe hairs make with a surface allows them to stick. As scientists watched films of geckos in action, they noticed that geckos curl and uncurl their toes to get them to stick to surfaces.

Why the big interest in gecko "glue"? Researchers believe that a human-made version would be an ideal dry adhesive that could be useful underwater or in space. Researchers have already made artificial hair tips that stick almost as well as the geckos' own. "Now we've got to make billions of them to get significant adhesive force," says engineer Ron Fearing.

One thing is certain—it'll be a super glue. A million tiny setae, **concentrated** in an area the size of a dime, would be strong enough to lift a 45-pound child!

A gecko clings upside-down to glass.

🦎 COCKROACH SCOUTS

Think before you squish: The next roach you step on could save your life. That, at least, is the goal of Jeff Brinker, a scientist at Sandia National Laboratories in Albuquerque, New Mexico. Brinker and his team have thought of a way to use these insects to detect chemical or biological dangers.

The idea isn't as strange as it may sound. The government is already exploring how to use everything from bug-sized robots to live wasps for similar tasks. Brinker once worked on a project that tried to train honeybees to sniff out explosives.

Roaches were a natural next step. "It's a very durable beast," Brinker says. "Plus they tend to explore nooks and crannies." The key, Brinker says, is to use yeast that has been genetically **altered**. The yeast cells are glued to the bug's body and will glow when they come in contact with something harmful.

American cockroach

Read Together	**Read Independently**
If your students need support to read this selection, use the prompts to guide comprehension and model how to complete the graphic organizer.	If your students can read this selection independently, have them read it and complete the graphic organizer. Remind students to use purposes to set or adjust their reading rate.

If your students need an alternate selection, choose the **Leveled Readers** that match their instructional level.

Technology

Selection available on **Listening Library Audio CD.**

Read

Main Selection   Student pages 70–71

📓 Preview and Predict

Have students read the title, preview the illustrations, and note questions and predictions about what may happen in the selection. Ask what they think this selection will be about. Have students write their predictions and questions they have about the selection.

Set Purposes

FOCUS QUESTION Discuss with students the question under the title of the article. Point out the Main Idea Web on **Leveled Practice Book** page 17. Explain that students will fill it in as they read.

Read *Gecko Glue, Cockroach Scouts, and Spider Silk Bridges*

1 **STRATEGY**
MAKE INFERENCES AND ANALYZE

Teacher Think Aloud I know from what I have read so far that scientists are studying geckos to figure out how to make a super glue. I think that the main idea of this article is that nature can provide inspiration for new products. Why might cockroaches and spiders be an important part of this article?

Student Think Aloud The subtitle of the article says that geckos, cockroaches, and spiders can make life better. I think the rest of the article will provide details about cockroaches and spiders that will support the main idea.

Develop Comprehension

2 DRAW CONCLUSIONS

Why are scientists interested in cockroaches, wasps, and honey bees? (They want to develop a way to use the insects to detect chemical dangers.)

3 MAIN IDEA AND DETAILS

Why do scientists want to use cockroaches as "scouts"? (Cockroaches are durable and naturally explore nooks and crannies)

4 MAIN IDEA AND DETAILS

What is the main idea of this nonfiction article? (Nature provides inspiration for scientists and researchers.) Work with students to fill in the Main Idea Web with details that support the main idea.

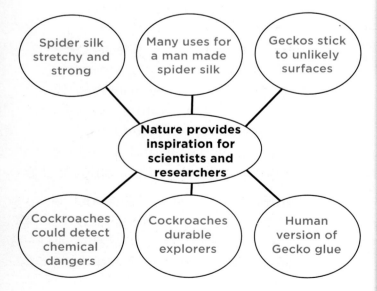

2 Living cells have several advantages over sensor machines, says Susan Brozik, a scientist working with Brinker. They're small, cheap, and very sensitive to their surroundings. Agent Roach
3 reporting for duty!

The silk in a spider web is both flexible and strong.

❧ THE ITSY-BITSY SPIDER IS A BIG BUILDER

Legend has it that when the mighty ruler Genghis Khan (JEN-gis KAHN) conquered Asia, his soldiers were protected from enemy arrows by very special clothing. These leather garments were interwoven with one of the strongest materials then known to humans—spider silk!

Eight hundred years later, scientists still can't make thread more durable than the stuff spiders use to make webs. But biologists trying to copy nature's strongest fiber are making great progress. The U.S. Army plans to use one of the Great Khan's tricks: making bulletproof vests woven with artificial spider silk.

What makes spider silk so remarkable is its unique combination of strength and stretch. Spider silk is as strong as the fiber now used to make bulletproof vests, but far more elastic. The

72

Ways to Confirm Meaning

Syntactic/Structural Cues

Explain Tell students that good readers sometimes use what they know about context clues and grammar to help them understand a difficult word.

Model Read the word *artificial* in context.

Think Aloud I know from the sentence that the word is an adjective because it tells me what kind of spider silk the U.S. Army plans to use. The sentence above says that biologists are trying to copy spider silk so I think that *artificial* means *made by people, not nature.*

Apply Encourage students to use grammatical clues to help them with other difficult words. For example, can they tell if the word is a noun or adjective or verb?

web of a golden silk spider is strong enough to trap a bird. Researchers have figured out that a web woven of spider silk the thickness of a pencil could stop a jet in midair!

"When you think about the size and speed of a flying bee, the web that catches it has to be able to **absorb** a lot of energy," says Jean Herbert, an Army scientist in Natick, Massachusetts. Herbert is researching ways to use the tough fiber in everyday objects. Among the possibilities: jeans that don't wear out, car and truck bumpers that resist dents, and bridges whose structures will not easily **erode** and can withstand earthquakes.

Unlike silkworms, spiders cannot be raised on farms. (One reason: they tend to eat one another!) So scientists are inventing ways of making spider silk without spiders.

The ability to spin a web is controlled by certain genes inside the cells of spiders. Researchers at two chemical companies have made copies of these genes and put them into certain easy-to-grow bacteria. The scientists' goal: bacteria that can churn out spider silk. Transplanting spider genes is a sticky business. The genes don't always act exactly the way they would in a living spider, so the silk is not as strong or elastic as the real stuff.

For now, the surest silk-production **4** method is the one that Genghis Khan supposedly used—spiders themselves. "I never step on spiders," says chemist John O'Brien. "I have too much respect for them."

Spider silk is strong enough to trap flies and bigger prey.

Think and Compare

1. What covers the feet of geckos and allows them to stick to walls?

2. Why are scientists interested in duplicating spider silk?

3. Of these three projects, which one will help the world the most? Explain your ideas.

4. How are the scientific innovations described in "How Long Will We Live?" on page 68 different from those in the gecko glue article?

73

Comprehension Check

TEST PREP

SUMMARIZE

Have partners summarize the main ideas and details of the selection *Gecko Glue, Cockroach Scouts, and Spider Silk Bridges.*

THINK AND COMPARE

Sample answers are given.

Tested

1. **Details:** Gecko feet are covered by millions of tiny setae that allow them to stick to surfaces.

2. **Analyze:** Scientists would like to use a strong and stretchy fiber like spider silk for making bulletproof vests.

3. **Text-to-World:** Students may select any of the three. If they select gecko glue, they should focus on adhesive qualities; if they select cockroach scouts, they should focus on durability; if they select spider silk, they should focus on the fiber's strength and elasticity.

4. **Text-to-Text:** Students should recognize that the ideas mentioned in the gecko glue article are all inspired by nature. The ideas mentioned in "How Long Will We Live?" are about "conquering" nature.

Quick Check   **Can students identify the main idea and details?**

During **Small Group Instruction**

If No → **Approaching Level** Leveled Reader Lesson, p. 77P

If Yes → **On Level** Options, pp. 77Q–77R

Beyond Level Options, pp. 77S–77T

Objectives

- Read accurately with good prosody
- Rate: 117–137 WCPM
- Identify main ideas and details

Materials

- Fluency Transparency 3
- Fluency Solutions
- Leveled Practice Books, p. 18

Transparency 3

> The ability to spin a web is controlled by certain genes inside the cells of spiders. Researchers at two chemical companies have made copies of these genes and put them into certain easy-to-grow bacteria. The scientists' goal: bacteria that can churn out spider silk. Transplanting spider genes is a sticky business. The genes don't always act exactly the way they would in a living spider, so the silk is not as strong or elastic as the real stuff.
>
> For now, the surest silk-production method is the one that Genghis Khan supposedly used—spiders themselves. "I never step on spiders," says chemist John O'Brien.

Fluency Transparency 3

Skills Trace

Main Idea and Details

Introduce	U1: 69A–69B
Practice/ Apply	U1: 70–73; Leveled Practice Books, 16–17
Reteach/ Review	U1: 77M–77T, 105A–105B, 106–119, 123M–123T; Leveled Practice Books, 30–31
Assess	Weekly Tests; Unit 1 Test; Benchmark Tests A, B
Maintain	U1: 73A, 119B; U2: 185A; U3: 309A

73A

Fluency
Repeated Reading: Punctuation

EXPLAIN/MODEL Use **Transparency 3** to model reading aloud the last two paragraphs on **Student Book** page 73. Use appropriate inflection or expression to model punctuation. Point out the punctuation used in the passage: periods, commas, and an em dash. Have students echo-read each sentence, paying careful attention to punctuation in the passage.

PRACTICE/APPLY Divide students into two groups to echo-read the passage. One group should read a few paragraphs, and the other group should echo each sentence. Groups may then switch roles. For additional practice, have students use **Leveled Practice Book** page 18 or the Fluency Solutions CD. Do a Quick Check to see which students need small group instruction.

Comprehension

MAINTAIN SKILL
MAIN IDEA AND DETAILS

EXPLAIN/MODEL Review with students:

- The main idea is the most important point an author makes. It is the most important information in a passage. The main idea may be stated in the author's own words near the beginning, or sometimes it may be stated elsewhere.

- The main idea may not be directly stated at all. Good readers should be able to infer what the main idea is by thinking about the information the author gives.

- Details support the main idea. They may help explain it, give examples, or embellish it.

PRACTICE/APPLY Put students in small groups to discuss the main idea and details in *Gecko Glue, Cockroach Scouts, and Spider Silk Bridges.*

- What is the main idea of each of the passages in the selection?

- What is the main idea of the selection itself?

- How does identifying the main idea of the individual passages help you identify the main idea of the selection?

Research
Study Skills

Using the Library and Media Center

EXPLAIN Tell students that if they are researching a topic such as nutrition, they can find the research materials they need at the library. A librarian can help them use technical information and other available resources to answer questions or solve problems.

Discuss how to use **card catalogs:**

- A card catalog lists all books, DVDs, and other library materials.

- Each book has three cards in the card catalog: the author card, the title card, and the subject card.

- The author card is used when you know the author of a book but not the title. The title card is used when you know the title but not the author. The subject card is used when you need a book on a particular topic and do not know any titles or authors.

- The call number tells you where to find the book.

Discuss how to use **electronic catalogs:**

- An electronic catalog gives three options for searching. You can search for a book by its author, title, and subject. To search by subject, you enter key words about the topic.

- A search result will show you a numbered list of titles. Type in the number of the book and press enter. The screen for a particular book will give the same information as in a card catalog. It will also tell you if the book is available.

MODEL

Think Aloud I want to find books about nutrition. I don't know any titles or authors, so I will choose S to search by subject. Then I enter *nutrition* as my key word. The next screen shows me four titles. The second title, *Vitamins, Nutrition, and You*, sounds right. I type in the number *2* and the screen shows me the book's call number, and that it is checked in.

PRACTICE/APPLY Have students use a library catalog to find a book on healthy living habits. Ask them to list the steps they used to find the book. If possible have students use both the card catalog and an electronic catalog to conduct their research. Remind them to record information about their sources so that they can give credit for all borrowed information in the notes at the end of their reports.

Objective

- Use library catalogs to research a topic

Materials

- Study Skills Transparency 1
- Leveled Practice Books, p. 19

 Transparency 1

SUBJECT SEARCH

Please type in the Subject that you are searching for below, and press the Return Key. Separate two or more words like this:

SPACE MISSIONS

SUBJECT: nutrition

SUBJECT SCREEN

Press a number key for more information on each title.

SUBJECT SEARCH: nutrition

1. Standard Values in Nutrition and Metabolism
2. Vitamins, Nutrition, and You
3. Mental Nutrition: Getting the Most Out of Education
4. American Medical Association: Council on Foods
5. High Performance Foods and Good Nutrition

Study Skills Transparency 1

 On Level Practice Book O, page 19

A library lists all its books, DVDs, and other materials in a card catalog. There are three cards in the card catalog for each book: an author card, a title card, and a subject card. If you know the author, the title, or the subject, you can flip through the appropriate section of the catalog.

An electronic catalog works the same way. However, you can also search by key words. For instance, you can enter an author's name and a subject, or even two or more subjects like *elephants* and *Indian*. An electronic search result will give you a numbered list of titles. Type in the number of the book and press enter. A screen for that particular book will come up, and give you the same information that you would find in a card catalog. It will also tell you if the book is available.

Look at the information on the following card. Then answer the questions below.

| J292.13M | Press, Geraldine. *Greek Myths.* Illustrated by Eirene Zagoreas. New York, Children's Publishers, 2003. 208 p. illus. Includes famous Greek myths, retold for younger readers. 1. Literature 2. Mythology 3. Ancient Greece |

1. What key words could you use to find this book? Greek mythology, Ancient Greek myths, Geraldine Press

2. Which row would house this book?
   a. J123.93–J292.01   b. J567.93–J890.23   c. J189.32–J301.78

3. What do you need to know to find this book? You need to know the title and the call number.

4. What kind of work is this? fiction, literature, mythology

 Approaching Practice Book A, page 19

Beyond Practice Book B, page 19

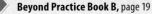

Answer Questions

Test Strategy: Right There

EXPLAIN

Good test takers realize that sometimes an answer to a question can be found right there in the selection.

- **Look for key words:** Sometimes the answer is written directly in the selection. Identify the most important words and phrases in the question. These are called *key words*. Then look for the key words in the selection.

- **Skim for clues:** Read the question carefully. Think about where you can find the answer in the selection. Then read quickly through the selection to find the key words.

MODEL

Remind students to record their answers on a separate sheet of paper.

Question 1 Read aloud the question and all of the answer choices.

Think Aloud Of the words in this question, I think the most important ones are *German* and *scientists*. I will skim the selection to look for the words. I found the phrase *German scientists* in the third sentence. It says their research "shows that getting enough sleep makes people better problem solvers." Answer A says the same thing. The other answers don't tell me what the research by German scientists proved.

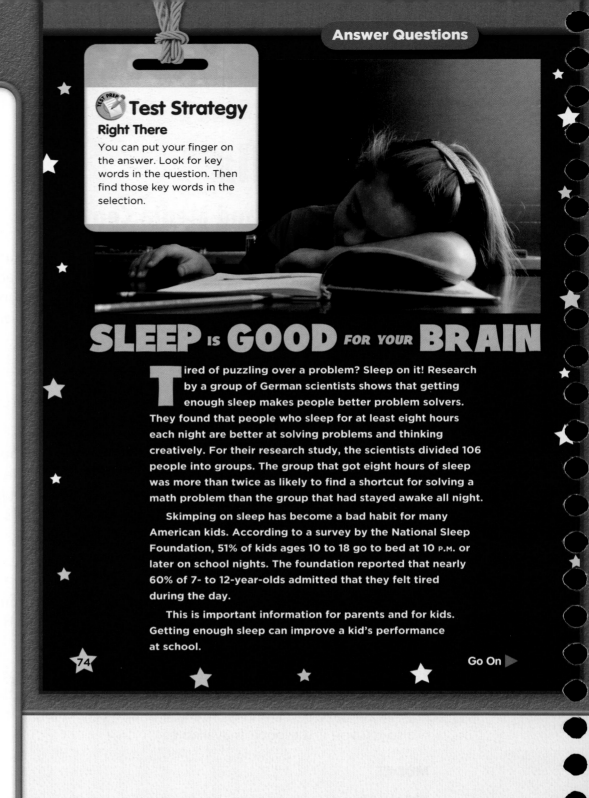

Answer Questions

Test Strategy
Right There
You can put your finger on the answer. Look for key words in the question. Then find those key words in the selection.

SLEEP IS GOOD FOR YOUR BRAIN

Tired of puzzling over a problem? Sleep on it! Research by a group of German scientists shows that getting enough sleep makes people better problem solvers. They found that people who sleep for at least eight hours each night are better at solving problems and thinking creatively. For their research study, the scientists divided 106 people into groups. The group that got eight hours of sleep was more than twice as likely to find a shortcut for solving a math problem than the group that had stayed awake all night.

Skimping on sleep has become a bad habit for many American kids. According to a survey by the National Sleep Foundation, 51% of kids ages 10 to 18 go to bed at 10 P.M. or later on school nights. The foundation reported that nearly 60% of 7- to 12-year-olds admitted that they felt tired during the day.

This is important information for parents and for kids. Getting enough sleep can improve a kid's performance at school.

74

Go On ▶

Directions: Answer the questions.

1. The research by a group of German scientists shows that

- **A** people who sleep enough are better problem solvers.
- **B** school administrators and parents should sleep more hours each night.
- **C** good math students do not require eight hours of sleep.
- **D** the National Sleep Foundation has 106 members.

2. According to the selection, how did the study group that got eight hours of sleep demonstrate that sleep improves performance?

- **A** They demonstrated more factual knowledge.
- **B** They found a quicker way to solve a math problem.
- **C** They scored much higher on standardized tests.
- **D** They did not doze off while taking the test.

3. Why is skimping on sleep bad for you?

- **A** American kids require more sleep.
- **B** Kids fail in school if they are not in bed by 8:00 P.M.
- **C** When you feel tired, you can't perform well at school.
- **D** Not getting enough sleep is good for your brain.

4. What is the main idea of this article?

5. Why do you think so many kids skimp on sleep?

Tip

Look for key words.

STOP   75

PRACTICE

Question 2 Read aloud the question and all of the answer choices.

Ask students:

Which are the most important words in the question? (group, eight and hours)

Skim Point out that the phrase *eight hours* appears twice by itself. Explain that the first time it appears it does not refer to a study *group*. Remind students that key words may appear more than once. The second time it appears it answers the question. Say:

The group that got eight hours of sleep was more than twice as likely to find a shortcut for solving a math problem. Answer B is best because it's another way of saying the same thing.

APPLY

Question 3 Read aloud the question and all of the answer choices.

Have the students use the **Right There** strategy to choose an answer. After the students have chosen an answer, ask:

What did you use as your key word? (skimping) Where did you find your key word? (at the beginning of the second paragraph) Where did you finally find the answer? (at the end of the second paragraph) So the best answer is C.

Have students answer questions 4 and 5.

Question 4 Answers will vary, but may be "Getting enough sleep makes people better problem-solvers."

Question 5 Answers will vary, and may be "kids stay up late doing homework."

Connect
Language Arts

WRITING
- **Tested Writing:** Expository
- **Expository Writing:** Article
- Research and Inquiry

WORD STUDY

- Words in Context
- Definitions
- **Phonics:** *ei* and *ie*
- Vocabulary Building

SPELLING
- Words with *ei* or *ie*

GRAMMAR
- Sentence Combining

SMALL GROUP OPTIONS
- Differentiated Instruction, pp. 77M–77V

Writing Prompt

EXPLAIN/MODEL

Help students analyze the writing prompt on Student Book page 76.

Determine the Mode and Form What type of writing is the prompt asking the student to write? (expository writing)

Determine the Purpose What clues tell what the writing should be about? *(benefits of getting a good night's sleep* and *details from the article to support your answer)*

Determine the Audience Does the prompt tell the student to whom he is writing? (no) To whom should he write? (the teacher)

Write to a Prompt

"Sleep Is Good for Your Brain" reports on the benefits of getting a good night's sleep. Do you think people are getting enough sleep? What might be the benefits of getting more sleep? Use details from the article to support your answer.

I used details from the article in my answer.

In Praise of Sleep

Scientific research says that sleep is good for us. People who get enough sleep think better and do better work. Research also shows that most of us don't get enough sleep and that a lot of kids feel tired during the day at school.

Getting enough sleep is like eating healthful foods or getting enough exercise. It is an important part of our daily life and something we all need to do.

It isn't always easy to go to bed early enough to get 8 hours of sleep. We have to make adjustments in our daily routines. One thing we can do is find ways to get our homework done earlier. It will only take a few nights to prove that it is worth it. Not only will kids do better in school, but they will also feel better.

A good night's sleep is an important part of our daily lives.

76

SCORING RUBRIC

4 Points	**3** Points	**2** Points	**1** Point
Writing is on topic and uses details from research to support the answer. There is a beginning, middle, and end. Writing shows accuracy in punctuation.	Writing is on topic. There is an attempt to sequence or show development of thought. The writing holds the reader's attention. May have errors but they do not interfere with reader's understanding.	Writing is generally on topic. There is an attempt to get sentences on paper. Sentences may be simple or incomplete with limited vocabulary. Errors may make understanding difficult.	Writing may show little or no development of topic, but may contain meaningful vocabulary. There is an attempt to get words on paper. Written vocabulary is limited. Writing shows no use of writing conventions.

Writing Prompt

Getting enough sleep is important, as the selection "Sleep Is Good for Your Brain" points out. The article describes the short-term effects of lack of sleep. But what might the long-term effects be? How important is sleep? Explain what the long-term consequences of not getting enough sleep could be for young people. Use research to support your answer.

Writer's Checklist

☑ Ask yourself, who is my audience?
☑ Think about your purpose for writing.
☑ Choose the correct form for your writing.
☑ Plan your writing before beginning.
☑ Be sure your ideas are clear and organized.
☑ Use your best spelling, grammar, and punctuation.

77

Picture Prompt

For further timed writing practice use the picture prompt on page 162 of the **Teacher's Resource Book**.

Teacher's Resource Book, page 162

Write to a picture prompt. Look at the picture below. Write a story about a science fair.

Writing Tips
• Use a graphic organizer to organize your thoughts.
• Write your story on lined paper.
• Proofread your story.

GUIDED PRACTICE

Have students read the writing prompt on **Student Book** page 77. Work with students to find the clues that determine the mode, form, purpose, and audience. Remind students that the expository mode of writing can take various forms, such as research reports, essays, and newspaper articles.

■ **Mode:** clues—*Explain, could be*

■ **Form:** clue—*Use research to support your answer.*

■ **Purpose:** clue—*Explain what the long-term consequences of not getting enough sleep could be for young people.*

■ **Audience:** no clues, so write the essay for your teacher

APPLY

Ask students to summarize the information they have found in the prompt and the clues they used. Be sure their summary includes the mode, form, purpose, and audience.

TIMED WRITING PRACTICE

You may wish to have students practice writing from the prompt, simulating a test-taking situation. After they have analyzed the prompt, tell students that they will have 45 minutes to write their opinion essays. Explain:

You may use scrap paper to organize your thoughts before you begin to draft your essay. I will tell you when to begin and tell you when you have 15 minutes left to finish the essay. Be sure to use the **Writer's Checklist** to make sure you have included all the necessary information.

Publishing Options

Have students use their best cursive to write their magazine articles. (See **Teacher's Resource Book** pages 168–173 for cursive models and practice.) Students may post their articles on a bulletin board or share them orally at an Invention Convention. See Speaking and Listening tips below.

Speaking and Listening

SPEAKING STRATEGIES

- Include an introduction, body, and conclusion.

- Support main ideas with facts, details, and examples.

- Invite the audience to ask questions.

- Use the information in your article and your general knowledge to respond to questions.

LISTENING STRATEGIES

- Look at the speaker.

- Focus on the speaker's main points.

- Jot down questions to ask after the speaker has finished.

4-Point Scoring Rubric

Use the scoring rubric on page 156 in the **Teacher's Resource Book**.

Writing Process

For a complete lesson, see Unit Writing pages 127A–127H.

Expository: Magazine Article

GENERATE QUESTIONS

Tell students that they will conduct research to write a magazine article about an invention. Have students turn to "Household Inventions Time Line" on **Student Book** page 69. Tell them that they may select one of the inventions listed as a topic or choose some other invention of interest. Direct students to use the Internet link below the time line on page 69 as they consider possible topics.

Suggest a topic of your own and model how to use a KWL chart. Work with students to fill in the first two columns of the chart. Explain that the third column should be filled in once research is completed. Have students create their own KWL charts to generate questions and narrow the focus of their topic. Direct them to think about the kinds of information they will need. Will they need facts? Opinions? Photos? Diagrams?

What I Know	What I Want to Know	What I Learned
Many people enjoy chewing gum.	Who invented chewing gum?	

FIND INFORMATION

Suggest that students look for information about their topic on the Internet. They can access the Internet at a library media center. Explain that the best way to find information online is to do a keyword search using a search engine. Emphasize that they should be specific. For example, if they are researching the cell phone, they should probably use the specific words *invention of cell phones*. Tell students to put the key words in quotation marks to narrow their search. Using quotation marks will help them find Web pages that contain those exact words.

ORGANIZE INFORMATION

Point out that organizing information is the next step after gathering information. Use the **Taking Notes** minilesson on page 77B and **Transparency 9** to teach students how to record the information. The **Outlining** minilesson and **Transparency 10** can help students organize notes.

SYNTHESIZE AND WRITE

Have students use their outlines to write a draft of their articles. Remind students to keep their purpose and audience in mind as they write. Show **Transparency 11** and discuss the draft. Then display **Transparency 12** and discuss the changes. Tell students that they may need to write several drafts. Urge them to read their draft carefully and check for errors.

Writer's Toolbox

Taking Notes

Once students have located information, they should take notes. Use **Transparency 9** to show students how to use the KWL chart to take notes. Offer these additional tips:

- Always record the source of your information. For print sources, list the author's name, the title of the book or article, publication information, and page numbers. For online sources, copy the URL of the Web site and note the date you visited it.

- Paraphrase the information—put it in your own words.

- Use quotation marks for any information you wish to quote directly from a source.

Tell students to review their notes to make sure they answer all their questions about their chosen topic. If students still have questions, urge them to continue researching their topic.

 Transparency 9

What I Know:	Many people enjoy chewing gum.
What I Want to Know:	Who invented chewing gum?
What I Learned:	Ancient Greeks, Mayans, and North American Indians all chewed gum made of sap from trees.
What I know:	Chewing gum is fun to chew.
What I Want to Know:	What is modern chewing gum made of?
What I learned:	Modern chewing gum is made from chicle, the sap of a sapodilla tree (from Mexico).
What I Know:	Things that are for sale were invented by someone.
What I Want to Know:	Who invented modern chewing gum?
What I Learned:	Thomas Adams invented modern chewing gum.

Writing Transparency 9

Outlining

Explain that outlining is one way to organize information. Have students use their notes to create an outline. Remind them that in an outline main ideas are numbered with Roman numerals, and details related to each main idea are listed under it with capital letters. Use **Transparency 10** as an example.

Transparency 10: **Outlining**

Research Tips

Evaluating Sources Emphasize the importance of using reliable sources when conducting research on the Internet. Have students use these questions to evaluate their sources:

- Is this information accurate?

- Is this information current?

- Where does the information come from?

- What are the author's credentials?

Connect
Word Study

Word Study

Objectives
- Apply knowledge of word meanings and context clues
- Look for definitions of unfamiliar words within a selection

Materials
- Vocabulary Transparency 5
- Vocabulary Strategy Transparency 6
- Leveled Practice Books, p. 20

Vocabulary

altered (p. 71) changed

erode (p. 73) to wear away

absorb (p. 73) to take in or soak up

concentrated (p. 71) accumulated in one place

innovations (p. 70) things that are newly introduced, changes

ELL

Reinforce Vocabulary
Point out that *altered* is the past tense of *alter*. Ask, *How do storms* alter *the land? How does a sponge* alter *when it* absorbs *water?*

Review
Vocabulary

 ## Words in Context

EXPLAIN/MODEL

Review the meanings of the vocabulary words. Display **Transparency 5.** Model how to use word meanings and context clues to fill in the missing word.

Think Aloud In the first sentence, I can tell from the punctuation and the word *or* that *changed* is a synonym or definition for the missing word. The missing word must be *altered,* which means about the same thing as *changed.*

Transparency 5

Vocabulary in Context
altered concentrated erode absorb innovations

A scientist (1) altered, or changed, some chemicals inside the bodies of round worms.

The salt was (2) concentrated, or accumulated, in the water. Over time, rivers and streams (3) erode, or wear away, rocks.

A sea creature might (4) absorb, or take in, minerals from the ocean.

Some of the greatest (5) innovations, or inventions, have been based on things found in nature.

Vocabulary Transparency 5

PRACTICE/APPLY

Access for All

Cooperative Learning

Instruct students to complete the remaining items on their own on a separate sheet of paper. Review students' answers as a class, or instruct students to check their answers with a partner.

Have You Ever. . .? Have students answer each of these questions, explain their answers to partners, and make up new questions. *Have you ever tried to* absorb *a lot of water using one paper towel? Have you ever* concentrated *all your efforts to achieve a goal? Have you ever* altered *your appearance?*

STRATEGY
CONTEXT CLUES: DEFINITIONS

EXPLAIN/MODEL

Review with students:

- The definition of an unfamiliar word often appears before or right after the word. If it appears after, there is usually a comma and the word *or*, followed by the definition.

- The definition is often a synonym of the unfamiliar word. The synonym is usually a simpler word that the reader already knows and can understand.

Read the following sentences on **Transparency 6.** Model how to use context clues to learn the meaning of an unfamiliar word.

 Transparency 6

Context Clues: Definitions

1. Scientists know that millions of tiny hairs called **setae,** cover a gecko's feet.

2. When my father buys a tool, he wants to make sure it will be **durable,** or tough and long-lasting.

3. Some illnesses are caused by microscopic organisms called **bacteria.**

4. The iron beams of a bridge will not easily wear away, or **erode.**

Vocabulary Strategy Transparency 6

PRACTICE/APPLY

Have students write sentences that contain definitions of the words *inspiration*, *method*, and *researchers*.

Quick Check **Do students understand word meanings? Do students understand how to use context clues to learn the meaning of a word?**

During **Small Group Instruction**

If No → **Approaching Level** Vocabulary pp. 77N–77O

If Yes → **On Level** Options, pp. 77Q–77R

Beyond Level Options, pp. 77S–77T

ELL **Access for All**

Context Clues On the board, write: *Here are a few of history's most amazing innovations, or inventions.* Point out how the author gives the meaning of *innovations* in the sentence. Help students share their thinking as they apply the strategy to other sentences.

■ **On Level Practice Book O,** page 20

When you read, you should use the surrounding text, which often gives you **definitions** in context, to help you determine the meaning of unfamiliar vocabulary. Just as its name implies, this kind of context clue actually states the meaning of the unfamiliar word.

Underline the definitions you find in the sentences. Write a sentence of your own using the defined word from each sentence.
Possible responses provided.
1. Astronauts used a powerful telescope to find out more about the cosmos, another name for the universe.
   In the desert on a clear, cold night, Danielle looked up at the cosmos.

2. The scientists at Mission Control, the place where the trip was supervised, were in constant contact with the astronauts who planned the repair of the telescope.
   The astronauts radioed back to Mission Control that they had accomplished the trip's goal.

3. So that the mission, the trip planned to fix the telescope, could succeed, the damaged part had to be replaced.
   Susan made it her mission to visit her grandmother's birthplace in Russia.

4. When the Endeavor was in place, the shuttle's robotic, or mechanical, arm was used to grab the damaged telescope.
   After Rebecca sprained her ankle, she had a robotic walk for several weeks.

5. Crew members left the shuttle through a small room with two hatches, or doors.
   Marta had to bend down to enter the submarine's hatches because they were so small.

 Approaching Practice Book A, page 20

Beyond Practice Book B, page 20

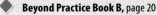

Word Study

Word Study

Objective

- Decode words with *ei* or *ie*

Materials

- Leveled Practice Books, p. 21
- Teacher's Resource Book, p. 7

ELL

Access for All

Identify Spelling Patterns On the board, write the words *piece* and *eight*. Say each word and have students repeat. Provide additional words for each pattern and practice saying them with students before students do the Practice activity.

On Level Practice Book O, page 21

The long *e* sound can be spelled by either *ei* or *ie*. The long *a* sound can be spelled by *ei*. To remember how to spell words with *ei* or *ie*, memorize the following sentence:

Place the *i* before *e* except after *c* or when sounding like *a* as in *neighbor* and *weigh*.

A. Read the sentences. Circle the words that contain the *ie* or *ei* digraphs. Then, in the space, write whether the sound is long e or long a.

1. The researcher mixed (eight) chemicals together. ___long *a*___
2. (Field) work can help find the medicine that will work. ___long *e*___
3. Researchers must (yield) to signs of danger when testing medicine. ___long *e*___
4. They must (weigh) everything carefully. ___long *a*___
5. Before they (receive) a new assignment, they must make thorough notes on the last one. ___long *e*___

B. Fill in the missing letters in each sentence.

6. The laboratory has many vents in the c___ei___ling to prevent dangerous gases from building up.
7. Researchers wear goggles as a way to sh___ie___ld their eyes from laboratory chemicals.
8. Chemicals shipped by fr___ei___ght have to be handled with caution.

⭐ **Approaching Practice Book A,** page 21
◆ **Beyond Practice Book B,** page 21

Phonics

Decode Words with *ei* and *ie*

EXPLAIN/MODEL Words with *ei* are often pronounced with the long *a* sound, as in *freight*. When *ie* appears in a word, it is often pronounced with the long *e* sound, as in *yield*. Sometimes the *ei* sound occurs after the /s/ sound, as in *seize*. Then *ei* is pronounced as the long *e* sound. Being able to recognize these spelling patterns can help you figure out an unfamiliar word. Write *shield*.

Think Aloud I see *ie* in the middle of the word. I know that when *ie* appears in a word it makes the long *e* sound. I know that the word *shield* is pronounced with the long *e* sound.

Access for All

PRACTICE/APPLY Write these words: *neighbor, field, weight, relief, fierce, vein, sleigh*. Have students make two columns, one for words with the long *a* sound and one for words with the long *e* sound. Students should sort the words into the two columns. The word *fierce* will be an exception.

Decode Multisyllabic Words Suffixes are words parts that are added at the end of a root word. A suffix has meaning. Write *-er* ("one who") on the board. Tell its meaning. Write *reviewer* on the board. Point out and say the root word *review* and the suffix *-er*. Draw a line between them. Say the word. Tell students that *reviewer* means "one who reviews." Display *wielder, believer, retriever,* and *foreigner*. Help students decode *wielder*. Then have students decode the other words. For more practice, see decodable passages on page 7 of the **Teacher's Resource Book**.

Cooperative Learning

Word Brainstorm Have groups of students write down as many *ei* and *ie* words that they can think of. At the end of three minutes have groups share their words. The group with the most *ei* and *ie* words is the winner.

Quick Check Can students decode words with *ei* and *ie*?

During **Small Group Instruction**

If No → **Approaching Level** Phonics, p. 77M

If Yes → **On Level** Options, pp. 77Q–77R

Beyond Level Options, pp. 77S–77T

Vocabulary Building

Oral Language

Expand Vocabulary Divide the class into three groups. Have students use the vocabulary words to write sentences about science, health, and fitness. Have each group present their ideas to the class.

Examples:

- Too much sugar will <u>erode</u> your teeth.

- Your body must <u>absorb</u> vitamins and nutrients to function properly.

- Medical <u>innovations</u> help keep us healthier.

Vocabulary Building

Suffixes Choose a suffix from one of the vocabulary words and add it to the other words to change their meaning. Have students use a dictionary to look up the definitions and to check the spelling of the words they create. Provide the following example for students:

> Take the suffix *-ion* from *innovation*:
> *altered* becomes *alteration*
> *erode* becomes *erosion*
> *absorb* becomes *absorption*
> *concentrated* becomes *concentration*

Apply Vocabulary

Write about the Future Have students use the words *altered, erode, absorb, concentrated,* and *innovations* to write a memo about the conditions on earth in the year 2100.

Memo:

Vocabulary Review

What's the Right Definition? Using vocabulary from this week and prior selections, have students choose a word and write two definitions for it. One definition should be made-up, and the other should be correct. When everyone has finished writing their definitions, call on students to read them aloud. Ask volunteers to select the correct definition from the two.

Technology

CD ROM

Vocabulary PuzzleMaker

LOG ON

For additional vocabulary and spelling games go to
www.macmillanmh.com

5 Day Spelling

Words with *ei* or *ie*

Spelling Words

reins	**ceiling**	reign
freight	retrieve	relieve
siege	grieve	niece
yield	sleigh	eighty
review	seize	wield
foreign	belief	diesel
shield	neither	

Review gaze, tile, bleach

Challenge receipt, leisure

Dictation Sentences

1. Jack pulled on the horse's <u>reins</u>.
2. The ship carries <u>freight</u>.
3. The city had been under <u>siege</u>.
4. To <u>yield</u> is to give way.
5. We have a weekly <u>review</u>.
6. You should study a <u>foreign</u> language if you can.
7. We used an umbrella to <u>shield</u> us.
8. Sasha painted her **ceiling** red.
9. Our dog can <u>retrieve</u> the paper.
10. Did you <u>grieve</u> over the loss?
11. The <u>sleigh</u> is blue.
12. Did she <u>seize</u> the shoe?
13. I cannot change your <u>belief</u>.
14. I chose <u>neither</u> of the dresses.
15. This is the <u>reign</u> of King George.
16. Aspirin will <u>relieve</u> a headache.
17. My <u>niece</u> is getting married in July.
18. My grandmother is <u>eighty</u> today.
19. Do not <u>wield</u> the scissors in class.
20. The truck runs on <u>diesel</u> fuel.

Review/Challenge Words

1. Did you <u>gaze</u> sadly at it?
2. The <u>tile</u> is blue and gold.
3. <u>Bleach</u> removes stains.
4. Where is the <u>receipt</u>?
5. I have no <u>leisure</u> time.

Note: Words in **bold** type are from *Gecko Glue, Cockroach Scouts,* and *Spider Silk Bridges*

Display the Spelling Words throughout the week.

Day 1 Pretest

ASSESS PRIOR KNOWLEDGE

Use the Dictation Sentences. Say the underlined word, read the sentence, and repeat the word. Have students write the words on **Spelling Practice Book** page 13, and then correct their own papers. For a modified list, use the first 17 Spelling Words and add three Review Words. For a more challenging list, use Spelling Words 3–20 and add the Challenge Words. Have students correct their own tests.

Have students cut apart the Spelling Word Cards BLM on **Teacher's Resource Book** page 68 and figure out a way to sort them. Have them save the cards for use throughout the week.

For **Leveled Word Lists,** go to
www.macmillanmh.com

Day 2 Word Sorts

TEACHER AND STUDENT SORTS

Review the Spelling Words, pointing out the words with *ei* or *ie,* and discuss meanings.

- Create a two-column chart on the board. Label one column *ie* and the other *ei.*

- Model how to sort several words, using cards for each pattern. Then pass out the cards and let each student tell where his or her word goes in the chart. Write the words on the board for students.

- Have pairs of students use their word cards to do the sort again. Discuss their completed word sorts.

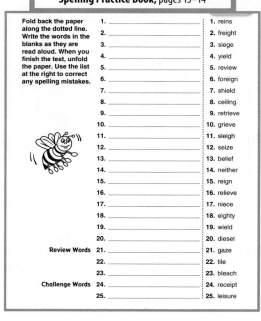

Spelling Practice Book, pages 13–14

Fold back the paper along the dotted line. Write the words in the blanks as they are read aloud. When you finish the test, unfold the paper. Use the list at the right to correct any spelling mistakes.

1. _____	1. reins
2. _____	2. freight
3. _____	3. siege
4. _____	4. yield
5. _____	5. review
6. _____	6. foreign
7. _____	7. shield
8. _____	8. ceiling
9. _____	9. retrieve
10. _____	10. grieve
11. _____	11. sleigh
12. _____	12. seize
13. _____	13. belief
14. _____	14. neither
15. _____	15. reign
16. _____	16. relieve
17. _____	17. niece
18. _____	18. eighty
19. _____	19. wield
20. _____	20. diesel
Review Words 21. _____	21. gaze
22. _____	22. tile
23. _____	23. bleach
Challenge Words 24. _____	24. receipt
25. _____	25. leisure

Spelling Practice Book, page 15

reins	review	retrieve	belief	niece
freight	foreign	grieve	neither	eighty
siege	shield	sleigh	reign	wield
yield	ceiling	seize	relieve	diesel

Write the spelling words with each of the spelling patterns below.

ei
1. reins
2. freight
3. foreign
4. ceiling
5. sleigh
6. seize
7. neither
8. reign
9. eighty

ie
10. siege
11. yield
12. review
13. shield
14. retrieve
15. grieve
16. belief
17. relieve
18. niece
19. wield
20. diesel

Alphabetical Order
Use the lines below to write the spelling words in alphabetical order.

belief	ceiling	diesel	eighty
foreign	freight	grieve	neither
niece	reign	reins	relieve
retrieve	review	seize	shield
siege	sleigh	wield	yield

Day 3 — Word Meanings

DEFINITIONS

Ask students to copy the list of words below. Then tell them to use a dictionary or thesaurus to find at least one synonym for each word.

1. review (check, analyze)
2. retrieve (fetch, reclaim)
3. leisure (free time, convenience)
4. seize (take, grab)
5. grieve (mourn)

■ Challenge students to write five sentences using the synonyms they found. Have them write the sentences in their word study notebook.

Day 4 — Review and Proofread

SPIRAL REVIEW

Have students sort their word cards from last week to review words with long vowels.

PROOFREAD AND WRITE

Write these sentences on the board including the misspelled words. Have students proofread, circle each misspelled word, and write the word correctly.

1. The fright was piled so high it reached the cieling of the train. (freight, ceiling)

2. Nither my neece nor my nephew can come next week. (neither, niece)

WORD SORT

To prepare students for the Posttest on Friday, have them sort this week's words again.

Day 5 — Assess and Reteach

POSTTEST

Use the Dictation Sentences on page 77G for the Posttest.

If students have difficulty with any words in the lesson, have them copy the words in a list entitled "Spelling Words I Want to Remember" in a word study notebook. Suggest that they write a context sentence for each word. Students should refer to their word lists during later writing activities.

WORD STUDY NOTEBOOK

Challenge students to look for other words with *ei* and *ie* spellings as they read this week's selections. Have them write the words in a word study notebook under the heading "Other words with *ie* and *ei*."

Spelling Practice Book, page 16

reins	review	retrieve	belief	niece
freight	foreign	grieve	neither	eighty
siege	shield	sleigh	reign	wield
yield	ceiling	seize	relieve	diesel

Sentence Completion

Fill in the blank with the appropriate spelling word.

1. Many of the everyday objects we use were invented in __foreign__ countries.
2. The __diesel__ engine was named after its inventor.
3. Water skiis were invented over __eighty__ years ago.
4. My __niece__ is working on an invention for my brother, her father.
5. __Neither__ of the Wright brothers gave up until they could fly.
6. The driver held the __reins__ as he drove the horses.

Synonyms

Write the spelling word that is a synonym for each word below.

7. rule __reign__
8. mourn __grieve__
9. grab __seize__
10. fetch __retrieve__
11. help __relieve__
12. surrender __yield__

Spelling Practice Book, page 17

There are five spelling mistakes in this letter. Circle the misspelled words. Write the words correctly on the lines below.

Dear Aunt Anita,

My vacation in Colorado is very enjoyable. We certainly are lucky that my father invented a new type of snow-making machine! Since I arrived, it feels like I have skied the mountain (aty) times. Last night, my mother and I took an old-fashioned (sliegh) ride in the snow. I even was allowed to hold the (rains) When I pulled them close to me, the horses would (yeild) It was loads of fun. I think tomorrow we are going to go sledding. I'll tell you all about it when I get home. I miss you.

Your (neice)

Julie

1. __eighty__
2. __sleigh__
3. __reins__
4. __yield__
5. __niece__

Writing Activity

Julie's father brought her family to Colorado because he invented a special kind of snow-making machine. What other inventions might require someone to go away on business? Write a postcard as if you were on such a trip. Use five spelling words in your postcard.

Students' writing should reflect the topic and include five spelling words.

Spelling Practice Book, page 18

Look at the words in each set below. One word in each set is spelled correctly. Use a pencil to fill in the circle next to the correct word. Before you begin, look at the sample set of words. Sample A has been done for you. Do Sample B by yourself. When you are sure you know what to do, you may go on with the rest of the page.

Sample A:
ⓐ tried
ⓑ tryed
ⓒ tride
ⓓ treid

Sample B:
ⓔ recieve
ⓕ reiceve
Ⓖ receive
ⓗ rieceve

1. ⓐ reins
   ⓑ reinz
   ⓒ riens
   ⓓ rienz
2. ⓔ frieght
   ⓕ freight
   Ⓖ freit
   ⓗ friet
3. ⓐ seige
   ⓑ siege
   ⓒ sieg
   ⓓ seig
4. ⓔ yeild
   ⓕ ield
   Ⓖ yield
   ⓗ ield
5. ⓐ reivew
   ⓑ review
   ⓒ rievew
   ⓓ reveiw

6. ⓔ foriegn
   ⓕ foreign
   Ⓖ forein
   ⓗ forien
7. ⓐ sheild
   ⓑ shield
   ⓒ shielde
   ⓓ sheilde
8. ⓔ cieling
   ⓕ celeing
   Ⓖ ceiling
   ⓗ celieng
9. ⓐ retreive
   ⓑ reitreve
   ⓒ retrieve
   ⓓ retrive
10. ⓔ greive
    ⓕ grevie
    Ⓖ grevei
    ⓗ grieve

11. ⓐ sleigh
    ⓑ sliegh
    ⓒ slei
    ⓓ slie
12. ⓔ seize
    ⓕ sieze
    Ⓖ sezie
    ⓗ sezei
13. ⓐ beilef
    ⓑ bielef
    ⓒ belief
    ⓓ beleif
14. ⓔ neither
    ⓕ niether
    Ⓖ netheir
    ⓗ nethier
15. ⓐ riegn
    ⓑ reign
    ⓒ rieghn
    ⓓ reighn

16. ⓔ relieve
    ⓕ reilive
    Ⓖ rielive
    ⓗ eleive
17. ⓐ neice
    ⓑ necie
    ⓒ niece
    ⓓ necei
18. ⓔ eigty
    ⓕ iegty
    Ⓖ eighty
    ⓗ eigthy
19. ⓐ weild
    ⓑ wield
    ⓒ weilde
    ⓓ wielde
20. ⓔ deisel
    ⓕ deseil
    Ⓖ desiel
    ⓗ diesel

Sentence Combining

Daily Language Activities

Use these activities to reinforce each day's lesson. Write the day's activities on the board, or use **Transparency 3.**

DAY 1
My father wants to move to California. My mother doesn't. (1. My father wants to move to California, but my mother doesn't.)

DAY 2
Aidan doesn't like soccer. Aidan doesn't like basketball either. (1. Aidan doesn't like soccer or basketball.)

DAY 3
Audrey can go to the movies on Friday. She can go on Saturday. (Audrey can go to the movies on Friday or Saturday.)

DAY 4
We cannot take a vacation this summer. In December we might take a vacation. (1. We cannot take a vacation this summer, but we might take one in December.)

DAY 5
Alex washed his new truck. His friend washed his old truck. (1. Alex washed his new truck; his friend washed his old truck.)

ELL   Access for All

Clarify Conjunctions
Co-construct examples of compound sentences using the words *and* and *but*. Use students' names and experiences. Point out the use of the comma. Afterwards, use these sentences to explain how a semicolon functions.

Day 1   Introduce the Concept

INTRODUCE CONJUNCTIONS AND COMPOUND SENTENCES

Present the following:

- A **conjunction** joins words or groups of words. *And* adds information; *but* shows contrast; *or* gives a choice.

- A **compound sentence** is two sentences joined with a comma and a conjunction.

- Use a semicolon to separate two parts of a compound sentence when they are not connected by a conjunction.

Explain that commas and semicolons show connection between sentences by using punctuation as a transition.

 See Grammar Transparency 11 for modeling and guided practice.

Grammar Practice Book, page 13

- A **conjunction** joins words or groups of words. *And* adds information; *but* shows contrast; *or* gives a choice.
- A **compound sentence** contains two sentences joined by a comma and *and*, *but*, or *or*.
- You can form a compound sentence by joining two related sentences.

Put an X in front of each sentence that is a compound sentence. For those sentences, write the word that joins the two shorter sentences.

1. __X__ Crayons were invented in 1903 by Edwin Binney and Harold Smith, and they were an instant success.
       __and__

2. __X__ Crossword puzzles can be diamond-shaped, or they can be square.
       __or__

3. _____ The first ferriswheel began operating on June 21, 1893 at the Chicago World's Fair.

4. __X__ It had 36 wooden cars that could each seat 40 people, but most modern ferriswheels are much smaller.
       __but__

5. _____ A kaleidoscope is a tube one can look into that makes beautiful, colorful patterns using mirrors.

6. _____ The kaleidoscope was invented by the Scottish physicist Sir David Brewster in 1817.

Day 2   Teach the Concept

REVIEW CONJUNCTIONS AND COMPOUND SENTENCES

Review how to combine related sentences using a conjunction.

INTRODUCE COMPOUND SUBJECT/ PREDICATE

Explain to students that a **compound subject** has two or more subjects that have the same predicate. A **compound predicate** has two or more predicates with the same subject. Two complete sentences can be combined by joining two subjects or two predicates with *and* or *or*.

Example:

I like to ski. Carlos likes to ski. Carlos and I like to ski.

 See Grammar Transparency 12 for modeling and guided practice.

Grammar Practice Book, page 14

- A **compound subject** contains two or more simple subjects that have the same predicate.
- A **compound predicate** contains two or more simple predicates that have the same subject.
- You can combine two sentences by joining two subjects or two predicates with *and*, *but*, or *or*.

Read the sentences. Write an S if it has a compound subject and P if it has a compound predicate. Write each compound subject and compound predicate below. Then put parentheses around the simple subjects or predicates in what you have written. (Not every sentence has a compound subject or compound predicate.)

1. My older sister, Selina, is studying hard and hopes to be an inventor one day. __P__
   (is) studying hard and (hopes) to be an inventor one day

2. Calculus, physics, and chemistry are her favorite subjects. __S__
   (Calculus), (physics), and (chemistry)

3. My preferred subject has always been English literature. _____

4. Selina rises early and arrives home late. __P__
   (rises) early and (arrives) home late

5. Selina's teachers and classmates believe she is marked for fame and fortune. __S__
   Selina's (teachers) and (classmates)

6. A big title and huge corner office are of no interest to Selina. __S__
   A big (title) and huge corner (office)

Day 3 | Review and Practice

REVIEW CONJUNCTIONS

Remind students that *and* adds information, *but* indicates contrast, and *or* separates a choice in compound sentences.

MECHANICS & USAGE

Punctuation creates a transition between sentences. Explain that students should use a comma before the conjunction in a compound sentence. If the parts of a compound sentence are not joined by a conjunction, students should use a semicolon to join the parts. For example:

Jared has a new car, but Siri does not.

Jared has a new car; Siri does not.

Day 4 | Review and Proofread

REVIEW COMPOUND SENTENCES

Ask students to explain the different ways to combine compound sentences using the Daily Language Activities for Days 1–4.

PROOFREAD

Have students correct errors in the following sentences.

1. Tanya has a cat and Jim has a turtle. (cat, and)

2. I won second place Cindy won first place. (place; Cindy)

3. Andrew likes rabbits but They make him sneeze. (rabbits, but they)

Day 5 | Assess and Reteach

ASSESS

Use the Daily Language Activity and page 17 of the **Grammar Practice Book** for assessment.

RETEACH

Have each student write pairs of simple sentences that can be combined into a compound sentence. Then, have them switch papers with partners and combine their partners' sentences using a conjunction.

Have students create mini-posters about the rules for punctuating compound sentences.

Use page 18 of the **Grammar Practice Book** for additional reteaching.

 See Grammar Transparency 13 for modeling and guided practice.

Grammar Practice Book, page 15

- Use a comma before the conjunction in a compound sentence.
- If two parts of a compound sentence are not joined by a conjunction, a semicolon is used to separate the parts.

Combine each set of sentences. Use a comma and a conjunction in the compound sentence.

1. Tic Tac Toe has been played in the United Kingdom for hundreds of years. There it is called Noughts and Crosses. **Tic Tac Toe has been played in the United Kingdom for hundreds of years, but there it is called Noughts and Crosses.**

2. A.S. Douglas was the first to put Noughts and Crosses on a software program. That was way back in 1949! **A.S. Douglas was the first to put Noughts and Crosses on a software program, and that was way back in 1949!**

3. In 1956, Noah and Joe McVicker invented play dough. It was promoted as a wallpaper cleaner first. **In 1956, Noah and Joe McVicker invented play dough, but it was promoted as a wallpaper cleaner first.**

4. Joe realized the child-safe type of clay would make a great toy. He became a millionaire almost overnight. **Joe realized the child-safe type of clay would make a great toy, and he became a millionaire almost overnight.**

5. Over 700 million pounds of play dough have been sold since it was first marketed. The formula is still a secret. **Over 700 million pounds of play dough have been sold since it was first marketed, but the formula is still a secret.**

 See Grammar Transparency 14 for modeling and guided practice.

Grammar Practice Book, page 16

- Use a comma before the conjunction in a compound sentence.
- If two parts of a compound sentence are not joined by a conjunction, use a semicolon to separate the parts.

Rewrite the passage below, correcting all capitalization and punctuation mistakes. Combine any sentences you find appropriate.

everyone knows that necessity is the mother of invention the woman who invented disposable diapers was both a woman and an inventor Marion Donovan invented the disposable diaper in 1950 she used a regular cloth diaper, lined it with pieces cut from a shower curtain, and called her invention "Boaters" since no company was interested in marketing her new invention Mrs. Donovan founded her own company today disposable diapers are big business

Everyone knows that necessity is the mother of invention, but the woman who invented disposable diapers was both a woman and an inventor. Marion Donovan invented the disposable diaper in 1950. She used a regular cloth diaper, lined it with pieces cut from a shower curtain, and called her invention "Boaters." Since no company was interested in marketing her new invention, Mrs. Donovan founded her own company, and today disposable diapers are big business.

 See Grammar Transparency 15 for modeling and guided practice.

Grammar Practice Book, pages 17–18

Revise the following paragraph so that it reads more clearly. Combine short sentences with a conjunction to form compound subjects, compound predicates, or compound sentences. Not every sentence needs to be combined or revised.

People put on their clothing every day. They do not think about how their pants stay put. They do not think about how their jackets stay put. Jackets have zippers. Pants have zippers. The zipper was invented in 1893 by Whitcomb L. Judson. He called his invention a "clasp-locker." In 1923, Mr. B.F. Goodrich coined the word "zipper." His company made rubber boots with zippers. His company sold rubber boots with zippers. Mr. Goodrich named them zippers because they made a zipping sound when opened and closed.

Possible answer is given.

People put on their clothing every day, but they do not think about how their pants and jackets stay put. Jackets and pants have zippers. The zipper was invented in 1893 by Whitcomb L. Judson. He called his invention a "clasp-locker." In 1923, Mr. B.F. Goodrich coined the word "zipper." His company made and sold rubber boots with zippers. Mr. Goodrich named them zippers because they made a zipping sound when opened and closed.

End-of-Week Assessments

Administer the Test

Weekly Reading Assessment,
Passages and questions, pages 29–36

ASSESSED SKILLS

- Main Idea and Details
- Vocabulary Words
- Context Clues: Definitions
- *ei* or *ie*
- Conjunctions and Compound Sentences

  Assessment Tool

Administer the **Weekly Assessment** online or on CD-ROM.

Weekly Assessment, 29–36

Fluency

Assess fluency for one group of students per week. Use the Oral Fluency Record Sheet to track the number of words read correctly. Fluency goal for all students:
117–137 words correct per minute (WCPM).

Approaching Level	Weeks 1, 3, 5
On Level	Weeks 2, 4
Beyond Level	Week 6

Fluency Assessment

Alternative Assessments

- **Leveled Weekly Assessment** for Approaching Level, pages 37–44
- **ELL Assessment,** pages 40–41

ELL Practice and Assessment, 40–41

Diagnose		Prescribe
	IF...	**THEN...**
VOCABULARY WORDS VOCABULARY STRATEGY Context Clues: Definitions Items 1, 2, 3, 4	0–2 items correct . . .	Reteach skills using the **Additional Lessons** page T6 **LOG ON** Reteach skills: Go to www.macmillanmh.com **CD ROM** Vocabulary PuzzleMaker Evaluate for Intervention.
COMPREHENSION Skill: Main Idea and Details Items 5, 6, 7, 8	0–2 items correct . . .	Reteach skills using the **Additional Lessons** page T2 Evaluate for Intervention.
GRAMMAR Conjunctions and Compound Sentences Items 9, 10, 11	0–1 items correct . . .	Reteach skills: **Grammar Practice Book** page 18
SPELLING *ei* or *ie* Items 12, 13, 14	0–1 items correct . . .	**LOG ON** Reteach skills: Go to www.macmillanmh.com
FLUENCY	109–116 WCPM	**AUDIO CD** Fluency Solutions
	0–108 WCPM	Evaluate for Intervention.

READING
Triumphs
AN INTERVENTION PROGRAM

Also Available

To place students in the Intervention Program, use the **Diagnostic Assessment** in the Intervention Teacher's Edition.

Gecko Glue, Cockroach Scouts, and Spider Silk Bridges   **77L**

Skills Focus ▶ Phonics

Objectives	Decode words with *ei* or *ie*
	Decode multisyllabic words with *ei* or *ie* in both familiar and unfamiliar text
Materials	• **Student Book** "How Long Will We Live?"

WORDS WITH *EI* OR *IE*

Model/Guided Practice

■ Write the letters *w, e, i, g, h, t* on the board. Segment the sounds: /w//ā//t/. Then blend the sounds: /wāt/. *Say the word with me:* weight. *When I say the word* weight, *I hear the long* a *sound. I know that many words with the vowel pair* ei *are pronounced with the long* a *sound.*

■ Write the word *field* on the board. Say the word. *I hear the long* e *sound when I say the word* field. *I know that when the vowel pair* ie *appears within a word, it makes the long* e *sound.*

■ Then write the word *seize* on the board. Say the word. *The vowel pair* ei *in the word* seize *doesn't make the long* a *sound as I expected. After the* s *sound, it makes a long* e *sound instead.*

■ Write the words *rein, piece,* and *receive* on the board. Ask students to say each word and explain what sound the vowel pair *ei* or *ie* makes in each. Ask students to provide their own examples of words with *ei* or *ie*. Provide constructive feedback.

MULTISYLLABIC WORDS WITH *EI* OR *IE*

■ Write the word *retriever* on the board. Draw lines to divide the word into syllables. Then say each syllable: /ri trē vər/. Have students work in small groups to decode longer words with *ei* or *ie*. Provide each group with the list of words below. *Say each word together. Draw a line under the syllable with* ei *or* ie. *Group the words with the same spellings and sounds together in a chart.*

neighborhood	yielding	believable	freighter
eighty	sleighing	reigning	relieving

■ Check each group for accuracy.

WORD SORT: WORDS WITH *EI* OR *IE* IN CONTEXT

■ Review the different sounds of the vowel pairs *ei* and *ie*.

■ Have groups of students search "How Long Will We Live?" for words with *ei* or *ie*. Tally the words to see if students found *twentieth, scientists, studies, believes, their, bodies, babies, healthier*. Have groups sort the words under the headings *long* a *sound* and *long* e *sound*. Groups should observe that *twentieth, scientists, their,* and *healthier* do not belong under either heading.

Additional Resources

For each skill below, additional lessons are provided. You can use these lessons on consecutive days after teaching the lessons presented within the week.
• Main Idea and Details, T2
• Context Clues, T6
• Using the Library, T10

Constructive Feedback

Isolate the error sound and repeat with students. If students say /ē/ in *rein*, for instance, point to the vowel pair *ei* and say:

To have a long e sound, the vowel pair *ei* has to follow an *s* sound. The *ei* in this word follows /r/, not an *s* sound. It has a long *a* sound, not a long *e* sound. Say it with me: /rān/.

Repeat as needed with other words with *ei*.

Decodable Text

To help students build speed and accuracy when reading multisyllabic words, use the additional decodable text on page 7 of the **Teacher's Resource Book**.

Skills Focus ▶ Fluency

Objective Read with increasing prosody and accuracy at a rate of 117–127 WCPM
Materials • **Approaching Practice Book A,** p. 18

MODEL EXPRESSIVE READING

Model reading the Fluency passage on page 18 of **Approaching Practice Book A**. Tell students to pay close attention and listen to your pauses and intonation as you read. Then read one sentence at a time and have students echo-read the sentence back, copying your pauses and intonation. Listen carefully to their reading, monitoring for accuracy.

REPEATED READING

Have students continue practicing reading the passage aloud as you circulate and provide constructive feedback. During independent reading time, have students work with a partner. Have one student read each sentence aloud, and the other repeat the sentence. Students should continue practicing the passage throughout the week.

TIMED READING

At the end of the week, tell students that they will do a timed reading of the passage that they have been practicing. With each student:

- Place the passage from **Approaching Practice Book A** page 18 facedown.
- When you say "Go," the student begins reading the passage aloud.
- When you say "Stop," the student stops reading the passage.

As students read, note any miscues. Stop each after one minute. Help students record and graph the number of words they read correctly.

Constructive Feedback

If students have difficulty saying the scientific terms included in the passage, write them on the board, read one aloud at a time, and have students echo-read each back to you. Then point to a word and call on a student at random to say it correctly.

Skills Focus ▶ Vocabulary

Objective Apply vocabulary word meanings
Materials • **Vocabulary Cards**

Tested

VOCABULARY WORDS

Divide the group into teams. Display the **Vocabulary Cards** for *altered, erode, absorb, concentrated,* and *innovations*. Ask volunteers to read the vocabulary words in "How Long Will We Live?" Review the meanings of each word. Challenge students to generate questions that use the vocabulary words: for example, *What is another word for* changed?

★ Approaching Practice Book A, page 18

As I read, I will pay attention to pronunciation of difficult and words.

How does a dolphin catch fish in deep, dark water where
11 it is hard to see? Dolphins have good eyesight. But the deep
23 ocean waters make it impossible for them to use eyesight
33 alone. Dolphins have a special ability called echolocation
41 (ek-oh-loh-KAY-shuhn). They use sound waves to locate
48 objects in the ocean. Dolphins use echolocation for hunting,
57 finding their enemies, and navigating.
62 The dolphin makes clicking noises. It uses a part of its
73 head called the melon to direct these sounds. The melon is
84 located above the dolphin's eyes and is filled with fat. That
95 is why a dolphin looks like it has a big bump on its head.
109 The clicking sounds made by the dolphin travel through
118 the water until they hit an object. Some of the sound waves
130 make an echo that returns to the dolphin. Then the dolphin
141 will make another click to measure how far away the object
152 is. 153

Comprehension Check

1. How do dolphins overcome the lack of light? **Main Idea and Details**
   Dolphins use echolocation to see.
2. How does the dolphin use echolocation? What is the effect? **Cause and Effect** Dolphins send out clicks and measure distance based on echo return time. They can hunt, avoid enemies, and navigate in the dark.

	Words Read	–	Number of Errors	=	Words Correct Score
First Read		–		=	
Second Read		–		=	

altered

erode

absorb

concentrated

innovations

Approaching Level Options

Small Group

Vocabulary

Review last week's words (*remote, escort, interpreter, vegetation, undergrowth, venomous, withstood, foretold*) and this week's words (*altered, erode, absorb, concentrated, innovations*). Have students write a sentence for each word.

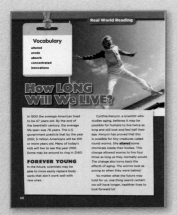

Student Book, or Transparency 3

ELL — Access for All

Have students use context clues to complete these sentences using the vocabulary words. 1. *The _____ helped make his work easier.* (innovations) 2. *Our plans were _____ when it snowed.* (altered) 3. *The needed medicine was _____ in one pill.* (concentrated) 4. *The rain began to _____ the riverbank.* (erode) 5. *This sponge can _____ all the water.* (absorb)

Skills Focus — Vocabulary

Objective Use context clues to figure out the meanings of words
Materials • **Student Book** *Gecko Glue, Cockroach Scouts, and Spider Silk Bridges*

CONTEXT CLUES: DEFINITIONS

- Have students write sentences containing context clues that help define each of this week's vocabulary words. For example: *The new formula has been* altered *by adding ammonia.* (new, adding)
- Have students exchange sentences and use the context clues to formulate a definition for the vocabulary word.

Skills Focus — Comprehension

Objective Identify main idea and details
Materials • **Student Book** "How Long Will We Live?" • **Transparency 3**

STRATEGY
MAKE INFERENCES AND ANALYZE

Review with students that they must make inferences when authors do not state all information directly.

SKILL
MAIN IDEA AND DETAILS

Explain/Model
- The main idea is the most important point an author makes.
- It is often stated at the beginning of a paragraph, but not always.
- The details illustrate, explain, or elaborate on the main idea.

Display **Transparency 3**. Reread the first paragraph of "How Long Will We Live?" Ask a volunteer to circle the main idea. Model identifying the main idea.

Think Aloud From the title and the first paragraph, I know that the main idea is about how long we will live. The sentence *The U.S. government predicts that by the year 2100, 5 million Americans will be 100 or more years old* is the main idea.

Practice/Apply

Reread the rest of "How Long Will We Live?" with students. Have them circle the main idea in the third paragraph and underline supporting details.

Leveled Reader Lesson

Objective Read to apply strategies and skills

Materials
- **Leveled Reader** *Technology and Nature: Water* • chart paper
- **Student Book** *Gecko Glue, Cockroach Scouts, and Spider Silk Bridges*

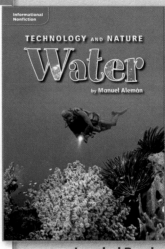

Leveled Reader

PREVIEW AND PREDICT

Have students read the title and preview the first chapter. Have students make predictions about what they will learn in this book and set a purpose for reading.

VOCABULARY WORDS

Before reading, review the vocabulary words as necessary. Tell students to look for the vocabulary words as they read.

STRATEGY
MAKE INFERENCES AND ANALYZE

Remind students that authors do not always state all information directly, but they do provide clues to help readers figure things out for themselves. Read pages 4–5 aloud, and model making inferences and analyzing.

Think Aloud The author gives readers a lot of information about dolphins and sonar. Although the author does not state directly how dolphins can tell different species of fish apart, or whether something is alive, I can infer that it must have something to do with the clicking sounds the dolphin makes.

SKILL
MAIN IDEA AND DETAILS

Discuss with students the ways that humans have made technological innovations by studying animals. Help students identify the main ideas and details. Work with them to begin a Main Idea Web on chart paper.

READ AND RESPOND

Students should read orally to the end of Chapter 2. Have students brainstorm other innovations that they think came from aquatic life. Then have them read the other chapters and complete the web.

MAKE CONNECTIONS ACROSS TEXTS

Invite students to compare *Gecko Glue, Cockroach Scouts, and Spider Silk Bridges* and *Technology and Nature: Water*. Ask them to name two innovations mentioned in *Gecko Glue, Cockroach Scouts, and Spider Silk Bridges* and *Technology and Nature: Water* that have changed our lives.

RESEARCH
Why It Matters

Studies of effective teachers show that they are more likely to use a mix of whole class and small group instruction; teachers who accomplished less learning with their students were less likely to do this.

Tim Shanahan

LOG ON For more information, go to Teacher Resources at www.macmillanmh.com

Skills Focus ▶ Vocabulary

Objective   Apply vocabulary words and use context clues

Materials   • **Student Book** *Gecko Glue, Cockroach Scouts, and Spider Silk Bridges*

VOCABULARY WORDS

Write this week's vocabulary words on the board. Work with students to create tongue twisters using some of the words.

CONTEXT CLUES: DEFINITIONS

Review with students that context clues can be found in surrounding words and in nearby sentences. Have students find three vocabulary words in *Gecko Glue, Cockroach Scouts, and Spider Silk Bridges*, and identify the context clues.

Student Book

Skills Focus ▶ Study Skill

Objective   Use an electronic card catalog

Materials   • computer with an Internet connection

USE AN ELECTRONIC CARD CATALOG

Review the following: *You can search an electronic catalog for a book by its author, title, or subject. A search result will show you a numbered list. Type in the number of the book and press enter. The screen will give you information about that book, including its call number.* Have students skim and scan a list of titles in order to find information quickly.

Skills Focus ▶ Fluency

On Level Practice Book O, page 18

As I read, I will pay attention to the tempo.

	Have you ever asked yourself how birds and insects fly?
10	Or why birds can fly, but other animals can't? Human beings
21	have long studied nature and its mysteries. Over time they
31	have found some amazing ways to use what they have learned.
42	Of course, human beings can't fly. But they have reached
52	the skies by using technology to invent flying machines.
61	Some of these ideas for flying machines have come from
71	animals like birds and insects.
76	Birds are not the only animals that humans have tried to
87	copy. Today we are able to track a plane from takeoff to
99	landing thanks to a system that bats and dolphins use to
110	navigate and hunt.
113	There are other animals that are useful to people. Bees
123	help people in lots of ways, providing them with many
133	valuable products. In this book you will learn about some
143	other ways in which humans have developed technology by
152	imitating nature. 154

Comprehension Check

1. What is the main idea of this passage? **Main Idea and Details** Human beings have found amazing ways to use what they have learned from nature.
2. How have other animals helped people to develop flying machines? **Main Idea and Details** People can track planes by using the same system dolphins and bats use to navigate and hunt.

	Words Read	–	Number of Errors	=	Words Correct Score
First Read		–		=	
Second Read		–		=	

Objective   Read accurately with a good tempo at a rate of 117–137 WCPM

Materials   • **On Level Practice Book O,** p. 18

REPEATED READING

Model reading the Fluency passage on page 18 of **On Level Practice Book O**. Afterward, have one student read a sentence, then invite the next student to join in. Repeat until all students are reading together.

During independent reading time, partners can take turns echo-reading the passage. Remind students to wait until their partner gets to the next punctuation mark before they correct a mistake. Listen carefully to their reading, monitoring for accuracy.

Timed Reading At the end of the week, have students read the passage and record their reading rate.

Leveled Reader Lesson

Objective Read to apply strategies and skills

Materials
- **Leveled Reader** *From Dragonflies to Helicopters: Learning from Nature*
- **Student Book** *Gecko Glue, Cockroach Scouts, and Spider Silk Bridges*

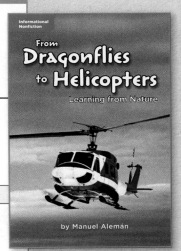

PREVIEW AND PREDICT

Show the cover and read the title of the book. Ask students what they think the selection is about.

STRATEGY
MAKE INFERENCES AND ANALYZE

Tell students that readers must often make inferences when authors do not state all information directly. Readers base their inferences on the information given and their own experiences.

Leveled Reader

SKILL
MAIN IDEA AND DETAILS

Review the following with students: Each paragraph in a selection has a main idea that is supported by details such as facts, examples, or quotations.

- Each section of a long piece of writing also has a main idea. The evidence that supports the section's main idea includes the main ideas of all the paragraphs within that section.

- The main idea may be stated or unstated.

Tell students that they will read the selection and then fill in information about the main idea and supporting details in a Main Idea Web.

READ AND RESPOND

Have students read Chapters 1 and 2 aloud. Discuss the technologies that have been inspired by animals that fly.

Continue with the other chapters. Discuss how to find the main idea and details in each paragraph and section.

VOCABULARY WORDS

After students finish reading, have them use the vocabulary words in questions and answers related to *From Dragonflies to Helicopters*.

MAKE CONNECTIONS ACROSS TEXTS

Have students summarize and compare the main ideas of *Gecko Glue, Cockroach Scouts, and Spider Silk Bridges* and *From Dragonflies to Helicopters*. Discuss how scientists look to designs found in nature for inspiration. Ask: *How do the two selections use details to support their main ideas?*

ELL
Leveled Reader
Go to pages
77U–77V.

Student Book

Beyond Practice Book B, page 18

As I read, I will pay attention to the pronunciation of difficult words.

	Do you know how many varieties of plants exist in nature? There are
13	more than 300,000 different species of plants known to exist on Earth!
25	There are huge plants like the giant sequoia tree and small plants like
38	mosses. Some of these plants can be used for medicine. Other plants
50	produce fruit. People use plants in many different ways.
59	Most of these plants live in tropical parts of Earth! These tropical
71	regions are close to the equator. Plants also grow in some places where
84	you wouldn't expect to see life.
90	Plants like yellow avens and lichens (LIGH-kuhns) grow in the Arctic
101	regions, the coldest places on Earth. There are also many plants
112	that grow underwater, such as algae, cattails, and sea grasses.
122	Plants and trees are like containers that store the sun's energy. They
134	are useful to people, animals, and life on Earth in many ways. Plants
147	produce the air we breathe through a chemical reaction that takes place in
160	their leaves. Trees also give people the materials they need to build many
173	things. Perhaps your house is made of wood. Even the paper this book is
187	written on comes from trees. 192

Comprehension Check

1. What habitats do plants occupy around the world? **Main Idea and Details** Many plants live in the tropics. Some live in the Arctic while others live underwater. Plants live just about everywhere on Earth.

2. How are plants useful? **Main Idea and Details** Plants produce air, building materials, medicine and food.

	Words Read	–	Number of Errors	=	Words Correct Score
First Read		–		=	
Second Read		–		=	

Skills Focus ▶ Vocabulary

Objective Apply understanding of vocabulary words

Materials • Word study notebooks

EXTEND VOCABULARY

Have students write in their word study notebooks about an invention that they would like to create. Have them use the vocabulary words to describe their invention. Invite them to choose a partner and edit each other's description.

Skills Focus ▶ Study Skill

Objective Use an electronic card catalog

Materials • Computer with an Internet connection

USE AN ELECTRONIC CARD CATALOG

Point out that an electronic card catalog gives three options. *You can search for a book by its author, title, or subject. To search by subject, you enter key words about the topic.* Have students pose a question related to this week's theme. Have them visit the Web site of a local library that uses an electronic card catalog. Ask students to find three books that would help answer their question. Remind students to skim and scan the listings to find information quickly.

Skills Focus ▶ Fluency

Objective Read accurately with a good tempo at a rate of 127–137 WCPM

Materials • **Beyond Practice Book B,** p. 18

REPEATED READING

Work with students to begin marking up the Fluency passage on page 18 of **Beyond Practice Book B**. Remind them that one slash means "pause" and should come after commas, dashes, and other places where they would naturally pause when reading or speaking. Two slashes mean "stop" and should come after end marks or semicolons. Partners can finish marking the passage on their own.

During independent reading time, partners can take turns reading the passage they have marked. Remind students to wait until their partner gets to the next punctuation mark before they correct a mistake.

Leveled Reader Library

Leveled Reader Lesson

Objective Read to apply strategies and skills
Materials • **Leveled Reader** *Plants: An Amazing Resource*

PREVIEW AND PREDICT

Have students preview *Plants: An Amazing Resource*, predict what it is about, and set a purpose for reading.

STRATEGY
MAKE INFERENCES AND ANALYZE

Tell students to use their own experiences and clues in the text when making inferences if the author does not state all information directly.

Tested

SKILL
MAIN IDEA AND DETAILS

Ask a volunteer to explain what a main idea is and what details are. Have students discuss where they might look for a main idea that is explicitly stated and how they can infer a main idea if it is not explicitly stated.

READ AND RESPOND

Have students read Chapters 1 and 2. Discuss how plants have influenced technological advances in our lives.

Have students finish reading the story. Discuss the main ideas and details of the last two chapters. Afterward, discuss which innovations students think are most important to us today.

Tested

VOCABULARY WORDS

Have students pay attention to vocabulary words as they come up during reading. Review definitions as needed.

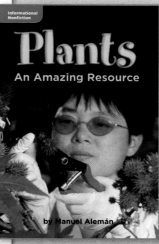

Informational Nonfiction

Plants
An Amazing Resource

by Manuel Alemán

Leveled Reader

Skills Focus

Self-Selected Reading

Objective Read independently to identify main idea and details
Materials • Leveled Readers or trade books at students' reading level

READ TO IDENTIFY MAIN IDEA AND DETAILS

Invite students to select a fiction book to read independently. For a list of theme-related titles, see pages T17–T18. As students read, have them take notes about the main idea of each section and include three details to support their conclusion.

ELL   **Access for All**

Questions and Answers
Ask students to summarize *Gecko Glue, Cockroach Scouts, and Spider Silk Bridges*. Explain that a nonfiction article like this one presents facts and information. Have each student write three questions about the article. Then have students work in pairs, taking turns asking and answering the written questions.

Academic Language

Throughout the week, the English language learners in your class will need help in building their understanding of the academic language used in daily instruction and assessment instruments. The following strategies will help to increase their language proficiency and comprehension of content and instructional words.

LOG ON Technology

For oral vocabulary development, go to
www. macmillanmh.com

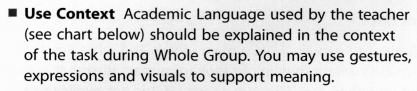

Strategies to Reinforce Academic Language

- **Use Context** Academic Language used by the teacher (see chart below) should be explained in the context of the task during Whole Group. You may use gestures, expressions and visuals to support meaning.

- **Use Visuals** Use charts, transparencies, and graphic organizers to explain key labels to help students understand classroom language.

- **Model** Demonstrate the task using academic language in order for students to understand instruction.

Academic Language Used in Whole Group Instruction

Content/Theme Words	Skill/Strategy Words	Writing/Grammar Words
altered (p. 68)	inferences (p. 69A)	conjunctions (p. 77I)
erode (p. 68)	main idea (p. 69A)	compound (p. 77I)
absorb (p. 68)	context clues (p. 72)	expository (p. 77A)
concentrated (p. 68)	strategy (p. 69)	comma (p. 77I)
innovations (p. 68)	search engine (p. 77A)	semicolon (p. 77J)

Leveled Reader Library

ELL Leveled Reader Lesson

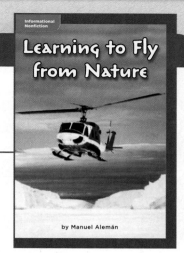

Informational Nonfiction

Learning to Fly from Nature

by Manuel Alemán

Before Reading

DEVELOP ORAL LANGUAGE

LOG ON

Build Background *What have human beings learned from animals that fly? How do birds and bees help us?* Brainstorm answers to these questions. Then point out how engineers have developed machines that imitate things certain animals do naturally.

Review Vocabulary Write the vocabulary and story support words on the board and discuss their meaning. Model using them in sentences. *Innovations have made airplanes safer and faster. Airplanes ride air currents when they fly.*

PREVIEW AND PREDICT

Point to the cover illustration and read the title aloud. *What is represented in this picture? How is this flying machine like a bird?* Have students set purposes for reading.

Set a Purpose for Reading Show the Main Idea Web and remind students they have used this web before. Ask them to fill in a similar web, as they identify details to support main ideas.

During Reading

Choose from among the differentiated strategies to support students' reading at all levels of language acquisition.

Beginning	**Intermediate**	**Advanced**
Shared Reading Do a shared reading. Pause to model how to identify the main idea and details in each chapter. Ask students to use the pictures and captions to gain information. *How do birds fly? What did people learn from watching birds fly?* Model filling in the web.	**Read Together** Read through Chapter 1. Help students identify the main idea and supporting details. Point out similarities and differences between birds and airplanes. Have students read the other chapters and identify other main ideas and details.	**Independent Reading** Have students read the book. Ask them to identify the main idea and details as they read each chapter. Tell them to use the information they've read to complete their web. Have them use their webs to write a summary of the book.

After Reading

Remind students to use the vocabulary and story words in their whole group activities.

Objective
- **To apply vocabulary and comprehension skills.**

Materials
- ELL Leveled Reader *Learning from Nature*

ELL 5 Day Planner

DAY 1	• Academic Language • Oral Language and Vocabulary Review
DAY 2	• Academic Language • ELL Leveled Reader
DAY 3	• Academic Language • ELL Leveled Reader
DAY 4	• Academic Language • ELL Leveled Reader
DAY 5	• Academic Language • ELL Leveled Reader Literacy Activities and Comprehension Check

Grade 6 • ELL TEACHER'S GUIDE

Treasures

English Language Learners

Macmillan/McGraw-Hill

ELL Teacher's Guide
for students who need additional instruction.

Weekly Literature

Week At A Glance

Whole Group

VOCABULARY
rummaged, undetected, chameleon, generosity, pathetic, ricocheting, famine, scrounging

Strategy: Use Context Clues/ Restatement

COMPREHENSION
Strategy: Make Inferences and Analyze
Skill: Character, Setting, Plot

WRITING
Personal Narrative

Social Studies Link

History

Small Group Options

Differentiated Instruction for Tested Skills

Tested Skills for the Week

Main Selection
Genre Folk Tale

Vocabulary/ Comprehension

Social Studies Link
Genre Informational Essay

Read-Aloud Anthology
• Listening Comprehension
• Readers Theater

78A

Resources for Differentiated Instruction

Leveled Readers

GR Levels S–Y

Genre Informational

- Same Theme
- Same Vocabulary
- Same Comprehension Skills

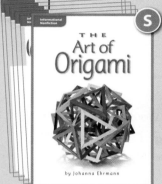
(S)
THE Art of Origami
by Johanna Ehrmann

Approaching Level

(V)
Arts of the Navajo
by Helen Byers

On Level

(Y)
The Tradition of Dance
by Johanna Ehrmann

Beyond Level

Navajo Indian Art
by Helen Byers

English Language Leveled Reader

On Level Reader sheltered for English Language Learner

ELL Teacher's Guide also available

Also Available
LEVELED READER PROGRAM

CLASSROOM LIBRARY

Genre Folk Tale

COME BACK, SALMON

Approaching

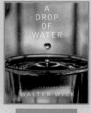
A DROP OF WATER
WALTER WICK

On Level

Interrupted Journey

Beyond

Trade books to apply Comprehension Skills

INTERVENTION ANTHOLOGY

- Phonics and Decoding
- Comprehension
- Vocabulary

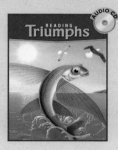
Reading Triumphs

Also available, *Reading Triumphs* Intervention Program

LEVELED PRACTICE

Practice Book A

Practice Book O

Practice Book B

ELL Practice and Assessment

Approaching   **On Level**   **Beyond**   **ELL**

Home-School Connection
Macmillan/McGraw-Hill

HOME-SCHOOL CONNECTION

- Family letters in English and Spanish
- Take-Home Stories

Technology

ONLINE INSTRUCTION
www.macmillanmh.com

AUDIO CD
- Listening Library
- Fluency Solutions

CD-ROM
- Vocabulary PuzzleMaker

The Magic Gourd **78B**

Suggested Lesson Plan

**Instructional Navigator
Interactive Lesson Planner**

The Magic Gourd, 82–93

Leveled Readers

Integrated **ELL** Support Every Day

Whole Group

ORAL LANGUAGE
- **Listening**
- **Speaking**
- **Viewing**

WORD STUDY
- **Vocabulary**
- **Phonics/Decoding**

READING
- **Develop Comprehension**

- **Fluency**

LANGUAGE ARTS
- **Writing**

- **Grammar**

- **Spelling**

ASSESSMENT
- **Informal/Formal**

**Turn the page for
Small Group Lesson Plan**

Day 1

Listening/Speaking/Viewing

❓ Focus Question Why do you think telling traditional stories is important to a culture?

Build Background, 78

Read Aloud: "Remember the Bridge," 79

Vocabulary

rummaged, undetected, chameleon, generosity, pathetic, ricocheting, famine, scrounging, 80

Practice Book A-O-B, 22

Strategy: Context Clues/ Restatement, 81

Read "Keira's Magical Moment," 80–81

Comprehension, 81A–81B
Strategy: Make Inferences and Analyze
Skill: Cause and Effect
Practice Book A-O-B, 23

Fluency Partner Reading, 78I
Model Fluency, 79

Student Book

Writing
Daily Writing Prompt: Write about the experiences you and your best friend have had.

Poem, 100–101B

Grammar Daily Language Activities, 101I
Clauses and Complex Sentences, 101I
Grammar Practice Book, 19

Spelling Pretest, 101G
Spelling Practice Book, 19–20

Quick Check Vocabulary, 80
Comprehension, 89

**Differentiated Instruction
101M–101V**

Day 2

Listening/Speaking

❓ Focus Question What is the cause of Chameleon's generosity?

Vocabulary
Review Vocabulary Words, 82

Phonics/Decoding
Decode Words with *r*-Controlled Vowels, 101E

Practice Book A-O-B, 28

Read *The Magic Gourd,* 82–93

Comprehension, 82–93
Strategy: Make Inferences and Analyze
Skill: Cause and Effect
Practice Book A-O-B, 24

Fluency Partner Reading, 78I
Read with Expression, 87

Student Book

Writing
Daily Writing Prompt: Which holiday is your favorite, and which of its traditions do you enjoy?

Poem, 100–101B

Grammar Daily Language Activities, 101I
Clauses and Complex Sentences, 101I
Grammar Practice Book, 20

Spelling *r*-Controlled Vowels, 101G
Spelling Practice Book, 21

Quick Check Comprehension, 89, 93
Phonics, 101E

**Differentiated Instruction
101M–101V**

78C

Skills/Strategies

Vocabulary	Comprehension	Writing
Vocabulary Words **Context Clues/** **Restatement**	**Strategy:** Make Inferences and Analyze **Skill:** Cause and Effect	**Personal Narrative** **Poem**

Turn the Page for
Small Group
Options

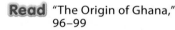

Day 3

Listing/Speaking

❓ Focus Question What do you think the role of a folk tale such as *The Magic Gourd* would have in Keira's great-grandmother's native culture?

Summarize, 95

Vocabulary

Review Words in Context, 101C
Strategy: Context Clues/Restatement, 101D
Practice Book A-O-B, 27

Phonics

Decode Multisyllabic Words, 101E

Read *The Magic Gourd*, 82–93

Comprehension

Comprehension Check, 95
Maintain Skill: Character, Setting, Plot, 95B

Student Book

Fluency Partner Reading, 78I
Repeated Reading, 95A
Practice Book A-O-B, 25

Writing

Daily Writing Prompt: Write a paragraph about families sharing traditions.

Writer's Craft: Precise Words, 101A
Poem, 100–101B

Grammar Daily Language Activities, 101I
Punctuating Complex Sentences: Comma vs. No Comma; Punctuating a Poem, 101H
Grammar Practice Book, 21

Spelling *r*-Controlled Vowels, 101H
Spelling Practice Book, 22

Quick Check Fluency, 95A

Differentiated Instruction
101M–101V

Day 4

Listening/Speaking/Viewing

❓ Focus Question Why did the pui of Gassire and the narrator in *The Magic Gourd* use animal characters?

Media Literacy: Animated Film, 88

Expand Vocabulary: Sharing Traditions, 101F

Vocabulary

Content Vocabulary: *origin, bolster, mythological*, 96
Restatement, 101 F
Apply Vocabulary to Writing, 101F

Read "The Origin of Ghana," 96–99

Comprehension

Informational Nonfiction, 96
Text Feature: Time Line, 96
Practice Book A-O-B, 26

Student Book

Fluency Partner Reading, 78I

Writing

Daily Writing Prompt: Think of a cultural tradition you've learned and write a paragraph describing the tradition.

Writing Trait: Ideas and Content, 101B
Poem, 100–101B

Grammar Daily Language Activities, 101I
Clauses and Complex Sentences, 101J
Grammar Practice Book, 22

Spelling *r*-Controlled Vowels, 101H
Spelling Practice Book, 23

Quick Check Vocabulary, 101D

Differentiated Instruction
101M–101V

Day 5
Review and Assess

Listening/Speaking/Viewing

❓ Focus Question How can origin stories help you understand a culture?

Speaking and Listening Strategies, 101A

Vocabulary

Spiral Review of Vocabulary Words, 101F

Read Self-Selected Reading, 78I

Comprehension

Connect and Compare, 99

Student Book

Fluency Partner Reading, 78I
Practice, 95A

Writing

Daily Writing Prompt: What country's traditions would you like to learn more about? Why?

Poem, 100–101B

Grammar Daily Language Activities, 101I
Clauses and Complex Sentences, 101J
Grammar Practice Book, 22–23

Spelling Posttest, 101H
Spelling Practice Book, 24

Weekly Assessment, 45–52

Differentiated Instruction
101M–101V

Differentiated Instruction

What do I do in small groups?

Teacher-Led Small Groups

Literacy Workstations

Independent Activities

Focus on Skills

 Skills Focus → Use your **Quick Check** observations to guide additional instruction and practice.

Phonics
r-Controlled Vowels

 Vocabulary
Words: chameleon, famine, generosity, pathetic, ricocheting, rummaged, scrounging, undetected
 Strategy: Context Clues: Restatement

Comprehension
Strategy: Make Inferences and Analyze
Skill: Cause and Effect

Fluency

Suggested Lesson Plan

 CD ROM
Instructional Navigator
Interactive Lesson Planner

	Day 1	Day 2
Approaching Level • **Additional Instruction/Practice** • **Tier 2 Instruction**	Fluency, 101N Vocabulary, 101N Comprehension, 101O	Phonics, 101M Vocabulary, 101O Leveled Reader Lesson, 101P • Vocabulary • Comprehension
On Level • **Practice**	Vocabulary, 101Q Leveled Reader Lesson, 101R • Comprehension **ELL** Leveled Reader, 101U–101V	Leveled Reader Lesson, 101R • Comprehension • Vocabulary
Beyond Level • **Extend**	Vocabulary, 101S Leveled Reader Lesson, 101T • Comprehension	Leveled Reader Lesson, 101T • Comprehension • Vocabulary

For intensive intervention see **READING Triumphs**

Small Group Options

Focus on Leveled Readers

Levels S–Y

Apply skills and strategies while reading appropriate leveled books.

Approaching
S

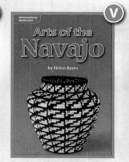
On Level
V

Beyond
Y

ELL

Additional Leveled Reader Resources

LOG ON

Leveled Reader Database
Go to www.macmillanmh.com

Search by
- Comprehension Skill
- Content Area
- Genre
- Text Feature
- Guided Reading Level
- Reading Recovery Level
- Lexile Score
- Benchmark Level

Subscription also available

Day 3

Phonics, 101M
Fluency, 101N
Vocabulary, 101O
Leveled Reader Lesson, 101P
- Comprehension

Fluency, 101Q
Vocabulary, 101Q
Leveled Reader Lesson, 101R
- Comprehension

Fluency, 101S
Vocabulary, 101S
Leveled Reader Lesson, 101T
- Comprehension

Day 4

Phonics, 101M
Leveled Reader Lesson, 101P
- Comprehension
ELL Cause and Effect, 101P

Text Feature, 101Q
Leveled Reader Lesson, 101R
- Comprehension

Text Feature, 101S
Leveled Reader Lesson, 101T
- Comprehension
ELL Time Line, 101T

Day 5

Fluency, 101N
Leveled Reader Lesson, 101P
- Make Connections
  Across Texts

Fluency, 101Q
Leveled Reader Lesson, 101R
- Make Connections
  Across Texts

Fluency, 101S
Self-Selected Reading, 101T

Managing the Class

What do I do with the rest of my class?

Class Management Tools

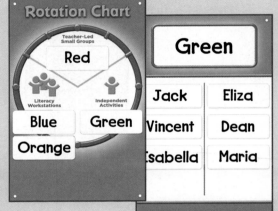

Includes:
- How-To Guides
- Rotation Chart
- Weekly Contracts

FOLDABLES™

Hands-on activities to reinforce weekly skills.

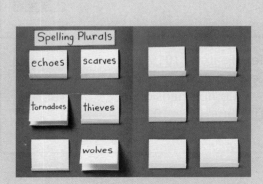

Matchbook Foldable

Word	Synonym	Antonym	Prefix or Suffix
normal	typical	unusual	normally

Folded Foldable

Independent Activities

Leveled Readers

For Repeated Readings and Literacy Activities

Approaching   **On Level**   **ELL**   **Beyond**

LEVELED PRACTICE

Skills: Vocabulary (p. 22), Comprehension: Cause and Effect (p. 23), Graphic Organizer (p. 24), Fluency (p. 25), Text Feature: Timeline (p. 26), Vocabulary Strategy: Restatement (p. 27), Phonics (p. 28)

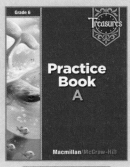

Approaching   **On Level**   **Beyond**   **ELL**

Technology

ONLINE INSTRUCTION www.macmillanmh.com

- Meet the Author/Illustrator
- Computer Literacy Lessons
- Research and Inquiry Activities

- Oral Language Activities
- Vocabulary and Spelling Activities
- Leveled Reader Database

LISTENING LIBRARY
Recordings of selections
- Main Selections
- Leveled Readers
- ELL Readers
- Intervention Anthology

FLUENCY SOLUTIONS
Recorded passages for modeling and practicing fluency

VOCABULARY PUZZLEMAKER
Activities providing multiple exposures to vocabulary, spelling, and high-frequency words including crossword puzzles, word searches, and word jumbles

Turn the page for Literacy Workstations.

Managing the Class

Literacy Activities
Collaborative Learning Activities

Reading

Objectives
- Time reading to practice fluency.
- Read passage fluently with expression.
- Select literature daily for reading enjoyment.

Word Study

Objectives
- Make restatement sentences.
- Group words with *r*-controlled vowels that rhyme and use words with *r*-controlled vowels in sentences.

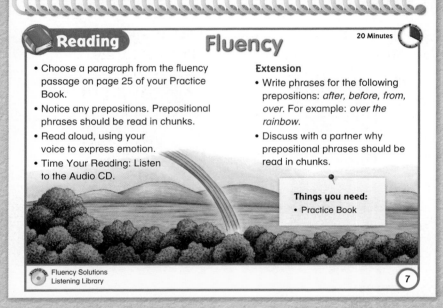

Reading — Fluency
20 Minutes

- Choose a paragraph from the fluency passage on page 25 of your Practice Book.
- Notice any prepositions. Prepositional phrases should be read in chunks.
- Read aloud, using your voice to express emotion.
- Time Your Reading: Listen to the Audio CD.

Extension
- Write phrases for the following prepositions: *after, before, from, over.* For example: *over the rainbow.*
- Discuss with a partner why prepositional phrases should be read in chunks.

Things you need:
- Practice Book

Fluency Solutions
Listening Library

7

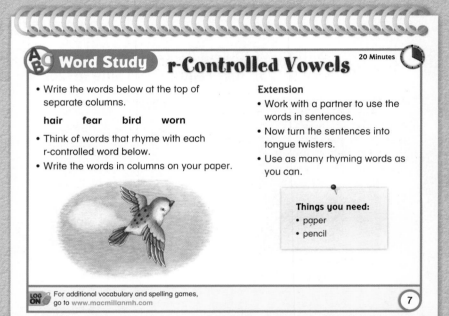

Word Study — r-Controlled Vowels
20 Minutes

- Write the words below at the top of separate columns.

  hair   fear   bird   worn

- Think of words that rhyme with each r-controlled word below.
- Write the words in columns on your paper.

Extension
- Work with a partner to use the words in sentences.
- Now turn the sentences into tongue twisters.
- Use as many rhyming words as you can.

Things you need:
- paper
- pencil

LOG ON For additional vocabulary and spelling games, go to www.macmillanmh.com

7

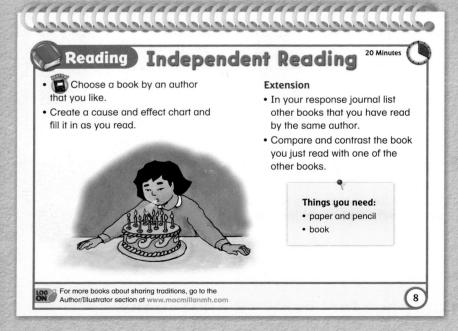

Reading — Independent Reading
20 Minutes

- Choose a book by an author that you like.
- Create a cause and effect chart and fill it in as you read.

Extension
- In your response journal list other books that you have read by the same author.
- Compare and contrast the book you just read with one of the other books.

Things you need:
- paper and pencil
- book

LOG ON For more books about sharing traditions, go to the Author/Illustrator section at www.macmillanmh.com

8

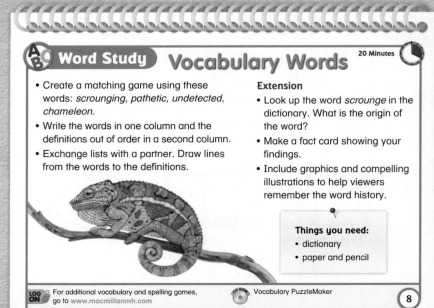

Word Study — Vocabulary Words
20 Minutes

- Create a matching game using these words: *scrounging, pathetic, undetected, chameleon.*
- Write the words in one column and the definitions out of order in a second column.
- Exchange lists with a partner. Draw lines from the words to the definitions.

Extension
- Look up the word *scrounge* in the dictionary. What is the origin of the word?
- Make a fact card showing your findings.
- Include graphics and compelling illustrations to help viewers remember the word history.

Things you need:
- dictionary
- paper and pencil

LOG ON For additional vocabulary and spelling games, go to www.macmillanmh.com   Vocabulary PuzzleMaker

8

Literacy Workstations

Writing

Objectives

- Write a poem about a personal tradition and illustrate the poem.
- Write and deliver an expository speech.

Content Literacy

Objectives

- Use reference books or the Internet to research healthy foods and make a chart to illustrate your findings.
- Use reference materials to find out the history of a food you normally eat and write a paragraph about your findings.

Writing — Sharing Traditions
20 Minutes

- Think of a tradition you share with others. What emotions does it evoke? Do you associate the tradition with any smells, flavors, textures, sights, or sounds?
- Write a poem, either free-form or rhyming, describing the tradition.

Extension

- Write your poem on a large sheet of paper.
- Use fancy writing—even calligraphy if you know how. Or, experiment with different styles of type using a computer. Include an illustration.

Things you need:
- paper and pencil
- colored markers
- construction paper

7

Science — A Healthy Diet
20 Minutes

- Use several reference sources of the Internet to research what kinds of food make a healthy diet.
- Create a chart listing the different types of foods and how many servings are needed a day.

Extension

Using your research on a healthy diet, write a menu for breakfast, lunch, and dinner.

Things you need:
- reference materials
- paper and pencil

LOG ON Internet Research and Inquiry Activity
Students can find more facts at www.macmillanmh.com

7

Writing — COMMUNITY TRADITIONS
20 Minutes

- Write a speech about a tradition in your community, such as a Fourth of July clambake or a Labor Day parade.
- Explain why the tradition makes your town unique.

Extension

- Deliver your speech to the class.
- Use the volume of your voice to make your opening dramatic.
- Try to speak clearly and slowly.
- Make good eye contact, and look at your notes as little as possible.

Things you need:
- paper
- pencil

8

Social Studies — You Are What You Eat
20 Minutes

- Work with a partner. Choose a food you both normally eat.
- Use reference materials to find out the history of that particular food. How long has is been around? Where did it come from?
- Write a paragraph based on your research.

Extension

- Create a poster with an illustration of the food you choose.
- List facts about the food below it.

Things you need:
- reference materials
- paper and pencil
- poster board
- colored markers

LOG ON Internet Research and Inquiry Activity
Students can find more facts at www.macmillanmh.com

8

Prepare

ORAL LANGUAGE
- Build Background
- Read Aloud
- Expand Vocabulary

VOCABULARY
- Context Clues
- Restatement

COMPREHENSION
- **Strategy:** Make Inferences and Analyze
- **Skill:** Cause and Effect

SMALL GROUP OPTIONS
- Differentiated Instruction, pp. 101M–101V

Oral Language

Build Background

ACCESS PRIOR KNOWLEDGE

Share information to help students think about this week's theme.

Every country has great traditions that people share. In the United Kingdom, people set off fireworks each year on November 5th, Guy Fawkes Day.

TALK ABOUT SHARING TRADITIONS

Discuss the weekly theme.

Why do you think people enjoy taking part in shared traditions?

 FOCUS QUESTION Ask a volunteer to read "Talk About It" on **Student Book** page 79 and describe the photo.

Why is it important to learn about the traditions of other cultures?

Sharing Traditions

78

ENGLISH LANGUAGE LEARNERS   Access for All

Beginning Name and Repeat Describe the photo: *The people are dancing. They are wearing masks. They are telling a story.* Ask students to point to items in the picture: *Point to the [masks].* Help students describe the photo.

Intermediate Share Ideas Have students talk about the picture. Share cultural traditions that you follow. Ask students to share their traditions. For Spanish speaking students, point out the cognates *tradition/tradición*.

Advanced Elaborate Do the Intermediate task. Model extending students' sentences. Simple: *We eat a special meal on New Year's Day.* Extended: *We eat a special meal with our relatives and friends on New Year's Day.*

78

Talk About It

Story telling is entertaining. Why do you think traditional stories are important to a culture?

LOG ON Find out more about sharing traditions at www.macmillanmh.com

79

Picture Prompt

Look at the picture. Write about what you see. You can write a story, a description, or use any other type of writing you like.

 **Technology**

For an extended lesson plan and Web site activities for **oral language development,** go to www.macmillanmh.com

Read Aloud
Read "Remember the Bridge"

GENRE: Poetry
Review features of poetry:

- composition in verse

- ideas organized into lines and stanzas

LISTENING FOR A PURPOSE

Read Aloud
pages 23–26

Ask students to listen carefully for reasons why retaining memories and sharing traditions is important as you read "Remember the Bridge" in the **Read-Aloud Anthology.** Choose from among the teaching suggestions.

Fluency Ask students to listen carefully as you read aloud. Tell students to listen to your phrasing, expression, and tone of voice.

RESPOND TO THE POEM

Ask students to write a poem urging their classmates not to forget something they feel is important to remember.

Expand Vocabulary

Have students write down words or phrases in the poem that relate to this week's theme of sharing traditions. Ask them to explain what they associate with these words. For example, students may write the word *dreams* and explain they associate dreams with looking toward the future every New Year's Day.

Vocabulary

TEACH WORDS IN CONTEXT

Use the following routine.

Routine

Define: If something is **rummaged** through, it has been searched thoroughly.
Example: Jenny rummaged through the bin to find a sweater.
Ask: Where have you rummaged through something? EXPLANATION

- Something **undetected** is not noticed. The mouse went undetected. What is a synonym for *undetected?* SYNONYM

- A **chameleon** is a lizard that changes color with its environment. I could barely see the chameleon on the rock. How would a chameleon look on a dead branch? EXAMPLE

 - **Generosity** is the quality of being kind and giving. We showed generosity by helping with the food drive. Why is generosity an important quality? EXPLANATION

- Characters that are **pathetic** cause others to feel sorry for them. The pathetic dog begged for scraps. What is an antonym of *pathetic?* ANTONYM

- If something is **ricocheting**, it is bouncing from surface to surface. The ball was ricocheting off everything it hit. Why might an object that is ricocheting be dangerous? EXPLANATION

- A **famine** is a time of extreme scarcity of food. Drought made the citizens victims of famine. Which countries have suffered from famine? PRIOR KNOWLEDGE

Vocabulary

rummaged	pathetic
undetected	ricocheting
chameleon	famine
generosity	scrounging

Context Clues

Context Clues provide hints to help readers figure out the meaning of an unfamiliar word. Restatement is a kind of context clue that gives a definition of the unfamiliar word.

"Her great-grandmother left her village because of a famine, a time of extreme scarcity of food."

80

- **Scrounging** for something means checking every available source. Cats were scrounging for food. What connotation does *scrounging* have? PRIOR KNOWLEDGE

Quick Check

Do students understand word meanings?

During **Small Group Instruction**

If No → **Approaching Level** Vocabulary, p. 101P

If Yes → **On Level** Options, pp. 101Q–101R

Beyond Level Options, pp. 101S–101T

Keira's Magical Moment

by Leonora Halvi

As Keira climbed into bed, she thought about tomorrow's field trip. Her class was going to a presentation by a West African traditional storyteller. Keira was excited because she was of West African descent. Her great-grandmother had come to the United States from Senegal. Until now, Keira hadn't thought much about her roots.

When her alarm went off, Keira **rummaged** through her closet. She was looking for something that showed her West African roots. She dug through every drawer, but she couldn't find anything that really stood out. Finally, she put on a white shirt and jeans. Despite her plain clothes, she hoped that her interest in her heritage would not go **undetected**.

At the community center, Keira was lucky enough to get a front-row seat. The first speaker talked about African writers and how they often use traditional stories with traditional characters, such as the Tortoise and the Spider. The speaker mentioned writers her mother and grandmother liked! Also, Tortoise was a favorite character in Keira's bedtime stories. Finally, the speaker mentioned Doudou N'Diaye Rose. He was Keira's favorite drummer. He was from Senegal. She began to realize just how much her West African heritage influenced her American life.

ELL   Access for All

Reinforce Vocabulary
Choose a student and reinforce the meaning of the word *generosity*, using his or her name. *Anna has her lunch. I don't have any. Anna shares her lunch with me. She shows me* <u>generosity</u>. *Generosity is when you are kind and share with others. When do you show generosity?*

Finally, the griot, or storyteller, took the stage. He told a story that explained how the **chameleon**, a small lizard, changed its colors. Then he introduced the tricksters Spider and Tortoise. They were known to fake **generosity** while actually looking for a handout. Some of the stories made these characters seem **pathetic** as they fought for every last scrap. However, they were simply naughty. They certainly did learn their lessons!

Keira couldn't keep her mind from **ricocheting** through all the different stories her mother had told. Her memory was bouncing around like a ball! She knew about everything the griot said.

After the presentation, the class talked to the griot. Keira told about how her great-grandmother had moved to the United States from Senegal. Her great-grandmother left her village because of a **famine**, a time of extreme scarcity of food. She had explained to Keira's grandmother that the villagers spent days **scrounging** for food. Her great-grandmother eventually came to the United States. Keira told the griot about the familiar bedtime stories.

When Keira was finished, the griot pointed out that she had just taken on his job. She had described her family and the stories they told. Keira could hardly wait to tell her mother and grandmother the news!

Reread for **Comprehension**

Make Inferences and Analyze
Cause and Effect
In a story, the actions of the characters often cause a series of events to unfold. Making inferences about a character's actions can help you identify cause-and-effect relationships between events in the story.

Use your Cause-and-Effect Chart to record important causes of events as you reread "Keira's Magical Moment."

| Cause → Effect |
| → |
| → |
| → |
| → |

81

On Level Practice Book O, page 22

A. Complete each sentence with a vocabulary word.

chameleon, rummaged, scrounging, pathetic, undetected, generosity, ricocheting, famine

1. Many folk tale characters are known for their kindness and _generosity_
2. African folk tales often feature insect and animal characters, such as a spider or a _chameleon_.
3. My grandmother _rummaged_ through her attic to find her favorite book from her childhood.
4. At one point in the story, the children were so hungry they were _scrounging_ for food.
5. The children in the story were very brave, but the enemy was _pathetic_.

B. Write sentences of your own, using the remaining vocabulary words.
6. Students should write sentences using the words ricocheting, undetected, and famine.
7.
8.

⭐ **Approaching Practice Book A,** page 22
◆ **Beyond Practice Book B,** page 22

Vocabulary

STRATEGY
CONTEXT CLUES

Restatement When you read, you should use the context, or surrounding words, to help determine the meaning of unfamiliar vocabulary. One kind of context clue is **restatement,** in which the meaning of a word is restated immediately after the word appears. By first using context clues and then looking for restatement, you can confirm the meaning of a word.

Point to the word *famine* in "Keira's Magical Moment" on **Student Book** page 81. Ask students to use surrounding words to figure out the meaning. Then ask them to identify the restatement in the example. (a time of extreme scarcity of food)

Read "Keira's Magical Moment"

As you read "Keira's Magical Moment" with students, ask them to use context clues to decide the meaning of each highlighted word in the story. Tell students they will read these words again in *The Magic Gourd.*

Objectives

- Make inferences and analyze logical text progression
- Identify cause-and-effect relationships

Materials

- Comprehension Transparencies 4a and 4b
- Graphic Organizer Transparency 4
- Leveled Practice Books, p. 23

Skills Trace

Cause and Effect	
Introduce	U1: 81A–81B
Practice/ Apply	U1: 82–95; Leveled Practice Books, 23–24
Reteach/ Review	U1: 101M–101T; U3: 305A–305B, 306–309, 313M–313T; Leveled Practice Books, 90–91
Assess	Weekly Tests; Unit 1, 2, 3 Tests; Benchmark Tests A, B
Maintain	U2: 147B

ELL

Access for All

Develop Concepts Write *cause* and *effect* on the board. Then write, *I get good grades because I study hard.* Say, *Studying hard is the* <u>cause</u> *of my good grades. Good grades are the* <u>effect</u> *of studying.* Next write, *I am sleepy because I stayed up too late.* Have students identify the cause and the effect in the sentence.

Reread for Comprehension

STRATEGY
MAKE INFERENCES AND ANALYZE

Authors do not always tell readers everything that takes place in a story. Good readers use information from the text as well as their own experiences to make inferences, or logical conclusions, about characters or events. Making inferences can also help readers to identify cause-and-effect relationships in a story.

SKILL
CAUSE AND EFFECT

A cause is an event or action that makes something happen. An effect is what happens because of an event or action. Cause-and-effect relationships help make up the events in a story, and are often marked by signal words and phrases such as *because, since, due to,* and *therefore.*

Transparency 4a

Vocabulary

rummaged — pathetic
undetected — ricocheting
chameleon — famine
generosity — scrounging

Context Clues

Context Clues provide hints to help readers figure out the meaning of an unfamiliar word. Restatement is a kind of context clue that gives a definition of the unfamiliar word.

"Her great-grandmother left her village because of a famine, a time of extreme scarcity of food."

Keira's Magical Moment

by Leonora Halvi

As Keira climbed into bed, she thought about tomorrow's field trip. Her class was going to a presentation by a West African traditional storyteller. Keira was excited because she was of West African descent. Her great-grandmother had come to the United States from Senegal. Until now, Keira hadn't thought much about her roots.

When her alarm went off, Keira **rummaged** through her closet. She was looking for something that showed her West African roots. She dug through every drawer, but she couldn't find anything that really stood out. Finally, she put on a white shirt and jeans. Despite her plain clothes, she hoped that her interest in her heritage would not go **undetected**.

At the community center, Keira was lucky enough to get a front-row seat. The first speaker talked about African writers and how they often use traditional stories with traditional characters, such as the Tortoise and the Spider. The speaker mentioned writers her mother and grandmother liked! Also, Tortoise was a favorite character in Keira's bedtime stories. Finally, the speaker mentioned Doudou N'Diaye Rose. He was Keira's favorite drummer. He was from Senegal. She began to realize just how much her West African heritage influenced her American life.

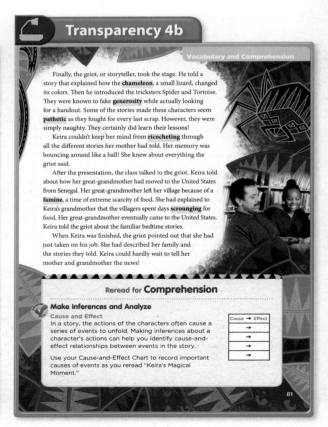

Transparency 4b

Vocabulary and Comprehension

Finally, the griot, or storyteller, took the stage. He told a story that explained how the **chameleon**, a small lizard, changed its colors. Then he introduced the tricksters Spider and Tortoise. They were known to fake **generosity** while actually looking for a handout. Some of the stories made these characters seem **pathetic** as they fought for every last scrap. However, they were simply naughty. They certainly did learn their lessons!

Keira couldn't keep her mind from **ricocheting** through all the different stories her mother had told. Her memory was bouncing around like a ball! She knew about everything the griot said.

After the presentation, the class talked to the griot. Keira told about how her great-grandmother had moved to the United States from Senegal. Her great-grandmother left her village because of a **famine**, a time of extreme scarcity of food. She had explained to Keira's grandmother that the villagers spent days **scrounging** for food. Her great-grandmother eventually came to the United States. Keira told the griot about the familiar bedtime stories.

When Keira was finished, the griot pointed out that she had just taken on his job. She had described her family and the stories they told. Keira could hardly wait to tell her mother and grandmother the news!

Reread for Comprehension

Make Inferences and Analyze

Cause and Effect
In a story, the actions of the characters often cause a series of events to unfold. Making inferences about a character's actions can help you identify cause-and-effect relationships between events in the story.

Use your Cause-and-Effect Chart to record important causes of events as you reread "Keira's Magical Moment."

Cause	→	Effect
	→	
	→	
	→	
	→	

Student Book pages 80–81 available on Comprehension Transparencies 4a and 4b

MODEL

Read aloud the first paragraph of "Keira's Magical Moment" from **Student Book** page 80.

Think Aloud Here is an example of a cause-and-effect relationship: Keira's class is going to hear a West African storyteller. This causes Keira to become excited because she is going to learn about her West African roots. Her anticipation sets the plot in motion.

GUIDED PRACTICE

Display the Cause and Effect Chart on **Transparency 4.** For Cause, write "A West African storyteller is coming to speak."

- Point out that cause-and-effect relationships are often merely implied by an author. The author does not always use one of the signal words or phrases.

- Cause-and-effect questions frequently begin with the word *why*. Therefore, students can practice this skill by asking themselves questions like: Why was Keira rummaging through her closet? Why was Keira lucky when she got to the community center?

- Explain that the event mentioned in the question is the **effect.** The answer to the question is the **cause.**

APPLY

Have students complete the Cause and Effect Chart. Then, ask them to explain Keira's new role at the end of the story. What are her new duties, and how do students think she will fulfill them? Remind students to ask themselves questions to better understand cause and effect.

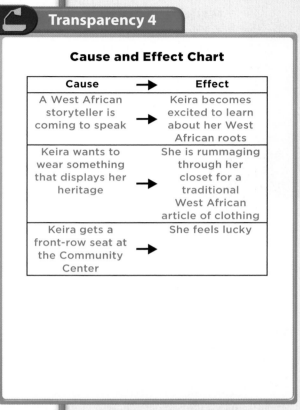

Transparency 4

Cause and Effect Chart

Cause	→	Effect
A West African storyteller is coming to speak	→	Keira becomes excited to learn about her West African roots
Keira wants to wear something that displays her heritage	→	She is rummaging through her closet for a traditional West African article of clothing
Keira gets a front-row seat at the Community Center	→	She feels lucky

Graphic Organizer Transparency 4

On Level Practice Book O, page 23

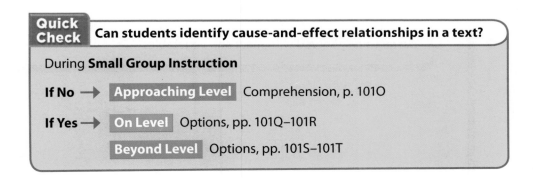

In stories and in real life, one event can make another event occur. For example, if your alarm does not go off then you might be late for school. The first event is the **cause,** and the second event is the **effect.** Authors use signal words or phrases such as *as a result, so, therefore, because, due to,* and *then* to show the relationships between events.

Read the following article. Underline the signal words or phrases that show the relationships between events. Then write the cause and effect of each situation as indicated by the signal words.
Possible responses provided.

Passing on traditions is very important to some families <u>because</u> they feel it keeps family memories alive. <u>When</u> an older relative tells the story of his father's immigration to America, he is passing on part of the family tradition. Traditions also accompany holiday gatherings. Every year special events, such as holiday dinners and celebrations, take place. <u>As a result,</u> familiarity with the events are passed on to the younger generations. <u>Then</u> these youngsters grow up and pass on their awareness of traditions. <u>Therefore,</u> family tradition survives through the centuries.

1. cause passing on traditions
   effect keeping family memories alive
2. cause An older relative tells the story of his father's immigration.
   effect passing on part of the family's tradition
3. cause Special events take place.
   effect Familiarity with events is passed on to the younger generations.
4. cause Youngsters grow up.
   effect They pass on their awareness of traditions, and family traditions survive.

★ **Approaching Practice Book A,** page 23

◆ **Beyond Practice Book B,** page 23

Quick Check Can students identify cause-and-effect relationships in a text?

During **Small Group Instruction**

If No → **Approaching Level** Comprehension, p. 101O

If Yes → **On Level** Options, pp. 101Q–101R

Beyond Level Options, pp. 101S–101T

Read

MAIN SELECTION
- *The Magic Gourd*

- **Skill:** Identify Cause and Effect

PAIRED SELECTION
- "The Origin of Ghana"
- **Text Feature:** Time Line

SMALL GROUP OPTIONS
- Differentiated Instruction, pp. 101M–101V

Comprehension

GENRE: FOLK TALE

Have a student read the definition of Folk Tale on **Student Book** page 82. As students read, they should look for features that show African traditions.

STRATEGY
MAKE INFERENCES

Authors do not always tell readers directly everything that takes place in a story. Good readers take what details the author does offer, analyze their own experiences, and infer or reasonably assume certain conclusions.

SKILL
IDENTIFY CAUSE AND EFFECT

Understanding **cause-and-effect relationships** can help students analyze events in a text. Cause-and-effect relationships are often marked by signal words such as *because*, *since*, and *therefore*.

Comprehension

Genre

A **Folk Tale** is a story based on the traditions of a people or region which is handed down from one generation to the next and becomes legendary.

Make Inferences and Analyze

Cause and Effect
As you read, use your Cause and Effect Chart.

Cause → Effect
→
→
→
→

Read to Find Out

What is the cause of Chameleon's generosity?

82

Vocabulary

Vocabulary Words Review the tested vocabulary words: **rummaged, undetected, chameleon, generosity, pathetic, ricocheting, famine,** and **scrounging.**

Story Word Students may find this word difficult. Pronounce the word and present the meaning as necessary.

couscous (p. 87): a North African dish of steamed semolina (small pasta) usually served with meat and vegetables

The Magic Gourd

by Baba Wagué Diakité

Award Winning
Author
and
Illustrator

83

Read Together	Read Independently
If your students need support to read the Main Selection, use the prompts to guide comprehension and model how to complete the graphic organizer.	If your students can read the Main Selection independently, have them read and complete the graphic organizer. Remind students to set and modify purposes when reading.

If your students need an alternate selection, choose the **Leveled Readers** that match their instructional level.

Technology

Story available on **Listening Library Audio CD.**

Preview and Predict

Ask students to read the title, preview the illustrations, and note questions and predictions about what may happen in the story. What kinds of characters does this story have?

Set Purposes

FOCUS QUESTION Discuss the "Read to Find Out" question on **Student Book** page 82. Remind students to look for the answer as they read.

Point out the Cause-and-Effect Chart in the student book and on **Leveled Practice Book** page 24. Explain that students will fill it in as they read.

Read *The Magic Gourd*

Use the questions and Think Alouds for additional instruction to support the comprehension strategy and skill.

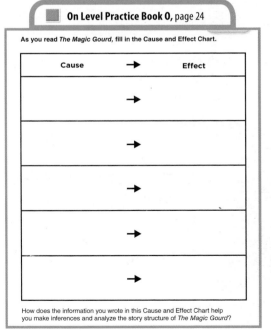

On Level Practice Book O, page 24

As you read *The Magic Gourd*, fill in the Cause and Effect Chart.

Cause	→	Effect
	→	
	→	
	→	
	→	
	→	

How does the information you wrote in this Cause and Effect Chart help you make inferences and analyze the story structure of *The Magic Gourd*?

★ **Approaching Practice Book A,** page 24
◆ **Beyond Practice Book B,** page 24

Develop Comprehension

1 STRATEGY
MAKE INFERENCES AND ANALYZE

Teacher Think Aloud In the opening of the story it says that the sun is not letting the clouds gather, so there is no rain. I see from the picture that the sun has arms and hands reaching for the clouds. I can make an inference from this image that the story is not going to be realistic, even though a drought could really happen. I can see that in this story I will have to make inferences to connect unrealistic events to real life lessons.

2 CAUSE AND EFFECT

Tested

In the story Rabbit faces the problem of a famine. Make inferences to figure out what caused the famine. How does the author show the cause-and-effect relationship? (The drought caused the famine. There was no rain, so the crops could not grow. This led to a shortage of food, which is why Rabbit and his family are starving. The author uses the word *then* to connect the two events.) Write this information in your Cause and Effect Chart.

Cause	→	Effect
There is a drought.	→	There is a famine, and Rabbit's family is starving.

It all began

1 when the sun refused to allow the clouds to gather, and there was no rain. First came drought. Then came **famine**. Everyone was hungry. And it was then that Brother Rabbit wandered around the parched countryside searching for wild roots

2 to feed his starving family. As he walked, he sang . . .

> *Feeyeh ku, feeyeh ku.*
> *Waara sa kun tay.*
> *Luck will come. Life will be good.*

84

Suddenly, Rabbit was interrupted by a sweet little voice that called out, "Dogo Zan! Dogo Zan! Rescue me from this thorny bush! My arms are being poked and scratched! Help me, and I will pay you well."

Rabbit was busy, but still he stopped. "I will help simply to avoid seeing my brother suffer," said Rabbit. Gently he lowered his hand between the thorny branches and saved the green **chameleon**. As Rabbit turned to leave, Chameleon called out to him once again.   **3**

4

"Dogo Zan! Don't go yet! Would you mind getting my gourd from the bush, too?"

"A gourd?" cried Brother Rabbit. "You want me to scratch myself again for a little gourd?"

"Please, Dogo Zan," begged Chameleon. "I will reward you well."

85

Develop Comprehension

3 **MAINTAIN**
CHARACTER AND PLOT

Who are the two main characters and what are their different problems? (The two main characters are Rabbit and Chameleon. There is a famine, and Brother Rabbit is trying to feed his starving family. Chameleon is trapped in a thorny bush and needs Rabbit's help.)

4 **USE ILLUSTRATIONS**

Look at the illustrations on pages 84 and 85. In the first illustration, how is the drought depicted? (The trees have no leaves, there is a skeleton in the middle, and the sun has many arms, as if reaching everywhere.) Where is Chameleon in the second illustration? What does this demonstrate about his character? (Chameleon blends in with the bushes. He seems to be a quiet and reserved character, observing most of the time.)

Comprehension

Monitor and Clarify: *Paraphrase*

Explain Remind students that paraphrasing means using their own words to restate something they've read. Successful paraphrasing must express the author's meaning accurately. It can help you realize what you did not understand so that you can reread for clarification.

Discuss *How can paraphrasing help you make inferences about characters and events?* (Answers will vary, but students might say that they understand a passage better when they restate it.)

Apply Have students paraphrase the second paragraph on page 85. (Paraphrases might be something like: "Rabbit was busy, but he didn't want chameleon to suffer. He reached in to pull Chameleon out of the thorns. Rabbit was leaving when Chameleon called him again.")

Develop Comprehension

5 STRATEGY
CONTEXT CLUES

How is the word *gourd* used in the second sentence? How can you use context clues to help you figure out its meaning? (A gourd is a squash, but the text says it is decorated. From the picture, it looks like a decorated bowl. Reading further on, it is clear that it must be a bowl, one which is probably made from the large end of a large dried squash.)

6 CAUSE AND EFFECT

What happened as a result of Rabbit's kindness? (Chameleon gave him a magic gourd.) Fill in the Cause and Effect Chart with your answers.

Cause	→	Effect
There is a drought.	→	There is a famine, and Rabbit's family is starving.
Rabbit kindly helps Chameleon.	→	Chameleon gives Rabbit a magic gourd.

Again, Rabbit's kind nature got the best of him, and he bent into the thorny bush and **rummaged** around.

5 Rabbit brought out a beautifully decorated gourd and handed it to Chameleon. But Chameleon just said, "Keep it. It's your reward."

"It's just an empty gourd," Rabbit cried.

"It's not *just* an empty gourd," Chameleon replied. "It's MAGIC!"

"*Ee ko dee!*" cried Rabbit. "A magic gourd?"

"Oh, yes!" said Chameleon. "Watch this: Magic Gourd, fill yourself up with insects!"

Brother Rabbit watched in amazement as Chameleon licked up a bowl full of insects.

"Why are you giving me such a valuable gift?" Rabbit asked.

6 "You were kind to me, Brother Rabbit," Chameleon said. "Besides, I have my own secret for catching insects," and he quickly unrolled his lo-o-o-o-o-ong tongue for Rabbit to admire.

Rabbit thanked Brother Chameleon and rushed home with his gourd.

Cause and Effect
What happened as a result of Rabbit's kindness?

86

STRATEGIES FOR EXTRA SUPPORT

Question 6 CAUSE AND EFFECT
Explain that the word *result* is a synonym of the word *effect*. Write these sentence frames on the board to help students use the words in their answers: *As a result of Rabbit's kindness, Chameleon _____. _____ is the effect of Rabbit's kindness.*

As soon as he arrived home, his entire family eagerly gathered around.

"An empty gourd?" they all gasped in disbelief.

"It's not *just* an empty gourd," said Brother Rabbit. "It's a magic gourd! Watch this: Magic Gourd!" he said. "Fill yourself up with carrots!"

To their astonishment, the gourd magically filled with carrots. Happily, they ate them all.

7

"Magic Gourd! Fill yourself up with couscous!" he said.

Again they ate until they were satisfied.

"Magic Gourd! Fill yourself up with water!" he said, and they drank deeply.

8

87

Fluency

Italics

Explain Authors frequently use italics to show that a word is emphasized. Sometimes the meaning of a sentence can be changed by stressing a different word. That's why it's important when reading aloud to stress words in italics.

Discuss What word is italicized for emphasis on this page? (just)

Apply Have students read the sentence aloud, stressing *just*. Then write the sentence on the board, using italics for *empty*. Ask students to read the sentence aloud stressing the italicized word. Repeat the procedure using italics for *gourd*. Have students decide which version makes the most sense.

Develop Comprehension

7 USE ILLUSTRATIONS

Look at the way the plates and bowls are painted in the illustrations on pages 86 and 87. How do the pictures enhance the story? (The large picture on page 86 shows Rabbit receiving the gourd. Chameleon's tongue is reaching toward insects, which is how he gets his food. There are three small bowls, one painted with insects, another with carrots, and one with water, the three things that the gourd first produces. The large picture on page 87 shows a plate filled with rabbit faces.)

8 STRATEGY
MAKE INFERENCES

Teacher Think Aloud As I read about the magic gourd, I can imagine all the good it can do for Rabbit's family. This gourd seems to come into Rabbit's life at the perfect time. What else can you infer about the magic gourd?

(Encourage students to apply the strategy in a Think Aloud.)

Student Think Aloud Let's see. So far the gourd has filled up with things that Rabbit and his family can eat and drink. I can infer, though, that the gourd can probably be filled with anything Rabbit wants, even though the author does not state this idea directly.

Develop Comprehension

9 PARAPHRASE

Restate the first two paragraphs in your own words. If you have difficulty paraphrasing, reread the selection. (Answers should mention how word spreads about the gourd. After a while, this information reaches the king, who wants it.)

10 CAUSE AND EFFECT

Tested

What happens when Rabbit decides to share the gourd with his neighbors? (Rabbit wants to keep the gourd a secret, but he does not want to see others go hungry. Because he shares, everyone starts to hear about it, including the king. The king is greedy and steals the gourd for himself, placing Rabbit back where he started.) Add this information to your Cause and Effect Chart.

Cause →	Effect
There is a drought. →	There is a famine, and Rabbit's family is starving.
Rabbit kindly helps Chameleon. →	Chameleon gives Rabbit a magic gourd.
The neighbors talk about Rabbit's gourd. →	The king steals the gourd to make gold and Rabbit is starving again.

Vocabulary

How would you describe what Rabbit was doing when he was **scrounging** for wild roots? (He was digging everywhere for them, searching wildly.)

From that day on, Brother Rabbit's family drank and ate well.

But as much as they wanted to keep the magic gourd a family secret, they also could not sit and watch friends and neighbors suffer. So they invited them **9** to share their meals every day.

And this is how word floated around from one to the other until it **10** came to the house of Mansa Jugu, the greedy king.

One day, the greedy king and his soldiers broke into Rabbit's compound and forced the little gourd away from him. Now, with the magic gourd in his possession, Mansa Jugu sat day and night commanding the little gourd to fill and refill with more and more gold.

Meanwhile, unable to get the magic gourd back, Rabbit returned once again to his poor life, **scrounging** for wild roots to feed his hungry family. Despite the hardships of the moment, he still had courage to sing . . .

*Feeyeh ku, feeyeh ku. Waara
sa kun tay.*

Luck will come. Life will be good.

Cause and Effect
What happened when Rabbit decided to share the gourd with his neighbors?

88

Media Literacy

Explain A folk tale like *The Magic Gourd* would probably make an excellent animated film.

Discuss What animated films featuring talking animals can you think of? Why is a story with talking animals a good subject for an animated film?

Help students complete their scenarios by asking the following questions: *How do you picture the characters? How do the characters move? What kinds of voices do they have? Should the movie be shot using hand-drawn or computer-generated animation?*

Apply Have students apply what they know about animated films to come up with a scenario for an animated film based on *The Magic Gourd*.

One day, while hunting for roots, Rabbit heard his name being called again.

"Dogo Zan, Dogo Zan!"

Recognizing the sweet little voice, he turned and looked in all directions. Slowly the chameleon came into view right next to him on a sparkling green rock.

"Dogo Zan! What has happened to you?" cried Chameleon. "You look skinny and **pathetic**!"

Rabbit told him all about the greedy king who stole the gourd. Again, Brother Chameleon offered a gift to Brother Rabbit. This time, it was the beautiful crystal rock he had been standing on.

"What is this, Brother Chameleon?" asked Rabbit.

"This is just a *fara*, a little rock!" As soon as the words came out of his mouth, the rock leaped into the air and bounced off his head.

"*Eee-heeeee! Fara!*" cried Rabbit. "Stop! Stop!"   **11**

Again, the rock knocked his head.

"Excuse me, Dogo Zan," said the chameleon. "You must call him by his name, *Fara-Ba*!" With that, the rock dropped silently to the ground. Rabbit thanked Chameleon for this unusual gift and returned home.   **12**

89

Extra Support

Cause and Effect

If students have difficulty determining causes and effects, have them reread the beginning of the story, and then ask them a series of simple "Why/Because" questions. For instance: Why was everyone hungry at the beginning of this story? (because there was a famine) Why did Rabbit decide to save Chameleon? (because Rabbit did not want to see a brother suffer) Why was Rabbit first amazed at the gourd? (because it filled up with insects)

Develop Comprehension

11 WRITER'S CRAFT: PRECISE WORDS

The author has used many words from the Bambara language of Mali, such as *fara*, or "little rock." Why do you think he chose to include these words? (Answers will vary, but should include that these words give the story a clear setting in Mali. The author can teach about another culture while he is telling a story that anyone can enjoy.)

12 MAKE PREDICTIONS

How do you think Rabbit will use Chameleon's new gift of the leaping rock? (Answers will vary. Rabbit might use the rock as a weapon against the king or he may find another use for it.)

Journal Have students respond to the selection by confirming or revising their predictions.

Quick Check   Can students determine causes and their effects? If not, see the **Extra Support** on this page.

Stop here if you wish to read this selection over two days.   STOP

Develop Comprehension

13 SUMMARIZE

List the main events in the story so far.
(Rabbit rescued Chameleon, who then gave Rabbit the magic gourd. Rabbit and his family thrived until the greedy king stole the gourd. As a result, Rabbit is poor and starving when he meets Chameleon again, who gives him a magic rock.)

14 DRAW CONCLUSIONS

What kind of a ruler is the king? (The king is really greedy. As king he should behave better toward his subjects. He made fun of Rabbit for his gift of the rock without trying to understand it. One can conclude that this is a king who has some things to learn about being a good ruler.)

RESEARCH
Why It Matters

"Summarizing has been shown to be a critical strategy for students to learn as they read. Summarizing helps students focus on the main ideas and leave out the irrelevant details. It forces students to pay closer attention to the text while they read, and it helps them return to the text to reread."

Janice A. Dole

 LOG ON For more information, go to Teacher Resources at **www.macmillanmh.com**

---

13 The next day, Brother Rabbit rolled the rock in a fresh *sheeyo* leaf and walked to the king's palace. "I have brought you a mysterious gift, your Majesty," said Brother Rabbit.

"*Aaa ha! Moondon!* What is it?" asked the king anxiously. Rabbit slowly unrolled the rock from the *sheeyo* leaf and showed it to Mansa Jugu.

"*Eeeeeeh! Fara doron?*" exclaimed the king. "A simple rock?"

And with that, the little rock began **ricocheting** off the head of the king.

"*A toh! A toh!* Stop this rock!" cried the king, but no one could capture it. All day and all night the little rock played music on the heads of the king and his soldiers. The annoyance continued and the king became troubled. Mansa Jugu was finally forced to call on Rabbit for help.

Cleverly, Brother Rabbit demanded his little gourd back first.

"You may take all the gold, but leave me the gourd," said the **14** greedy king.

90

CHECK COMPREHENSION

Ask, *What does it mean to be greedy? What examples of being greedy can you find in this story so far?* People are greedy when they do not share what they have or help others in need. People who are greedy do not show generosity. *How does the King show his greediness?*

"But the gourd was a gift to me," replied Rabbit.

"Then take all my food from my royal storage bins, but leave me the gourd," cried the annoyed king.

"*Ee dusu dah*. Let us bargain," countered Rabbit. "My little gourd is my prize."

The king angrily shouted, "*U-TAH, U-TAH*—TAKE IT ALL! Take the gold, the food, and the little gourd!"

Rabbit took the gourd, but left the gold and the food behind. And before he turned to flee, he shouted, "*Fara-Ba!*"

Calmly, the little rock dropped into Rabbit's hand.

Fearing revenge from the king, Rabbit's family escaped to the country to join their faithful friend Chameleon. From Chameleon's great lessons in disguises, Brother Rabbit learned the skill of hiding in the bush. Today Dogo Zan and his family are masters at going **undetected**. One could be hiding in your backyard right now. **15**

91

Develop Comprehension

15 CAUSE AND EFFECT

What chain of events caused Rabbit to move to the country? (Rabbit uses the rock to punish the king, and gets his gourd back. Because the king might seek revenge, Rabbit takes his family to the country and becomes good at hiding.) Fill in the Cause and Effect Chart with your answers.

Cause →	Effect
There is a drought. →	There is a famine, and Rabbit's family is starving.
Rabbit kindly helps Chameleon. →	Chameleon gives Rabbit a magic gourd.
The neighbors talk about Rabbit's gourd. →	The king steals the gourd to make gold and Rabbit is starving again.
Rabbit uses a rock to punish the king. →	Rabbit gets his gourd back.
The king might seek revenge. →	Rabbit moves to the country and hides.

ELL   Access for All

STRATEGIES FOR EXTRA SUPPORT

Question 15 CAUSE AND EFFECT
Explain the phrase *chain of events*. Draw or show a chain. Explain that each event is connected to the other just like in a chain. Help your students talk about the events using cause and effect words such as *so, as a result,* and *because*.

Develop Comprehension

16 | **STRATEGY**
MAKE INFERENCES

What inference can you make about the way the king will rule in the future?

Student Think Aloud The king was surprised that Rabbit was not as greedy as he was. Rabbit only wanted his gourd returned and did not steal the king's food. Because Rabbit was kind, the king seems to learn the value of kindness. The king may be more generous in the future.

17 | **GENRE: FOLK TALE**

The Magic Gourd is an origin story. How does the plot of the story help to explain the behaviors of rabbits and chameleons today? What lessons does the story teach? What other stories do you know that have a similar theme? (The story teaches that because of this event long ago, rabbits live in the country and are very good at hiding. Chameleons still blend in with their surroundings. The story teaches that kindness is more effective than bullying for getting help.)

Vocabulary

Read the last sentence on page 92, which contains the word **chameleon**. Ask students to replace the word *chameleon* with a word that has a similar meaning. *(lizard, reptile)*

92

Mansa Jugu, the greedy king, and his soldiers felt embarrassed by their defeat at the hand of a rabbit and a small rock. The king could not believe that in his moment of weakness, he had given away the wealth of his kingdom. Exhausted and hungry, the king sat down to eat before pursuing Brother Rabbit for revenge. Upon opening his storage bins, he was surprised to discover that all of his wealth and food remained.

"Come eat!" he called to his soldiers and servants. "Let us appreciate what we have been given."

16   From this final kind act of Rabbit, the greedy king, Mansa Jugu, began to learn the importance of **generosity** and friendship.

As for Rabbit and Chameleon, they have always understood that loyal friendships are the true treasures that make one rich.

And for their many good deeds, all sang a song of praise to Rabbit and Chameleon.

17

Glossary

Here are some words from the story that are in Bambara, the national language of Mali.

Dogo Zan (DOE-go ZAHN) - Brother Rabbit

Mansa Jugu (MAHN-sah JOO-goo) – greedy king (mansa means ruler; jugu means greedy)

＊**Ee dusu dah** (ee du-SU dah) – Let us bargain; calm down

＊**Ee ko dee** (EE ko DEE) – exclamation of surprise when a person doesn't believe what they have just heard (What did you say?)

Fara (FAH-rah) – rock

＊**Fara-ba** (FAH-rah BAH) – Mr. Rock (title of respect)

Fara doron (FAH-rah DOH-ron) – a simple rock

Moondon (MOON-don) – What is it?

Sheeyo (SHEE-yoh) – a bush with large leaves found in Mali

A toh! (ah TOH) – Stop!

U-tah (OO-tah) – Take it all!

＊**Feeyeh ku, feeyeh ku**. (FEE-yeh koo) **Waara sa kun tay**. (WA-rah sah KOON-teh) – This is a chant of encouragement to give hope for survival in difficult times.

(Note: Bambara is a metaphorical language, so the English translation is not always literal.)

＊ Not a literal translation

93

Develop Comprehension

RETURN TO PREDICTIONS AND PURPOSES

Review students' predictions and purposes. Were they correct? Did they discover the cause of Chameleon's generosity? (Chameleon repays Rabbit's kindness to him.)

REVIEW READING STRATEGIES

How did making inferences about cause and effect help you to understand the story?

PERSONAL RESPONSE

Ask students to think of a time they were kind and the kindness was repaid, or when someone was kind to them and they showed gratitude in response.

Quick Check	Can students identify cause and effect?

During **Small Group Instruction**

If No → Approaching Level Leveled Reader Lesson, p. 101P

If Yes → On Level Options, pp. 101Q–101R

Beyond Level Options, pp. 101S–101T

Author and Illustrator

MEET THE STORYTELLER

Have students read the biography of author-illustrator Baba Wagué Diakité.

DISCUSS

Ask students:

- Why do you think Baba Wagué Diakité decided to write *The Magic Gourd* after hearing it told at his family's evening meals?

- How does he use traditional West African designs to tell the story of Rabbit and Chameleon?

WRITE ABOUT IT

Discuss how Rabbit and Chameleon know that loyal friendships are treasures that make them rich. Invite students to identify the most important quality they seek in friends. List their responses on the board. Have students write about someone they know who exhibits one or several of the qualities listed.

Author's Purpose

Remind students that the genre can offer a clue to the author's main purpose. A folk tale is fiction and is usually meant to entertain. Here, Diakité entertains the reader by giving animals personalities and the power of speech. Students should recognize that rabbits need to hide to protect themselves from predators.

LOG ON Technology

Tell students they can find more information about Baba Wagué Diakité at www.macmillanmh.com

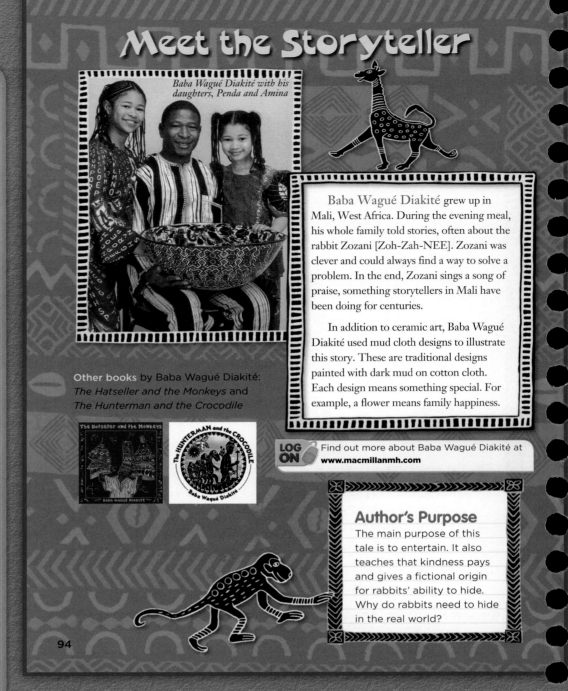

Meet the Storyteller

Baba Wagué Diakité with his daughters, Penda and Amina

Baba Wagué Diakité grew up in Mali, West Africa. During the evening meal, his whole family told stories, often about the rabbit Zozani [Zoh-Zah-NEE]. Zozani was clever and could always find a way to solve a problem. In the end, Zozani sings a song of praise, something storytellers in Mali have been doing for centuries.

In addition to ceramic art, Baba Wagué Diakité used mud cloth designs to illustrate this story. These are traditional designs painted with dark mud on cotton cloth. Each design means something special. For example, a flower means family happiness.

Other books by Baba Wagué Diakité: *The Hatseller and the Monkeys* and *The Hunterman and the Crocodile*

LOG ON Find out more about Baba Wagué Diakité at www.macmillanmh.com

Author's Purpose
The main purpose of this tale is to entertain. It also teaches that kindness pays and gives a fictional origin for rabbits' ability to hide. Why do rabbits need to hide in the real world?

94

Author's Craft
Dialogue

Baba Wagué Diakité uses dialogue to reveal information not stated directly in the story.

- A dialogue is a conversation between or among characters that is set off by quotation marks. For example:

  "Why are you giving me such a valuable gift?" Rabbit asked.

  "You were kind to me, Brother Rabbit," Chameleon said.

- Through dialogue, the author reveals that Chameleon and Rabbit recognize each other's kindness.

Discuss how dialogue can reveal information about a character, the plot, and the setting. Have students write a dialogue between two characters that provides information about a person, place or event.

Comprehension Check

Summarize

Use your Cause and Effect Chart to help you summarize *The Magic Gourd*. What causes Brother Chameleon to give Brother Rabbit the gourd? What effect does the gourd have on Brother Rabbit and the King?

Cause → Effect
→
→
→
→

Think and Compare

1. Something unexpected takes place at the end of *The Magic Gourd*. What is it? What causes this event to happen? How does this event help you understand the moral of the story? **Make Inferences and Analyze: Cause and Effect**

2. How does the weather affect the characters in the story? Use examples from the text to support your answers. **Synthesize**

3. Think of a time when you did a good deed for someone. What happened? How did your **generosity** help? How did it make you feel? **Evaluate**

4. Who gets the bigger reward from the gourd: the King or Brother Rabbit? Explain why. **Analyze**

5. In "Keira's Magical Moment" on pages 80-81, Keira says her great-grandmother left Senegal because of a famine. What do you think the role of a folk tale such as *The Magic Gourd* would have in Keira's great-grandmother's native culture? **Reading/Writing Across Texts**

95

Strategies for Answering Questions

Author and Me

Model the Author and Me strategy with questions 2 and 4.

The answer to this question is not directly stated in the text, but there may be clues. Connect these text clues with what you know to answer the question.

Question 2: Think Aloud The author doesn't directly state this idea, but I think the lack of rain starts the story rolling. Brother Rabbit would not have had to go looking for wild roots and would not have met Chameleon if there had not been a famine.

Question 4: Think Aloud If I think about the story, I have to say that Brother Rabbit gets the bigger reward. The king keeps his riches, but Brother Rabbit figures out that family and friendship are life's true treasures.

Comprehension Check

SUMMARIZE

Tested

Have students reread and then summarize *The Magic Gourd* in their own words. Remind students to use the Cause-and-Effect Chart they completed to help them organize their summaries.

THINK AND COMPARE

Sample answers are given.

Tested

1. **Cause and Effect:** The king calls all of his servants and subjects to eat and celebrate because Brother Rabbit leaves the king's riches and food. This event shows us the moral of the story: It is important not to be selfish and to help those less fortunate than we are.

2. **Analyze:** The weather causes hunger and poverty. Students should point to the beginning of the story, in which the narrator describes the famine caused by lack of rain. USE AUTHOR AND ME

3. **Text to Self:** Answers should include the idea that helping another person made students feel good about themselves.

4. **Text to World:** Though the king keeps his riches and food supply, Brother Rabbit gets the bigger reward because he keeps the magic gourd and helps his people to get food. USE AUTHOR AND ME

FOCUS QUESTION

5. **Text to Text:** *The Magic Gourd* serves to provide hope for the Senegalese facing the challenge of a famine; it teaches a lesson about generosity and survival.

Objectives
- Read accurately with good prosody
- Rate: 117–137 WCPM

Materials
- Fluency Transparency 4
- Fluency Solutions Audio CD
- Leveled Practice Books, p. 25

On Level Practice Book O, page 25

As I read, I will pay attention to punctuation.

	The Navajo (NAH-vah-hoh) Indians call themselves the
6	*Dineh* (dee-NAY). In Navajo, their name means "The People."
14	Over 255,000 Navajos live in the United States today. Their
23	nation is the largest in the country.
30	For generations the Navajo have made beautiful weavings,
38	baskets, and jewelry. Their arts reflect their traditions, their
47	history, and their modern life.
52	Centuries ago, the Navajo settled in a part of the Southwest
63	now called the Four Corners. It's called that because the
73	borders of four states meet in one spot.
81	The Four Corners area has beautiful canyons, mesas, rivers,
90	and rock formations. But the high desert climate is harsh and
101	dry. The Navajo lived in hogans. They moved often to find
112	grass for their sheep and horses. When the climate permitted,
122	they planted corn, squash, and melons. At times, on the brink
133	of famine, they have to be good farmers to get by.
144	In 1868, the United States and the Navajo signed a treaty.
154	The treaty promised them their own government, called the
163	Navajo Nation. It also created the huge Navajo Reservation in
173	the Four Corners area. 177

Comprehension Check

1. How does the climate affect the Navajo? **Cause and Effect**
The Navajo live in a harsh desert climate, which often makes farming or grazing difficult.
2. Why is art important to the Navajo? **Draw Conclusions**
Art is a way for them to pass down their tradition and history.

	Words Read	–	Number of Errors	=	Words Correct Score
First Read		–		=	
Second Read		–		=	

★ **Approaching Practice Book A,** page 25
◆ **Beyond Practice Book B,** page 25

95A

Fluency
Repeated Reading: *Punctuation*

EXPLAIN/MODEL Read the entire passage on **Transparency 4.** Then reread it, one sentence at a time. Have students pay attention to the punctuation in each sentence while you read. Reread the passage, and have students echo-read each sentence.

 Transparency 4

Rabbit was busy, but still he stopped. "I will help simply to avoid seeing my brother suffer," said Rabbit. Gently he lowered his hand between the thorny branches and saved the green chameleon. As Rabbit turned to leave, Chameleon called out to him once again.

"Dogo Zan! Don't go yet! Would you mind getting my gourd from the bush, too?".

Fluency Transparency 4 from *The Magic Gourd*, page 85

Think Aloud When I see a period, my voice stays even. I take a short pause when I see a comma, and my voice goes up when I see a question mark. I also see an exclamation point, and I will use emphasis when I read that sentence. The quotation marks tell me that the characters are speaking.

PRACTICE/APPLY Divide the class into two groups. Have groups echo-read each sentence in the passage on **Transparency 4.** Remind students to pay attention to punctuation marks. Have students use **Leveled Practice Book** page 25 or Fluency Solutions Audio CD.

Quick Check | **Can students read accurately with good prosody?**

During **Small Group Instruction**

If No → **Approaching Level** Fluency, p. 101N

If Yes → **On Level** Options, pp. 101Q–101R

Beyond Level Options, pp. 101S–101T

Comprehension

MAINTAIN SKILL
CHARACTER, SETTING, PLOT

EXPLAIN/MODEL

Review with students:

- **Story structure** is the way the story events are organized into a **plot.** The plot includes a problem that the main **character** has to solve and a **setting** in which the story takes place. Identifying the main problem and how the character tries to solve it helps the reader better understand the story structure.

- Understanding **character** helps the reader relate to the character's feelings and predict how he or she will behave. As students read, they should think about the character's thoughts, feelings, words, actions, and motivations. Students should look for a description of the character in the text or in an illustration.

PRACTICE/APPLY

Discuss the story structure in *The Magic Gourd*. Ask students:

- Who is the main character and what are some of the problems he faces? What effect does the setting have on the events of the plot?

- How does Brother Rabbit respond when the king steals the magic gourd?

- How effective was Brother Rabbit's solution to his problem?

Have students work in groups to compare Brother Rabbit's motivations with those of Chameleon and the king. How are they alike? How are they different? Groups should use story details to support their answers and compare answers when finished.

Objective

- Analyze character, setting, and plot

Skills Trace

Character, Setting, Plot	
Introduce	U1: 19A–19B
Practice/ Apply	U1: 20–35; Leveled Practice Books, 2–3
Reteach/ Review	U1: 39M–39T; 43A–43B, 44–59, 65M–65T; Leveled Practice Books, 9–10
Assess	Weekly Tests; Unit 1, 3 Tests; Benchmark Tests A, B
Maintain	U1: 35B, 59B, 95B; U2: 171B; U3: 249A–249B, 250–267, 273M–273T; Leveled Practice Books, 76–77

Informational Text: Social Studies

GENRE: INFORMATIONAL ESSAY

Have students read the bookmark on **Student Book** page 96. Explain that an essay:

- focuses on a single subject

- often includes the author's opinions and point of view as well as facts and details about the topic

Text Feature: Time Line

Explain that a **time line** is a graphic device that helps a reader see the sequence of events at a glance. Remember to:

- read a time line from left to right.

- match events to the dates on the time line to see the order in which things occur.

APPLY

Have students identify the title of the time line on page 98 and the events and dates it contains. Discuss why more events and dates are not included. (Only those dates significant to Ghana's origin are included.)

Social Studies

Genre

An **Informational Essay** is a short composition about a single subject written from a particular point of view.

Text Feature

A **Time Line** is marked with dates to help you see when events happened in history.

Content Vocabulary

origin
bolster
mythological

By the 700s, the empire of Ghana was already a major power in Africa. It grew rich and powerful as a source of gold for the Mediterranean world.

THE ORIGIN OF GHANA

by Patricia and Fredrick McKissack

The first of the great Western Sudanese empires to emerge was Ghana, peopled by a Mande-speaking group called the Soninke or Sarakulle.

1 The oldest account of Ghana's **origin** is contained in the Soninke's oral tradition. Soninke's oral history, like that of most African cultures, has been passed from one generation to another by bards, or griots (GREE-ohs).

96

Content Vocabulary

Review the spelling and meaning of each content vocabulary word in "The Origin of Ghana" on **Student Book** page 96: *origin, bolster, mythological.*

- To **bolster** is to boost. How might you bolster your courage if you were lost?

- **Mythological** means "make-believe" or "legendary." Most myths explain natural or historical phenomena. Name a mythological character.

- The **origin** is what something begins or comes from. What is the origin of your family?

For centuries the griots have combined history, music, poetry, dance, and drama to entertain and teach their audiences. They can be compared with ancient Greek bards, like Homer, who were fascinating storytellers but so much more. Before the Soninke had a written language, the griots were the historians, the keepers of memories. Every village had a griot, and so did every clan. The royal family and other important families sometimes hired a personal griot to record their actions. Griots kept mental records of all memorable events—feasts and ceremonies, royal coronations, births, deaths, marriages, victories, and defeats. Some of their presentations were as long and artful as *The Iliad* and *The Odyssey*.

According to legend, Gassire was the first griot from whom all other Soninke griots are descended. He invented the *pui*, which is a poem about a hero, also called a praise-song.

97

Informational Text

Read "The Origin of Ghana"

Access for All

As you read, remind students to apply what they have learned about reading a time line. Also, have them identify clues to the meanings of the highlighted words.

Develop Comprehension

1 VOCABULARY

What synonym might the author have chosen for the word *origin*? (beginning, start)

Informational Text

2 TEXT FEATURE: TIME LINE

According to the time line, what important event happened in 1067? (Al-Bakri was writing about Ghana's great wealth.)

3 TEXT FEATURE: TIME LINE

Why doesn't this time line show anything that happened in modern times? (The time line only goes up to 1600.)

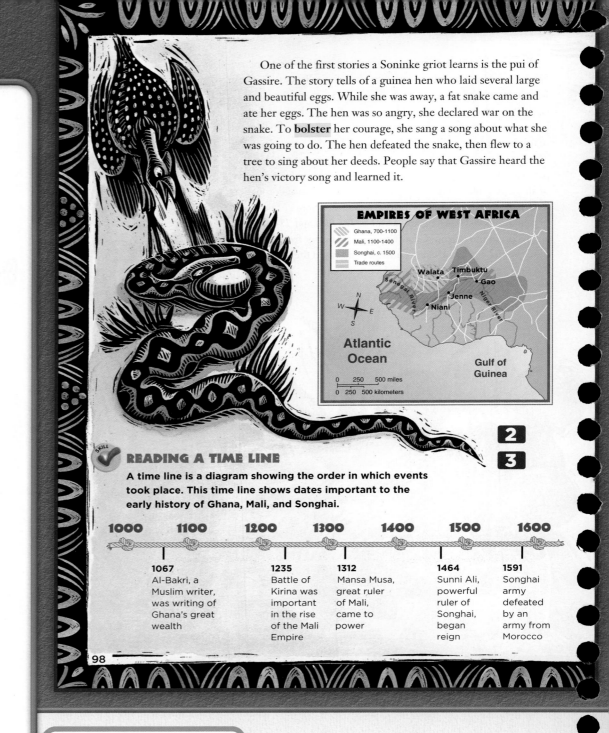

One of the first stories a Soninke griot learns is the pui of Gassire. The story tells of a guinea hen who laid several large and beautiful eggs. While she was away, a fat snake came and ate her eggs. The hen was so angry, she declared war on the snake. To **bolster** her courage, she sang a song about what she was going to do. The hen defeated the snake, then flew to a tree to sing about her deeds. People say that Gassire heard the hen's victory song and learned it.

EMPIRES OF WEST AFRICA

Ghana, 700-1100
Mali, 1100-1400
Songhai, c. 1500
Trade routes

Walata Timbuktu Gao
Senegal River Jenne
Niani Niger River

Atlantic Ocean Gulf of Guinea

0   250   500 miles
0   250   500 kilometers

READING A TIME LINE

A time line is a diagram showing the order in which events took place. This time line shows dates important to the early history of Ghana, Mali, and Songhai.

1000	1100	1200	1300	1400	1500	1600

1067 Al-Bakri, a Muslim writer, was writing of Ghana's great wealth

1235 Battle of Kirina was important in the rise of the Mali Empire

1312 Mansa Musa, great ruler of Mali, came to power

1464 Sunni Ali, powerful ruler of Songhai, began reign

1591 Songhai army defeated by an army from Morocco

98

On Level Practice Book O, page 26

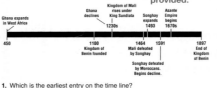

A **time line** organizes information chronologically, or in time order. Time lines are divided into spans of years. The time moves from the earliest on the left to the latest on the right. Events are listed on the time line in the year they occurred.

Use the time line below to answer the questions. Possible responses provided.

Ghana expands in West Africa
Ghana declines
Kingdom of Mali rises under King Sundiata 1230s
Songhay expands 1493
Asante Empire begins 1670s

450
1100 Kingdom of Benin founded
1464 Mali defeated by Songhay
1591 Songhay defeated by Moroccans. Begins decline.
1897 End of Kingdom of Benin

1. Which is the earliest entry on the time line?
   Ghana expands in West Africa in 450.

2. About what year did Ghana begin to decline?
   It began to decline in the 1230s.

3. About how long did Mali exist?
   Mali existed from the 1230s to 1464, about 230 years.

4. Which is the longest-lived kingdom on the time line?
   Kingdom of Benin

5. When were the Songhay defeated?
   They were defeated in 1591.

6. When did the Asante Empire begin?
   It began in the 1670s.

 Approaching Practice Book A, page 26

Beyond Practice Book B, page 26

Historians believe this pui is a **mythological** retelling of Ghana's origin. The hen represents the early Soninke people who overthrew an enemy who was more powerful.

By the middle of the 1000s, Ghana had attracted many rivals who sought to share in the wealth of the gold trade. The new empire Mali (MAH lee) had great influence by about 1250. After 1337 the rulers of Mali grew weaker. They were unable to control the empire and its gold trade. Mali was replaced by an even stronger empire, the Songhai (SOHNG hi). By the late 1490s, Songhai included Mali and parts of present-day Benin, Niger, and Nigeria.

This West African brass weight was used with a scale to measure the weight of gold.

Connect and Compare

1. Use the time line to find the year the Songhai army lost power. **Reading a Time Line**

2. Why do you think that the griots are still important today? **Analyze**

3. Why did the pui of Gassire and the narrator in *The Magic Gourd* use animal characters? **Reading/Writing Across Texts**

Social Studies Activity

Research one of the early West African kingdoms. Write and illustrate a fact card using the interesting facts you discovered during your research.

 Find out more about griots at **www.macmillanmh.com**

99

Informational Text

Connect and Compare

SUGGESTED ANSWERS

1. The Songhai army was defeated in 1591. READING A TIME LINE

2. Griots help to continue the passage of cultural history from generation to generation. ANALYZE

FOCUS QUESTION

3. Animals have specific traits that don't need explanation. For example, snakes are sneaky, and rabbits are clever. READING/ WRITING ACROSS TEXTS

Social Studies Activity

Encourage students to use multiple sources as they conduct their research. Display students' fact cards throughout the classroom.

LOG ON Technology

Internet Research and Inquiry Activity
Students can find more facts about griots at **www.macmillanmh.com**

Research and Inquiry

Theme: Sharing Traditions

Dramatizing, or acting out stories, has been an important source of information among people for thousands of years. In addition, drama is used to transmit culture as well as to entertain and persuade people.

Students might be interested in exploring one of these traditional Anglo-American, African-American, and Native American storytelling genres. Your school librarian may be able to supply them with examples of each of the following types of folk tales: Appalachian Lore, Grandfather Tales, Jack Tales, Coyote Tales, Br'er Rabbit.

Other students might enjoy writing to the National Storytelling Network (132 Boone Street, Suite 5, Jonesborough, TN 37659) for additional information about American storytelling. Provide class time for students to share what they learn.

Connect
Language Arts

WRITING
- Poem
- **Writer's Craft:** Precise Words

WORD STUDY
- Words in Context
- **Context Clues:** Restatement
- **Phonics:** *r*-Controlled Vowels
- Vocabulary Building

SPELLING
- Words with *r*-Controlled Vowels

GRAMMAR
- Clauses and Complex Sentences

SMALL GROUP OPTIONS
- Differentiated Instruction, pp. 101M–101V

Writing

Precise Words

READ THE STUDENT MODEL

Read the bookmark about using precise and colorful words in poems and other writing. Explain that specific, vivid words help readers understand better what a writer means.

Have students identify five examples of precise or colorful words in the selection on pages 80–81.

Then read aloud Jaycee's **poem** and discuss the callouts. Tell students they will write a poem about a lesson they learned or an important friendship. Students will choose precise and colorful words to describe the topic of their poem and make it come alive for readers.

100

Writer's Craft

Precise Words

Choose **precise words** to describe your topic and to show how you feel about it. Using colorful words can help bring a poem or other writing to life.

> I used the words *friends forever* to appeal to my readers' emotions.

> I used words like *long, floppy ears* and *round, pink belly* to help readers imagine what my puppy looked like.

Write a Poem

My Best Buddy

by Jaycee L.

I met you seven years ago at a
    stranger's house.
When I looked at you,
I knew we would be friends forever.

Quickly, I ran across the room
And gathered you in my arms.
I petted your long, floppy ears.
I tickled your round, pink belly.
I smelled your sweet puppy breath.

After eight long weeks passed,
You came to live with me.
We ran through the green grass.
We played hide-and-seek.
We swam in the cool stream.

Now you are older and slower,
But you are still there for all I do.
I share my secrets with you.
I spend my happiest days with you.
I will love you forever,
My best buddy.

Features of a Poem

A writer may tell a story in a narrative poem or capture emotions in a lyric poem. Readers must use reasoning skills, both inductive and deductive, to analyze poems. Different kinds of poems often share some basic features.

- A poem is often organized in lines and stanzas.
- It may use sound techniques such as rhyme, rhythm, and alliteration.
- A poem can express the writer's feelings.
- It includes precise, colorful words and appeals to the reader's ear.

Your Turn

Write a poem about a lesson you learned or an important friendship. You might write a narrative poem that tells a story. Or you might choose to write a lyric poem that captures the feeling of a friendship or presents a lesson you learned. Be sure to include precise and colorful words to bring your poem to life for readers. Remember to punctuate sentences within the poem. Use the Writer's Checklist to review your poem.

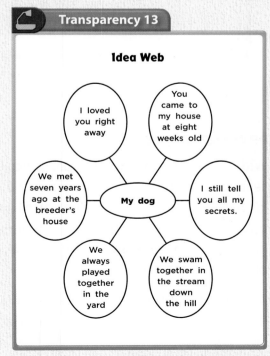

Writer's Checklist

✓ **Ideas and Content:** Did I precisely describe a lesson I learned or an important friendship?

☑ **Organization:** Did I divide my poem into stanzas? Did I use logical line breaks?

✓ **Voice:** Does my poem capture the emotion I feel about my topic?

 ☑ **Word Choice:** Did I use colorful and **precise words** to bring the poem to life?

☑ **Sentence Fluency:** Did I include complete sentences and a variety of sentence lengths?

☑ **Conventions:** Did I punctuate within the poem properly? Did I check my spelling?

101

Transparency 13: **Idea Web**
Transparency 14: **Draft**
Transparency 15: **Revision**

Transparency 13

Idea Web

I loved you right away

You came to my house at eight weeks old

We met seven years ago at the breeder's house

My dog

I still tell you all my secrets.

We always played together in the yard

We swam together in the stream down the hill

Writing Transparency 13

PREWRITE

Read the writing prompt on page 101. Discuss the difference between a narrative poem, which tells a story, and a lyric poem, which captures thoughts and feelings. Have students jot down possible topics in their writer's notebook. Tell them to think about their audience and their purpose.

Display **Transparency 13**. Discuss how Jaycee used the center oval for the topic of her poem. Around it she noted some details about her dog. Have students use an idea web to plan their poems. See page 101B for **Ideas and Content** and **Selecting Mode and Topic** tips.

DRAFT

Display **Transparency 14**. Discuss the words Jaycee chose from her idea web to describe her dog. Invite students to include precise words in their writing.

Before students begin writing, present the lesson on **Precise Words** on page 101A. Then direct students to use their webs to draft their poems. Remind them to choose colorful words.

REVISE

Display **Transparency 15**. Ask students where they think descriptive words are needed. Discuss the vivid details Jaycee added. Students can revise their drafts or place them in writing portfolios to work on later.

If students choose to revise, have them work with a partner and use the Writer's Checklist on page 101. Have them **proofread** their writing. For **Publishing Options** see page 101A.

For lessons on **Complex Sentences** and **r-Controlled Vowels** see page 101B and **5 Day Spelling** and **5 Day Grammar** on pages 101G–101J.

Writer's Craft

Precise Words

EXPLAIN/MODEL

Good writers look for precise and colorful words to describe their feelings and get their meaning across to readers. The careful choice of descriptive words, especially words that appeal to the senses, helps readers feel they are sharing an experience with the writer. Good writers consider their choice of words while both drafting and revising their writing. Display **Transparency 16.**

Think Aloud The colorful words *aromas, waft,* and *swirl* in the first stanza make me feel like I am in the writer's house on Thanksgiving Day. I can almost see the aromas coming up the stairs and smell the turkey, potatoes, and pie myself.

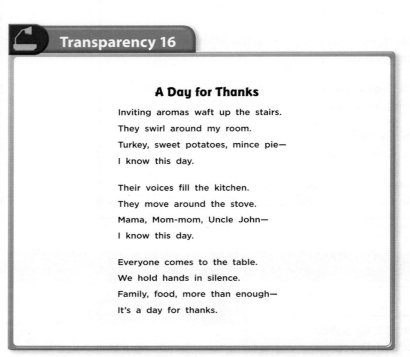

Transparency 16

A Day for Thanks

Inviting aromas waft up the stairs.
They swirl around my room.
Turkey, sweet potatoes, mince pie—
I know this day.

Their voices fill the kitchen.
They move around the stove.
Mama, Mom-mom, Uncle John—
I know this day.

Everyone comes to the table.
We hold hands in silence.
Family, food, more than enough—
It's a day for thanks.

Writing Transparency 16

PRACTICE/APPLY

With students brainstorm more precise words to insert in the second stanza of the poem. (Example: *Their conversation rings in the kitchen. They waltz around the stove.*) Have students work in small groups to choose more colorful words for the third stanza. Then have groups find examples of precise, descriptive words in poems or other writing they have read.

As students write their poems, remind them to use precise words that will convey their feelings and meaning to readers.

Writer's Toolbox

Writing Trait: Ideas and Content

Explain/Model Imagery is often an important part of narrative and lyric poetry. It can help a reader use his or her imagination to experience the poem with all the senses. The most successful poets can help their readers imagine the sights, sounds, tastes, and smells the poem describes.

Practice/Apply Ask students to describe their favorite use of imagery in Jaycee's poem. Does the imagery appeal to their sense of sight, hearing, touch, taste, or smell?

Selecting Own Mode and Topic

Purpose and Audience When choosing a topic and mode of writing, writers think about their purpose and audience. Personal narrative is one mode of writing. Explain that one of Jaycee's purposes in writing her poem was to entertain. Her audience was probably her classmates. Discuss how Jaycee's topic and mode of writing fit her purpose and audience. Tell students to keep their purpose and audience in mind when they choose their topic and as they write their poem.

Technology

Have students use the ruler and other features of their word processor to indent lines and set off stanzas in their poems.

Clauses and Complex Sentences

Explain/Model Differentiate between independent clauses and dependent clauses. An independent clause forms a complete thought and can stand alone as a sentence. A dependent clause does not form a complete thought and cannot stand alone; its meaning depends on the independent clause. A complex sentence is made up of one independent and one or more dependent clauses. Have students look at the complex sentence in the first two lines of the third stanza in the poem on page 100. Identify *After eight long weeks passed* as a dependent clause and *You came to live with me* as an independent clause.

Practice/Apply Have students identify independent and dependent clauses in complex sentences in other selections they have read. For a complete lesson on clauses and complex sentences, see pages 101I–101J.

Mechanics Point out that a comma follows a dependent clause at the beginning of a sentence, such as *When I looked at you* in line 2 of Jaycee's poem. Commas are also used to set off a dependent clause that is not essential: *My dog, who is in the yard, is seven years old*. Have students check for commas with clauses as they proofread.

Spelling Words with *r*-Controlled Vowels

Contrast the sounds of *a* in *stranger's* (line 1 of the poem on page 100) and *gathered* (line 5). Note that the *r* in *stranger's* makes the letter *a* sound like long *a*. Remind students to pay attention when they spell words with vowels followed by *r*. Students can use a print or online dictionary to check spelling in their drafts. For a complete lesson on *r*-controlled vowels, see pages 101G–101H.

Objective
- Apply knowledge of word meanings and context clues

Materials
- Vocabulary Transparency 7
- Vocabulary Strategy Transparency 8
- Leveled Practice Books, p. 27

Vocabulary

8. **rummaged** (p. 86) made an active search by moving, turning, or looking through the contents of a place or container

1. **undetected** (p. 91) gone unseen or unnoticed

6. **chameleon** (p. 85) a lizard that can vary the color of its skin

3. **generosity** (p. 92) readiness in giving

7. **pathetic** (p. 89) causing one to feel tenderness, pity, or sorrow

2. **ricocheting** (p. 90) bouncing off at an angle

5. **famine** (p. 84) an extreme shortage of food

4. **scrounging** (p. 88) checking every available source

ELL

Demonstrate/Use Visuals Demonstrate *rummaged* and *scrounging*. Illustrate on the board what happens when something is *ricocheting*. Using a map, discuss where *famines* happen.

Review
Vocabulary

Words in Context

EXPLAIN/MODEL

Review the meanings of the vocabulary words. Display **Transparency 7.** Model how to use word meanings and context clues to fill in the missing words in the first sentence.

Think Aloud I think the missing word in the first example is *rummaged*, which means to search for something. The context clues *searched through* and *around for a while* support the meaning of *rummage* and the word makes sense in the sentence.

Transparency 7

Vocabulary in Context
rummaged undetected chameleon generosity

Rabbit bent down and searched through the thick brush. After he (1) <u>rummaged</u> around for a while in the thorny bush he found the gourd.

Because they are so good at hiding, Dogo Zan and his family may go (2) <u>undetected</u> right in your own backyard.

When the (3) <u>chameleon</u> rested on the brown tree bark, no one could see it.

Rabbit left food for the greedy king in a kind act of (4) <u>generosity</u>.

Vocabulary Transparency 7

  PRACTICE/APPLY

Tell students to complete sentences 2–4. Then have students write sentences with context clues for the rest of the vocabulary words: *pathetic, ricocheting, famine, scrounging.* Ask students to leave a blank where the vocabulary word should go. Have students exchange papers with a partner and fill in the blanks. Tell them to underline the context clues they used to figure out the missing word.

Word Relationships Ask students to work as partners to generate and answer questions about vocabulary words. *What would happen to people during a* famine? (They would not have enough food.) *If people show* generosity, *what would they most likely do?* (They would probably share their wealth.)

STRATEGY
USE CONTEXT CLUES

EXPLAIN/MODEL

Tell students:

■ Writers often restate, or paraphrase, a word they have just used to make the word's meaning clearer. A restatement is a different way of saying a word or phrase.

■ Restatements are sometimes used as context clues to help the reader understand difficult vocabulary.

Read the following sentence aloud to students: *During the famine, there was a shortage of food all over the country.* Model how to use restatement to determine the meaning of *famine*.

 **Transparency 8**

Context Clues: Restatement

chameleon *noun* **1.** a lizard that can vary the color of its skin. *The chameleon, which had been a bright green lizard when it lounged on the grass, turned into a pale brown one as it crawled onto the sand.*

rummaged *verb* **1.** to make an active search by moving, turning, or looking through the contents of a place or container. *As Rabbit rummaged in the bush, his search turned up a beautiful bowl.*

Vocabulary Strategy Transparency 8

 PRACTICE/APPLY

Have students read the definitions of the two vocabulary words on **Transparency 8.** Ask for volunteers to come up and underline examples of restatement on the transparency.

Quick Check Can students identify the correct vocabulary words?
Can students use context clues to identify word meanings?

During **Small Group Instruction**

If No → **Approaching Level** Vocabulary, pp. 101N–101O

If Yes → **On Level** Options, pp. 101Q–101R

Beyond Level Options, pp. 101S–101T

 ELL **Access for All**

Paraphrase
Explain that paraphrasing is something that writers do to make their meaning clearer. Write on the board: *The chameleon ran under the door and into the house.* Have students take turns paraphrasing this sentence.

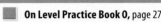 **On Level Practice Book O,** page 27

When you read, you should use the context, or surrounding words, to help you determine the meaning of unfamiliar vocabulary. One kind of context clue is **restatement,** in which the meaning of a word is restated after the word appears. Look at the example:

The country was afflicted by famine. It suffered from an extreme scarcity of food.

The meaning of the word *famine* is restated in the sentence that follows it.

Read each sentence. Circle the word whose meaning is restated. Then write the meaning on the line. Possible responses provided.

1. Passing on cultural traditions is important to (Malians), the people who live in Mali. people who live in Mali

2. Often storytelling is accompanied by (djembes), which are drums that people play as others tell stories, dance, or sing. drums that people play

3. The (Dogon), a tribe of people in Mali who live at the base of the Bandiagara Cliffs, have rituals of their own. a tribe of people who live in Mali

4. The (Dama dance), which is religious, is part of the Dogon tradition. a religious dance that is part of the Dogon tradition

5. Part of the Dama dance is done on (stilts), which are long poles people can stand on to mimic the long legs of a water bird. long poles that people stand on

★ **Approaching Practice Book A,** page 27
◆ **Beyond Practice Book B,** page 27

Word Study

Objective
- Decode *r*-controlled vowels

Materials
- Leveled Practice Books, p. 28
- Teacher's Resource Book, p. 8

ELL **Access for All**

Pronunciation
Pronouncing the *r*-controlled vowel sound /ûr/ will be difficult for many speakers. Provide extra practice by having students listen to the sound in isolation and in words. Have students take turns saying and spelling the words.

On Level Practice Book O, page 28

When a vowel is followed by the letter *r* it has a different sound than a vowel that is short or long, for example, the sound *âr* in *cart*. This is called an **r-controlled vowel.** The *r*-controlled sound can be spelled in different ways, for example: *surf, bird,* or *work.*

Read each clue. Provide an answer that uses an *r*-controlled vowel sound. Then use each word you found in a sentence.
Possible responses provided.

1. Something that is ripped is this. _____ torn _____
   Karina's recipe was carefully torn out of the newspaper.

2. This is on the side of your head. _____ ear _____
   Keith tugged on his ear to tell Lori to steal second base.

3. You can play games, eat hot dogs, and see farm animals here. _____ fair _____
   Last year, Chambliss won a blue ribbon for his calf at the county fair.

4. This is something you can do in the ocean. _____ surf _____
   Jill and Grace like to surf the waves early in the morning.

5. This is the opposite of far. _____ near _____
   Without his glasses, Brian could see only objects that were near him.

6. You can brush it, curl it, or put it in braids. _____ hair _____
   Carrie pulled her hair through an elastic band to make a ponytail.

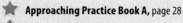

★ **Approaching Practice Book A,** page 28

◆ **Beyond Practice Book B,** page 28

Phonics
Decode Words with *r*-Controlled Vowels

EXPLAIN/MODEL When the letter *r* follows a vowel, the sound changes. The letters *air, are, ear,* and *ere* can stand for the /âr/ sound, as in *lair, blare, pear,* and *where.* The letters *ar* can also stand for the /är/ sound, as in *sharp.* The letters *ear, eer, eir,* and *ier* can stand for the /îr/ sound, as in *fear, steer, weird,* and *tier.* The letters *or* and *our* can stand for the /ôr/ sound, as in *short* and *gourd.* The letters *ear, er,* and *ur* can stand for the /ûr/ sound, as in *search, nerve,* and *surf.* Write the word *earnest.*

Think Aloud I see the letters *ear* in this word. I know that *ear* can have the /âr/ sound, as in *bear,* the /îr/ sound, as in *clear,* or the /ûr/ sound, as in *search.* I will try all three ways of saying *ear* in this word and see which one makes sense. When I try the /âr/ sound, I get /ârnəst/. That doesn't make sense. When I try the /îr/ sound, I get /îrnəst/. That doesn't make sense either. When I try the /ûr/ sound, I get /ûrnəst/. *Earnest* is a word I know.

 PRACTICE/APPLY

List these words on the board. Ask students to sort them by the sounds /âr/, /är/, /îr/, /ôr/, and /ûr/, organizing them into five columns.

1. starve (/är/)
2. servant (/ûr/)
3. urge (/ûr/)
4. sphere (/îr/)
5. pursue (/ûr/)
6. veer (/îr/)
7. pierce (/îr/)
8. search (/ûr/)
9. wharf (/ôr/)
10. year (/îr/)
11. torch (/ôr/)
12. mourn (/ôr/)

Decode Multisyllabic Words Remind students that *-ing* and *-ed* are endings added to the end of a root word; *-ing* shows an action that is happening in the present and *-ed* shows an action that happened in the past. Write *searched* on the board. Say *search* and the ending *-ed.* Draw a line between them. Tell students that the *-ed* means that the action was done in the past. Display *rewarded, pursued, starving, mourning, piercing, urging, courted,* and *veering.* Together with students decode *rewarded.* Then have students decode the remaining words. For more practice, see the decodable passages on page 8 of the **Teacher's Resource Book**.

Quick Check Can students decode words with *r*-controlled vowels?

During **Small Group Instruction**

If No → **Approaching Level** Phonics, p. 101M

If Yes → **On Level** Options, pp. 101Q–101R

Beyond Level Options, pp. 101S–101T

Vocabulary Building

Oral Language

Expand Vocabulary Ask students to list words that are meaningful in the traditions of their family. Then challenge each student to use his or her words in a sentence. Have students read their sentences aloud. Students' sentences should include restatement clues to aid classmates for whom the original words might be unfamiliar.

Spiral Review

Vocabulary Concentration Let pairs of students work together and play a matching game. Have each pair write the vocabulary words from Weeks 1 and 2 on small cards. On a matching set of cards, have them write synonyms of the vocabulary words. Have students shuffle the cards and spread them out on the table face down. The first player turns over a pair of cards. If the pair includes a vocabulary word and its correct synonym, the student earns one point and may take another turn. If not, the second player takes a turn. Play until all the cards are face up. The student with the highest number of points is the winner.

Apply Vocabulary

Write a Song Remind students that at the end of the story the animals sang a song of praise to Rabbit and Chameleon for their good deeds. Ask students to write their own song of praise, using the vocabulary words from the lesson. The original songs should tell about Rabbit's and Chameleon's good deeds. Encourage students to use at least two vocabulary words in their song, and to circle them.

Vocabulary Building

Restatement Have each student choose a favorite vocabulary word from the selection. Ask students to write their chosen word in a circle in the middle of a blank page. On lines that extend from the circle, ask them to write words or phrases that could be used as restatement clues for their word. Finally, encourage students to write full sentences using their chosen word and one or more of their restatements. Have students share their sentences with a partner. Each partner should try to guess the meaning of the word based on restatement clues.

anxiety foretold abruptly

Technology

Vocabulary PuzzleMaker

LOG ON **For additional vocabulary and spelling games go to** www.macmillanmh.com

r-Controlled Vowels

Spelling Words

search	pursue	urge
starve	**servant**	wharf
thorn	torch	court
reward	earnest	weird
sparkle	mourn	veer
bargain	fierce	burnt
parched	pierce	

Review freight, yield, seize

Challenge sphere, aeronautics

Dictation Sentences

1. Let's **search** for the keys.
2. Without food, people **starve**.
3. A **thorn** is sharp.
4. Jake wanted no **reward**.
5. Look at the diamond **sparkle**!
6. The new car was a real bargain!
7. The runner was **parched**.
8. How long did he **pursue** the issue?
9. A firefighter is a public **servant**.
10. The torch is lit at night.
11. Danielle was earnest about the topic.
12. People mourn the passing of the family.
13. The lion was fierce.
14. You can pierce a lid with a knife.
15. I have an urge for pizza.
16. The boats docked at the wharf.
17. Dad went to court for a ticket.
18. We heard weird howls.
19. The driver had to veer to the left.
20. He burnt the toast

Review/Challenge Words

1. The freight arrived today.
2. You must yield to pedestrians.
3. Police seize contraband.
4. A globe is shaped like a sphere.
5. The study of aeronautics is fun.

Note: Words in **bold** type are from *The Magic Gourd.* Display the Spelling Words throughout the week.

Day 1 — Pretest

ASSESS PRIOR KNOWLEDGE

Use the Dictation Sentences. Say the underlined word, read the sentence, and repeat the word. Have students write the words on **Spelling Practice Book** page 19. For a modified list, use the first 17 Spelling Words and the Review Words. For a more challenging list, use Spelling Words 3–17 and the Challenge Words. Have students correct their own tests.

Have students cut apart the Spelling Word Cards BLM on Teachers Resource Book page 69 and figure out a way to sort them. Have them save the cards for use throughout the week.

For **Leveled Word Lists,** go to **www.macmillanmh.com**

Day 2 — Word Sorts

TEACHER AND STUDENT SORTS

- Use the words *servant, starve, thorn,* and *weird* as column headings for a word sort. Write them on the board or on cards attached to a bulletin board. Take a card, say the word, and ask students to listen for the vowel sound.

- Then have each student take a card, say the word, tell where it goes on the sort, and write or place it there.

- Then have students use their own word cards. After placing the key words on their desks, they can sort the words three times. Have students write their last sort on **Spelling Practice Book** page 21.

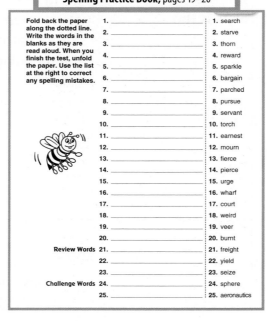

Spelling Practice Book, pages 19–20

Fold back the paper along the dotted line. Write the words in the blanks as they are read aloud. When you finish the test, unfold the paper. Use the list at the right to correct any spelling mistakes.

1.	1. search
2.	2. starve
3.	3. thorn
4.	4. reward
5.	5. sparkle
6.	6. bargain
7.	7. parched
8.	8. pursue
9.	9. servant
10.	10. torch
11.	11. earnest
12.	12. mourn
13.	13. fierce
14.	14. pierce
15.	15. urge
16.	16. wharf
17.	17. court
18.	18. weird
19.	19. veer
20.	20. burnt
Review Words 21.	21. freight
22.	22. yield
23.	23. seize
Challenge Words 24.	24. sphere
25.	25. aeronautics

Spelling Practice Book, page 21

search	sparkle	servant	fierce	court
starve	bargain	torch	pierce	weird
thorn	parched	earnest	urge	veer
reward	pursue	mourn	wharf	burnt

Write the spelling words with each of the spelling patterns below.

är spelled:

ar
1. starve
2. sparkle
3. bargain
4. parched

ir spelled:

ier
5. fierce
6. pierce

eir
7. weird

eer
8. veer

ôr spelled:

or
9. thorn
10. torch

ar
11. reward
12. wharf

our
13. mourn
14. court

ûr spelled:

ear
15. search
16. earnest

ur
17. pursue
18. urge
19. burnt

er
20. servant

Day 3 Word Meanings

WORD CONNECTIONS

- Have students do a word hunt in their reading materials for words that have the same spelling pattern as this week's words. Ask students to add the words to the word sort in their Word Study notebook.

- Read aloud the following list of words. Then have students write a Spelling Word that is related in some way to each word.

1. flame (torch)
2. maid (servant)
3. diamonds (sparkle)
4. sale (bargain)

Day 4 Review and Proofread

SPIRAL REVIEW

Have students use their spelling sort from last week to review the CVVC spelling pattern for words with *ie* or *ei*. Have students work in pairs to add more words to the sort.

Write the sentences below on the board, including the misspelled words. Ask students to proofread each sentence. Have them circle the incorrect spellings and write the correct spellings.

1. Have you been on a basketball cort? (court)
2. Who likes bernt food? (burnt)
3. Would you touch a thourn? (thorn)
4. Have you ever walked on a whorf? (wharf)
5. Did you serch for words this week? (search)

Day 5 Assess and Reteach

POSTTEST

Use the Dictation Sentences on page 101G for the Posttest.

If students have difficulty with any words in the lesson, have them place them on a list called "Spelling Words I Want to Remember" in a word study notebook.

WORD STUDY NOTEBOOK

Challenge students to search for other words with r-Controlled vowels in their reading for the week and write them in a word study notebook under the heading "Other Words with r-Controlled Vowels."

Spelling Practice Book, page 22

search	sparkle	servant	fierce	court
starve	bargain	torch	pierce	weird
thorn	parched	earnest	urge	veer
reward	pursue	mourn	wharf	burnt

Analogies
Write the spelling word that completes each analogy.

1. **Dock** is to _____wharf_____ as **park** is to **garage**.
2. **Open** is to **close** as **retreat** is to _____pursue_____.
3. **Thirst** is to **drink** as _____starve_____ is to **eat**.
4. **Teacher** is to **classroom** as **judge** is to _____court_____.
5. **Laugh** is to **chortle** as _____mourn_____ is to **grieve**.

Completions
Use a spelling word to complete the following sentences.

6. He lost control of his car and it started to _____veer_____ off the road.
7. She offered a _____reward_____ to anyone with information about their lost family heirloom.
8. Our customs seemed _____weird_____ to Uta.
9. In Egypt, it is common to _____bargain_____ with the street vendors.
10. The _____fierce_____ weather conditions allow them to spend more time at home, inside with their families.

Students' writing should include a spelling word in each analogy.

More Analogies
Write some analogies of your own on the lines below. Use at least one spelling word in each analogy.

11. Search is to find as investigate is to discover.
12. Surgeon is to operating room as judge is to court.

Spelling Practice Book, page 23

There are five spelling mistakes in this story. Circle the misspelled words. Write the words correctly on the lines below.

Long ago when James was a young boy, he worked as a mayor's (servent) and lived in a shed behind their mansion. Late one night, the mayor's wife came to James's door with an (ernest) request. Her husband had gone for a walk and had not yet returned hours later. She didn't need to (urge) James to find her husband. James took a (torch) and went to (serch) for him. Hours later, James found and rescued the mayor. The next day the news was all over the small town, and James became a hero. Over the years, the story of James's adventure grew until it became a grand tale.

1. servant
2. earnest
3. urge
4. torch
5. search

Writing Activity
How might the story of James's simple adventure have changed over the years? Write a tale that might have grown from it. Use five spelling words in your story.

Students' writing should reflect the topic and include five spelling words.

Spelling Practice Book, page 24

Look at the words in each set below. One word in each set is spelled correctly. Use a pencil to fill in the circle next to the correct word. Before you begin, look at the sample set of words. Sample A has been done for you. Do Sample B by yourself. When you are sure you know what to do, you may go on with the rest of the page.

Sample A:
- Ⓐ sport
- Ⓑ spart
- Ⓒ sporte
- Ⓓ sphort

Sample B:
- Ⓔ bork
- Ⓕ barke
- Ⓖ bark
- Ⓗ bohrk

1. Ⓐ search
   Ⓑ sirch
   Ⓒ sertch
   Ⓓ seartch
2. Ⓔ starv
   Ⓕ starfe
   Ⓖ starve
   Ⓗ storv
3. Ⓐ thorne
   Ⓑ thorn
   Ⓒ thornn
   Ⓓ thohrn
4. Ⓔ reworde
   Ⓕ reeward
   Ⓖ reeword
   Ⓗ reward
5. Ⓐ sporkle
   Ⓑ sparkle
   Ⓒ sporkel
   Ⓓ sparkel
6. Ⓔ bargain
   Ⓕ borgen
   Ⓖ bargen
   Ⓗ borgain
7. Ⓐ partched
   Ⓑ portched
   Ⓒ parched
   Ⓓ porched
8. Ⓔ pursoo
   Ⓕ porsoo
   Ⓖ pursue
   Ⓗ porsue
9. Ⓐ survunt
   Ⓑ survent
   Ⓒ servant
   Ⓓ servent
10. Ⓔ tortch
    Ⓕ torche
    Ⓖ torch
    Ⓗ tohrch
11. Ⓐ ernest
    Ⓑ erneast
    Ⓒ ernast
    Ⓓ earnest
12. Ⓔ mourn
    Ⓕ morne
    Ⓖ moarn
    Ⓗ moorn
13. Ⓐ feerce
    Ⓑ feirce
    Ⓒ fierce
    Ⓓ ferce
14. Ⓔ peirce
    Ⓕ pearce
    Ⓖ pierce
    Ⓗ perce
15. Ⓐ urge
    Ⓑ urg
    Ⓒ oorge
    Ⓓ erge
16. Ⓔ worf
    Ⓕ wharf
    Ⓖ warf
    Ⓗ whorf
17. Ⓐ cort
    Ⓑ corte
    Ⓒ court
    Ⓓ coart
18. Ⓔ wierd
    Ⓕ weerd
    Ⓖ weird
    Ⓗ werde
19. Ⓐ vier
    Ⓑ veir
    Ⓒ veer
    Ⓓ vere
20. Ⓔ burnet
    Ⓕ burnt
    Ⓖ boornt
    Ⓗ burnte

Clauses and Complex Sentences

Daily Language Activities

Use these activities to introduce each day's lesson. Write the day's activities on the board or use **Transparency 4.**

DAY 1
chameleon was releved when he saw Brother Rabbit? (1: Chameleon; 2: relieved; 3: Rabbit.)

DAY 2
Brother rabbit retreved the gourd from the bush (1: Rabbit; 2: retrieved; 3: bush.)

DAY 3
The man, who teaches the computer class, got a lone from the bank. (1: man who; 2: class got; 3: loan)

DAY 4
Mr. Mukura whom we all love will be missed, when he retires. (1: Mukura,; 2: love,; 3: missed when)

DAY 5
My Dad plays golf, when the weather is nicer. (1: dad; 2: golf when; 3: nice)

ELL — Access for All

Introduce Clauses Write on the board: *Rabbit was busy, but still he stopped.* Invite volunteers to underline the subject and the verb. Explain the word *clause* and have students circle the clauses. Repeat with other sentences.

Day 1 Introduce the Concept

INTRODUCE CLAUSES

Present the following:

- A clause is a group of words that includes a subject and a verb.
- An independent clause forms a complete thought and can stand alone as a sentence.
- A dependent clause does not form a complete thought and thus cannot stand alone as a sentence.
- The meaning of a dependent clause depends on the independent clause that it precedes or follows.

Access for All
Example:

After she went to the store, Mom made dinner. (independent: Mom made dinner; dependent: after she went to the store)

 See Grammar Transparency 16 for modeling and guided practice.

Grammar Practice Book, page 19

Day 2 Teach the Concept

REVIEW CLAUSES

Discuss with students the difference between dependent and independent clauses.

INTRODUCE COMPLEX SENTENCES

Present the following:

- A sentence is a group of words that expresses a complete thought.
- A complex sentence is made up of one independent clause and one or more dependent clauses.

Example:

Although my friend invited me to the party, I did not want to go. (independent: I did not want to go; dependent: Although my friend invited me to the party)

 See Grammar Transparency 17 for modeling and guided practice.

Grammar Practice Book, page 20

101l

Day 3 — Review and Practice

REVIEW COMPLEX SENTENCES

Ask students to identify the dependent clause in the following sentence.

1. The doctor who operated on my mom came to dinner. (who operated on my mom; no commas)

MECHANICS AND USAGE: PUNCTUATING COMPLEX SENTENCES

- Some dependent clauses are essential to the meaning of a sentence. Do not use commas to set off these clauses.

- Some clauses are nonessential. They do not affect the basic meaning of the sentence. Use commas to set off these clauses.

 See Grammar Transparency 18 for modeling and guided practice.

Grammar Practice Book, page 21

- When a dependent clause comes at the beginning of a sentence, use a comma after the dependent clause.
- When a dependent clause comes at the end, a comma is not usually necessary.

Read the following interview. Rewrite each line, adding commas to the dialogue where they are needed. Remove any unnecessary commas.

REPORTER: When your first novel was published were you nervous?
When your first novel was published, were you nervous?

FAMOUS WRITER: On the contrary I felt elated.
On the contrary, I felt elated.

REPORTER: As you work, on your next book do you find yourself writing to please your readers?
As you work on your next book, do you find yourself writing to please your readers?

FAMOUS WRITER: No, I always write to please myself because I write what I feel, and believe.
No, I always write to please myself because I write what I feel and believe.

Day 4 — Review and Practice

REVIEW COMPLEX SENTENCES

Have students look at the corrected sentences for the previous days. Ask students to identify the complex sentences. Then have them underline the dependent clauses and double underline the independent clauses.

PROOFREAD

Have students add commas as needed to the following sentences.

1. After we left the party last night we went to get dinner. (night,;)

2. The movie that we watched last week is on TV now.

3. Emma who is my best friend lives in Texas. (Emma,; friend,)

 See Grammar Transparency 19 for modeling and guided practice.

Grammar Practice Book, page 22

- A **complex sentence** contains an independent clause and one or more dependent clauses.
- When a dependent clause comes at the beginning of a sentence, use a comma after the dependent clause.
- When a dependent clause comes at the end, you usually do not use a comma.

Rewrite the passage. Draw a line under the complex sentences. Correct the capitalization and punctuation mistakes, adding punctuation as needed.

although every family has its own traditions, ours is my favorite on Sunday nights we all sit around the kitchen table with a bowl of roasted walnuts hazelnuts peanuts, and almonds as we crack the nuts each family member tells one good thing and one bad thing that happened to them that week this family time not only teaches us about each other but also lets us see the many good things in our lives.

Although every family has its own traditions, ours is my favorite. On Sunday nights, we all sit around the kitchen table with a bowl of roasted walnuts, hazelnuts, peanuts, and almonds. As we crack the nuts, each family member tells one good thing and one bad thing that happened to them that week. This family time not only teaches us about each other, but also lets us see the many good things in our lives.

Day 5 — Assess and Reteach

ASSESS

Use the Daily Language Activity and page 23 of the **Grammar Practice Book** for assessment.

RETEACH

Write the following words and phrases on the board: *as long as, because, if, that, unless, whenever, while, who.* Divide students into small groups and have each group write five complex sentences using the words. Then, have groups write their sentences on the board. As a class, check each sentence to make sure it is complex.

Use page 24 of the **Grammar Practice Book** for additional reteaching.

 See Grammar Transparency 20 for modeling and guided practice.

Grammar Practice Book, pages 23–24

Each question begins with a sentence that, when joined with the correct response, will result in a complex sentence. Circle the letter of your answer. Hint: The correct answer will be a clause.

1. We have an unusual family tradition at our house
   a. every night.
   b. when tired.
   c. that every family should adopt.

2. Every Memorial Day, we have a family fire drill
   a. that my parents carefully organize.
   b. and barbeque.
   c. only once.

3. every person knows what to do and where to go.
   a. Today
   b. If a fire starts,
   c. In this case,

Try making sentences from the different answers. Choose the answer that gives you a complex sentence with correct punctuation. Circle the letter of your answer.

4. Isaac takes little Maria by the hand
   a. first of all.
   b. for safety sake.
   c. before he walks her safely across the street.

5. Everyone meets on the neighbors' lawn
   a. that night.
   b. so we can have a big barbeque.
   c. across the street.

End-of-Week Assessments

Administer the Test

Weekly Reading Assessment,
Passages and questions, pages 45–52

ASSESSED SKILLS

- Cause and Effect
- Vocabulary Words
- Context Clues: Restatement
- *R*-controlled Vowels
- Clauses and Complex Sentences

 **Assessment Tool**

Administer the **Weekly Assessment** online or on CD-ROM.

Weekly Assessment, 45–52

Fluency

Assess fluency for one group of students per week. Use the Oral Fluency Record Sheet to track the number of words read correctly. Fluency goal for all students:
117–137 words correct per minute (WCPM).

Approaching Level	Weeks 1, 3, 5
On Level	Weeks 2, 4
Beyond Level	Week 6

Fluency Assessment

Alternative Assessments

- **ELL Assessment,** pages 44–45

ELL Practice and Assessment, 44–45

Diagnose	IF...	Prescribe — THEN...
VOCABULARY WORDS VOCABULARY STRATEGY Context Clues: Restatement Items 1, 2, 3, 4	0–2 items correct . . .	Reteach skills using the **Additional Lessons** page T7 **LOG ON** Reteach skills: Go to **www.macmillanmh.com** **CD ROM** Vocabulary PuzzleMaker Evaluate for Intervention.
COMPREHENSION Skill: Cause and Effect Items 5, 6, 7, 8	0–2 items correct . . .	Reteach skills using the **Additional Lessons** page T3 Evaluate for Intervention.
GRAMMAR Clauses and Complex Sentences Items 9, 10, 11	0–1 items correct . . .	Reteach skills: **Grammar Practice Book** page 24
SPELLING *R*-controlled Vowels Items 12, 13, 14	0–1 items correct . . .	**LOG ON** Reteach skills: Go to **www.macmillanmh.com**
FLUENCY	109–116 WCPM 0–108 WCPM	**AUDIO CD** Fluency Solutions Evaluate for Intervention.

READING
Triumphs
AN INTERVENTION PROGRAM

Also Available

To place students in the Intervention Program, use the **Diagnostic Assessment** in the Intervention Teacher's Edition.

Approaching Level Options

Small Group

Skills Focus ▶ Phonics

Objective	Decode one-syllable and multisyllabic words that include *r*-controlled vowels in both familiar and unfamiliar text
Materials	• **Student Book** "Keira's Magical Moment"

WORDS WITH *r*-CONTROLLED VOWELS

Model/Guided Practice

- Write the word *shape. Say the word with me:* shape. *In the word* shape, *the* e *at the end is silent, and the vowel* a *has the long* a *sound.* Write the word *share* on the board. *Say the word:* /shâr/. *The word* share *includes the vowel* a, *like* shape, *but the vowel sound is a little different. That's because it's followed by the letter* r. *Vowels followed by* r *change a little in sound.*

- Write the words *beat* and *bear* on the board. *Try it yourself. Say the first word. What sound does the vowel pair have? Say the second word. How does the vowel pair* ea *sound when it's followed by the letter* r? Ask students to provide their own examples of words with vowels whose sound the letter *r* changes. Provide constructive feedback.

MULTISYLLABIC WORDS WITH *r*-CONTROLLED VOWELS

- Write the words *unfair* and *aquarium* on the board, and draw lines to divide each into syllables. *Listen to how the* r *changes the vowel sound in each word. Say the words:* /un fâr/, /ə kwâr ē əm/. *Now say the words with me:* unfair, aquarium.

- Have students work in pairs to decode longer words with *r*-controlled vowels. Give each pair the list of words below. *Take turns saying each word, syllable by syllable. Listen for the vowel sound changed by* r. *Circle the vowel or vowels in the word that come before the letter* r. *Then group the words with the same vowel sounds.*

surroundings	victory	heartbeat	backward
adore	compare	pursue	personal
entertain	capture	storage	starving

- Check each pair's work for accuracy.

WORD HUNT: WORDS WITH *r*-CONTROLLED VOWELS IN CONTEXT

- Have students choose partners and search "Keira's Magical Moment" for words with *r*-controlled vowels. Tell them to list the words they find and then practice pronouncing them.

- Students' lists may include the following: *Keira, tomorrow, storyteller, great-grandmother, alarm, drawer, shirt, interest, heritage, center, first, speaker, writers, stories, characters, Tortoise, Spider, favorite, drummer, her, American, lizard, colors, tricksters, generosity, however, were, certainly, learn, their, different, memory, around, scarcity, villagers, familiar, hardly.* Call on pairs to come to the board, write a word from their list, underline the *r*-controlled vowel or vowel pair it contains, and say the word. Repeat until students have exhausted their lists.

Additional Resources

For each skill below, additional lessons are provided. You can use the lessons on consecutive days after teaching the lessons presented within the week.
• Cause and Effect, T3
• Context Clues, T7
• Time Lines, T10

Constructive Feedback

Isolate the error sound and repeat with students. If students say /ē/ in *bear*, for instance, point to the letter *r* and say:

Pay attention to the *r* in *bear*. In *beat*, the vowel pair *ea* has the long *e* sound. But in *bear*, the letter *r* changes the sound of *ea*. Say the word with me: /bâr/.

Repeat as needed with other words with *r*-controlled vowels.

Decodable Text

To help students build speed and accuracy when reading multisyllabic words, use the additional decodable text on page 8 of the **Teacher's Resource Book**.

101M

Skills Focus ▶ Fluency

Objective	Read with increasing prosody and accuracy at a rate of 117–127 WCPM
Materials	• **Approaching Practice Book A,** p. 25

MODEL EXPRESSIVE READING

Model reading the Fluency passage in **Approaching Practice Book**, page 25. Tell students to pay close attention and listen to your pauses and intonation as you read. Then read one sentence at a time and have students echo-read the sentence back, copying your pauses and intonation. Listen for accuracy.

REPEATED READING

Have students continue to practice reading the passage aloud as you circulate and provide constructive feedback. During independent reading time, have students work with a partner. Have one student read aloud, and the other repeat each sentence. Students should continue practicing the passage throughout the week.

TIMED READING

At the end of the week, tell students that they will do a timed reading of the passage that they have been practicing. With each student:

- Place the passage from **Approaching Practice Book A** page 25 facedown.
- When you say "Go," the student begins reading the passage aloud.
- When you say "Stop," the student stops reading the passage.

As students read, note any miscues. Stop each after one minute. Help students record and graph the number of words they read correctly.

Skills Focus ▶ Vocabulary

Objective	Apply vocabulary word meanings
Materials	• **Vocabulary Cards** • **Transparencies 4a and 4b**

VOCABULARY WORDS

Display the Vocabulary Cards for *famine, rummaged, pathetic, scrounging, chameleon, undetected, generosity,* and *ricocheting*. Help students locate and read the vocabulary words in "Keira's Magical Moment" on **Transparencies 4a and 4b**. Ask students to circle context clues for each on the transparency and use the clues to suggest a definition for the word.

Constructive Feedback

Pronunciation of unfamiliar proper nouns and new vocabulary may slow or interrrupt the tempo of oral reading. Write the phonetic spellings of potentially troublesome words from the selection on the board for students' reference. Say the words aloud with students before reading. During reading have students refer quickly to the board for the correct pronunciation of difficult words.

★ **Approaching Practice Book A,** page 25

As I read I will pay attention to punctuation.

	How can you take a piece of paper and turn it into a cup,
14	a boat, or a bird? You can do it with *origami*
25	(awr-i-GAH-MEE). You don't need any special tools. All
33	you need is a design, your hands, and paper. The instructions
44	aren't hard. And there's no limit to the number of things you
56	can make. Once you get a little practice, you can even create
68	your own designs!
71	The word *origami* is Japanese. It comes from the words
81	for "to fold" and "paper." The word *origami* was coined in
92	the 1880s. It described playful folded forms. The art of
102	origami is much older, though. It goes back over a 1,000
113	years.
114	This book will tell you more about the history of origami.
125	You'll also learn about new ways to create origami designs.
135	And you'll read about the greatest paper folder of modern
155	times. To top it off, you'll get to fold your own origami
167	crane, which is a very special bird. 174

Comprehension Check

1. How does origami's simplicity make it popular? **Cause and Effect** Origami is popular because it is easy for many people to make. All you need is a design, your hands, and paper.]
2. Why is origami considered art? **Draw Conclusions** Origami is art because you can use your hands to make creative designs.

	Words Read	–	Number of Errors	=	Words Correct Score
First Read		–		=	
Second Read		–		=	

The Magic Gourd 101N

Vocabulary

Review last week's words (*altered, erode, absorb, concentrated, innovations*) and this week's words (*rummaged, undetected, chameleon, generosity, pathetic, ricocheting, famine, scrounging*). Have students write a story using the words.

Student Book, or Transparencies 4a and 4b

Skills Focus ▶ Vocabulary

Objective	Use context clues to figure out the meanings of words
Materials	• **Student Book** "Keira's Magical Moment"

CONTEXT CLUES: DEFINITIONS

Using this week's vocabulary words, create sentences that include a restatement of a word's meaning. For example: *I was so hungry I was scrounging in the refrigerator.* (I was so hungry that I searched every shelf for something to eat.) Then have students create their own sentences that include restatement as a context clue to word meanings.

Skills Focus ▶ Comprehension

Objective	Analyze cause and effect in a story
Materials	• **Student Book** "Keira's Magical Moment" • **Transparencies 4a and 4b**

STRATEGY
MAKE INFERENCES AND ANALYZE

Review with students that they must use both their own experience and the text to figure out information when authors do not tell them directly everything that takes place in a story.

SKILL
CAUSE AND EFFECT

Explain/Model

- A cause makes something happen. It often answers the question *Why did this happen?* An effect is what happens. It often answers the question *What happened as a result, or because, of this?*

- Signal words and phrases such as *because, since, as a result,* and *therefore* may point to causes and effects in a story.

Display **Transparencies 4a and 4b**. Reread the first paragraph of "Keira's Magical Moment." Ask: *Why was Keira excited?* Have students identify two causes of Keira's excitement, and circle them on the transparency. Then point out that the author also hints at an effect of Keira's excitement in the first paragraph of the story. Underline the last sentence of the paragraph and challenge students to describe the effect. Lead them to infer that Keira begins to think more about her roots as a result of her excitement about the upcoming presentation.

Practice/Apply

Reread the rest of "Keira's Magical Moment" with students and have them continue circling causes and underlining effects.

Leveled Reader Lesson

Objective Read to apply strategies and skills

Materials
- **Leveled Reader** *The Art of Origami* • chart paper
- **Student Book** *The Magic Gourd*

Leveled Reader

PREVIEW AND PREDICT

Have students read the title and preview the first chapter. Ask students what they think this book will be about, and set a purpose for reading.

VOCABULARY WORDS

Tell students to look for the vocabulary words as they read. Discuss the meaning of each word in context. To check understanding, have students use each word in a meaningful sentence.

STRATEGY

MAKE INFERENCES AND ANALYZE

Remind students that an author does not always tell readers directly everything that takes place. They must use their own experience as well as the text to figure out missing information.

Think Aloud I learned that events in a story are often examples of cause and effect. Where the author does not state causes and effects directly, I can figure them out on my own based on my own experience and the information the author does provide.

SKILL

CAUSE AND EFFECT

Discuss cause-and-effect relationships in *The Art of Origami*. Ask, *Why was origami practiced by only a few people? Which events made origami popular?*

Have students begin a Cause and Effect Chart on chart paper.

READ AND RESPOND

Have students read orally to the end of Chapter 2. Help students make inferences as they read. Ask students to identify developments as causes or effects. After completing the book, invite students to share personal responses. Have students research and make their own origami.

MAKE CONNECTIONS ACROSS TEXTS

Invite students to compare *The Art of Origami* and *The Magic Gourd*.

- What do these two selections have in common? What is different about the selections?

- What cause-and-effect relationships can you find in these selections?

ELL Access for All

Cause and Effect
Point out that *The Art of Origami* includes examples of cause and effect. Ask: *What are some examples of cause and effect?* Write this cause on the board: *It rained on Saturday.* Ask: *What might an effect be?* Then write this effect on the board: *I felt happy.* Ask: *What might the cause be?*

Student Book

Student Book

Skills Focus ▶ **Vocabulary**

Objective	Apply vocabulary words and use context clues
Materials	• **Student Book** "Keira's Magical Moment"

VOCABULARY WORDS

Write the vocabulary words on the board. Call for a volunteer to begin a story by using a vocabulary word in a sentence. Challenge the group to continue, using a different vocabulary word in each sentence.

CONTEXT CLUES: RESTATEMENT

Explain that the definition of a word might be set off in a text by commas. For example, in "Keira's Magical Moment," the word *chameleon* is defined by the phrase *a small lizard*. Have students write sentences that include restatements.

Skills Focus ▶ **Text Feature**

Objective	Use a time line
Materials	• **Student Book** "The Origin of Ghana" • history articles

TIME LINE

Discuss the purpose and importance of a time line in "The Origin of Ghana." Then have students look through history articles from books, magazines, or their textbook. Ask them to find and interpret a time line or create one.

Skills Focus ▶ **Fluency**

Objective	Read accurately with a good tempo at a rate of 117–137 WCPM
Materials	• **On Level Practice Book O,** p. 25

REPEATED READING

Model reading the Fluency passage on page 25 of **On Level Practice Book O.** Work with students to begin marking up the passage to indicate proper phrasing. Remind students that one slash means "pause" and should come after commas, dashes, and other places where they would naturally pause when reading or speaking. Two slashes mean "stop" and should come after end marks or semicolons.

During independent reading time, have students practice reading the passage to each other. Circulate and provide feedback.

Timed Reading At the end of the week, have students do a timed reading to check how many words they read correctly in one minute.

On Level Practice Book O, page 25

As I read, I will pay attention to punctuation.

	The Navajo (NAH-vah-hoh) Indians call themselves the
6	*Dineh* (dee-NAY). In Navajo, their name means "The People."
14	Over 255,000 Navajos live in the United States today. Their
23	nation is the largest in the country.
30	For generations the Navajo have made beautiful weavings,
38	baskets, and jewelry. Their arts reflect their traditions, their
47	history, and their modern life.
52	Centuries ago, the Navajo settled in a part of the Southwest
63	now called the Four Corners. It's called that because the
73	borders of four states meet in one spot.
81	The Four Corners area has beautiful canyons, mesas, rivers,
90	and rock formations. But the high desert climate is harsh and
101	dry. The Navajo lived in hogans. They moved often to find
112	grass for their sheep and horses. When the climate permitted,
122	they planted corn, squash, and melons. At times, on the brink
133	of **famine,** they have to be good farmers to get by.
144	In 1868, the United States and the Navajo signed a treaty.
154	The treaty promised them their own government, called the
163	Navajo Nation. It also created the huge Navajo Reservation in
173	the Four Corners area. 177

Comprehension Check

1. How does the climate affect the Navajo? **Cause and Effect**
   The Navajo live in a harsh desert climate, which often makes farming or grazing difficult.
2. Why is art important to the Navajo? **Draw Conclusions**
   Art is a way for them to pass down their tradition and history.

	Words Read	–	Number of Errors	=	Words Correct Score
First Read		–		=	
Second Read		–		=	

Leveled Reader Lesson

Objective   Read to apply strategies and skills
Materials   • **Leveled Reader** *Arts of the Navajo* • chart paper

PREVIEW AND PREDICT

Show the cover of *Arts of the Navajo*, and read the title of the book. Ask students what kind of art they think the Navajo make, and have students set a purpose for reading.

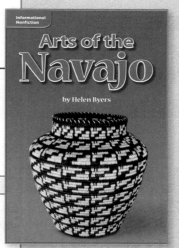

Leveled Reader

STRATEGY
MAKE INFERENCES AND ANALYZE

Remind students to use both their own experience and the text to figure out information when authors do not tell them directly everything that takes place in a selection.

SKILL
CAUSE AND EFFECT

Read the introduction. Pause to discuss the history of the Navajo and ask: *Do you think that knowing Navajo history will help you understand Navajo art? Why or why not?* At the end of the first chapter, have students fill in a Cause and Effect Chart on chart paper.

READ AND RESPOND

Have students finish reading the selection. Ask: *Why did the Navajo call their area Four Corners? Why did the Navajo move often?* Have students give an artistic interpretation of Navajo art.

VOCABULARY WORDS

Discuss the vocabulary words as they are used in the story. Have students use the words in questions and answers about the reading.

ELL
Leveled Reader
Go to pages
101U–101V.

MAKE CONNECTIONS ACROSS TEXTS

Invite students to summarize and draw connections between "The Origin of Ghana," *Arts of the Navajo,* and *The Magic Gourd.* Ask: *What cause-and-effect relationships can you identify in either the story events or the information presented in each of these selections?*

Beyond Level Options

Student Book

Beyond Practice Book B, page 25

As I read, I will pay attention to punctuation.

	Dance has been an important art form since ancient times. People
11	wrote music to accompany dance. They designed masks and costumes to
22	better express their dances. Dances were a way for people to tell stories.
35	Words were not necessary.
39	Why do people dance? People in some cultures have used dance as a
52	ritual. They might have danced to end a drought that caused a **famine**.
65	Other dances celebrated the harvest. Some traditional dances hoped to
75	cure or heal someone.
79	Add costumes, music, and masks to a dance and you have more than
97	just movement; you also have a story. Today many dances are performed
109	for entertainment. Ballets often retell fairy tales. Modern dances might
119	retell a myth or demonstrate a feeling. All dances show the
130	dancer's artistry.
132	No matter where you travel in the world, you will almost always find
145	dance. Dances might be traditional and part of a festival or modern with
158	people moving in time to their favorite music. Dance is an art form that
172	people continue to use to express themselves. 179

Comprehension Check

1. Why might people perform rituals? What effect do they hope to receive? **Cause and Effect** People performed rituals because they hoped to cure a sick person or make it rain.
2. How do people express themselves in dance? **Character** People express themselves by telling stories through dance. They also use masks and costumes.

	Words Read	–	Number of Errors	=	Words Correct Score
First Read		–		=	
Second Read		–		=	

Objective   Create sentences using content vocabulary words

Materials   • **Student Book** "The Origin of Ghana"

EXTEND VOCABULARY

Write the content words on the board: *origin, bolster, mythological.* Divide the group into two teams. Have a member of the first team use a word in an original sentence. Continue back and forth until one student cannot think of an original sentence. The other team scores a point. Continue by having a member of the second team pick another word.

Objective   Use a time line

Materials   • textbooks

TIME LINE

Point out that time lines are an effective way to convey a lot of information quickly. Have students select a historical passage from a textbook that does not include a time line. As them to create a time line that illustrates the information.

Objective   Read accurately with good prosody and tempo at a rate of 127–137 WCPM

Materials   • **Beyond Practice Book B,** p. 25

REPEATED READING

Model reading the Fluency passage on page 25 of **Beyond Practice Book B.** Then work with students to begin marking up the passage. Remind them that one slash means "pause," and should come after commas, dashes, and other places where they would naturally pause when reading. Two slashes mean "stop," and should come after end marks or semicolons. Partners can finish marking the passage on their own.

During independent reading time, have partners take turns reading the passage. Listen carefully to their reading, monitoring for accuracy.

Leveled Reader Lesson

Objective   Read to apply strategies and skills
Materials   • **Leveled Reader** *The Tradition of Dance*

PREVIEW AND PREDICT

Have students preview *The Tradition of Dance*, predict what it is about, and set a purpose for reading.

VOCABULARY WORDS

Review vocabulary words with students as needed.

STRATEGY
MAKE INFERENCES AND ANALYZE

Tell students to use their own experience and the text to make inferences when authors do not tell them directly everything in a story.

SKILL
CAUSE AND EFFECT

Ask a volunteer to define the terms *cause* and *effect*. Have students discuss how understanding cause-and-effect relationships will help them better understand an informational book.

READ AND RESPOND

Have students read Chapters 1 and 2. Discuss the examples of cause and effect. Have students predict what effect the events will have on the story.

After students finish reading the selection, have them share their personal responses. Then have students choreograph a dance based on the selection.

- How did the events affect the outcome of the story?
- Did making inferences about cause and effect help you understand the selection better? Explain.

Leveled Reader

ELL   Access for All

Time Line Say, *A time line is a good tool for showing a lot of information in one place.* Tell students that they will be creating a time line about someone they have read about. Have students think of the five important events of the person's life. Then have them draw a time line including those events.

Skills Focus

Self-Selected Reading

Objective   Read independently to identify cause and effect
Materials   • Leveled Readers or trade books at students' reading level

READ TO IDENTIFY CAUSE AND EFFECT

Invite students to select a fiction book to read independently. For a list of theme-related titles, see pages T17–T18. As students read, have them take notes about at least five causes and effects they encounter while reading.

Academic Language

Throughout the week, the English language learners in your class will need help in building their understanding of the academic language used in daily instruction and assessment instruments. The following strategies will help to increase their language proficiency and comprehension of content and instructional words.

Oral Language For oral vocabulary development, go to www.macmillanmh.com

Strategies to Reinforce Academic Language

- **Use Context** Academic Language used by the teacher (see chart below) should be explained in the context of the task during Whole Group. You may use gestures, expressions and visuals to support meaning.

- **Use Visuals** Use charts, transparencies, and graphic organizers to explain key labels to help students understand classroom language.

- **Model** Demonstrate the task using academic language in order for students to understand instruction.

Academic Language Used in Whole Group Instruction

Content/Theme Words	Skill/Strategy Words	Writing/Grammar Words
origin (p. 96)	essay (p. 96)	clauses (p. 101l)
bolster (p. 96)	time line (p. 96)	complex (p. 101l)
mythological (p. 96)	cause (p. 81A)	precise (p. 100)
folk tale (p. 82)	effect (p. 81A)	colorful (p. 100)
traditions (p. 78)		paraphrase (p. 101D)
informational (p. 96)		

ELL Leveled Reader Lesson

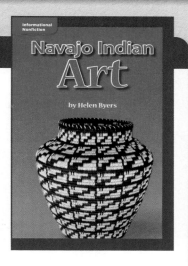

Informational Nonfiction

Navajo Indian Art

by Helen Byers

Before Reading

ORAL LANGUAGE

LOG ON

Build Background Show pictures of Native American people. Focus on the Navajo and the Four Corners area of the Southwest. *What Native American cultures do you know?* Brainstorm a list of crafts and traditions.

Review Vocabulary Write the vocabulary and story support words on the board and discuss their meaning. Model using them in sentences. *The Navajo live in a* Reservation *in the Four Corners area.*

PREVIEW AND PREDICT

Point to the cover illustration and read the title aloud. Encourage students to describe what they see and predict what they will learn about Navajo arts.

Set a Purpose for Reading Show the Cause and Effect Chart and remind students they have used this chart before. Ask them to identify causes and effects in the development of Navajo arts and fill in a similar chart.

During Reading

Choose from among the differentiated strategies to support students' reading at all levels of language acquisition.

Beginning	Intermediate	Advanced
Shared Reading Do a shared reading of the story. Model how to identify cause and effect relationships. Check students' comprehension and use vocabulary and support words. *What was one effect of Spider Woman's generosity?*	**Read Together** Read through the first chapter. Review events and help students identify them as causes or effects. Write results on the chart. Have students take turns identifying causes and effects as they read about basket and jewelry making.	**Independent Reading** Have students read the story with a partner. After reading each day, ask them to identify causes and effects and record these on their charts. Then ask students to discuss their favorite Navajo design and write a description.

After Reading

Remind students to use the vocabulary and story words in their whole-group activities.

Objective
- **To apply vocabulary & comprehension skills.**

Materials
- **ELL Leveled Reader** *Navajo Indian Art*
- **pictures of Native American peoples**

ELL 5 Day Planner

DAY 1	• Academic Language • Oral Language and Vocabulary Review for the ELL Leveled Reader
DAY 2	• Academic Language • ELL Leveled Reader
DAY 3	• Academic Language • ELL Leveled Reader
DAY 4	• Academic Language • ELL Leveled Reader Comprehension Check
DAY 5	• Academic Language • ELL Leveled Reader Literacy Activities

Grade 6 • ELL TEACHER'S GUIDE

English Language Learners

Treasures

Macmillan/McGraw-Hill

ELL Teacher's Guide for students who need additional instruction.

Weekly Literature

Weekly Theme: Protecting Wildlife

Week At A Glance

Whole Group

VOCABULARY
vital, conserve, dehydrated, analyzing, speculated, embedded, sedated, propelled

Strategy: Use Analogies/ Antonyms

COMPREHENSION
Strategy: Make Inferences and Analyze

Skill: Main Idea and Details

WRITING
Personal Narrative

Science Link

Life Science
Life Cycles

Small Group Options

Differentiated Instruction for Tested Skills

Tested Skills for the Week

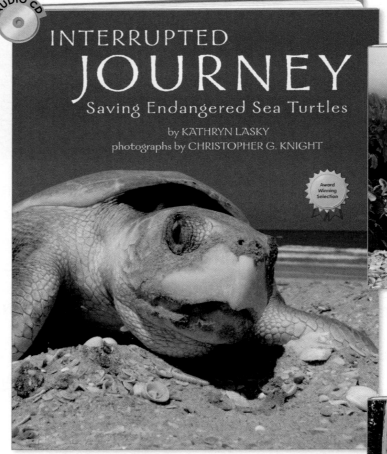

Science Link
Main Selection

Genre Informational Nonfiction

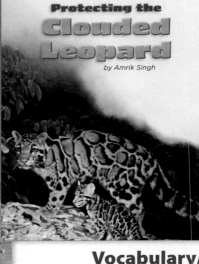

Vocabulary/ Comprehension

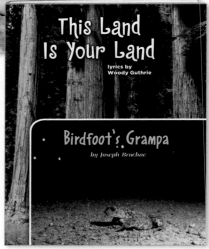

Genre Poetry/Song Lyrics

Read-Aloud Anthology
• Listening Comprehension
• Readers Theater

Leveled Readers

Leveled Reader Library

GR Levels T–Y

Genre Informational

- • Same Theme
- • Same Vocabulary
- • Same Comprehension Skills

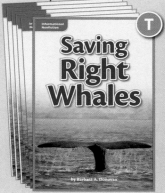

T

Saving Right Whales
by Barbara A. Donovan

V

SAVING Peregrine FALCONS
by Barbara A. Donovan

Y

SAVING Alligators
by Barbara A. Donovan

Approaching Level

On Level

Beyond Level

The King OF BIRDS
by Barbara A. Donovan

On Level Reader sheltered for English Language Learner

ELL Teacher's Guide also available

English Language Leveled Reader

Also Available LEVELED READER PROGRAM

CLASSROOM LIBRARY

Genre Informational

COME BACK, SALMON

A DROP OF WATER
WALTER WICK

Interrupted Journey

Approaching

On Level

Beyond

Trade books to apply Comprehension Skills

INTERVENTION ANTHOLOGY

- • Phonics and Decoding
- • Comprehension
- • Vocabulary

Also available, *Reading Triumphs* Intervention Program

READING Triumphs

LEVELED PRACTICE

Grade 6 Treasures
Practice Book A
Macmillan/McGraw-Hill

Grade 6 Treasures
Practice Book O
Macmillan/McGraw-Hill

Grade 6 Treasures
Practice Book B
Macmillan/McGraw-Hill

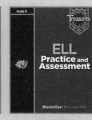

Grade 6 Treasures
ELL Practice and Assessment
Macmillan/McGraw-Hill

Approaching

On Level

Beyond

ELL

Grade 6 Treasures
Home-School Connection
• Parent Letters
• Homework Activities
• Take-Home Stories
Macmillan/McGraw-Hill

HOME-SCHOOL CONNECTION

- • Family letters in English and Spanish
- • Take-Home Stories

Technology

ONLINE INSTRUCTION
www.macmillanmh.com

AUDIO CD
- • Listening Library
- • Fluency Solutions

CD-ROM
- • Vocabulary PuzzleMaker

Suggested Lesson Plan

 **Instructional Navigator**
Interactive Lesson Planner

Interrupted Journey, 106–117

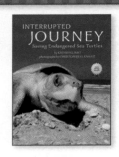   

Leveled Readers

 Integrated ELL Support Every Day

Whole Group

ORAL LANGUAGE
- **Listening**
- **Speaking**
- **Viewing**

WORD STUDY
- **Vocabulary**
- **Phonics/Decoding**

READING
- **Develop Comprehension**

- **Fluency**

LANGUAGE ARTS
- **Writing**

- **Grammar**

- **Spelling**

ASSESSMENT
- **Informal/Formal**

Turn the page for Small Group Lesson Plan

Day 1

Listening/Speaking/Viewing

❓ Focus Question In what ways do people protect wildlife? What kinds of things can harm wildlife?

Build Background, 102

Read Aloud: "Bringing Back Salmon," 103

Vocabulary

vital, conserve, dehydrated, analyzing, speculated, embedded, sedated, propelled, 104

Practice Book A-O-B, 29

Strategy: Analogies/Antonyms, 105

Read "Protecting the Clouded Leopard," 104–105

Comprehension 105A–105B
  Strategy: Make Inferences and Analyze
  Skill: Main Idea and Details

  Practice Book A-O-B, 30

Fluency Partner Reading, 102I
Model Fluency, 103

Student Book

Writing

Daily Writing Prompt: Write a paragraph about any species of wild animal you would choose to protect.

Personal Narrative: Diary, 122–123B

Grammar Daily Language Activities, 123I
Run-On Sentences, 123I
Grammar Practice Book, 25

Spelling Pretest, 123G
Spelling Practice Book, 25–26

Quick Check Vocabulary, 14
Comprehension, 105B

Differentiated Instruction 123M–123V

Day 2

Listening/Speaking

❓ Focus Question How did volunteers help save the endangered sea turtles?

Vocabulary
  Review Vocabulary Words, 106

Phonics/Decoding
  Decode Compound Words, 123E

  Practice Book A-O-B, 35

Read *Interrupted Journey,* 106–117

Comprehension, 106–117
  Strategy: Make Inferences and Analyze
  Skill: Main Idea and Details

  Practice Book A-O-B, 31

Fluency Partner Reading, 102I

 Student Book

Writing

Daily Writing Prompt: Why do you think conservation groups focus on big animals? Explain.

Personal Narrative: Diary, 122–123B

Grammar Daily Language Activities, 123I
Run-On Sentences, 123I
Grammar Practice Book, 26

Spelling Compound Words, 123G
Spelling Practice Book, 27

Quick Check Comprehension, 111, 117
Phonics, 123E

Differentiated Instruction 123M–123V

Skills/Strategies

Vocabulary
Vocabulary Words
Analogy/Antonyms

Comprehension
Strategy: Make Inferences and Analyze
Skill: Main Idea and Details

Writing
Personal Narrative
Diary

Turn the Page for
Small Group Options

Day 3

Listening/Speaking

❷ Focus Question Read "Protecting the Clouded Leopard" on pages 104–105. Compare and contrast the conservation project detailed in this selection with the one in *Interrupted Journey*.

Summarize, 119

Vocabulary
Review Words in Context, 123C
Strategy: Analogies/Antonyms, 123D
Practice Book A-O-B, 34

Phonics
Decode Multisyllabic Words, 123E

Read *Interrupted Journey*, 106–117

Student Book

Comprehension
Comprehension Check, 119
Maintain Skill: Main Idea, 119B

Fluency Partner Reading, 102I
Repeated Reading, 119A
Practice Book A-O-B, 32

 Writing

Daily Writing Prompt: If you were an endangered bird and you could talk, what would you say to people?

Writer's Craft: Transition Words, 123A
Personal Narrative: Diary, 122–123B

Grammar Daily Language Activities, 123I
Correcting Fragments and Run-On Sentences, 123J
Grammar Practice Book, 27

Spelling Compound Words, 123H
Spelling Practice Book, 28

Quick Check Fluency, 119A

Day 4

Listening/Speaking/Viewing

❷ Focus Question How are Max Nolan's attitudes toward wildlife in *Interrupted Journey* and the grandpa's attitudes in "Birdfoot's Grampa" similar?

Expand Vocabulary: Protecting Wildlife, 123F

Vocabulary
Vocabulary Sentences, 123F
Apply Vocabulary to Writing, 123F

Read "Birdfoot's Grampa" and "This Land is Your Land," 120–121

Student Book

Comprehension
Poetry, 120
Literary Elements: Alliteration and Imagery
Practice Book A-O-B, 33

Fluency Partner Reading, 102I

 Writing

Daily Writing Prompt: Write an editorial for your local newspaper about protecting wildlife.

Writing Trait: Ideas and Content, 123B
Personal Narrative: Diary, 122–123B

Grammar Daily Language Activities, 123I
Run-On Sentences, 123J
Grammar Practice Book, 28

Spelling Compound Words, 123H
Spelling Practice Book, 29

Quick Check Vocabulary, 123D

Day 5
Review and Assess

Listening/Speaking/Viewing

❷ Focus Question What common attitude toward nature and wildlife do all of this week's selections have?

Speaking and Listening Strategies, 123A

Vocabulary
Spiral Review of Vocabulary Words, 123F

Read Self-Selected Reading, 102

Student Book

Comprehension
Connect and Compare, 121

Fluency Partner Reading, 102I
Practice, 119A

Writing

Daily Writing Prompt: What questions would you ask a conservationist?

Personal Narrative: Diary, 122–123B

Grammar Daily Language Activities, 123I
Run-On Sentences, 123J
Grammar Practice Book, 29–30

Spelling Posttest, 123H
Spelling Practice Book, 30

Weekly Assessment, 53–60

Differentiated Instruction 123M–123V

Differentiated Instruction 123M–123V

Differentiated Instruction 123M–123V

Differentiated Instruction

What do I do in small groups?

Teacher-Led Small Groups

Literacy Workstations

Independent Activities

 **Skills Focus** Use your **Quick Check** observations to guide additional instruction and practice.

Phonics
Compound Words

 Vocabulary
Words: analyzing, conserve, dehydrated, embedded, propelled, sedated, speculated, vital
 Strategy: Analogy: Antonyms

Comprehension
Strategy: Make Inferences and Analyze
Skill: Main Idea and Details

Fluency

Suggested Lesson Plan

 Instructional Navigator
Interactive Lesson Planner

Approaching Level
- **Additional Instruction/Practice**
- **Tier 2 Instruction**

On Level
- **Practice**

Beyond Level
- **Extend**

Day 1

Fluency, 123N
Vocabulary, 123N
Comprehension, 123O
ELL Vocabulary in Context, 123O

 Saving Right Whales

Vocabulary, 123Q
Leveled Reader Lesson, 123R
- Comprehension
ELL Leveled Reader, 123U–123V

Vocabulary, 123S
Leveled Reader Lesson, 123T
- Comprehension

Day 2

Phonics, 123M
Vocabulary, 123O
Leveled Reader Lesson, 123P
- Vocabulary
- Comprehension

 Saving Right Whales

Leveled Reader Lesson, 123R
- Comprehension
- Vocabulary

Leveled Reader Lesson, 123T
- Comprehension
- Vocabulary

For intensive intervention see **READING Triumphs**

102E

Small Group Options

Focus on Leveled Readers

Apply *Tested* **skills and strategies while reading appropriate leveled books.**

Leveled Reader Library

Levels T–Y

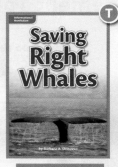 T

 V

 Y

Approaching

On Level

Beyond

ELL

Additional Leveled Reader Resources

LOG ON

Leveled Reader Database

Go to **www.macmillanmh.com**

Search by

- Comprehension Skill
- Content Area
- Genre
- Text Feature

- Guided Reading Level
- Reading Recovery Level
- Lexile Score
- Benchmark Level

Subscription also available

Day 3

Phonics, 123M
Fluency, 123N
Vocabulary, 123O
Leveled Reader Lesson, 123P
- Comprehension

Fluency, 123Q
Vocabulary, 123Q
Leveled Reader Lesson, 123R
- Comprehension

Fluency, 123S
Vocabulary, 123S
Leveled Reader Lesson, 123T
- Comprehension

Day 4

Phonics, 123M
Leveled Reader Lesson, 123P
- Comprehension

Literary Elements, 123Q
Leveled Reader Lesson, 123R
- Comprehension

Literary Elements, 123S
Leveled Reader Lesson, 123T
- Comprehension
ELL Poetic Language, 123S

Day 5

Fluency, 123N
Leveled Reader Lesson, 123P
- Make Connections
Across Texts

Fluency, 123Q
Leveled Reader Lesson, 123R
- Make Connections
Across Texts

Fluency, 123S
Self-Selected Reading, 123T

Managing the Class

What do I do with the rest of my class?

Teacher-Led Small Groups

Literacy Workstations

Independent Activities

Class Management Tools

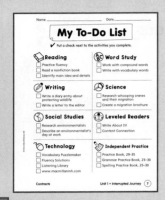

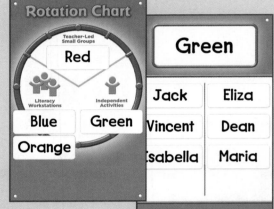

Includes:
- How-To Guides
- Rotation Chart
- Weekly Contracts

FOLDABLES™

Hands-on activities to reinforce weekly skills

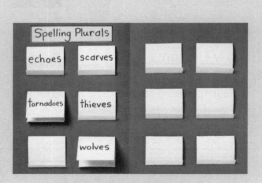

Matchbook Foldable

Word	Synonym	Antonym	Prefix or Suffix
normal	typical	unusual	normally

Folded Foldable

Independent Activities

Leveled Readers

For Repeated Readings and Literacy Activities

 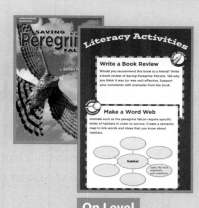  

Approaching | **On Level** | **ELL** | **Beyond**

LEVELED PRACTICE

Skills: Vocabulary (p. 29), Comprehension: Main Ideas and Details (p. 30), Graphic Organizers (p. 31), Fluency (p. 32), Literary Elements: Alliteration and Imagery (p. 33), Vocabulary Strategy: Antonyms (p. 34), Phonics (p. 35)

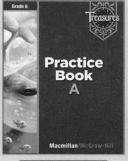  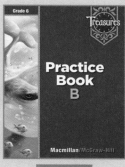 

Approaching | **On Level** | **Beyond** | **ELL**

Technology

ONLINE INSTRUCTION www.macmillanmh.com

- Meet the Author/Illustrator
- Computer Literacy Lessons
- Research and Inquiry Activities

- Oral Language Activities
- Vocabulary and Spelling Activities
- Leveled Reader Database

 LISTENING LIBRARY
Recordings of selections
- Main Selections
- Leveled Readers
- ELL Readers
- Intervention Anthology

 FLUENCY SOLUTIONS
Recorded passages for modeling and practicing fluency

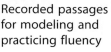 **VOCABULARY PUZZLEMAKER**
Activities providing multiple exposures to vocabulary, spelling, and high-frequency words including crossword puzzles, word searches, and word jumbles

Turn the page for Literacy Workstations.

Literacy Activities

Collaborative Learning Activities

Reading

Objectives

- Time reading to practice fluency.
- Read passage fluently with expression.
- Identify main idea and supporting details.
- Select a book and read for enjoyment.

Word Study

Objectives

- Divide compound words into two separate words and then alphabetize them.
- Look up vocabulary words.

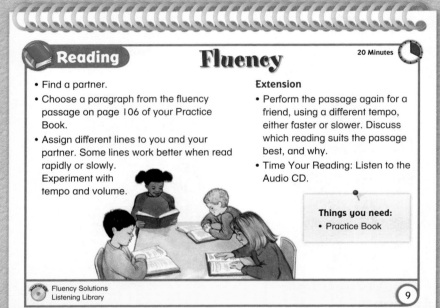

Reading — **Fluency** — 20 Minutes

- Find a partner.
- Choose a paragraph from the fluency passage on page 106 of your Practice Book.
- Assign different lines to you and your partner. Some lines work better when read rapidly or slowly. Experiment with tempo and volume.

Extension

- Perform the passage again for a friend, using a different tempo, either faster or slower. Discuss which reading suits the passage best, and why.
- Time Your Reading: Listen to the Audio CD.

Things you need:
- Practice Book

Fluency Solutions
Listening Library

9

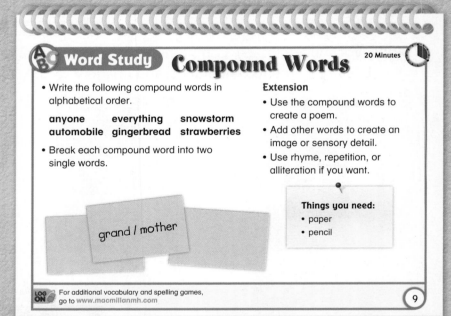

Word Study — **Compound Words** — 20 Minutes

- Write the following compound words in alphabetical order.

anyone	**everything**	**snowstorm**
automobile	**gingerbread**	**strawberries**

- Break each compound word into two single words.

Extension

- Use the compound words to create a poem.
- Add other words to create an image or sensory detail.
- Use rhyme, repetition, or alliteration if you want.

grand / mother

Things you need:
- paper
- pencil

For additional vocabulary and spelling games, go to www.macmillanmh.com

9

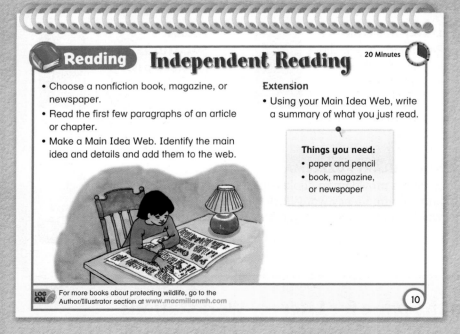

Reading — **Independent Reading** — 20 Minutes

- Choose a nonfiction book, magazine, or newspaper.
- Read the first few paragraphs of an article or chapter.
- Make a Main Idea Web. Identify the main idea and details and add them to the web.

Extension

- Using your Main Idea Web, write a summary of what you just read.

Things you need:
- paper and pencil
- book, magazine, or newspaper

For more books about protecting wildlife, go to the Author/Illustrator section at www.macmillanmh.com

10

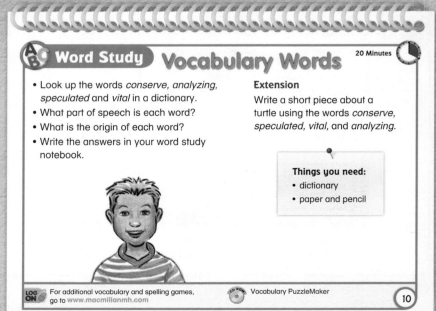

Word Study — **Vocabulary Words** — 20 Minutes

- Look up the words *conserve, analyzing, speculated* and *vital* in a dictionary.
- What part of speech is each word?
- What is the origin of each word?
- Write the answers in your word study notebook.

Extension

Write a short piece about a turtle using the words *conserve, speculated, vital,* and *analyzing.*

Things you need:
- dictionary
- paper and pencil

For additional vocabulary and spelling games, go to www.macmillanmh.com

Vocabulary PuzzleMaker

10

Literacy Workstations

 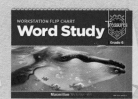  

Writing

Objectives

- Write a diary entry about protecting wildlife and a letter from the opposite point of view.
- Write a letter to the editor taking a particular stand and then argue the opposite point of view.

Content Literacy

Objectives

- Use an encyclopedia to research whooping cranes.
- Use an encyclopedia to research an environmentalist's job and schedule an imaginary work day.

Writing — PROTECTING WILDLIFE
20 Minutes

- What are your feelings about protecting wildlife? Are you passionate about saving animals? Or not?
- Write a diary entry describing your views.

Extension
- Now pretend you are someone who holds opposing views.
- Write a letter to an editor describing your views.
- Explain why you think others are wrong.

Things you need:
- paper
- pencil

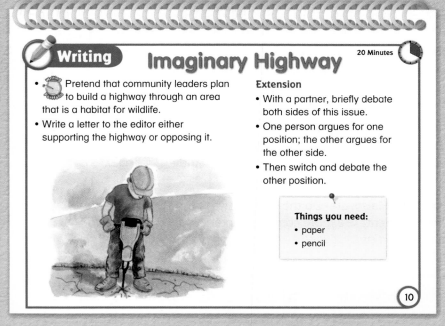

9

Science — Whooping Cranes and Ultra-light Aircraft
20 Minutes

- Find information on how scientists are helping endangered cranes learn to migrate to new areas using ultra-light aircraft.
- Use several different sources to research the information.
- Take notes on your findings.

Extension
- Use your notes to create a brochure that describes the process.
- Include colorful drawings.

Things you need:
- reference materials
- paper and pencil
- colored markers

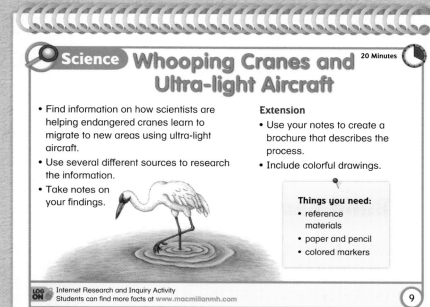

LOG ON — Internet Research and Inquiry Activity
Students can find more facts at www.macmillanmh.com

9

Writing — Imaginary Highway
20 Minutes

- Pretend that community leaders plan to build a highway through an area that is a habitat for wildlife.
- Write a letter to the editor either supporting the highway or opposing it.

Extension
- With a partner, briefly debate both sides of this issue.
- One person argues for one position; the other argues for the other side.
- Then switch and debate the other position.

Things you need:
- paper
- pencil

10

Social Studies — Save the Environment
20 Minutes

- Look up the term *environmentalist* in a dictionary and encyclopedia. What kind of environmentalists are there? What do environmentalists do?
- Write a paragraph based on the information you find.

Extension
- Now pretend that you are an environmentalist.
- Create a daily schedule that shows what you might do in a typical day.

Things you need:
- reference materials
- paper and pencil

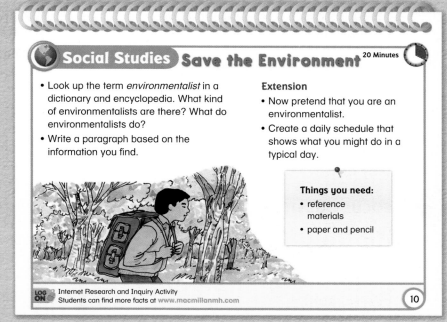

LOG ON — Internet Research and Inquiry Activity
Students can find more facts at www.macmillanmh.com

10

Prepare

ORAL LANGUAGE
- Build Background
- Read Aloud
- Expand Vocabulary

 **VOCABULARY**
- Teach Words in Context
- **Analogy:** Antonyms

COMPREHENSION
- **Strategy:** Make Inferences and Analyze
- **Skill:** Main Idea and Details

SMALL GROUP OPTIONS
- Differentiated Instruction, pp. 123M–123V

Oral Language

Build Background

ACCESS PRIOR KNOWLEDGE

Share information to help students think about this week's theme.

The U.S. Fish and Wildlife Service manages more than 500 wildlife refuges and thousands of wetlands.

TALK ABOUT PROTECTING WILDLIFE

Discuss the weekly theme.

Do you think human beings should intervene to help save animal species? Why or why not?

 FOCUS QUESTION Ask a volunteer to read "Talk About It" on **Student Book** page 103 and describe the photo.

What do you think is happening in the photograph?

ENGLISH LANGUAGE LEARNERS

Beginning Name and Repeat Have students say what they can about the photo. Provide language as needed. Say, *The whale is in the net. The man is helping the whale.* Have students repeat. Next, have students point to items. Then ask, *What is the man doing?*

Intermediate Prior Knowledge Discuss the meaning of the word *wildlife* and brainstorm examples. Discuss what it means to protect something. Explain the words *species* and *extinct*. Discuss why some wildlife need protection.

Advanced Elaborate Do the same task as in the Intermediate box. Help students use more complex sentences as they talk: *Some fish need protection because the water they live in is too polluted. They are dying.*

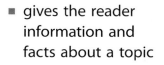

Talk About It

In what ways do people protect wildlife? What kinds of things can harm wildlife?

Find out more about protecting wildlife at **www.macmillanmh.com**

Protecting Wildlife

103

Picture Prompt

Look at the picture. Write about what you see. You can write a story or a description, or use any other type of writing you like.

Technology

For an extended lesson plan and Web site activities for **oral language development,** go to **www.macmillanmh.com**

Read Aloud
Read "Bringing Back Salmon"

GENRE: Informational Nonfiction
Review features of informational nonfiction:

- gives the reader information and facts about a topic

- has a main idea and supporting details

Read Aloud pages 27–30

LISTENING FOR A PURPOSE

Ask students to listen carefully for the steps taken by the students at Shasta Union Elementary School to help save the fish as you read "Bringing Back Salmon" in the **Read-Aloud Anthology.** Choose from among the teaching suggestions.

Fluency Ask students to listen carefully as you read aloud. Tell students to listen to your phrasing, expression, and tone of voice.

RESPOND TO THE STORY

Ask students to write a response to this question: What plant or animal species would you most want to save if it were threatened by extinction, and why?

Expand Vocabulary

Ask students to find words or phrases in "Bringing Back Salmon" that relate to the weekly theme "Protecting Wildlife." Have them use various resources and strategies to identify word meanings, spellings, and pronunciations. Have them record new words in a word study notebook.

Vocabulary

TEACH WORDS IN CONTEXT

Use the following routine.

Routine

Define: A **speculated**³ idea is assumed to be true without complete proof.
Example: The doctor speculated that my runny nose was caused by allergies.
Ask: What is a synonym for *speculated*?
SYNONYM

- When you **conserve**⁴ something, you save it. Lower your thermostat to conserve electricity. How could you conserve something? **EXPLANATION**

- When **analyzing**⁶ something, you examine its parts. By analyzing the plot of the story, I understood it. What kinds of things require analyzing? **EXAMPLE**

- Something that is **vital**⁵ can be of great importance. It was vital that the class president attend the meeting. What vital role does nutrition play in good health? **EXPLANATION**

- If something is **propelled**¹, it is pushed forward. The boat was propelled through the water by its engine. How is being propelled different from simply moving? **COMPARE AND CONTRAST**

- When a person or animal is **sedated**⁷, it is calmed using medicine. Jamal was sedated before he had his tooth pulled. When might an animal need to be sedated? **PRIOR KNOWLEDGE**

- If someone is **dehydrated**², he or she has lost water. Drink water so you won't become dehydrated. When might you be at risk of becoming dehydrated? **EXAMPLE**

- If something is **embedded**, it is made a central part of a thing. The fossil was embedded in the stone. Tell how something could become embedded in your memory. **DESCRIPTION**

8. *to placed or planted firmly within the central part of a thing.*

Quick Check Do students understand word meanings?

During **Small Group Instruction**

If No → **Approaching Level** Vocabulary, p. 123N

If Yes → **On Level** Options, pp. 123Q–123R

Beyond Level Options, pp. 123S–123T

Vocabulary

speculated	propelled
conserve	sedated
analyzing	dehydrated
vital	embedded

STRATEGY SKILL

Analogies

Analogies compare two pairs of words. Sometimes analogies use **Antonyms**, words with opposite meanings.

Conserve is to *waste* as *assist* is to *hinder*.

Protecting the Clouded Leopard

by Amrik Singh

Not many people know about the clouded leopard. Even scientists don't know much about the animal in the wild because it is so private. We do know that the clouded leopard isn't actually a leopard. It is a species of its own. However, it does have spots like a leopard. They help it blend into the background in the forest.

What else do we know about the cat? It is one of the best climbers of all wild cats. This skill is clearly imprinted in the kittens early on by their mothers and by instinct. In the wild,

104

ELL Access for All

Clarify Vocabulary Say: *Some scientists are studying sea turtles. They are <u>analyzing</u> how turtles live. <u>Analyzing</u> means studying something. What are we <u>analyzing</u> in science and social studies?*

Say, *The sea turtles are in danger. It is <u>vital</u> that people help them. <u>Vital</u> means very important. Why is air <u>vital</u>? Why is studying <u>vital</u>?*

the cat lives in the tropical rain forests of Asia. It hunts small animals, such as squirrels and monkeys. It is listed on the United States Endangered Species Act. This protects it from being hunted. Scientists have **speculated** that the wild population is getting smaller, but no actual numbers are available.

The Clouded Leopard Project works to **conserve** and protect the population of these cats. The project teaches about clouded leopards, **analyzing** their habits in captivity by watching their behaviors and interactions. The project realizes it is **vital** to the cats' survival to breed the animals in zoos. If more clouded leopards aren't born, the population will be **propelled** quickly into extinction.

The Clouded Leopard Project has recently begun a conservation effort in Thailand. It is a natural home of the clouded leopard. Funds will be given to the Khao Kheow Open Zoo to help with the breeding of these cats. Part of the money also will help save the habitat of the wild cats. People will work to monitor these wild cats. They will be photographed instead of being **sedated**, or drugged, to be tagged. Sedating clouded leopards could cause the cats' bodies to lose too much water and become **dehydrated**, or worse.

The project has had some great successes in the last few years. Two cubs were born in the United States, and two were born in Thailand.

Members of the Clouded Leopard Project hope the urge to protect such species will become **embedded** in people. They sponsor several education programs at zoos. They also sponsor programs to directly help the cats. Through their work they ultimately will increase the population of this species.

Reread for **Comprehension**

Make Inferences and Analyze
Main Idea and Details
To understand a text, the reader must make inferences and analyze information. This will help the reader understand the main idea. Authors use various details to help readers understand the main idea.

Use a Main Idea Web to help you record the main idea and details as you reread "Protecting the Clouded Leopard."

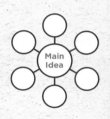

105

On Level Practice Book O, page 29

Write each word next to its definition.

vital	conserve	sedated	analyzing
speculated	embedded	dehydrated	propelled

1. examining carefully and in detail in order to understand something — analyzing
2. moved or driven forward — propelled
3. avoid waste; save or preserve — conserve
4. of greatest importance — vital
5. medicated to calm or go to sleep — sedated
6. thought of reasons or answers — speculated
7. dried out due to lost water or moisture — dehydrated
8. set into surrounding matter — embedded

Write four sentences using one of the vocabulary words in each sentence. **Possible responses provided.**
9. Jing wanted to be sedated when the dentist pulled her tooth.
10. Even a cactus can become dehydrated if it doesn't get enough water.
11. Padma embedded the seedling in the ground and then watered it.
12. Jake wanted to conserve water, so he turned his front yard into a rock garden.

★ **Approaching Practice Book A,** page 29
◆ **Beyond Practice Book B,** page 29

Vocabulary

STRATEGY
USE ANALOGIES

Antonyms Explain to students that using analogies requires them to understand how words relate to each other. Antonyms, words that have opposite or nearly opposite meanings, are one way an author can show the relationship between words. Sometimes antonyms can be used as context clues.

Ask students what *vital* means in "Protecting the Clouded Leopard." Then ask for an antonym for *vital*. (unimportant, unnecessary, trivial) Have students write an analogy using *vital* and one of its antonyms.

Read "Protecting the Clouded Leopard"

As you read "Protecting the Clouded Leopard" with students, ask them to use context clues to decide the meaning each highlighted word has in the story. Tell students they will read these words again in *Interrupted Journey*.

Objectives

- Make inferences and analyze
- Use academic language: *main idea* and *details*
- Identify the main idea and details

Materials

- Comprehension Transparencies 5a, 5b
- Graphic Organizer Transparency 5
- Leveled Practice Books, p. 31

Skills Trace

Main Idea and Details

Introduce	U1: 69A–69B
Practice/ Apply	U1: 70–73; Leveled Practice Books, 16–17
Reteach/ Review	U1: 77M–77T, 105A–105B, 106–119, 123M–123T; Leveled Practice Books, 30–31
Assess	Weekly Tests; Unit 1 Tests; Benchmark Tests A, B
Maintain	U1: 73A, 119B; U2: 185A; U3: 309A

ELL

Access for All

Develop Concepts
Model how to identify the main idea in the first few paragraphs through a Think Aloud. Discuss with students how you choose which sentence is the main idea. Invite students to share their thinking with you. Write the steps you follow on the board.

105A

Reread for
Comprehension

STRATEGY
MAKE INFERENCES AND ANALYZE

Authors do not always tell readers everything that takes place in a story or selection, but they do provide details that allow readers to figure things out for themselves. Good readers use information from the text as well as their own prior knowledge to make inferences, or logical decisions, about characters and events. Making inferences can help readers identify the main idea in a selection.

SKILL
MAIN IDEA AND DETAILS

- The main idea is the most important point an author makes about a topic. It is often found in a sentence at the beginning of a paragraph or selection. The sentences that follow give details about the main idea that help explain or support it.

- Sometimes an author does not state the main idea directly. Good readers then put together details in the text to help them figure out the main idea. They ask, *What is this selection or paragraph mostly about?*

Student Book pages 104–105 available on Comprehension transparencies 5a and 5b.

MODEL

Read aloud the first paragraph of "Protecting the Clouded Leopard" from **Student Book** page 104.

Think Aloud After reading the first paragraph, I can infer that one reason scientists don't know much about clouded leopards is because they blend into the background in the forest and are hard to find. After reading the first four paragraphs I can tell that the main idea is that the Clouded Leopard Project is trying to save these animals.

GUIDED PRACTICE

Explain to students that they will be filling in the Main Idea Web as they read the selection. Tell students:

- A good way to find the main idea of an entire selection is to think about the main ideas of the individual paragraphs or sections.

Display the Main Idea Web on **Transparency 5.**

- The main idea of a paragraph or section is often found in the opening sentence. But this is not always the case. Sometimes an author places the main idea in the middle or at the end of a paragraph or section.

- Authors do not always state the main idea directly. Sometimes readers must infer the main idea from details the author includes.

Work with students to fill in the center of the Main Idea Web and one of the supporting details.

APPLY

Have students work together to complete the Main Idea Web. Ask students to explain the final goal of the Clouded Leopard Project. Do students believe the goal will be reached? Why or why not?

Quick Check	**Can students identify the main idea and details in the selection?**

During **Small Group Instruction**

If No → Approaching Level Comprehension, p. 123O

If Yes → On Level Options, pp. 123Q–123R

Beyond Level Options, pp. 123S–123T

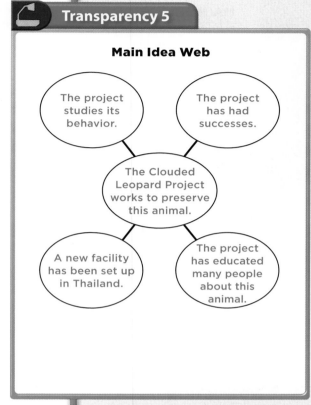

Transparency 5

Main Idea Web

- The project studies its behavior.
- The project has had successes.
- The Clouded Leopard Project works to preserve this animal.
- A new facility has been set up in Thailand.
- The project has educated many people about this animal.

Graphic Organizer Transparency 5

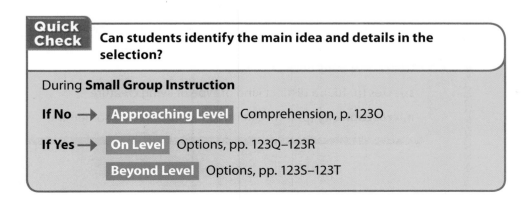

On Level Practice Book, page 30

Read the paragraph. Then answer the questions.

The Florida Everglades are home to many birds, reptiles, and mammals. The Everglades provide a variety of habitats. They are vital to the wildlife they support, supplying particular environmental conditions that can be found only in the Everglades. Birds and other animals are protected by the sawgrass prairies. Crocodiles and alligators live together in the swamps and water. People must protect and preserve this land in order to nurture and protect the wildlife that make the Everglades their home.

Possible responses provided.
1. What is the main idea of this paragraph?
   People must protect the Everglades to protect the wildlife that live there.

2. Where is the main idea of this paragraph located?
   at the end of the paragraph

3. Why do you think it is located there?
   It is at the end in order to persuade people to help.

4. What purpose do the first and second sentences serve?
   They provide details to support the main idea.

5. Why are the Everglades vital to wildlife?
   They provide particular environments not found elsewhere.

★ **Approaching Practice Book A,** page 30

◆ **Beyond Practice Book B,** page 30

Read

MAIN SELECTION
- *Interrupted Journey*
- **Skill:** Main Idea and Details

PAIRED SELECTION
- "Birdfoot's Grampa" and "This Land is Your Land"
- **Literary Elements:** Alliteration and Imagery

SMALL GROUP OPTIONS
- Differentiated Instruction, pp. 123M–123V

Comprehension

GENRE: INFORMATIONAL NONFICTION

Have a student read the definition of Informational Nonfiction on **Student Book** page 106. As students read, they should look for real situations and factual information.

STRATEGY
MAKE INFERENCES AND ANALYZE

When students make inferences, they use their own prior knowledge and experiences as well as clues from the text. Making inferences can help a reader identify a selection's main idea and details.

SKILL
MAIN IDEA AND DETAILS

The main idea is the most important point an author makes about his or her topic. Details support the main idea.

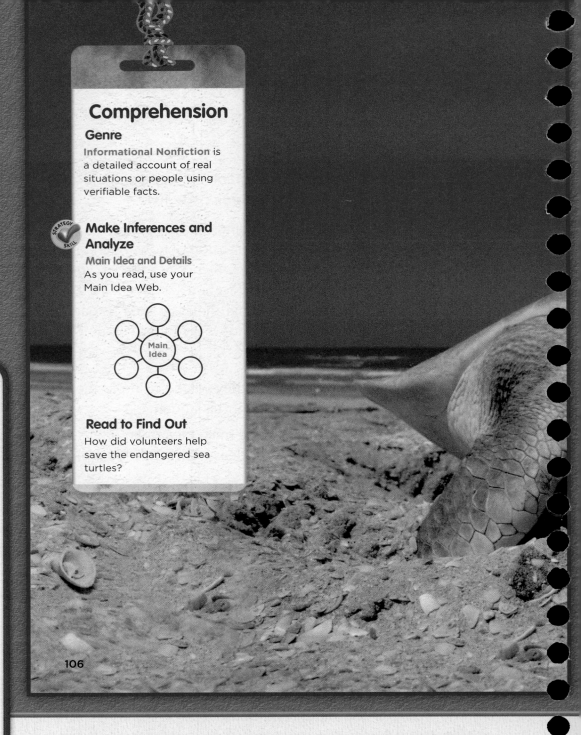

Comprehension

Genre

Informational Nonfiction is a detailed account of real situations or people using verifiable facts.

Make Inferences and Analyze

Main Idea and Details
As you read, use your Main Idea Web.

Read to Find Out

How did volunteers help save the endangered sea turtles?

106

Vocabulary

Vocabulary Words Review the tested vocabulary words: **analyzing, conserve, dehydrated, embedded, propelled, sedated, speculated,** and **vital.**

Selection Words Students may find these words difficult. Pronounce the words and present the meanings as necessary.

plankton (p. 108): very small animals and plants that float or swim weakly in a body of water

species (p. 109): a distinct kind or type of living creature

microscopically (p. 111): relating to the smallness of something

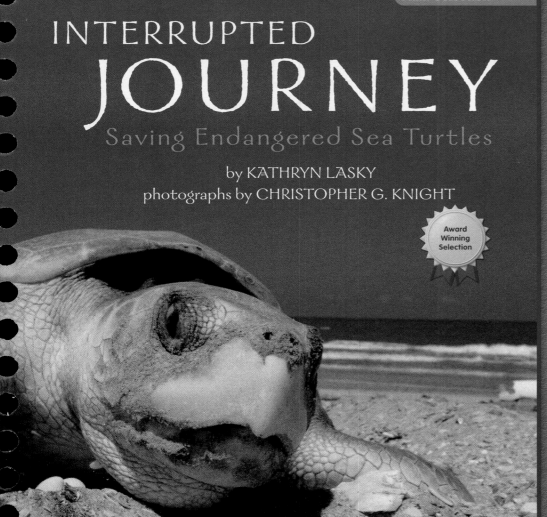

INTERRUPTED JOURNEY
Saving Endangered Sea Turtles

by KATHRYN LASKY

photographs by CHRISTOPHER G. KNIGHT

Award Winning Selection

107

Read Together

If your students need support to read the Main Selection, use the prompts to guide comprehension and model how to complete the graphic organizer.

Read Independently

If your students can read the Main Selection independently, have them read and complete the graphic organizer. Remind students to set and modify purposes when reading and adjust their reading rate as needed.

If your students need an alternate selection, choose the **Leveled Readers** that match their instructional level.

Technology

Story available on **Listening Library Audio CD**

Preview and Predict

Ask students to read the title, preview the photographs, and note questions and predictions about what may happen in the story. Ask: What do you think the title refers to?

Set Purposes

FOCUS QUESTION Discuss the "Read to Find Out" question on **Student Book** page 106. Remind students to look for the answer as they read.

Point out the Main Idea Web in the Student Book and on **Leveled Practice Book** page 31. Explain that students will use the web to keep track of events in the selection.

Read *Interrupted Journey*

Use the questions and Think Alouds for additional instruction to support the comprehension strategy and skill.

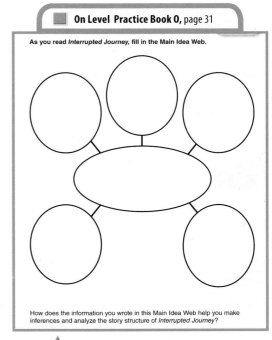

On Level Practice Book O, page 31

As you read *Interrupted Journey*, fill in the Main Idea Web.

How does the information you wrote in this Main Idea Web help you make inferences and analyze the story structure of *Interrupted Journey*?

⭐ **Approaching Practice Book A,** page 31

◆ **Beyond Practice Book B,** page 31

Develop Comprehension

1 STRATEGY
MAKE INFERENCES AND ANALYZE

Teacher Think Aloud I can infer from the heading "Stranded" that something or someone is going to be stranded in this selection. I can see in the photos on these pages that a boy is holding a sea turtle. So, I think that the turtle will be stranded. I'll continue reading to find out if this is part of the main idea.

2 MAIN IDEA AND DETAILS

What is the main idea in the second paragraph? (Volunteers help save turtles.)

3 CAUSE AND EFFECT

What is the cause-and-effect relationship between the first two paragraphs on this page? (The first paragraph describes a turtle's journey into winter, which puts the turtle in danger. The second paragraph describes the effect—efforts by people to save the endangered turtles.)

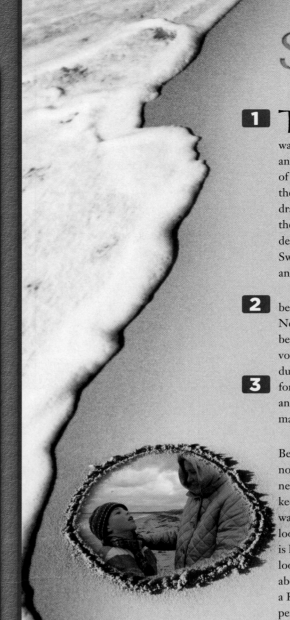

Stranded

1 The young turtle has been swimming for three months now in the same warm shallow bay, grazing on small crabs and plankton, basking in an endless dream of calm water and plentiful food. But as the days begin to shorten and the light drains out of the sky earlier and earlier, the water grows colder. It drops to fifty degrees Fahrenheit. The turtle is confused. Swimming is harder. Its heartbeat slows—and almost stops.

2 Ten days before Thanksgiving, on a beach where Pilgrims once walked, Max Nolan, a ten-year-old boy, and his mother begin their patrol. The Nolans are among volunteers who walk Cape Cod's beaches during November and December to search **3** for turtles who are often cold and stunned and seem dead—turtles whose lives they may be able to save.

It is a blustery day on Ellis Landing Beach. At twenty-five knots the bitter northwest wind stings Max's face like sharp needles. It makes his eyes water but he keeps looking—looking above the high-water mark through the clumps of seaweed, looking below the tide line where the sand is hard and sleek and lapped by surf—looking for a dark greenish-brown mound about the size of a pie plate, looking for a Kemp's ridley turtle that is dying and perhaps can be saved.

108

Ways to Confirm Meaning

Semantic/Meaning Cues

Explain Tell students that good readers check their understanding by making sure what they read makes sense. One way to do this is by using context, meaning, and background knowledge to confirm meaning.

Model Discuss the word *stunned* on **Student Book** page 108. *I'm not sure what the word* stunned *means, but I know that the turtles are cold and often seem to be dead.* Stunned *probably means that the turtle is unconscious. If I replace the word* stunned *with the word* unconscious, *the sentence still makes sense.*

Apply Encourage students to use context clues and their background knowledge to help them with other difficult words and phrases as they read.

Max and his mother and the other volunteers work for a **vital** cause. All sea turtles are threatened or endangered; Kemp's ridleys are the most endangered of all. Right now on our planet there are fewer than eight thousand Kemp's ridley turtles left. They are a vanishing species.

On Ellis Landing Beach, snow squalls begin to whirl down. The waves are building, and as they begin to break, the white froth whips across their steep faces. So far there is no sign of a turtle.

Max is far ahead of his mother when he sees the hump in the sand being washed by the surf. He runs up to it and shouts to his mom, "Got one!" The turtle is cold. Its flippers are floppy. Its eyes are open, but the turtle is not moving at all. It might be dead, but then again, it might not.

Main Idea
What is the main idea on pages 108–109? What details support it?

109

ELL

Access for All

STRATEGIES FOR EXTRA SUPPORT

Question 5 MAIN IDEA AND DETAILS
Remind students of the steps in identifying the main idea and detail: *Read through the paragraph first to get the general idea. Then reread each sentence to decide which one identifies the main idea.* You may need to explain the following words in the text: *endangered, cause, volunteers, vanishing.*

Develop Comprehension

4 CHARACTER

What words would you use to describe Max Nolan and his mother? (Answers will vary but should include that Max and his mother are kind, compassionate people who care about animals. Even though the wind stings Max's face, he and his mother keep looking for turtles they may be able to save.)

5 MAIN IDEA AND DETAILS

Tested

What is the main idea on pages 108–109? What details support it? (Answers may vary but should include information such as *The Nolans are among many volunteers who work to save endangered turtles.* Details should include *As the water grows colder, a turtle's heartbeat slows; all sea turtles are threatened or endangered; Kemp's ridleys are the most endangered of all; Max finds a turtle that may or may not be dead.*) Add this information to your main idea web.

All sea turtles are threatened or endangered.

Kemp's ridleys are the most endangered of all.

The Nolans are among many volunteers who work to save endangered turtles.

As the water grows colder, a turtle's heartbeat slows.

Max finds a turtle that may or may not be dead.

Develop Comprehension

6 **USE PHOTOGRAPHS**

Which photograph goes with the paragraph on this page? What caption would you write for the photograph? (The photograph at the lower left of the page. The caption could be "Max covers the turtle with seaweed to protect it from the wind.")

7 **GENRE: INFORMATIONAL NONFICTION**

How can you tell that this selection is nonfiction? (The selection includes real events, such as finding a dying turtle; real people, such as Max Nolan; and real places, such as Ellis Landing Beach. The photographs also make clear that the selection is nonfiction.)

6

Max remembers the instructions given to all rescuers. He picks up the turtle, which weighs about five pounds, and moves it above the high-tide mark to keep it from washing out to sea. Then he runs to find seaweed to protect it from the wind. He finds a stick to mark the spot, and next, he and his mother go to the nearest telephone and call the sea-turtle rescue line of the Massachusetts Audubon Society.

7

110

Comprehension

Word Study: *Analogies*

Explain An analogy shows how two ideas are alike. For instance, an analogy might read as follows: *still* is to *moving* as *near* is to _____. Think of the first idea as the part of the sentence that comes before the word as: "*still* is to *moving*." They should realize that the words are opposites, or *antonyms*.

Discuss The second part of the analogy is the part of the sentence following the word *as*. Have students find an antonym for *near*. (far)

Apply Ask students to create other analogies, similar to the above example. Remind them that the first half of the analogy sentence must contain both a word and its antonym. Create teams, have the students ask one another the questions they have created. Award one point for each correct answer.

Within an hour the turtle has been picked up and taken to the Wellfleet Bay Wildlife Sanctuary on Cape Cod. Robert Prescott, the director of the Sanctuary, examines the turtle. "It sure does look dead," he says softly. "But you never can tell." If the turtle is really alive, it must be brought out of its cold, stunned condition. That is a task for the New England Aquarium with its medical team who, over the years, have made a specialty of treating turtles.

Robert puts the new turtle in a plastic wading pool with another turtle that is quite lively. Max crouches by the edge and watches his turtle. It is as still as a stone. He gently touches a flipper. Nothing moves. Then after about twenty minutes, he thinks he might see a flicker in the turtle's left eyelid. He leans closer. "Hey, it's moving!" It wasn't just the eyelid. He saw the right rear flipper move a fraction of an inch. Over the next five minutes, he sees the turtle make three or four microscopically small motions with its right rear flipper. Soon, the rescue team from the New England Aquarium arrives. **8**

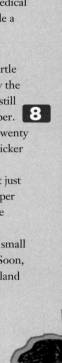

111

Develop Comprehension

8 MAIN IDEA AND DETAILS

What is the unstated main idea in this selection? What details on this page support this idea? (Answers may vary but should include a statement such as *It's difficult to tell whether the turtle is alive or dead.* Details could include *the turtle is not moving; eyelid flickers; flipper moves slightly.*) Fill in your main idea web with this information.

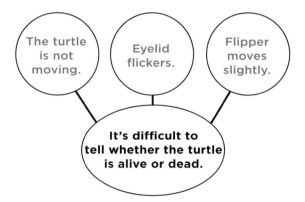

The turtle is not moving.

Eyelid flickers.

Flipper moves slightly.

It's difficult to tell whether the turtle is alive or dead.

 Have students respond to the selection by confirming or revising their predictions.

Quick Check Can students identify a main idea and details on this page? If not, see the **Extra Support** on this page.

Extra Support

Main Idea and Details

If students have difficulty identifying the main idea in a passage, have them reread the second paragraph on page 111. Then help them determine the main idea. Ask, *Does one sentence determine what this passage is mostly about? Do other sentences give details to support it?* Since there isn't one sentence in this paragraph that states the main idea, ask, *What is Max doing? What do the sentences tell about, explain, or describe?* Use the details students mention to help them determine the unstated main idea.

Stop here if you wish to read this selection over two days.

Develop Comprehension

9 **MONITOR AND CLARIFY: ADJUST READING RATE**

What does the new heading indicate? Why might this affect your reading rate? (A new heading has been introduced. Earlier, the information in the selection was under the heading "Stranded." Now, the heading is "Emergency." The vets have come and begun to take care of the turtle. The reading pace should slow even more because the information is becoming more scientific.)

10 **MAIN IDEA AND DETAILS**

Tested

What is the main idea of this paragraph? Find two details to support your answer. (The vets treat the turtles as emergency cases. They take the turtles' temperatures and check their heartbeats.)

Emergency

9 Beth Chittick is a vet at the New England Aquarium. When the turtles arrive she is ready for them. The turtles are taken immediately into the examination room. Beth is joined by head veterinarian, Howard Crum. They insert a thermometer into the cloaca, the opening under the turtle's tail. The temperature of the turtle Max found is fifty degrees Fahrenheit. **10** Normal temperature for a turtle is usually about seventy-five degrees. Howard next tries to find a heartbeat. He listens intently. "I think I can hear a faint sound . . . " He holds the stiff turtle against his ear as one might hold a seashell. "Why, gee whiz, I can hear the ocean," he jokes.

> **STRATEGY SKILL**
> **Main Idea**
> What is the main idea of this paragraph? Find two details to support your answer.

112

112

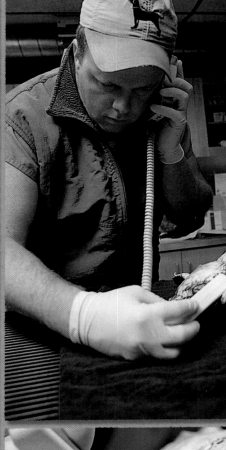

113

Howard is still not convinced that the turtle is dead. "With turtles," Howard says, "death is a relative term." Turtles can operate, can survive, even when their hearts slow down for periods of time. Events that might damage the larger, more complicated brains of other animals will not always prove fatal to turtles.

In fact, a turtle's heartbeat naturally slows down at times to just one or two beats per minute in order to **conserve** oxygen and keep vital organs like the brain working. So Howard won't give up on this **11** turtle yet. The turtle does not seem **dehydrated**. The skin on its limbs is not wrinkled—a good sign.

An assistant swabs down an area on the turtle's neck, from which a blood sample will be taken. By **analyzing** the blood, Howard and Beth will be able to see how the turtle's kidneys and other organs are functioning. **12**

Main Selection   Student page 113

Develop Comprehension

11 STRATEGY
USE ANALOGIES

Complete the following analogy, which uses two words from the selection: Vital is to unimportant as conserve is to _____. This analogy uses antonyms, or opposites. The opposite of vital is unimportant or unnecessary. (The opposite of conserve is waste.)

12 SUMMARIZE

What steps have been taken so far in rescuing a turtle? (Max, a volunteer, spotted the turtle and called the Sanctuary. People from the Sanctuary picked up the turtle and began treating it. The turtle was then taken by the New England Aquarium and was examined.)

Cross-Curricular Connection

EXTINCTION BY THE NUMBERS

Scientists and other people interested in conservation must always think in terms of numbers. When studying endangered species, it is important to know the answers to these mathematical questions:

• *About how many individual animals are estimated to be alive?*

• *How long does it take the baby to grow to adulthood?*

• *How many babies does the typical mother have each year?*

Research and Inquiry Have students select an endangered species of their own choosing. Help the class research the answers to the questions listed above. Did their research offer any other important statistics about their species?

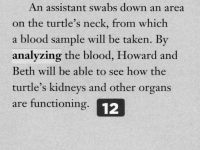

Develop Comprehension

13 MAKE INFERENCES AND ANALYZE

Teacher Think Aloud I can tell from the vets' behavior that they know much more about the turtle's condition. Why do you think the fluids they give the turtle are at a temperature higher than the turtle's body?

Encourage students to apply the strategy in a Think Aloud.

Student Think Aloud I know that the turtle is stunned because the ocean water was growing colder. That's why its heartbeat was slowing down. So the fluids must be a higher temperature than the turtle's body because the vet is trying to warm the turtle's blood.

14 MAIN IDEA AND DETAILS

Tested

What is the main idea of this page? (The vets still aren't sure about the status of the turtle.) What details support this main idea? (The movements aren't definite signs of life. The vets are still not sure the turtle is alive.)

Let's add the details to our web.

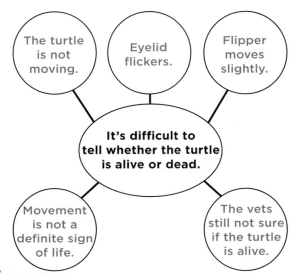

The turtle is not moving.

Eyelid flickers.

Flipper moves slightly.

It's difficult to tell whether the turtle is alive or dead.

Movement is not a definite sign of life.

The vets still not sure if the turtle is alive.

114

13 Next the turtle is cleaned. The algae are washed and wiped from its shell. The doctors detect movement in its tail and then see some of the same movements that Max saw in its flippers. They are the motions a turtle makes when it swims. They do not necessarily mean that it is alive, though. It has been **speculated** that these movements could be what are sometimes called vestigial motions, echoes of long-ago actions, fossil behaviors **embedded** in the brain of an ancient creature. The turtle could be swimming in death or swimming toward life.

14 Nonetheless, the vets hook up the turtle to an intravenous needle through which fluids will be pumped very slowly at a temperature slightly higher than the turtle's body. Beth and Howard have learned much about the condition of this turtle but they are still not sure if it is really alive or dead.

114

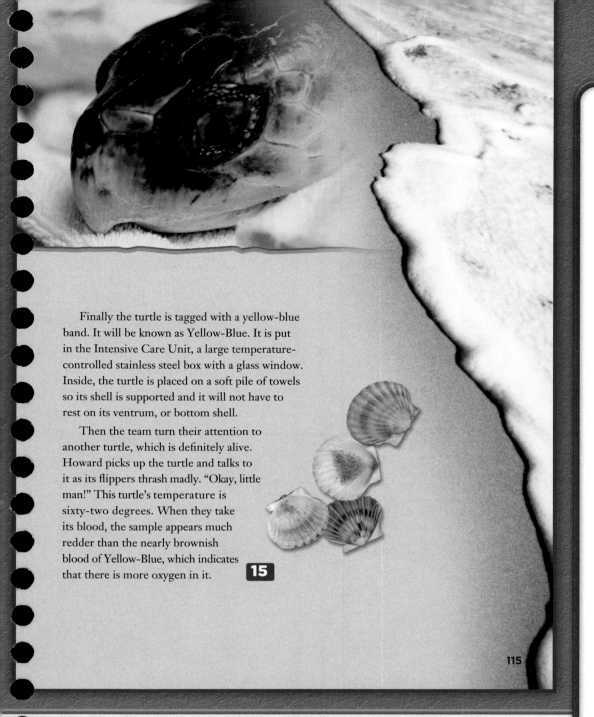

Finally the turtle is tagged with a yellow-blue band. It will be known as Yellow-Blue. It is put in the Intensive Care Unit, a large temperature-controlled stainless steel box with a glass window. Inside, the turtle is placed on a soft pile of towels so its shell is supported and it will not have to rest on its ventrum, or bottom shell.

Then the team turn their attention to another turtle, which is definitely alive. Howard picks up the turtle and talks to it as its flippers thrash madly. "Okay, little man!" This turtle's temperature is sixty-two degrees. When they take its blood, the sample appears much redder than the nearly brownish blood of Yellow-Blue, which indicates that there is more oxygen in it. **15**

115

Develop Comprehension

15 **GENRE: INFORMATIONAL NONFICTION**

This selection is mostly straightforward and informational in tone. How does the author make the vets seem more human and real? (The author puts in a bit of humor, especially in spoken words, such as "Okay, little man" and, earlier, "Why, gee whiz, I can hear the ocean.")

Vocabulary

Word Structure Clues: *Prefixes*

Explain/Model Prefixes are word parts added to the beginning of a root or base word. Prefixes change a word's meaning. When readers identify a prefix and know the meaning and pronunciation of the root or base word and the prefix, they can figure out the word's meaning. The prefix *intra-* means "within." Write *intravenous* on the board.

Think Aloud I see the root word *venous* and the prefix *intra-*. I know that *intra-* means "within," so *intravenous* probably means "within the vein."

Practice/Apply Display the words *intrastate* and *intramuscular*. Have students identify the prefix and root or base word in each and use the meaning of the prefix to tell the meaning of the word. Point out to students that they must look for a root or base word when they see *intra-*.

Vocabulary

What are some synonyms the author might have used for **speculated**? (*guessed, thought, supposed, hypothesized*)

Develop Comprehension

16 **DRAW CONCLUSIONS**

Based on what you have read so far, what conclusions can you draw about the future of the Kemp's ridley sea turtles? (Unless people continue to make cooperative efforts to rescue and treat the turtles, the turtles might experience a tremendous drop in population or possibly even become extinct.)

17 **MAIN IDEA AND DETAILS**

What is the main idea of the entire selection? What details support this main idea? (The main idea is that many people doing different tasks can cooperate to save the turtles. Supporting details are that some people search, transport, treat, and clean the turtles. Others watch for signs of life and recovery.)

Vocabulary

What does it mean to say that the turtle needs to be **sedated**? What other words or phrases could the author have used? (relaxed, put "under" or put "out," tranquilized)

But as lively as this one is, Howard gives it only a fifty-percent survival rate. There is a good chance that pneumonia could still develop. They insert an intravenous tube for rehydration. Then they tag the animal with a plain yellow band.

16   There are other turtles also being treated. One, Orange, needs to have its eyes lubricated and then be weighed and examined. The turtle is feisty and needs to be **sedated**. This is done without drugs, simply by shielding the top of its head from the ceiling lights. There is a gland inside a turtle's head that is sensitive to light, and it is speculated that when the gland is covered, it helps the turtle settle down into a relaxed, near-sleeping state.

116

Cultural Perspectives

TURTLES IN MYTH AND LEGEND

In prehistoric times, people thought a turtleshell stood for the universe. The curved top of the shell looked to them like the sky, and the flat bottom of the shell looked like the earth (which primitive people believed was flat). Turtles live for many years and move very purposefully, thus symbolizing a long, "solid" life. Because turtles carry their "homes" wherever they go, they often represent adaptability.

ACTIVITY

Turtles appear as symbols in folk art all over the world. Have students draw or paint scenes in which a turtle is used as a symbol for one of the ideas mentioned above.

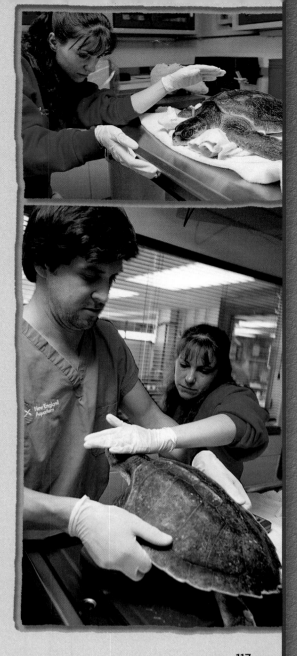

In this peaceful state, Orange begins to "swim" on the table, its flippers making the paddling motions that have since birth **propelled** it through thousands of miles of sea. Its heart rate, at thirty-six beats a minute, is good. Its respiration rate is still slow. It takes only one breath every minute. Its temperature is near seventy degrees. Orange is x-rayed for signs of pneumonia. The lungs are clear.

Whatever the outcome for these three turtles, Beth, Howard, Robert, Max, and his mother all know they are doing their part to help return the turtles to health, to help return them to the sea. **17**

117

Develop Comprehension

RETURN TO PREDICTIONS AND PURPOSES

Review students' predictions and purposes. Were they correct? How did making inferences and analyzing details help students to identify the main idea of this selection?

REVIEW READING STRATEGIES

Discuss how making inferences about the main idea and supporting details in this selection helped students clarify their understanding of the events in the selection.

PERSONAL RESPONSE

Ask students to write about an animal that they think might need help from people in order to survive.

Quick Check Can students identify the main ideas and supporting details?

During **Small Group Instruction**

If No → **Approaching Level**
Leveled Reader Lesson, p. 123P

If Yes → **On Level** Options, Instruction, pp. 123Q–123R

Beyond Level Options, Instruction, pp. 123S–123T

ELL   Access for All

Practicing Language Reread the final paragraph on page 117. Ask, *How do Max and his mother help the turtles? How do Beth and Howard help?* Point out that they help the turtles in different ways. Say, *They are doing their part to help. How can you do your part to help?* Discuss the meaning of the expression "to do your part."

Author and Illustrator

TAKE A JOURNEY WITH KATHRYN LASKY AND CHRISTOPHER G. KNIGHT

Have students read the biographies of the author and the photographer.

DISCUSS

Ask students:

- Why might Kathryn Lasky have wanted to write about the Nolans and their desire to help endangered sea turtles?

- How is Christopher G. Knight's sense of adventure communicated through his photographs?

WRITE ABOUT IT

Ask students to write about an animal they would like to protect or preserve. They should explain how they would approach this task.

Author's Purpose

To help students understand how the photographs add to the text, ask them to imagine that the text had appeared on plain white pages. Would students have been able to picture the people, places, and events as clearly? Would they have understood what Kemp's ridley turtles look like? Students should understand that the photos add visual detail to the text and help readers connect with the people and events.

LOG ON Technology

Tell students they can find out more about Kathryn Lasky and Christopher G. Knight at **www.macmillanmh.com**

Take a Journey with Kathryn Lasky and Christopher G. Knight

Kathryn Lasky has written more than 100 books in all genres. You would think she wouldn't have time for anything else, but twice she has sailed with her husband across the Atlantic Ocean in a small sailboat. Even when she was seasick, Kathryn loved watching the birds and the dolphins . . . and maybe she even saw a sea turtle!

Christopher G. Knight is Kathryn Lasky's husband. He is also a photographer and an adventurer. He has paddled a kayak from Alaska to Seattle and canoed through seven countries in Europe. Then he met Kathryn. They have two children and have done seventeen books together.

Other books by Kathryn Lasky: *The Man Who Made Time Travel* and *A Voice of Her Own*

LOG ON Find out more about Kathryn Lasky and Christopher G. Knight at **www.macmillanmh.com**

118

Author's Purpose

Kathryn Lasky's purpose here is to inform. She tells about real people doing real things and documents those acts with photographs. How do the photos add to the text?

Author's Craft

Imagery

Kathryn Lasky uses imagery to help the reader picture the action and events in her writing.

- Imagery is the use of descriptive words and phrases to create vivid pictures or images in the reader's mind. For example: "At twenty-five knots the bitter northwest wind stings Max's face like sharp needles." (p. 108)

- Does this image help you feel the cold weather on the beach? What other images might the author have used?

Have students identify passages that use imagery to convey a sense of setting or emotion. Also discuss how fiction writers use imagery to develop the plot.

Comprehension Check

Summarize

Use your Main Idea Web to help you summarize *Interrupted Journey*. State the main idea in one or two sentences.

Think and Compare

1. What are some important details that Kathryn Lasky includes to explain why the sea turtles need assistance? **Make Inferences and Analyze: Main Idea and Details**

2. Do you think the yellow-blue turtle will live? Explain why or why not. Use information from the text to support your answer. **Evaluate**

3. Max and his mother are volunteers. What kind of volunteer work would you like to do? Are volunteers **vital** to your community? Why or why not? **Synthesize**

4. What facts from *Interrupted Journey* would you choose to show if you were to give a presentation about conservation? Explain your choices. **Apply**

5. Read "Protecting the Clouded Leopard" on pages 104-105. Compare and contrast the conservation project detailed in this selection with the one in *Interrupted Journey*. How are the two projects similar? How are their methods different? **Reading/Writing Across Texts**

119

Strategies for Answering Questions

Author and Me

Model the Author and Me strategy with question 2.

The answer is not directly stated in the selection, but the author provides some of the information. You have to think about what you already know and link it to what you know from the text.

Question 2: Think Aloud At the beginning of the selection, Robert Prescott of the Bay Wildlife Sanctuary says Yellow-Blue "sure does look dead, but you never can tell." Then Max sees movement in the turtle's flippers. Yellow-Blue receives fluids to raise its body temperature and is placed in an Intensive Care Unit. Howard Crum says that with turtles, "death is a relative term." I think there is a good chance the turtle will live because of the care it is receiving.

Comprehension Check

SUMMARIZE

Have students reread and then summarize *Interrupted Journey* by paraphrasing the main ideas and key concepts, events, and supporting details. Remind students to use the Main Idea Web to help them organize their summaries.

THINK AND COMPARE

Sample answers are given.

1. **Main Idea and Details:** Kathryn Lasky mentions that the turtles have difficulty surviving in the cold weather and that while all sea turtles are endangered, Kemp's ridley turtles are the most threatened.

2. **Evaluate:** Answers will vary. Students may say that the yellow-blue turtle will live because Howard Crum says that "with turtles, death is a relative term," and because the turtle is receiving expert care. USE ON MY OWN

3. **Text to Self:** Answers will vary, but should include the idea that volunteers are important because they do work that helps their communities.

4. **Text to World:** Answers will vary. Students may include the fact that there are less than 8,000 Kemp's ridley turtles left.

FOCUS QUESTION

5. **Text to Text:** Students may write that the two projects are similar because they both seek to protect an endangered species from extinction.

Objectives
- Read accurately with correct tempo
- Rate: 117–137 WCPM

Materials
- Fluency Transparency 5
- Audio CD
- Leveled Practice Books, p. 32

ELL Access for All

Fluency Discuss the passage. Practice saying the following phrases in isolation and then in the sentences in which they occur: *whirl down, white froth whips,* and *flippers are floppy.* You may also have students read along with the recording on the Audio CD.

On Level Practice Book O, page 32

As I read, I will pay attention to tempo.

	The peregrine falcon is a raptor, a bird of prey. It has a
13	body that is designed for hunting.
19	The falcon's eyes are set forward in its head. That gives it
31	depth perception. Its vision is excellent. It can spot a bird in
43	flight from a great distance away.
49	Inside its nostrils are baffles. Scientists have **speculated**
57	that these small walls slow the air rushing into the falcon's
68	lungs as it dives. They let the falcon breathe. They also keep
80	its lungs from bursting.
84	Like all raptors, the falcon's beak is curved. It's designed
94	for tearing its prey's flesh. Unlike other raptors, the falcon
104	also has a "tooth." This special notch on its beak breaks its
116	prey's back.
118	The falcon's legs, feet, and curved talons are strong
127	weapons. They can deliver a powerful blow to prey. Then, as
138	the falcon flies away, it can grasp its prey.
147	Peregrine falcon's wings are long, narrow, and pointed.
155	They help give this bird its incredible speed in a dive. In level
168	flight its wings flap rapidly to keep it aloft. 177

Comprehension Check

1. What is the main idea of the passage? **Main Idea and Details** Peregrine falcons have bodies that are designed for hunting.
2. What natural weapons does the peregrine falcon have? **Main Idea and Details** The falcon has a curved beak to tear flesh, a special notch to break its prey's back, and strong legs, feet and talons to strike its prey.

	Words Read	−	Number of Errors	=	Words Correct Score
First Read		−		=	
Second Read		−		=	

★ **Approaching Practice Book A,** page 32

◆ **Beyond Practice Book B,** page 32

Fluency
Repeated Reading: *Tempo/Pacing*

EXPLAIN/MODEL Model reading the entire passage on **Transparency 5** and then read one sentence at a time. Increase the speed the second and third time through the sentences. Ask students to pay attention to the tempo.

 Transparency 5

On Ellis Landing Beach, snow squalls begin to whirl down. The waves are building, and as they begin to break, the white froth whips across their steep faces. So far there is no sign of a turtle.

Max is far ahead of his mother when he sees the hump in the sand being washed by the surf. He runs up to it and shouts to his mom, "Got one!" The turtle is cold. Its flippers are floppy. Its eyes are open, but the turtle is not moving at all. It might be dead, but then again, it might not.

Fluency Transparency 5 from *Interrupted Journey,* page 109

Think Aloud When I recite a sentence, I try to read at an appropriate tempo, or speed. When I increase the tempo, I check if the sentences sound more like the way I talk. If the sentences sound natural, then my tempo is probably good.

PRACTICE/APPLY Have students take turns rereading the passage with partners. Encourage partners to give each other feeback, including positive reinforcement. For additional practice, have students use **Leveled Practice Book** page 32 or the Fluency Solutions Audio CD.

Quick Check **Can students read accurately with correct tempo?**

During **Small Group Instruction**

If No → **Approaching Level** Fluency, p. 123N

If Yes → **On Level** Options, pp. 123Q–123R

Beyond Level Options, pp. 123S–123T

Comprehension

MAINTAIN SKILL
MAIN IDEA AND DETAILS

EXPLAIN

The **main idea** is the most important point an author makes about his or her topic. Nonfiction selections are often based upon a main idea, with supporting details. The details help explain or support the main idea.

PRACTICE/APPLY

Form three groups. Each group should discuss one of the following questions and present their answers to the class.

- Discuss the details the author includes in *Interrupted Journey,* and how they support the main idea of the text.

- Suppose the author's viewpoint concerning sea turtles was that too much effort was being put toward their survival. How might the main idea of the article be different?

- Discuss what other kinds of details would support the main idea, and what additional details would weaken the selection.

For comprehension practice use the Graphic Organizers on **Teacher's Resource Book** pages 40–64.

Objective

- Identify and analyze the main idea and details of the selection

Skills Trace

Main Idea and Details	
Introduce	U1: 69A–69B
Practice/ Apply	U1: 70–73; Leveled Practice Books, 16–17
Reteach/ Review	U1: 77M–77T, 105A–105B, 106–119, 123M–123T; Leveled Practice Books, 30–31
Assess	Weekly Tests; Unit 1 Tests; Benchmark Tests A, B
Maintain	U1: 73A, 119B; U2: 185A; U3: 309A

Poetry

GENRE: FREE VERSE AND SONG LYRICS

Have students read the bookmark on **Student Book** page 120. Explain that poetry

- uses lines and stanzas rather than sentences and paragraphs

- uses imagery to paint a picture in a reader's mind

- is sometimes set to music

Literary Elements: Alliteration and Imagery

EXPLAIN Remind students that poets must express a lot in a few words.

- Poets play with language, using such devices as alliteration—the repetition of beginning sounds—to add interest to their writing.

- They often use vivid verbs, adjectives, and adverbs to create imagery that helps their reader sense what they are describing.

PRACTICE/APPLY Have students create examples of alliteration and imagery. Write their ideas on the board. Remind them as they read and listen to the poems to be aware of the sounds of language.

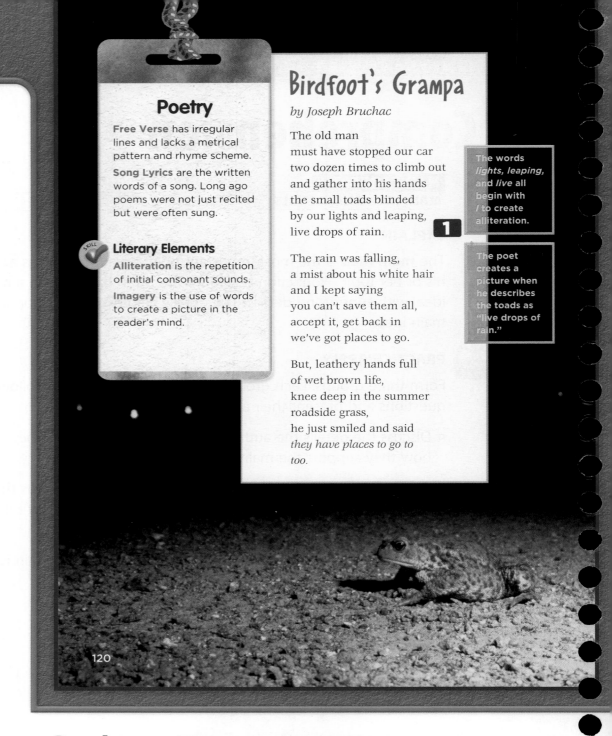

Poetry

Free Verse has irregular lines and lacks a metrical pattern and rhyme scheme.

Song Lyrics are the written words of a song. Long ago poems were not just recited but were often sung.

Literary Elements

Alliteration is the repetition of initial consonant sounds.

Imagery is the use of words to create a picture in the reader's mind.

Birdfoot's Grampa
by Joseph Bruchac

The old man
must have stopped our car
two dozen times to climb out
and gather into his hands
the small toads blinded
by our lights and leaping,
live drops of rain.

The rain was falling,
a mist about his white hair
and I kept saying
you can't save them all,
accept it, get back in
we've got places to go.

But, leathery hands full
of wet brown life,
knee deep in the summer
roadside grass,
he just smiled and said
*they have places to go to
too.*

1 The words *lights, leaping,* and *live* all begin with *l* to create alliteration.

The poet creates a picture when he describes the toads as "live drops of rain."

120

Read "Birdfoot's Grampa" and "This Land Is Your Land"

As students read, encourage them to apply what they have learned about alliteration and imagery to help their understanding of the selections. After they finish reading, have them describe, orally or in writing, how reading song lyrics differs from reading other types of literature.

This Land Is Your Land

lyrics by Woody Guthrie

This land is your land, this land is my land
From California to the New York island;
From the redwood forest to the Gulf Stream waters,
This land was made for you and me.

As I was walking that ribbon of highway,
I saw above me that endless skyway;
I saw below me that golden valley,
This land was made for you and me.

The lyricist uses imagery when he compares a highway to a ribbon.

Connect and Compare

1. Find another example of imagery in "Birdfoot's Grampa" or "This Land Is Your Land." How does the image appeal to one of your senses? **Imagery**

2. What kind of person is Birdfoot's grandfather? Give examples from the poem. **Analyze**

3. How are Max Nolan's attitudes toward wildlife in *Interrupted Journey* and the grampa's attitudes in "Birdfoot's Grampa" similar? **Reading/Writing Across Texts**

LOG ON Find out more about poetry at **www.macmillanmh.com**

121

LITERARY ELEMENTS: ALLITERATION

What consonant sound is repeated in lines 6 through 7 of "Birdfoot's Grampa"? (the /l/ sound)

2 LITERARY ELEMENTS: IMAGERY

In what way does Woody Guthrie compare the sky to the highway? (He calls it a "skyway," and suggests that both are endless.)

Connect and Compare

SUGGESTED ANSWERS

1. Answers will vary. Most of the images appeal to the sense of sight. **IMAGERY**

2. Birdfoot's grandfather is kind and compassionate; he is more concerned with saving the toads than with reaching his own destination. **ANALYZE**

FOCUS QUESTION

3. Like Max Nolan, the grandfather is interested in making sure endangered animals reach their rightful destinations. **READING/ WRITING ACROSS TEXTS**

LOG ON Technology

Students can find out more about poetry at **www.macmillanmh.com**

Connect
Language Arts

WRITING
- Personal Narrative
- **Writer's Craft:** Transitions—Cause and Effect

WORD STUDY
- Words in Context
- **Analogies:** Antonyms
- **Phonics:** Compound Words
- Vocabulary Building

SPELLING
- Compound Words

GRAMMAR
- Run-on Sentences

SMALL GROUP OPTIONS
- Differentiated Instruction, pp. 123M–123V

Writing

Transition Words

READ THE STUDENT MODEL

Read the bookmark about using transition words in sentences to signal cause and effect. Explain that words such as *because* and *as a result* help readers identify cause and effect.

Have students turn to page 104. Discuss cause and effect in the second sentence.

Then have students read the **diary entry** and discuss the callouts. Tell students they will write a diary entry and also learn to use cause-and-effect signal words.

Writer's Craft

Transition Words

Use **transition words** in sentences to show cause and effect. Words such as *because* and *as a result* can make your writing clearer.

Write a Diary Entry

"As a result" explains why it was cold in July.

I included the word *because* here to explain why we stopped during the hike.

July 15

Dear Diary,

My hike to Black Lake in the Rocky Mountains was incredible and a unique experience! I went with a group from the parks department last Saturday.

We met early on Saturday morning and took a bus to the Glacier Gorge Trail Head. Even though it's July, it was pretty cool. This was as a result of being so high up, more than 9,000 feet above sea level. We decided to climb a lot higher! In fact, we climbed 1,000 feet more.

First, we stopped at Mills Lake. It was really quiet in the middle of the mountains. I have never felt so small in my life! From Mills Lake, we kept going up. Because the climb became harder and harder, the guide let us stop every few minutes to rest. During the last part of the hike, we actually walked through snow! Black Lake was beautiful! It was well worth the trip.

122

Features of a Diary Entry

Writers keep diaries to record observations, feelings, and personal experiences on a daily basis. In addition to writing about the events of the day, they express their thoughts and feelings about what happened.

- A diary entry tells about a writer's day.
- It is written in the first person, using words such as *I*, *me*, and *my*.
- A diary entry often describes the writer's feelings.
- It is written by the writer for him or herself.

Your Turn

Write a diary entry about a personal experience with nature or a conservation group. You can describe a real experience or one you would like to have. Remember that this writing is about how you feel. Include transition words to show cause and effect. Use the Writer's Checklist to review your diary entry.

Writer's Checklist

☑ **Ideas and Content:** Did I clearly describe my experience and my reactions to it?

☑ **Organization:** Did I organize my ideas logically?

☑ **Voice:** Does my diary entry capture my feelings about the experience?

☑ **Word Choice:** Did I use **transition words** to show cause and effect?

☑ **Sentence Fluency:** Did I avoid using run-on sentences? Did I vary the length of my sentences?

☑ **Conventions:** Did I correct run-on sentences by combining them with commas and conjunctions, or by writing them as two separate sentences? Did I check my spelling?

123

Transparency 17: **Event/Feeling Chart**
Transparency 18: **Draft**
Transparency 19: **Revision**

Transparency 17

Events/Feelings Chart

Event	Feeling
We met early on Saturday morning.	I was excited to get going.
We took the bus to Glacier Gorge Trail Head.	It was pretty cool, even though it's the middle of July.
We were more than 9,000 feet above sea level.	Yikes! We were really high up!

Writing Transparency 17

PREWRITE

Read aloud the writing prompt on page 123. Emphasize that this diary entry may describe either a real experience or an experience students would like to have. Have students meet in groups to list ideas.

Display **Transparency 17**. Discuss how the writer used an Event/Feeling chart to make notes for his diary entry. Have students use a similar chart to make notes for their diary entries. Have them discuss their ideas with a classmate. See page 123B for **Ideas and Content** and **Conferencing Tips**.

DRAFT

Display **Transparency 18**. Discuss how the writer used his chart to include events and feelings in his diary entry.

Before students begin writing, present the lesson on **Transitions: Cause and Effect** on page 123A. Then have students use their charts to draft their diary entries. Remind them to include transition words.

REVISE

Display **Transparency 19**. Point out that transition words could be added to show connections among events. Discuss the other revisions. Students can revise their drafts or place them in writing portfolios to work on later.

If students choose to revise, tell them to work with a partner to use the Writer's Checklist on page 123. Have students **proofread** their writing. For **Publishing Options** see page 123A.

For lessons on **Run-on Sentences** and **Compound Words** see page 123B and **5 Day Spelling** and **5 Day Grammar** on pages 123G–123J.

Writer's Craft

Transitions: Cause and Effect

Publishing Options

Students may wish to read their diary entries aloud to the class. See Speaking and Listening tips below. Have students use their best cursive to write their entries. (See **Teacher's Resource Book** pages 168–172 for cursive models and practice.) Suggest that students publish their diary entries online as blogs.

Speaking and Listening

SPEAKING STRATEGIES

- Practice your oral presentation beforehand.
- Speak loudly and clearly.
- Look at the audience.

LISTENING STRATEGIES

- Look at the speaker.
- Sit quietly and listen carefully.
- After the speaker has finished, ask questions and ask for restatement or explanations to clarify meaning.

4- and 6-Point Scoring Rubrics

Use the rubrics on pages 127G–127H to score published writing.

Writing Process

For a complete lesson, see Unit Writing pages 127A–127H.

EXPLAIN/MODEL

Writers use transition words to help readers understand relationships among ideas and events. Explain that the words *because, as a result, since,* and *so* are often used to signal causes or effects. Good writers clearly show cause-and-effect relationships by including transition words while drafting their writing or by inserting them later during revision. Display **Transparency 20.**

Think Aloud I wondered why the writer was wearing a fleece jacket on a summer morning. Then I saw the word *because.* This word told me the writer was going to explain why he or she needed a fleece jacket. The fog was the reason, or cause.

Transparency 20

> August 10
>
> Dear Diary,
>
> Today started out like almost every day this summer. I headed down to the bay as soon as I woke up. As I went out the door, I pulled on my fleece jacket because the fog never lifts before noon. I ran down the short path through the brambles to the water.
>
> I scanned the shoreline of the bay. It was empty. It was high tide, so no one was raking clams. It was just me, the water, and the sky. A few gulls dipped toward me to say good morning.
>
> Then I saw it lying by the water's edge. I can't believe I missed it at first. Its white-grey feathers stood out against the black-brown seaweed. It was huge. I knew it was an osprey. I could see that it was injured. I didn't know how badly. I didn't get any closer.

Writing Transparency 20

PRACTICE/APPLY

With students' help, identify details in the diary entry. Circle the details on the transparency. Guide students in identifying a transition word that signals cause or effect in the second paragraph. Then have student pairs suggest where two cause-and-effect transition words might be added in the third paragraph. Also challenge student pairs to find examples of such transition words in other writing they have read.

As students write their diary entries, remind them to use cause-and-effect transition words to show relationships among ideas and events.

Writer's Toolbox

Writing Trait: Ideas and Content

Explain/Model Writers sometimes use suspense to heighten readers' interest. Suspense is a feeling of excitement about how a story will end. To create suspense, writers provide information little by little. Have students look at the diary entry on **Transparency 20** and discuss how the writer could create suspense.

Practice/Apply As students draft their diary entries, suggest that they add suspense by not revealing all the information about their topic at once. Have students review and critique the use of suspense in each other's diary entries.

Conferencing Tips

Peer Conferencing Have students read each other's Event/Feeling charts. Encourage them to share ideas about which events and feelings listed are especially interesting and which are not. Suggest that students consider these questions as they review each other's charts:

• Have I ever done this?

• Have I ever felt this?

• Would I write about this event or feeling in a diary? Why or why not?

Run-on Sentences

Explain/Model Point out that a run-on sentence occurs when one independent clause is allowed to "run on," or continue, into the next. The clauses may be separated by only a comma or have no punctuation between them. Give students this example of a run-on sentence: *We met on Saturday morning we took a bus to the Glacier Gorge Trail Head*. Discuss two ways of correcting this sentence.

Practice/Apply Remind students to check their diary entries and other writing for run-on sentences and insert punctuation and coordinating conjunctions as needed. For a complete lesson on run-on sentences, see pages 123I–123J.

Mechanics Explain that in compound sentences a comma is used before the coordinating conjunction to separate the independent clauses. Have students check for commas with compound sentences as they proofread.

Compound Words

Explain that a compound word is made up of two words. Point out that compound words are spelled in one of three ways. Open compounds are spelled as two separate words: *sea turtle*. Closed compounds are spelled as one word: *zookeeper*. Hyphenated compounds include a hyphen: *brother-in-law*. Remind students to pay attention to these three spelling patterns when they use compound words. Students can use a print or online dictionary to check the spelling of compound words in their drafts. For a complete lesson on compound words, see pages 123G–123H.

Objective
- Apply knowledge of word meanings and context clues

Materials
- Vocabulary Transparency 9
- Vocabulary Strategy Transparency 10
- Leveled Practice Books, p. 34

Vocabulary

speculated (p. 114) thought or wondered about a subject

conserve (p. 113) to use carefully; to keep in a safe or sound state

analyzing (p. 113) studying or finding out the nature and relationship of parts of something

vital (p. 109) concerned with or necessary for the continuation of life

propelled (p. 117) pushed or driven usually forward or onward

sedated (p. 116) made quiet in manner or conduct

dehydrated (p. 113) lost water or body fluids

embedded (p. 114) enclosed in or as if in a surrounding mass

ELL   Access for All

Generate Sentences As you review vocabulary, help students make statements using the vocabulary words. Restate what they say in complete sentences and write the sentences on the board.

Review
Vocabulary

Words in Context

EXPLAIN/MODEL

Review the meanings of the vocabulary words. Display **Transparency 9.** Model how to use word meanings and context clues to fill in the missing words in the first sentence.

Think Aloud In the first sentence, I learn that a turtle's heartbeat slows down and that this has to do with oxygen needed for the brain. Since *conserve* means *to use carefully,* I think this is the missing word.

Transparency 9

Vocabulary In Context

speculated conserve analyzing vital propelled

A turtle's heartbeat slows down in order to (1) <u>conserve</u> oxygen which is needed to keep the brain working.

Your brain is considered a (2) <u>vital</u> organ because it is needed for life to continue.

Scientists can learn how a turtle's organs are working by (3) <u>analyzing</u> its blood.

People who have studied turtles have often (4) <u>speculated</u> about the flipper motions of a turtle's tail.

The turtle's flippers made paddling motions that (5) <u>propelled</u> it through miles of sea.

Vocabulary Transparency 9

PRACTICE/APPLY

Have students use context clues to find the missing words for sentences 2–5. Ask students to work with a partner to check their answers and to explain the context clues they used to find the missing words. Then have students create sentences for *sedated, dehydrated,* and *embedded.* Remind them to include context clues.

Complete the Idea Ask a student to set up a completion frame by saying something such as, *The patient was* dehydrated *so he* _____; *We* speculated *about the* _____. *The donated blood was* vital *for* _____. Have a volunteer finish each sentence and then set up the next one.

STRATEGY
USE ANALOGIES: ANTONYMS

EXPLAIN/MODEL

Tell students that identifying the relationship between two words is one way to find the meaning of a word. An analogy is a comparison of two sets of words that are related in the same way.

Understanding analogies that show opposite relationships of words is a strategy that is helpful in finding a word's meaning. Antonyms are words that have the opposite or nearly opposite meanings.

Help students identify the relationship between *conserve* and *waste*. Model how to figure out that *waste* is an antonym of *conserve*. Work with students to help them think of an antonym for *vital*.

Transparency 10

Analogies

1. Conserve : waste :: vital : _____ (unimportant).

2. Swift : slow :: finish : _____ (start, begin).

3. Find : lose :: build : _____ (demolish).

4. Ascend : descend :: forward : _____ (backward).

5. Careful : careless : thoughtful : _____ (thoughtless).

Vocabulary Strategy Transparency 10

PRACTICE

Have students work with a partner to complete analogies 2–5. Ask students to check their work by making sure that the analogies show relationships that are opposites.

Quick Check

Can students identify the correct vocabulary words?
Can students complete the analogies?

During **Small Group Instruction**

If No → **Approaching Level** Vocabulary, pp. 123N–123O

If Yes → **On Level** Options, pp. 123Q–123R

Beyond Level Options, pp. 123S–123T

ELL
Access for All

Analogies Explain the meanings of the words used in the analogies. Then help students "read" the analogies aloud: Conserve *is the opposite of* waste *and* vital *is the opposite of* unimportant. Have students work in small groups to complete the analogies.

On Level Practice Book O, page 34

Using analogies requires you to understand how words relate to each other.

Analogies are written like this: up : down :: conserve : waste.

They are read like this: "Up *is to* down *as* conserve *is to* waste."

One relationship that is often used is opposites, or **antonyms**, as in the example given above. Choose the best word to complete the analogy.

A. Circle the letter of the correct answer.

1. open : closed :: wild : _____
   a. savage   b. quiet   c. tame   d. barbaric

2. advance : retreat :: comedy : _____
   a. tragedy   b. music   c. jokes   d. laughter

3. agree : disagree :: feast : _____
   a. Thanksgiving   b. famine   c. festival   d. hunger

4. remain : leave :: allow : _____
   a. permit   b. decide   c. request   d. prohibit

5. defeat : victory :: lazy : _____
   a. weary   b. ambitious   c. aggressive   d. decent

B. Write three analogies, using antonyms, of your own. Possible responses provided.

6. float : sink :: clean : dirty

7. fresh : stale :: new : old

8. pull : push :: shove : grab

 Approaching Practice Book A, page 34

 **Beyond Practice Book B,** page 34

Objective

- Understand and pronounce compound words

Materials

- Leveled Practice Books, p. 35
- Teacher's Resource Book, p. 9

ELL **Access for All**

Compound Words Check that students understand the meanings of the two words that make up the compound words as well as the compound words themselves. Before students play the game, allow them to brainstorm compound words for each base word (*ball, light, book,* etc.) in groups.

On Level Practice Book O, page 35

Compound words are words that are made of up two or more words.

apple + sauce = applesauce

When you find compound words, you can use the single words that make them up to help you pronounce the larger word. For example, look at the word *homework*. First, you need to determine that the word is made up of the words *home* and *work*. Then you can apply what you know about pronunciation to sound out the word. You know the VCe uses a silent *e* to make a long *o* sound in *home*. And you know that a vowel followed by an *r* has a specific *r*-controlled sound.

Read each compound word. Put a slash through the word to divide it into single words. Then write a sentence using the word.

1. every/body Everybody I know loves ice cream.
2. down/pour Jessica didn't have an umbrella, so the downpour soaked her.
3. flash/bulb The flashbulb was so bright, Heather's eyes were closed in the photograph.
4. some/thing Nya knew something exciting was about to happen.
5. week/end Pilar's mom promised to take the family camping over the weekend.
6. mountain/side Drew took the ski lift up the mountainside.
7. beach/front Allison jogs along the beachfront during the summer.
8. wild/life Stacy removed all the trash so that no wildlife could scatter it.

 Approaching Practice Book A, page 35

 Beyond Practice Book B, page 35

Phonics
Compound Words

EXPLAIN/MODEL Tell students that a compound word is made up of two words. Understanding the meaning of the two smaller words often provides hints at the meaning and pronunciation of the compound word. Write *flashbulb*.

Think Aloud When I see the word *flashbulb*, I see the two words *flash* and *bulb* together. A flash is a sudden burst of light. A bulb is a glass container that holds the filament for a light. *Flashbulb* probably means "a lightbulb that flashes" and is probably used when taking pictures with a camera.

PRACTICE/APPLY Ask a volunteer to explain the meaning of *applesauce*. (a sauce made of apples) Then write the following words and ask volunteers to explain how the word parts hint at the meaning of each word: *windshield, heartbeat, seaweed*.

Decode Multisyllabic Words To read long words, students can use their knowledge of phonics patterns and word parts—prefixes, suffixes, and endings—that are added to root words. They can sound out and blend together the word parts and use context to make sure they are right. Display these words: *teenager, old-fashioned, self-respect, after-school*. Have students decode the word *teenager*. Help them as necessary. Have them decode the remaining words. For more practice, see the decodable passages on page 9 of the **Teacher's Resource Book**.

 Access for All

 Cooperative Learning

Compound Word Baseball Set up a "baseball diamond." Divide the class into two teams and "pitch" one part of a compound word to the batter on the first team. If the batter can think of another word to create a compound word, he or she may go to first base. If not, the batter is "out." After three outs the second team is up to bat. The team with the most points after the first round wins. Use the following words: *ball* (baseball, basketball, ballpark) *light* (skylight, stoplight, headlight), *book* (notebook, bookshelf, bookmark), *walk* (boardwalk, walkway, sleepwalk), *room* (bedroom, cloakroom, classroom), *father* (grandfather, father-in-law, stepfather), *drum* (eardrum, drumstick, drumbeat).

Quick Check **Can students decode compound words?**

During **Small Group Instruction**

If No → **Approaching Level** Phonics, p. 123M

If Yes → **On Level** Options, pp. 123Q–123R

Beyond Level Options, pp. 123S–123T

Vocabulary Building

Oral Language

Expand Vocabulary Discuss with students what they might do to help protect wildlife. Challenge them to use words that would be common in such a discussion. Some examples might be: *environment, habitat, conservation,* and *endangered.* List these words on the board and ask students to look up their definitions in a dictionary.

Vocabulary Building

Vocabulary Sentences Write the vocabulary words on the board. Ask the class to define each word. Then challenge students to think of a way to use each word in a sentence that is not about conservation.

 Apply Vocabulary

Write a News Report Tell students that they will be reporters for a day. Have students read through *Interrupted Journey* taking notes as they go along. Ask students to use vocabulary words and their notes to write a news report that could be broadcast on television.

Vocabulary Review

Picture Clues Divide the class into two teams. Place the Vocabulary Cards for Weeks 1, 2, and 4 face down near the board. Have a member of the first team select the first Vocabulary Card. He or she has thirty seconds to create a drawing that hints at the right word. If the team guesses the word, it earns a point; if not, the other team may try. The teams alternate drawing, regardless of the outcome. The game is over when all Vocabulary Cards have been used. The team with the most points wins.

Technology

 Vocabulary PuzzleMaker CD–ROM

LOG ON **For additional vocabulary and spelling games go to** www.macmillanmh.com

Interrupted Journey **123F**

Compound Words

Spelling Words

heartbeat	nearsighted	self-respect
northwest	brother-in-law	flashbulb
seaweed	old-fashioned	after-school
eyelid	full-time	teenager
seashell	windshield	fingernail
twenty-five	watermelon	question mark
wading pool	science fiction	

Review fierce, urge, bargain

Challenge barbed wire, fire escape

Dictation Sentences

1. Her **heartbeat** is fast.
2. It rains a lot in the **northwest.**
3. Some turtles eat **seaweed.**
4. An **eyelid** is a fold of skin.
5. I saw a pink **seashell.**
6. Ms. Woo is **twenty-five** years old.
7. Kids splash in the **wading pool.**
8. The nearsighted boy has glasses.
9. My brother-in-law is a chef.
10. My grandmother is old-fashioned.
11. Janis works a full-time job.
12. The windshield is cracked.
13. A watermelon has many seeds.
14. Job loves to read science fiction.
15. He lost self-respect by cheating.
16. I need a flashbulb for my camera.
17. My brother is in an after-school program.
18. A teenager is still growing.
19. Lyn painted one fingernail blue.
20. Put a question mark at the end.

Review/Challenge Words
1. The wind outside is fierce.
2. Paolo had an urge to travel.
3. I like to shop at the bargain table.
4. Be careful of the barbed wire!
5. The family ran down the fire escape.

Note: Words in **bold** type are from *Interrupted Journey.*

Display the Spelling Words throughout the week.

Day 1 Pretest

ASSESS PRIOR KNOWLEDGE

Use the dictation sentences. Say the underlined word. Read the sentence and repeat the word. Have students write the words on **Spelling Practice Book** page 25, and then correct their own papers. For a modified list, use the first 17 Spelling Words and the Review Words. For a more challenging list, use Spelling Words 3–20 and the Challenge Words.

Have students cut apart the Spelling Words Cards BLM on **Teacher's Resource Book** page 70. Have them use the cards throughout the week to do word sorts.

For **Leveled Word Lists,** go to **www.macmillanmh.com**

Day 2 Word Sorts

TEACHER AND STUDENT SORTS

- Write the words *wading pool, heartbeat,* and *nearsighted* on the board. Point out the patterns for spelling compound words: as two separate words (open), as one word (closed), or with a hyphen.

- Demonstrate sorting compound words. Draw a card, say the word, and show it to students. Help students identify the spelling pattern. For example, *fingernail* has the same closed-compound word pattern as *heartbeat.* Write *fingernail* in the word sort on the board.

- Give each student a chance to draw a card, say the word, and tell where it belongs in the sort.

- Have students sort their word cards, using the same key words. Discuss the completed word sorts.

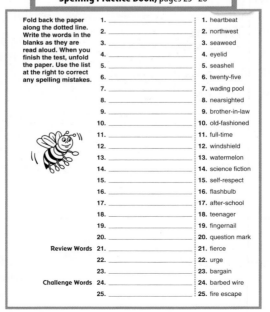

Spelling Practice Book, pages 25–26

Fold back the paper along the dotted line. Write the words in the blanks as they are read aloud. When you finish the test, unfold the paper. Use the list at the right to correct any spelling mistakes.

1. _____	1. heartbeat
2. _____	2. northwest
3. _____	3. seaweed
4. _____	4. eyelid
5. _____	5. seashell
6. _____	6. twenty-five
7. _____	7. wading pool
8. _____	8. nearsighted
9. _____	9. brother-in-law
10. _____	10. old-fashioned
11. _____	11. full-time
12. _____	12. windshield
13. _____	13. watermelon
14. _____	14. science fiction
15. _____	15. self-respect
16. _____	16. flashbulb
17. _____	17. after-school
18. _____	18. teenager
19. _____	19. fingernail
20. _____	20. question mark
Review Words 21. _____	21. fierce
22. _____	22. urge
23. _____	23. bargain
Challenge Words 24. _____	24. barbed wire
25. _____	25. fire escape

Spelling Practice Book, page 27

heartbeat	seashell	brother-in-law	watermelon	after-school
northwest	twenty-five	old-fashioned	science fiction	teenager
seaweed	wading pool	full-time	self-respect	fingernail
eyelid	nearsighted	windshield	flashbulb	question mark

Sort each spelling word according to whether it is written as one word, as two words, or with a hyphen. Write each word on the appropriate line below.

One Word:
1. heartbeat
2. northwest
3. seaweed
4. eyelid
5. seashell
6. nearsighted
7. windshield
8. watermelon
9. flashbulb
10. teenager
11. fingernail

Two Words:
12. wading pool
13. science fiction
14. question mark

Hyphenated:
15. twenty-five
16. brother-in-law
17. old-fashioned
18. full-time
19. self-respect
20. after-school

Students' writing should include a compound word in each sentence.
Write two sentences using as many compound words as you can in each sentence.

21. In a heartbeat my nearsighted brother-in-law, who is a teenager, found a watermelon by the light of a flashbulb.
22. It was good for my self-respect to accept an after-school job that turned out to be a full-time position.

Day 3 — Word Meanings

DEFINITIONS

- Read aloud the following groups of words. Ask students to copy the words in their word study notebook, adding a Spelling Word to each group.

1. eyelash, eyebrow, _____
   (eyelid)

2. banana, orange, _____
   (watermelon)

3. tires, hood, _____
   (windshield)

4. infant, adult, _____
   (teenager)

5. period, comma, _____
   (question mark)

- Invite students to select 10 words to illustrate. Have them draw and label their pictures in their word study notebook.

Day 4 — Review and Proofread

SPIRAL REVIEW

Review *r*-controlled vowels. Write *fierce, urge,* and *bargain* on the board. Have students identify the *r*-controlled vowels.

PROOFREAD AND WRITE

Write a paragraph on the board. Include misspelled words and have students proofread to find them. Ask students to circle six misspelled words and write the correct spellings.

WORD SORT

To prepare students for the Posttest on Friday, have them sort this week's words again. Remind students of the different ways to spell compound words.

Day 5 — Assess and Reteach

POSTTEST

Use the Dictation Sentences on page 123G for the Posttest.

If students have trouble with any words in the lesson, have them create personal lists of troublesome words in their word study notebook.

WORD STUDY NOTEBOOK

Challenge students to search for other compound words in their reading for the week and write them in a word study notebook under the heading "Compound Words."

Spelling Practice Book, page 28

heartbeat	seashell	brother-in-law	watermelon	after-school
northwest	twenty-five	old-fashioned	science fiction	teenager
seaweed	wading pool	full-time	self-respect	fingernail
eyelid	nearsighted	windshield	flashbulb	question mark

Finish the Set

Write the spelling word that belongs in each group.

1. pupil, lashes, _____ eyelid
2. toddler, adult, _____ teenager
3. period, comma, _____ question mark
4. knuckle, palm, _____ fingernail
5. three, fourteen, _____ twenty-five
6. antique, classical, _____ old-fashioned
7. apple, peach, _____ watermelon
8. south, east, _____ northwest
9. sister, nephew, _____ brother-in-law
10. pulse, breathing, _____ heartbeat

Write About It

Use one of the sets of words above in a short piece of writing about a topic of your choice.

Students' writing should reflect a topic of their choice and include one of the sets of words above.

Spelling Practice Book, page 29

There are five misspelled spelling words in this story. Circle the misspelled words. Write the words correctly on the lines below.

Manuel lost his glasses at his (fulltime) job. Manuel is (near-sited) and so he had great difficulty driving home. He was headed home when suddenly he felt a big bump under his car, and something red splattered against the (winsheeld). He thought he had hit an animal, so his (hartbeat) began to race. He pulled over to the side of the road to see what he had hit. Squinting to get a better look, Manuel let out a chuckle. In the middle of the road was a crushed (water-melon).

1. full-time
2. nearsighted
3. windshield
4. heartbeat
5. watermelon

Writing Activity

If you were a conservationist, what kind of adventures might you have? Write about a day in the life of a conservationist. Use five spelling words in your writing.

Students' writing should reflect the topic of their choice and include five spelling words.

Spelling Practice Book, page 30

Look at the words in each set below. One word in each set is spelled correctly. Use a pencil to fill in the circle next to the correct word. Before you begin, look at the sample set of words. Sample A has been done for you. Do Sample B by yourself. When you are sure you know what to do, you may go on with the rest of the page.

Sample A:
- (A) firsthand
- (B) fursthend
- (C) foorsthand
- (D) fuhrsthand

Sample B:
- (E) bloobery
- (F) blooberry
- (G) blueberry
- (H) bluberry

1.
- (A) heart beat
- (B) heartbeat
- (C) heart-beat
- (D) heartbeet

2.
- (E) north west
- (F) north-west
- (G) northwest
- (H) noorthwest

3.
- (A) seaweed
- (B) sea weed
- (C) sea-weed
- (D) seewead

4.
- (E) eye lid
- (F) eye-lid
- (G) ayelid
- (H) eyelid

5.
- (A) seeshel
- (B) sea-shell
- (C) seashell
- (D) sea shell

6.
- (E) twenty-five
- (F) twenty five
- (G) twentyfive
- (H) tuentee-five

7.
- (A) wading pool
- (B) wading-pool
- (C) wadingpule
- (D) wadingpool

8.
- (E) near sited
- (F) nearsited
- (G) nearsighted
- (H) near sighted

9.
- (A) brother in law
- (B) brotherinlaw
- (C) brother in-law
- (D) brother-in-law

10.
- (E) old fashioned
- (F) old-fashioned
- (G) old-fashioned
- (H) oldfashioned

11.
- (A) full time
- (B) fulltime
- (C) fultime
- (D) full-time

12.
- (E) windshield
- (F) wind shield
- (G) wind sheeld
- (H) wind-shield

13.
- (A) water melon
- (B) water-melon
- (C) watermelon
- (D) wattermellon

14.
- (E) sciencefiction
- (F) science-fiction
- (G) science fiction
- (H) scisense fiction

15.
- (A) self-respect
- (B) selfrespect
- (C) self respect
- (D) self respact

16.
- (E) flash bulb
- (F) flash-bolb
- (G) flashbulb
- (H) flash-bulb

17.
- (A) afterschool
- (B) after-school
- (C) after skool
- (D) after school

18.
- (E) teen-ager
- (F) teen ager
- (G) tenager
- (H) teenager

19.
- (A) finger nail
- (B) finger-nail
- (C) finger nale
- (D) fingernail

20.
- (E) questionmark
- (F) question mark
- (G) queschunmark
- (H) question-mark

5 Day Grammar

Run-on Sentences

Daily Language Activities

Use these activities to introduce each day's lesson. Write the day's activities on the board or use **Transparency 5.**

DAY 1
when the days shorten the water of the ocean grows colder (1. When; 2. shorten,; 3. colder.)

DAY 2
turtles that dwel in the ocean can die in the cold water but they might be rescued. (1. Turtles; 2. dwell; 3. water)

DAY 3
dr. Crum treated the turtle we found he clensed its shell. (1. Dr.; 2. found. or found;; 3. cleansed)

DAY 4
Mr. Bond revued the book *Maniac Magee,* it is my favorite book. (1. reviewed; 2. Magee.; 3. It)

DAY 5
I rode my bicycle to the warf I chained it to a bike rack, before I went fishing. (1. wharf,; 2. and; 3. rack before)

ELL **Access for All**

Create Sentences Have a student tell you what he or she did over the weekend. Write what he/she says in run on sentences on the board. Have the class help you circle the subjects and verbs and break up the text into individual sentences.

Day 1 — Introduce the Concept

INTRODUCE RUN-ON SENTENCES

Present the following:

- A run-on sentence results from two main clauses separated by only a comma without a coordinating conjunction.

- There are three main kinds of run-on sentences:
  - two main clauses separated by only a comma
  - two main clauses with no punctuation between them
  - two main clauses with no comma before the coordinating conjunction.

Example:

The turtle I saw on the beach was moving slowly and it was in distress.

 See Grammar Transparency 21 for modeling and guided practice.

Grammar Practice Book, page 25

- A **run-on sentence** joins together two or more sentences that should be written separately.
- You can correct a run-on sentence by separating two complete ideas into two sentences.

Put an X in front of each run-on sentence. Then correct the sentences in the space provided.

X **1.** The kiwi bird is a strange-looking animal it is part of a group of endangered species.
The kiwi bird is a strange-looking animal. It is part of a group of endangered species.

___ **2.** These animals have died or been killed in such large numbers that there are very few left.

X **3.** The kiwi's body is covered with fluffy feathers unlike other birds, the kiwi has no tail.
The kiwi's body is covered with fluffy feathers. Unlike other birds, the kiwi has no tail.

X **4.** Kiwis are the size of a chicken their eggs are as large as ostriches' eggs!
Kiwis are the size of a chicken. Their eggs are as large as ostriches' eggs!

___ **5.** The kiwi's "cousin," the dodo bird, is already extinct.

X **6.** There are no dodos left anywhere in the world no other dodos will ever be born.
There are no dodos left anywhere in the world. No other dodos will ever be born.

Day 2 — Teach the Concept

REVIEW RUN-ON SENTENCES

Review that a run-on sentence occurs when one main clause is allowed to "run on" into the next. Ask what might cause students to make errors in their writing.

INTRODUCE COMMA SPLICES

Explain to students:

- The use of a comma in a run-on sentence that has two main clauses is called a **comma splice** or **comma fault.**

Example:

My sister went to the beach, she rode her bicycle there.

My sister went to the beach. She rode her bicycle there.

 See Grammar Transparency 22 for modeling and guided practice.

Grammar Practice Book O, page 26

- A **run-on sentence** may be rewritten as a compound or complex sentence.

Read these sentences. If the sentence is correct, write C on the line next to it. If it is a run-on sentence, write R. Rewrite each run-on sentence.

C **1.** The platypus has feet like a duck's.

R **2.** Many scientists have studied the platypus dark brown fur covers its body.
Many scientists have studied the platypus. Dark brown fur covers its body.

C **3.** Platypuses live on land, although these odd animals also swim very well.

R **4.** The female platypus lays eggs the mother sits on the eggs like a bird.
The female platypus lays eggs; the mother sits on the eggs like a bird.

R **5.** The platypus has survived for millions of years many scientists call it a living fossil.
The platypus has survived for millions of years, and many scientists call it a living fossil.

R **6.** Unlike ducks platypuses have bills that are soft and feel for food underwater.
Unlike ducks, platypuses have bills that are soft. They can feel for food underwater.

R **7.** Australia is the home of the platypus it prefers fresh water to the salt water that surrounds the island. **Australia is the home of the platypus, and it prefers fresh water to the salt water that surrounds the island.**

Day 3 Review and Practice

REVIEW COMMA SPLICE

Review the definition of a comma splice. Show students how to correct this type of error.

MECHANICS & USAGE: CORRECTING FRAGMENTS AND RUN-ON SENTENCES

- A run-on sentence can be corrected by making two sentences out of the run-on.

- It can be corrected by making it a compound sentence connected by a comma and a coordinating conjunction.

- It can be corrected by inserting a semicolon and possibly a conjunction.

 See Grammar Transparency 23 for modeling and guided practice.

Grammar Practice Book, page 27

- A **sentence fragment** does not express a complete thought. You can sometimes correct a sentence fragment by adding a subject or predicate.
- Use a comma before the conjunction in a compound sentence. If there is no conjunction, use a semicolon.
- Use a comma after a dependent clause at the beginning of a sentence.

Rewrite each run-on sentence or sentence fragment using proper capitalization, commas, and end punctuation. Possible answers are given.

1. scientists study wildlife in order to protect it the study of the cheetah is an example **Scientists study wildlife in order to protect it; the study of the cheetah is an example.**

2. is found mainly in northern Africa
The cheetah is found mainly in northern Africa.

3. its feet have hard pads with sharp edges these special pads help the cheetah to grip the ground
Its feet have hard pads with sharp edges, and these special pads help the cheetah to grip the ground.

4. the cheetah has been called a natural running machine it is able to reach a speed of 71 miles per hour
The cheetah has been called a natural running machine; it is able to reach a speed of 71 miles per hour.

5. it may be the fastest animal on Earth we must protect this amazing cat
It may be the fastest animal on Earth. We must protect this amazing cat.

6. the cheetah is an endangered species it is even extinct in India and northern Africa
The cheetah is an endangered species, and it is even extinct in India and northern Africa.

Day 4 Review and Proofread

REVIEW RUN-ON SENTENCES

Ask students to explain the ways that run-on sentences are formed. Then, ask them to provide possible ways to fix each kind of run-on sentence.

PROOFREAD

Have students correct each of the following run-on sentences.

1. I swam in the ocean for hours, I came home and slept like a baby. (hours. or hours;)

2. I don't know what kind of bicycle to get there are so many different choices. (get. There)

3. Ursula began to write a story about an alien and then she changed the main character to a human being. (alien; then)

 See Grammar Transparency 24 for modeling and guided practice.

Grammar Practice Book, page 28

- A **sentence fragment** does not express a complete thought. You can sometimes correct a sentence fragment by adding a subject or predicate.
- A **run-on sentence** joins together two or more sentences that should be written separately.
- You can correct run-on sentences in three different ways:
  1. Separate two complete ideas in a run-on sentence into two sentences.
  2. Rewrite the run-on sentence as a compound sentence.
  3. Rewrite the run-on sentence as a complex sentence.

Correct any sentence fragments or run-on sentences in the diary entry below. Rewrite the passage with correct punctuation and capitalization.

today I joined a group of students on a bird-watching walk i wanted to see a snail kite because I read that this bird is in trouble the snail kite eats only one thing it eats the meat of the apple snail when builders drain swampland to put up buildings, the apple snails die out. then the snail kites have nothing to eat we must put a stop to putting buildings where endangered animals live

Today I joined a group of students on a bird-watching walk. I wanted to see a snail kite because I read that this bird is in trouble. The snail kite eats only one thing; it eats the meat of the apple snail. When builders drain swampland to put up buildings, the apple snails die out, and then the snail kites have nothing to eat! We must put a stop to putting buildings where endangered animals live.

Day 5 Assess and Reteach

ASSESS

Use the Daily Language Activity and page 29 of the **Grammar Practice Book** for assessment.

RETEACH

Divide students into four groups. Have the first group write a run-on sentence on the board. Then, allow each of the three remaining groups an opportunity to correct the sentence. Continue the exercise with the next group constructing a run-on sentence and the remaining groups correcting the sentence. If time permits, have groups complete the same activity only with sentence fragments.

Use page 30 of the Grammar Practice Book for additional reteaching.

 See Grammar Transparency 25 for modeling and guided practice.

Grammar Practice Book, pages 29–30

Rewrite each run-on sentence, adding the punctuation and conjunctions shown in parentheses.

1. The Florida manatee has been one of the most protected animals on earth it may now be in danger. (Add a comma and the conjunction *but*.)
The Florida manatee has been one of the most protected animals on Earth, but it may now be in danger.

2. The marine mammal is listed as endangered it is protected by the federal Marine Mammal Act. (Add a comma and the conjunction *and*.)
The marine mammal is listed as endangered, and it is protected by the federal Marine Mammal Act.

3. Scientists with the Florida Fish and Wildlife Commission may reevaluate the protected status of the manatee the commission plans to act soon. (Add a semicolon.)
Scientists with the Florida Fish and Wildlife Commission may reevaluate the protected status of the manatee; the commission plans to act soon.

4. Recreational boaters in Florida believe the manatee population has increased enough environmentalists disagree. (Add a semicolon, a comma and the conjunction *however*.)
Recreational boaters in Florida believe the manatee population has increased enough; however, environmentalists disagree.

5. Manatee lovers admit that the populations have increased in some areas populations in other areas are low. (Add a comma and the conjunction *but*.)
Manatee lovers admit that the populations have increased in some areas, but populations in other areas are low.

End-of-Week Assessments

Administer the Test

 Weekly Reading Assessment,
Passages and questions, pages 53–60

ASSESSED SKILLS

- Main Idea and Details
- Vocabulary Words
- Analogy: Antonyms
- Compound Words
- Run-on Sentences

 Progress Reporter Macmillan/McGraw-Hill    **Assessment Tool**

Administer the **Weekly Assessment** online or on CD-ROM.

Weekly Assessment, 53–60

 ## Fluency

Assess fluency for one group of students per week. Use the Oral Fluency Record Sheet to track the number of words read correctly. Fluency goal for all students:
117–137 words correct per minute (WCPM).

Approaching Level	Weeks 1, 3, 5
On Level	Weeks 2, 4
Beyond Level	Week 6

Fluency Assessment

 ## Alternative Assessments

- **Leveled Weekly Assessment** for Approaching Level, pages 61–68
- **ELL Assessment,** pages 48–49

ELL Practice and Assessment, 48–49

Diagnose	IF...	Prescribe — THEN...
VOCABULARY WORDS **VOCABULARY STRATEGY** Analogy: Antonyms Items 1, 2, 3, 4	0–2 items correct . . .	Reteach skills using the **Additional Lessons** page T8 **LOG ON** Reteach skills: Go to www.macmillanmh.com **CD ROM** Vocabulary PuzzleMaker Evaluate for Intervention.
COMPREHENSION **Skill:** Main Idea and Details Items 5, 6, 7, 8	0–2 items correct . . .	Reteach skills using the **Additional Lessons** page T2 Evaluate for Intervention.
GRAMMAR Run-on Sentences Items 9, 10, 11	0–1 items correct . . .	Reteach skills: **Grammar Practice Book** page 30
SPELLING Compound Words Items 12, 13, 14	0–1 items correct . . .	**LOG ON** Reteach skills: Go to www.macmillanmh.com
FLUENCY	109–116 WCPM	**AUDIO CD** Fluency Solutions
	0–108 WCPM	Evaluate for Intervention.

Skills Focus — Phonics

Objective Decode compound words in both familiar and unfamiliar text
Materials • **Student Book** "Protecting the Clouded Leopard"

COMPOUND WORDS

Model/Guided Practice

- Write the word *bookend* on the board. Draw a line between the words *book* and *end*. Say: *When I look at the word* bookend, *I see two words:* book *and* end. *A word made up of two or more words is a compound word. I can use the two smaller words to figure out its meaning. I know what a* book *is. An* end *is a place where something starts or stops. I think a* bookend *is something you put where a row of books starts or stops.*

- *Now you try it. Look at the compound word* lighthouse. *Say the word and divide it into two smaller words. What does each word mean? What do you think the compound word means?* Have students brainstorm other compound words. Extend the review to include different patterns for spelling compound words: as one word (closed), as two separate words (open), or with a hyphen.

MORE MULTISYLLABIC WORDS AS COMPOUNDS

- Write the words *windy* and *windshield* on the board, circling the words in each. Say: Windy *has two parts:* wind *and* y. Wind *is a word, but* -y *is not.* Windy *is not a compound word, because it contains only one word.* Windshield *also has two parts:* wind *and* shield. *Both are words. That makes* windshield *a compound word.*

- Have students work in small groups and give each group the list of words below. *Say each word. Circle the words within each word. Tell whether the word is a compound word.*

aircraft	homework	furthermore
assignment	bodyguard	sympathetic
discourage	extremely	mountain lion
civilization	forecast	twenty-one

- Check each group's work for accuracy. Provide constructive feedback.

WORD HUNT AND SORT: COMPOUNDS IN CONTEXT

- Have student pairs search "Protecting the Clouded Leopard" and other selections in this book to find examples of closed, open, and hyphenated compounds. Have them sort the words by spelling pattern.

- Call on student pairs to share their findings. Under the headings *Closed, Open,* and *Hyphen,* list the compounds. (They will include examples such as *clouded leopard, however,* and *rain forests.*)

Additional Resources

For each skill below, additional lessons are provided. You can use these lessons on consecutive days after teaching the lessons presented within the week.
• Main Ideas and Details, T2
• Analogies: Antonyms, T8

Constructive Feedback

Isolate the incorrectly identified compound and discuss. If students say *discourage* is a compound, for instance, point to the prefix *dis-* and say:

Courage is a word, but *dis-* is not. *Discourage* is a multisyllabic word, but not a compound. Remember a compound is made up of two or more words.

Repeat as needed with other multisyllabic words that are not compound words.

Decodable Text

To help students build speed and accuracy when reading multisyllabic words, see the additional decodable text on page 9 of the **Teacher's Resource Book**.

Skills Focus ▸ Fluency

Objective   Read with increasing prosody and accuracy at a rate of 117–127 WCPM
Materials   • **Approaching Practice Book A,** p. 32

MODEL EXPRESSIVE READING

Model reading the fluency passage on **Approaching Practice Book A** page 32. Tell students to pay close attention and listen to your pauses and intonation as you read. Then read one sentence at a time and have students echo-read the sentence back, copying your pauses and intonation. Listen carefully to their reading, monitoring for accuracy.

REPEATED READING

Have students continue to practice reading the passage as you circulate and provide constructive feedback. During independent reading time, have students work with a partner. Have one student read aloud, and the other repeat each sentence. Students should continue practicing the passage throughout the week.

TIMED READING

At the end of the week, tell students that they will do a timed reading of the passage that they have been practicing. With each student:

- Place the passage from **Approaching Practice Book A** page 32 facedown.
- When you say "Go," the student begins reading the passage aloud.
- When you say "Stop," the student stops reading the passage.

Stop each student after one minute. Review students' miscues and help them record and graph the number of words they read correctly.

Constructive Feedback

Suggest that students who are having difficulty with pacing and pronunciation practice reading aloud smaller chunks of the selection, such as several sentences, then a single paragraph, building up slowly to a fluent reading of the entire article. Students may work independently or with a partner.

Skills Focus ▸ Vocabulary

Objective   Apply vocabulary word meanings
Materials   • **Vocabulary Cards**   • **Transparencies 5a and 5b**

VOCABULARY WORDS

Display the **Vocabulary Cards** for *vital, analyzing, speculated, embedded, conserve, sedated, dehydrated,* and *propelled.* Help students locate and read these words in "Protecting the Clouded Leopard" on **Transparencies 5a** and **5b**. Review each word's meaning. Then have students choose partners and write messages to each other using all the vocabulary words. Tell students that their messages can be silly as long as they use all the words correctly.

 Approaching Practice Book A, page 32

As I read, I will pay attention to tempo.

	A mother right whale floats lazily on the surface of the
11	water. Her calf swims close by and then rests by its mother
23	with its tail across the mother's back. Neither mother nor
33	calf sees danger steaming closer, closer, and closer still.
42	Even with their excellent hearing, neither whale seems
50	bothered by the ship heading through their nursery. Will they
60	swim away or dive deep? Will the ship avoid them?
70	Maybe. Maybe not.
73	Today right whales face many threats. Ship strikes
81	and fishing gear are threats. Right whales are slow
90	swimmers. They spend most of their days on top of the
101	water, and that's a dangerous place to be. Ships and fishing
112	gear can hurt them.
116	These whales are endangered. The few that are left could
126	become extinct in your lifetime. That's why it's **vital** for you
137	and others to learn about these whales. You can join the fight
149	to save them. 152

Comprehension Check

1. What problem do whales face today? **Main Idea and Details** Ship strikes and fishing gear can kill whales.
2. What is the author's purpose? **Author's Purpose** The author wants to persuade people to help right whales.

	Words Read	–	Number of Errors	=	Words Correct Score
First Read		–		=	
Second Read		–		=	

Vocabulary

Review last week's words (*rummaged, undetected, chameleon, generosity, pathetic, ricocheting, famine, scrounging*) and this week's words (*speculated, conserve, analyzing, vital, propelled, sedated, dehydrated, embedded*). Have students write a sentence for each word.

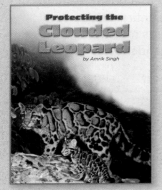

Student Book, or Transparencies 5a and 5b

ELL

Access for All

Have students use context clues to choose the vocabulary word that completes each sentence frame. 1. *I was _____ forward by the power of the waves.* (propelled) 2. *Without anything to drink, I became _____.* (dehydrated) 3. *The elephant was _____ before it was examined.* (sedated) 4. *The jewel was _____ in the ring.* (embedded) 5. *This problem needs _____ before it can be solved.* (analyzing)

Skills Focus ▶ Vocabulary

Objective Use analogies with antonyms to understand the meanings of words
Materials • **Student Book** *Interruped Journey* • **Vocabulary Cards**

ANALOGIES: ANTONYMS

Review with students that an antonym has the opposite meaning of another word and that an analogy shows the relationship between two pairs of words. Model how to use a **Vocabulary Card** to make analogies. For example: *vital* is to *weak* as *strong* is to *feeble*. Have students work in small groups to use the cards to create their own analogies with antonyms. Ask groups to share their analogies.

Skills Focus ▶ Comprehension

Objective Identify main idea and details
Materials • **Student Book** "Protecting the Clouded Leopard" • **Transparencies 5a and 5b**

STRATEGY
MAKE INFERENCES AND ANALYZE

Review with students that when certain information is not stated directly in a selection, good readers combine the information that is provided with what they know from their own experience to make inferences.

SKILL
MAIN IDEA AND DETAILS

Explain/Model

- The main idea is the most important point an author makes. Details support or provide more information about the main idea.
- If the main idea is not stated directly in the text, readers must put together details to figure out the unstated main idea.

Display **Transparencies 5a and 5b**. Reread the second paragraph of "Protecting the Clouded Leopard." Model how to identify the main idea.

Think Aloud The first place to look for the main idea of a paragraph is a sentence at or near the beginning. Here the first sentence says: *What else do we know about the cat?* The other sentences in the paragraph tell what we know about this animal. The topic sentence is not stated exactly, but it could be *This is what we know about the clouded leopard.*

Practice/Apply

Reread the rest of "Protecting the Clouded Leopard" with students. Have volunteers underline the main idea of each paragraph if it is stated, or state it if it is implied, and then find supporting details.

Leveled Reader Lesson

Objective Read to apply strategies and skills
Materials
- **Leveled Reader** *Saving Right Whales* • chart paper
- **Student Book** *Interrupted Journey*

PREVIEW AND PREDICT

Have students read the title and preview the first chapter. Ask students to make predictions about what they will learn in this book, and set purposes for reading.

VOCABULARY WORDS

To reinforce students' grasp of the words, have them write a synonym/antonym sentence for each word following this model: *Vital* means the opposite of _____ but means the same as _____ . (unnecessary, important)

STRATEGY
MAKE INFERENCES AND ANALYZE

Remind students that authors do not always state directly everything that takes place in a selection. Good readers consider the information the author does provide, analyze their own experiences, and infer, or reasonably assume, certain conclusions.

Think Aloud After reading the introduction, I learn that right whales face many threats. The author says they are also endangered. Although she doesn't state directly why the whales are endangered, I can infer that it's because of the dangers the whales face from ships and fishing gear.

SKILL
MAIN IDEA AND DETAILS

Discuss the different ways groups are trying to save endangered species. Ask, *What is the main idea of the first chapter? Is it stated or unstated? Which details support or help explain the main idea?* Have students begin a Main Idea Web on chart paper.

READ AND RESPOND

Have students read orally to the end of Chapter 2. Have them discuss the details the author provides about the main idea. After students complete the book, discuss their personal responses.

MAKE CONNECTIONS ACROSS TEXTS

Invite students to compare *Interrupted Journey* and *Saving Right Whales*. Ask, *What is the main idea of each selection, and what important details help support and provide more information about these ideas?*

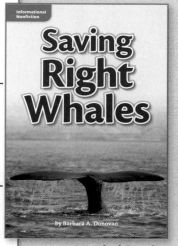

Leveled Reader

This Land Is Your Land
lyrics by
Woody Guthrie

Birdfoot's Grampa
by Joseph Bruchac

Student Book

Skills Focus ▶ Vocabulary

Objective	Use vocabulary words and create analogies
Materials	• **Vocabulary Cards**

VOCABULARY WORDS

Distribute the **Vocabulary Cards** upside down, equally between two teams. Have team members turn over one of their cards and write a sentence using the word. The first team to write an acceptable sentence wins a point. The team with the most points after all of the cards are turned over wins.

ANALOGIES: ANYONYMS

Ask students to find a vocabulary word to complete the following analogy: *Full* is to *empty* as *soaked* is to _____. (dehydrated) Have student pairs create other analogies to demonstrate their understanding of the vocabulary words.

Skills Focus ▶ Literary Elements

Objective	Use alliteration and imagery
Materials	• Poetry books
	• **Student Book** "Birdfoot's Grampa" and "This Land Is Your Land"

ALLITERATION AND IMAGERY

Discuss the purpose and importance of alliteration in "Birdfoot's Grampa" and imagery in poems. Have students look through poetry books to find examples of alliteration and/or imagery. Have students write their own poem using alliteration and imagery.

Skills Focus ▶ Fluency

On Level Practice Book O, page 32

As I read, I will pay attention to tempo.

	The peregrine falcon is a raptor, a bird of prey. It has a
13	body that is designed for hunting.
19	The falcon's eyes are set forward in its head. That gives it
31	depth perception. Its vision is excellent. It can spot a bird in
43	flight from a great distance away.
49	Inside its nostrils are baffles. Scientists have **speculated**
57	that these small walls slow the air rushing into the falcon's
68	lungs as it dives. They let the falcon breathe. They also keep
80	its lungs from bursting.
84	Like all raptors, the falcon's beak is curved. It's designed
94	for tearing its prey's flesh. Unlike other raptors, the falcon
104	also has a "tooth." This special notch on its beak breaks its
116	prey's back.
118	The falcon's legs, feet, and curved talons are strong
127	weapons. They can deliver a powerful blow to prey. Then, as
138	the falcon flies away, it can grasp its prey.
147	Peregrine falcon's wings are long, narrow, and pointed.
155	They help give this bird its incredible speed in a dive. In level
168	flight its wings flap rapidly to keep it aloft. 177

Comprehension Check

1. What is the main idea of the passage? **Main Idea and Details** Peregrine falcons have bodies that are designed for hunting.
2. What natural weapons does the peregrine falcon have? **Main Idea and Details** The falcon has a curved beak to tear flesh, a special notch to break its prey's back, and strong legs, feet and talons to strike its prey.

	Words Read	–	Number of Errors	=	Words Correct Score
First Read		–		=	
Second Read		–		=	

Objective	Read accurately with a good tempo at a rate of 117–137 WCPM
Materials	• **On Level Practice Book O,** p. 32

REPEATED READING

Model reading the Fluency passage on page 32 of **On Level Practice Book O**. Work with students to begin marking up the passage. Remind students that one slash means "pause" and should come after commas, dashes, and other places where they would naturally pause when reading or speaking. Two slashes mean "stop" and should come after end marks or semicolons.

During independent reading time, have students practice reading the passage to each other. Circulate and provide feedback.

Timed Reading At the end of the week, have students read the passage and record their reading rate.

Leveled Reader Lesson

Objective   Read to apply strategies and skills
Materials   • **Leveled Reader** *Saving Peregrine Falcons* • chart paper

PREVIEW AND PREDICT

Show the cover and read the title of the book. Ask students if they have heard of peregrine falcons. Have students predict what the story is going to be about and set purposes for reading.

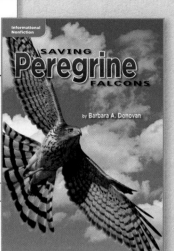

Leveled Reader

STRATEGY
MAKE INFERENCES AND ANALYZE

Remind students that when all information is not stated directly by the author, readers should combine any information provided with their own experiences to make inferences.

SKILL
MAIN IDEA AND DETAILS

Review that details are facts or ideas that explain or support the main idea. Have students begin a Main Idea Web on chart paper.

READ AND RESPOND

Have students read Chapters 1 and 2. Discuss the main idea and details. At the end of Chapter 2, have students add to their Main Idea Web. After students finish reading the story, have them share personal responses.

- Would you recommend this book to a friend? Why or why not?
- How did the details help reveal the main idea of the story?

VOCABULARY WORDS

Discuss the vocabulary words as they are used in the story. To extend students' understanding of the words, have each student make a word map for a vocabulary word that includes synonyms, antonyms, and examples.

ELL
Leveled Reader
Go to pages 123U–123V.

MAKE CONNECTIONS ACROSS TEXTS

Have students summarize and compare *Interrupted Journey* and *Saving Peregrine Falcons*.

- What kind of details does the author of each selection provide to support the main ideas in each paragraph? Which do you find most effective?
- How does the author use the main idea and details to structure *Saving Peregrine Falcons*? How can you use a similar structure when you write nonfiction?

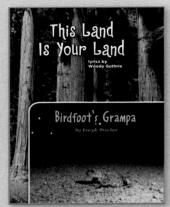

Student Book

Vocabulary

Objective Examine origins of vocabulary words

Materials • **Vocabulary Cards**

EXTEND VOCABULARY

Break students into four groups and assign one **Vocabulary Card** to each group. Have groups brainstorm possible histories of their word and then do research to find out the word's actual origin and history. Have students share their findings with the rest of the class.

Literary Elements

Objective Use alliteration and imagery

Materials • Poetry anthologies

ALLITERATION AND IMAGERY

Point out that alliteration is the repetition of the same initial letter, sound, or group of sounds in a series of words. Poets and other authors use imagery to create vivid pictures in the reader's mind.

- Have students find a poem that uses alliteration and contains imagery.
- Have them describe or draw the pictures the poet painted with words. Discuss whether the image was effective for them.

Have students write their own poems using alliteration and imagery. Allow them time to read their work aloud to the class.

ELL

Access for All

Poetic Language

Say: *Listen to this example of alliteration:* The funny fat frog told a fable. Explain that alliteration is a device that poets and authors use to get the reader's attention. Have students practice alliteration. Give them one letter at a time and have them think of at least three words beginning with that letter that will form an example of alliteration.

◆ **Beyond Practice Book B,** page 32

As I read, I will pay attention to tempo.

	It floats with only its eyes, ears, and nostrils above the
11	water. It's on the lookout for prey—and it will eat just about
24	anything. This is an American alligator. Physically, this
32	creature hasn't changed much since the age of the dinosaurs.
42	Its wet habitat hasn't changed much either. The alligator
51	makes its home in fresh water wetlands that range from
61	North Carolina to Texas to Arkansas.
67	Alligators are important to the ecosystems in which they
76	live. They're so **vital** that they're known as keystone species.
86	That means that what happens to them affects many other
96	animals and plants in their habitat. That's why we must keep
107	a close eye on their populations. Protecting them helps us
117	protect others in their environment.
122	Alligators dominate their food chain. Except for humans,
130	they have no real predators. For hundreds of years, alligators
140	were hunted for their meat and their skins. They were hunted
151	to a point of near extinction. Recent laws protected them,
161	and people worked to save these ancient creatures. Now the
171	American alligator has made a comeback. Its population is
180	growing, but it's still facing threats from humans. 188

Comprehension Check

1. Why are alligators important to the ecosystem? **Summarize** If alligators die, it affects other animals and plants in their habitats.

2. Why have alligators come close to extinction and what have people tried to do about it? **Cause and Effect** People have over hunted alligators. Now people are passing laws to keep them safe.

	Words Read	−	Number of Errors	=	Words Correct Score
First Read		−		=	
Second Read		−		=	

Fluency

Objective Read accurately with good prosody and tempo at a rate of 127–137 WCPM

Materials • **Beyond Practice Book B,** p. 32

REPEATED READING

Model reading the Fluency passage on page 32 of **Beyond Practice Book B**. Tell students to pay close attention and listen to your pauses and intonation as you read. Then read one sentence at a time and have students echo-read the sentence back, copying your pauses and intonation. Listen carefully to their reading, monitoring for accuracy.

During independent reading time, partners can take turns reading the passage. Have one student read aloud and the other repeat each sentence. You may wish to have students do a timed reading at the end of the week.

Leveled Reader Lesson

Objective Read to apply strategies and skills

Materials • **Leveled Reader** *Saving Alligators*

PREVIEW AND PREDICT

Have students preview *Saving Alligators,* predict what it is about, and set a purpose for reading.

STRATEGY
MAKE INFERENCES AND ANALYZE

Tell students to combine the information provided with what they already know from their own experience to make inferences.

SKILL
MAIN IDEA AND DETAILS

Ask a volunteer to explain main ideas and details. Have students discuss where they might look for a main idea that is explicitly stated and how they can infer a main idea if it is not explicitly stated.

READ AND RESPOND

Have students read Chapters 1 and 2. Discuss the main plot events. After students finish reading the story, have them share personal responses.

■ How did details support the main idea?

■ Was the story easy to follow? Where you able to make inferences?

VOCABULARY WORDS

Review with students the meanings of vocabulary words as needed. Ask students to write a journal entry by a person working to save an endangered species. Tell them to use the vocabulary words in their entry.

Skills Focus ▶ Self-Selected Reading

Objective Read independently to identify main idea and details

Materials • Leveled Readers or trade books at students' reading level

READ TO IDENTIFY MAIN IDEA AND DETAILS

Invite students to select a fiction book to read independently. For a list of theme-related titles, see pages T17–T18. As students read, have them take notes about the main idea and the details that support it.

Have students research and create an article using a main idea that is similar to the selection they have read. Remind students to include strong supporting details.

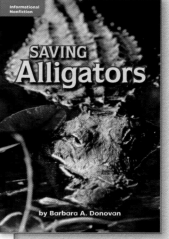

Informational Nonfiction

SAVING Alligators

by Barbara A. Donovan

Leveled Reader

Academic Language

Throughout the week, the English language learners in your class will need help in building their understanding of the academic language used in daily instruction and assessment instruments. The following strategies will help to increase their language proficiency and comprehension of content and instructional words.

LOG ON Technology

Oral Language For oral vocabulary development go to www.macmillanmh.com

Strategies to Reinforce Academic Language

- **Use Context** Academic Language used by the teacher (see chart below) should be explained in the context of the task during Whole Group. You may use gestures, expressions and visuals to support meaning.

- **Use Visuals** Use charts, transparencies, and graphic organizers to explain key labels to help students understand classroom language.

- **Model** Demonstrate the task using academic language in order for students to understand instruction.

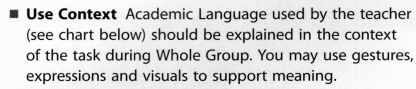

Academic Language Used in Whole Group Instruction

Content/Theme Words	Skill/Strategy Words	Writing/Grammar Words
refuge (p. 102)	main idea/details (p. 105A)	diary (p. 122)
protecting (p. 103)	make inferences (p. 105A)	transition words (p. 122)
wildlife (p. 103)	alliteration (p. 120)	voice (p. 123)
conserve (p. 104)	imagery (p. 120)	run-on (p. 123I)
	free verse (p. 120)	fragments (p. 123I)
	antonyms (p. 105)	
	analogy (p. 105)	

ELL Leveled Reader Lesson

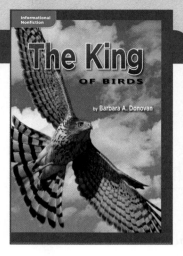

The King OF BIRDS
by Barbara A. Donovan

Before Reading

ORAL LANGUAGE

Build Background *Why are some animals in danger of disappearing?* Ask student to name causes and review the concept of *endangered species*. Brainstorm ways to protect such animals and save them from extinction.

Review Vocabulary Write the vocabulary and story support words on the board and discuss their meaning. Model using them in sentences. *Pets can become* dehydrated. *Make sure a pet in captivity always has water.*

PREVIEW AND PREDICT

Point to the cover illustration and read the title aloud. Encourage students to describe the falcon. Have them read the Table of Contents and make more predictions.

Set a Purpose for Reading Show the Main Idea Web and remind students they have used this web before. Ask them to use a similar web, as they identify the main ideas and the details.

During Reading

Choose from among the differentiated strategies to support students' reading at all levels of language acquisition.

Beginning	Intermediate	Advanced
Shared Reading Do a shared reading. Pause after each section to model the strategy. *Why is the peregrine falcon a mighty hunter?* Have students fill in the web with their responses. Ask questions after each section to guide students to identify the main idea and details.	**Read Together** Read through the first chapter. Have students recall as many details of peregrine falcons as they can. Have them write them on the main idea web. Ask students to continue to read with a partner and identify additional details to add to their webs.	**Independent Reading** Have students read the story. Ask them to identify the main idea and details and fill in their web as they read each day. Encourage them to use information from pictures and captions in their web.

After Reading

Remind students to use the vocabulary and story words in their whole-group activities.

Objective

- **To apply vocabulary & comprehension skills.**

Materials

- **ELL Leveled Reader *The King of Birds***

5-Day Planner

DAY 1	• Academic Language
	• Oral Language and Vocabulary Review
DAY 2	• Academic Language
	• ELL Leveled Reader
DAY 3	• Academic Language
	• ELL Leveled Reader
DAY 4	• Academic Language
	• ELL Leveled Reader
DAY 5	• Academic Language
	• ELL Leveled Reader Comprehension Check and Literacy Activities

ELL Teacher's Guide for students who need additional instruction.

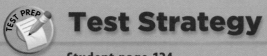
Answer Questions

Test Strategy: Think and Search

EXPLAIN

Good test takers think about where in the selection they are most likely to find the best answer to a question.

- **Think** about what the question is asking you to find.

- **Search** the selection for the part or parts that will give you the correct answer.

- **Keep reading:** Often information you need is in more than one place so you should read the entire selection.

MODEL

Remind students to record their answers on a separate sheet of paper.

Question 1 Read aloud the question and all of the answer choices.

Think Aloud The capitalized word "BEST" shows me that more than one answer might be possible, so I'll have to read carefully. The question asks me to describe the author's tone. I'll have to think about the whole play, not just one or two lines. The title is a humorous play on words. Eddie's dialogue has a few jokes; at one point, he says "my mummy's waiting." Of the four choices, I would say that choice B, *light-hearted,* is the best description of the author's tone.

 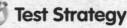

Don't Tell My Mummy,
A Radio Play

Test Strategy

Think and Search
The answer is in more than one place. Keep reading to find the answer.

EDDIE: *(voiceover)* It was midnight. Just when I was expecting to get some shut-eye, I got the call instead about a stolen ruby, a museum, and a four thousand-year-old mummy. My name is Eddie Grimes, and I solve crimes.

(Sounds: Crowds, cameras snapping.)

EDDIE: *(voiceover)* I showed up at the crime scene and found my good friend Sergeant Tommy Drake of the Victory City Police Department. The museum had reporters crawling all over it.

DRAKE: What can I do for you, Grimes?

EDDIE: Tell me what you know about this ruby business.

DRAKE: It's the Isis Ruby. It's been stolen. The ruby is a rare gem on loan from a London museum. The place was locked. There are guards on every door. Nobody could get in or out after closing.

EDDIE: You're wrong, Tommy. Nobody was supposed to get in or out, but someone did. Hey, this coffin looks interesting.

(Sounds: Footsteps on a marble floor, then a creaky door.)

DR. BLOOM: What do you think you are doing? That's a priceless artifact. I am Dr. Donald Bloom, head curator of the Victory City Museum.

DRAKE: Sorry, Dr. Bloom. This is Eddie Grimes, private investigator.

124   **Go On** ▶

Genre: Plays

Plays are stories that are intended to be performed.

- **Characters:** The people or animals in the story.
- **Setting:** When and where the story occurs.
- **Stage directions:** The text in parentheses that describes characters' actions and feelings.
- **Dialogue:** The text that shows what the characters say.
- **Scenes:** The different sections that make up a play.

Dr. Bloom: No one opens the sarcophagus except to restore it. The coffin stays shut. The precious paintings on the inside must not be exposed to light. Their green pigment is already flaking off.

Eddie: So this coffin thing is part of the same exhibit as the ruby?

Dr. Bloom: Yes. We just got it back from the restoration department, and I haven't even seen the inside of the sarcophagus yet.

Eddie: Restoration, eh? Who does the restoring?

Dr. Bloom: Why, that's Dr. Peterson. Her office is across the street.

Eddie: Thanks, Doc. It was nice to meet you.

(Sounds: Two pairs of footsteps.)

Drake: What's up, Eddie?

Eddie: I want to talk to this art restorer.

(Sounds: Street sounds, a knock, then the door opens.)

Eddie: You must be Dr. Peterson. My name is Eddie Grimes, private investigator.

Dr. Peterson: You must be looking into the missing ruby.

Eddie: What do you know about it?

Dr. Peterson: I know that its value is beyond measure. But I don't know how the thief got into and out of the museum.

Eddie: *(voiceover)* I took a stroll around the place. There were books on mummies, and jewels, and magic tricks. Magic tricks? A pair of old boots sat under her desk. There were flecks of green paint on the side of one boot. That was strange. But what was even stranger was that these were men's boots. Then, right in the middle of a work bench, I spotted the largest ruby I had ever seen.

Drake: The Isis Ruby!

Dr. Peterson: No, just a glass copy. I was preparing to replace the real ruby until it is found. Excuse me, sir. I really have a lot to do before the exhibit opens.

Eddie: Don't let me keep you. Besides, my mummy's waiting.

Eddie: *(voiceover)* I went back to my office to check my messages. I thought about what Dr. Bloom had said when I was messing with his creaky old coffin. Then it hit me.

(Sound: Bells to indicate a flashback.)

Go On   125

PRACTICE

Question 2 Read aloud the question and all of the answer choices.

Tell students the question is asking the reader how the ruby was smuggled out of the museum. Point out Dr. Bloom's original comments about the sarcophagus and their repetition in flashback. Ask:

Is Eddie suspicious about Dr. Bloom and the sarcophagus? (yes) How can you be sure that the ruby was smuggled in a false compartment of the sarcophagus? (keep reading)

Read aloud the dialogue beginning after the flashback on page 126 to students. Ask: Does Eddie figure out exactly how the ruby was smuggled out of the museum? (yes) How was it done? (It was hidden in a false compartment inside the sarcophagus). So which letter is the best answer? (C)

APPLY

Question 3 Read aloud the question and all of the answer choices.

Have students use the **Think and Search** strategy to choose an answer.

After the students have chosen an answer, ask: What did you think the question was asking you to do? (figure out whose boots were in Dr. Peterson's office) What did you search for to find the answer? (the word *boots*) Did the word *boots* appear more than once? (yes) So to be sure you chose the best answer, what did you need to do? (keep reading) So the best answer is B.

Have students answer questions 4 and 5.

Question 4 Answers will vary. Eddie knows who stole the ruby and wants to confront both Dr. Peterson and Dr. Bloom. He is being sarcastic when he calls them "the good doctors."

Question 5 Answers will vary, but should mention that the author wants to draw attention to Dr. Bloom's comments. By doing so, the author is helping the reader (or listener) solve the mystery along with Eddie Grimes.

DR. BLOOM: No one opens the sarcophagus except to restore it. The coffin stays shut. The precious paintings on the inside must not be exposed to light. Their green pigment is already flaking off.

EDDIE: *(voiceover)* And then. . .

DR. BLOOM: We just got it back from the restoration department, and I haven't even seen the inside of the sarcophagus yet.

(Sound: Bells to indicate end of flashback.)

EDDIE: *(voiceover)* That was it! I had the answer. I called Drake and told him to round up the good doctors and meet me at Dr. Peterson's office and to have the sarcophagus moved there.

DR. BLOOM: What's the meaning of this? I was sleeping soundly.

EDDIE: You'll sleep in prison, Dr. Bloom. You stole the ruby.

DR. BLOOM: This is outrageous. Where's your proof?

(Sounds: Harsh squeal of hinges, a thump.)

EDDIE: This Egyptian sarcophagus has a false back wall.

DR. PETERSON: That's a lie.

EDDIE: The magic books tipped me off. Doing a little research into disappearing tricks, Doc?

DR. BLOOM: I knew she did it!

EDDIE: Not so fast, Dr. Bloom. You said you hadn't seen the inside of the sarcophagus yet, but you also said that the paintings inside were flaking. How would you know unless you had seen the inside? You snuck out of the museum with the ruby hidden inside this coffin when it was sent for restoration. Those size-thirteen boots under her desk aren't Dr. Peterson's. They're yours! Drake, stop Dr. Peterson, that ruby isn't glass, it's the real thing.

DR. PETERSON: Let me go!

DRAKE: Good work, Grimes.

(Music: Dramatic climax.)

EDDIE: *(voiceover)* It was just another night in the big city. I'm Eddie Grimes, and I solve crimes.

THE END

Go On ▶

Directions: Answer the questions.

Tip

Keep reading. The answer may be in more than one place.

1. **Which word BEST describes the author's tone in the play?**

   A grim
   B light-hearted
   C sad
   D serious

2. **How was the Isis Ruby smuggled out of the museum?**

   A in Dr. Peterson's pocket
   B in Dr. Bloom's boots
   C in a false compartment inside the sarcophagus
   D in Dr. Peterson's work bench

3. **To whom do the boots in Dr. Peterson's office belong?**

   A Dr. Peterson
   B Dr. Bloom
   C Eddie Grimes
   D Isis

4. **Why does Eddie call Drake and ask him to "round up the good doctors"?**

5. **What is the most likely reason the author included a flashback in the play? Write two paragraphs, and include examples from the selection.**

   Writing Prompt

   Think of a problem or mystery in your own life. Write a friendly letter to someone asking for help in solving your problem. Your letter should be at least two paragraphs.

STOP 127

Writing Prompt

EXPLAIN

Explain to students that before they begin, they will need to find the following information.

- What is the **mode** or **type** of writing described in the prompt?
- What is the **purpose** for my writing?
- Does the prompt tell me the **form** or **format** for my writing?
- Who is the **audience** I am writing for?

MODEL/PRACTICE

Determine the Writing Mode Read the prompt aloud emphasizing the phrase *your own life.* Who is the prompt asking you to write about? (you) What clue tells you that you are writing about a real event? (the phrase *in your own life*) So you're being asked to write about a real problem or mystery in your own life.

Determine the Purpose Why are you writing? (to ask for help in solving a problem)

Determine the Form What clues in the prompt tell you the form in which to write? (the phrase *a friendly letter*)

Determine the Audience Since your writing will be a letter, who is its audience? (the person to whom the letter is addressed)

APPLY

Have students summarize the information they have found in the prompt and the clue words they used.

Objectives

- **Identify features of a personal narrative**
- **Plan and organize ideas for a personal narrative**
- **Draft and revise a personal narrative**
- **Proofread, publish and present a personal narrative**

Materials

- **Unit Writing Transparencies 1–6**

Features of a Personal Narrative

- It tells the story of a **personal experience** from the writer's own life.
- It expresses the writer's **feelings.**
- It is written from the **first-person point of view,** using words such as *I, me, my,* and *we.*
- It chronicles a sequence of three or more events.
- It uses **time-order words** to tell the sequence of events.

ELL · Access for All

Analyze Structure
Provide copies of the passage. Before you read, ask students what they know about baseball. Write important terms from the story and explain them. After you read the passage, have students underline the sensory details. Explain and demonstrate words as needed. Then students locate and circle the time order words. Discuss how they help understand the events.

Personal Narrative

Read Like a Writer

Read aloud the following passage. Explain to students that this excerpt is a personal narrative—a true story a writer tells about his or her own experiences. Ask students to listen for:

- events that happened in the writer's life.
- how the writer feels.
- how the writer uses *I, me,* and *my.*
- the **time-order words** the writer uses to tell the sequence of events.

Batter Up!

Nervously, I stepped up to bat. The other team's pitcher was very good, I'd heard. She must have sensed my tension, because she took her time, making me even more nervous. First she tossed the ball back and forth between her bare hand and her glove. Then she smiled at her catcher and called "easy out!" Next, she grinned right at me, showing me how confident she was. My heart was in my mouth as the ball finally zoomed across the plate. Strike one.

That was too easy for her, I thought. I swung with all my might at her second pitch. Strike two.

I was determined not to let my team down. After taking a few deep breaths, I gritted my teeth and waited for the third pitch.

Discuss the Features

After reading, discuss the following questions with students.

- **Who tells this story?** (a first-person narrator, in this case, the author)
- **How do you know?** (words such as *I, me,* and *my* are used)
- **What sensory details does the author use to suggest his feelings?** (*nervous, tension, my heart was in my mouth, heartbroken, I gritted my teeth*)
- **What time-order words does the author use to show the sequence of events?** (*first, then, next, finally, after*)

Prewrite

Set a Purpose Tell students that one purpose for writing a personal narrative is to share feelings about an experience. Another purpose is to entertain.

Know the Audience Explain that students will need to think about their readers as they write. Are they writing for family, classmates, or other people?

Choose a Topic Have students brainstorm ideas about a time they had to take action in a helpful way. Ask:

- Who needed help? What action did you have to take?
- What did you do first? Next? Last?
- When and where did you take this action?
- What were your feelings at the time?

Alternatively allow students to self-select a topic. For example, they may choose to develop one of their weekly writing pieces.

Mini Lesson | Organization

Display **Transparency 1.** With students, point out the following details in Maria M.'s Cluster Map:

- She writes a **personal experience** in the center circle.
- She uses **first-person** words like *I* and *my*.
- She includes her **feelings** about being scared and glad and **sensory details** to draw the reader into the narrative.
- She includes **time-order** words to show the order of events.

Organize Ideas Ask students to create their own Cluster Maps to record the events of their narratives. Use Transparency 1 to demonstrate how to organize ideas. Remind students to apply what they have learned about topic sentences and details as they brainstorm ideas for their Cluster Maps.

Peer Review

Think, Pair, Share Have students discuss their Cluster Maps with a partner. As they share their Cluster Maps, have them consider whether each lists events in the correct order. Have partners encourage one another to express their feelings about the event.

Flexible Pairing Option Consider pairing students with a partner who took a similar action.

Writing Topic

Write a personal narrative about a time you took action to help someone such as a teammate, family member, friend, or person in your community. Include details about how you felt before, during, and after the action you took. Remember to order the events in your story properly.

Transparency 1

Cluster Map

- I was five years old.
- I found Gran on the floor in the bedroom.
- I saved my grandma's life.
- I was really scared, but knew I had to call for help.
- Later, I was glad to hear the siren of the ambulance.
- Then I told the operator where we lived.
- First I dialed really carefully.

Unit Writing Transparency 1

ELL **Access for All**

Ask Questions Ask students to think about a time they helped someone. Then pose questions to help them generate an attention-getting first sentence. Ask: *Who was in need and why did you decide to help? If you were telling this story to a friend, what would you say to generate interest in hearing it?*

Transparency 2

The Day I Saved a Life
by Maria M.

Once, I saved my grandmother's life. She was visiting us for a week. I was the only one home with her.

Gran and I had a great breakfast. She went into the geust bedroom to get her purse. I waited and waited. I knocked on the door. There was no sound. I opened the door and peaked in. Gran lay on the carpet. At first I couldnt do anything. My body had turned to stone.

Then I remembered what Gran had taught me. I went to the refrigerater. There was 911. I picked up the telephone. I looked carefully for the 9. I punched 1 twice. When the operator answered I took a deep breath and told him where we lived. Later, I heard a loud siren when the paramedics arrived. "We'll get your grandmother all better, a guy said. You saved her by calling us."

Unit Writing Transparency 2

Draft

Mini Lesson First-Person Point of View

Display **Transparency 2** and read it with students. As you discuss Maria M.'s draft, point out the following features:

- It is clear from reading this draft that Maria M. is writing about something that happened to her. She relates a true **personal experience** about saving her grandma.

- She uses **first-person words** like *I, me, my,* and *we.*

- She expresses her **feelings** with **sensory** words and phrases such as *my body had turned to stone* and *hands shaking.*

Note that Maria M. will revise and proofread her draft later.

Review Your Cluster Map Encourage students to refer to their Cluster Maps frequently to make sure they are including important details.

Write the Draft Remind students that the purpose of writing a first draft is to express their ideas on paper. Share these tips:

- Tell a true story about a personal experience using first person words such as *I, me,* and *my.*

- Write good paragraphs. Begin with an attention-getting first sentence that makes your reader want to hear more about what happened. Then write sentences that add important supporting details.

- Describe your feelings using sensory words and phrases.

- Tell events in the correct sequence using time-order words like *first, next,* and *finally.*

Writer's Resources
Use Primary Sources

Writers of first-person narratives often sift through old photographs, letters, journals, diaries, and other sources of personal information before writing. Evaluating these primary sources can help a writer to recall details about the past.

Have students bring photographs, letters, and other mementos to class and jot down ideas and memories. Students can include these notes as details in their narratives or save their ideas in a writing notebook for use throughout the year.

Revise

Mini Lesson | Word Choice

Display **Transparency 3** and point out how Maria M. revises her personal narrative to make it excellent.

- She adds the time-order phrases *when I was five* and *after we finished* to clarify the order of events. She also uses the transition word *because* to show cause and effect. (Organization)

- In the second paragraph, she adds colorful words like *impatiently* and *nervously* to express how she felt. (Word Choice)

- She substitutes more precise words for vague ones such as *great, went,* and *guy.* (Word Choice)

- She combines sentences to vary her sentence lengths. (Sentence Fluency)

You may want to note that Maria M. will need to proofread her personal narrative to make final corrections.

Advise students to think about the following writing traits as they revise their personal narratives.

> **Organization** Do you use **time-order words** to clarify the sequence of events? Do you use **transition words** to help show cause and effect? Does your personal narrative have a clear beginning, a middle, and an end?
>
> **Voice** Do you speak directly to your audience? Is it clear that your **personal experience** was important to you?
>
> **Word Choice** Do you use colorful, precise words? Do your words express your **feelings**?

Peer Review

Think, Pair, Share Ask students to read their revised drafts aloud to partners. Direct listeners to summarize the narrative they heard and to write down any questions they have.

Flexible Pairing Option Pair students of similar abilities and encourage them to share what they liked best about each other's drafts.

ELL — Access for All

Build Descriptive Language Ask students to look at their drafts and choose two words for which they would like to find more precise substitutes. Put students in groups and have them take turns briefly explaining their stories and reading the sentences in which the words appear. Have the groups help decide on more precise words. Provide additional help as needed.

Transparency 3

The Day I Saved a Life
by Maria M.

When I was five
Once, I saved my grandmother's life. She was
my parents and me
visiting us for a week. I was the only person one home
with her.
big, delicious   After we finished
Gran and I had a great breakfast. She went
into the geust bedroom to get her purse. I waited
impatiently Eventually,   but
and waited. I knocked on the door. There was no
Nervously,
sound. I opened the door and peaked in. Gran lay
on the carpet. At first I couldnt do anything. My
body had turned to stone.
Then I remembered what Gran had taught me.
dashed   in big red print were the numbers   Hands shaking,
I went to the refrigerater. There was 911. I picked
and   Next
up the telephone. I looked carefully for the 9. I
punched 1 twice. When the operator answered I
took a deep breath and told him where we lived.
Moments
Later, I heard a loud siren when the paramedics
arrived. "We'll get your grandmother all better, a
paramedeic   Because you called us, you saved her life
guy said. You saved her by calling us."

Speaking and Listening

Have students read their personal narratives aloud. Share these strategies.

SPEAKING STRATEGIES

- Speak loudly and clearly, using correct vocabulary and language.
- Don't rush while reading.
- Make eye contact with members of the audience.

LISTENING STRATEGIES

- Set a purpose for listening, such as to learn how people help others.
- Identify and evaluate the speaker's tone, mood, and emotion as conveyed through verbal and nonverbal communication.

Transparency 4

The Day I Saved a Life
by Maria M.

When I was five

~~Once,~~ I saved my grandmother's life. She was
visiting ~~us~~ for a week. I was the only ~~one~~ home
with her.
  Gran and I had a ~~great~~ breakfast. She went
into the ~~geust~~ bedroom to get her purse. I waited
and ~~waited.~~ I knocked on the door. There was no
sound. I opened the door and ~~peaked~~ in. Gran lay
on the carpet. At first I couldnt do anything. My
body had turned to stone.
  Then I remembered what Gran had taught me.
I ~~went~~ to the refrigerater. There ~~was~~ 911. I picked
up the telephone. I looked carefully for the 9. I
punched 1 twice. When the operator answered, I
took a deep breath and told him where we lived.
Later, I heard a loud siren when the paramedics
arrived. "We'll get your grandmother all better, a
~~guy~~ said. You saved her by calling us."

Unit Writing Transparency 4

Proofread

Mini Lesson | Conventions

Display **Transparency 4** to point out examples of Maria M.'s proofreading corrections.

- She corrects spelling errors. She adds commas after opening clauses like *after we finished* and *when the operator answered*.
- She fixes her quotation marks to surround the speaker's dialogue.

Have students proofread their personal narratives. Review the use of proofreading marks on **Teacher's Resource Book** page 152. Have students apply them as they proofread. Discuss other resources students can use to help them proofread, such as a print or electronic dictionary.

Peer Review

Think, Pair, Share Have partners review each other's edited drafts and identify additional corrections that should be made. Remind students to look for missing punctuation.

TEACHER CONFERENCE

As students finalize their stories, ask:

- What words indicate the first-person point of view?
- How did you express your feelings in your narrative?
- How effectively did you use time-order words?

Publish

Ask students to write or type a final draft of their personal narratives. Remind students to use appropriate spacing between words, sentences, and paragraphs.

PRESENTATION

Ask students to give a presentation of their work. Suggest that they pass around any illustrations or photos that they have included.

Author's Chair Invite students with strong personal narratives to share their stories from the Author's Chair.

Encourage students to publish one of their weekly writing assignments as well.

Raising Scores

READ AND SCORE

Display **Transparency 5** and invite a volunteer to read it aloud. Then direct student groups to use the scoring rubric on page 153 of the **Teacher's Resource Book** to assess the writing sample. Explain to students that the personal narrative is a fair writing sample that would score a 2 on the scoring rubric and that they will work together to improve it.

RAISE THE SCORE

Point out the following weaknesses in the writing sample:

> **Organization** The writer does not use sequential order and does not make cause and effect clear.
>
> **Word Choice** The writer uses colorless, imprecise words.
>
> **Voice** The writer lacks enthusiasm. There is no personal voice.

Ask students to work in small groups to revise the narrative to raise the score. Remind them to refer to the student rubric.

SHARE AND COMPARE

Have groups share their revised versions with the class, explaining how they improved the writing. Then display **Transparency 6** to show the same personal narrative written at an excellent level. Have each group compare their revised versions. Remind students that there can be more than one way to improve the writing sample and make it an excellent personal narrative. Then have students review their own personal narratives to raise their scores.

Objective

- Revise a personal narrative to raise the writing score from a 2 to a 4

CREATE A RUBRIC

Make copies of the blank rubric form on page 159 or 160 in the **Teacher's Resource Book** and distribute to students. Remind students that the rubric should assess whether the personal narrative tells about a personal experience, includes the writer's feelings, is written in the first person, and relates events in sequence. Students should include the following four levels to assess writing: Excellent, Good, Fair, and Unsatisfactory.

 Transparency 6

My Name in the Newspaper
by Jason W.

About two months ago, I picked up the newspaper and saw my name, but the story wasn't about me. Who was this other Jason Walker? I hoped he hadn't done anything embarrassing!

As I read, I learned that he was a student in Greenville, about 50 miles away. The library at his school had lost all its books in a flood. The reporter had interviewed students to see how they felt. Jason, an avid reader like me, said he was heartbroken. I would have been, too.

Immediately, I thought of a mystery novel I had recently devoured. I hoped the other Jason would cheer up if I sent it to him. Then I had a brainstorm. What if every kid in my school donated a book? So I sent an e-mail to all my classmates. Before long, they had also written e-mails to their relatives and friends. When my teacher and principal heard about the project, they were delighted to give it the go-ahead.

Yesterday, my class presented over 5,000 books to Jason's school. This time, both Jason Walkers were photographed and interviewed by the newspaper.

Unit Writing Transparency 6

4-Point Rubric

Use this four-point rubric to assess student writing.

SCORING RUBRIC FOR PERSONAL NARRATIVE

4 Excellent	**3 Good**	**2 Fair**	**1 Unsatisfactory**
Ideas and Content Creates a clear, entertaining account of a personal experience; includes the writer's thoughts and feelings	**Ideas and Content** Relates a personal experience; includes some thoughts and feelings about events	**Ideas and Content** Relates a personal experience, but lacks focus; sometimes wanders from topic	**Ideas and Content** Does not share a personal experience and writing is unfocused
Organization Details unfold in a logical, easy-to-follow sequence	**Organization** Tells the story in the correct sequence	**Organization** Some events are told out of order	**Organization** Events are told out of order and the sequence is confusing
Voice Relates events in the first person; clearly expresses the writer's personality and feelings	**Voice** Events told mostly in the first person; somewhat expresses the writer's personality and feelings	**Voice** Strays from first person; conveys insufficient amount of feeling	**Voice** Not in first person; does not express the feelings or personality of the writer
Word Choice Consistently uses first-person pronouns and many time-order words	**Word Choice** Uses first-person pronouns and time-order words	**Word Choice** Lacks sufficient number of first-person pronouns; not enough time-order words to guide readers	**Word Choice** Missing first-person and time-order words
Sentence Fluency Writes complete, easily understood sentences that vary in length and structure	**Sentence Fluency** Includes both simple and compound sentences; some sections have rhythm and flow	**Sentence Fluency** Uses simple sentences, but reader may have to reread in order to follow the meaning	**Sentence Fluency** Sentences are fragmented, run-on, or otherwise difficult to read
Conventions Narrative is free or almost entirely free from mechanical, grammatical, and spelling errors	**Conventions** Spelling, capitalization, punctuation, and usage are mostly correct; incorrect elements do not interfere with meaning	**Conventions** Frequent errors in spelling, punctuation, and usage interfere with a clear understanding of the narrative	**Conventions** Significant errors in spelling, punctuation, and usage
Presentation Text is easy to read whether word-processed or handwritten; spacing and the use of white space allow the reader to focus on the message without distractions	**Presentation** Text is readable; spacing is mostly uniform; margins are present	**Presentation** Text is readable, but variations in size, slant, or font are distracting; margins are attempted	**Presentation** Text is difficult to read due to slant, font, or size; spacing is random or confusing

Refer to Anchor Papers for personal narratives on pages 192–195 in the **Unit and Benchmark Assessment** for a sample of each writing level.

6-Point Rubric

Use this six-point rubric to assess student writing.

SCORING RUBRIC FOR PERSONAL NARRATIVE					
6 Exceptional	**5 Excellent**	**4 Good**	**3 Fair**	**2 Poor**	**1 Unsatisfactory**
Ideas and Content Crafts an appealing, well-detailed story drawn from personal experience; ideas are focused and flow naturally	**Ideas and Content** Original ideas are developed with a clear focus and supported with well-chosen details	**Ideas and Content** Develops adequate ideas that move the story along in a natural way	**Ideas and Content** Shows some difficulty in developing ideas that are clear and focused	**Ideas and Content** Writing is vague; may present events without a clear focus	**Ideas and Content** Does not relate a personal experience; shows no effort to develop clear and interesting ideas
Organization Has an engaging opening sentence and thoughtful ending; clearly establishes when and where events took place	**Organization** Has an engaging beginning and ending, relates events in a logical sequence; consistently well-developed paragraphs and clarity of purpose	**Organization** Relates events in sequence; has a clear introduction, conclusion, and a consistent structure	**Organization** Weak introduction or conclusion, and confusing sequences hinder reader understanding	**Organization** Events are haphazardly related; narrative displays minimal attempts at an introduction or conclusion	**Organization** Account is so random or confused that narrative thread is indiscernible
Voice Expresses first-person voice that effectively communicates personality and feeling	**Voice** Displays originality and demonstrates awareness of audience; communicates feelings and personality	**Voice** Makes a strong effort to share feelings; expresses the writer's personality	**Voice** Makes an effort to employ first-person voice, but the writing style does not communicate feelings effectively	**Voice** Inconsistent use of first-person voice; does not communicate writer's feelings or personality	**Voice** Not in first person; makes no attempt to convey feeling
Word Choice Consistent use of first-person pronouns; abundance of time-order words; chooses words that are colorful and precise to create a compelling picture of events	**Word Choice** Uses many first-person pronouns and time-order words; imaginative language reflects a sophisticated vocabulary	**Word Choice** Adequate use of first-person pronouns and time-order words; chooses words that are expressive and clear	**Word Choice** Insufficient use of first-person pronouns and time-order words; uses predictable wording	**Word Choice** Missing first-person pronouns and time-order words; chooses inaccurate words	**Word Choice** Contains no first-person pronouns and time-order words; uses words incorrectly, or employs indecipherable terms
Sentence Fluency Sentences have power and sureness of style, vary in length and type, and flow easily	**Sentence Fluency** Crafts varied sentences that sound natural	**Sentence Fluency** Crafts varied sentences that sound mostly natural	**Sentence Fluency** Crafts sentences with some variation, although sometimes sounds labored	**Sentence Fluency** Includes fragments or rambling sentences that are extremely difficult to follow	**Sentence Fluency** Consists largely of awkward or incomplete sentences that do not flow together
Conventions Demonstrates a strong grasp of standard writing conventions	**Conventions** Shows control of most spelling, punctuation, capitalization, and usage conventions	**Conventions** Some proofreading is necessary, but errors do not interfere with meaning or flow	**Conventions** Includes some errors in convention that disrupt the reading of the text	**Conventions** Demonstrates an unfamiliarity with, or lack of understanding of, writing conventions; much proofreading necessary	**Conventions** Serious and frequent errors in grammar, usage, and spelling interfere with readability
Presentation Form and presentation of text enhance the reader's ability to relate to and understand the text	**Presentation** Shows creative, clear design that makes reading the text pleasing	**Presentation** Creates an appropriate layout that makes it possible to focus on the message while reading	**Presentation** Text is readable, but discrepancies in form and spacing make some parts easier to read than others	**Presentation** Text is difficult to read due to crowding or inappropriate font and sizing choices	**Presentation** Variability in handwriting, lack of proper spacing, and inappropriate multiple fonts make text indecipherable

Refer to Anchor Papers for personal narratives on pages 192–195 in the **Unit and Benchmark Assessment** for a sample of each writing level.

Unit 1 Computer Literacy

Objectives

- Use the Internet to find information
- Read to follow multi-step directions to complete a complex task
- Use specific search techniques to narrow a search
- Learn to cite URLs properly

Materials

- www.macmillanmh.com/reading

Vocabulary

URL (Uniform Resource Locator) the location or address of a Web page that starts with the abbreviation http://

search engine a computer program that finds items in files or databases electronically

browser a computer program that enables a person to explore the Internet

keyword search a type of search where a key word is used to help find information on a specific topic

hits requests to a Web site from a Web browser

cite: to quote a passage or author

Searching on the Internet

ACCESS PRIOR KNOWLEDGE

Discuss with students:

- What topics have you researched on the Internet?

- How do you make sure you get the best search results? *(use key words, use search terms like "and" or "or", use quotes, etc.)*

EXPLAIN

Introduce the lesson vocabulary by writing each word on the board and asking for a definition.

- Tell students that when they research a topic online they should open an Internet **browser** and type in the **URL** of a **search engine.**

- Help students brainstorm topics to search and write down possible **keyword searches** for students.

- Students can search using "or" between words to find Web pages that contain any of their key words.

- They can use "and" between key words to find Web pages that contain all of the key words. Different types of searches will produce various numbers of **hits.**

MODEL

- Show students how to find a **search engine** on the Internet.

- Choose a **keyword search** from the list and show students how to conduct a search. Narrow down the results by adding an "and" or "or." Point out the number of **hits** each search produces.

Using Citations

- Explain that students must be able to **cite URLs** in their writing to avoid plagiarism.

- Post an example of a correct **URL** citation for students to refer to: Author's name. "Title of Article or Link." Name of the Web Page. Date of Update. Name of Organization Associated with the Site. Access Date. <Web Address>.

GUIDED PRACTICE

Have students connect to www.macmillanmh.com/reading and go to Computer Literacy Lesson Grade 6 Unit 1.

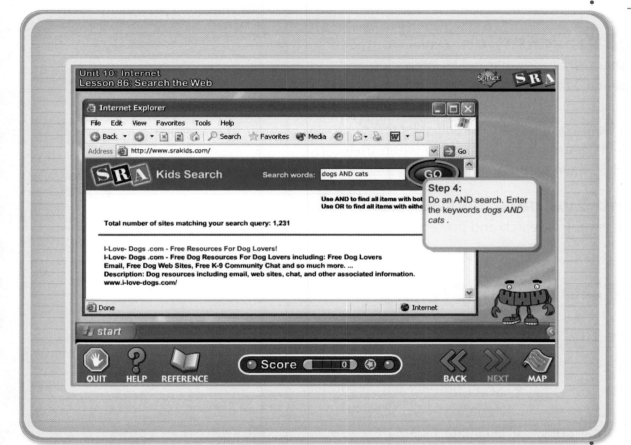

 The online practice lesson is an excerpt from SRA TechKnowledge. For information about the full SRA TechKnowledge program, go to **www.sratechknowledge.com**.

Leveled Practice

Approaching	On Level	Beyond Level
Have students choose a search topic and use search techniques to find information. They can record the number of hits they get for each type of search.	Have students choose a search topic, use search techniques to find information, and record the number of hits they get. Have them write down a piece of information they found and cite the URL where they found it.	Have students choose a search topic and effectively search the Internet for information. Ask students to write a paragraph about the topic using information that is accurately cited from at least two different Web sites.

Theme Project Wrap-Up

Research and Inquiry

After students complete steps 1, 2, 3, and 4, have them work on the following:

 Step 5 Create the Presentation Explain to students that they will share what they learned by preparing and delivering a speech. Provide students with information on a Student Checklist so they can review their work.

After students have completed their self-selected or cross-curricular projects, plan a Take Action Day when they can present what they have learned.

> How can people stop pollution?
>
> Land: Reduce, Reuse, Recycle

 Step 6 Review and Evaluate Use these questions to help you and students evaluate their research and presentation.

Teacher Checklist

Assess the Research Process

Planning the Project
- ✔ Participated in theme discussion
- ✔ Formulated research questions
- ✔ Identified and located multiple sources

Doing the Project
- ✔ Used primary and secondary sources
- ✔ Evaluated sources
- ✔ Synthesized information
- ✔ Evaluated information learned through inquiry

Assess the Presentation

Speaking
- ✔ Included a clear introduction, development, and conclusion
- ✔ Selected details appropriate for informing

Representing
- ✔ Made note cards
- ✔ Used visual media
- ✔ Visuals illustrated or enhanced important ideas.

Assess the Listener

Listening
- ✔ Made eye contact with the presenter
- ✔ Asked relevant, thoughtful questions and asked for clarification
- ✔ Gave helpful feedback
- ✔ Listened actively and responded appropriately

Student Checklist

Research Process
- ✔ Did you write questions you could research?
- ✔ Did you use at least three primary and secondary sources?

Presenting

Speaking
- ✔ Did you use note cards to help you remember important information?
- ✔ Could you answer your classmates' and teacher's questions?

Representing
- ✔ Did you use visuals to help listeners understand what you found out?
- ✔ Did you use statistics or quotes relevant to your topic?

SCORING RUBRIC FOR THEME PROJECTS

4 Excellent	**3** Good	**2** Fair	**1** Unsatisfactory
The student: • Presents the information in a clear and interesting way. • Uses words and (where relevant) visuals that effectively present important information. • May offer sophisticated reflections.	The student: • Presents the information in a fairly clear way. • Uses words and (where relevant) visuals that present relevant information. • May offer thoughtful reflections.	The student: • Struggles to present the information clearly. • May use adequate words and (where relevant) visuals. • May offer irrelevant reflections.	The student: • May not grasp the task. • May present sketchy information in a disorganized way. • May have extreme difficulty with research.

 Home-School Connection

Invite family members, other students, and members of the community to attend students' presentations of their projects on Take Action Day. Try to include some people who have taken a public action.

■ Introduce each guest by name and relationship to the community.

■ Videotape the presentations for family members to borrow or to show at the parent/teacher conferences.

Administer the Test

Unit 1 Reading Assessment,
pp. 9–24

TESTED SKILLS AND STRATEGIES

COMPREHENSION STRATEGIES AND SKILLS

- Strategies: Analyze story structure, make inferences and analyze
- Skills: Character and setting, plot, mood, tone, main idea and details, cause and effect

VOCABULARY STRATEGIES

- Dictionary
- Word parts
- Context clues
- Analogies

TEXT FEATURES AND STUDY SKILLS

- Photos and captions
- Social Studies textbook
- Using the library/media center
- Time lines

GRAMMAR, MECHANICS, USAGE

- Sentence types and fragments
- Subjects and predicates
- Conjunctions and compound sentences
- Clauses and complex sentences
- Run-on sentences
- End punctuation
- Using proper punctuation while writing a letter

WRITING

- Personal narrative

Using Multiple Assessments for Instructional Planning

To create instructional profiles for your students, look for patterns in the results from any of the following assessments.

Fluency Assessment

Plan appropriate fluency-building activities and practice to help all students achieve the following fluency goal:
117–137 WCPM

Running Records

Use the instructional reading level determined by the Running Record calculations for regrouping decisions.

Benchmark Assessment

Administer tests three times a year as an additional measure of both student progress and the effectiveness of the instructional program.

Technology

- Administer the **Unit Assessment** electronically.
- Score all tests electronically.
- Available online or on CD-ROM.

Analyze the Data

Use information from a variety of informal and formal assessments, as well as your own judgment, to assist in your instructional planning. Students who consistently score at the lowest end of each range should be evaluated for Intervention. Use the **Diagnostic Assessment** in the Intervention Teacher's Edition.

Diagnose		Prescribe
ASSESSMENTS	**IF...**	**THEN...**
UNIT TEST	0–23 questions correct	Reteach tested skills using the **Additional Lessons** (pp. T1–T10)
FLUENCY ASSESSMENT		
Oral Reading Fluency	109–116 WCPM	Fluency Solutions
	0–108 WCPM	Evaluate for Intervention.
RUNNING RECORDS	Level 50 or below	Reteach comprehension skills using the **Additional Lessons** (pp. T1–T10). Provide additional Fluency activities.

Glossary

Introduce students to the Glossary by reading through the introduction and looking over the pages with them. Encourage the class to talk about what they see.

Words in a glossary, like words in a dictionary, are listed in **alphabetical order.** Point out the **guide words** at the top of each page that tell the first and last words appearing on that page.

ENTRIES

Point out examples of **main entries,** or entry words, and entries. Read through a simple entry with the class, identifying each part. Have students note the order in which information is given: entry word(s), definition(s), example sentence(s), syllable division, pronunciation respelling, part of speech, plural/verb/adjective forms.

Note if more than one definition is given for a word, the definitions are numbered. Note the format used for a word that is more than one part of speech.

Review the **parts of speech** by identifying each in a sentence:

Inter.	*article*	*n.*	*conj.*	*article*	*n.*
Wow!	A	dictionary	and	a	glossary

v.	*adv.*	*pron.*	*prep.*	*n.*
tell	almost	everything	about	words!

HOMOGRAPHS/HOMOPHONES/HOMONYMS

Point out that some entries are for multiple-meaning words called **homographs.** Homographs have the same spellings but have different origins and meanings, and, in some cases, different pronunciations.

Explain that students should not confuse homographs with **homophones** or **homonyms.** Homophones are words that have the same pronunciation but have different spellings and meanings. Homonyms are words that have the same pronunciation and spelling but have different meanings. Provide students with examples.

PRONUNCIATION KEY

Explain the use of the pronunciation key (either the short key, at the bottom of every other page, or the long key, at the beginning of the Glossary). Demonstrate the difference between primary stress and secondary stress by pronouncing a word with both. Pronounce the words both correctly and incorrectly to give students a clearer understanding of the proper pronunciations.

WORD HISTORY

The Word History feature explains the **etymology** of select words. Explain that *etymology* is the history of a word from its origin to its present form. A word's etymology explains which language it comes from and what changes have occurred in its spelling and/or meaning. Many English words are derivatives of words from other languages, such as Latin or Greek. Derivatives are formed from base or root words.

Glossary

What Is a Glossary?

A glossary can help you find the **meanings** of words in this book that you may not know. The words in the glossary are listed in **alphabetical order**. **Guide words** at the top of each page tell you the first and last words on the page.

Each word is divided into syllables. The way to pronounce the word is given next. You can understand the pronunciation respelling by using the **pronunciation key**. A shorter key appears at the bottom of every other page. When a word has more than one syllable, a dark accent mark (´) shows which syllable is stressed. In some words, a light accent mark (ʹ) shows which syllable has a less heavy stress. Sometimes an entry includes a second meaning for the word.

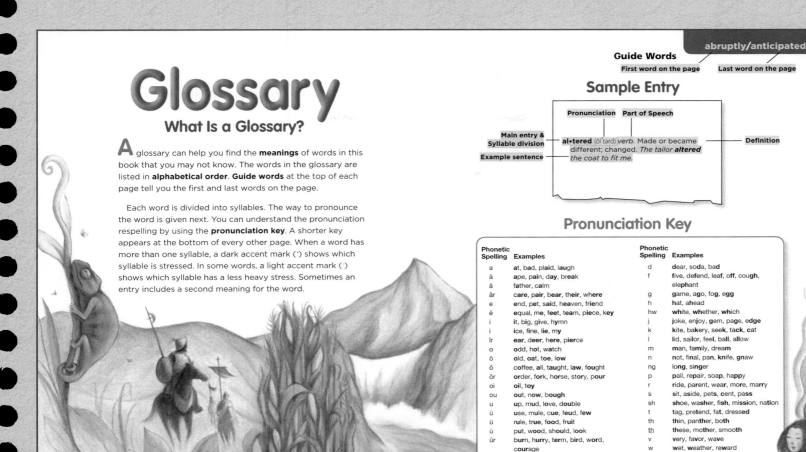

Guide Words
First word on the page — **abruptly/anticipated** — Last word on the page

Sample Entry

Pronunciation — **Part of Speech**
Main entry & Syllable division — **al•tered** (ôl´tərd) *verb*. Made or became different; changed. *The tailor **altered** the coat to fit me.* — **Definition**
Example sentence

Pronunciation Key

Phonetic Spelling	Examples
a	at, bad, plaid, laugh
ā	ape, pain, day, break
ä	father, calm
âr	care, pair, bear, their, where
e	end, pet, said, heaven, friend
ē	equal, me, feet, team, piece, key
i	it, big, give, hymn
ī	ice, fine, lie, my
îr	ear, deer, here, pierce
o	odd, hot, watch
ō	old, oat, toe, low
ô	coffee, all, taught, law, fought
ôr	order, fork, horse, story, pour
oi	oil, toy
ou	out, now, bough
u	up, mud, love, double
ū	use, mule, cue, feud, few
ü	rule, true, food, fruit
u̇	put, wood, should, look
ûr	burn, hurry, term, bird, word, courage
ə	about, taken, pencil, lemon, circus
b	bat, above, job
ch	chin, such, match

Phonetic Spelling	Examples
d	dear, soda, bad
f	five, defend, leaf, off, cough, elephant
g	game, ago, fog, egg
h	hat, ahead
hw	white, whether, which
j	joke, enjoy, gem, page, edge
k	kite, bakery, seek, tack, cat
l	lid, sailor, feel, ball, allow
m	man, family, dream
n	not, final, pan, knife, gnaw
ng	long, singer
p	pail, repair, soap, happy
r	ride, parent, wear, more, marry
s	sit, aside, pets, cent, pass
sh	shoe, washer, fish, mission, nation
t	tag, pretend, fat, dressed
th	thin, panther, both
th	these, mother, smooth
v	very, favor, wave
w	wet, weather, reward
y	yes, onion
z	zoo, lazy, jazz, rose, dogs, houses
zh	vision, treasure, seizure

714

715

Aa

a•brupt•ly (ə brupt´lē) *adverb*. Happening in a quick way or without warning. *Ben **abruptly** dropped the hot potato onto the floor.*

ab•sorb (ab sôrb´, ab zôrb´) *verb*. To soak up or take in. *Use a towel to **absorb** the spilled water.*

ac•ces•si•ble (ak ses´ə bəl) *adjective*. Able to be reached, entered, or approached. *Ramps make buildings **accessible** to those who cannot climb stairs.*

a•dept (ə dept´) *adjective*. Highly skilled, expert. *Bonnie is **adept** on the balance beam in gymnastics.*

ad•min•is•ter (ad min´ə stər) *verb*. To give or provide something. *The nurse will **administer** first aid.*

ad•verse (ad vûrs´, ad´vûrs) *adjective*. Not helpful to what is wanted; not favorable. *The football game was played under **adverse** conditions because of the heavy rain.*

aer•o•nau•tics (âr´ə nô´tiks) *noun*. The science or art of flight. *The pilots studied **aeronautics**.*

ag•o•nized (ag´ə nīzd´) *verb*. Experienced great discomfort, pain, or stress. *The owner **agonized** over money problems after he closed the store for the day.*

al•loy (al´oi) *noun*. A metal formed by fusing two or more metals, or a metal and another substance. *Brass is an **alloy** of copper and zinc.*

an•thro•pol•o•gists (an´thrə pol´ə gists) *noun, plural*. Students or experts in the science that deals with physical, cultural, and social development of humans. *Several **anthropologists** showed up at the construction site after the workers found the artifacts.*

an•tic•i•pat•ed (an tis´ə pā´tid) *verb*. Expected or looked forward to. *All day we **anticipated** getting our test scores from our teacher.*

al•tered (ôl´tərd) *verb*. Made or became different; changed. *The tailor **altered** the coat to fit me.*

am•bi•tious (am bish´əs) *adjective*. Eager to succeed. *The **ambitious** assistant would work all weekend in hopes of becoming a manager someday.*

am•pu•tat•ed (am´pyə tā´tid) *verb*. Having had any limb or digit cut off by surgery. *After her arm was crushed in the car accident, it was **amputated**.*

an•a•lyz•ing (an´ə lī´zing) *verb*. Examining carefully and in detail in order to understand something. *By **analyzing** the soil sample, the scientist learned that the land was safe for a playground.*

a•nat•o•my (ə nat´ə mē) *noun*. The branch of science dealing with the structure of animals or plants and the relationships of their parts. *The teacher held classes in **anatomy**.*

a•non•y•mous (ə non´ə məs) *adjective*. Of unknown origin or authorship; without any name given. *All the donations were **anonymous**, so the hospital did not know whom to thank for all the money.*

Word History

Anonymous comes from the Greek word *anōnymos*. *Onyma* means "name," and the *a-* placed at the beginning means "without."

an•tique (an tēk´) *adjective*. Of, belonging to, or in the style of long ago; dating from an early time period. *My grandmother had an **antique** dining room table that was worth a lot of money.*

anx•i•e•ty (ang zī´i tē) *noun*. A feeling of fearful uneasiness or worry about what may happen. *The family felt **anxiety** when no one could find the lost dog.*

ap•pa•rat•us (ap´ə rat´əs, ap´ə rā´təs) *noun*. A device or mechanism used for a particular purpose. *One of the **apparatus** in the gym required repairing.*

aq•ue•ducts (ak´wə dukts´) *noun, plural*. Large pipes or other channels that carry water over a long distance. ***Aqueducts** were built for easier access to the water supply through the village.*

ar•id (ar´id) *adjective*. Dry; lifeless. *After the long drought, the ground was **arid**.*

ar•ray (ə rā´) *noun*. A large collection or display. *The shop window offered a wide **array** of objects for the home.*

ar•ti•fi•cial (är´tə fish´əl) *adjective*. Produced by humans; made in imitation or as a substitute. *The **artificial** knee my uncle received worked as well as his natural one.*

as•pir•ing (ə spīr´ing) *verb*. Wanting or trying very hard to achieve some goal. *John is **aspiring** after fame and fortune.*

auc•tion (ôk´shən) *noun*. A public sale at which property or possessions are sold to the highest bidder. *My brother bid twenty dollars for some lamps at an **auction**.*

awe•some (ô´səm) *adjective*. Inspiring great wonder combined with fear or respect. *The Grand Canyon is an **awesome** sight.*

ax•is (ak´sis) *noun*. A real or imaginary straight line through the center of an object, around which the object turns. *Earth rotates on its **axis** once every twenty-four hours.*

Bb

ben•e•fit (ben´ə fit) *noun*. Something that helps or betters a person or thing. *We all knew the **benefit** of eating fresh green vegetables.*

be•wil•der•ing (bi wil´də ring) *verb*. Confusing or puzzling. *This math problem is **bewildering** to me.*

bi•ased sam•ple (bī´əst sam´pəl) *noun*. A group of subjects in a survey that does not represent the total group. *In order for Kim to get the results she wanted in her survey, she polled a **biased sample**.*

bil•low (bil´ō) *verb*. To rise in waves. *Watch the curtains **billow** in the breeze.*

bi•on•ics (bī on´iks) *noun*. The study of the parts of the bodies of humans and other animals in order to devise improvements in various machines, especially computers and artificial limbs. *Since I am so interested in sports and computers, I decided to study **bionics** at college.*

at; āpe; fär; câre; end; mē; it; īce; pîerce; hot; ōld; sông; fôrk; oil; out; up; ūse; rüle; pu̇ll; tûrn; chin; sing; shop; thin; this; hw in white; zh in treasure.

The symbol ə stands for the unstressed vowel sound in about, taken, pencil, lemon, and circus.

716

717

board (bôrd) *noun.* Meals provided regularly for pay or in exchange for services. *The student received room and* ***board*** *for a reasonable fee.*

bol•ster (bōl′stər) *verb.* To support or strengthen. *The sight of land can* ***bolster*** *a sailor's low spirits after many days at sea.*

broad•cast (brôd′kast′) *noun.* Information or entertainment that is sent out by radio or television. *We all listened to Rita's* ***broadcast*** *of the news and the weather.*

Cc

ca•lam•i•ties (kə lam′i tēz) *noun, plural.* Disasters causing great destruction and loss. *The relief agency helped people through many kinds of* ***calamities****.*

cal•cu•la•tions (kal′kyə lā′shənz) *noun, plural.* The products or results of a mathematical process. *By performing careful* ***calculations****, the astronomer was able to locate a new star.*

can•vass (kan′vəs) *verb.* To examine or discuss carefully or thoroughly. *I had to* ***canvass*** *my class to find out who the most popular person was.*

cas•cade (kas kād′) *noun.* A waterfall or series of small waterfalls; anything resembling this. *The clothes fell out of the suitcase in a* ***cascade*** *down the staircase.*

ce•ram•ics (sə ram′iks) *noun.* The art or technique of making objects by shaping clay and then baking it at a high temperature. *Connie displayed beautiful* ***ceramics*** *throughout her home.*

Word History

The word **ceramics** comes from the Greek *keramikos*, which stems from *keramos* meaning "potter's clay" or "pottery."

cha•me•leon (kə mēl′yən) *noun.* Any of various small, slow-moving lizards that can change the color of their skin to match their surroundings. Also used in reference to a person who is very changeable. *Since he tended to look different every time we saw him, we called him a* ***chameleon.***

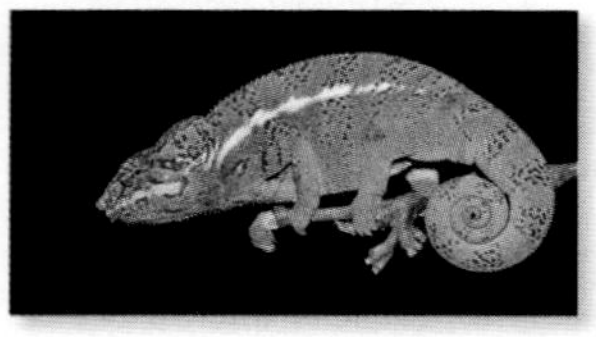

char•is•mat•ic (kar′iz mat′ik) *adjective.* Having the rare personal quality of attracting the loyalty and devotion of a large following of people. *People are drawn to* ***charismatic*** *politicians.*

chro•nol•o•gy (krə nol′ə jē) *noun.* The arrangement of events in the order in which they happened. *In class the teacher showed us the* ***chronology*** *of events that led to the War of Independence.*

civ•i•lized (siv′ə līzd′) *adjective.* No longer savage or primitive; educated. *He was a very* ***civilized*** *young man and had excellent manners.*

clock•wise (klok′wīz′) *adverb.* Going in the direction that the hands of a clock move. *The popular new dance involved spinning around* ***clockwise*** *several times.*

co•in•ci•den•ces (kō in′si dən ses) *noun, plural.* Remarkable occurrences of events or circumstances at the same time and apparently by chance. *A series of* ***coincidences*** *led me to meet my group of friends in the museum.*

col•lec•tive (kə lek′tiv) *adjective.* Of, relating to, or done by a group of persons or things; united. *The book was written by a* ***collective*** *effort; all the writers added something.*

com•mis•sioned (kə mish′ənd) *verb.* Being assigned to create a work of art. *My art teacher was* ***commissioned*** *to paint a huge mural at the new hotel.*

com•mit•ment (kə mit′mənt) *noun.* The act of devoting oneself; an obligation. *Since joining the drama club was a huge time* ***commitment****, I had to think twice before signing up.*

con•cen•trat•ed (kon′sən trā′tid) *verb.* Close together in one place. *The population of our country is* ***concentrated*** *in the cities.*

con•quis•ta•do•res (kon kēs′tə dôr′ēz) *noun, plural.* The Spanish conquerors in Mexico and Peru during the sixteenth century. *In history class we are learning about Hernando Cortés and the* ***conquistadores*** *who conquered the Aztec Empire.*

con•scious (kon′shəs) *adjective.* **1.** Knowing or realizing; aware. *Linda was* ***conscious*** *of her own tendency to exaggerate.* **2.** Awake. *Despite the blow to his head, Al remained* ***conscious****.*

con•serve (kən sûrv′) *verb.* To preserve. ***Conserve*** *your strength.*

con•tin•u•ous (kən tin′ū əs) *adjective.* Unbroken or without a break. *The* ***continuous*** *screaming of the baby ruined our lunch at the restaurant.*

con•vic•tions (kən vik′shənz) *noun, plural.* Firm beliefs or opinions. *Many people voted for the politician because of his deep* ***convictions****.*

Dd

da•ta (dā′tə, dat′ə) *noun, plural.* Information from which conclusions can be drawn; facts and figures. *The* ***data*** *from the reports must be accurate.*

de•but (dā bū′, dā′bū) *noun.* A first public appearance. *It was difficult to get tickets to the* ***debut*** *of the movie because of the great advance reviews it received.*

dec•ades (dek′ādz) *noun, plural.* Periods of ten years. *At my grandmother's party, she told stories that spanned the eight* ***decades*** *of her life.*

Word History

The word **decade** comes from the Greek word, *deka*, which means "ten."

de•crease (di krēs′) *verb.* To lessen or reduce. *Our class made a list of ways to* ***decrease*** *pollution in our state.*

de•fi•ance (di fī′əns) *noun.* Bold or open resistance to authority or opposition. *The general was getting very angry at the strong* ***defiance*** *of the small number of enemy troops.*

at; āpe; fär; câre; end; mē; it; īce; pîerce; hot; ōld; sông; fôrk; oil; out; up; ūse; rüle; pu̇ll; tûrn; chin; sing; shop; thin; this; hw in white; zh in treasure.

The symbol ə stands for the unstressed vowel sound in about, taken, pencil, lemon, and circus.

deft•ly (deft′lē) *adverb.* In a skillful or nimble way. *The dancer* ***deftly*** *performed her moves across the stage.*

de•hy•drat•ed (dē hī′drā tid) *adjective.* To have had water or moisture removed. *The marathon runner was* ***dehydrated*** *after the race because she sweated so much.*

de•ject•ed•ly (di jek′tid lē) *adverb.* Showing disheartened, downcast, or low spirits. *I* ***dejectedly*** *kicked the ball against the wall after we lost the soccer game.*

dem•on•stra•tion (dem′ən strā′shən) *noun.* Something that proves clearly; an explaining or showing by the use of visible examples. *It's a thrill when scientists prove a new theory in a* ***demonstration.***

de•ri•sion (di rizh′ən) *noun.* Scornful contempt; ridicule; mockery. *The bully treated all the class with* ***derision.***

de•scend•ing (di sen′ding) *verb.* Moving or coming from a higher place to a lower one. *They were* ***descending*** *the mountain on skis.*

de•spon•dent•ly (di spon′dənt lē) *adverb.* In a way that shows having lost heart; in a depressed or dejected way. *As the team lost more points, they walked* ***despondently*** *along the sidelines.*

des•ti•na•tion (des′tə nā′shən) *noun.* A place to which a person or thing is going. *The train conductor asked us what our* ***destination*** *was when we boarded the train.*

de•te•ri•o•rat•ed (di tîr′ē ə rā′tid) *verb.* Lessened in character, quality, condition, or value; worsened. *The newspaper* ***deteriorated*** *rapidly in the rain.*

dev•as•tat•ing (dev′ə stā′ting) *adjective.* Wreaking or capable of wreaking complete destruction; ruinously destructive. *The hurricane proved to be* ***devastating****; it completely destroyed 1000 houses.*

di•lap•i•dat•ed (di lap′i dā′tid) *adjective.* Fallen into ruin or decay. *Everyone on our street decided to help paint the* ***dilapidated*** *old house on the corner.*

drow•sy (drou′zē) *adjective.* Feeling sleepy. *The guard was* ***drowsy*** *after working extra shifts every day of the week.*

dwell•ing (dwel′ing) *noun.* A place where a person lives. *While walking along the beach, the children found an old* ***dwelling*** *made of wood and canvas.*

Ee

eaves (ēvz) *noun, plural.* The overhanging edge or edges of a sloping roof. *The new window was placed upstairs under the* ***eaves****.*

e•con•o•mists (i kon′ə mists) *noun, plural.* Students of or experts in economics or money matters. *Many* ***economists*** *predicted that sales during the holiday season would be low.*

edg•y (ej′ē) *adjective.* Very nervous or impatient. *Sam felt* ***edgy*** *when he was called down to the principal's office.*

e•lab•o•rate (*adjective,* i lab′ər it; *verb,* i lab′ə rāt′) *adjective.* Worked out with great care and great detail. *The committee spent one year planning the* ***elaborate*** *ceremony.* —*verb.* To give additional or fuller treatment to something spoken or written. *I was too tired to* ***elaborate*** *on the events of the trip, so I just gave a basic account of it.*

em•barked (em bärkt′) *verb.* To begin or set out, as on an adventure. *The vacationers* ***embarked*** *on a two-week cruise in the Caribbean.*

em•bar•rass•ment (em bar′əs mənt) *noun.* The act or state of feeling uncomfortable or ashamed. *Aunt Tillie's crass behavior at the dinner party was an* ***embarrassment*** *to the whole family.*

em•bed•ded (em be′did) *verb.* To set in surrounding matter; to place or plant firmly. *The seeds were deeply* ***embedded*** *in the soil.*

em•ploy•ee (em ploi′ē) *noun.* A person who works for a person or business for pay. *A good* ***employee*** *is one who always does his or her best on the job.*

en•coun•ter (en koun′tər) *noun.* Any kind of meeting between friends, enemies, or colleagues. *My grandfather told me about the violent* ***encounter*** *when he was wounded in the war.*

en•gulf (en gulf′) *verb.* To swallow up or completely surround. *The flames may* ***engulf*** *the whole hillside unless we put the fire out soon.*

en•thralled (en thrôld′) *verb.* Held spellbound; charmed. *The crowd was* ***enthralled*** *by the magician and his bag of magic tricks.*

en•vi•sioned (en vizh′ənd) *verb.* Formed a picture in the mind. *The principal* ***envisioned*** *a big, new gym for his school.*

ep•i•dem•ic (ep′i dem′ik) *noun.* **1.** The rapid spread of a disease among people at the same time. *The elementary school experienced an* ***epidemic*** *of chicken pox last winter.* **2.** The rapid spread or sudden, widespread appearance of anything. *An* ***epidemic*** *of burglaries hit our town.*

e•qua•tor (i kwā′tər) *noun.* An imaginary line around Earth halfway between the North and South poles. *The United States and Canada are north of the* ***equator****.*

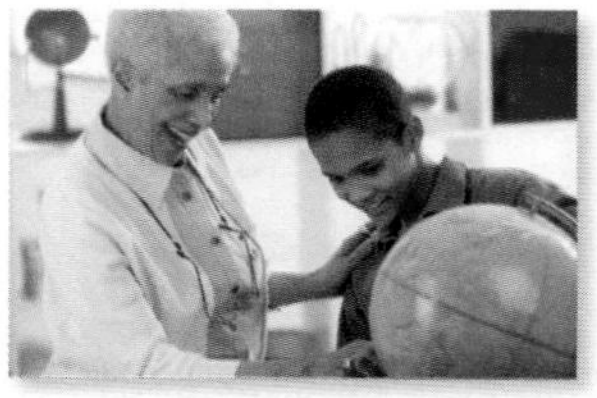

e•rode (i rōd′) *verb.* To wear or wash away slowly. *Ocean waves will* ***erode*** *the shore.*

es•cort (es′kôrt) *noun.* A person or persons who go along with another as a courtesy or for protection. *Cinderella's stepsisters wanted the prince to be their* ***escort*** *to the ball.*

es•tab•lished (e stab′lisht) *verb.* Set up permanently. *The restaurant where we ate lunch was* ***established*** *in 1897!*

es•ti•mate (*verb,* es′tə māt′; *noun,* es′tə mit) *verb.* To come to a conclusion by reasoning or an educated guess. *We* ***estimate*** *that the trip will take an hour, but it might take longer if there is heavy traffic.* —*noun.* An approximate judgment or calculation. *The painters gave me an* ***estimate*** *of what the job would cost.*

e•vac•u•ate (i vak′ū āt′) *verb.* To leave or cause to leave. *Firefighters must* ***evacuate*** *the people from the burning building.*

ev•i•dent (ev′i dənt) *adjective.* Easily seen or understood. *It was* ***evident*** *to everyone that the thief had stolen the money.*

at; āpe; fär; câre; end; mē; it; īce; pîerce; hot; ōld; sông; fôrk; oil; out; up; ūse; rüle; pu̇ll; tûrn; chin; sing; shop; thin; this; hw in white; zh in treasure.

The symbol ə stands for the unstressed vowel sound in about, taken, pencil, lemon, and circus.

ex·ca·vate (eks'kə vāt') *verb.* To uncover by digging. *The miners work to **excavate** coal.*

ex·cel (ek sel') *verb.* To do very well; to succeed. *The teacher told us that it takes a lot of studying to **excel** in our classes.*

ex·cep·tion·al (ek sep'shə nəl) *adjective.* Unusual or out of the ordinary. *I liked the **exceptional** architecture of the building.*

ex·trav·a·gant (ek strav'ə gant) *adjective.* Lavish or wasteful in the spending of money. *Mary made many **extravagant** purchases that she really could not afford.*

Ff

fam·ine (fam'in) *noun.* A great lack of food in an area or country. *The **famine** affected nearly all the people in the village.*

feat (fēt) *noun.* An act or deed that shows great courage, strength, or skill. *Climbing that mountain was quite a **feat**.*

fidg·et (fij'it) *verb.* To be nervous or make restless movements. *The girl tried not to **fidget** in the long line.*

fire·re·sist·ant (fīr ri zis'tant) *adjective.* Being constructed specifically against getting set on fire at a certain temperature and certain amount of time. *The **fire-resistant** outfit worked well.*

fleet·ing (flē'ting) *adjective.* Passing very quickly. *We only had a **fleeting** look at the famous actress as she hurried into the theater.*

flour·ish (flûr'ish) *verb.* To grow or develop strongly or prosperously; thrive. *In order for a child to grow and **flourish**, he or she must eat nutritious food and get lots of rest and exercise.*

fore·man (fôr'mən) *noun.* A worker who supervises a group of workers, as in a factory or on a farm. *The **foreman** was in charge of seeing that the cars came off the assembly line on time.*

fore·told (fôr tōld') *verb.* Told of ahead of time. *The game played out just as my coach **foretold**: we won the championship!*

for·mal·ly (fôr'mə lē) *adverb.* Acting with stiff, proper, or polite behavior. *The governor **formally** welcomed the guests to the party.*

for·ma·tions (fôr mā'shəns) *noun, plural.* Something that is formed. *The tourists took a boat to see the strange rock **formations** in the lake.*

ful·fill (fúl fil') *verb.* To carry out or bring to completion; cause to happen. *Miguel was able to **fulfill** his promise as a musician by mastering the piano.*

fur·rowed (fûr'ōd) *adjective.* Having deep wrinkles. *Whenever I asked for money, my dad's brow looked **furrowed**.*

Word History

The word furrow comes from the Old English *furh* which is "a channel made by a plow."

Gg

gen·er·ate (jen'ə rāt') *verb.* To bring about or produce. *That machine will **generate** electricity.*

gen·er·os·i·ty (jen'ə ros'i tē) *noun.* Willingness to give or share freely. *We thanked the community for its **generosity** and helpfulness during the crisis.*

glee·ful·ly (glē'fə lē) *adverb.* In a joyous or merry way. *The children **gleefully** ran toward the ice-cream truck.*

glid·er (glī'dər) *noun.* An aircraft that flies without a motor and rides on currents of air. *We entered a contest to see who could build a model **glider** that could fly the farthest.*

gloat·ed (glō'tid) *verb.* Thought about with satisfaction or, sometimes, mean-spirited pleasure. *The town **gloated** over its team's victory in the state tournament.*

glum·ly (glum'lē) *adverb.* To act in a sad or depressed manner. *Vincent **glumly** walked home after he got his bad report card.*

gri·maced (grim'əst) *verb.* To twist the face to show disgust, pain, or displeasure. *The carpenter **grimaced** when he stepped on a nail.*

grit·ted (gri'tid) *verb.* Ground or held tightly clamped together, as with the teeth. *The weightlifter **gritted** her teeth as she lifted 300 pounds.*

grouch·y (grou'chē) *adjective.* In a bad mood; irritable; sulky. *Working with **grouchy** people is no fun at all.*

guid·ance (gī'dəns) *noun.* The act or process of guiding; giving direction or leading. *Before embarking on a law career, Maria sought **guidance** from lawyers she had met.*

guilds (gildz) *noun, plural.* In the Middle Ages, a group of merchants or artisans in one trade or craft, organized to maintain standards of work and to protect the interests of members. *Representatives from all the **guilds** went to a meeting to discuss work conditions.*

Hh

ham·per[1] (ham'pər) *verb.* To interfere or slow the action or progress of something. *The rain did not **hamper** people from enjoying themselves at the outdoor concert.*

ham·per[2] (ham'pər) *noun.* A large basket or container, usually with a cover. *After getting caught in the rain, I threw my wet clothes in the laundry **hamper**.*

hob·bled (hob'əld) *verb.* Moved or walked awkwardly with a limp. *After he sprained his ankle, Brad **hobbled** around for three weeks.*

hon·or·a·ble (on'ər ə bəl) *adjective.* Characterized by or having a sense of what is right or moral. *The young girl was considered very **honorable** when she returned the wallet she found.*

hov·er·ing (huv'ə ring) *verb.* Remaining in the same spot for a period of time. *The bees were **hovering** above the chocolate cake at our picnic.*

at; āpe; fär; câre; end; mē; it; īce; pîerce; hot; ōld; sông; fôrk; oil; out; up; ūse; rūle; púll; tûrn; chin; sing; shop; thin; <u>th</u>is; hw in white; zh in treasure.

The symbol ə stands for the unstressed vowel sound in about, taken, pencil, lemon, and circus.

Ii

il·le·gal·ly (i lē'gə lē) *adverb.* Acting in an unlawful manner. *The police officer wrote tickets for all the cars that were parked **illegally**.*

im·mense (i mens') *adjective.* Very large or huge. *The crowd at the outdoor concert left an **immense** amount of garbage on the ground.*

im·mi·grat·ed (im'i grā'tid) *verb.* Entered a country or region in which one was not born in order to make a permanent home there. *Saskia's parents **immigrated** here from Russia about fifteen years ago.*

in·no·va·tions (in'ə vā'shənz) *noun, plural.* Things or ideas that are of value and newly introduced. *The development of the first antibiotic was one of the great **innovations** in medicine.*

in·scribed (in skrībd') *verb.* Written, carved, engraved, or marked on something. *The stone walls were **inscribed** with the names of people who had given money to the museum.*

in·stinc·tive·ly (in stingk'tiv lē) *adverb.* Of or relating to a natural tendency. *Birds **instinctively** feed their young in the nest.*

in·tact (in takt') *adjective.* Not damaged and in one whole piece. *The flower vase was still **intact** after it was found in the bottom of the box.*

in·ter·cept (in'tər sept') *verb.* To stop on the way; to stop the course or progress of. *The defensive back managed to **intercept** the quarterback's pass.*

Word History

Intercept comes from the Latin, *interceptus*, which is the past participle of *intercipere*, meaning "interrupt" or "to catch between."

in·te·ri·or (in tîr'ē ər) *noun.* The inside of something. *The **interior** of the building was very cool compared to the heat outside.*

in·ter·pret·er (in tûr'pri tər) *noun.* One who helps to make something clear or understandable. *The **interpreter** at the United Nations translated English into Swahili.*

in·ter·sec·tion (in'tər sek'shən, in'tər sek'shən) *noun.* A place of intersecting, especially where two or more roads or streets meet or cross. *We stopped our car at the **intersection** of 70th Street and Second Avenue.*

Ll

la·ment·ed (lə men'təd) *verb.* Expressed sorrow, grief, or regret. *We all **lamented** the loss of the best player on the team to a knee injury.*

la·va (lä'və, lav'ə) *noun.* Very hot, melted rock that comes out of an erupting volcano. *The **lava** destroyed everything in its path as it flowed out of the volcano.*

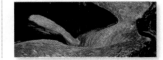

leg·a·cy (leg'ə sē) *noun.* Something handed down by custom or tradition. *The mansion was passed down to my uncle by a **legacy** specifying that he never modernize it.*

lim·ou·sine (lim'ə zēn') *noun.* A large sedan, often with a glass partition between the front and back seats, often driven by a chauffeur. *When the **limousine** pulled up, a crowd gathered to see the movie star.*

lounge (lounj) *verb.* To lean, sit, or lie lazily. *During the summer, I love to **lounge** around the pool and read magazines.* —*noun.* **1.** A place for sitting, waiting, or relaxing within a public setting. *In the Victorian era, there was a ladies' and a gentlemen's **lounge** at the railway station.* **2.** A couch or sofa. *I sat on a comfortable **lounge**.*

lures (lúrz) *noun, plural.* Artificial bait used in fishing. *The **lures** were in the tackle box.*

lux·u·ry (luk'shə rē, lug'zhə rē) *noun.* Something that adds to a person's comfort or pleasure but is not really necessary. *A yacht is a **luxury** that most of us cannot afford.*

Mm

maize (māz) *noun.* A grain that grows on the ears of a tall plant. ***Maize** is usually called corn.*

Word History

Maize comes from the Spanish word *maíz* which means "Indian corn" and originates from the native South American Taino tribe's word *mahiz*.

ma·neu·vered (mə nü'vərd) *verb.* Used skillful or clever moves or plans. *Jackson **maneuvered** the large boat skillfully past the smaller ones.*

man·u·scripts (man'yə skripts') *noun, plural.* The handwritten versions of books, articles, or other works, especially ones from before the invention of printing presses. *The editor spent the weekend reading the **manuscripts** available in the museum's library.*

mar·veled (mär'vəld) *verb.* To become filled with wonder or astonishment. *The class **marveled** at Henry's ability to answer math problems so quickly and accurately.*

ma·tu·ri·ty (mə chùr'i tē) *noun.* The state or quality of reaching full physical and mental development, or full growth. *The crops are ready to be harvested when they have reached **maturity**.*

me·di·e·val (mē'dē ē'vəl, mid ē'vəl) *adjective.* Belonging to or happening in the Middle Ages, the period of European history from about the fifth century to the middle of the fifteenth century. *James came to class in a **medieval** costume to present his report on tenth-century Europe.*

at; āpe; fär; câre; end; mē; it; īce; pîerce; hot; ōld; sông; fôrk; oil; out; up; ūse; rūle; púll; tûrn; chin; sing; shop; thin; <u>th</u>is; hw in white; zh in treasure.

The symbol ə stands for the unstressed vowel sound in about, taken, pencil, lemon, and circus.

mem•o•ra•bil•i•a (mem'ər ə bil'ē ə) *noun, plural.* Things that are worth being collected or recorded. *At the flea market there was a lot of* ***memorabilia***.

mi•grant (mī'grənt) *adjective.* Moving from one region to another in search of work. *The* ***migrant*** *worker returned every April.*

mim•ics (mim'iks) *verb.* To imitate the speech, manners, or gestures of; to copy closely or reproduce. *The way Lucy* ***mimics*** *Harpo Marx is a classic bit of comedy.*

min•i•a•ture (min'ē ə chər) *adjective.* Greatly reduced in size or very small. *On their vacation, my parents bought me a* ***miniature*** *model of the Eiffel Tower.*

mis•treat•ed (mis trē'tid) *verb.* To be treated badly. *The veterinarian said the dog we found had been* ***mistreated*** *by its owner.*

mit•i•gate (mit'i gāt') *verb.* To make milder or less severe or painful. *The nurse tried to* ***mitigate*** *the suffering of the patient.*

mod•er•ate (*adjective,* mod'ər it; *verb,* mod'ə rāt) *adjective.* Not extreme; balanced. *We have had* ***moderate*** *temperatures this winter.* —*verb.* To preside over or at. *My class wanted me to* ***moderate*** *the middle school debate, but I was too shy.*

mo•men•tum (mō men'təm) *noun.* The force or speed resulting from motion. *I was gaining* ***momentum*** *as I rode down the hill.*

muf•flers (muf'lərz) *noun, plural.* Scarves of wool or other material worn around the neck for warmth. *The children were dressed in hats, coats, and* ***mufflers*** *so they could play in the snow.*

myth•o•log•i•cal (mith'ə loj'i kəl) *adjective.* Of, relating to, or found in mythology. *The* ***mythological*** *character of Zeus was the ruler of all the gods on Mount Olympus.*

Nn

non•re•new•a•ble (non'ri nü'ə bəl, non'ri nū'ə bəl) *adjective.* Easily used up or exhausted. *Coal and petroleum are* ***nonrenewable*** *natural resources.*

nour•ish•ing (nûr'ə shing) *adjective.* Promoting health and growth. *So that I could grow up to be healthy and strong, my mother made me eat many* ***nourishing*** *foods.*

nui•sance (nü'səns, nū'səns) *noun.* A person, thing, or action that annoys or offends. *The bees were a huge* ***nuisance*** *during the picnic.*

Oo

ob•sta•cles (ob'stə kəlz) *noun, plural.* Persons or things that get in the way of or block progress. *After the big storm, there were many* ***obstacles*** *in the road that blocked traffic.*

op•pres•sion (ə presh'ən) *noun.* The act of controlling or governing by cruel and unfair use of force. *The citizens protested against the* ***oppression*** *of their strict leader.*

or•deals (ôr dēlz') *noun, plural.* Very difficult tests or painful experiences. *Auditioning for the two ballet companies made for exhausting* ***ordeals***.

or•i•gin (ôr'i jin, or'i jin) *noun.* **1.** The source from which something begins. *What is the* ***origin*** *of that folk song?* **2.** Parentage; ancestry. *Settlers of European* ***origin*** *arrived in Plymouth, Massachusetts, in 1620.*

out•skirts (out'skûrts') *noun, plural.* The regions or sections surrounding or at the edge of an area, as in a city. *On the* ***outskirts*** *of the town we discovered beautiful woodland.*

Pp

par•tic•i•pate (pär tis'ə pāt') *verb.* To take part in an activity with others. *My teacher asked me to* ***participate*** *in the class discussion about NATO.*

pa•thet•ic (pə thet'ik) *adjective.* Bringing about pity, sadness, or sympathy. *The lost puppy looked so* ***pathetic***, *we brought him home.*

pe•des•tri•ans (pə des'trē ənz) *noun, plural.* Persons who travel on foot; walkers. *At busy intersections,* ***pedestrians*** *must cross only when the light stops traffic.*

Word History

The word **pedestrians** stems from the Latin word *pedester* that originally comes from the Latin *pes*, meaning "foot."

pen•nant (pen'ənt) *noun.* A long, often triangular flag, used especially for school or team identification. *Each fan carried a* ***pennant*** *saying, "Go Panthers!"*

pen•ni•less (pen'ē lis) *adjective.* Very poor or having no money. *The man was* ***penniless*** *after the fire destroyed his business.*

pe•ri•od•ic (pîr'ē od'ik) *adjective.* Happening at regular times. *There was a rainbow in the sky between the* ***periodic*** *showers.*

pe•riph•er•al (pə rif'ər əl) *adjective.* Relating to, located at, or forming the outermost part or edge. *Even though Ivan was facing the window, he saw in his* ***peripheral*** *vision that Karen had come in the door.*

per•sist•ent (pər sis'tənt) *adjective.* Continuing firmly and steadily in spite of opposition or difficulty. *The* ***persistent*** *fan finally got his favorite actor's autograph after trying for two months.*

per•suade (pər swād') *verb.* To cause someone to believe or do something by pleading or arguing. *The manager tried to* ***persuade*** *her employees to work extra hours during the holidays.*

phase (fāz) *noun.* A stage of development of a person or thing. *On the third* ***phase*** *of the journey, we traveled by sea.*

phi•los•o•pher (fə los'ə fər) *noun.* An expert in or student of the purpose of humanity, the universe, and life itself. *Many people showed up to listen to the* ***philosopher*** *speak on the human condition.*

at; āpe; fär; câre; end; mē; it; īce; pîerce; hot; ōld; sông; fôrk; oil; out; up; ūse; rüle; pu̇ll; tûrn; chin; sing; shop; thin; this; hw in white; zh in treasure.

The symbol ə stands for the unstressed vowel sound in about, taken, pencil, lemon, and circus.

plight (plīt) *noun.* A bad situation or condition. *The drought created a terrible* ***plight*** *for farmers.*

pon•der•ing (pon'də ring) *noun.* The act of thinking something through. *Before deciding which summer camp to attend, Lisa spent a week of* ***pondering***.

pores (pôrz) *noun, plural.* Very small openings. *The* ***pores*** *in the fabric occur naturally.*

port•a•ble (pôr'tə bəl) *adjective.* Able to be moved easily or carried by hand. *The manager brought a* ***portable*** *television to the store so he could watch the baseball game while he worked.*

post•marked (pōst'märkt') *verb.* Stamped with an official mark to cancel the postage stamp, showing the date and place of mailing. *The tax return must be* ***postmarked*** *no later than midnight on April 15.*

pre•car•i•ous (pri kâr'ē əs) *adjective.* Dependent on chance or circumstance; dangerous. *The climber was in a* ***precarious*** *position on the cliff.*

pre•cede (pri sēd') *verb.* To go or come before or ahead of. *The bridesmaids* ***precede*** *the bride down the aisle.*

pref•er•enc•es (pref'ər əns əz) *noun, plural.* That which is preferred, liked better. *My* ***preferences*** *didn't seem to count when my family opted to go to the seashore rather than the mountains.*

pre•sum•a•bly (pri zü'mə blē) *adverb.* Likely, probably, or taken for granted. *Many students* ***presumably*** *stayed home when they saw all the snow this morning.*

pre•vail (pri vāl') *verb.* **1.** To be greater in power or influence; triumph or succeed. *We must try to* ***prevail*** *over everyday obstacles.* **2.** To be widespread; persist. *Colds still* ***prevail*** *in our school during the winter.*

priv•i•leged (priv'ə lijd) *adjective.* A special person, group, or class enjoying or possessing special rights, advantages, or benefits. *Several of Maria's* ***privileged*** *classmates were invited to a special dinner by the mayor.*

pro•ce•dure (prə sē'jər) *noun.* A particular course of action, especially one that follows a definite series of steps. *The children followed the correct* ***procedure*** *during the fire drill.*

pro•hib•it (prō hib'it) *verb.* To forbid or prevent. *We need to* ***prohibit*** *smoking on the bus.*

pro•long (prə lông') *verb.* To make longer, especially in time. *The host was happy to* ***prolong*** *the dinner, since the guests were having such a good time.*

prom•e•nade (prom'ə nād', prom' ə näd') *noun.* A leisurely walk, especially one taken in a public place for pleasure or display. *The ladies made their evening* ***promenade*** *to show off their finery.*

prom•i•nent (prom'ə nənt) *adjective.* Well-known or important; very noticeable. *Mr. Rodriguez and Mr. Johnson are* ***prominent*** *community leaders.*

pro•pelled (prə peld') *verb.* Caused to move forward or onward; kept in motion. *The engine blast* ***propelled*** *the rocket into space.*

pro•por•tion (prə pôr'shən) *noun.* The relation of one thing to another with respect to size, number, degree or amount. *The number of seats in the gym was not in* ***proportion*** *to the number of students who arrived.*

pros•pered (pros'pərd) *verb.* Having had success, wealth, or good fortune. *The owners of the business finally* ***prospered*** *after years of hard work.*

Qq

quar•an•tine (kwôr'ən tēn', kwor'ən tēn') *noun.* The isolation of persons, animals, ships, or goods exposed to infectious disease, to prevent the spread of the disease. *The doctors placed the family under* ***quarantine*** *when influenza broke out.*

quick•ened (kwik'ənd) *verb.* To move more rapidly. *Sally* ***quickened*** *her pace so she wouldn't miss her bus.*

qui•pu (kē'pü) *noun.* A device consisting of a cord with knotted strings of various colors attached, used by the ancient Peruvians for recording events, keeping accounts, etc. *Our teacher brought in a* ***quipu*** *today to show us how ancient Peruvians kept track of their accounts.*

Rr

raft•ers (raf'tərz) *noun, plural.* The sloping beams that support a roof. *Termites caused a lot of damage to the* ***rafters*** *in our house.*

ran•chos (ranch'ōs) *noun, plural.* The Spanish term for ranches. *The* ***ranchos*** *of Old California were known for their fertile land.*

ran•dom sam•ple (ran'dəm sam'pəl) *noun.* In statistics, a sampling technique where a group of subjects (sample) is selected by chance from a larger group (population) for study. Every possible sample that could be selected has the same probability of being selected. *We conducted a survey on Americans' opinions about recycling, so we used a* ***random sample*** *of men and women from the ages of 18 to 85.*

rav•aged (rav'ijd) *verb.* Laid waste to, destroyed. *The flooding caused by the heavy rains* ***ravaged*** *the town.*

rec•om•mend (rek'ə mend') *verb.* To suggest or advise favorably. *I would* ***recommend*** *pizza if you go to that restaurant.*

reg•u•late (reg'yə lāt') *verb.* To control, manage, or set. *The mayor wanted to* ***regulate*** *the amount of traffic on some streets.*

reg•u•la•tion (reg'yə lā'shən) *adjective.* Required by law or rule. *The teacher issued* ***regulation*** *PE uniforms to the students.* —*noun.* A rule or order prescribed by authority. *There was a* ***regulation*** *dealing with excessive lateness at the elite prep school.*

rem•e•dies (rem'i dēz) *noun, plural.* Things that relieve, heal, or improve a disease, disorder, or other ailment. *The village doctor had many jars of* ***remedies***.

re•mote (ri mōt') *adjective.* Located out of the way, secluded. *It was a* ***remote*** *part of the mountains where few ever go.*

Ren•ais•sance (ren'ə säns') *noun.* A revival of art, intellectual, and scientific learning that took place in Europe from the fourteenth through the sixteenth centuries. *This weekend I need to finish my paper on the Italian* ***Renaissance***.

at; āpe; fär; câre; end; mē; it; īce; pîerce; hot; ōld; sông; fôrk; oil; out; up; ūse; rüle; pu̇ll; tûrn; chin; sing; shop; thin; this; hw in white; zh in treasure.

The symbol ə stands for the unstressed vowel sound in about, taken, pencil, lemon, and circus.

ren•dez•vous (rän′də vü′) *adjective.* Of or relating to an appointment to meet at a fixed place or time; the place chosen for such a meeting. *The* ***rendezvous*** *point for the members of the sewing club was set for the local café.*

Word History

Rendezvous comes directly from the French *rendezvous* which also means "appointment" or "place of meeting."

re•new•a•ble (ri nü′ə bəl) *adjective.* Able to be replaced or restored. *The lease to the apartment was* ***renewable*** *after three years.*

rep•re•sent•a•tive sam•ple (rep′ri zen′tə tiv sam′pəl) *noun.* In statistics, when the group sampled represents a typical example or specimen. *Our survey was about school activities, so we chose a* ***representative sample*** *from all grades.*

rep•u•ta•tion (rep′yə tā′shən) *noun.* The public's opinion or reception of something or someone. *The scholar's* ***reputation*** *was ruined when he was caught cheating.*

re•sem•blance (ri zem′bləns) *noun.* A similarity, as of physical appearance; likeness. *There is often a close physical* ***resemblance*** *among members of the same family.*

res•o•nat•ed (rez′ə nā′tid) *verb.* Exhibited or produced fullness and richness of sound. *The actor's voice* ***resonated*** *throughout the large theater.*

re•vived (ri vīvd′) *verb.* Gave new strength or freshness. *It was so humid that I felt* ***revived*** *when I drank the glass of iced-tea.*

rev•o•lu•tion (rev′ə lü′shən) *noun.* In astronomy, the turning of a celestial body on its axis. *Earth makes one complete* ***revolution*** *every 24 hours.*

ric•o•chet•ing (rik′ə shā′ing, rik′ə shā′ing) *verb.* Bouncing of an object off the surface that it strikes at an angle. *The hail stones were* ***ricocheting*** *off cars during the storm.*

rum•maged (rum′ijd) *verb.* Having searched through (something) thoroughly by moving about its contents. *We* ***rummaged*** *around the attic until we found Grandma's old toys.*

rup•tured (rup′chərd) *verb.* To break open or apart. *The pipe* ***ruptured*** *in the basement and caused a flood that ruined the carpet.*

Ss

sat•el•lites (sat′ə līts′) *noun, plural.* **1.** In astronomy, celestial bodies that revolve around planets; moons. *Jupiter has many* ***satellites***. **2.** Persons or things that depend on, accompany, or serve someone or something else. *The king's* ***satellites*** *were so numerous that they had to have separate lodgings.*

scribes (skrībz) *noun.* Before the invention of the printing press, the people whose profession was writing down or copying letters, manuscripts, contracts, or other documents. *The* ***scribes*** *spent several months copying the Athenian bylaws.*

scroung•ing (skrounj′ing) *verb.* Gathering or collecting with effort or difficulty. *After school, I found my brother* ***scrounging*** *around the cupboards for something to eat.*

se•dat•ed (si dā′tid) *verb.* Made calm. *The nervous patient was* ***sedated*** *so she could sleep.*

sen•sa•tion•al (sen sā′shə nəl) *adjective.* Arousing or intending to arouse great excitement or interest; outstanding or extraordinary. *The* ***sensational*** *news story was, in fact, an exaggeration.*

sev•ered (sev′ərd) *verb.* Separated by cutting or breaking. *The hose was* ***severed*** *when the gardener hit it by accident.*

shak•i•ly (shāk′i lē) *adverb.* Moving quickly to and fro, up and down, or side to side. *The little boy* ***shakily*** *picked up the heavy box.*

sheep•ish•ly (shē′pish lē) *adverb.* In an awkward, shy, or embarrassed way. *After slipping on the floor, the man* ***sheepishly*** *got up and left the room.*

sig•nif•i•cance (sig nif′i kəns) *noun.* Of special value or importance. *The flag of any nation holds* ***significance*** *for its people.*

sleuth•ing (slü′thing) *verb.* The act of detecting or investigating. *Ramona's* ***sleuthing*** *led her to solve the mystery.*

sou•ve•nir (sü′və nîr′, sü′və nîr′) *adjective.* Reminder of a person, place, or event; keepsake. *Mom kept the* ***souvenir*** *baseball we bought at the championship game.*

spe•cial•ists (spesh′ə lists) *noun, plural.* Persons who focus on or specialize in a particular branch of a profession or field of study. *When faced with a disease, it is helpful to consult* ***specialists***.

spec•ta•tors (spek′tā tərz) *noun, plural.* People who observe. *The spectators cheered for their team.*

spec•u•lat•ed (spek′yə lā′tid) *verb.* Thought carefully or seriously about; thought of reasons or answers for. *Because there were so few fish in the lake, the community* ***speculated*** *on the possibility of pollution.*

spic•y (spī′sē) *adjective.* Seasoned with a spice or spices, such as pepper or cinnamon. *At first Mia was afraid to try the* ***spicy*** *food, but when she did, she loved it.*

spon•sor•ing (spon′sə ring) *verb.* Assuming responsibility for or support of another person or thing. *Ms. Kaplan will be* ***sponsoring*** *the newspaper next year.*

spon•ta•ne•ous (spon tā′nē əs) *adjective.* On the spur of the moment; unplanned. *Since I like to control everything, I am not a* ***spontaneous*** *person.*

starch (stärch) *noun.* A carbohydrate used for stiffening cloth. *Stiffen that tablecloth with* ***starch***.

sta•tis•tics (stə tis′tiks) *noun.* Numerical facts or data or the study of such. ***Statistics*** *show that American women vote in greater numbers than do American men.*

stead•fast•ly (sted′fast′lē) *adverb.* In an unchanging, unwavering way; faithfully. *The crew was* ***steadfastly*** *loyal to their captain.*

sum•mit (sum′it) *noun.* The highest part or point. *The climbers reached the* ***summit*** *of the mountain and had a fabulous view.*

sump•tu•ous (sump′chü əs) *adjective.* Expensive and lavish, richly done. *The castle had* ***sumptuous*** *furnishings.*

su•per•sti•tious (sü′pər stish′əs) *adjective.* Having beliefs based on an unreasoning fear of the unknown. *Many architects of tall buildings are* ***superstitious*** *and never include a thirteenth floor.*

sweet•en (swē′tən) *verb.* To make or become sweet or sweeter. *Because the batter was bitter, the cook had to* ***sweeten*** *it with honey.*

at; āpe; fär; câre; end; mē; it; īce; pîerce; hot; ōld; sông; fôrk; oil; out; up; ūse; rüle; pu̇ll; tûrn; chin; sing; shop; thin; <u>th</u>is; hw in white; zh in treasure.

The symbol ə stands for the unstressed vowel sound in about, taken, pencil, lemon, and circus.

swiv•eled (swiv′əld) *verb.* Turned something on a base. *The principal* ***swiveled*** *around in her chair when she heard me enter her office.*

sym•me•try (sim′i trē) *noun.* An arrangement of parts that are alike on either side of a central line; beauty, proportion, and harmony of form. *The starfish shows a lovely* ***symmetry*** *in its shape.*

Tt

tech•nol•o•gy (tek nol′ə jē) *noun.* Methods and machines used in doing things in science or industry. *The surgeons used the newest* ***technology*** *during the operation.*

ter•rac•ing (ter′i sing) *verb.* To form raised, level platforms of earth with vertical or sloping fronts or sides. *The farmers were* ***terracing*** *their land to conserve the soil.*

ter•rain (tə rān′) *noun.* A region or tract of land. *The* ***terrain*** *was not easy to climb; it was muddy and very steep.*

tink•er•ing (ting′kə ring) *verb.* To busy oneself in a trifling or aimless way; putter. *The farmer had been* ***tinkering*** *with the engine of his tractor all morning.*

trench•es (trench′əz) *noun, plural.* Long, narrow ditches. *We dug* ***trenches*** *around the road to put in new sewer lines.*

tri•ples (trip′əlz) *noun, plural.* Hits in baseball when a batter reaches third base. *Sara hit two* ***triples*** *during the game.*

tur•bu•lence (tûr′byə ləns) *noun.* Violent disorder or commotion. *There was so much* ***turbulence*** *on the flight that the attendants had to walk carefully in the aisles.*

typ•i•cal (tip′i kəl) *adjective.* Showing the qualities of a particular type; usual. *Jake's joking response was* ***typical****; he likes to get me to laugh about my problems.*

Uu

un•bear•a•ble (un bâr′ə bəl) *adjective.* That which cannot be endured or tolerated. *When there are presents to open, the wait can be* ***unbearable****!*

un•der•growth (un′dər grōth′) *noun.* The growth of small plants beneath the large trees of a forest. *The hikers had to make a trail in the woods by cutting down the* ***undergrowth***.

un•de•tec•ted (un′di tek′tid) *verb.* Not being noticed or discovered. *The secret plot was* ***undetected*** *for some time, but the police soon learned the truth.*

un•done (un dun′) *adjective.* Unfastened; untied; open. *The ribbon on the package came* ***undone****, and Chris was tempted to open it!*

un•i•mag•i•na•ble (un′i maj′ə nə bəl) *adjective.* Unable to be imagined; hard to imagine. *That the whole class could fail the test was* ***unimaginable***.

u•ni•ver•sal•ly (ū′nə vûr′sə lē) *adverb.* In every instance or place; without exception. *The movie was* ***universally*** *criticized for its horrible acting and ridiculous plot.*

un•sat•is•fac•to•ry (un′sat is fak′tə rē) *adjective.* Not good enough to meet a need or desire; not satisfactory. *Builders cannot risk doing* ***unsatisfactory*** *work because the safety of many is in their hands.*

un•stead•y (un sted′ē) *adjective.* Shaky or not firm. *Everyone was nervous when Michael climbed up the* ***unsteady*** *ladder to get on the roof.*

u•ten•sils (ū ten′səlz) *noun, plural.* An object that is useful in doing or making something. *One third of the world eats with its fingers, one third with chopsticks, and one third with metal* ***utensils***.

ut•tered (ut′ərd) *verb.* To express aloud. *The teacher got very angry when someone* ***uttered*** *the answer during the test.*

Vv

va•pors (vā′pərz) *noun, plural.* Visible particles of matter suspended in the air, such as mist or smoke. *Our teacher told us that some of the* ***vapors*** *from the science experiment were harmful.*

veg•e•ta•tion (vej′i tā′shən) *noun.* Plant life. *The fields and forests are full of* ***vegetation***.

ven•om•ous (ven′ə məs) *adjective.* Able to inflict a poisonous wound, especially by biting or stinging. *Some snakes are* ***venomous****, so be careful not to get too close!*

vic•to•ri•ous (vik tôr′ē əs) *adjective.* Having won a contest or conflict. *The* ***victorious*** *team was given a parade when they returned home.*

vig•il (vij′əl) *noun.* The act or period of remaining awake to guard or observe something. *Ka-Po's mom kept a* ***vigil*** *all night to be sure the fever came down.*

vig•or•ous•ly (vig′ər əs lē) *adverb.* Done in a powerful or forceful way; with healthy strength. *The lawyer* ***vigorously*** *defended the U.S. Constitution.*

vi•tal (vī′təl) *adjective.* Of greatest importance. *The information was* ***vital*** *to everyone who wanted the project to succeed.*

Word History

Vital comes from the old French *vital* meaning "having or supporting life."

Ww

with•stood (with stůd′) *verb.* Held out against or fought against successfully. *The beach house* ***withstood*** *the force of the hurricane.*

wrath (rath) *noun.* Extreme or violent anger. *The football player tried extra hard in the game to avoid the* ***wrath*** *of his coach.*

wreck•age (rek′ij) *noun.* The remains of anything that has been destroyed. *A lot of* ***wreckage*** *from the sunken ship washed up on the beach.*

at; āpe; fär; câre; end; mē; it; īce; pîerce; hot; ōld; sông; fôrk; oil; out; up; ūse; rüle; pu̇ll; tûrn; chin; sing; shop; thin; <u>th</u>is; hw in white; zh in treasure.

The symbol ə stands for the unstressed vowel sound in about, taken, pencil, lemon, and circus.

Additional Lessons and Resources

CONTENTS

Additional Lessons

Comprehension: Character, Setting, Plot T1

Comprehension: Main Idea and Details T2

Comprehension: Cause and Effect T3

Vocabulary: Multiple-Meaning Words T4

Vocabulary: Word Parts (Compound Words) T5

Vocabulary: Context Clues (Definitions) T6

Vocabulary: Context Clues (Restatement) T7

Vocabulary: Analogies (Antonyms) T8

Study Skills: Photos/Captions and Text Features . . .T9

Study Skills: Library/Media Center
    and Time Lines T10

Classroom Library Lessons T11

Theme Bibliography T17

Author/Illustrator Awards T19

Word Lists T20

Scope & Sequence T26

Index T34

Comprehension Skill

Objective: Identify plot, character and setting

Character, Setting and Plot

Intervention/Remediation

Materials "Sam's Summer Search," pp.18–19

Explain Say: *All stories have three elements in common: characters, setting and plot. Characters are the people or animals that the story is about. Setting is where the story takes place. Plot is how the events in the story unfold.*

Model Read aloud the story "Sam's Summer Search" on pages 18–19 of the Student Book. Say: *To identify a story's characters, I ask myself, "Who is this story about?" To determine the setting, I ask, "Where and when does the story take place?" To find the plot, I ask, "What problem does the character face?"*

Guided Practice Say: *First, I'll look for character names. I see Sam, Champ, and Sam's mother. Are there any other characters?* (José, Tasha and Jamal) *The first setting is Sam's yard in the present day. What is the next setting?* (the neighborhood) Ask students to identify the plot by having them identify Sam's problem and how he solves it.

> ### Constructive Feedback
> If students have trouble identifying character, setting and plot review their definitions.

Practice Ask students to identify the main character, setting and plot of a familiar story such as *Little Red Riding Hood*.

> ### Constructive Feedback
> If students are having trouble with the skill after they complete the practice activity, repeat the definition and ask students to restate it in their own words.

Character, Setting and Plot

Materials pencils, paper

Explain Write the following on the board: *It was late at night and Dr. Pitt was still working in the lab. She was trying to find a new formula for a soft drink.* Read the sentences with students. Tell them that they will practice identifying character, setting, and plot in this activity.

Guided Practice Lead a class discussion about the story elements described in the sentence. Ask: *What is the character's name?* (Dr. Pitt) *What is the setting?* (a lab) *What is the story problem?* (She wants to find a new formula for a soft drink.)

Practice Add to the story by reading the following aloud: *Dr. Pitt accidentally spilled some of the mixture she was testing on a hair brush. She tried to pick up the brush, but it wouldn't budge. "Oh my!" Dr. Pitt cried. "I've discovered a formula for a fast-drying glue."* Have students restate the complete plot. Auditory

Changing Characters

Materials pencils, paper

Explain Tell students that they will show how the plot of "Sam's Summer Search" would change if the main character had different traits.

Guided Practice/Practice Have students think about Sam and list three of his character traits. Then have them think of three different character traits and write a paragraph about how the story might change if Sam had these traits instead. Invite students to read their paragraphs aloud to the class. Auditory

Comprehension Skill

Objective: Identify main idea and details

Main Idea and Details

Intervention/Remediation

Materials "Where Did All That Salt Come From?", page 69

Explain Say: *The main idea is the most important point an author makes about a topic. Supporting details are the sentences that give more information about the main idea.*

Model Say: *Sometimes the title or subtitle of a selection gives you a hint about the main idea.* Read aloud the title, "Where Did All That Salt Come From?" Ask: *Does this title give you a hint about the main idea?* (yes)

Guided Practice Ask students to read the passage and write some details they learn about salt in the ocean. When they have listed the details, ask them to think of a one-sentence statement of the main idea.

Constructive Feedback

Remind students that the main idea is what a passage is about. Ask them to think of a different title this passage might have had.

Practice Have students read the first sentence of the second paragraph aloud: "Want a little more information?" Ask students to determine if this is an important detail.

Constructive Feedback

If students have trouble identifying details, or identify superfluous ones, ask them to think again about the whole selection. Point out that some of the information on a page might not help readers understand the *main idea.*

Main Idea and Details

Materials pencils, paper

Explain Write the following on the board: *I love to go to the movies.* Read the sentence with students. Tell them: *This sentence tells what your paragraph should be about.*

Guided Practice Work with students to list three details that might support the main idea. Ask: *What information can you give me to show why you love to go to the movies?*

Practice Have students write their own paragraphs and create a movie poster for one movie they particularly like. Visual

Put a Title On It

Explain Say: *Check details and come up with an appropriate title for a paragraph.*

Guided Practice/Practice Have students read aloud paragraphs they have written. Ask each student to come up with a title that helps express the main idea. Auditory

Comprehension Skill

Objective: Identify cause and effect

Cause and Effect

Intervention/Remediation

Materials The Magic Gourd, pages 84–86

Explain Tell students that knowing why things happen helps them follow the events in a story. Say: *A cause is an event or action that makes something happen. An effect is what happens because of an event or action.*

Model Read the paragraph on page 84 up to the words "... starving family." Say: *When I am looking for connections between events, I ask myself, "Why did this happen?" or "Why did the character do that?" The answer tells me the cause (or causes) of an event. Why was Brother Rabbit's family starving?* (because there was a drought, and everyone was hungry)

Guided Practice Read the first two paragraphs on page 85. Say: *Chameleon asked Rabbit for help, but Rabbit was busy looking for food to feed his family. So what caused Rabbit to stop and help?* (Rabbit said he wanted to avoid seeing his brother suffer.)

Constructive Feedback

If students have trouble identifying the cause, tell them to ask themselves, "Why did this happen?"

Practice Have students read the rest of page 85 and page 86. Say: *Why do you think Chameleon gave Rabbit the Magic Gourd? What was the cause?* (Chameleon wanted to show that he was grateful.)

Constructive Feedback

Remind students that the cause tells why something happened. The effect is what happens as a result of the cause.

Cause and Effect

Materials pencils, paper

Explain Write the following on the board: *Mark's mother bought him a nature guidebook because he wanted to learn about birds.*

Guided Practice Discuss the cause-and-effect relationship presented in the sentence. Point out to students that the effect is listed before the cause. Draw students' attention to the clue word *because.*

Practice Ask students to draw a cause-and-effect relationship, such as what happens when a balloon is pricked by a pin.
Visual

Act It Out

Materials familiar stories

Explain Tell students that they will be working in groups of 4 or 5 to perform skits that show how events in a story would change if one major event changed.

Guided Practice/Practice Assign each group a familiar story, such as Little Red Riding Hood, or a story from their Student Book. Have students think about what might have been different if one of the events in their story was changed. Ask: *What other changes might that one change cause? What kind of chain reaction might occur that would change the story's ending?* Have groups put on a skit, showing a new version of their story in which one changed event changes the ending. Ask the student audience what event was different in the skit and how the change caused a different outcome. Kinesthetic

Take Action **T3**

Additional Lessons

Vocabulary Strategy

Objective: Identify multiple-meaning words

Dictionary: Multiple-Meaning Words

Intervention/Remediation

Materials "Sam's Summer Search," page 18

Explain Say: *Multiple–meaning words are spelled the same but have different meanings. The only way to tell which meaning a writer intends is to read the word in context.*

Model Read aloud the first sentence in the second paragraph in "Sam's Summer Search" on page 18 in the Student Book. Say: *The word* table *is a multiple-meaning word. It can mean a piece of furniture or it can mean a list of facts or information. I can tell from the word* picnic *that in this sentence it means a piece of furniture.*

Guided Practice Write these sentences on the board: *The dance class was held until noon on Saturdays. The hiker climbed up the steep hill to study a special class of plants.*

Read aloud the sentences. Say: *What word has a different meaning in each sentence?* (class) *How would you figure out which meaning the writer means?* (look for context clues in the sentences)

Constructive Feedback

If students have trouble defining the word, underline clues in the sentences.

Practice Assign the multiple-meaning word *train* to students and ask them to write two sentences with *train* using context clues.

Constructive Feedback

Have students look for context clues to each meaning and use those clues to define *train*.

Multiple-Meaning Words

Materials Dictionary

Explain Say: *Multiple–meaning words are spelled the same but have different meanings.*

Guided Practice Write the following sentence pair on the board: *The charge for the phone call was only twenty cents. The bull began to charge directly at me, so I ran.* Tell students they should use context clues in the sentences to determine the meaning of *charge* in each. Ask students to look closely at the first sentence. Say: *Twenty cents is an amount of money. So I can figure out that the charge must be the cost.* Ask students to look in the second sentence for two clues. Ask a volunteer to say the clues (bull and I ran).

Practice Have students write two sentences for the multiple-meaning word *trip* using context clues to show each meaning. Auditory

Picture This

Materials paper and colored markers

Explain Tell students that you will give them a multiple-meaning word and that they will draw two pictures showing two different meanings of the word.

Guided Practice/Practice Say: *If I say the word* nail *what are two different meanings for that word?* (covering at the tip of a finger, metal spike) Ask students to draw two different pictures for the word *nail* illustrating the different meanings of the word. Visual

Additional Lessons

T4

Vocabulary Strategy

Objective: Identify the two smaller words in a compound word

Word Parts: Compound Words

Intervention/Remediation

Materials "An Inca City," page 43

Explain Say: *A compound word is a word that is formed by joining two or more words.* Have students repeat this definition.

Model Write the following sentence on the board: *As my brother spread out the picnic blanket, the rest of the family worried about the clouds overhead.* Say: *I see the compound word* (overhead). *I think* overhead *means above us.*

Guided Practice Ask students to turn to page 43 in their Student Book. Ask students to look at the highlighted vocabulary words and say which ones are compound words. (undergrowth, withstood, foretold)

Constructive Feedback

If students have difficulty identifying compound words, read the vocabulary words with them and help them identify the compound words.

Practice Write the following sentence on the board. *He hung from the ledge by his fingertips.* Ask students to identify the compound word in the sentence.

Constructive Feedback

If students cannot identify the compound word in the sentence, review the definition of compound words with them and ask them what two smaller words make up the word *fingertips.*

Compound Words

Explain Write the following on the board: *We built a fancy doghouse with a skylight.*

Guided Practice Ask students to identify the compound words in the sentence on the board. (doghouse, skylight) Then, ask them to define the compounds based on the component words.

Practice Have students write and say three sentences, using at least one compound word in each. If necessary, students can use a dictionary to come up with ideas for compound words. Auditory

Creative Compounds

Materials pencils, paper

Explain Tell students that they will write and act out a story using compound words.

Guided Practice/Practice Ask students to write a brief story about any subject they like. They must use at least four compound words in their story. Give them this example: *Barbara woke up because she thought she heard a loud <u>thunderstorm</u>. She ran to the window, and looked out at clear <u>moonlight</u>. There was no rain <u>outside</u>. Then she realized that the noise was coming from the TV in her brother's <u>bedroom</u>. He was watching scary movies, long after his <u>bedtime</u>!* Have students read their stories aloud with appropriate gestures and expression. Ask the class to raise their hands when they hear a compound word. Auditory/ Kinesthetic

Vocabulary Strategy

Objective: Use context clues to help determine the meanings of unfamiliar words

Context Clues: Definitions

Intervention/Remediation

Explain Say: *Context clues are words or phrases that help you figure out the meaning of an unfamiliar word. Context clues often provide definitions of the word.* Ask students to explain what a definition is.

Model Say: *When I encounter an unfamiliar word, I read the sentence that contains it—and the following sentence—very carefully. The writer may have defined the word for me.*

Guided Practice Write the following sentences on the board:

1. John dreamed of visiting a remote island. He saw himself in a faraway, secluded place.

Ask: *Can you find a definition of* remote *in number 1?* (faraway, secluded)

Constructive Feedback
Remind students that most writers want to be understood by readers. To make sure readers understand unfamiliar words, many writers supply definitions.

Practice Have students look for definitions of the underlined words in numbers 2 and 3.

2. There is lots of vegetation in my grandmother's yard because she loves to grow all kinds of plants.
3. Sandra was so thirsty that she said she felt dehydrated, or completely dried out.

Constructive Feedback
Remind students that context clues help readers picture what the word means.

Context Clues: Definition

Materials pencils, paper

Explain Listen to these two sentences: *I inquired about our homework. "When do we have to hand it in?" I asked.*

Guided Practice Tell students they should use context clues to figure out the meaning of *inquired*. Say: *I do see a clue.* Ask: *What context clue have I found?* (The clue is *asked*. It gives a definition for the unfamiliar word.)

Practice Have students choose three vocabulary words from this unit. Ask them to write a sentence using each vocabulary word, providing context clues to its meaning. Have students read their sentences aloud and have volunteers identify the context clues. Auditory

The "Or" Technique

Explain Point out that the simplest kind of definition clue uses the word *or*.

Guided Practice/Practice Write this sentence: *Alfredo was a numismatist, or coin-collector.* Ask: *What is a numismatist?* (a coin-collector) *How do you know?* (The writer supplied a definition.) Have students write and read aloud sentences using the *or* technique. Auditory

Vocabulary Strategy

Objective: Use context clues to help determine the meanings of unfamiliar words

Context Clues: Restatement

Intervention/Remediation

Explain Say: *Context clues help you figure out the meaning of an unfamiliar word.*

Model *Context clues often restate the unfamiliar word in a different word or phrase.* Ask: *Who can tell me the definition of* context clues?

Guided Practice Write the following on the board:

1. The man <u>rummaged</u> through his backpack, looking for his keys. He searched through his things until he found the familiar red keychain.

2. Many people work to <u>conserve</u> the Earth. They want to save the land from pollution.

3. The <u>terrain</u> was muddy. Because of the rain, the land was wet and slippery.

Read aloud the first item. Say: *When I come across an unfamiliar word, I look for clues to its meaning. First I look in the same sentence. If I don't find a clue, then I look in nearby sentences. Which word in the second sentence probably means about the same thing as* rummaged? (searched)

Constructive Feedback

If students have trouble recognizing context clues remind them that they are words that restate an unfamiliar word.

Practice Have students repeat the exercise with items number 2 and 3.

Constructive Feedback

Remind students to find a word that means about the same thing as the unfamiliar word.

Context Clues: Restatement

Materials thesaurus

Explain Write this sentence on the board: *My cold was not too bad, so I was able to go to school even with my <u>ailment</u>.*

Guided Practice Tell students they should use context clues to figure out the meaning of *ailment*. Ask students to look through the sentence for a clue. Say: *I see a context clue at the beginning of the sentence.* Ask: *Who can find the context clue?* (The clue is *cold*.)

Practice Have students use a thesaurus to find simple synonyms for any three vocabulary words. Then ask them to write a sentence using each vocabulary word, providing a context clue that restates it. Auditory

Context Clue Chart

Materials pencils, paper

Explain Tell students that they will make a chart to help them identify unfamiliar words.

Guided Practice/Practice Make up four or five sentences, similar to the ones on this page, using restatement context clues for vocabulary or other difficult words. Write these sentences on the board, underlining the unfamiliar words. Ask students to create a two-column chart with these headings: *Unfamiliar Word, Context Clue.* Then call for a volunteer to read aloud the first item. Ask students to suggest how to fill in the first line in their chart. Then have students finish filling in their charts for the rest of the items. Visual/Auditory

Vocabulary Strategy

Objective: Use antonyms to complete analogies

Analogies: Antonyms

Intervention/Remediation

Materials paper, markers or colored pencils

Explain Say: *Sometimes we want to compare two words to each other. We find their relationship.*

Model Say: *Some words, like* hot *and* cold, *are related to each other because they mean opposite things. They are* antonyms. *Antonyms are words with opposite meanings.*

Guided Practice Ask: *What's the opposite of* tall? (short) *So what's an antonym for* tall? (short) *What's an antonym for* old? (young) *Who can define* antonym *and give another example?*

Constructive Feedback

If students have difficulty finding antonyms, you might suggest that they draw a small picture to illustrate the word and write a simple caption. Then ask students to draw another picture showing the opposite and write a caption for the second picture.

Practice Have students think of antonyms for each of the following words:

shout (whisper)	high (low)
cloudy (sunny)	beginning (ending)
happy (sad)	excellent (terrible)
serious (silly)	neat (messy)

Constructive Feedback

Some students may have difficulty thinking of antonyms. Explain that the two words should be related in the same way.

Analogies: Antonyms

Explain Say: *Sometimes we want to compare two* sets *of words. We look at one set of words and see how they are related. Then we look at the second set and make sure they relate to each other the same way. This is called an* **analogy**.

Guided Practice Write the following on the board, and read it aloud: *Wide is to* narrow *as* thick *is to* _____. Discuss how *wide* and *narrow* are related. (They are antonyms, words with opposite meanings.) Remind students that the second word pair in an analogy must have the same relationship as the first word pair. Say: *Can you suggest a word that means the opposite of* thick? (thin)

Practice Write the following analogies on the board:

Male is to female as boy is to _____. (girl)

Small is to big as tiny is to _____. (huge)

Comic is to tragic as laugh is to _____. (cry)

Summer is to winter as boiling is to _____. (freezing)

Have students read and complete the analogies aloud. Visual/Auditory

Antonym Game

Explain Students will play a game of creating analogies using antonyms.

Guided Practice/Practice Organize students into two teams. Have a volunteer from Team A come to the board and write the first half of an analogy using antonyms. Then have a volunteer from Team B come to the board and complete the second half. Continue in this manner, limiting time for each round. The team with the highest score at the end of 10 rounds wins. Kinesthetic

 # Study Skill

Photos with Captions/Text Features

Intervention/Remediation

Materials captioned photographs from newspapers

Explain Say: *Captions accompany photographs to explain or give information about them.* Ask: *What kind of information might be given in a caption for a newspaper photograph?*

Guided Practice/Practice Have students turn to a page in a newspaper that has a caption with a photograph. Ask: *What information is given in the caption? How does the caption help you understand the photograph?* Show students several newspaper photographs with captions. Work with them to answer the preceding questions for each.

Give students a photo without a caption. Have students use their creativity to write a caption for the photograph. Remind them that a caption usually gives information that a reader cannot figure out just by looking at the picture.

Constructive Feedback

If students have difficulty writing a caption, review the purpose of captions with them.

Intervention/Remediation

Materials social studies or science textbook

Explain Point out that textbooks use a variety of text features to help readers navigate complicated material. Headings and subheadings tell about and divide the information into manageable sections. Changes in print may also divide sections of text. They may show where an original or primary source begins and ends. Key words are often written in bold face type. Captions and labels provide more information about photographs, illustrations and diagrams.

Guided Practice/Practice Point to the beginning of a chapter in a textbook. Ask students to read the headings and subheadings and explain what the chapter will be about. Then have them identify any key words in the text.

Ask them if there are any changes in print other than subheadings that divide the text. Have students turn to a new chapter, tell what the chapter is about and identify the text features. Ask them to write a sentence summarizing the topics that are covered within the chapter.

Constructive Feedback

If students have difficulty in identifying text features, point out each of the text features in a chapter of a textbook and review what they are.

 **Study Skill**

Objectives: Use the library and read a time line

Using the Library/Time Lines

Intervention/Remediation

Materials Study Skills Transparency 1

Explain Tell students that card and electronic catalogues list all the books, DVDs, and other materials found in a library. In a card catalogue, there is an author card, title card, and a subject card for each book. The author card is used when you know the author of a book but not the title. The title card is used when you know the title but not the author. The subject card is used when you need books about a particular subject.

An electronic catalogue gives three options for searching. You can search by author, title, or subject. To search by subject, you enter key words about the topic.

Guided Practice/Practice Display Study Skills Transparency 1. Ask students what kind of card catalogue is being used. (electronic) Say: *This person wanted to find books about nutrition and he or she did a subject search. What key word was entered?* (nutrition) *If you wanted to learn more about the title,* Vitamins, Nutrition, and You *what number would you type in?* (3) Ask students to what key words they might use if they wanted to find information about how the toaster was invented.

Constructive Feedback

If students have difficulty understanding how to do a subject search in an electronic card catalog, review Study Skills Transparency 1 with them.

Intervention/Remediation

Materials copies of a time line from a social studies Student Book

Explain Say: *A time line shows events in the order that they took place, from first to last. Time lines are usually read from left to right, in the same direction that we read.* Ask: *In what order are events shown on a time line?*

Guided Practice/Practice Distribute the time line. Point out that a time line is divided into segments of time. These segments of time show an *interval*. An interval might be a month, a year, ten years, a century, or any other convenient division. Ask students to identify events shown on the time line and tell when each event occurred. Then give students a date shown on the time line and ask them to name an event that occurred at that time.

Constructive Feedback

If students have difficulty understanding the time line, help them create a time line of their lives. The time line should begin the year they were born, be organized into one-year intervals, and end with the current year. They should show the most important events from their own lives.

Come Back, Salmon

by Molly Cone

Before Reading

BUILD BACKGROUND

Ask students to discuss what they know about fish in general and salmon in particular. List the information in a web. Explain that salmon swim great distances through treacherous conditions to reach their birthplace in order to lay eggs. If obstacles are in their way, or the spawning ground is destroyed, the population decreases accordingly.

- What activities do humans do that prevent salmon from returning upstream?
- How can a spawning ground be destroyed?
- Once a stream or river is polluted, can it be cleaned up? How?

PREVIEW AND SET PURPOSES

Have students read the title and subtitle on the cover. Ask them to preview the cover photographs and the table of contents. Invite volunteers to explain what they think this book will be about and whether it is fiction or nonfiction. Then ask them to set a purpose for reading, such as to find out what it took to get the salmon back to Pigeon Creek.

During Reading

APPLY COMPREHENSION SKILLS AND STRATEGIES

Following are suggestions for dividing the reading into manageable sections. For each section, think alouds and discussion questions are provided. Use these to review comprehension strategies and skills taught in this unit.

Chapters 1–2

STRATEGY

MAKE INFERENCES AND ANALYZE

Teacher Think Aloud An author doesn't always tell me everything I need to know when I read a book. Sometimes I have to use what I already know and combine it with what I read to make logical decisions about things that are not directly stated. I think Mr. King must be a very good teacher. His actions lead me to believe that he must be pretty inspiring to his class.

Main Ideas and Details The main idea in Chapter 2 is that the students had to work together to make the dream of restoring the salmon a reality. What are some details that support this idea? (Together they cleaned up the creek. Groups of students patrolled the shores to keep trash dumpers away. They wrote letters to the mayor and the city council.)

Objectives

- **Make inferences and analyze**
- **Identify the main idea and details**
- **Identify cause and effect**

Genre Informational Nonfiction

Approaching Level

Summary

The fifth-grade classes at Jackson Elementary in Everett, Washington, are dismayed to hear that the filthy stream near their school was once the spawning ground for salmon. With the help of their teachers, they educate the community and work hard to bring salmon back to Pigeon Creek. This nonfiction book shows that when people work together and put their minds to it, they can accomplish a goal.

 for your information

Throughout the text, there are informational sidebars that give the reader the background science needed to understand what the students are observing in their classroom and the environment. A glossary at the back of the book helps readers with unfamiliar terminology.

Cross–Curricular Connection

Salmon Life Cycle
Students can use information in the book and additional facts they find in other sources to create a salmon life cycle poster. Remind students to include all the stages of the salmon's life and label each stage with vocabulary they learned from their research.

Cross–Curricular Connection

Community

Clean-Up Invite small groups to consider an area of their own community that could use some attention. Ask students to write a paragraph that identifies a place that needs to be cleaned up, why it should be cleaned up, and who or what will benefit. Suggest that students come up with a step-by-step plan that explains what needs to be done and who else they need to involve. Have groups present their plans to the class.

Chapters 3–4

STRATEGY
MAKE INFERENCES AND ANALYZE

Teacher Think Aloud As I read, I use prior knowledge and story clues to make inferences. I think the students must have really studied to know what to do with the fish eggs. I know that sometimes the conditions have to be just right to get eggs to hatch. The students must do many things right because a great number of the eggs hatch.

Cause and Effect What happens when the empty egg casings begin to float through the water? What does this cause to happen? (The casings begin to clog the filters. As a result, the filters need to be cleaned more and more often.)

Chapters 5–6

STRATEGY
MAKE INFERENCES AND ANALYZE

Teacher Think Aloud I know that salmon return to their spawning ground to lay eggs. I think the salmon will not return until they are adults, old enough to lay eggs. I read that the children watched for the salmon, but it is not until two years later that some of the salmon returned. It must have been really hard not to get discouraged.

Main Idea and Details Reread the fourth paragraph on page 32. What sentence states the main idea? Where is it located? ("To return to its home stream to spawn is the goal of an adult salmon's life." It is the last sentence of the paragraph.)

After Reading

LITERATURE CIRCLES
Use page 174 in the **Teacher's Resource Book** to review Listening and Speaking guidelines for a discussion. Have students discuss the books in small groups using questions such as these:

- When you first started reading this book, did you think the students would reach their goal? Why or why not?

- Why is it necessary for humans to help with an environmental problem?

- If you could choose only one job to do, out of all the tasks mentioned in the book, what would it be? Explain.

Write About It
Have students write a letter to the students in Mr. King's class asking them questions about their experiences with Pigeon Creek. Suggest that they think of what else they would like to know that was not fully described in the book. Remind students to use the correct punctuation and form for a friendly letter, including the commas.

A Drop of Water
by Walter Wick

Before Reading

BUILD BACKGROUND
Explain that water is what makes our planet unique. Without water, there is no life. Remind students that the water we see today is the same water that was on the planet when dinosaurs roamed Earth. Brainstorm what students know about water and its properties. List the responses. Ask students:

- What do we call the different stages of the water cycle?
- In one day, how many different ways do you use water?
- What would happen if water did not freeze into ice or evaporate into vapor?

PREVIEW AND SET PURPOSES
Ask students to read the title of the book and preview the cover illustration. Ask them to describe, in detail, what this photograph shows. Then show them the back cover photographs. Invite students to predict what they might learn in this nonfiction text. Have them set a purpose for reading, such as to find out how a snowflake is formed.

During Reading

APPLY COMPREHENSION SKILLS AND STRATEGIES
Following are suggestions for dividing the reading into manageable sections. For each section, think alouds and discussion questions are provided. Use these to review comprehension strategies and skills taught in this unit.

Pages 6–17

STRATEGY
MAKE INFERENCES AND ANALYZE

Teacher Think Aloud When I read I use my own prior knowledge and evidence in the text to make logical decisions about information that is not directly stated. On page 10, the photograph shows a pin floating on the surface of the water. It looks like the water has a skin. I read that this is called the water's surface tension. Although the author does not say so, I can infer that this tension can hold up objects as long as they are light enough and do not pierce the water's surface. The egg shown on page 11 is too heavy to sit on the surface.

Cause and Effect On page 13, three tubes sit in a puddle of water. Each has a different level of water. Why? (The levels of water are due to capillary action. The water clings to the sides of the glass. The narrower the tube, the higher it climbs.)

Objectives
- Make inferences and analyze
- Identify the main idea and details
- Identify cause and effect

Genre Expository Nonfiction

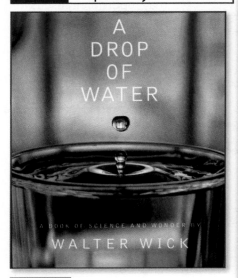

On Level

Summary
In this nonfiction book of stunning photography, readers can examine the many amazing states of water: as ice, snowflakes, steam, frost, and dew.

 for your information

The author of this book is also the photographer. After looking at many children's books of simple experiments, he used these as ideas for the shots he included in this book. On pages 38–39, there is a list of the experiments he used when setting up the shots. Readers can try these experiments themselves.

Classroom Library

Classroom Library

Cross–Curricular Connection

Experiments Have small groups of students choose and perform one of the experiments described on pages 38–40. Students may report their results in writing, or demonstrate their experiments for the class.

Cross–Curricular Connection

Water Still Life Look again at how water beads up on a surface by reviewing the images on pages 7, 22, and 27. Challenge students to capture their own dramatic photos with a digital camera. Suggest that students find interesting background materials such as an old CD or a flower, for example. Print and display their chosen images.

Cross–Curricular Connection

Precipitation Graph Have students collect data on precipitation in their region and display it in a line graph that compares the amounts over time. Students can collect data about rainfall amounts on their own, or they can use the Internet or an almanac to find out the precipitation amounts for a certain range of time. Have students display their completed graphs and discuss what they show.

Pages 18–27

STRATEGY
MAKE INFERENCES AND ANALYZE

Teacher Think Aloud When I read, I take all the ideas that I learn and I put them together to help me understand a new idea. I learned how water changes to a solid, a liquid, and a gas. When I read about how clouds form, I understand that these changes of state help form the clouds.

Main Idea and Details What is the main idea of this section? Name some details that support this main idea. (The main idea of this section is that water molecules are always moving and take different states. Some details: dye dropped into water will eventually color all of the water without stirring; ice is the solid form of water; water vapor is the gas form of water.)

Pages 28–37

STRATEGY
MAKE INFERENCES AND ANALYZE

Teacher Think Aloud The author tells me what I am seeing in the snowflake photographs, but he doesn't tell me how he made these pictures. I can infer that he used a lens to magnify the snowflake because he says this image is 60 times its actual size. I can also infer that he had to work fast and keep the snowflakes very cold.

Cause and Effect Snowflakes are mostly six-sided structures. Why does this happen? (As the water molecules freeze, they join at angles that make six-sided shapes.)

After Reading

LITERATURE CIRCLES

Use page 174 in the **Teacher's Resource Book** to review Listening and Speaking guidelines for a discussion. Have students discuss the books in small groups using questions such as these:

- What was the most amazing thing that you saw or learned?
- Describe experiments you have done with water.
- In what ways can you see the water cycle at work?

Write About It

Review with students the characteristics of cinquain or haiku poetry. Have them revisit the photographs in *A Drop of Water* and select one as the inspiration for a poem. Using the poetry form of their choice, ask them to write a poem using details they see in the photograph. Display the poems on a bulletin board. Remind students to use correct punctuation appropriate for their poetry form.

Interrupted Journey

by Kathryn Lasky

Before Reading

BUILD BACKGROUND

Discuss endangered animals with students. Ask them to define what it means to be endangered. List the information in a chart. Explain that many species of sea turtles are endangered.

- What do you know about turtles? What characteristics and behaviors do they have?

- How are sea turtles different from other turtle species?

- What are some other endangered species? What has made them endangered?

PREVIEW AND SET PURPOSES

Have students read the title and subtitle and the names of the author and illustrator. Ask them to preview the cover photograph and predict what the turtle is doing. Invite them to predict what the author means by "Interrupted Journey." Then have students set a purpose for reading, such as to find out what people are doing to save the sea turtles.

During Reading

APPLY COMPREHENSION SKILLS AND STRATEGIES

Following are suggestions for dividing the reading into manageable sections. For each section, think alouds and discussion questions are provided. Use these to review comprehension strategies and skills taught in this unit.

Pages 1–10

STRATEGY
MAKE INFERENCES AND ANALYZE

Teacher Think Aloud I know I have to use what I read and what I know to infer information the author doesn't state directly. I read that Max and his mother are volunteers. That means they don't get paid to patrol the beaches for stranded turtles. I also read that they do this in November and December. That has to be a very cold time of the year to be at the beach! I can infer that Max and his mother are dedicated to saving sea turtles.

Cause and Effect How can researchers tell if a turtle is dehydrated? (The skin on its limbs would be wrinkled.)

Genre | Informational Nonfiction

Interrupted Journey
Saving Endangered Sea Turtles

Kathryn Lasky • photographs by Christopher G. Knight

Beyond Level

Summary

This book follows the activities of dedicated groups of volunteer researchers who help rescue sea turtles in trouble. Sea turtles around the world are endangered because their annual trip onto the beach to lay eggs makes them extremely vulnerable.

 **for your information**

The Kemp's ridley sea turtle are the most endangered of all sea turtles. In part, this is because the females of this species lay their eggs only on a five-mile strip of beach in Mexico and no other place in the world. Scientists are hoping to train a number of captured Kemp's ridley turtles to lay their eggs on a beach in Texas.

Classroom Library

Cross-Curricular Connection

Rescue Instructions

Volunteers who patrolled the beaches had certain instructions. Review the first four pages of Interrupted Journey. Suppose you are training volunteers. What instructions will you give them? Write a memo in which you tell them how to patrol the beach and what to do when or if they cite a turtle.

Visit the Aquarium

Have students visit the New England Aquarium's Web site. To get an update on current "patients," click on "Animal Rescue." Ask individuals or small groups to report on any recent rescues or the status of rescued animals now being cared for at the Aquarium. Encourage them to relate what they learned in Interrupted Journey to any new information at the site.

Pages 11–20

STRATEGY
MAKE INFERENCES AND ANALYZE

Teacher Think Aloud I learn that the turtles sometimes become too cold and dazed off of Cape Cod, and that they do many things on instinct. I also learn that it is usually juvenile turtles that are stranded. I can infer that these young turtles may not know their migration patterns well enough.

Cause and Effect Even if the team manages to get the turtle's body temperature back up, what can still happen? (There is a good chance it can develop pneumonia.)

Pages 21–end

STRATEGY
MAKE INFERENCES AND ANALYZE

Teacher Think Aloud I learn that Richie Moretti owns a motel, and that from the money he earns at the motel, he runs a hospital for turtles. I also learn that the motel pool is filled with injured sea turtles. I can infer that guests staying at the motel like to see or perhaps help with the turtles. Otherwise, I don't think they would stay at the motel.

Main Idea and Details What is the main idea of the section titled "Release"? What are some details that support this idea? (Richie Moretti helps injured sea turtles and releases them into the sea is the main idea. Details that support this idea include information about Moretti's motel and hospital.)

After Reading

LITERATURE CIRCLES

Use page 174 in the **Teacher's Resource Book** to review Listening and Speaking guidelines for a discussion. Have students discuss the books in small groups using questions such as these:

- What new facts did you learn about the sea turtles?
- Why do you think the author wrote this book? Explain.
- Why do you think the researchers spend so much time measuring and marking the turtles for identification?
- What else would you like to learn about sea turtles?

Write About It

Review with students the events that occurred from the moment Max and his mother saw the turtle to the time it is placed on a soft pile of towels. Then, have students think creatively as they write a narrative of events from the turtle's point of view. Ask them to include details about what the turtle is thinking or feeling. Remind students to use a variety of sentence types and to punctuate complex sentences.

Additional Readings:

By the Authors and Illustrators

Byars, Betsy. *The Midnight Fox.* **Puffin, 1996.** Tom dislikes spending the summer with his aunt on her farm until he discovers a fox and tracks it to its den.
`ON LEVEL`

Lewin, Ted. *Elephant Quest.* **HarperCollins, 2000.** Botwana's Moremi Reserve is the setting for this beautifully illustrated adventure story that introduces us to the region's wildlife and ecology.
`ON LEVEL`

Related to the Theme

Byars, Betsy. *The Summer of the Swans.* **Puffin, 1996.** Since their mother died six years ago, Sara, her brother, and sister have been living with their Aunt Willie. The siblings take great interest in and grow to love the swans that live near their pond.
`APPROACHING *`

Donkin, Andrew. *DK Readers: Atlantis, The Lost City.* **DK, 2000.** Follow the evolution of a mystery that has sparked human curiosity from Ancient Greece to the present day.
`APPROACHING`

Redmond, Ian. *The Elephant Book.* **Candlewick, 2001.** Fascinating close-up photographs reveal the world of the African elephant and threats to its survival.
`APPROACHING`

Ganeri, Anita. *Emperors and Gladiators.* **Peter Bedrick, 2001.** Readers will gain insight into ancient cultures through the eyes of those who lived and worked in them.
`APPROACHING`

Blumberg, Rhoda. *Shipwrecked! The True Adventures of a Japanese Boy.* **HarperCollins, 2001.** The amazing life of a 14-year-old fisherman in 19th-century Japan who is brought to the United States after being shipwrecked.
`ON LEVEL`

Tanaka, Shelley. *The Buried City of Pompeii.* **Hyperion, 1997.** A fictionalized account of the life of an estate steward that describes the ancient city of Pompeii during the eruption of Mount Vesuvius in A.D. 79.
`ON LEVEL`

Lawrence, Ian. *The Wreckers.* **Delacorte, 1998.** A young boy, John Spencer, survives a shipwreck only to find that life on land is more treacherous than any storm at sea.
`ON LEVEL`

Sutcliff, Rosemary. *Black Ships Before Troy: The Story of the Iliad.* **Frances Lincoln Children's Books, 2000.** The mythic story of the Trojan War is brought into sharp focus and amazingly told with all its dramatic action and terror.
`ON LEVEL`

Harlow, Joan Hiatt. *Star in the Storm.* **Aladdin, 2000.** There's a new law forbidding the ownership of non-sheepherding dogs in her Newfoundland village and Maggie tries to keep her dog safe by hiding him.
`BEYOND`

McCaughrean, Geraldine. *1001 Arabian Nights.* **Oxford University Press, 2000.** This illustrated edition brings together all of the Arabian Nights tales in this original retelling by McCaughrean.
`BEYOND`

O'Brien, Robert C. *Mrs. Frisby and the Rats of NIMH.* **Aladdin, 2000.** Mrs. Frisby, a widowed mouse, is helped by the extraordinary rats of NIMH.
`BEYOND`

Osborne, Mary Pope. *Favorite Medieval Tales.* **Scholastic, 2002.** This storybook is a great introduction to medieval art and literature and to the development of the English language.
`BEYOND`

*Main Selection from Student Book

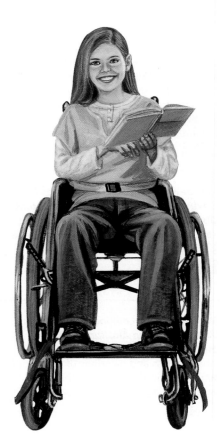

Theme Bibliography

Theme Bibliography

WEEK 3	WEEK 4	WEEK 5
Editors of TIME for Kids. *TIME for Kids: Spiders.* **HarperTrophy, 2005.** A visually appealing format with eye-popping photos will attract students who are reluctant readers. `APPROACHING`	**Diakité, Baba Wagué.** *The Hatseller and the Monkeys.* **Scholastic, 1999.** Here is the West African version of the familiar tale of a peddler whose hats are stolen by monkeys. The beautiful ceramic tile paintings are lively and add to the fun. `ON LEVEL`	**Lasky, Kathryn.** *A Voice of Her Own: The Story of Phillis Wheatley, Slave Poet.* **Candlewick. 2003.** Phillis Wheatley, who was enslaved, became the first African American woman to have her poetry published. `ON LEVEL`
Arnosky, Jim. *Watching Desert Wildlife.* **National Geographic, 1998.** A journey through the American Southwest to observe the diverse wildlife with beautiful illustrations that bring the deserts to life. `APPROACHING`	**Kipling, Rudyard.** *Just So Stories.* **HarperCollins, 1996.** Kipling's fanciful stories of animal escapades in Africa and India are clever and entertaining and serve as a good introduction to this important writer and the Victorian times in which he lived. `APPROACHING`	**Lasky, Kathryn.** *Shadows in the Dawn: The Lemurs of Madagascar.* **Gulliver, 1998.** In this engaging photo-essay, the author introduces us to the scientist, Alison Jolly, and her team of researchers as they study the habits of this unusual animal. `APPROACHING`
Hehner, Barbara. *First On the Moon.* **Hyperion, 1999.** An account of the first moon landing of Apollo 11 in 1969. `APPROACHING`	**Muth, Jon J.** *Zen Shorts.* **Scholastic, 2005.** The author incorporates short Buddhist tales into a story about three contemporary children. The lush watercolors will draw the reader into the story line. `APPROACHING`	**Rylant, Cynthia.** *Every Living Thing.* **Alladin, 1988.** The author offers up the stories of twelve people whose lives are improved because of their contact with animals. `APPROACHING`
Camper, Cathy. *Bugs Before Time: Prehistoric Insects and Their Relatives.* **Simon & Schuster, 2002.** Fascinating facts, characteristics, and habits of prehistoric bugs are detailed in this history of insects and how they continue to survive. `ON LEVEL`	**Freedman, Russell.** *Confucius: The Golden Rule.* **Scholastic, 2002.** The wonderful illustrations and informative text capture the mystery of the great Chinese philosopher. `ON LEVEL`	**Kurlansky, Mark.** *The Cod's Tale.* **Putnam, 2001.** An entertaining history of an influential fish and how important cod has been to people through the ages. The full-color illustrations add to the tale. `ON LEVEL`
Jenkins, Steve. *Life on Earth.* **Houghton, 2002.** Dramatic paper-cut illustrations tell the story of plants and animals from cells to dinosaurs. `ON LEVEL`	**Rodowsky, Colby.** *The Turnabout Shop.* **Farrar, 1998.** Here is a story about the acceptance of loss and change and how Livvy learns to go on after her mother's death to find new happiness in a different family. `ON LEVEL`	**Matthews, Tom L.** *Light Shining Through the Mist: A Photobiography of Dian Fossey.* **National Geographic, 1998.** A vivid portrayal of the naturalist renowned for her ground-breaking work with mountain gorillas. `ON LEVEL`
Kramer, Stephen. *Hidden Worlds: Looking Through a Scientist's Microscope.* **Houghton, 2001.** Amazing colorized photography enhances this fascinating study of very small living things. `BEYOND`	**Burns, Khephra.** *Mansa Musa: The Lion of Mali.* **Gulliver, 2001.** An engrossing account of one of the greatest kings of Mali based on fact with breathtaking illustrations by Leo and Diane Dillon. `BEYOND`	**Goodall, Jane.** *The Chimpanzees I Love: Saving Their World and Ours.* **Scholastic, 2001.** A compelling personal narrative by the renowned scientist with remarkable photographs. `BEYOND`
Marrin, Albert. *Secrets from the Rocks: Dinosaur Hunting with Roy Chapman Andrews.* **Dutton, 2002.** The amazing adventures of the man who revolutionized paleontology during his expeditions to Mongolia in the 1920s. `BEYOND`	**Kurtz, Jane.** *The Storyteller's Beads.* **Harcourt, 1998.** In this harrowing tale set in the 1980s in Ethiopia, two girls, one Christian and one Jewish, overcome cultural prejudices to survive a dangerous trek through their devastated country. `BEYOND`	**Webb, Sophie.** *Looking for Seabirds: Journal from an Alaskan Voyage.* **Houghton, 2004.** A scientist shares her observations and paintings of tufted puffins and other northern birds in this beautiful and engaging book. `BEYOND`

Selection Honors, Prizes, and Awards

The Summer of the Swans

Unit 1, p. 20
by *Betsy Byars*

Newbery Medal (1971)

Author: *Betsy Byars,* winner of the Regina Medal (1987); National Book Award (1981) for *The Night Swimmers;* ALA Notable Children's Book (1992), School Library Journal Best Book of the Year (1992), Edgar Allan Poe Mystery Writers Award (1992) for *Wanted...Mud Blossom;* ALA Notable Children's Book (1995) for *The Golly Sisters Ride Again*

Lost City: The Discovery of Machu Picchu

Unit 1, p. 44
by *Ted Lewin*

Author: *Ted Lewin,* winner of the Caldecott Honor Book Award (1994) for *Peppe, the Lamplighter;* ALA Notable Children's Book (1994) for *I Was A Teenage Professional Wrestler*

The Magic Gourd

Unit 1, p. 82
by *Baba Wagué Diakité*

African Studies Association Children's Africana Honor Book (2004), NCTE Notable Children's Book in the Language Arts (2004)

Author/Illustrator: *Baba Wagué Diakité,* winner of the Coretta Scott King Award Honor Book (1998), Chicago Public Library's Best of the Best (1997), Children's Literature Choices List (1998) for *The Hunterman and the Crocodile*

Unit 1

Word List

Week		Vocabulary	Spelling			
1	**The Summer of the Swans** *Leveled Books:* *The Lost Cave* *Rachel's Choice* *Surprises in the Desert*	abruptly anxiety conscious intersection engulf procedure souvenir cascade	gram clash dense dread prank	strict drill swan prod shrunk	scuff clutch threat dwell fund	text rank brink mock plaid
			Review Words: stuff		batch	sense
			Challenge Words: guest		cleanse	
2	**Lost City** *Leveled Books:* *I Discover Pompeii, or How I Spent My Summer Vacation* *Queen Pu-Abi's Royal Tomb* *The Ancient Secret of Cliff Canyon*	remote escort interpreter vegetation undergrowth venomous withstood foretold	slope acute remote bathe gaze	rhyme keen tile fuse bleach	loan tote foal foe coax	bleak cue pave meek shrine
			Review Words: gram		dread	shrunk
			Challenge Words: trait		capsule	
3	**Gecko Glue, Cockroach Scouts, and Spider Silk Bridges** *Leveled Books:* *Technology and Nature: Water* *From Dragonflies to Helicopters: Learning from Nature* *Plants: An Amazing Resource*	altered erode absorb concentrated innovations	reins freight siege yield review	foreign shield ceiling retrieve grieve	sleigh seize belief neither reign	relieve niece eighty wield diesel
			Review Words: gaze		tile	bleach
			Challenge Words: receipt		leisure	
4	**The Magic Gourd** *Leveled Books:* *The Art of Origami* *Arts of the Navajo* *The Tradition of Dance*	rummaged undetected chameleon generosity pathetic ricocheting famine scrounging	search starve thorn reward sparkle	bargain parched pursue servant torch	earnest mourn fierce pierce urge	wharf court weird veer burnt
			Review Words: freight		yield	seize
			Challenge Words: sphere		aeronautics	
5	**Interrupted Journey** *Leveled Books:* *Saving Right Whales* *Saving Peregrine Falcons* *Saving Alligators*	speculated conserve analyzing vital propelled sedated dehydrated embedded	heartbeat northwest seaweed eyelid seashell	twenty-five wading pool nearsighted brother-in-law old-fashioned	full-time windshield watermelon science fiction self-respect	flashbulb after-school teenager fingernail question mark
			Review Words: fierce		urge	bargain
			Challenge Words: barbed wire		fire escape	

Key Spelling words in bold appear in the selection.

Go to www.macmillanmh.com for **Leveled Spelling Lists**.

T20

Unit 2

Week		Vocabulary	Spelling			
1	**How Tía Lola Came to Stay** *Leveled Books:* *A Sound Move* *The Right Move* *A Good Move*	enthralled embarrassment pennant regulation grouchy resemblance inscribed postmarked	echoes photos data scarves volcanoes	shelves media bacteria wolves dominoes	solos thieves wives cuffs staffs	buffaloes sheriffs tornadoes sopranos loaves
			Review Words: old-fashioned	windshield	question mark	
			Challenge Words: halves	wharves		
2	**The Night of the Pomegranate** *Leveled Books:* *Around the Sun: Our Solar System* *Stargazers: Astronomers in Ancient Times* *Stargazing:The History of the Telescope*	spicy unsatisfactory undone ravaged broadcast calculations vigil marveled	sloped stifling marveled sipped encouraged	permitting orbiting credited labored patrolling	referred regretting totaled unraveling uttered	reviving glimmering accused confiding hovered
			Review Words: echoes	shelves	media	
			Challenge Words: interpreted	swiveling		
3	**Zoo Story** *Leveled Books:* *The Wildfires of 2000* *The Great Flood of 1993* *Waiting for Rain: Drought in Ethiopia*	calamities mitigate devastating evacuate administer	vault slouch poise scrawl noodle	blouse boost sooty fraud sought	scowl employ thaw groove corduroy	browse rookie scoot avoid snoozed
			Review Words: slipped	credited	regretting	
			Challenge Words: drowsy	boisterous		
4	**Rumpelstiltskin's Daughter** *Leveled Books:* *Peter Humbug and The White Cat* *The Princess and the Gnome* *The Two Sinbads*	sheepishly coincidences sumptuous sweeten phase mufflers hobbled prospered	factor banner victim mental formal	pantry ballot prosper pumpkin muffler	ragged kingdom barren necklace wallet	ponder funnel dwelling snapshot fabric
			Review Words: blouse	employ	thaw	
			Challenge Words: verdict	garment		
5	**The Great Serum Race** *Leveled Books:* *Rescue Dog Heroes* *Sled Dog Heroes* *Canine War Heroes*	pedestrians outskirts unbearable rendezvous intercept quarantine epidemic plight	brutal secure panic cabins fever	voter vanish nylon detect resist	labor focus rival recite topic	amid unit rotate vital lament
			Review Words: victim	snapshot	wallet	
			Challenge Words: mural	civic		

Unit 3

Week		Vocabulary	Spelling			
1	**Juan Verdades** *Leveled Books:* *Searching for Gold* *The Secrets of Old Mesilla* *A Maidu Home*	foreman employee gritted fulfill gloated flourish vigorously gleefully	ignore wealthy fulfill healthy enroll	accept parchment dismay debate prepare	repair applaud forlorn shoulder abroad	flounder saunter falter install bounty
			Review Words: voter		recite	topic
			Challenge Words: jaunty		cauldron	
2	**Nothing Ever Happens on 90th Street** *Leveled Books:* *How the Library Lost Its Books* *The Great American Hometown Homework* *Lazy Acres Wakes Up*	limousine sensational precarious extravagant unimaginable lamented promenade embarked	actor stroller scatter gutter platter	customer ancestor flavor mirror vinegar	bachelor behavior calendar waiter singular	maneuver observer wander traitor janitor
			Review Words: healthy		accept	prepare
			Challenge Words: clamor		rescuer	
3	**Building Green** *Leveled Books:* *Energy: Powering Our World* *Energy: Problems and Solutions* *Energy: A Bright Future?*	nonrenewable renewable adverse generate apparatus	burden carton hasten cable civil	dwindle gallon fumble normal novel	basin whistle villain urban organ	satin curtain peril gravel dangle
			Review Words: customer		flavor	calendar
			Challenge Words: vertical		veteran	
4	**The Emperor's Silent Army** *Leveled Books:* *Buried Palace Brought to Light* *Rock Art from the Stone Age* *Rediscovery Cultures: Lost and Found*	utensils superstitious civilized excavate trenches steadfastly precede prolong	unknown incredible superhuman prolong outpost	independent incomplete enlist enrich enlarge	superstar supermarket outfield outlaw outstanding	outcry proclaim uncommon untangle unhook
			Review Words: cable		gallon	curtain
			Challenge Words: indistinct		unequal	
5	**The Case of the Phantom Poet** *Leveled Books:* *Starring Frankie Smithers* *Will the Show Go On?* *What Happened to the Music?*	charismatic sleuthing mimics array significance despondently sponsoring anonymous	inspire inspiration consult consultation separate	separation illustrate illustration instruct instruction	observe observation react reaction connect	connection hesitate hesitation represent representation
			Review Words: incomplete		supermarket	outfield
			Challenge Words: evaporate		evaporation	

Key Spelling words in bold appear in the selection.

Go to **www.macmillanmh.com** for **Leveled Spelling Lists**.

Unit 4

Week		Vocabulary	Spelling			
1	**Seeing Things His Own Way** *Leveled Books:* *The Only Game in Town* *Marla Runyan: In It for the Long Run* *Seabiscuit: The Horse Nobody Wanted*	typical specialists peripheral guidance deteriorated maturity summit awesome	admit admission permit permission explain	explanation exclaim exclamation include inclusion	explode explosion divide division decide	decision omit omission collide collision
			Review Words: separation		instruction	connection
			Challenge Words: expand		expansion	
2	**Exploring the Titanic** *Leveled Books:* *Eugenie Clark* *Jacques Cousteau* *Robert Ballard: Underwater Adventurer*	edgy clockwise hovering interior formations intact severed wreckage	vocalize explosive recognize passage storage	modernize positive negative criticize organize	creative realize advantage attractive percentage	emphasize wreckage specialize sympathize secretive
			Review Words: permission		explanation	decision
			Challenge Words: progressive		scrutinize	
3	**Saving Grace** *Leveled Books:* *Achievements in Business: Amadeo Giannini* *Achievements in Education: Mary McLeod Bethune* *Achievements in Health: Annie Dodge Wauneka*	bewildering moderate hamper prohibit accessible	unfairness disgraceful unsuccessful outlandish outsider	discouragement incorrectly enforcement reminder enclosure	unselfish delightful unevenly disapproval disappointment	repayment designer departure unhappiness enjoyment
			Review Words: positive		passage	realize
			Challenge Words: displeasure		informal	
4	**Mayor Taylor: Champion Cyclist** *Leveled Books:* *Tony Hawk: A Skating Legend* *Lance Armstrong: Racing Into Bicycling History* *Jesse Owens: Racing into History*	spectators demonstration prominent luxury prevail maneuvered collective adept	compete competition metal metallic final	finality nation national moment momentous	crime criminal reside resident origin	original ignite ignition refer reference
			Review Words: incorrectly		departure	unhappiness
			Challenge Words: acquire		acquisition	
5	**A Single Shard** *Leveled Books:* *Arts and Crafts in Feudal Japan* *Crafts in Medieval Europe* *Building a Cathedral*	derision ceramics furrowed eaves arid deftly symmetry benefit	crumb crumble design designate solemn	solemnity muscle muscular reject rejection	create creation public publicity prejudice	prejudicial magic magician office official
			Review Words: competition		criminal	resident
			Challenge Words: complicate		complication	

Unit 5

Week	Vocabulary	Spelling			
1 **Breaking Through** *Leveled Books:* Rafi's Secret Micaela Moves Abuela Sews	reputation uttered quickened migrant mistreated wrath illegally ruptured	lesson lessen aisle isle I'll	navel naval pain pane miner	minor vain vane vein principal	principle idle idol sheer shear
		Review Words: crumble		rejection	publicity
		Challenge Words: hanger		hangar	
2 **Ta-Na-E-Ka** *Leveled Books:* Zach's Best Shot Stacey's Winning Move A Fair Trade	participate ordeals nourishing encounter grimaced anticipated dejectedly victorious	audience benefit factory flexible reduce	credit dictionary section incredible structure	insect audio introduce prediction destruction	education inject reflection objection dejected
		Review Words: lessen		aisle	principle
		Challenge Words: manufacture		dictate	
3 **Many Countries, One Currency** *Leveled Books:* Money Talks Behind the Scenes at the Treasury The Stock Market Crash of 1929	economists continuous chronology debut periodic	aerial aerospace autobiography paragraph biography	biology diagram microwave hydrant grammar	catalog thermometer microscope microphone chronic	program hydrogen dialogue thermos symphony
		Review Words: credit		dictionary	education
		Challenge Words: graphic		logical	
4 **Honus and Me** *Leveled Books:* 50 Quarters: One for Every State The Baseball Hall of Fame The Smithsonian: America's Attic	instinctively decrease swiveled shakily dilapidated auction decades rafters	terrible impossible valuable noticeable considerable	available horrible believable audible predictable	remarkable reversible changeable reliable acceptable	probable admirable dependable profitable lovable
		Review Words: biography		programs	microphone
		Challenge Words: eligible		legible	
5 **Let It Shine** *Leveled Books:* Barbara Jordan: One Woman Taking a Stand César Chávez Thurgood Marshall: Civil Rights Champion	defiance evident resonated persistent convictions oppression momentum remedies	experience evident persistent intelligent defiance	constant violence permanent president incident	important excellent fragrance acquaintance conference	disappearance occurrence nuisance observant hesitant
		Review Words: terrible		profitable	noticeable
		Challenge Words: elegance		diligent	

Key Spelling words in bold appear in the selection.

LOG ON Go to **www.macmillanmh.com** for **Leveled Spelling Lists**.

Unit 6

Week		Vocabulary	Spelling			
1	**Leonardo's Horse** *Leveled Books:* *The Taj Mahal* *Stories on the Ceiling* *A New Pyramid for Paris*	Renaissance commissioned proportion miniature philosopher elaborate envisioned recommend	co-worker commission transformation proportion cooperate **Review Words:** **Challenge Words:**	intersection profession transparent submit interrupt experience profound	postpone companion submarine postwar transform intelligent subscribe	suburb combine interfere transfer copilot persistent
2	**Lafff** *Leveled Books:* *Field Trip* *Speed Dial* *The Trees of Time Past*	glumly tinkering honorable formally destination immigrated unsteady fidget	democrat democracy physician zoology telepathy **Review Words:** **Challenge Words:**	sympathy technology biologist pianist geologist cooperate electrician	musician ecology apology politician tourist profession mythology	heroism technician novelist archaeology specialist suburb
3	**These Walls Can Talk** *Leveled Books:* *Talking Pictures: Signs, Symbols, and Systems* *Talking Pictures: A Mystery in Peru* *Talking Pictures: The Mayan Mystery*	anthropologists presumably immense portable nuisance	immigrate impatiently accompany announce arrive **Review Words:** **Challenge Words:**	collect arrest irregular illuminate accommodate musician impractical	collaborate immature suffix illogical immigration democracy suffocate	suppress illegal support correspond assembly sympathy
4	**Breaking into Print** *Leveled Books:* *Stories Told Through the Ages* *Spread the Word– Become a Publisher* *From Papyrus to Paper*	established scribes obstacles penniless privileged manuscripts guilds alloy	iris nectar cosmetics chaos solar **Review Words:** **Challenge Words:**	geography mania titanic romance geometry announce lethal	helicopter nocturnal psychology phobia terrain collect hypnotize	amnesia tantalize hygiene mercury marathon illegal
5	**The Dog of Pompeii** *Leveled Books:* *River of Destruction* *Eruption on the Mountain* *Besieged by Lava*	ambitious drowsy lounge agonized revived dwelling pondering vapors	bazaar bronco sombrero caribou denim **Review Words:** **Challenge Words:**	gong plaza igloo pizza barbecue solar gondola	canoe chocolate pajamas plateau poodle geography kindergarten	apricot balcony yacht cruise ballet marathon

Scope and Sequence

	K	1	2	3	4	5	6
READING: FOUNDATIONS FOR LITERACY							
Concepts of Print							
Recognize own name							
Understand directionality (tracking print from left to right; return sweep)							
Understand that print provides information							
Develop print awareness (concept of letter, word, sentence)							
Understand that spoken words consist of phonemes							
Understand that written words are represented in written language by a specific sequence of letters							
Distinguish between letters, words, sentences							
Identify and distinguish paragraphs							
Match oral and written words							
Distinguish uppercase and lowercase letters							
Understand correct book handling							
Recognizes parts of a book; recognize that parts of a book contain information							
READING: ALPHABETICS							
Phonemic Awareness							
Identify spoken sounds, words, and sentences							
Recognize and produce rhyming words; distinguish between rhyming and nonrhyming		✔					
Segment word into phonemes, sentence into words	✔	✔					
Identify, segment, and combine syllables		✔					
Blend and segment onsets and rimes	✔	✔					
Add, delete, and substitute phonemes	✔	✔					
Identify and isolate initial, medial, and final consonants	✔	✔					
Blend phonemes to make a spoken word	✔	✔					
Categorize phonemes							
Understand alliteration							
Count and track sounds in syllables, syllables in words							
Decoding Phonics Analysis							
Understand the Alphabetic Principle							
Sound/letter association	✔						
Blend sounds to make syllables and words; blend word families: including CVC, CVCe, CVVC words	✔	✔	✔				
Initial consonant blends		✔	✔	✔			
Final consonant blends		✔	✔	✔			
Initial and medial short vowels	✔	✔	✔	✔	✔	✔	
Long vowels		✔	✔	✔	✔	✔	
Variant vowels		✔	✔	✔	✔	✔	✔
r–Controlled vowels		✔	✔	✔	✔	✔	✔
Hard/soft consonants			✔	✔	✔	✔	
Initial digraphs		✔	✔	✔	✔	✔	✔
Medial and final digraphs		✔	✔	✔	✔	✔	✔
Diphthongs		✔	✔	✔	✔	✔	✔

KEY ✔ = Assessed Skill
Tinted panels show skills, strategies, and other teaching opportunities.

	K	1	2	3	4	5	6
Silent letters			✔	✔	✔	✔	✔
Schwa words			✔	✔	✔	✔	✔
Inflected endings			✔	✔	✔	✔	✔
Triple-consonant clusters			✔	✔	✔	✔	✔
Decoding Structural Analysis							
Common spelling patterns (word families)							
Common syllable patterns							
Inflectional endings: including plurals		✔	✔	✔	✔	✔	✔
Contractions		✔		✔	✔		
Compound words		✔	✔	✔	✔	✔	✔
Prefixes and suffixes		✔	✔	✔	✔	✔	✔
Root or base words		✔			✔	✔	✔
Comparatives, superlatives		✔	✔	✔	✔	✔	✔
Greek and Latin roots			✔	✔	✔	✔	✔

READING: FLUENCY

	K	1	2	3	4	5	6
Fluency							
Read regularly on independent and instructional levels							
Read orally with fluency from familiar texts (choral, echo, partner, Readers Theater)							
Read silently and independently							
Use appropriate pace, expression, intonation, and phrasing		✔	✔	✔	✔	✔	✔
Read with automaticity (accurately and effortlessly)		✔	✔	✔	✔	✔	✔
Use punctuation cues in reading							
Adjust reading rate to purpose							
Repeated readings							
Timed readings							
Self-Selected Reading							
Use personal criteria to choose own reading: including favorite authors, genres, recommendations from others							
Read a variety of literature for assigned tasks as well as for enjoyment							

READING: VOCABULARY/WORD IDENTIFICATION

	K	1	2	3	4	5	6
Word Meaning Skills and Strategies							
Identify academic language							
Identify persons, places, things, actions							
Classify and categorize words	✔	✔	✔				
Synonyms, antonyms, and opposites	✔	✔	✔	✔	✔	✔	✔
High-frequency words	✔	✔					
Use context clues: word, sentence, paragraph; definition, example, restatement		✔	✔	✔	✔	✔	✔
Use word identification strategies		✔	✔	✔	✔	✔	✔
Unfamiliar words		✔		✔	✔		
Multiple-meaning words	✔	✔	✔	✔	✔	✔	✔
Use dictionary to locate meanings, pronunciation, and derivatives		✔	✔	✔	✔	✔	✔
Compound words					✔	✔	✔
Words ending in -er and -est			✔	✔	✔		
Prefixes and suffixes			✔	✔	✔	✔	✔
Greek and Latin roots			✔	✔	✔	✔	✔

KEY	✔ = Assessed Skill
	Tinted panels show skills, strategies, and other teaching opportunities.

Scope and Sequence

	K	1	2	3	4	5	6
READING: VOCABULARY/WORD IDENTIFICATION (continued)							
Word Meaning Skills and Strategies (continued)							
Denotation and connotation			✔	✔	✔	✔	✔
Word families			✔	✔	✔	✔	✔
Inflected-ending words and plurals		✔	✔	✔	✔		
Use thesaurus					✔	✔	✔
Use reference sources for word meaning		✔	✔	✔	✔	✔	✔
Homographs					✔	✔	✔
Homophones					✔	✔	✔
Contractions				✔			
Figurative language				✔			
Idioms					✔	✔	✔
Analogies					✔	✔	✔
Word origins					✔	✔	✔
READING: COMPREHENSION							
Prereading Strategies							
Build background							
Use prior knowledge							
Preview and predict							
Set and adjust purpose for reading							
Comprehension Strategies							
Analyze		✔	✔	✔	✔	✔	✔
Evaluate		✔	✔	✔	✔	✔	✔
Generate questions							
Inferences, making	✔	✔	✔	✔	✔	✔	✔
Monitor comprehension: including reread, adjust reading rate, paraphrase, self-correct, read ahead, seek help							
Summarize		✔	✔	✔	✔	✔	✔
Story structure, analyzing		✔	✔	✔	✔	✔	✔
Text structure, analyzing		✔	✔	✔	✔	✔	✔
Visualize							
Comprehension Skills							
Author's perspective					✔	✔	✔
Author's purpose		✔	✔	✔	✔	✔	✔
Cause and effect	✔	✔	✔	✔	✔	✔	✔
Character	✔	✔	✔	✔	✔	✔	✔
Compare and contrast	✔	✔	✔	✔	✔	✔	✔
Classify and categorize	✔	✔	✔				
Conclusions, drawing	✔	✔	✔		✔	✔	✔
Description as text structure			✔	✔	✔	✔	✔
Fact and opinion					✔	✔	✔
Fantasy and reality; fact and fiction	✔	✔	✔	✔			
Generalizations, making					✔	✔	✔
Illustrations	✔	✔	✔				
Inferences, making	✔	✔	✔	✔	✔	✔	✔
Judgments, making			✔	✔	✔	✔	✔
Main idea and supporting details	✔	✔	✔	✔	✔	✔	✔

KEY ✔ = Assessed Skill
Tinted panels show skills, strategies, and other teaching opportunities.

	K	1	2	3	4	5	6
Persuasion/persuasive techniques					✔	✔	✔
Plot	✔	✔	✔	✔	✔	✔	✔
Predictions, making/confirming	✔	✔	✔				
Problem and solution		✔	✔	✔	✔	✔	✔
Sequence	✔	✔	✔	✔	✔	✔	✔
Setting	✔	✔	✔	✔	✔	✔	✔
Summarize, retell	✔	✔	✔	✔	✔	✔	✔
Theme				✔	✔	✔	✔

LITERATURE

Genre: Fiction

	K	1	2	3	4	5	6
Drama/play							
Fantasy							
Historical fiction							
Humorous fiction							
Mystery							
Picture book							
Realistic fiction							
Rhyming story							
Science fiction							
Short story							
Traditional stories: fairy tale, fable, folk tale, tall tale, myth							

Genre: Nonfiction

	K	1	2	3	4	5	6
Biography/autobiography							
Diary/journal							
Encyclopedia							
Expository text							
Functional text							
How-to							
Informational text							
Letter							
Nonfiction							
Narrative							
Newsletter							
Newspaper							
Science article							
Personal essay							
Persuasive essay							
Photo essay							

Genre: Poetry

	K	1	2	3	4	5	6
Forms (refrain, cinquain, free verse, haiku, limerick, lyric, narrative, simple)							
Literary elements							

Literary Devices and Elements

	K	1	2	3	4	5	6
Alliteration			✔	✔	✔	✔	✔
Consonance and assonance				✔	✔	✔	✔
Dialect						✔	
Figurative language (metaphors, similes, personification)		✔	✔	✔	✔	✔	✔
Foreshadowing; flashback					✔	✔	✔

KEY	✔ = Assessed Skill
	Tinted panels show skills, strategies, and other teaching opportunities.

	K	1	2	3	4	5	6
LITERATURE (continued)							
Literary Devices and Elements (continued)							
Imagery			✔	✔	✔	✔	✔
Meter					✔	✔	✔
Onomatopoeia			✔	✔	✔	✔	✔
Repetition		✔	✔	✔	✔	✔	✔
Rhyme/rhyme schemes		✔	✔	✔	✔	✔	✔
Rhythm			✔	✔	✔	✔	✔
Sensory words and details					✔	✔	✔
Symbolism					✔	✔	✔
Author and Illustrator Craft							
Analyze author and illustrator craft							
Analyze role of author and illustrator							
Analyze how illustrations enhance and interpret text							
Literary Response							
Reflect and respond to text							
Connect and compare text characters, events, ideas to self							
Connect and compare text characters, events, ideas across texts							
Connect and compare text characters, events, ideas to world							
Connect literary texts to other curriculum areas							
Identify cultural elements of text							
Identify historical elements of text							
Read to understand and perform tasks and activities							
Interpret text through creative response							
Interpret text ideas through writing, discussion, media, research							
STUDY SKILLS, RESEARCH AND INFORMATIONAL LITERACY							
Study Skiills							
Directions: read, write, give, follow		✔	✔	✔			
Evaluate directions for sequence and completeness							
Use library/media center		✔	✔	✔	✔	✔	✔
Use parts of book to locate information		✔	✔	✔	✔	✔	✔
Interpret information from graphic aids		✔	✔	✔	✔	✔	✔
Use graphic organizers to organize information and comprehend text							
Use functional, everyday documents				✔	✔	✔	✔
Apply study strategies: skimming and scanning, note-taking, outlining, K-W-L							
Apply test prep and test-taking strategies							
Text Features							
Recognize and identify text and organizational features of nonfiction texts		✔	✔	✔	✔	✔	✔
Recognize and identify text features of poetry, fiction, drama		✔	✔	✔	✔	✔	✔
Captions and labels, headings, subheadings, footnotes, endnotes, key words, bold print		✔	✔	✔	✔	✔	✔
Graphics: including photographs, illustrations, maps, charts, diagrams, graphs, time lines			✔	✔	✔	✔	✔
Research and Informational Literacy							
Generate and revise questions for research							
Narrow focus of research							
Find and locate information using print and electronic resources							

KEY	✔ = Assessed Skill
	Tinted panels show skills, strategies, and other teaching opportunities.

	K	1	2	3	4	5	6
Record information systematically (note-taking, outlining)							
Develop a systematic research plan							
Evaluate reliability, credibility, usefulness of sources and information							
Use primary sources to obtain information				✔	✔	✔	✔
Synthesize, evaluate, and draw conclusions from information							
Cite and list sources of information							
Technology							
Use computer, Internet, CD-ROM, and technology resources to access information			✔	✔	✔	✔	✔
Use text and organizational features of electronic resources: including search engines, keywords, e-mail, hyperlinks, URLs, Web pages, databases, graphics				✔	✔	✔	✔
WRITING							
Modes and Forms							
Descriptive writing			✔	✔	✔	✔	✔
Explanatory writing		✔	✔	✔	✔	✔	✔
Expository writing		✔	✔	✔	✔	✔	✔
Narrative writing: Personal and Fictional			✔	✔	✔	✔	✔
Persuasive writing		✔	✔	✔	✔	✔	✔
Writing that compares			✔	✔	✔	✔	✔
Prompts							
Determine the audience and purpose		✔	✔	✔	✔	✔	✔
Determine the mode		✔	✔	✔	✔	✔	✔
Timed writing		✔	✔	✔	✔	✔	✔
Writer's Craft							
Topic sentence, details							
Write a good paragraph							
Beginning, middle, end							
Strong opening, strong conclusion							
Precise words							
Informal and formal language							
Figurative language							
Dialogue							
Tone, mood							
Fact and opinion							
Transitions							
Writing Traits							
Organization, ideas and content, word choice, conventions		✔	✔	✔	✔	✔	✔
Sentence fluency, voice		✔	✔	✔	✔	✔	✔
Processes							
Prewriting, drafting, revising, editing, publishing							
Evaluating, Rubrics, assessment							
Penmanship							
Write uppercase and lowercase letters using correct formation and spacing							
Write using left-to-right and top-to-bottom directionality							
Write using appropriate spacing between words, letters, sentences							
Write using appropriate margins and indentations							
Write legibly in manuscript or cursive							

KEY ✔ = Assessed Skill
Tinted panels show skills, strategies, and other teaching opportunities.

WRITING (continued)

	K	1	2	3	4	5	6
Grammar, Mechanics, and Usage							
Sentence concepts: statements, questions, exclamations, commands		✔	✔	✔	✔	✔	✔
Complete and incomplete sentences; sentence fragments				✔	✔	✔	✔
Nouns: including common, proper, singular, plural, irregular plural, possessive		✔	✔	✔	✔	✔	✔
Verbs: including action, helping, linking, irregular		✔	✔	✔	✔	✔	✔
Verb tenses: including past, present, future, perfect, and progressive		✔	✔	✔	✔	✔	✔
Pronouns: including possessive, subject and object, pronoun-verb agreement		✔	✔	✔	✔	✔	✔
Adjectives: including articles		✔	✔	✔	✔	✔	✔
Adverbs: including telling how, when, where; comparative; superlative; irregular			✔	✔	✔	✔	✔
Subject, predicate				✔	✔	✔	✔
Subject-verb agreement				✔	✔	✔	✔
Contractions		✔	✔	✔	✔	✔	✔
Conjunctions				✔	✔	✔	✔
Prepositions and prepositional phrases					✔	✔	✔
Negatives, correcting double negatives					✔	✔	✔
Use correct capitalization in sentences, proper nouns, titles, abbreviations		✔	✔	✔	✔	✔	✔
Use correct punctuation (periods, questions marks, exclamation marks, commas, apostrophes, quotation marks, colons, hyphens, or semicolons)		✔	✔	✔	✔	✔	✔
Antecedents					✔	✔	✔
Homophones						✔	
Spelling							
Spell independently by using pre-phonetic knowledge							
Use spelling approximations and some conventional spelling							
Spell own name and write high-frequency words							
Words with short vowels		✔	✔	✔	✔	✔	✔
Words with long vowels		✔	✔	✔	✔	✔	✔
Words with digraphs, blends, consonant clusters, double consonants		✔	✔	✔	✔	✔	✔
Words with variant and ambiguous vowels		✔	✔	✔	✔	✔	✔
Words with diphthongs		✔	✔	✔	✔	✔	✔
Words with r-controlled vowels		✔	✔	✔	✔	✔	✔
Schwa words			✔	✔	✔	✔	✔
Words with silent letters			✔	✔	✔		✔
Words with hard and soft letters			✔	✔	✔	✔	
Inflectional endings: including plural, past tense, drop final e and double consonant when adding -ed and -ing)		✔	✔	✔	✔	✔	✔
Compound words			✔	✔	✔	✔	✔
Homonyms/homophones				✔	✔	✔	✔
Prefixes and suffixes				✔	✔	✔	✔
Root and base words			✔		✔	✔	✔
Syllables: patterns, rules, accented, stressed, closed, open					✔	✔	✔
Words with Greek and Latin roots					✔	✔	✔
Words from mythology						✔	✔
Words from around the world							✔
Words with spelling patterns, word families		✔	✔	✔	✔	✔	✔

KEY	✔ = Assessed Skill
	Tinted panels show skills, strategies, and other teaching opportunities.

LISTENING, SPEAKING, VIEWING, REPRESENTING

	K	1	2	3	4	5	6
Listening							
Identify musical elements of language							
Determine the purpose for listening (for information, to solve problems, for enjoyment)		✔	✔	✔	✔	✔	✔
Understand and follow directions		✔	✔	✔	✔	✔	✔
Develop oral vocabulary and concepts							
Listen responsively, attentively, and critically							
Listen to distinguish fact from fiction; fact from opinion							
Listen responsively to oral presentation: stories, poems, skits, songs, personal accounts, speeches, classic and contemporary works							
Ask and answer relevant questions (for clarification; to follow up on ideas)							
Apply comprehension strategies and skills in listening activities							
Interpret speaker's verbal and nonverbal messages, purposes, and perspectives							
Speaking							
Use repetition, rhyme, and rhythm in oral texts: including songs, poems, and stories							
Participate in classroom activities and discussions							
Ask and answer questions							
Stay on topic when speaking							
Use language appropriate to situation, purpose, and audience							
Use nonverbal communications such as eye contact, gestures, and props							
Use verbal communication in effective ways							
Retell a story or spoken message by summarizing							
Clarify and support spoken ideas with evidence and examples							
Oral presentations: focus, organizational structure, audience, purpose; types: narrative, persuasive, informational, descriptive							
Give and follow directions							
Consider audience when speaking or preparing a presentation							
Viewing							
Various media genres: including posters, pictures, videos, slide shows, technology							
Summarize the main idea or message from visuals, graphics, and media							
Use graphics, illustrations to analyze and interpret information							
Identify structural features of popular media and use the features to obtain information: including newspapers, magazines, and online information							
Distinguish between fact and opinion in visuals and media							
Analyze media source; recognize effects of media in one's mood and emotion							
Make informed judgments about print and nonprint media							
Representing							
Select, organize, or produce visuals to complement or extend meaning							
Select, organize, and create media compositions for various purposes							
Show how language, medium, and presentation contribute to the message							
Use technology, media, multimedia to present information							
Use technology/media to compare ideas information and viewpoints							

KEY	✔ = Assessed Skill Tinted panels show skills, strategies, and other teaching opportunities.

Aa

Abbreviations, 151J

Academic language, 19A–19B, 39U, 39V, 43A–43B, 65U, 65V, 69A–69B, 77U, 77V, 81A–81B, 101U, 101V, 105A–105B, 123U, 123V, 131A–131B, 151U, 151V, 155A–155B, 177U, 177V, 181A–181B, 189U, 189V, 193A–193B, 217U, 217V, 221A–221B, 241U, 241V, 249A–249B, 273U, 273V, 277A–277B, 301U, 301V, 305A–305B, 313U, 313V, 317A–317B, 335U, 335V, 339A–339B, 359U, 359V, 367A–367B, 387U, 387V, 391A–391B, 413U, 413V, 417A–417B, 425U, 425V, 449U, 449V, 475U, 475V, 483A–483B, 503U, 503V, 507A,–507B 529U, 529V, 533A–533B, 541U, 541V, 545A–545B, 567U, 567V, 571A–571B, 591U, 591V, 599A–599B, 621U, 621V, 625A–625B, 645U, 645V, 649A–649B, 657U, 657V, 661A–661N, 683U, 683V, 687A–687B, 709U, 709V

Accelerated Reader Quizzes. *See* Technology: CD-ROM.

Access for All. *See* English Language Learners.

Accessing prior knowledge, 16, 39V, 40, 65V, 66, 77V, 78, 101V, 102, 123V, 128, 151V, 152, 177V, 178, 189V, 190, 217V, 218, 241V, 246, 273V, 274, 301V, 302, 313V, 314, 335V, 336, 359V, 364, 387V, 388, 413V, 414, 425V, 426, 449V, 450, 475V, 480, 503V, 504, 529V, 530, 541V, 542, 567V, 568, 591V, 596, 621V, 622, 645V, 646, 657V, 658, 683V, 684, 709V

Acknowledgments, 6.1: T60-T62, **6.2:** T53–T55, **6.3:** T53–T55, **6.4:** T53–T55, **6.5:** T54–T56, **6.6:** T54–T56

Additional Lessons, 6.1: T1–T10, **6.2:** T1–T11, **6.3:** T1–T11, **6.4:** T1–T11, **6.5:** T1–T12, **6.6:** T1–T12

Adjectives. *See* Grammar: adjectives.

Adverbs. *See* Grammar: adverbs.

Advertisements, analyzing, 364I

Affixes. *See* Phonics/Spelling; Spelling; Vocabulary: prefixes, suffixes.

Alliteration. *See* Literary devices: alliteration.

Almanac, 148–149, 151Q, 151S

Analogies, 105, 110, 113, 123D, 123O, 123Q, 339, 352, 359D, 359F, 359O, 359Q, 449D, 449F, 449O, 449Q, **6.1:** T8, **6.3:** T9, **6.4:** T8. *See also* Vocabulary: analogies.

Analyzing. *See* Comprehension strategies; analyze.

Antonyms. *See* Vocabulary: antonyms.

Apostrophes, 217I–217J, 245E

Appositives. *See* Grammar: appositives.

Approaching Level Options, 39M–39P, 65M–65P, 77M–77P, 101M–101P, 123M–123P, 151M–151P, 177M–177P, 189M–189P, 217M–217P, 241M–241P, 273M–273P, 301M–301P, 313M–313P, 335M–335P, 359M–359P, 387M–387P, 413M–413P, 425M–425P, 449M–449P, 475M–475P, 503M–503P, 529M–529P, 541M–541P, 567M–567P, 591M–591P, 621M–621P, 645M–645P, 657M–657P, 683M–683P, 709M–709P

  comprehension, 39O, 39P, 65O, 65P, 77O, 77P, 101O, 101P, 123O, 123P, 151O, 151P, 177O, 177P, 189O, 189P, 217O, 217P, 241O, 241P, 273O, 273P, 301O, 301P, 313O, 313P, 335O, 335P, 359O, 359P, 387O, 387P, 413O, 413P, 425O, 425P, 449O, 449P, 475O, 475P, 503O, 503P, 529O, 529P, 541O, 541P, 567O, 567P, 591O, 591P, 621O, 621P, 645O, 645P, 657O, 657P, 683O, 683P, 709O, 709P

    strategies, 39O, 65O, 77O, 101O, 123O, 151O, 177O, 189O, 217O, 241O, 273O, 301O, 313O, 335O, 359O, 387O, 413O, 425O, 449O, 475O, 503O, 529O, 541O, 567O, 591O, 621O, 645O, 657O, 683O, 709O

  fluency, 39M, 39N, 65M, 65N, 77M, 77N, 101M, 101N, 123M, 123N, 151M, 151N, 177M, 177N, 189M, 189N, 217M, 217N, 241M, 241N, 273M, 273N, 301M, 301N, 313M, 313N, 335M, 335N, 359M, 359N, 387M, 387N, 413M, 413N, 425M, 425N, 449M, 449N, 475M, 475N, 503M, 503N, 529M, 529N, 541M, 541N, 567M, 567N, 591M, 591N, 621M, 621N, 645M, 645N, 657M, 657N, 683M, 683N, 709M, 709N

  phonics, 39M, 65M, 77M, 101M, 123M, 151M, 177M, 189M, 217M, 241M, 273M, 301M, 313M, 335M, 359M, 387M, 413M, 425M, 449M, 475M, 503M, 529M, 541M, 567M, 591M, 621M, 645M, 657M, 683M, 709M

  vocabulary, 39N, 39O, 65N, 65O, 77N, 77O, 101N, 101O, 123N, 123O, 151N, 151O, 177N, 177O, 189N, 189O, 217N, 217O, 241N, 241O, 273N, 273O, 301N, 301O, 313N, 313O, 335N, 335O, 359N, 359O, 387N, 387O, 413N, 413O, 425N, 425O, 449N, 449O, 475N, 475O, 503N, 503O, 529N, 529O, 541N, 541O, 567N, 567O, 591N, 591O, 621N, 621O, 645N, 645O, 657N, 657O, 683N, 683O, 709N, 709O

Assessment, 39K–39L, 65K–65L, 77K–77L, 101K–101L, 123K–123L, 151K–151L, 177K–177L, 189K–189L, 217K–217L, 241K–241L, 273K–273L, 301K–301L, 313K–313L, 335K–335L, 359K–359L, 387K–387L, 413K–413L, 425K–425L, 449K–449L, 475K–475L, 503K–503L, 529K–529L, 541K–541L, 567K–567L, 591K–591L, 621K–621L, 645K–645L, 657K–657L, 683K–683L, 709K–709L

  alternative, 39K, 65K, 77K, 101K, 123K, 151K, 177K, 189K, 217K,

Key 6.1 = Grade 6, Book 1

241K, 273K, 301K, 313K, 335K, 359K, 387K, 413K, 425K, 449K, 475K, 503K, 529K, 541K, 567K, 591K, 621K, 645K, 657K, 683K, 709K

fluency, 35A, 39K, 59A, 65K, 73A, 77K, 95A, 101K, 119A, 123K, 147A, 151K, 171A, 177K, 185A, 189K, 211A, 217K, 237A, 241K, 267A, 273K, 295A, 301K, 309A, 313K, 331A, 335K, 355A, 359K, 381A, 387K, 407A, 413K, 421A, 425K, 445A, 449K, 471A, 475K, 497A, 503K, 525A, 529K, 537A, 541K, 561A, 567K, 587A, 591K, 615A, 621K, 639A, 645K, 653A, 657K, 679A, 683K, 703A, 709K

formal/informal, 16F, 128F, 246F, 364F, 480F, 596F

National Test Alignment chart, 16G, 128G, 246G, 364G, 480G, 596G

Quick Check and observational assessments. *See individual skills listings for* **Comprehension skills, Comprehension strategies, Fluency, Grammar, Phonics/Spelling, Vocabulary, Writing.**

scoring rubrics, 39A, 65A, 76, 77A, 101A, 123A, 127G, 127H, 127L, 151A, 177A, 188, 189A, 217A, 241A, 245G, 245H, 245L, 273A, 301A, 312, 313A, 335A, 359A, 363G, 363H, 363L, 387A, 413A, 424, 425A, 449A, 475A, 479G, 479H, 479L, 503G, 503A, 529A, 540, 541A, 567A, 591A, 595G, 595H, 595L, 621A, 645A, 656, 657A, 683A, 709A, 713G, 713H, 713L

Test Prep, 74–77, 186–189, 310–313, 422–425, 538–541, 654–657

Test Strategy
   Author and Me, 35, 95, 147, 171, 186–187, 211, 242–244, 331, 360–362, 381, 422–423, 445, 471, 476–478, 497, 525, 561, 587, 592–594, 615, 639

   On My Own, 59, 119, 267, 295, 355, 407, 538–539, 679, 703, 710–712

Right There, 74–75
   Think and Search, 124–126, 237, 310–311, 654–655
   writing prompts, 76–77, 127, 188–189, 245, 312–313, 363, 424–425, 479, 540–541, 595, 656–657, 713

Theme Project, 16H–16I, 127K–127L, 128H–128I, 245K–245L, 246H–246I, 363K–363L, 364H–364I, 479K–479L, 480H–480I, 595K–595L, 596H–596I, 713K–713L

Timed-reading, 39N, 65N, 77N, 101N, 123N, 151N, 177N, 189N, 217N, 241N, 273N, 301N, 313N, 335N, 335Q, 359N, 387N, 387Q, 359Q, 413N, 413Q, 425N, 425Q, 449N, 449Q, 475N, 475Q, 503N, 529N, 541N, 567N, 591N, 591Q, 621N, 645N, 657N, 683M, 683N, 683Q, 709N, 709Q

Timed-writing, 77, 189, 313, 425, 541, 657

unit, 127M–127N, 245M–245N, 363M–363N, 479M–479N, 595M–595N, 713M–713N

weekly reading, 39K–39L, 65K–65L, 77K–77L, 101K–101L, 123K–123L, 151K–151L, 177K–177L, 189K–189L, 217K–217L, 241K–241L, 273K–273L, 301K–301L, 313K–313L, 335K–335L, 359K–359L, 387K–387L, 413K–413L, 425K–425L, 449K–449L, 475K–475L, 503K–503L, 529K–529L, 541K–541L, 567K–567L, 591K–591L, 621K–621L, 645K–645L, 657K–657L, 683K–683L, 709K–709L

writing, 16C, 76–77, 128C, 188–189, 246C, 312–313, 364C, 424–425, 480C, 540–541, 596C, 656–657

Assonance, 446–447, 449Q, 449S. *See also* **Literary devices: assonance; Poetry.**

Author/illustrator biographies, 34, 58, 94, 118, 146, 170, 210, 236, 266, 294, 330, 354, 380, 406, 444, 470, 496, 524, 560, 586, 614, 638, 678, 702

Author's Craft, 34, 58, 94, 118, 146, 170, 210, 236, 266, 294, 330, 354, 380, 406, 444, 470, 496, 524, 560, 586, 614, 638, 678, 702

   alliteration, 146
   character development, 34
   descriptive detail, 170
   dialogue, 94, 354, 524
   dramatization, 330
   figurative language, 638
   humor, 294
   hyperbole, 560
   idioms, 210
   imagery, 118, 444
   jargon, 406
   onomatopoeia, 236
   personification, 702
   point of view, 380, 496, 614
   repetition, 586
   simile, 470, 638
   suspense, 58, 266
   transitional devices, 678

Authors, main selection
   Alvarez, Julia, 132–145, 146
   Ballard, Robert D., 392–405, 406
   Byars, Betsy, 20–33, 34
   Cline-Ransome, Lesa, 430–443, 444
   Diakité, Baba Wagué, 82–93, 94
   English, Karen, 340–353, 354
   Fritz, Jean, 600–613, 614
   Gutman, Dan, 546–559, 560
   Hayes, Joe, 250–265, 266
   Jiménez, Francisco, 484–495, 496
   Kaminsky, Marty, 368–379, 380
   Krensky, Stephen, 662–677, 678
   Lasky, Kathryn, 106–117, 118
   Lewin, Ted , 44–57, 58
   McKissack, Patricia and Fredrick, 96–99, 96
   Miller, Debbie S., 222–235, 236
   Namioka, Lensey, 626–637, 638
   O'Connor, Jane, 318–329, 330
   Odom, Karen, 296–299
   Park, Linda Sue, 454–469, 470
   Pinkney, Andrea Davis, 572–585, 586
   Schotter, Roni, 278–293, 294
   Stanley, Diane, 194–209, 210
   Untermeyer, Louis, 688–701, 702
   Whitebird, Mary, 508–523, 524
   Wynne–Jones, Tim, 156–169, 170

Index

Author's Perspective. *See* Comprehension skills: author's perspective.

Author's Purpose. *See* Comprehension skills: author's purpose.

Autobiographies, 392, 484–495, 659

Bb

Base words. *See* Vocabulary: base words.

Beyond Level Options, 39S–39T, 65S–65T, 77S–77T, 101S–101T, 123S–123T, 151S–151T, 177S–177T, 189S–189T, 217S–217T, 241S–241T, 273S–273T, 301S–301T, 313S–313T, 335S–335T, 359S–359T, 387S–387T, 413S–413T, 425S–425T, 449S–449T, 475S–475T, 503S–503T, 529S–529T, 541S–541T, 567S–567T, 591S–591T, 621S–621T, 645S–645T, 657S–657T, 683S–683T, 709S–709T

   comprehension, 39T, 65T, 77T, 101T, 123T, 151T, 177T, 189T, 217T, 241T, 273T, 301T, 313T, 335T, 359T, 387T, 413T, 425T, 449T, 475T, 503T, 529T, 541T, 567T, 591T, 621T, 645T, 657T, 683T, 709T

   fluency, 39S, 65S, 77S, 101S, 123S, 151S, 177S, 189S, 217S, 241S, 273S, 301S, 313S, 335S, 359S, 387S, 413S, 425S, 449S, 475S, 503S, 529S, 541S, 567S, 591S, 621S, 645S, 657S, 683S, 709S

   vocabulary, 39S, 39T, 65S, 65T, 77S, 77T, 101S, 101T, 123S, 123T, 151S, 151T, 177S, 177T, 189S, 189T, 217S, 217T, 241S, 241T, 273S, 273T, 301S, 301T, 313S, 313T, 335S, 335T, 359S, 359T, 387S, 387T, 413S, 413T, 425S, 425T, 449S, 449T, 475S, 475T, 503S, 503T, 529S, 529T, 541S, 541T, 567S, 567T, 591S, 591T, 621S, 621T, 645S, 645T, 657S, 657T, 683S, 683T, 709S, 709T

Bibliographies, using, 245K, 479C

Biographies, 365, 368–379, 430–443, 476–478, 572–585

Book, parts of, 421B, 425A, 425Q, 425S, 537B, 541Q, 541S

Build Background, 16, 39V, 40, 65V, 66, 77V, 78, 101V, 102, 123V, 128, 151V, 152, 177V, 178, 189V, 190, 217V, 218, 241V, 246, 273V, 274, 301V, 302, 313V, 314, 335V, 336, 359V, 364, 387V, 388, 413V, 414, 425V, 426, 449V, 450, 475V, 480, 503V, 504, 529V, 530, 541V, 542, 567V, 568, 591V, 596, 621V, 622, 645V, 646, 657V, 658, 683V, 684, 709V

Cc

Capitalization. *See* Grammar: capitalization.

Captions. *See* Text features: captions.

Cause and effect. *See* Comprehension skills: cause and effect; Writing forms and modes.

Character. *See* Comprehension skills: character.

Character Building, 16I, 128I, 246I, 364I, 480I, 596I

Charts. *See* Graphic organizers: charts; Study skills; Text features: charts.

Chronology. *See* Comprehension skills: sequence; Writing traits: organization.

Citations. *See* Computer literacy; Research and Inquiry; Study skills: citing sources.

Classroom Library, 16K, 40B, 66B, 78B, 102B, 128K, 152B, 178B, 190B, 218B, 246K, 274B, 302B, 314B, 336B, 364K, 388B, 414B, 426B, 450B, 480K, 504B, 530B, 542B, 568B, 596K, 622B, 646B, 658B, 684B, **6.1:** T11–T16; **6.2:** T12–T17; **6.3:** T12–T17; **6.4:** T12–T17; **6.5:** T13–T18; **6.6:** T13–T18

Clauses. *See* Grammar: clauses.

Colons, 151J, 301J, 359J, 529J, 709J. *See also* **Grammar: punctuation.**

Commas, 65B, 65J, 77I–77J, 101B, 101J, 123B, 123J, 127E, 177J, 241B, 241I–241J, 245E, 301J, 425J, 503B, 595E, 683J. *See also* **Grammar: punctuation.**

Compare and contrast. *See* Comprehension skills: compare/contrast.

Compound sentences. *See* Grammar: sentences.

Compound words. *See* Phonics/Spelling; Spelling; Vocabulary.

Comprehension skills

   author's perspective, 239, 453A–453B, 454–469, 471, 475O, 475P, 475R, 475T, 497B, 522, 525B, 551, **6.4:** T4

   author's purpose, 34, 58, 94, 118, 146, 170, 210, 236, 266, 294, 330, 354, 367A–367B, 368–379, 380, 381, 387O, 387P, 387R, 387T, 406, 442, 444, 445B, 470, 471B, 483A–483B, 484–495, 496, 497, 497B, 499, 503O, 503P, 503R, 503T, 514, 524, 553, 558, 560, 561B, 586, 614, 638, 670, 678, 690, 702 **6.4:** T1, **6.5:** T1

   cause/effect, 81A–81B, 82–93, 95, 101O, 101P, 101R, 101T, 108, 135, 147B, 214, 230, 269, 305A–305B, 306–309, 313O, 313P, 313R, 313T, 321, 373, 399, 438, 499, 585, 632, 652, 675, **6.1:** T3, **6.3:** T3

   character, 19A–19B, 20–33, 35, 35B, 39O, 30P, 39R, 39T, 43A–43B, 44–57, 65O, 65P, 65R, 65T, 95B, 134, 136, 167, 171B, 206, 249A–249B, 250–265, 267, 273O, 273P, 273R, 273T, 287, 350, 352, 439, 466, 520, 603, **6.1:** T1, **6.3:** T1

   compare/contrast, 166, 199, 417A–417B, 418–421, 425O, 425P, 425R, 425T, 440, 507A–507B, 508–523, 525, 529O, 529P, 529R, 529T, 536, 552, 604, 615B, 676, , **6.4:** T3, **6.5:** T2

conclusions, drawing, 56, 62, 90, 116, 173, 174, 184, 226, 277A–277B, 278–293, 295, 301O, 301P, 301R, 301T, 323, 331B, 339A–339B, 340–353, 355, 357, 359O, 359P, 359R, 359T, 384, 396, 407B, 409, 463, 511, 517, 576, 606, 617, 631, 639B, **6.3:** T2

description as text structure, 661A–661B, 662–677, 679, 683O, 683P, 683R, 683T, **6.6:** T4

fact and opinion, 391A–391B, 392–405, 407, 413O, 413P, 413R, 413T, 429A–429B, 430–443, 445, 449O, 449P, 449R, 449T, 537A, 606 **6.4:** T2

generalizations, making, 181A–181B, 182–185, 189O, 189P, 189R, 189T, 599A–599B, 600–613, 615, 621O, 621P, 621R, 621T, 672, 679B, **6.2:** T2, **6.6:** T1

inferences, making, 23, 48, 54, 131A–131B, 132–145, 147, 149, 151O, 151P, 151R, 151T, 155A–155B, 156–169, 171, 177O, 177P, 177R, 177T, 200, 204, 211B, 229, 231, 254, 260, 267B, 328, 346, 376, 384, 395, 402, 421A, 436, 461, 464, 488, 520, 552, 554, 665, 667, 670, 674, 692, 695, **6.2:** T1

judgments, making, 159, 232, 545A–545B, 546–559, 561, 564, 567O, 567P, 567R, 567T, 578, 581, 587B, 603, 633, **6.5:** T4

main ideas and details, 69A–69B, 70–73, 77O, 77P, 77Q, 77R, 77T, 105A–105B, 106–117, 119, 119B, 123O 123P, 123R, 123T, 174, 185A, 308, 309A, **6.1:** T2

persuasion, techniques of, 533A–533B, 534–537, 541O, 541P, 541R, 541T, 653A, **6.5:** T3

plot, 19A–19B, 20–33, 35, 35B, 39O, 39P, 39R, 39T, 43A–43B, 44–57, 59, 65O, 65P, 65R, 65T, 95B, 142, 171B, 211, 249A–249B, 250–265, 267, 273O, 273P, 273R, 273T **6.1:** T1, **6.3:** T1

predictions, making. *See* **Predictions, making.**

problem and solution, 193A–193B, 194–209, 211, 217O, 217P, 217R, 217T, 224, 228, 237B, 282, 293, 295B, 326, 518, 608, 634, 649A–649B, 650–653, 650, 652, 657O, 657P, 657R, 657T, 667, **6.2:** T3, **6.6:** T3

sequence, 221A–221B, 222–235, 237, 241O, 241P, 241R, 241T, 371, 399, 527, 625A–625B, 626–637, 639, 645O, 645P, 645R, 645T, 703B, **6.2:** T4

setting, 19A–19B, 20–33, 35, 35B, 39O, 39P, 39R, 39T, 43A–43B, 44–57, 59, 59B, 65O, 65P, 65R, 65T, 95B, 134, 171B, 249A–249B, 250–265, 267, 273O, 273P, 273R, 273T, 491, 518, 694, **6.1:** T1, **6.3:** T1

summarize, 28, 35, 52, 59, 73, 90, 95, 113, 119, 140, 147, 171, 185, 211, 237, 267, 295, 317A–317B, 318–329, 331, 335O, 335P, 335R, 335T, 350, 355, 355B, 373, 381, 381B, 407, 421, 445, 461, 471, 492, 497, 516, 525, 537, 555, 561, 571A–571B, 572–585, 587, 591O, 591P, 591R, 591T, 606, 615, 639, 653, 669, 679, 699, 703, **6.3:** T4, **6.5:** T5, **6.6:** T2

theme, 162, 168, 589, 687A–687B, 688–701, 703, 709O, 709P, 709R, 709T, **6.6:** T5

Comprehension strategies

analyze, 19A–19B, 20–33, 35, 39O, 43A–43B, 44–57, 59, 65O, 106–117, 123O, 171, 185, 211, 237, 249A–249B, 250–265, 273O, 295, 305A–305B, 306–309, 313O, 381, 429A–429B, 430–443, 445, 471, 497, 615, 639

    story structure, , 19A–19B, 20–33, 39O, 43A–43B, 44–57, 65O, 95B, 142, 249A–249B, 250–265, 273O

    text structure, 305A–305B, 306–309, 313O

evaluate, 147, 367A–367B, 368–379, 387O, 391A–391B, 392–405, 407, 413O, 453A–453B, 454–469, 471, 475O, 483A–483B, 484–495, 503O, 525, 533A–533B, 534–537, 541O, 545A–545B, 546–559, 561, 567O, 679

generate questions, 131A–131B, 132–145, 149, 151O, 155A–155B, 156–169, 177O, 181A–181B, 182–185, 189O, 563, 599A–599B, 600–613, 615, 621O, 625A–625B, 626–637, 639, 645O, 661A–661B, 662–677, 679, 683O

inferences, making, 69A–69B, 70–73, 77O, 81A–81B, 82–93, 101O, 105A–105B, 106–117, 123O, 417A–417B, 418–421, 425O, 429A–429B, 430–443, 449O

monitor comprehension, 277A–277B, 278–293, 301O, 317A–317B, 318–329, 335O, 339A–339B, 340–353, 359O, 507A–507B, 508–523, 529O, 571A–571B, 572–585, 587, 591O. *See also* **Monitor and Clarify.**

summarize, 193A–193B, 194–209, 217O, 221A–221B, 222–235, 241O, 649A–649B, 650, 687A–687B, 688–701, 709O

Computer Literacy, 127I–127J, 245I–245J, 363I–363J, 479I–479J, 595I–595J, 713I–713J. *See also* **Internet; Technology.**

  avoiding plagiarism, 127I–127J

  avoiding viruses, 245I–245J

  browser, 127I-127J

  citations, 127I–127J, 128H

  databases, creating, 189T, 595I–595J

  electronic thesaurus and spell check, 363I–363J

  e-mail, 245I–245J

  field names, 595I-595J

  fields, 595I-595J

  graphs, 479I, 479J

  hardware and software issues, 595I

  hits, 127I-127J

  hyperlinks, 640–643, 645Q, 645S

  Internet, 52, 127I–127J, 185B, 189A, 189Q, 189S, 640–643, 713I–713J, **6.2:** T11. *See also* **Research and Inquiry.**

  key words, 60–63, 127I–127J, 128H, 185B, 246I, 640–643, 645Q, 645S, **6.2:** T11

Index

protecting computers and networks, 245I–245J

safety alerts, 127J, 245J, 363J, 479J, 595J, 713J

search engines and search techniques, 127I–127J, 185B, 189Q, 189S, 246H, 246I

site maps, 127I–127J

spreadsheets, 479I–479J

URLs, 127I–127J

viruses, 245I

vocabulary, 127I, 245I, 363I, 479I, 595I, 713I

Web addresses and Web sites, 185B, 189Q, 189S, 653B

Web pages, creating, 713I–713J

word-processing tools, 363I–363J

writing process and, 363I–363J

Conclusions, drawing. *See* Comprehension skills: conclusions, drawing.

Concrete poetry, 446–447. *See also* Poetry.

Conjunctions. *See* Grammar: conjunctions.

Connect and Compare, 37, 63, 99, 121, 149, 175, 215, 239, 271, 299, 333, 357, 385, 411, 447, 473, 501, 527, 565, 589, 619, 643, 681, 707. *See also* Informational text; Text connections.

Connections, making. *See* Text connections.

Connotation and denotation, 134, 625, 645D, 645F, 645Q. *See also* Vocabulary.

Consonance, 332–333, 335Q, 335S. *See also* Literary devices; Poetry.

Constructive Feedback. *See individual skiill listings for* Additional Lessons; Fluency; Phonics/Spelling.

Content Area Reading, 36–37, 60–63, 70–73, 96–99, 148–149, 172–173, 182–183, 268–271, 296–299, 306–309, 356–357, 382–385, 418–421, 472–473, 498–501, 534– 537, 562–565, 616–619, 640–643, 650–653, 704–707

Context clues. *See* Vocabulary: context clues.

Context, teaching words in. *See* Vocabulary: teach words in context.

Contractions. *See* Grammar: contractions.

Cooperative learning, 35A, 39C, 39E, 59A, 65C, 65E, 77C, 77E, 73A, 95A, 101C, 101E, 119A, 123C, 123E, 147A, 151C, 151E, 171A, 177C, 177E, 185A, 189C, 189E, 211A, 217C, 217E, 237A, 241C, 241E, 267A, 273C, 273E, 295A, 301C, 301E, 309A, 313C, 313E, 331A, 335C, 335E, 355A, 359C, 359E, 381A, 387C, 387E, 407A, 413C, 413E, 413L, 421A, 425C, 425E, 445A, 449C, 449E, 471A, 475C, 475E, 497A, 503C, 503E, 525A, 529C, 529E, 537A, 541C, 541E, 561A, 567C, 567E, 587A, 591C, 591E, 615A, 621C, 621E, 631C, 631E, 639A, 645C, 645E, 653A, 657C, 657E, 679A, 683C, 683E, 703A 709C, 709E

Cross-Curricular connections

art, 16I, 164, 246I, 323, 364I, 457, 512, **6.1:** T14, **6.3:** T17

health, 136

language arts, 364I, 596I

math, 113, 149, 357, 401, 557, 565

music, 53

science, 16S, 31, 40J, 66J, 78J, 102J, 128I, 128S, 152J, 175, 178J, 190J, 218J, 246I, 246S, 274J, 302J, 314J, 336J, 364S, 385, 388J, 414J, 426J, 439, 450J, 480S, 504J, 530J, 542J, 568J, 596S, 603, 622J, 629, 643, 646J, 658J, 684J, 694, 707, **6.1:** T12, T14, T16, **6.3:** T17, **6.4:** T15

social studies, 16S, 37, 40J, 63, 66J, 78J, 99, 102J, 128I, 128S, 152J, 178J, 190J, 202, 218J, 234, 246S, 258, 271, 274J, 289, 299, 302J, 314J, 336J, 364S, 378, 388J, 414J, 426J, 450J, 473, 480I, 480S, 490, 501, 504J, 522, 530J, 542J, 568J, 580, 596S, 619, 622J, 646J, 658J, 672, 684J, **6.1:** T12

workstations, 16R–16S, 40I–40J, 66I–66J, 78I–78J, 102I–102J, 128R–128S, 152I–152J, 178I–178J, 190I–190J, 218I–218J, 246R–246S, 274I–274J, 302I–302J, 314I–314J, 336I–336J, 364R–364S, 388I–388J, 414I–414J, 426I–426J, 450I–450J, 480R–480S, 504I–504J, 530I–530J, 542I–542J, 568I–568J, 596R–596S, 622I–622J, 646I–646J, 658I–658J, 684I–684J

Cultural Perspectives, 52, 116, 137, 205, 291, 328, 347, 402, 468, 510, 556, 558, 630, 636, 669, 692

Dd

Daily Language Activities, 39I, 65I, 77I, 101I, 123I, 151I, 177I, 189I, 217I, 241I, 273I, 301I, 313I, 335I, 359I, 387I, 413I, 425I, 449I, 475I, 503I, 529I, 541I, 567I, 591I, 611I, 645I, 657I, 683I, 709. *See also* **Grammar.**

Decodable Passages, 39E, 39M, 77E, 77M, 123E, 123M, 151E, 151M, 177E, 177M, 189E, 189M, 217E, 217M, 241E, 341M, 273E, 273M, 301E, 301M, 313E, 313M, 335E, 335M, 359E, 359M, 387E, 387M, 413E, 413M, 425E, 425M, 449E, 449M, 475E, 475M, 529E, 529M, 541E, 541M, 591E, 591M, 621E, 621M, 645E, 645M, 657E, 657M, 683E, 683M, 709E, 709M

Decoding. *See* Decodable Passages; Phonics/Spelling.

Denotation, 134, 625, 645D, 645O, 645Q. *See also* Vocabulary: denotation.

Description. *See* Comprehension skills: description as text structure.

Diagram. *See* Graphic organizers: diagrams; Text features.

Dialogue, 26, 94, 246S, 300–301, 301A–301B, 336I, 336J, 354, 358, 359, 363A, 363C, 363D, 363E, 408–411, 413Q, 413S, 524, 552

Dictionary, using, 19, 31, 39D, 39F, 39O, 39Q, 123F, 134, 155, 162, 177D, 177O, 177Q, 189F, 193, 217D, 217O, 217Q, 221, 241Q, 277, 283, 301D, 301O, 301Q, 363Q, 417, 425D, 425O, 425Q, 453, 475D, 475F, 475O, 475Q, 537B, 541A, 541R, 621F, 645F, 687, 693, 709D, 709O, 709Q, **6.5:** T11

Differentiated instruction, 16K, 16N–16O, 40B, 40E–40F, 66B, 66E–66F, 78B, 78E–78F, 102B, 102E–102F, 128K, 128N–128O, 152B, 152E–152F, 178B, 178E–178F, 190B, 190E–190F, 218B, 218E–218F, 246K, 246N–246O, 274B, 274E–274F, 302B, 302E–302F, 314B, 314E–314F, 336B, 336E–336F, 364K, 364N–364O, 388B, 388E–388F, 414B, 414E–414F, 426B, 426E–426F, 450B, 450E–450F, 480K, 480N–480O, 504B, 504E–504F, 530B, 530E–530F, 542B, 542E–542F, 568B, 568E–568F, 596K, 596N–596O, 622B, 622E–622F, 646B, 646E–646F, 658B, 658E–658F, 684B, 684E–684F. *See also* **Approaching Level Options; Beyond Level Options; ELL; Leveled Reader Lessons; On Level Options; Small Group Options.**

Direct and indirect objects. *See* **Grammar: direct and indirect objects.**

Directions, writing and following, 521, 610, 620–621B

Dramatic monologue, 597

Ee

Encyclopedia, 472–473, **6.4:** T11

English Language Learners
   advanced/beginning/
      intermediate, 18, 19A, 35A, 39C, 39D, 39E, 39I, 39V, 42, 43A, 59A, 65C, 65D, 65E, 65I, 65V, 68, 69A, 77C, 77D, 77E, 77I, 77V, 80, 81A, 95A, 101C, 101D, 101E, 101I, 101V, 104, 105A, 119A, 123C, 123D, 123E, 123I, 123V, 130, 131A, 147A, 151C, 151D, 151E, 151I, 151V, 154, 171A, 155A, 177C, 177D, 177E, 177I, 177V, 180, 181A, 189C, 189D, 189E, 189I, 189V, 192, 193A, 211A, 217C, 217D, 217E, 217I, 217V, 220, 221A, 237A, 241C, 241D, 241E, 241I, 241V, 248, 249A, 267A, 273C, 273D, 273E, 273I, 273V, 276, 277A, 295A, 301C, 301D, 301E, 301I, 301V, 304, 305A, 313C, 313D, 313E, 313I, 313V, 316, 317A, 331A, 335C, 335D, 335E, 335I, 335V, 338, 339A, 355A, 359C, 359D, 359E, 359I, 359V, 366, 367A, 381A, 387C, 387D, 387E, 387I, 387V, 390, 391A, 407A, 413C, 413D, 413E, 413I, 413V, 416, 417A, 425C, 425D, 425E, 425I, 425V, 428, 429A, 445A, 449C, 449D, 449E, 449I, 449V, 452, 453A, 471A, 475C, 475D, 475E, 475I, 475V, 482, 483A, 497A, 503C, 503D, 503E, 503I, 503V, 506, 507A, 525A, 529C, 529D, 529E, 529I, 529V, 532, 533A, 541C, 541D, 541E, 541I, 541V, 544, 545A, 561A, 567C, 567D, 567E, 567I, 567V, 570, 571A, 587A, 591C, 591D, 591E, 591I, 591V, 598, 599A, 615A, 621C, 621D, 621E, 621I, 621V, 624, 625A, 639A, 645C, 645D, 645E, 645I, 645V, 648, 649A, 657C, 657D, 657E, 657I, 657V, 660, 661A, 679A, 683C, 683D, 683E, 683I, 683V, 686, 687A, 703A, 709C, 709D, 709E, 709I, 709V

   comprehension, 19A, 39V, 43A, 65V, 69A, 77V, 81A, 101V, 105A, 123V, 131A, 151V, 155A, 177V, 181A, 189V, 193A, 217V, 221A, 241V, 249A, 273V, 277A, 301V, 305A, 313V, 317A, 335V, 339A, 359V, 367A, 387V, 391A, 413V, 417A, 425V, 429A, 449V, 453A, 475V, 483A, 503V, 507A, 529V, 533A, 541V, 545A, 567V, 571A, 591V, 599A, 621V, 625A, 645V, 649A, 657V, 661A, 683V, 687A, 709V

   fluency, 35A, 59A, 95A, 119A, 147A, 171A, 211A, 237A, 267A, 295A, 331A, 355A, 381A, 407A, 445A, 471A, 497A, 525A, 561A, 587A, 615A, 639A, 679A, 703A

   grammar, 39I, 65I, 77I, 101I, 123I, 151I, 177I, 189I, 217I, 241I, 273I, 301I, 313I, 335I, 359I, 387I, 413I, 425I, 449I, 475I, 503I, 529I, 541I, 567I, 591I, 621I, 645I, 657I, 683I, 709I

   oral language, 16, 39V, 40, 65V, 66, 77V, 78, 101V, 102, 123V, 128, 151V, 152, 177V, 178, 189V, 190, 217V, 218, 241V, 246, 273V, 274, 301V, 302, 313V, 314, 335V, 336, 359V, 364, 387V, 388, 413V, 414, 425V, 426, 449V, 450, 475V, 480, 503V, 504, 529V, 530, 541V, 542, 567V, 568, 591V, 596, 621V, 622, 645V, 646, 657V, 658, 683V, 684, 709V

   phonics, 39E, 65E, 77E, 101E, 123E, 151E, 177E, 189E, 217E, 241E, 273E, 301E, 313E, 335E, 359E, 387E, 413E, 425E, 449E, 475E, 503E, 529E, 541E, 567E, 591E, 621E, 645E, 657E, 683E, 709E

   vocabulary, 18, 39C, 39D, 39V, 42, 65C, 65D, 65V, 68, 77C, 77D, 77V, 80, 101C, 101D, 101V, 104, 123C, 123D, 123V, 130, 151C, 151D, 151V, 154, 177C, 177D, 177V, 180, 189C, 189D, 189V, 192, 217C, 217D, 217V, 220, 241C, 241D, 241V, 248, 273C, 273D, 273V, 276, 301C, 301D, 301V, 304, 313C, 313D, 313V, 316, 335C, 335D, 335V, 338, 359C, 359D, 359V, 366, 387C, 387D, 387V, 390, 413C, 413D, 413V, 416, 425C, 425D, 425V, 428, 449C, 449D, 449V, 452, 475C, 475D, 475V, 482, 503C, 503D, 503V, 506, 529C, 529D, 529V, 532, 541C, 541D, 541V, 544, 567C, 567D, 567V, 570, 591C, 591D, 591V, 598, 621C, 621D, 621V, 624, 645C, 645D, 645V, 648, 657C, 657D, 657V, 660, 683C, 683D, 683V, 686, 709C, 709D, 709V

Evaluating. *See* **Comprehension strategies: evaluate.**

Everyday communications, 653B, 657Q, 657S

Evidence and sources. *See* Comprehension skills: evidence and sources.

Exaggeration, 247, 408, 411. *See also* Hyberbole.

Expository nonfiction. *See* Genre: reading nonfiction.

Extra Support, 29, 51, 89, 111, 140, 163, 203, 229, 259, 287, 325, 349, 375, 399, 437, 461, 489, 515, 553, 579, 605, 633, 671, 697

Ff

Fable, 526–527

Fact and opinion. *See* Comprehension skills: fact and opinion.

Fairy tale, 194–209, 217F

Fantasy, 278–293

Figurative language. *See* Author's Craft; Literary devices: figurative language; Poetry; figurative language; Writer's Craft; Writing traits: word choice.

First person point-of-view, 253, 380, 511, 575, 631

Fix-up strategies. *See* Monitor and Clarify; Predictions, making.

Fluency, 16R, 17, 30, 35A, 39K, 39L, 39N, 39Q, 39S, 40I, 41, 59A, 65K, 65L, 65N, 65Q, 65S, 66I, 67, 73A, 77K, 77L, 77N, 77Q, 77S, 78I, 79, 87, 95A, 101K, 101L, 101N, 101Q, 101S, 102I, 103, 119A, 123K, 123L, 123N, 123Q, 123S, 128R, 129, 147A, 151K, 151L, 151N, 151Q, 151S, 152I, 153, 171A, 177K, 177L, 177N, 177Q, 177S, 178I, 179, 185A, 189K, 189L, 189N, 189Q, 189S, 190I, 191, 211A, 217K, 217L, 217N, 217Q, 217S, 218I, 219, 237A, 241K, 241L, 241N, 241Q, 241S, 246R, 247, 262, 267A, 273K, 273L, 273N,

273Q, 273S, 274I, 275, 295A, 301K, 301L, 301N, 301Q, 301S, 302I, 303, 309A, 313K, 313L, 313N, 313Q, 313S, 314I, 315, 331A, 335K, 335L, 335N, 335Q, 335S, 336I, 337, 355A, 359K, 359L, 359N, 359Q, 359S, 364R, 365, 371, 381A, 387K, 387L, 387N, 387Q, 387S, 388I, 389, 407A, 413K, 413L, 413N, 413Q, 413S, 414I, 415, 421A, 425I, 425K, 425L, 425N, 425Q, 425S, 426I, 427, 445A, 449K, 449L, 449N, 449Q, 449S, 450I, 451, 471A, 475K, 475L, 475N, 475Q, 475S, 480R, 481, 497A, 503K, 503L, 503N, 503Q, 503S, 504I, 505, 525A, 529K, 529L, 529N, 529Q, 529S, 530I, 531, 537A, 541K, 541L, 541N, 541Q, 541S, 542I, 543, 561A, 567K, 567L, 567N, 567Q, 567S, 568I, 569, 587A, 591K, 591L, 591N, 591Q, 591S, 596R, 597, 615A, 621K, 621L, 621N, 621Q, 621S, 622I, 623, 639A, 645K, 645L, 645N, 645Q, 645S, 646I, 647, 653A, 657K, 657L, 657N, 657Q, 657S, 658I, 659, 679A, 683K, 683L, 683N, 683Q, 683S, 684I, 685, 703A, 709K, 709L, 709N, 709Q, 709S. *See also* **Self-selected reading.**

accuracy, speed, prosody, 35A, 39L, 59A, 65L, 73A, 77L, 95A, 101L, 119A, 123L, 147A, 151L, 171A, 177L, 185A, 189L, 211A, 217L, 237A, 241L, 267A, 273L, 295A, 301L, 309A, 313L, 331A, 335L, 355A, 359L, 381A, 387L, 407A, 413L, 421A, 425L, 445A, 449L, 471A, 475L, 497A, 503L, 525A, 529L, 537A, 541L, 561A, 567L, 587A, 591L, 615A, 621L, 639A, 645L, 653A, 657L, 679A, 683L, 703A, 709L

Approaching Level Options for, 39M, 39N, 65M, 65N, 77M, 77N, 101M, 101N, 123M, 123N, 151M, 151N, 177M, 177N, 189M, 189N, 217M, 217N, 241M, 241N, 273M, 273N, 301M, 301N, 313M, 313N, 335M, 335N, 359M, 359N, 387M, 387N, 413M, 413N, 425M, 425N, 449M, 449N, 475M, 475N, 503M, 503N, 529M, 529N, 541M, 541N, 567M, 567N, 591M, 591N, 621M,

621N, 645M, 645N, 657M, 657N, 683M, 683N, 709M, 709N

Beyond Level Options, 39S, 65S, 77S, 101S, 123S, 151S, 177S, 189S, 217S, 241S, 273S, 301S, 313S, 335S, 359S, 387S, 413S, 425S, 449S, 475S, 503S, 529S, 541S, 567S, 591S, 621S, 645S, 657S, 683S, 709S

choral reading, 35A, 151N, 189Q, 189S, 267A, 335N, 359N. 387N, 449N, 561A, 567N, 567Q

cooperative learning, 35A, 59A, 73A, 95A, 119A, 147A, 171A, 185A, 211A, 237A, 267A, 295A, 309A, 331A, 355A, 381A, 407A, 413L, 421A, 445A, 471A, 497A, 525A, 537A, 561A, 587A, 615A, 639A, 653A, 679A, 703A

echo reading, 35A, 39N, 40I, 59A, 65N, 73A, 77N, 95A, 123N, 151N, 177N, 185A, 211A, 217N, 217Q, 217S, 218I, 237A, 301N, 309A, 313N, 355A, 388I, 407A, 413N, 421A, 425Q, 425S, 449N, 471A 475N, 475Q, 503N, 503Q, 503S, 525A, 529N, 529Q, 537A, 541N, 541Q, 561A, 587A, 591N, 615A, 621N, 639A, 645N, 645Q, 645S, 653A, 657N, 657Q, 679A, 683N, 703A, 709N, 709Q

ELL, 35A, 59A, 95A, 119A, 147A, 171A, 211A, 237A, 267A, 295A, 331A, 355A, 381A, 407A, 445A, 471A, 497A, 525A, 561A, 587A, 615A, 639A, 679A, 703A

explain/practice, 35A, 59A, 73A, 95A, 119A, 147A, 171A, 185A, 211A, 237A, 267A, 295A, 309A, 331A, 355A, 381A, 407A, 421A, 445A, 471A, 497A, 525A, 537A, 561A, 587A, 615A, 639A, 653A, 679A, 703A

Fluency Solutions Audio CD, 35A, 39L, 59A, 65L, 73A, 77L, 95A, 101L, 119A, 123L, 147A, 151L, 171A, 177L, 185A, 189L, 211A, 217L, 237A, 241L, 267A, 273L, 295A, 301L, 309A, 313L, 331A, 335L, 355A, 359L, 381A, 387L, 407A, 413L, 421A, 425L, 445A, 449L, 471A, 475L, 497A, 503L, 525A, 529L, 537A, 541L, 561A,

Key 6.1 = Grade 6, Book 1

567L, 587A, 591L, 615A, 621L, 639A, 645L, 653A, 657L, 679A, 683L, 703A, 709L

group reading, 35A, 73A, 95A, 147A, 185A, 309A, 355A, 381A, 421A, 445A, 449N, 497A 537A, 541Q, 561A, 653A

modeling fluent reading, 39N, 65N, 77N, 101N, 123N, 151N, 177N, 189N, 217N, 241N, 273N, 301N, 313N, 335N, 359N, 387N, 413N, 425N, 449N, 475N, 503N, 529N, 541N, 567N, 591N, 621N, 645N, 657N, 683N, 709N

On Level Options for, 39Q, 65Q, 77Q, 101Q, 123Q, 151Q, 177Q, 189Q, 217Q, 241Q, 273Q, 301Q, 313Q, 335Q, 359Q, 387Q, 413Q, 425Q, 449Q, 475Q, 503Q, 529Q, 541Q, 567Q, 591Q, 621Q, 645Q, 657Q, 683Q, 709Q

partner reading, 39N, 39S, 65N, 77N, 101N, 101S, 123N, 123S, 128R, 151N, 151Q, 151S, 177Q, 177S, 189N, 217S, 246R, 301Q, 313Q, 335N, 335S, 359N, 359S, 387S, 413S, 414I, 425N, 425S, 449N, 449S, 471A, 475S, 525A, 541N, 541Q, 567Q, 615A, 670A, 703A, 709N

pauses, stops, and intonation, 35A, 39N, 39Q, 39S, 59A, 65N, 65Q, 77N, 77Q, 77S, 101N, 101Q, 123N, 123Q, 151Q, 151S, 161, 177N, 177Q, 177S, 217N, 217S, 267A, 273Q, 273S, 301N, 301S, 313N, 313Q, 313S, 335N, 335Q, 335S, 359Q, 359S, 381A, 387N, 387Q, 387S, 413N, 413Q, 425N, 425Q, 475N, 497A, 503Q, 503S, 525A, 561A, 587A, 591Q, 615A, 621S, 639A, 703N, 709N, 709Q

phrase-cued text, 35A, 65Q, 65S, 67, 101Q, 101S, 147A, 211B, 262, 267A, 295A, 337, 387Q, 387S, 388I, 475S, 497A, 587A, 591Q, 685

pronunciation, 59A, 185A, 189N, 189S, 237A, 274I, 309A, 313S, 314I, 331A, 421A, 425S, 537A, 541N, 541Q, 541S, 591N, 621Q, 653A, 657N, 657Q, 657S, 703A

punctuation, 16S, 39S, 40I, 65A, 65Q, 65S, 73A, 77Q, 77S, 95A, 101Q, 101S, 123Q, 123S, 128R, 151N, 151Q, 151S, 152I, 161, 171A, 177Q, 177S, 241Q, 241S, 246R, 273Q, 274I, 301Q, 301S, 335S, 364R, 387S, 407A, 413S, 413Q, 449N, 471A, 475N, 503N, 503Q, 503S, 525A, 529N, 529Q, 561A, 587A, 591N, 591Q, 621N, 621Q, 621S, 639A, 645N, 645Q, 645S, 696

reading with expression and intonation, 30, 39N, 77N, 78I, 101N, 102I, 151N, 177N, 178I, 217N, 218I, 241N, 246S, 262, 265N, 273N, 335N, 336I, 337, 359N, 371, 381A, 387N, 425N, 475S, 497A, 503N, 503Q, 519, 645N, 696

repeated reading, 35A, 39N, 39Q, 39S, 59A, 65N, 65Q, 65S, 73A, 77N, 77Q, 77S, 95A, 101N, 101Q, 101S, 119A, 123N, 123Q, 123S, 147A, 151N, 151Q, 151S, 171A, 177N, 177Q, 177S, 185A, 189N, 189Q, 189S, 211A, 217N, 217Q, 217S, 237A, 241N, 241Q, 241S, 267A, 273N, 273Q, 273S, 295A, 301N, 301Q, 301S, 309A, 313N, 313Q, 313S, 331A, 335N, 335Q, 335S, 355A, 359N, 359Q, 359S, 381A, 387N, 387Q, 387S, 407A, 413M, 413Q, 413S, 421A, 425N, 425Q, 425S, 445A, 449N, 449Q, 449S, 471A, 475N, 475Q, 475S, 497A, 503N, 503Q, 503S, 525A, 529M, 529Q, 529S, 537A, 541N, 541Q, 541S, 561A, 567N, 567Q, 567S, 587A, 591N, 591Q, 591S, 615A, 621N, 621Q, 621S, 639A, 645M, 645Q, 645S, 653A, 657N, 657Q, 657S, 679A, 683N, 683Q, 683S, 703A, 709N, 709Q, 709S

tempo and pace, 77Q, 102I, 119A, 123N, 123Q, 151Q, 177Q, 177S, 190I, 211A, 217N, 217Q, 217S, 273S, 301S, 336I, 355A, 359N, 387Q, 407A, 421A, 425N, 445A, 449N, 449Q, 449S, 503N, 503Q, 541S, 567N, 567Q, 567S, 587A, 615A, 639A, 645Q, 679A, 683N, 683Q, 683S, 709Q

timed reading, 39N, 39Q, 65N, 77N, 77Q, 101N, 101Q, 123N, 123S, 151N, 177N, 189N, 189Q, 217N, 217Q, 241N, 273N, 273Q, 301N, 301Q, 313N, 313Q, 335N, 335Q, 359N, 387N, 387Q, 359Q, 413N, 413Q, 425N, 425Q, 449N, 449Q, 475N, 475Q, 503N, 529N, 529Q, 541N, 567N, 567Q, 591N, 591Q, 621N, 645N, 645Q, 657N, 657Q, 683N, 683N, 683Q, 709N, 709Q

Focus question, 16, 35, 37, 40, 59, 63, 66, 78, 95, 102, 119, 121, 128, 133, 147, 149, 152, 171, 178, 190, 211, 218, 223, 237, 239, 246, 251, 267, 271, 274, 276, 295, 299, 302, 314, 331, 336, 341, 355, 364, 381, 388, 407, 414, 426, 445, 450, 471, 480, 497, 504, 525, 527, 530, 542, 561, 565, 568, 587, 589, 596, 615, 622, 639, 646, 658, 679, 681, 684, 703, 707

Folk tale, 82–93, 191, 250–265, 505

Free verse, 120–121

Functional documents, 653B, 657Q, 657S

Gg

Generalizations, making. *See* **Comprehension skills: generalizations, making.**

Genre. *See also* **Informational text; Poetry.**

features of, 17, 36, 41, 60, 67, 79, 96, 103, 120, 129, 148, 153, 172, 179, 191, 219, 238, 247, 268, 275, 303, 315, 332, 337, 356, 365, 382, 389, 415, 427, 446, 451, 472, 481, 498, 505, 531, 543, 562, 569, 588, 597, 616, 623, 640, 647, 659, 685, 680, 704

reading fiction
    dramatic monologue, 597
    fable, 526–527
    fairy tale, 194–209
    fantasy, 278–293

folk tale, 82–93, 191, 250–265, 505

historical fiction, 44–57, 454–469

humorous fiction, 196, 198

mystery, 346

myth, 153, 212–215

novel excerpt, 20–33

parody, 196, 198

personal essay, 129

play, 340–353

realistic fiction, 20–33, 132–145, 156–169, 415, 505, 508–523, 546–559

science fiction, 626–637

short story, 156–169, 688–701

song lyrics, 120–121

tall tale, 247, 408–411

reading nonfiction. *See also* Informational text.

almanac, 148–149

autobiography, 392, 484–495, 659

biographical sketch, 430–443

biography, 365, 368–379, 476–478, 572–585

critique, 337

encyclopedia, 472–473

expository nonfiction, 219, 222–235

historical text, 427

informational essay, 96–88

informational nonfiction, 17, 36–37, 41, 60–63, 67, 70–73, 103, 106–117, 129, 148–149, 172–175, 179, 182–185, 219, 222–235, 268–271, 296–299, 306–309, 315, 318–329, 337, 356–357, 365, 368–379, 382–385, 392, 418–421, 427, 430–443, 451, 472–473, 481, 484–495, 498–501, 531, 534–537, 543, 562–565, 569, 600–613, 616–619, 640–643, 650–653, 659, 662–677, 685, 704–707

Internet article, 640–643

interview, 296–299

letters to editor, 498–501

newspaper article, 36–37

personal essay, 129

primary sources, 616–619

science articles, 172–175, 382–385, 640–643, 704–707

social studies article, 36–37, 60–63, 96–99, 472–473, 498–501, 616–619

speech, 569

textbook, 60–63

reading poetry, 79, 120–121, 238–239, 275, 303, 332–333, 389, 446–447, 588–589, 623, 647, 680–681. *See also* **Poetry.**

Grammar, 39I–39J, 65I–65J, 77I–77J, 101I–101J, 123I–123J, 151I–151J, 177I–177J, 189I–189J, 217I–217J, 241I–241J, 273I–273J, 301I–301J, 313I–313J, 335I–335J, 359I–359J, 387I–387J, 413I–413J, 425I–425J, 449I–449J, 475I–475J, 503I–503J, 529I–529J, 541I–541J, 567I–567J, 591I–591J, 621I–621J, 645I–645J, 657I–657J, 683I–683J, 709I–709J

adjectives

articles, 529B, 529I–529J

indefinite and definite, 529I–529J

comparing with *good* and *bad,* 591B, 591I–591J

demonstrative, 503B, 503I–503J

irregular comparative forms, 591I, 591J

predicate, 335B, 335I–335J

proper adjectives, 503B, 503J

superlative, 541I–541J, 591I, 591J

that compare, 541I–541J, 567B, 567I–567J, 591B, 591I–591J

usage, 541J

vs. adverbs, 621I–621J

adverbs

intensifiers, 621I–621J, 713E

that compare, 645B, 645I–645J

superlative, 645B, 645I–645J

that tell *how, when, where,* 621B, 621I–621J

using *good* and *well,* 621I–621J

vs. adjective, 621I–621J

antecedents, 387I–387J

appositives, 241B, 241I–241J

capitalization

first word in sentence, 39B, 39I–39J, 65B, 65J, 479E

in letters, 64–65, 65J, 151, 151F, 151J

proper nouns and adjectives, 151I, 503B, 503J, 595E

titles, 151I

clauses, 101B, 101I–101J, 123I–123J

conjunctions, 77I–77J, 123J, 123B

coordinating, 123B, 123J

contractions, 245E, 475J

direct and indirect objects, 273B, 273I–273J

interjections, 300, 517

mechanics and usage, 39B, 39J, 65B, 65J, 77J, 101B, 101J, 123B, 123J, 151B, 151J, 177B, 177J, 189J, 217B, 217J, 241B, 241J, 273B, 273J, 301B, 301J, 313J, 335B, 335J, 359B, 359J, 387B, 387J, 413B, 413J, 425J, 449B, 449J, 475B, 475J, 503B, 503J, 529B, 529J, 541J, 567B, 567J, 591B, 591J, 621B, 621J, 645J, 657J, 683B, 683J, 709B, 709J

negatives, 657I–657J

double, 157I–157J

nouns

common, 151I–151J, 217I–217J, 245E, 363E

plural, 128R, 176B, 177I–177J, 189I–189J, 217I–217J

irregular, 189I–189J

possessive, 217I–217J

predicate, 335B, 335I–335J

proper, 151I–151J, 217I–217J, 503B, 503J

singular, 176B, 177I–177J, 217I

plurals, 177I–177J, 189I–189J

possessives, 217B, 217I–217J, 425I–425J, 475J

prepositions and prepositional phrases, 683B, 683I–683J, 709I–709J

Key 6.1 = Grade 6, Book 1

pronouns

   antecedents, 387B, 387I–387J

   demonstrative, 475I

   indefinite, 449B, 449I–449J, 475B

   interrogative, 475I

   object, 413B, 413I–413J

   plural, 475I–475J

   possessive, 425I–425J, 475J, 479E

   pronoun–antecedent agreement, 387I–387J

   pronoun–verb agreement, 475B, 475I–475J

   relative, 475I

   subject, 413B, 413I–413J

punctuation

   apostrophes, 217I–217J, 245E

   colon, 151J, 301J, 359J, 529B, 529J, 709B, 709J

   commas, 65B, 65J, 77I–77J, 101B, 101J, 123B, 123J, 127E, 177J, 241B, 241I–241J, 245E, 301J, 425J, 503B, 595E, 683J

      in dates, 151B

      in a series, 177J

      in sentences, 39I–39J, 65B, 77J, 101B, 101I–101J, 123B, 123J, 301J

      splice or fault, 123I–123J

      to separate introductory words, prepositional phrases, interrupters, transitions, nonrestrictive relative clauses, 101B, 123B, 127E, 177J, 503B, 683J

      with appositives, 241B, 241I–241J

   compound words, 541J

   dialogue, 301B, 301J, 359J

   hyphens, 449J, 541J

   italics, 335J, 359J, 479D

   letter, 64–65, 65A–65B, 65J, 150–151, 151A–151B, 151J, 529B

   parenthesis, 359J

   period, 39J, 359J

   quotation marks, 301J, 335J, 425J, 529J, 709B, 709J

   semicolon, 77J, 123J, 301J, 529B, 709B, 709J

   sentence, 39B, 39I–39J

   titles, 335J

   underlining, 335, 335J

sentences

   combining, 77I–77J, 790B, 709I–709J

   complete, 39I–39J, 65I

   complex, 101B, 101I–101J

   compound, 77I–77J, 123J

   fragments, 39B, 39I–39J, 123J

   run-ons, 123B, 123I–123J

   subjects and predicates, 65B, 65I–65J

   types, 39B, 39I–39J

subject–verb agreement, 273B, 273J, 475I–475J

verbs

   action, 273B, 273I–273J

   direct and indirect objects, 273B, 273I–273J

   helping, 313I–313J

   irregular, 301B, 359I–359J

   linking, 335B, 335I–335J

   main, 313I–313J

   tenses, 301B, 301I–301J, 313I–313J, 387B

Graphic aids, 704–707, 709Q, 709S. *See also* **Text features.**

Graphic organizers

   charts

      author's purpose chart, 369, 370, 372, 375, 376, 378, 485, 486, 491, 492, 493, 494, 495

      cause and effect chart, 84, 86, 88, 91, 308

      character, setting, plot chart, 45, 46, 49, 53, 55

      conclusion chart, 279, 280, 286, 288, 292, 341, 344, 347, 349, 351

      fact and opinion chart, 391B, 393, 394, 395, 398, 400, 403, 432, 435, 438, 442

      generalization chart, 184, 601, 604, 609, 610

      inferences chart, 133, 135, 137, 143, 145

      judgment chart, 547, 548, 551, 554, 557

      K–W–L, 16H, 189A, 313A, 425A, 541A, 657A

      persuasion chart, 536

      problem and solution chart, 195, 200, 203, 208, 652

      sequence chart, 223, 226, 230, 232, 233, 234, 627, 628, 629, 635, 636

      summary chart, 251, 254, 258, 264, 319, 322, 325, 327, 573, 575, 579, 582, 584

      theme chart, 689, 692, 695, 699, 700

   diagrams

      inferences diagram, 158, 157, 163, 168

      Venn diagram, 158, 163, 168, 420, 509, 511, 521, 595B

   maps

      story map, 21, 22, 24, 32, 39N

   pyramids, persuasion, 240-241

   webs

      author's perspective web, 458, 462, 465, 467, 468

      descriptive web, 663, 664, 665, 666, 668, 673

      main idea web, 72, 109, 111, 114

Greek roots. *See* **Phonics/Spelling; Vocabulary: Greek roots.**

Guided Practice. *See* **Comprehension Skills; Fluency: practice; Phonics/Spelling; Vocabulary.**

Hh

Haiku, 238–239. *See also* **Poetry.**

Handwriting. *See* **Penmanship.**

Higher level thinking, 35, 37, 59, 63, 95, 99, 119, 121, 147, 149, 171,

175, 211, 215, 237, 239, 267, 271, 295, 299, 331, 333, 355, 357, 381, 385, 407, 411, 445, 447, 471, 473, 497, 501, 525, 527, 561, 565, 587, 589, 615, 619, 639, 643, 679, 681, 703, 707. *See also* Comprehension skills; Comprehension strategies; Text connections.

Historical fiction, 44–57, 454–469

Home-School Connection, 127L, 245L, 363L, 479L, 595L, 713L

Homographs. *See* Vocabulary: homographs.

Homophones. *See* Phonics/ Spelling; Spelling; Vocabulary.

Humorous fiction, 196, 198. *See also* Genre.

Hyperbole, 26, 212–215, 217Q, 217S, 408–411, 413Q, 413S

Hyperlinks, 640–643, 645Q, 645S, **6.6:** T1 *See also* Computer literacy.

Ii

Idioms, 26, 141, 193, 199, 210, 217D, 217Q, 217S. *See also* Author's Craft: idioms; Literary devices: idioms; Vocabulary: idioms.

Illustrations/photographs, using, 47, 85, 87, 138, 161, 201, 207, 226, 252, 255, 290, 322, 371, 374, 399, 404, 487, 510, 550. *See also* Picture prompt.

Illustrators and photographers

Begay, Shonto, 524
Brooker, Kyrsten, 279
Christensen, Bonnie, 678
Colon, Raul, 638
Diakité, Baba Wagué, 94
Fiedler, Joseph Daniel, 266
Kim, Julie, 470
Knight, Christopher G., 118
Lewin, Ted, 58
Ransome, James E., 444
Rowe, John, 21
Tadgell, Nicole, 354

Talbott, Hudson, 614
Zyle, Jon Van, 236

Imagery, 26, 118, 120–121, 123Q 123Q, 444, 588–589. *See also* Author's Craft; Literary devices.

Independent Practice for Managing the Class, 16P–16Q, 40G–40H, 66G–66H, 78G–78H, 102G–102H, 128P–128Q, 152G–152H, 178G–178H, 190G–190H, 218G–218H, 246P–246Q, 274G–274H, 302G–302H, 314G–314H, 336G–336H, 364P–364Q, 388G–388H, 414G–414H, 426G–426H, 450G–450H, 480P–480Q, 504G–504H, 530G–530H, 542G–542H, 568G–568H, 596P–596Q, 622G–622H, 646G–646H, 658G–658H, 684G–684H

Independent Workstations. *See* Cross-Curricular connections: workstations.

Inferences, making. *See* Comprehension skills: inferences, making; Comprehension strategies: inferences, making.

Inflectional endings. *See* Phonics/ Spelling; Vocabulary.

Information and Media literacy. *See* Computer literacy; Informational text; Media literacy; Research and Inquiry; Technology.

Informational literacy. *See* Genre; Informational Text; Research and Inquiry.

Informational text

connect and compare, 37, 63, 99, 121, 149, 175, 215, 239, 271, 299, 333, 357, 385, 411, 447, 473, 501, 527, 565, 589, 619, 643, 681, 707

content vocabulary, 36–37, 60–63, 70–73, 96–99, 148–149, 172–175, 182–183, 268–271, 296–299, 306–309, 356–357, 382–385, 418–421, 472–473, 498–501, 534–537, 562–565, 616–619, 640–643, 650–653, 704–707

features of, 36–37, 60–63, 96–99, 148–149, 172–175, 268–271, 296–299, 356–357, 382–385, 472–473, 498–501, 562–565, 616–619, 640–643, 704–707

types
encyclopedia article, 472–473

informational nonfiction, 36–37, 60–63, 70–73, 96–99, 148–149, 172–173, 182–183, 268–271, 296–299, 306–309, 356–357, 382–385, 418–421472–473, 498–501, 534–537, 562–565, 616–619, 640–643, 650–653, 704–707

letter to the editor, 498–501

math article, 148–149, 562–565

newspaper article, 36–37

nonfiction article, 36–37, 60–63, 70–73, 96–99, 148–149, 172–173, 182–183, 268–271, 296–299, 306–309, 356–357, 382–385, 418–421, 472–473, 498–501, 534–537, 562–565, 616–619, 640–643, 650–653, 704–707

science article, 172–175, 382–385, 640–643, 704–707

social studies article, 36–37, 60–63, 96–99, 472–473, 498–501, 616–619

textbook article, 60–63

Instructional Navigator Interactive CD-ROM. *See* Lesson plan, suggested weekly; Technology: CD-ROM.

Internet. *See* Computer Literacy; Research and Inquiry; Study skills; Technology.

Intervention Program, 39L, 65L, 77L, 101L, 123L, 151L, 177L, 189L, 217L, 241L, 273L, 301L, 313L, 335L, 359L, 387L, 413L, 425L, 449L, 475L, 503L, 529L, 541L, 567L, 591L, 621L, 645L, 657L, 683L, 709L

Interview, 296–299, 301F, 364H, 529F, 565

Jj

Journal writing, 21, 29, 33, 45, 51, 57, 71, 73, 83, 89, 93, 107, 111, 117, 133, 140, 145, 157, 169, 183, 185, 195, 209, 223, 229, 235, 251, 259, 265, 279, 293, 307, 309, 319, 329, 341, 353, 369, 379, 393, 405, 419, 421, 431, 443, 455, 469, 485, 495, 509, 515, 523, 535, 537, 547, 553, 559, 573, 579, 585, 601, 605, 613, 627, 633, 637, 651, 653, 663, 677, 689, 701

Judgments, making. *See* Comprehension skills: judgments making.

Ll

Latin roots. *See* Phonics/Spelling; Vocabulary: Latin roots.

Lesson Plans, suggested weekly, 16L–16O, 40C–40F, 66C–66F, 78C–78F, 102C–102F, 128L–128O, 152C–152F, 178C–178F, 190C–190F, 218C–218F, 246L–246O, 274C–274F, 302C–302F, 314C–314F, 336C–336F, 364L–364O, 388C–388F, 414C–414F, 426C–426F, 450C–450F, 480L–480O, 504C–504F, 530C–530F, 542C–542F, 568C–568F, 596L–596O, 622C–622F, 646C–646F, 658C–658F, 684C–684F

Letters. *See* Writing forms and modes: letters.

Leveled Reader Lessons

Approaching Level Options, 39P, 65P, 77P, 101P, 123P, 151P, 177P, 189P, 217P, 241P, 273P, 301P, 313P, 335P, 359P, 387P, 413P, 425P, 449P, 475P, 503P, 529P, 541P, 567P, 591P, 621P, 645P, 657P, 683P, 709P

Beyond Level Options, 39T, 65T, 77T, 101T, 123T, 151T, 177T, 189T, 217T, 241T, 273T, 301T, 313T, 335T, 359T, 387T, 413T, 425T, 449T, 475T, 503T, 529T, 541T, 567T, 591T, 621T, 645T, 657T, 683T, 709T

ELL, 39V, 65V, 77V, 101V, 123V, 151V, 177V, 189V, 217V, 241V, 273V, 301V, 313V, 335V, 359V, 387V, 413V, 425V, 449V, 475V, 503V, 529V, 541V, 567V, 591V, 621V, 645V, 657V, 683V, 709V

On Level Options, 39R, 65R, 77R, 101R, 123R, 151R, 177R, 189R, 217R, 241R, 273R, 301R, 313R, 335R, 359R, 387R, 413R, 425R, 449R, 475R, 503R, 529R, 541R, 567R, 591R, 621R, 645R, 657R, 683R, 709R

Library or media center, using, 73B, 77A, 77Q, 75S, 596H. *See also* Study skills.

Limerick, 623

Listening

active and attentive listening, 16H, 16I, 39A, 65A, 77A, 101A, 123A, 127E, 127K–127L, 128H, 128I, 151A, 177A, 189A, 217A, 241A, 245E, 245K–245L, 246H, 246I, 273A, 301A, 313A, 335A, 359A, 363E 363I–363J, 364H, 364I, 387A, 413A, 425A, 449A, 475A, 479E, 479K–479L, 480H, 480I, 481, 503A, 529A, 541A, 543, 567A, 591A, 595E, 595K–595L, 596H, 586I, 621A, 645A, 657A, 683A, 709A, 713E, 713K–713L

comprehension. *See* Listening comprehension.

discussion and conversation guidelines, 246I, 479K, 480I, 596I, 713L

focusing on the speaker, 39A, 65A, 77A, 101A, 151A, 189A, 387A, 413A, 475A, 503A, 541A, 591A, 621A, 645A, 709A

for a purpose, 17, 41, 53, 67, 78, 79, 102, 103, 129, 153, 179, 191, 219, 247, 275, 303, 314, 315, 336, 337, 363E, 363K, 365, 389, 415, 427, 451, 481, 505, 531, 543, 569, 597, 623, 647, 659, 685

formulate questions, 16, 77A, 101A, 123A, 127K, 129, 151A, 177A, 217A, 241A, 273A, 301A, 314, 363E, 387E, 413A, 449A, 503A, 529A, 567A, 591A, 683A, 709A

Listening Library, 21, 45, 71, 83, 107, 133, 157, 183, 195, 223, 251, 279, 307, 319, 341, 369, 393, 419, 431, 455, 485, 509, 535, 547, 573, 601, 627, 651, 663, 689

strategies for, 16H, 16I, 39A, 65A, 77A, 101A, 123A, 127E, 127K–127L, 128H, 128I, 151A, 177A, 189A, 217A, 241A, 245E, 245K–245L, 246H, 246I, 273A, 301A, 313A, 335A, 359A, 363E, 363I–363J, 364H, 364I, 387A, 413A, 425A, 449A, 475A, 479E, 479K–479L, 480H, 480I, 481, 503A, 529A, 541A, 543, 567A, 591A, 595E, 595K–595L, 596H, 586I, 621A, 645A, 657A, 683A, 709A, 713E, 713K–713L

to develop oral language, 16, 17, 40, 41, 66, 67, 78, 79, 102, 103, 128, 129, 152, 153, 178, 179, 190, 191, 218, 219, 246, 247, 274, 275, 302, 303, 314, 315, 336, 337, 364, 365, 388, 389, 414, 415, 426, 427, 450, 451, 480, 481, 504, 505, 530, 531, 542, 543, 568, 569, 596, 597, 622, 623, 646, 647, 658, 659, 684, 685

to interpret speaker's verbal and nonverbal messages, 16I, 17, 39A, 41, 65A, 67, 77A, 79, 101A, 103, 123A, 127E, 128I, 129, 151A, 153, 177A, 179, 189A, 191, 217A, 219, 241A, 245E, 246I, 247, 273A, 275, 301A, 303, 313A, 315, 335A, 337, 359A, 363E, 363I, 364I, 365, 387A, 389, 413A, 415, 425A, 427, 449A, 451, 475A, 479E, 480I, 481, 503A, 505, 529A, 531, 541A, 543, 567A, 569, 591A, 595E, 586I, 597, 621A, 623, 645A, 647, 657A, 659, 683A, 685, 709A, 713E

to presentations, 16H–16I, 39A, 65A, 77A, 101A, 102, 123A, 127E, 127K–127L, 128H–128I, 151A, 152, 177A, 178, 189A, 217A, 241A, 245E, 245K–245L, 246H–246I, 273A, 301A, 302, 313A, 335A, 359A, 363E, 364H–364I, 387A, 413A, 425A, 449A, 475A, 479E, 479K–479L, 480H–480I, 503A, 529A, 541A, 567A, 591A, 595E, 595K–595L, 596H–586I, 621A, 645A, 657A, 683A, 709A, 713E, 713K–713L

Index

Listening Library, 21, 45, 71, 83, 107, 133, 157, 183, 195, 223, 251, 279, 307, 319, 341, 369, 393, 419, 431, 455, 485, 509, 535, 547, 573, 601, 627, 651, 663, 689

Literary devices

alliteration, 26, 100, 120, 121, 123Q, 123S, 146, 675

analogies, 139

assonance, 446–447, 449Q, 449S

conflict resolution, 142

consonance, 332–333, 335Q, 335S

descriptive language, 397, 492

dialogue, 26, 408–411, 413Q, 413S, 552

exaggeration, 247

figurative language

  imagery, 26, 118, 120–121, 123Q, 123S, 588–589

  metaphor, 26, 139, 144, 238–239, 241Q, 241S, 446, 589

  personification, 139, 526–527, 529Q, 529S, 680–681, 683Q, 683S, 702

  simile, 26, 28, 139, 144, 583, 588–589, 591Q, 591S, 606, 638, 698

flashback, 25, 26, 27, 35B, 165, 490, 513,

foreshadowing, 46, 50, 256, 555, 696

hyperbole, 26, 212–215, 217Q, 217S, 408–411, 413Q, 413ST

idioms, 26, 217D, 631

italics, 552

meter, 332–333, 335Q, 335S

mood, 22, 26, 28, 32, 33, 488, 491, 588-589

moral, 212–215, 217Q, 217S, 526–527, 529Q, 529S

onomatopoeia, 236, 446–447, 449Q, 449S, 604, 705

repetition, 578, 588, 589, 591Q, 591S

rhyme/rhyme scheme, 100, 332, 588–589, 591Q, 591S, 623, 680–681, 683Q, 683S

satire, 26

sensory words and details, 26

sound techniques, 26, 100, 120, 121, , 123Q, 123S, 146, 236, 332, 446–447, 566

suspense, 266, 436, 441

symbolism, 238–239, 241Q, 241S

tone, 26, 201, 202

Literary response. *See also* **Text connections.**

personal, 33, 57, 73, 93, 117, 145, 169, 185, 209, 235, 259, 265, 293, 309, 329, 353, 379, 405, 421, 443, 469, 495, 523, 537, 559, 585, 613, 637, 653, 677, 701

reading and responding, 39P, 39R, 39T, 65P, 65R, 65T, 77P, 77R, 77T, 101P, 101R, 101T, 123P, 123R, 123T, 151P, 151R, 151T, 177P, 177R, 177T, 189P , 189R, 189T, 217P, 217R, 217T, 241P, 241R, 241T, 273P, 273R, 273T, 301P, 301R, 301T, 313P, 313R, 313T, 335P, 335R, 335T, 359P, 359R, 359T, 387P, 387R, 387T, 413P, 413R, 413T, 425P, 425R, 425T, 449P, 449R, 449T, 475P, 475R, 475T, 503P, 503R, 503T, 529P , 529R, 529T, 541P, 541R, 541T, 567P, 567R, 567T, 591P, 591R, 591T, 621P, 621R, 621T, 645P, 645R, 645T, 657P, 657R, 657T, 683P, 683R, 683T, 709P, 709R, 709T

respond to read alouds, 17, 41, 67, 79, 103, 129, 153, 179, 191, 219, 247, 275, 303, 315, 337, 365, 389, 415, 427, 451, 481, 505, 531, 543, 569, 597, 623, 647, 659, 685

response journal, 33, 57, 73, 93, 117, 145, 169, 185, 209, 235, 265, 293, 309, 329, 353, 379, 405, 421, 443, 469, 495, 523, 537, 559, 585, 613, 637, 653, 677, 701

Literature selections, main

Breaking into Print: Before and After the Printing Press (Krensky), 662–677

Breaking Through (Jiménez), 484–495

"Building Green," 306–309

The Case of the Phantom Poet (English), 340–353

The Dog of Pompeii (Untermeyer), 688–701

The Emperor's Silent Army (O'Connor), 318–329

Exploring the Titanic (Ballard), 392–405

"Gecko Glue, Cockroach Scouts, and Spider Silk Bridges," 70–73

The Great Serum Race (Miller), 222–235

Honus and Me (Gutman), 546–559

How Tia Lola Came to Stay (Alvarez), 132–145

Interrupted Journey (Lasky), 106–117

Juan Verdades: The Man Who Couldn't Tell a Lie (Hayes), 250–265

LAFFF (Namioka), 626–637

Leonardo's Horse (Fritz), 600–613

Let it Shine: Black Women Freedom Fighters (Pinkney), 572–585

Lost City: The Discovery of Machu Picchu (Lewin), 44–57

The Magic Gourd (Diakité), 82–93

Major Taylor (Cline-Ransome), 430–443

"Many Countries, One Currency: Europe and the Euro," 534–537

"The Night of the Pomegranate" (Wynne-Jones), 156–169

Nothing Ever Happens on 90th Street (Schotter), 278–293

Rumpelstiltskin's Daughter (Stanley), 194–209

"Saving Grace," 418–421

Seeing Things His Own Way (Kaminsky), 368–379

A Single Shard (Park), 454–469

The Summer of the Swans (Byars), 20–33

Ta-Na-E-Ka (Whitebird), 508–523

"These Walls Can Talk," 650–653

"Zoo Story," 182–185

Literature selections, paired

"Amazing Artificial Limbs" (Glassman), 382–385

"Baseball by the Numbers," 148–149

"Bicycle Riding" (Liatsos), 446

"Birdfoot's Grampa" (Bruchac), 120

"Caged Bird" (Angelou), 588

"Cool Collections," 562–565

"Earth and the Sun," 172–175

Key 6.1 = Grade 6, Book 1

"Empire in the Andes," 60–63
Encyclopedias, 472–473
"A Fable by Aesop" (Pinkney), 526–527
"Future Bookmaker," 680–681
"The Golden Touch," 212–215
"Haiku," 238–239
"How to Conduct a Survey," 356–357
"I Dream a World" (Hughes), 589
"In The Days of the Vaqueros: America's First True Cowboys," 268–271
"Leonardo da Vinci," 616–619
"Mentoring Matters," 498–501
"Old Stormalong Finds a Man-Sized Ship" (Walker), 408–411
"The Origin of Ghana" (McKissack and McKissack), 96–99
"Ozymandias" (Shelley), 332–333
"Reading Online About Time Travel," 640–643
"The Sidewalk Racer or on the Skateboard" (Morrison), 447
"Storm Surprises Maine Students" (MacQuarrie), 36–37
"Student Interview with Author Karen Odom," 296–299
"This Land is Your Land" (Guthrie), 121
"Volcano!," 704–707

Literature selections, vocabulary
18–19, 42–43, 68–69, 80–81, 104–105, 130–131, 154–155, 180–181, 192–193, 220–221, 248–249, 276–277, 304–305, 316–317, 338–339, 366–367, 390–391, 416–417, 428–429, 452–453, 482–483, 506–507, 532–533, 544–545, 570–571, 598–599, 624–625, 648–649, 660–661, 686–687

Lyric, song, 120–121, 332–333, 446–447, 588–589

Mm

Magazine article. *See* **Writing forms and modes.**

Main ideas and details. *See* **Comprehension skills: main ideas and details.**

Mechanics and usage. *See* **Grammar: mechanics and usage.**

Media Literacy, 16I, 33, 56, 88, 144, 208, 230, 264, 350, 364I, 404, 442, 480I, 487, 548, 563, 584, 607, 700

   advertising and, 364I, 700

   analyzing and evaluating media and media forms, 16I, 33, 56, 88, 144, 208, 246I, 350, 364I, 404, 442, 480I, 487, 548, 563, 584, 607

   creating multi-media presentations, 595K-595L

   identifying role of, 56, 88, 487, 700

   persuasive techniques in media, 166, 364I, 480I, 700

   uses of media, 16I, 33, 56, 144, 208, 230, 264, 404, 487, 584

Metacognitive strategies. *See* **Monitor and Clarify.**

Metaphor, 26, 139, 144, 238–239, 241Q, 241S, 446, 589. *See also* **Literary devices: figurative language, metaphor; Poetry: metaphor.**

Meter, 332–333, 335Q, 335S. *See also* **Poetry.**

Modeling. *See* **Comprehension; Fluency; Phonics/Spelling; Vocabulary.**

Monitor and Clarify. *See also* **Paraphrasing; Predictions, making; Ways to Confirm Meaning.**

   adjust reading rate, 48, 50, 61, 112, 328. *See also* **Reading rate.**

   generate questions, 21, 45, 48, 50, 61, 71, 83, 107, 112, 131A–131B, 132–145, 151O, 151R, 155A–155B, 156–169, 177O, 177R, 181A–181B, 182–185, 189O, 189R, 195, 223, 251, 279, 307, 319, 328, 341, 369, 393, 419, 431, 455, 485, 509, 535, 547, 563, 573, 599A–599B, 600–613, 621O, 621R, 625A–625B, 626–637, 641, 645O, 645R, 651, 661A–661B, 662–677, 679, 683O, 683R, 689

   monitor comprehension, 277A–277B, 278–293, 301O, 301R, 317A–317B, 328–329, 335O, 335R, 339A–339B, 340–353, 359O, 359R, 507A–507B, 508–523, 529O, 529R, 571A–571B, 572–585, 591O, 591R

   paraphrase, 85, 88, 197, 214, 261, 298, 421, 511, 525, 529O, 529R, 567O, 567R, 591O, 591R, 641

   read ahead, 159, 162, 256, 343, 460

   reread, 226, 233, 320, 323, 326, 328, 409, 641

   seek help, 370, 372

   self-correct, 139, 436

   self-question, 23, 26

   visualize, 283, 291, 397, 629

Moral, 212–215, 217P, 217R, 217T, 526–527, 529Q, 529S. *See also* **Literary devices.**

Multiple-meaning words, 17, 19, 31, 39D, 39F, 39O, 39R, 687, 693, 709D, 709O, 709Q. *See also* **Vocabulary: multiple-meaning words.**

Mystery, 346

Myth, 153, 212–215

Nn

Narrative poetry, 680–681. *See also* **Poetry.**

Narratives. *See* **Genre; Writing forms and modes: fictional narratives, personal narratives.**

Narrator, 253, 257, 511, 631, 691. *See also* **Point of view.**

Negatives. *See* **Grammar: negatives.**

Newspaper article. *See* **Genre; Writing forms and modes.**

Nonfiction. *See* **Genre: reading nonfiction.**

Note taking, 16H, 77B, 123F, 144, 189B, 258, 309B, 313A, 313B, 313Q, 313S, 364H, 364S, 475, 479B, 480H, 541B

Nouns. *See* **Grammar: nouns.**

Oo

On Level Options, 39Q–39R, 65Q–65R, 77Q–77R, 101Q–101R, 123Q–123R, 151Q–151R, 177Q–177R, 189Q–189R, 217Q–217R, 241Q–241R, 273Q–273R, 301Q–301R, 313Q–313R, 335Q–335R, 359Q–359R, 387Q–387R, 413Q–413R, 425Q–425R, 449Q–449R, 475Q–475R, 503Q–503R, 529Q–529R, 541Q–541R, 567Q–567R, 591Q–591R, 621Q–621R, 645Q–645R, 657Q–657R, 683Q–683R, 709Q–709R

   comprehension skill, 39R, 65R, 77R, 101R, 123R, 151R, 177R, 189R, 217R, 241R, 273R, 301R, 313R, 335R, 359R, 387R, 413R, 425R, 449R, 475R, 503R, 529R, 541R, 567R, 591R, 621R, 645R, 657R, 683R, 709R

   fluency, 39Q, 65Q, 77Q, 101Q, 123Q, 151Q, 177Q, 189Q, 217Q, 241Q, 273Q, 301Q, 313Q, 335Q, 359Q, 387Q, 413Q, 425Q, 449Q, 475Q, 503Q, 529Q, 541Q, 567Q, 591Q, 621Q, 645Q, 657Q, 683Q, 709Q

   vocabulary, 39Q, 39R, 65Q, 65R, 77R, 101Q, 101R, 123Q, 123R, 151R, 177R, 189Q, 189R, 217Q, 217R, 241Q, 241R, 273R, 301Q, 301R, 313Q, 313R, 335Q, 335R, 359Q, 359R, 387Q, 387R, 413Q, 413R, 425Q, 425R, 449Q, 449R, 475Q, 475R, 503Q, 503R, 529Q, 529R, 541Q, 541R, 567R, 591Q, 591R, 621Q, 621R, 645Q, 645R, 657Q, 657R, 683Q, 683R, 709Q, 709R

Onomatopoeia, 236, 446–447, 449Q, 449S, 604, 70. *See also* **Author's Craft; Literary devices: onomatopoeia.**

Oral Language, 16–17, 39F, 39V, 40–41, 65F, 65V, 66–67, 77F, 77V, 78–79, 101F, 101V, 102–103, 123F, 123V, 128–129, 151F, 151V, 152–153, 177F, 177V, 178–179, 189F, 189V, 190–191, 217F, 217V, 218–219, 241F, 241V, 246–247, 273F, 273V, 274–275, 301F, 301V, 302–303, 313F, 313V, 314–315, 335F, 335V, 336–337, 359F, 359V, 364–365, 387F, 387V, 388–389, 413F, 413V, 414–415, 425F, 425V, 426–427, 449F, 449V, 450–451, 475F, 475V, 480–481, 503F, 503V, 504–505, 529F, 529V, 530–531, 541F, 541V, 542–543, 567F, 567V, 568–569, 591F, 591V, 596–597, 621F, 621V, 622–623, 645F, 645V, 646–647, 657F, 657V, 658–659, 683F, 683V, 684–685, 709F, 709V

Outlining, 77B, 189B, 274J, 302J, 313B, 336J, 364I, 364S, 425A, 425B, 479C, 541B, 657B

Pp

Paraphrasing, 85, 88, 197, 214, 261, 298, 421, 511, 525, 529Q, 529S, 567Q, 567S, 591Q, 591S, 641

Parts of a book, 421B, 425A, 425Q, 425S, 537B, 541Q, 541S. *See also* **Study skills.**

Penmanship, 39B, 65B, 77B, 101B, 123B, 151B, 177B, 189B, 217B, 241B, 273B, 301B, 313B, 335B, 359B, 387B, 413B, 425B, 449B, 475B, 503B, 529B, 541B, 567B, 591B, 621B, 645B, 657B, 683B, 709

Personification, 139, 526–527, 529Q, 529S, 680–681, 683Q, 683S, 702 *See also* **Author's Craft; Literary devices: personification.**

Persuasion, techniques of. *See* **Comprehension skills; Media literacy; Writing forms and modes: persuasive.**

Phonics/Spelling, 39E, 39G-39H, 39M, 65E, 65G-65H, 65M, 77E, 77G-77H, 77M, 101E, 101G-101H, 101M, 123E, 123F, 123H, 123M, 151E, 151G, 151H, 151M, 177E, 177G, 177H, 177M, 189E, 189G, 189H, 189M, 217E, 217G-217H, 241E, 241G-241H, 241M, 273E, 273G-273H, 273M, 301E, 301G-301H, 313E, 313G-313H, 313M, 335E, 335G-335H, 337M, 359E, 359G-359H, 359M, 387E, 387G-387H, 387M, 413E, 413G-413H, 413M, 425E, 425G-425H, 425M, 449E, 449G-449H, 449M, 475E, 503E, 503G-503H, 503M, 529E, 529G-529H, 529M, 541E, 541G-541H, 541M, 567E, 567H-567H, 567M, 591E, 591G-591H, 591M, 621E, 621G-621H, 621M, 645E, 645G-645H, 645M, 657E, 657G-657H, 657M, 683E, 683G-683H, 683M, 709E, 709G-709H, 709M. *See also* **Spelling.**

   compound words, 123E, 123G-123H, 123M

   decodable passages, 39E, 39M, 77E, 77M, 123E, 123M, 151E, 151M, 177E, 177M, 189E, 189M, 217E, 217M, 241E, 341M, 273E, 273M, 301E, 301M, 313E, 313M, 335E, 335M, 359E, 359M, 387E, 387M, 413E, 413M, 425E, 425M, 449E, 449M, 475E, 475M, 529E, 529M, 541E, 541M, 591E, 591M, 621E, 621M, 645E, 645M, 657E, 657M, 683E, 683M, 709E, 709M

   decode multisyllabic words, 39E, 39M, 77E, 77M, 123E, 123M, 151E, 151M, 177E, 177M, 189E, 189M, 217E, 217M, 241E, 341M, 273E, 273M, 301E, 301M, 313E, 313M, 335E, 335M, 359E, 359M, 387E, 387M, 413E, 413M, 425E, 425M, 449E, 449M, 475E, 475M, 529E, 529M, 541E, 541M, 591E, 591M, 621E, 621M, 645E, 645M, 657E, 657M, 683E, 683M, 709E, 709M

   homophones, 503E, 503G-503H, 503M

   words ending -ed and -ing, 177E, 177G-177H, 177M

   words from around the world, 709E, 709G-709H, 709M

   words from mythology, 683E, 683G-683H, 683M

Key 6.1 = Grade 6, Book 1

words with absorbed prefixes, 645E, 645G-645H, 645M

words with accented syllables, 273E, 273G-273H, 273M

words with base words, 425E, 425G-425H, 425M

words with suffixes with consonant alternation, 475E, 475G-475H, 475M

words with *ei* or *ie,* 77E, 77G-77H, 77M

words with final schwa
　final /əl/, /ən/, 313E, 313G-313H, 313M
　final /ər/, 301E, 301G-301H, 301M

words with Greek roots, 541E, 631E, 631G-631H, 631M

words with Latin roots, 529E, 529G-529H, 529M, 621E, 621G-621H, 621M

words with long vowels, 65E, 65G-65H, 65M

words with /o/ou/oi/oo/, 189E, 189G-189H, 189M

words with plurals *s* and *es, y* to *i,* 151E, 151G-151H, 151M

words with plurals adding *-ed* and *-ing,* 177E, 177G-177H, 177M

words with prefixes, 335E, 335G-335H, 335M, 425E, 425G-425H, 425M, 621E, 621G-621H, 621m, 657E, 657G-657H, 657M

　Greek and Latin prefixes *co-, con-, post-, pro-, sub-,* 621E, 621G-621H, 621M

words with prefixes, suffixes, base words, 425E, 425G-425H, 425M

words with r-controlled vowels, 101E, 101G-101H, 101M

words with short vowels, 39E, 39G-39H, 39M

words with suffix and vowel alternation, 449E, 449G-449H, 449M

words with suffixes, 359E, 359G-359H, 359M, 387E, 387G-387H, 387M, 425E, 425G-425H, 425M,

591E, 591G-591H, 591M, 657E, 657G-657H, 657M

words with *-able, -ible,* 567E, 567G-567H, 567M

words with *ant ent, -ance, -ence,* 591E, 591G-591H, 591M

words with Greek suffixes, 657E, 657G-657H, 657M

words with *-ion, -ation,* 359E, 359G-359H, 359M, 387E, 387G-387H, 387M

words with *-ive, -age, -ize,* 413E, 413G-413H, 413M

words with variant ambiguous vowels, 189E, 189G-189H, 189M

words with vccv and vcccv pattern, 217E, 217G-217H, 217M

words with v/cv and vc/v pattern, 241E, 241G-241H, 241M

words with vowel alternation, 449E, 449G-449H, 449M

words with vowel patterns in accented syllables, 273E, 273G-273H, 273M

Phonics/Structural analysis. *See* Phonics/Spelling.

Photo essay. *See* Genre.

Picture prompt, 17, 41, 67, 79, 103, 129, 153, 179, 191, 219, 247, 275, 303, 315, 337, 365, 389, 415, 427, 597, 623, 647, 659, 685

Plagiarism, 127I–127J, 128H, 425B, 541B, 657B

Plays. *See* Genre; Writing forms and modes.

Plurals. *See* Grammar: plurals; Vocabulary.

Plot. *See* Comprehension skills: plot.

Poetry
　features of, 120, 238, 303, 332, 446, 588, 680
　forms of
　　concrete, 446–447
　　free verse, 120–121
　　haiku, 238–239
　　limerick, 623

lyric/song, 120–121, 332–333, 446–447, 588–589

narrative, 680–681

literary elements in
　alliteration, 100, 120, 121, 123Q, 123S
　assonance, 446–447, 449Q, 449S
　consonance, 332–333
　figurative language in
　　imagery, 120, 121, 123Q, 123S, 588-589
　　metaphor, 238–239, 446
　　personification, 680–681
　　simile, 588–589, 591Q, 591S
　meter, 303, 332–333, 389
　onomatopoeia, 446–447
　repetition, 588–589, 591Q, 591S
　rhyme/rhyme schemes, 100, 303, 389, 588–589, 591P, 591R, 591T, 623, 680–681
　symbolism, 238–239, 241Q, 241S
structures of, 100–101, 101A–101B, 389, 566–567, 567A–567B, 588–589

Point of view
　first person, 253, 380, 511, 575, 631
　narrator, 253, 257, 511
　omniscient, 253, 257, 691
　third person, 253

Possessives. *See* Grammar: possessives.

Predictions and purposes, return to, 33, 57, 73, 93, 117, 145, 169, 185, 209, 235, 265, 293, 309, 329, 353, 379, 405, 421, 443, 469, 495, 523, 537, 559, 585, 613, 637, 653, 677, 701

Predictions, making, 21, 29, 39P, 39R, 39T, 45, 53, 65P, 65R, 65T, 65V, 71, 77P, 77R, 77T, 77V, 83, 89, 101P, 101R, 101T, 101V, 107, 123P, 123R, 123T, 123V, 133, 151P, 151R, 151T, 151V, 157, 159, 177P, 177R, 177T, 177V, 183, 189P, 189R, 189T, 189V, 195, 202, 217P, 217R, 217T, 217V, 223, 228, 241P, 241R, 241T, 241V, 251, 263, 273P, 273R, 273T, 273V, 279, 301P, 301R, 301T, 301V, 307, 313P, 313R, 313T, 313V, 319, 335P,

335R, 335T, 335V, 341, 359P, 359R, 359T, 359V, 369, 387P, 387R, 387T, 387V, 393, 413P, 413R, 413T, 413V, 419, 425P, 425R, 425T, 425V, 431, 433, 449P, 449R, 449T, 449V, 455, 475P, 475R, 475T, 475V, 485, 503P, 503R, 503T, 503V, 509, 515, 529P, 529R, 529T, 529V, 535, 541P, 541R, 541T, 541V, 547, 555, 567P, 567R, 567T, 567V, 573, 591P, 591R, 591T, 591V, 601, 609, 621P, 621R, 621T, 621V, 627, 632, 645P, 645R, 645T, 645V, 651, 657P, 657R, 657T, 657V, 663, 672, 683P, 683R, 683T, 683V, 689, 696

Prefixes. *See* Phonics/Spelling; Spelling; Vocabulary.

Prepositions and prepositional phrases. *See* Grammar, mechanics and usage.

Prereading strategies. *See* Predictions, making; Previewing literature; Setting purposes for reading.

Previewing literature, 21, 39P, 39R, 39T, 39V, 45, 65P, 65R, 65T, 65V, 71, 77P, 77R, 77T, 77V, 83, 101P, 101R, 101T, 101V, 107, 123P, 123R, 123T, 123V, 133, 151P, 151R, 151T, 151V, 157, 177P, 177R, 177T, 177V, 183, 189P, 189R, 189T, 189V, 195, 217P, 217R, 217T, 217V, 223, 241P, 241R, 241T, 241V, 251, 273P, 273R, 273T, 273V, 279, 301P, 301R, 301T, 301V, 307, 313R, 313T, 313V, 313V, 319, 335P, 335R, 335T, 335V, 341, 359P, 359R, 359T, 359V, 369, 387P, 387R, 387T, 387V, 393, 413P, 413R, 413T, 413V, 419, 425P, 425R, 425T, 425V, 431, 449P, 449R, 449T, 449V, 455, 475P, 475R, 475T, 475V, 485, 503P, 503R, 503T, 503V, 509, 529P, 529R, 529T, 529V, 535, 541P, 541R, 541T, 541V, 547, 567P, 567R, 567T, 567V, 573, 591P, 591R, 591T, 591V, 601, 621P, 621R, 621T, 621V, 627, 645P, 645R, 645T, 645V, 651, 657P, 657R, 657T, 657V, 663, 683P, 683R, 683T, 683V, 689

Primary sources, 16H, 127C, 246H, 404, 613, 616–619, 621Q, 621S, **6.6:** T11

Problem and solution. *See* Comprehension skills: problem and solution.

Pronouns. *See* Grammar: pronouns.

Pronunciation. *See* Fluency: pronunciation.

Punctuation. *See* Fluency: punctuation; Grammar: punctuation.

Purposes, setting for reading. *See* Setting purposes for reading.

Qq

Questions. *See* Comprehension strategies: generate questions; Monitor and Clarify: generate questions; Research and Inquiry: generating questions for.

Quotation marks, 301J, 335J, 425J, 529J, 709B, 709J. *See also* Dialogue; Grammar: punctuation.

Rr

Read Alouds, 17, 41, 67, 79, 103, 129, 153, 179, 191, 219, 247, 275, 303, 315, 337, 365, 389, 415, 427, 451, 481, 505, 531, 543, 569, 597, 623, 647, 659, 685

Reader's Theater, 40I, 218I, 414I, 622I, 530I

Reading and responding, 39P, 39R, 39T, 65P, 65R, 65T, 77P, 77R, 77T, 101P, 101R, 101T, 123P, 123R, 123T, 151P, 151R, 151T, 177P, 177R, 177T, 189P, 189R, 189T, 217P, 217R, 217T, 241P, 241R, 241T, 273P, 273R, 273T, 301P, 301R, 301T, 313P, 313R, 313T, 335P, 335R, 335T, 359P, 359R, 359T, 387P, 387R, 387T, 413P, 413R, 413T, 425P, 425R, 425T, 449P, 449R, 449T, 475P, 475R, 475T, 503P, 503R, 503T, 529P, 529R, 529T, 541P, 541R, 541T, 567P, 567R, 567T, 591P, 591R, 591T,

621P, 621R, 621T, 645P, 645R, 645T, 657P, 657R, 657T, 683P, 683R, 683T, 709P, 709R, 709T

Reading independently, 16R, 21, 39P, 39R, 39T, 40I, 45, 65P, 65R, 65T, 66I, 71, 77I, 77P, 77R, 77T, 83, 101P, 101R, 101T, 107, 123P, 123R, 123T, 128R, 133, 151P, 151R, 151T, 152I, 157, 177P, 177R, 177T, 178I, 183, 189P, 189R, 189T, 190I, 195, 217P, 217R, 217T, 218I, 223, 241P, 241R, 241T, 246R, 251, 273P, 273R, 273T, 274I, 279, 301P, 301R, 301T, 307, 313P, 313R, 313T, 314I, 319, 335P, 335R, 335T, 336I, 341, 359P, 359R, 359T, 364R, 369, 387P, 387R, 387T, 388I, 393, 413P, 413R, 413T, 414I, 419, 425P, 425R, 425T, 426I, 431, 449P, 449R, 449T, 455, 475P, 475R, 475T, 485, 503P, 503R, 503T, 504I, 509, 529P, 529R, 529T, 530I, 535, 541P, 541R, 541T, 542I, 547, 567P, 567R, 567T, 568I, 573, 591P, 591R, 591T, 596I, 601, 621P, 621R, 621T, 622I, 627, 645P, 645R, 645T, 646I, 651, 657P, 657R, 657T, 658I, 663, 683P, 683R, 683T, 684I, 689

Reading rate, 21, 45, 48, 50, 61, 71, 112, 133, 157, 183, 195, 223, 279, 307, 319, 341, 369, 393, 419, 431, 455, 529Q, 535, 567N, 591Q, 601, 627, 651, 663, 689

Reading together, 21, 45, 71, 83, 107, 133, 157, 183, 195, 223, 251, 279, 307, 319, 341, 369, 393, 419, 431, 455, 485, 509, 535, 547, 573, 601, 627, 651, 663, 689

Realistic fiction. *See* Genre: reading fiction.

Reference sources and resources, using. *See* Research and Inquiry; Study Skills; Vocabulary: dictionary, using.

Repetition, 578, 588, 589, 591Q, 591S. *See also* Literary devices; Poetry.

Reread for Comprehension. *See* Comprehension skills; Comprehension strategies.

Research and Inquiry, 16H, 16I, 16S, 37, 40J, 53, 63, 66J, 77A, 78J, 99, 102J, 113, 121, 127K, 127L, 128H, 128I, 128S, 137, 149, 152J, 175, 178J, 190J, 215, 218J, 239, 245K, 245L, 246H, 246I, 246S, 271, 274J, 299, 302J, 314J, 333, 336J, 357, 363K, 363L, 364H, 364I, 364S, 385, 388J, 411, 414J, 426J, 447, 450J, 473, 479K, 479L, 480H, 480I, 480S, 501, 504J, 527, 530J, 542J, 565, 568J, 589, 595K, 595L, 596H, 596I, 596S, 619, 622J, 643, 646J, 658J, 681, 684J, 707, 713K, 713L. *See also* **Cross-Curricular connections; Cultural Perspectives; Note taking; Skimming and scanning.**

  citing and evaluating sources, 16H, 63, 77B, 127I–127J, 128H, 189B, 189Q, 189S, 246H, 313B, 425B, 480H, 541B, 619, 657A, 657B

  creating outlines, 77B, 189B, 274J, 302J, 313B, 336J, 364I, 364S, 425A, 425B, 479C, 541B, 657B

  creating presentations, 16H, 16I, 39A, 65A, 77A, 101A, 123A, 127B, 127E, 127K, 128H, 128I, 151A, 177A, 189A, 217A, 241A, 245B, 245E, 245K, 245L, 246H, 246I, 273A, 301A, 313A, 335A, 359A, 363A, 363B, 353K, 363L, 364H, 364I, 387A, 413A, 425A, 449A, 475A, 479B, 479E, 479K, 479, 480H, 480I, 503A, 529A, 541A, 567A, 591A, 595B, 595E, 595K, 595L, 595H, 596I, 621A, 645A, 657A, 683A, 709A, 713B, 713K, 713L, 713E

  finding information, 16H, 16I, 63, 77A, 128H, 128I, 175, 189A, 215, 246H, 246I, 271, 313A, 364H, 364I, 425A, 447, 479, 480H, 480I, 501, 527, 541A, 596H, 596I, 619, 643, 657A, 681, 707

  generating questions, 16H, 16I, 77A, 128H, 128I, 189A, 246H, 246I, 313A, 364H, 364I, 425A, 447, 480H, 480I, 541A, 596H, 596I, 657A

  narrowing focus of research, 16H, 16I, 77A, 128H, 128I, 189A, 246H, 246I, 313A, 364H, 364I, 425A, 480H, 480I, 541A, 596H, 596I, 657A

  organizing information, 16H, 73A, 73B, 128H, 185A, 185B, 246H, 309A, 309B, 364H, 421A, 421B, 473, 479K, 480H, 537A, 537B, 596H, 653A, 653B

  paraphrasing, 77B, 189B, 313B, 425B, 541B, 657B

  quotations in, 425B

  research strategies, 16H, 128H, 245K, 246H, 363K, 364H, 479K, 480H, 596H

  understanding plagiarism, 127I–127J, 128H, 425B, 541B, 657B

  using key words and questions, 16H, 60–63, 77A, 127I–127J, 128H, 185B, 189A, 189Q 189S, 246H, 313A, 364H, 425A, 480H, 541A, 596H, 640–643, 657A, 763C

  using print, Internet and other electronic resources, 16H, 16I, 37, 53, 63, 77A, 99, 113, 121, 127K, 127L, 128H, 128I, 137, 149, 175, 189A, 215, 239, 245K, 245L, 246H, 246I, 271, 299, 313A, 333, 357, 363K, 363L, 364H, 364I, 385, 411, 425A, 447, 473, 479K, 479L, 480H, 480I, 501, 527, 541A, 565, 589, 595K, 595L, 596H, 596I, 619, 643, 657A, 681, 707, 713K, 713L. *See also* **Cultural Perspectives; Cross-Curricular connections.**

Research and study skills. *See* **Study skills; Text features.**

Research: Why It Matters, vi, 23, 65O, 77N, 90, 151N, 177N, 193, 211B, 240, 260, 295B, 335D, 350N, 387N, 413E, 449O, 456, 591N, 545

Response to Literature. *See* **Literary response.**

Return to predictions and purposes. *See* **Predictions and purposes, return to.**

Rhyme/rhyme schemes. *See* **Literary devices and elements: rhyme.**

Rhythm. *See* **Literary devices and elements: rhythm.**

Root words. *See* **Phonics/Spellling;**

Spelling; Vocabulary: root words.

Rubrics. *See* **Scoring rubrics.**

Ss

Science article, 172–175, 382–385, 640–643, 704–707

Science fiction, 177F, 626–637

Scoring rubrics

  creating, 127F, 245F, 363F, 479F, 595F, 713F

  theme project, 127L, 245L, 363L, 479L, 595L, 713L

  writing, 39A, 65A, 76, 77A, 101A, 123A, 127G, 127H, 151A, 177A, 188, 189A, 217A, 241A, 245G, 245H, 273A, 301A, 312, 313A, 335A, 359A, 363G, 363H, 387A, 413A, 424, 425A, 449A, 475A, 479G, 479H, 503A, 529A, 540, 541A, 567A, 591A, 595G, 595H, 621A, 645A, 656, 657A, 683A, 709A, 713G, 713H

Self-correction strategies. *See* **Monitor and Clarify.**

Self-monitoring strategies. *See* **Monitor and Clarify.**

Self-Selected Reading, 16R, 39T, 40I, 65T, 66I, 77T, 78I, 101T, 102I, 123T, 128R, 151T, 152I, 177T, 178I, 189T, 190I, 217T, 218I, 241T, 246R, 273T, 274I, 301T, 302I, 313T, 314I, 335T, 336I, 359T, 364R, 387T, 388I, 413T, 414I, 425T, 426I, 449T, 450I, 475T, 480R, 503T, 504I, 529T, 530I, 541T, 542I, 567T, 568I, 591T, 596R, 621T, 622I, 645T, 646I, 657T, 658I, 683T, 684I, 709T

Semicolons, 77J, 123J, 301J, 529B, 709B, 709. *See also* **Grammar: punctuation.**

Sentences. *See* **Grammar: sentences; Writing traits: sentences.**

Sequence. *See* **Comprehension skills: sequence; Writing traits: organization.**

Setting purposes for reading, 21, 39P, 39R, 39T, 39V, 45, 65P, 65R, 65T, 65V, 71, 77P, 77R, 77T, 77V, 83, 101P, 101R, 101T, 101V, 107, 123P, 123R, 123T, 123V, 133, 151P, 151R, 151T, 151V, 157, 177P, 177R, 177T, 177V, 183, 189P, 189R, 189T, 189V, 195, 217P, 217R, 217T, 217V, 223, 241P, 241R, 241T, 241V, 251, 273P, 273R, 273T, 273V, 279, 301P, 301R, 301T, 301V, 307, 313R, 313T, 313V, 313V, 319, 335P, 335R, 335T, 335V, 341, 359P, 359R, 359T, 359V, 369, 387P, 387R, 387T, 387V, 393, 413P, 413R, 413T, 413V, 419, 425P, 425R, 425T, 425V, 431, 449P, 449R, 449T, 449V, 455, 475P, 475R, 475T, 475V, 485, 503P, 503R, 503T, 503V, 509, 529P, 529R, 529T, 529V, 535, 541P, 541R, 541T, 541V, 547, 567P, 567R, 567T, 567V, 573, 591P, 591R, 591T, 591V, 601, 621P, 621R, 621T, 621V, 627, 645P, 645R, 645T, 645V, 651, 657P, 657R, 657T, 657V, 663, 683P, 683R, 683T, 683V, 689

Short story, 156–169, 187F, 334–335, 335A–335B, 683F, 688–701

Similes, 26, 28, 139, 144, 583, 588–589, 591Q, 591S, 606, 638, 69. *See also* Literary devices: simile; Poetry: figurative language.

Simple poetry. *See* Poetry.

Skills Trace, 19A, 35B, 43A, 59B, 69A, 81A, 95B, 105A, 119B, 131A, 147B, 155A, 171B, 181A, 193A, 211B, 221A, 237B, 249A, 267B, 277A, 295B, 305A, 317A, 331B, 339A, 355B, 367A, 381B, 391A, 407B, 417A, 445B, 429A, 453A, 471B, 483A, 497B, 507A, 525B, 533A, 545A, 561B, 571A, 587B, 599A, 615B, 625A, 639B, 649A, 661A, 679B, 687A, 703B

Skimming and scanning, 246H, 309B, 313Q, 313S

Small Group Options, 39M–39V, 65M–65V, 77M–77V, 101M–101V, 123M–123V, 151M–151V, 177M–177V, 189M–189V, 217M–217V, 241M–241V, 273M–273V, 301M–301V, 313M–313V, 335M–335V, 359M–359V, 387M–387V, 413M–413V, 425M–425V, 449M–449V,

475M–475V, 503M–503V, 529M–529V, 541M–541V, 567M–567V, 591M–591V, 621M–621V, 645M–645V, 657M–657V, 683M–683V, 709M–709V. *See also* **Approaching Level Options; Beyond Level Options; ELL; On Level Options.**

Speaking. *See also* **Listening.**

checklists and rubrics, 127K–127L, 245K–245L, 363K–363L, 479K–479L, 595K–595L, 713K–713L

discussion, 34, 39P, 39R, 39T, 58, 65P, 65R, 65T, 77P, 77R, 77T, 94, 101P, 101R, 101T, 118, 123P, 123R, 123T, 146, 151P, 151R, 151T, 170, 177P, 177R, 177T, 189P, 189R, 189T, 210, 217P, 217R, 217T, 236, 241P, 241R, 241T, 266, 273P, 273R, 273T, 294, 301P, 301R, 301T, 313P, 313R, 313T, 330, 335P, 335R, 335T, 354, 359P, 359R, 359T, 380, 387P, 387R, 387T, 406, 413P, 413R, 413T, 425P, 425R, 425T, 444, 449P, 449R, 449T, 470, 475P, 475R, 475T, 496, 503P, 503R, 503T, 524, 529P, 529R, 529T, 541P, 5431R, 541T, 560, 567P, 567R, 567T, 586, 591P, 591R, 591T, 614, 621P, 621R, 621T, 638, 645P, 645R, 645T, 657P, 657R, 657T, 678, 683P, 683R, 683T, 702, 709P, 709R, 709T

oral presentations, 39A, 65A, 77A, 101A, 123A, 127E, 127K–127L, 151A, 177A, 189A, 217A, 241A, 245E, 245K–245L, 273A, 301A, 313A, 335A, 359A, 363E, 363K–363L, 387A, 413A, 425A, 449A, 475A, 479E, 479K–479L, 503A, 529A, 541A, 567A, 591A, 595E, 595K–595L, 621A, 645A, 657A, 683A, 709A, 713E, 713K–713L

strategies, 39A, 65A, 77A, 101A, 123A, 127B, 127E, 127K–127L, 151A, 177A, 189A, 217A, 241A, 245B, 245E, 245K–245L, 273A, 301A, 313A, 335A, 359A, 363B, 363B, 363K–363L, 387A, 413A, 425A, 449A, 475A, 479B, 479E, 479K–479L, 503A, 529A, 541A, 567A, 591A, 595B, 595E, 595K–595L, 621A, 645A, 657A, 683A, 709A, 713B, 713E, 713K–713L

using appropriate language, 39A, 65A, 77A, 101A, 123A, 127B, 127E, 127K, 151A, 177A, 189A, 217A, 241A, 245B, 245E, 273A, 301A, 313A, 335A, 359A, 363A, 363B, 387A, 413A, 425A, 449A, 475A, 479B, 479E, 503A, 529A, 541A, 567A, 591A, 595B, 595E, 621A, 645A, 657A, 683A, 709A, 713B, 713E

using props and visuals, 39A, 65A, 77A, 101A, 123A, 127B, 127E, 151A, 177A, 189A, 217A, 241A, 245B, 245E, 273A, 301A, 313A, 335A, 359A, 363K, 413A, 425A, 449A, 475A, 479B, 479E, 479K, 503A, 529A, 541A, 567A, 591A, 595B, 595E, 621A, 645A, 657A, 683A, 709A, 713B, 713E

using verbal and nonverbal techniques, 16I, 39A, 65A, 77A, 101A, 123A, 127B, 127E, 127K–127L, 151A, 177A, 189A, 217A, 241A, 245B, 245E, 245K–245L, 273A, 301A, 313A, 335A, 359A, 363A, 363K–363L, 387A, 413A, 425A, 449A, 475A, 479B, 479E, 479K–479L, 503A, 529A, 541A, 567A, 591A, 595B, 595E, 595K–595L, 621A, 645A, 657A, 683A, 709A, 713B, 713E, 713K–713L

Speech. *See* **Genre: speech; Writing forms and modes: speech.**

Spelling, 39B, 39G–39H, 65B, 65G–65H, 77G–77H, 101B, 101G–101H, 123B, 123G–123H, 151B, 151G–151H, 177B, 177G–177H, 189G–189H, 217B, 217G–217H, 241B, 241G–241H, 273B, 273G–273H, 301B, 301G–301H, 313G–313H, 335B, 335G–335H, 359B, 359G–359H, 387B, 387G–387H, 413B, 413G–413H, 425G–425H, 449B, 449G–449H, 475B, 475G–475H, 503B, 503G–503H, 529B, 529G–529H, 541G–541H, 567B, 567G–567H, 591B, 591G–591H, 621B, 621G–621H, 645B, 645G–645H, 657G–657H, 683B, 683G–683H, 709B, 709G–709H. *See also* **Phonics/Spelling; Writer's Toolbox.**

challenge words, 39G, 65G, 77G, 101G, 123G, 151G, 177G, 189G,

217G, 241G, 273G, 301G, 313G, 335G, 359G, 387G, 413G, 425G, 449G, 475G, 503G, 529G, 541G, 567G, 591G, 621G, 645G, 657G, 683G, 709G

compound words, 123B, 123G–123H

dictation sentences, 39G, 65G, 77G, 101G, 123G, 151G, 177G, 189G, 217G, 241G, 273G, 301G, 313G, 335G, 359G, 387G, 413G, 425G, 449G, 475G, 503G, 529G, 541G, 567G, 591G, 621G, 645G, 657G, 683G, 709G

homophones, 503B, 503G–503H

posttest, 39H, 65H, 77H, 101H, 123H, 151H, 177H, 189H, 217H, 241H, 273H, 301H, 313H, 335H, 359H, 387H, 413H, 425H, 449H, 475H, 503H, 529H, 541H, 567H, 591H, 621H, 645H, 657H, 683H, 709H

pretest, 39G, 65G, 77G, 101G, 123G, 151G, 177G, 189G, 217G, 241G, 273G, 301G, 313G, 335G, 359G, 387G, 413G, 425G, 449G, 475G, 503G, 529G, 541G, 567G, 591G, 621G, 645G, 657G, 683G, 709G

spiral review, 39H, 65H, 77H, 101H, 123H, 151H, 177H, 189H, 217H, 241H, 273H, 301H, 313H, 335H, 359H, 387H, 413H, 425H, 449H, 475H, 503H, 529H, 541H, 567H, 591H, 621H, 645H, 657H, 683H, 709H

teacher and student word sorts, 39G, 65G, 77G, 101G, 123G, 151G, 177G, 189G, 217G, 241G, 273G, 301G, 313G, 335G, 359G, 387G, 413G, 425G, 449G, 475G, 503G, 529G, 541G, 567G, 591G, 621G, 645G, 657G, 683G, 709G

words ending -ed and -ing, 177B, 177G–177H

words from around the world, 709B, 709G–709H

words from mythology, 683B, 683G–683H

word study notebook, 39H, 65H, 77H, 101H, 123H, 151H, 177H, 189H, 217H, 241H, 273H, 301H, 313H, 335H, 359H, 387H, 413H,

425H, 449H, 475H, 503H, 529H, 541H, 567H, 591H, 621H, 645H, 657H, 683H, 709H

words with absorbed prefixes, 645B, 645G–645H

words with accented syllables, 273G–273H, 650

words with base words, 425G–425H

words with consonant alternation, 475B, 475G–475H

words with ei or ie, 77G–77H

words with final schwa
final /əl/, /ən/, 313G-313H
final /ər/, 301B, 301G-301H

words with Greek roots, 541G–541H, 621B, 621G–621H, 657G–657H

words with Latin roots, 529B, 529G–529H, 621G–621H

words with long vowels, 65B, 65G–65H

words with plurals adding -ed and -ing, 177B, 177G–177H

words with plurals s and es, y to i, 151B, 151G–151H

words with prefixes, 335B, 335G–335H, 621B, 621G–621H, 645B, 645G–645H

  words with Greek and Latin prefixes co-, con-, post-, pro-, sub-, 621B, 621G–621H

words with prefixes, suffixes, base words, 425G–425H

words with r-controlled vowels, 101B, 101G–101H

words with short vowels, 39B, 39G–39H

words with suffixes, 359B, 359G–359H, 387B, 387G–387H, 657G–657H

  words with -able, -ible, 567B, 567G–57H

  words with -ant -ent, -ance, -ence, 591B, 591G–591H

  words with Greek suffixes, 657G–657H

  words with -ion, -ation, 359B, 359G–359H, 387B, 387G–387H

words with -ive, -age, -ize, 413B, 13G–413H

words with variant ambiguous vowels, 189G–189H

words with vccv and vcccv pattern, 217B, 217G–217H

words with v/cv and vc/v pattern, 241B, 241G–241H

words with vowel alternation, 449B, 449G–449H

words with vowel patterns in accented syllables, 273B, 273G–273H

Spiral Review, 39F, 39H, 39O, 65F, 65H, 65O, 77F, 77H, 77O, 101F, 101H, 101O, 123F, 123H, 123O, 151F, 151H, 151O, 177F, 177H, 177O, 189F, 189H, 189O, 217F, 217H, 217O, 241F, 241H, 241O, 273F, 273H, 273O, 301F, 301H, 301O, 313F, 313H, 313O, 335F, 335H, 335O, 359F, 359H, 359O, 387F, 387H, 387O, 413F, 413H, 413O, 425F, 425H, 425O, 449F, 449H, 449O, 475F, 475H, 475O, 503F, 503H, 503O, 529F, 529H, 529O, 541F, 541H, 541O, 567F, 567H, 567O, 591F, 591H, 591O, 621F, 621H, 621O, 645F, 645H, 645O, 657F, 657H, 657O, 683F, 683H, 683O, 709F, 709H, 709O

Story structure. See Comprehension strategies: analyze, story structure.

Structural analysis. See Phonics/Spelling; Vocabulary.

Study skills, 73B, 185B, 309B, 421B, 537B, 653B, 6.1: T9–T10, 6.2: T10–T11, 6.3: T10–T11, 6.4: T10–T11, 6.5: T11–T12, 6.6: T11–T12. See also Text features.

  almanacs, charts, graphs, 6.2: T10

  dictionary, 537B, 6.5: T11

  encyclopedia, 6.4: T11

  functional documents/forms, 653B, 657Q, 657S, 6.6: T12

    applicants and applicant information, 653B

    document heading, 653B

Index

Internet, using, 73B, 77A, 77Q, 77S, 185B, 189Q, 189S, 596H, **6.2:** T11. *See also* **Computer literacy; Research and Inquiry.**

  evaluating sources, 185B, 189Q, 189S

  keywords, 73B, 185B, **6.1:** T10, **6.2:** T11

  refine search, 185B

  search engines, 185B, 189Q, 189S

interview, **6.3:** T10

library and media center, using, 73B, 77A, 77Q, 77S, 596H, **6.1:** T10

  author and title, subject searches, 73B , 77A, 77Q, 77S, 596H

  call number, 596H

  electronic and print card catalogs, 73B, 77A, 77Q, 77S, 596H, **6.1:** T10

  Internet and key word searches, 73B, 77A,77Q, 77S, 185B, 596H

parts of a book, 421B, 425A, 425Q, 425S, 537B, 541Q, 541S, , **6.4:** T10

  copyright page, 421B, 425A, 425Q, 425S

  entry words, 537B

  guide words, 537B

  index, 421B, 425A, 425Q, 425S

  pronunciation key, 537B

  range of pages, 421B

  table of contents, 421B, 425A, 425Q, 425S

  title, 421B

  title page, 421B

study strategies, 309B, 313Q, 313S, **6.3:** T11

  locating sources of information, 309B, 313Q, 313S, 541A, 541Q, 541S, **6.3:** T11

  skimming and scanning,309B, 313Q, 313S, **6.3:** T11

  taking notes, 309B, 313Q, 313S, **6.3:** T11. *See also* **Note taking.**

thesaurus, 537B, 541Q, 541S, **6.5:** T11.

Subjects and predicates. *See* **Grammar: subjects and predicates.**

Subject–verb agreement. *See* **Grammar: subject-verb agreement.**

Suffixes. *See* **Phonics/Spelling: words with suffixes; Vocabulary.**

Suggested weekly lesson plan. *See* **Lesson plan, suggested weekly.**

Summarizing. *See* **Comprehension skills: summarize; Comprehension strategie: summarize.**

Symbolism, 238–239, 241Q, 241S *See also* **Literary devices; Poetry.**

Synonyms. *See* **Vocabulary: synonyms.**

Synthesize, 211, 267, 313B, 355, 703

Tt

Tall tale, 247, 408–411

Technology, 16K, 40B, 66B, 78B, 102B, 128K, 152B, 178B, 190B, 218B, 246K, 274B, 302B, 314B, 336B, 364K, 388B, 414B, 426B, 450B, 480K, 504B, 530B, 542B, 568B, 596K, 622B, 646B, 658B, 684B. *See also* **Computer Literacy; Research and Inquiry; Study skills.**

  audio CDs, 16K, 40B, 66B, 78B, 102B, 128K, 152B, 178B, 190B, 218B, 246K, 274B, 302B, 314B, 336B, 364K, 388B, 414B, 426B, 450B, 480K, 504B, 530B, 542B, 568B, 596K, 622B, 646B, 658B, 684B. *See also* **Fluency: Fluency Solutions audio CD; Listening Library.**

  CD-ROMs, 16K, 40B, 66B, 78B, 102B, 128K, 152B, 178B, 190B, 218B, 246K, 274B, 302B, 314B, 336B, 364K, 388B, 414B, 426B, 450B, 480K, 504B, 530B, 542B, 568B, 622B, 646B, 658B, 684B

Instructional Navigator Interactive CD-ROM. *See* **Suggested lesson plan; Technology: CD-ROM**

online instruction

  author/illustrator information, 34, 58, 94, 118, 146, 170, 210, 236, 266, 294, 330, 354, 380, 406, 444, 470, 496, 524, 560, 586, 614, 638, 678, 702

  computer literacy, 127I–127J, 245I–245J, 363I–363J, 479I–479J, 595I–595J, 713I–713J

  for lesson plans, 17, 41, 67, 79, 103, 129, 153, 179, 191, 219, 247, 275, 303, 315, 337, 365, 389, 415, 427, 451, 481, 505, 531, 543, 569, 597, 623, 647, 659, 685

  oral language development, 17, 41, 67, 79, 103, 129, 153, 179, 191, 219, 247, 275, 303, 315, 337, 365, 389, 415, 427, 451, 481, 505, 531, 543, 569, 597, 623, 647, 659, 685

  vocabulary and spelling, 16K, 40B, 66B, 78B, 102B, 128K, 152B, 178B, 190B, 218B, 246K, 274B, 302B, 314B, 336B, 364K, 388B, 414B, 426B, 450B, 480K, 504B, 530B, 542B, 568B, 596K, 622B, 646B, 658B, 684B

  Vocabulary PuzzleMaker, 39F, 65F, 77F, 101F, 123F, 151F, 177F, 189F, 217F, 241F, 273F, 301F, 313F, 335F, 359F, 387F, 413F, 425F, 449F, 475F, 503F, 529F, 541F, 567F, 591F, 621F, 645F, 657F, 683F, 709F

Test Prep. *See* **Assessment: Test Prep.**

Test Strategy

  Author and Me, 35, 95, 147, 171, 186–187, 211, 242–244, 331, 360–362, 381, 422–423, 445, 471, 476–478, 497, 525, 561, 587, 592–594, 615, 639

Key 6.1 = Grade 6, Book 1

On My Own, 59, 119, 267, 295, 355, 407, 538–539, 679, 703, 710–712

Right There, 74–75

Think and Search, 124–126, 237, 310–311, 654–655

writing prompts, 76–77, 127, 188–189, 245, 312–313, 363, 424–425, 479, 540–541, 595, 656–657, 713

Text connections

connect and compare, 37, 63, 99, 121, 149, 175, 215, 239, 271, 299, 333, 357, 385, 411, 447, 473, 501, 527, 565, 589, 619, 643, 681, 707

making connections across texts, 39P, 39R, 39T, 65P, 65R, 65T, 77P, 77R, 77T, 101P, 101R, 101T, 123P, 123R, 123T, 151P, 151R, 151T, 177P, 177R, 177T, 189P, 189R, 189T, 217P, 217R, 217T, 241P, 241R, 241T, 273P, 273R, 273T, 301P, 301R, 301T, 313P, 313R, 313T, 335P, 335R, 335T, 359P, 359R, 359T, 387P, 387R, 387T, 413P, 413R, 413T, 425P, 425R, 425T, 449P, 449R, 449T, 475P, 475R, 475T, 503P, 503R, 503T, 529P, 529R, 529T, 541P, 541R, 541T, 567P, 567R, 567T, 591P, 591R, 591T, 621P, 621R, 621T, 645P, 645R, 645T, 657P, 657R, 657T, 683P, 683R, 683T, 709P, 709R, 709T

reading/writing across texts, 37, 63, 99, 121, 149, 175, 215, 239, 271, 299, 333, 357, 385, 411, 447, 473, 501, 527, 565, 589, 619, 643, 681, 707

text to self, 35, 59, 95, 119, 147, 171, 185, 211, 237, 267, 295, 331, 355, 381, 407, 445, 471, 497, 525, 537, 561, 587, 615, 639, 653, 679, 703

text to text, 35, 59, 73, 95, 119, 147, 171, 185, 211, 237, 267, 295, 331, 355, 381, 407, 445, 471, 497, 525, 537, 561, 587, 639, 653, 679, 703

text to world, 35, 59, 73, 95, 119, 147, 171, 211, 237, 267, 295, 331, 355, 381, 407, 445, 471, 497, 525, 561, 587, 615, 639, 679, 703

Text features. *See also* **Informational text; Study skills.**

almanac, 148–149, 151Q, 151S **6.2:** T10

captions, 36–37, 39Q, 39S, 60–63, 65Q, 65S, 562–565, 567Q, 567S, 704–707, 709Q, 709S,, **6.1:** T9, **6.5:** T1

charts, 148–149, 151Q, 151S, **6.2:** T10

diagrams, 382–385, 387Q, 387S, 420, 511, 517, 521, 611, , **6.4:** T10

dialogue, 359J, 408

forms, 653B

graphs and graphic aids, 172–175, 177Q, 177S, 268–271, 556, 704–707, 709Q, 709S, **6.2:** T10, **6.6:** T12

headings and subheadings,16H, 65Q, 65S, 128H

headlines, 36, 230, 442

hyperlinks, 640–643, 645Q, 645S, **6.6:** T11

key words, 60–63, 65Q, 65S, 246I, 640–643, 645Q, 645S

labels, 60–63, 65Q, 65S, 382–385, 387Q, 387S, **6.4:** T10

maps, 24, 32, 268–271, 273Q, 273S, 704–707, 709Q, 709S, **6.3:** T10

newspaper, 487, 563

parts of a book, 421B, 425A, 425Q, 425S, 537B, 541Q, 541S. *See also* **Study skills: parts of a book.**

photos, 16H, 36–37, 39Q, 39S, 56, 60–63, 65Q, 65S, 110, 562–565, 567Q, 567S, 621Q, 621S, 705, 706, 704–707, 709Q, 709S **6.1:** T9, **6.5:** T12

play, 357, 359B, 359J

primary source, 616–619, 621Q, 621S, **6.6:** T11

print, bold, colored,60–63, 65Q, 65S

questions and answers, 296–299, 301Q, 301S

schedules, 498–501, 503Q, 503S,, **6.5:** T11

subheading, 704–707, 709Q, 709ST

tables, 356–357, 359Q, 359S, **6.3:** T11

time lines, 96–99, 101Q, 101S, 677, 677, **6.1:** T10

type faces, 472–473, 475Q, 475S

Text structure, analyzing. *See* **Comprehension strategies: analyzing, text structure.**

Theme. *See also* **Comprehension skills: theme; Theme projects.**

introduction to, 16, 40, 66, 78, 102, 128, 152, 178, 190, 218, 246, 274, 302, 314, 336, 364, 388, 414, 426, 450, 480, 504, 530, 542, 568, 596, 622, 646, 658, 684

Theme projects,16H–16I, 127K–127L, 128H–128I, 245K–245L, 246H–246I, 363K–363L, 364H–364I, 479K–479L, 480H–480I, 595K–595L, 596H–596I, 713K–713

Thesaurus, using, 189, 189F, 221, 225, 241D, 241F, 241O, 241R, 245C, 387F, 425F, 449F, 537B, 541A, 541F, 541Q, 545, 549, 567O, 567Q, 625, 628, 645D, 645F, 645O, 645Q, **6.5:** T11

Think and compare, 35, 59, 73, 95, 119, 147, 171, 185, 211, 237, 267, 295, 309, 331, 355, 381, 407, 421, 445, 471, 497, 525, 537, 561, 587, 615, 639, 653, 679, 703

Timed Reading, 16R, 39N, 39Q, 65N, 65Q, 66I, 77N, 77Q, 78I, 101N, 101Q, 102I, 123N, 123Q, 128R, 151N, 151Q, 152I, 177N, 177Q, 178I, 189N, 189Q, 190I, 217N, 217Q, 241N, 241Q, 273N, 273Q, 301N, 301Q, 313N, 313Q, 335N, 335Q, 359N, 359Q, 364R, 387N, 387Q, 388I, 413N, 413Q, 425N, 425Q, 426I, 449N, 449Q, 450I, 475N, 475Q, 480R, 503N, 503Q, 504I, 529N, 529Q, 541N, 541Q, 542I, 567N, 567Q, 568I, 591N, 591Q, 596R, 621N, 621Q, 640I, 645N, 645Q, 657N, 658I, 657Q, 683N, 683Q, 685I, 709N, 709Q

Timed Writing Practice, 77, 189, 313, 425, 541, 657

Index

Uu

Time for Kids
"Building Green," 306–309
"Gecko Glue, Cockroach Scouts, and Spider Silk Bridges," 70–73
"Many Countries, One Currency: Europe and the Euro, 534–537
"Saving Grace," 418–421
"These Walls Can Talk," 650–653
"Zoo Story," 182–185

Time lines, 96–99, 101Q, 101S, 677, 677, **6.1:** T10. *See also* **Text features.**

Unit Projects. *See* **Research and Inquiry; Theme Projects.**

Vv

Venn diagram. *See* **Graphic organizers: Venn diagrams.**

Verbs. *See* **Grammar: verbs.**

Vocabulary. *See also* **Word Study.**
analogies, 105, 110, 113, 123D, 123O, 123Q, 339, 352, 359D, 359F, 359O, 359Q, 449D, 449F, 449O, 449Q, **6.1:** T8, **6.3:** T9, **6.4:** T8

antonyms, 105, 110, 113, 123D, 123O, 123Q, 425F, 449F, 545, 549, 567D, 567F, 567O, 567Q

Approaching Level Options for. *See* Approaching Level Options: vocabulary.

base words/root words, 249, 253, 273D, 273O, 273Q, 286, 359G, 413D, 425E, 425G–425H, 503F, **6.3:** T5

Beyond Level Options for. *See* Beyond Level Options: vocabulary.

compound words, 43, 47, 65D, 65F, 65O, 65Q, 102I, 123E

content, 36–37, 60–63, 70–73, 96–99, 148–149, 172–173, 182–183, 268–271, 296–299, 306–309, 356–357, 382–385, 418–421, 472–473, 498–501, 534–537, 562–565, 616–619, 640–643, 650–653, 704–707

context clues, 69, 77D, 81, 101D, 181, 189D, 189O, 189Q, 305, 313D, 367, 373, 383, 387D, 387O, 387Q, 571, 577, 591D, 591Q, 642, 705, **6.1:** T6, **6.3:** T7, **6.4:** T5, **6.5:** T10

definitions, 69, 77D, 77O, 77Q, 86, 189D, 297, 472

description/explanation, 69, 77D, 77O, 77Q, 297, 383, 472, 577, 591Q, 642, 705

examples, 142, 571, 591D, 591O, 591Q

restatement, 81, 101D, 101F, 101O, 101Q

sentence and paragraph clues, 69, 181, 189D, 189O, 189Q, 305, 313D, 313O, 313Q, 383

denotation, 134, 625, 645D, 645O, 645Q

derivations and origins, 277, 301O, 301Q, 709G–709H

dictionary, 19, 31, 39D, 39F, 39O, 39Q, 123F, 134, 151F, 155, 162, 177D, 177O, 177Q, 189F, 193, 217D, 217O, 217Q, 221, 241Q, 273F, 277, 283, 301D, 301O, 301Q, 363C, 363Q, 417, 425D, 425O, 425Q, 453, 475D, 475F, 475O, 475Q, 537B, 541A, 541Q, 621F, 645F, 687, 693, 709D, 709O, 709Q, **6.5:** T11

expand, 17, 39F, 41 65F, 67, 77F, 79, 101F, 103, 123F, 129, 151F, 153, 177F, 179, 189F, 191, 217F, 219, 241F, 247, 273F, 275, 301F, 303, 313F, 315, 335F, 337, 359F, 365, 387F, 389, 413F, 415, 425F, 427, 449F, 451, 475F, 481, 503F, 505, 529F, 531, 541F, 543, 567F, 569, 591F, 597, 621F, 623, 645F, 647, 657F, 659, 683F, 685, 709F

explain/model/practice, 39C, 39D, 65C, 65D, 77C, 77D, 101C, 101D, 123C, 123D, 151C, 151D, 177C, 177D, 189C, 189D, 217C, 217D, 241C, 241D, 273C, 273D, 301C, 301D, 313C, 313D, 335C, 335D, 359C, 359D, 387C, 387D, 413C, 413D, 425C, 425D, 449C, 449D, 475C, 475D, 503C, 503D, 529C, 529D, 541C, 541D, 567C, 567D, 591C, 591D, 621C, 621D, 645C, 645D, 657C, 657D, 683C, 683D, 709C, 709D

extend, 39T, 77T, 123T, 151T, 177T, 189T, 217T, 241T, 273T, 301T, 313T, 335T, 359T, 387T, 413T, 425T, 449T, 475T, 529T, 541T, 591T, 621T, 645T, 657T, 683T, 709T

games, 39F, 65F, 77F, 101F, 123F, 151F, 177F, 189F, 217F, 241F, 273F, 301F, 313F, 335F, 359F, 387F, 413F, 425F, 449F, 475F, 503F, 529F, 541F, 567F, 591F, 621F, 645F, 657F, 683F, 709F

Greek roots, 530I, 533, 541D, 541O, 541Q, 596R, 599, 610, 621D, 621F, 621O, 621Q, 649, 657D, 657O, 657Q

homographs, 417, 425D, 425O, 425Q

homophones, 453, 462, 475D, 475F, 475O, 475Q, 480R, 503F, 567F

idioms, 193, 199, 210, 217D, 217O, 217Q

inflectional endings, 131, 151D, 151F, 151O, 151Q, 152I, 177E, 249, 273D

Latin roots, 507, 513, 529D, 529O, 529Q, 596R, 649, 657D, 657O, 657Q, 661, 669, 683D, 683O, 683Q

multiple-meaning words, 17, 19, 23, 31, 39D, 39F, 39O, 39Q, 687, 693, 709D, 709O, 709Q

On Level Options for. *See* On Level Options: vocabulary.

prefixes, 115, 249, 273D, 314I, 317, 324, 335D, 335O, 335Q, 425E, 425G, 425H, 503D, 529F, 596R, 646I

pronunciation and meaning, 123F, 155, 162, 177D, 177O, 177Q, 221, 475F, 541A

pronunciation key, 155, 162, 177D, 177O, 277

relationships, 113, 352, 359D, 359F, 429, 449D, 449F, 449O, 449Q

semantic/meaning cues, 108, 520, 582, 634

Spiral Review, 65F, 65O, 77F, 77O, 101F, 101O, 123F, 123O, 151F, 151O, 177F, 177O, 189F, 189O, 217F, 217O, 241F, 241O, 273F, 273O, 301F, 301O, 313F, 313O, 335F, 335O, 359F, 359O, 387F, 387O, 413F, 413O, 425F, 425O, 449F, 449O, 475F, 475O, 503F, 503O, 529F, 529O, 541F, 541O, 567F, 567O, 591F, 591O, 621F, 621O, 645F, 645O, 657F, 657O, 683F, 683O, 709F, 709O

strategies, 19, 39D, 43, 65D, 69, 77D, 81, 101D, 105, 123D, 131, 151D, 155, 177D, 181, 189D, 193, 217D, 221, 241D, 249, 273D, 277, 301D, 305, 313D, 317, 335D, 339, 367, 387D, 391, 413D, 417, 425D, 429, 449D, 453, 475D, 483, 503D, 507, 529D, 533, 541D, 545, 567D, 571, 591D, 599, 621D, 625, 645D, 657D, 661, 683D, 687, 709D, **6.1:** T4–T8, **6.2:** T5–T9, **6.3:** T5–T9, **6.4:** T5–T9, **6.5:** T6–T10, **6.6:** T6–T10

suffixes, 77F, 198, 273D, 396, 391, 413D, 413F, 413O, 413Q, 425E, 425G, 425H, 503D

synonyms, 97, 189C, 189D, 221, 241D, 241F, 241O, 241Q, 339, 352, 359D, 359O, 359Q, 367, 373, 387D, 387F, 387O, 387Q, 425F, 449F, 545, 591P, 625, 645D, 645F, 645O, 645Q

syntactic/structural cues, 72, 159, 190, 233, 308, 353, 434, 608

teach words in context, 18, 39C, 42, 65C, 68, 77C, 80, 101C, 104, 123C, 130, 151C, 154, 177C, 180, 189C, 192, 217C, 220, 241C, 248, 273C, 276, 301C, 304, 313C, 316, 335C, 338, 359C, 366, 387C, 390, 413C, 416, 425C, 428, 449C, 452, 475C, 482, 503C, 506, 529C, 532, 541C, 544, 567C, 570, 591C, 598, 621C, 624, 645C, 648, 657C, 660, 683C, 686, 709C

thesaurus, 189, 189F, 221, 225,

241D, 241F, 241O, 241Q, 245C, 387F, 425F, 449F, 537B, 541A, 541F, 541Q, 545, 549, 567D, 567O, 567Q, 625, 628, 645D, 645F, 645O, 645Q, **6.5:** T11

using resources to acquire, 19, 31, 39D, 39F, 39O, 39Q, 43, 47, 65D, 65F, 65O, 65Q, 123F, 134, 151F, 155, 177D, 177O, 177Q, 189, 189F, 193, 217D, 217O, 217Q, 221, 225, 241D, 241**F**, 241Q, 249, 253, 273D, 273F, 273O, 273Q, 277, 283, 301D, 301O, 301Q, 313F, 347, 387F, 417, 425F, 425D, 425F, 425O, 425Q, 453, 475D, 475F, 475O, 475Q, 483, 503D, 503F, 503O, 503Q, 529F, 541A, 541F, 545, 549, 567D, 567O, 567Q, 591F, 621F, 625, 628, 645D, 645F, 645O, 645Q, 657F, 687, 693, 709D, 709O, 709Q

word families, 483, 503D, 503F, 503O, 503Q, **6.5:** T6

word parts, 43, 47, 65D, 131, 140, 151D, 151O, 151Q, 249, 253, 273C, 273O, 273R, 317, 324, 335D, 335O, 335Q, 391, 396, 413D, 413O, 413R, 483, 503D, 503O, 507, 513, 529D, 529O, 533, 541D, 541O, 621D, 649, 661, 669, 683D, **6.1:**T5; **6.2:** T5; **6.3** T5, T8; **6.4:** T6; **6.5:** : T6, T7, T8; **6.6:** T6, T8, T9

words from around the world, 684I

words from mythology, 658I

word structural clues, 115, 198, 256

Vocabulary PuzzleMaker. *See* **Technology: Vocabulary PuzzleMaker.**

Ww

Ways to confirm meaning, 72, 108, 233, 308, 324, 353, 434, 520, 555, 582, 608, 634

Weekly Contract, 16N, 40E, 66E, 78E, 102E, 128N, 152E, 178E, 190E, 218E, 246N, 274E, 302E, 314E, 336E,

364N, 388E, 414E, 426E, 450E, 480N, 504E, 530E, 542E, 568E, 596N, 622E, 646E, 658E, 684E

Word Study, 16R, 39C–39F, 65C–65F, 66I, 77C–77F, 78I, 101C–101F, 123C–123F, 151C–151F, 177C–177F, 189C–189F, 190I, 217C–217F, 241C–241F, 246R, 273C–273F, 274I, 301C–301F, 313C–313F, 314J, 335C–335F, 336I, 359C–359F, 387C–387F, 388I, 413C–413F, 414I, 425C–425F, 425I, 449C–449F, 475C–475F, 480R, 503C–503F, 529C–529F, 530I, 541C–541F, 542I, 567C–567F, 568I, 591C–591F, 596R, 621C–621F, 622I, 645C–645F, 646I, 657C–657F, 658I, 683C–683F, 684I, 709C–709F. *See also* **Vocabulary; Ways to Confirm Meaning.**

Write About It. 34, 58, 94, 118, 146, 170, 210, 236, 266, 294, 330, 354, 380, 406, 444, 470, 496, 524, 560, 586, 614, 638, 678, 702, **6.1:** T12, T14, T16, **6.2:** T13, T15, T17, **6.3:** T13, T15, T17, **6.4:** T13, T15, T17, **6.5:** T14, T16, T18, **6.6:** T14, T16, T18

Write and respond, 38–39, 64–65, 76–77, 100–101, 122–123, 150–151, 176–177, 188–189, 216–217, 240–241, 272–273, 300–301, 312–313, 334–335, 358–359, 386–387, 412–413, 424–425, 448–449, 474–475, 502–503, 528–529, 540–541, 566–567, 590–591, 620–621, 644–645, 656–657, 682–683, 708–709

Writer's checklist, 39, 65, 77, 101, 123, 151, 177, 189, 217, 241, 249, 301, 359, 363, 387, 503, 529, 567, 591, 621, 645, 683, 709

Writer's Craft

beginning, middle, end, 334, 335A

denotation and connotation, 150, 151A

dialogue, 300, 301A

facts and opinions, 412, 413A

figurative language, 555, 566, 567A

formal and informal language, 488, 502, 503A

good paragraph, 27, 36, 37A

good topic, 176, 177A

important and unimportant details, 62, 64, 65A, 448, 449A

mood, 590, 591A

multiple paragraphs, 474, 475A

precise words, 100, 101A, 687, 708, 709A

rearrange ideas, 522, 528, 529A

strong conclusion, 386, 387A

strong opening, 205, 216, 217A

time-order words, 609, 620, 621A

tone, 358, 359A

topic sentence, 62, 64, 65A, 448, 449A

transitions, 122, 123A, 644, 645A

    between paragraphs, 644, 645A

    cause and effect, 122, 123A

transition words, 122, 123A, 634

unimportant details,

vary sentences, 240, 241A

voice, 272, 273A

word choice, 672, 682, 683A

Writer's Resources, 127C, 245C, 363C, 479B, 479C, 595C, 713C

Writer's Toolbox, 39B, 65B, 77B, 101B, 123B, 151B, 177B, 189B, 217B, 241B, 273B, 301B, 313B, 335B, 359B, 387B, 413B, 425B, 449B, 475B, 503B, 529B, 541B, 567B, 591B, 621B, 645B, 657B, 683B, 709B. *See also* **Writing traits.**

Writing. *See also* **Cross-Curricular connections, Scoring rubrics: writing; Timed Writing Practice; Write About It; Write and respond; Writer's checklist; Writer's Craft; Writer's Resources; Writer's Toolbox; Writing forms and modes; Writing process; Writing traits; Writing Workshop.**

    audience and purpose, 127B, 245B, 363B, 479B, 595B, 713B

    Author's Chair, 127E, 245E, 363E, 479E, 595E, 713E

    daily, 16L–16M, 40C–40D, 66C–66D, 78C–78D, 102C–102D, 128L–128M, 152C–152D, 178C–178D, 190C–190D, 218C–218D, 246L–246M, 274C–274D, 302C–302D, 314C–314D, 336C–336D, 364L–364M, 388C–388D, 414C–414D, 426C–426D, 450C–450D, 480L–480M, 504C–504D, 530C–530D, 542C–542D, 568C–568D, 596L–596M, 622C–622D, 646C–646D, 658C–658D, 684C–684D

    features of writing, 38, 64, 100, 122, 127A, 150, 176, 216, 240, 245A, 272, 300, 334, 358, 363A, 386, 412, 448, 474, 479A, 502, 528, 566, 590, 595A, 620, 644, 682, 708, 713A

    guided practice, 77, 189, 313, 425, 540, 657

    independent. *See* **Picture prompts; Write About It; Writing: daily; Writing forms and modes.**

    literary devices in, 101B, 123A, 335B, 359B, 555, 566, 567A, 567B, 591B

    options for student writing, 38, 64, 100, 122, 150, 176, 216, 240, 272, 300, 334, 358, 386, 412, 448, 474, 502, 528, 566, 590, 620, 644, 682, 708

    peer review, 127B, 127D, 127E, 245B, 245D, 245E, 363B, 363D, 363E, 479D, 479E, 595B, 595D, 595E, 713B, 713D, 713E

    purpose, 127B, 245B, 363B, 479B, 595B, 713B

    student models for, 38, 64, 100, 122, 127A, 150, 176, 216, 240, 245A, 272, 300, 334, 358, 363A, 386, 412, 448, 474, 479A, 502, 528, 566, 590, 595A, 620, 644, 682, 708, 713A

    teacher conference, 127E, 245E, 363E, 479E, 595E, 713E

    using graphic organizers for, 39B, 77B, 127B, 189B, 245B, 313B, 363B, 425B, 479B, 541B, 595B, 657B, 713B

    using technology in, 39B, 65B, 77B, 101B, 123B, 151B, 177B, 189B, 217B, 241B, 273B, 301B, 313B, 335B, 359B, 387B, 413B, 425B, 449B, 475B, 503B, 529B, 541B, 567B, 591B, 621B, 657B, 683B, 709B

Writing forms and modes

    advertisement, 364I

    articles, 48R, 77A–77B, 189A–189B, 425A–425B, 448–449, 449A–449B, 474–475B, 541A–541B, 620–621, 621A–621B, 682–683, 683A–683B

    cause and effect, 309B, 405, 591F

    character sketch, 246S, 272–273B

    compare-and-contrast, 528–529B, 595A–595H, **6.5:** T18

    descriptive/expressive writing, 480S, 502–503B, 504I, 542J, 590–591B, 763A–767F

    dialogue, 246S, 274J, 300–301B, 336J, 357

    diary entry, 39F, 102J, 122–123B, 622J, 684J

    directions, 620-621, 621A–621B

    documentary, 684J

    editorial, 176–177B

    e-mail, 245I–245J

    essays, 190J, 218J, 240–241B, 245A-245H312–313, 528–529B, 568J, 595A–H, 644–645B, 646J

    explanatory writing, 596S, 620–621B, 622J, 644–645B, 658J, 682–683B, 708–709B, 713A–713H

        explain a process, 682-683B

        explanation for two audiences, 708-709B

    expository writing, 66J, 77A–77B, 78J, 189A–189B, 302J, 313A–313B, 386–387B, 412–413B, 425A–425B, 448–449B, 450J, 474-475B, 479A–479H, 541A–541B, 657A–657B, 658J

    eyewitness account, 568J, 590–591B

    fact cards, 246S

    fairy tale, 217F

    fictional narrative, 272–273B, 300–301B, 334–335B, 358–359B, 363A–363H, 479F

    flyer, 336F

Key 6.1 = Grade 6, Book 1

how-to writing, 620–621B, 713A-713H

informational pamphlet, 336J

interview, 241F, 301F, 386–387B, 450J, 529F

journal entry, 39F, 313F, 413F. *See also* **Journal.**

letters

  business letters, 102J, 128S, 150–151B, 151F, 152J, 425J, 596S

  friendly letters, 40J, 64–65B, 335F, 480S, 504J, 621F, 622J, 646J

  persuasive, 102J, 150–151, 151A–151B, 151F, 426J, 622J

list, 40J, 274J, 414J, 530J

magazine and news articles, 37, 123F, 189A–189B, 448–449B, 474–475B, 620–621B

memo, 77F, 425F

outlines, 77B, 189B, 274J, 302J, 313B, 336J, 364I, 364S, 425B, 479C, 541B, 657B

paragraph, 66J, 178J, 388J, 414J, 426J, 530J, 542J, 568J, 684J

poster, 16S

personal essay, 364S

personal narrative, 16S, 38–39B, 64-65B, 122-123B, 127A-127H, 190J

persuasive, 150–151B, 176–177B, 216–217B, 240–241B, 245A–245H, 312–313, 568J, 709F

photo essay, 388J

plan, 596S

play, scene, 358–359B

poem, 78J, 100-101B, 541F, 566–567B, 658J

point of view essay, 216–217B, 312–313

proposal, 314J

question/answer format, 31, 216, 363K

research report, 63, 123F, 364S, 479A–479H, 658J

review, 503F, 607

science fiction, 177F

scientific observation, 175, 412–413B

script, 449F

short story, 187F, 314J, 334–335B, 683F

song, 101F

speech, 16S, 78J, 502–503B, 568J, 591F, 657F

story, 65F, 274J, 314J, 359F, 363A–363H, 414J, 645F, 709F

summary, 31, 128I

Writing portfolio, 127G, 245G, 363G, 479G, 595G, 713G

Writing process

  drafting, 39, 65, 101, 123, 127C, 151, 177, 217, 241, 245C, 273, 301, 335, 359, 363C, 387, 413, 449, 475, 479C, 503, 529, 567, 591A, 595C, 621, 645, 683, 709, 713C

  presenting, 39A, 65A, 77A, 101A, 123A, 127B, 127E, 151A, 177A, 189A, 217A, 241A, 245B, 245E, 273A, 301A, 313A, 335A, 359A, 363A, 363B, 387A, 413A, 425A, 449A, 475A, 479B, 479E, 503A, 529A, 541A, 567A, 591A, 595B, 595E, 621A, 645A, 657A, 683A, 709A, 713E

  prewriting, 39, 65, 77, 101, 123, 127B, 151, 177, 189, 217, 241, 245B, 273, 301, 313, 335, 359, 363B, 387, 413, 425, 449, 475, 479B, 503, 529, 541, 567, 591A, 595B, 621, 645, 657, 683, 709, 713B

  proofreading and editing, 39, 65, 77, 101, 123, 127E, 151, 177, 189, 217, 241, 245E, 273, 301, 313, 335, 359, 363E, 387, 413, 425, 449, 475, 479E, 503, 529, 541B, 567, 591, 595E, 621, 645, 657, 683, 709, 713E

  publishing, 39, 65, 77, 101, 123, 127E, 151, 177, 189, 217, 241, 245E, 273, 301, 313, 335, 359, 363E, 387, 413, 425, 449, 475, 479E, 503, 529, 541, 567, 591, 595E, 621, 645, 657, 683, 709, 713E

  revising, 39, 65, 101, 123, 151, 177, 217, 241, 245D, 273, 301, 313, 335, 359, 363D, 387, 413, 449, 475, 503, 529, 541, 567, 591, 621, 645, 683, 709

Writing prompts, 76–77, 188–189, 312–313, 424–425, 540–541, 656–657

  determine audience, 76, 188, 312, 424, 540, 656

  determine mode and form, 76, 188, 312, 424, 540, 656

  determine purpose, 76, 188, 312, 424, 540, 656

  practice, 77, 189, 313, 425, 541, 676

  timed writing, 77, 189, 313, 425, 541, 676

Writing traits, 39B, 65B, 77B, 101B, 123B, 127D, 151B, 177B, 189B, 217B, 241B, 245D, 273B, 301B, 313B, 335B, 359B, 363D, 387B, 413B, 425B, 449B, 475B, 479D, 503B, 529B, 541B, 567B, 591B, 595D, 621B, 645B, 657B, 683B, 709B, 713D. *See also* **Writer's checklist; Writer's Craft; Writing Workshop.**

  conventions, 127E, 151B, 245E, 301B, 363E, 479E, 529B, 595E, 621B, 683B, 713E. *See also* **Writer's Toolbox.**

  ideas and content, 39B, 101B, 123B, 241B, 245D, 335B, 359B, 363D, 387B, 475B, 479D, 595D, 713D

  organization, 127B, 127D, 217B, 245B, 245D, 363B, 363D, 413B, 479B, 479C, 595C, 595D, 713B, 713C

  sentence fluency, 273B, 363D, 449B, 479D, 595D, 645B, 713D

  voice, 127D, 177B, 363D, 479D, 591B, 595D, 709B, 713D

  word choice, 65B, 127D, 363D, 479D, 503B, 567B, 595D, 713D

Writing Workshop, 127A–127H, 245A–245H, 363A–363H, 479A–479H, 595A–595H, 713A–713H

Acknowledgments

Illustration Credits

039U: Meryl Treatner. 065U: Meryl Treatner. 77C: (tl) Elizabeth Wolf; (tr) Barbara Spurll; (br) Elizabeth Wolf. 077U: Meryl Treatner. 101U: Meryl Treatner. 123U: Meryl Treatner.

Photography Credits

All photographs are by Macmillan/McGraw Hill (MMH) and Ken Karp for MMH except as noted below:

16I: Lori Adamski Peek/Getty Images. 119B: Carl Miller/Peter Arnold Inc. 127C: Ryan McVay/Getty Images. 127F: Jim Cummins/CORBIS. 127G: Royalty-Free/CORBIS.

Acknowledgments

The publisher gratefully acknowledges permission to reprint the following copyrighted material:

"After Apple Picking" by Robert Frost is from NORTH OF BOSTON. Copyright © 1915. Reprinted by permission of Henry Holt and Company.

"Amazing Artificial Limbs" includes information from "Bionic Arms for 11-Year-Old." *BBC News.* March 15, 2001. http://news.bbc.co.uk/1/hi/health/1222642.stm.

"Baseball by the Numbers" chart is from THE NEW YORK TIMES 2004 ALMANAC edited by John W. Wright. Copyright © 2003 by The New York Times Company. Used by permission of the Penguin Group Penguin Putnam Inc.

"Bicycle Riding" is from CRICKET by Sandra Liatsos. Copyright © 1984 by Sandra Liatsos. Reprinted by permission of Marion Reiner for the Author.

"Birdfoot's Grampa" is from NATIVE AMERICAN STORIES by Joseph Bruchac, illustrated by John Kahionhes Fadden. Text copyright © 1991 by Joseph Bruchac. Illustrations copyright © 1991 by John Kahionhes Fadden.

"Breaking into Print: Before and After the Invention of the Printing the Press" is from BREAKING INTO PRINT: BEFORE AND AFTER THE INVENTION OF THE PRINTING PRESS by Stephen Krensky, illustrations by Bonnie Christensen. Text copyright © 1996 by Stephen Krensky. Illustrations copyright © 1996 by Bonnie Christensen. Published simultaneously in Canada by Little, Brown & Company (Canada) Limited.

"Breaking Through" is from BREAKING THROUGH by Francisco Jiménez. Copyright © 2001 by Francisco Jiménez. Reprinted by permission of Houghton Mifflin Company.

"Caged Bird" is from MAYA ANGELOU: POEMS by Maya Angelou. Copyright © 1986 by Bantam Books. Reprinted by permission of Random House, Inc.

"Cool Collections" from "Smithsonian Kids Collecting." http://smithsonianeducation.org//students/idealabs/amazing_collections.html.

"The Crow and the Pitcher" is from AESOP'S FABLES by Jerry Pinkney. Copyright © 2000 by Jerry Pinkney. Reprinted by permission of SeaStar Books, a division of North-South Books, Inc.

"The Dog of Pompeii" is from THE DONKEY OF GOD by Louis Untermeyer, illustrated by James MacDonald. Text copyright © 1999 The Estate of Louis Untermeyer. This permission is expressly granted by Laurence S. Untermeyer.

"Earth and the Sun" includes information from McGRAW-HILL SCIENCE. Copyright © 2002 by Macmillan/McGraw-Hill.

"The Emperor's Silent Army: Terracotta Warriors of Ancient China" is from THE EMPEROR'S SILENT ARMY: TERRACOTTA WARRIORS OF ANCIENT CHINA by Jane O'Connor. Copyright © Jane O'Connor, 2002. Reprinted by permission of Viking, a division of Penguin Putnam Books for Young Readers.

"Empire in the Andes" includes information from LOST CITY OF THE INCAS by Hiram Bingham and New World News. Copyright © 2001 by Labyrinthina.

"Exploring the *Titanic*" is from EXPLORING THE *TITANIC* by Robert D. Ballard, cover illustration by Ken Marshall. Text copyright © Odyssey Corporation 1998. Illustration copyright © 1988 Madison Publishing Inc. Used by permission of Scholastic Inc.

"The Golden Touch: The Story of Bacchus and King Midas" is from FAVORITE GREEK MYTHS by Mary Pope Osborne. Copyright © 1989 by Mary Pope Osborne. Reprinted by permission of Scholastic Inc.

"The Great Serum Race: Blazing the Iditarod Trail" is from THE GREAT SERUM RACE: BLAZING THE IDITAROD TRAIL by Debbie S. Miller, illustrations by Jon Van Zyle. Text copyright © 2002 by Debbie S. Miller. Illustrations copyright © 2002 by Jon Van Zyle. Used by permission of Walker & Company.

"Haiku" is from JAPANESE HAIKU by Boncho. Translated by Peter Beilenson. Copyright © 1955, 1956 by Peter Pauper Press. Reprinted by permission of Peter Pauper Press.

"Honus and Me" is from HONUS AND ME by Dan Gutman. Copyright © 1997 by Dan Gutman. Used by permission of HarperCollins Children's Books.

"How Tía Lola Came to Visit Stay" is from HOW TÍA LOLA CAME TO VISIT STAY by Julia Alvarez. Text copyright © 2001 by Julia Alverez. Jacket Illustration copyright © by Sally Wern Comport. Reprinted by permission of Alfred A. Knopf, a division of Random House.

"How to Conduct a Survey" is from MACMILLAN/McGRAW-HILL MATH. Copyright © 2005 by Macmillan/McGraw-Hill.

"Interrupted Journey: Saving Endangered Sea Turtles" is from INTERRUPTED JOURNEY: SAVING ENDANGERED SEA TURTLES by Kathryn Lasky. Copyright © 2001 by Kathryn Lasky. Used by permission of Candlewick Press.

"I Dream a World" by Langston Hughes is from THE COLLECTED POEMS OF LANGSTON HUGHES edited by Arnold Rampersad and David Roessel. Copyright © 1994 by the Estate of Langston Hughes.

"In the Days of the Vaqueros: America's First True Cowboys" is from IN THE DAYS OF THE VAQUEROS: AMERICA'S FIRST TRUE COWBOYS by Russell Freedman. Text copyright © 2001 by Russell Freedman. Reprinted by permission of Houghton Mifflin Company.

"Juan Verdades: The Man Who Couldn't Tell a Lie" is from JUAN VERDADES: THE MAN WHO COULDN'T TELL A LIE by Joe Hayes, illustrated by Joseph Daniel Fiedler. Text copyright © 2001 by Joe Hayes. Illustrations copyright © 2001 by Joseph Daniel Fiedler. Used by permission of Orchard Books, an imprint of Scholastic Inc.

"LAFFF" is from LAFFF by Lensey Namioka, illustrations by Raúl Colón. Copyright © 1993 by Lensey Namioka. Used by permission.

"Leonardo da Vinci" is from LEONARDO DA VINCI by Diane Stanley. Copyright © 1996 by Diane Stanley. Used by permission of William Morrow and Company, Inc.

"Leonardo da Vinci" caption from http://www.museoscienza.org/english/leonardo/vitc.html.

"Leonardo's Horse" is from LEONARDO'S HORSE by Jean Fritz, illustrated by Hudson Talbott. Text copyright © 2001 by Jean Fritz. Illustrations copyright © 2001 by Hudson Talbott. Reprinted by permission of G.P. Putnam's Sons, a division of Penguin Putnam Books for Young Readers.

"Let It Shine" is from LET IT SHINE by Andrea Davis Pinkney, illustrated by Stephen Alcorn. Text copyright © by Andrea Davis Pinkney. Illustrations copyright © 2000 by Stephen Alcorn. Used by permission of Harcourt.

"Lost City: The Discovery of Machu Picchu" is from LOST CITY: THE DISCOVERY OF MACHU PICCHU by Ted Lewin. Copyright © 2003 by Ted Lewin. Reprinted by permission of Philomel Books, a division of Penguin Putnam Books for Young Readers.

"The Magic Gourd" is from THE MAGIC GOURD by Baba Wagué Diakité. Text and art copyright © 2003 by Baba Wagué Diakité. Used by permission of Scholastic Press, a division of Scholastic Inc.

"Major Taylor: Champion Cyclist" is from MAJOR TAYLOR: CHAMPION CYCLIST by Lesa Cline-Ransome, illustrated by James E. Ransome. Text copyright © 2004 by Lesa Cline-Ransome. Illustrations copyright © 2004 by James E. Ransome. Reprinted by permission of Atheneum Books for Young Readers, an Imprint of Simon & Schuster Children's Publishing Division.

"The Night of the Pomegranate" is from SOME OF THE KINDER PLANETS by Tim Wynne-Jones. Copyright © 1993 by Tim Wynne-Jones. Used by permission of Puffin Books.

"Nothing Ever Happens on 90th Street" is from NOTHING EVER HAPPENS ON 90TH STREET by Roni Schotter, illustrated by Kyrsten Brooker. Text copyright © 1997 by Roni Schotter. Illustrations copyright © 1997 by Kyrsten Brooker. Reprinted by permission of Orchard Books.

"Old Stormalong Finds a Man-Sized Ship" is from BIG MEN, BIG COUNTRY by Paul Robert Walker, illustrations by James Bernardin. Text copyright © 1993 by Paul Robert Walker. Illustration copyright © 1993 by James Bernardin. Reprinted by permission of Harcourt, Inc.

734

"The Origin of Ghana" is from THE ROYAL KINGDOMS OF GHANA, MALI, AND SONGHAY: LIFE IN MEDIEVAL AFRICA by Patricia and Fredrick McKissack. Copyright © 1994 by Patricia and Fredrick McKissack. Reprinted by permission of Henry Holt and Company.

"Rumpelstiltskin's Daughter" is from RUMPELSTILTSKIN'S DAUGHTER by Diane Stanley. Copyright © 1997 by Diane Stanley. Used by permission of Morrow Junior Books, a division of William Morrow & Company, Inc.

"Seeing Things His Own Way" is from UNCOMMON CHAMPIONS: FIFTEEN ATHLETES WHO BATTLED BACK by Marty Kaminsky. Copyright © 2000 by Marty Kaminsky. Reprinted by Boyds Mills Press, Inc., a Highlights Company.

"The Sidewalk Racer or On the Skateboard" is from THE SIDEWALK RACER AND OTHER POEMS OF SPORTS AND MOTION by Lillian Morrison. Copyright © 1977 by Lillian Morrison. Reprinted by permission of the author in Macmillan McGraw-Hill Reading (Grade 5) copyright © 2003, 2001.

"A Single Shard" is from A SINGLE SHARD by Linda Sue Park. Text copyright © 2001 by Linda Sue Park. Used by permission of Clarion Books.

"The Storm" by Chora, and "Winter" by Shiki are from AN INTRODUCTION TO HAIKU by Harold G. Henderson. Copyright © 1958 by Harold G. Henderson. Reprinted by permission of Random House.

"Storm Surprises Maine Students After Anxious Night, All Found Cold, Tired" is from The Boston Globe by Brian MacQuarrie. Copyright © 2003 Globe Newspaper Company.

"The Summer of the Swans" is from THE SUMMER OF THE SWANS by Betsy Byars. Copyright © 1970 by Betsy Byars. All rights reserved. Reprinted by permission of Puffin Books.

"TA-NA-E-KA" by Mary Whitebird, illustrated by Shonto Begay. Published in SCHOLASTIC VOICE, December 13, 1973. Copyright © 1973 by Scholastic, Inc.

"This Land is Your Land" by Woody Guthrie. Copyright © 1956, 1958, and 1970 by Ludlow Music Inc. Used by permission of Ludlow Music, Inc., New York.

"Volcano!" is from Ranger Rick by Forrest Gale, as told to Lora Gale. Copyright © 2003 by the National Wildlife Federation.

ILLUSTRATIONS
Cover Illustration: Anton Petrov

C20:Art Thompson.20-35: John Rowe. 44-59: Ted Lewin. 80-81: Stephan Daigle. 82-95: Baba Wagué Dakité. 96-97: Jennifer Hewitson. 98: (tr) Mike DiGiorgio. 98-99: (bkgd) Jennifer Hewitson. 108-119: Royalty Free. 132-147: Lester Coloma. 140: Brian Dugan. 156-171: Elizabeth Sayles. 174: Mike DiGiorgio. 181: Rick Nease for TFK. 194-211: Diane Stanley. 212-215: Carol Heyer. 222-237: Jon Vanzyle. 238-239: (Oki Han. 250-267: Joseph Daniel Fielder. 269: (bc) Arvis Stewart; (c) John Hovell. 276-277: Antonio Cangemi. 278-295: Kyrsten Brooker. 319-331: Royalty Free. 338-339: (bkgd) Peter Thornton. 340-355: Nicole Tadgell. 360: Getty Images. 383: Mike DiGiorgio. 392-393: Ken Marschall. 395: Pronk&Associates. 398: Ken Marschall. 399: Pronk&Associates. 404-405: Ken Marschall. 406: Pronk&Associates. 408-411: Carol Heyer. 430-445: James E. Ransome. 454-471: Julie Kim. 482-483: Colin Bootman. 508-525: (bkgd) Shonto Begay. 526-527: Jerry Pinkney. 546-560: Ned Shaw. 626-629,638-639: Raúl Colón. 645: Tim Haggerty. 648: Rick Nease for TFK. 649: Charles Reasoner. 678-679: Bonnie Christensen. 688-689,702-703: Michael Jaroszko. 704: Reprinted from the June 2003 issue of Ranger Rick magazine, with the permission of the publisher, the National Wildlife Federation. Copyright 2003 by the National Wildlife Federation. 714-715: Elizabeth Sayles.

PHOTOGRAPHY
All photographs by Macmillan/McGraw-Hill except where noted below.

16-17: (bkgd) Charles O'Rear/CORBIS. 17: (inset)Photodisc. 18: Paul Barton/CORBIS. 19: PhotoDisc/Getty Images, Inc. 34: Edward Byars. 36: (tr) Portland Press Herald. 36-37: (bkgd) Greg Probst/CORBIS. 38: Barbara Penoyar/Getty Images, Inc. 39: Lori Adamski Peek/Stone/ Getty Images, Inc 40-41: (bkgd) Nadia Molinari/ Alamy. 41: (inset) C. Sherburne/ Photolink/Getty Images, Inc. 42: (bc) Adalberto Rios Szalay/Sexto Sol/Getty Images, Inc. 42-43: (bkgd) Frank Siteman/ AGE Fotostock. 43: Werner Forman/Art Resource. 58: Courtesy of Ted Lewin. 60: (tr) Jamie Marshall/ Alamy. 60-61: (bkgd) Galen Rowell/CORBIS. 62: (tl) The Granger Collection, New York 62-63: (t) Kevin Schafer/CORBIS;(b) Pablo Corral Vega/CORBIS. 63: (tl) Wolfgang Kaehler. 64: Rubberball Productions/Getty Images, Inc. 65: Courtesy Columbus Center of Science and Industry. 66-67: Scott T. Baxter/Photodisc/Getty Images, Inc.68: VEER. 69: (tl) C Squared Studios/Photodisc/Getty Images, Inc.; (tc) The Granger Collection; (tr) The Granger Collection;(c) C Squared Studios/Photodisc/Getty Images, Inc.;(bl) Image 100/Punchstock;(bc) Kurt Strazdins/KRT/ NewsCom. 70: Mark Moffett/Minden Pictures.71: (tl) Jonathan Searle/ Reuters;(br) Creatas/ Punchstock.72: Tony Bennett/Getty Images.73: Ernst Haas/Getty Images, Inc. 74: David Buffington/ Photodisc/Getty Images, Inc. 76: Amos Morgan/Photodisc/Getty Images, Inc. 77: (l) Burke/Triolo Productions/Alamy; (br) Photodisc/ Getty Images, Inc. 78-79: (bkgd) Steve Allen/ Brand X Pictures/ Picture Quest.79: (inset) C Squared Studios/Getty Images, Inc. 81: Dana White/Photo Edit Inc. 94: Leo Arfer. 99: The Art Archive. 100: Alan Levenson/AGE Fotostock. 101: G.K. and Vikki Hart/Getty Images, Inc. 102-103: (bkgd) ROMEO-VISUAL&WRITTEN/Bruce Coleman. 103: (inset) James Gritz/Getty Images, Inc.104-105: (bkgd) Royalty-Free/CORBIS; (b) Tom Brakefield/CORBIS. 106-107: Christopher G. Knight. 108: (l) Royalty-Free/CORBIS; (bl) Larry Williams/CORBIS; (inset) Christopher G. Knight.108-109: (tc) Kennan Ward/CORBIS. 109: Christopher G. Knight. 110: (tr) Christopher G. Knight; (l) Royalty-Free/CORBIS; (r) Christopher G. Knight. 112: (l) Royalty-Free/ CORBIS; (bc) Christopher G. Knight. 112-113: (tc) Alan Towse/CORBIS. 113: (r) Christopher G. Knight. 114: (t) Alan Towse/CORBIS; (cr) David Muench/CORBIS; (b) Christopher G. Knight. 115: (tc) Christopher G. Knight; (r) Royalty-Free/CORBIS; (bcr) David Muench/CORBIS. 116: (l) Royalty-Free/CORBIS; (b) Christopher G. Knight. 117: (r) Christopher G. Knight; (bl) Kevin Schafer/CORBIS. 118: (l) Royalty-free/ CORBIS;(tcr) Larry Williams/CORBIS;(cl) Larry Williams/CORBIS; (inset) Courtesy of Candlewick Press. 119: (bcl) Christopher Knight;(bl) Kennan Ward/CORBIS; (br) Alan Towse/CORBIS. 120: Michael Leach/NHPA. 121: Royalty-Free/CORBIS. 122: Photolibrary. com/Photonica. 123: Konrad Wothe/Minden Pictures. 124: Getty Images, Inc. 125: Jeff Greenberg/Photo Edit Inc.128-129: (bkgd) Lori Adamski Peek/Getty Images, Inc. 129: (inset) Photodisc/Getty Images, Inc. 130: (l) Françoise Gervais/CORBIS; (bl) Minnesota Historical Society/CORBIS; (bcl) National Baseball Hall of Fame and Museum. 131: (tr) Minnesota Historical Society/CORBIS;(cr) Royalty-Free/CORBIS. 146: © copyright by Bill Eichner. Reprinted by permission of Susan Bergholz Literary Services, New York. All rights reserved. 148: Bettmann/CORBIS. 150: (cl) Photomondo/Photodisc/ Getty Images, Inc. 151: (tr) PhotoDisc/Getty Images, Inc.; (br) Royalty-Free/CORBIS. 152-153: (bkgd) Steve Bloom/ Steve Bloom Images/ Alamy. 153: (inset) Stock Trek/Getty Images, Inc. 154: (tr) Carson Ganci/AGE Fotostock. 170: (tl) Courtesy of Tim Wynne-Jones. 172-173: (bkgd) Getty Images, Inc. 173: (tr) Peter Sherrard/Getty Images, Inc.; (bl) Bettman/CORBIS. 174-175: Denis Scott/Getty Images, Inc. 176: Stephen Marks/Getty Images, Inc. 177: EPA/NASA/Landov. 178-179: AP-Wide World Photos. 180: Burke/Triolo Productions/Brand X/Getty Images, Inc. 181: Andy Newman/Florida Keys News Bureau. 182: (tr) Brian Smith/Corbis Outline; (bcr) Digital Vision/PictureQuest. 183-185: Brian Smith/Corbis Outline. 186: Jameson Simpson. 188: Amos Morgan/Photodisc/Getty Images, Inc. 189: Dian Lofton for TFK. 190-191: (bkgd) Premium Stock/CORBIS. 191: (inset) PhotoDisc/Getty Images, Inc. 192-193: (bkgd) Ken Karp for MMH. 210: Karen Sachar. 216: (tr) Bob Rowan/Progressive Image/CORBIS;(cl) Amos Morgan/ Getty Images, Inc. 218-219: (bkgd) Jeff Schultz/Alaska Stock Images. 219: (inset) Photo Link/Getty Images, Inc. 220-221: (b) Paul A. Sauders/CORBIS. 236: (tcl) Courtesy of Walker and Company; (tcr) Jeff Schultz. 238-239: C Squared Studios/Getty Images, Inc. 240: Brad Wilson/Photonica. 241: (tr) Bob Daemmrich/The Image Works, Inc. 242-243: (tr) Michael S. Yamashita/CORBIS. 244: (tl) Jose Manuel Ribeiro/Reuters/CORBIS. 246-247: (bkgd) California Historical Society Collection at the University of Southern California. 247: (inset) PhotoDisc/Getty Images, Inc. 248: (bl) Dewitt Jones/CORBIS. 248-249: George H.H. Huey/CORBIS. 266: (tcl) Jack Kotz for MMH; (tcr) Courtesy of Joseph Daniel Fiedler. 268-269: David Stoecklein/CORBIS. 270: (tl) Christie's Images/CORBIS. 270-271: (bkgd) Tom Bean/Getty Images, Inc. 272: Comstock/Getty Images, Inc. 274-275: (bkgd) Frederic Neema/ CORBIS SYGMA. 275: (inset) C Squared Studios/Getty Images, Inc. 294: Courtesy of Scholastic 296: (tc) Courtesy of Karen Odom; (tcr) Courtesy of Perry Faulkner. 296-297: (bkgd) Ken Karp for MMH. 298: (bc) Paul Barton/ CORBIS. 298-299: (bkgd) Ken Karp for MMH. 300: Gabe Palmer/ CORBIS. 301: Graham French/Masterfile. 302-303: ML Sinibadi/ CORBIS. 303: (tcl) Greg Locke/Reuters/NewsCom; (tcr) Otoo Rogge/ CORBIS. 305: Tom McHugh/Photo Researchers Inc. 306: Emory Kristof/National Geographic Image Collection. 307: Martin Bond/ Science Photo Library. 308: Claudio Santini. 309: David Eisenberg. 310: Dean Abramson. 312: Brand X Pictures. 313: (r) Dian Lofton for TFK; (bl) Photodisc/Getty Images, Inc. 314-315: (bkgd) Randy Olson/ National Geographic/Getty Images, Inc. 315: (inset) Don Farrall/

Getty Images, Inc. 316: AP-Wide World Photos. 317: Bojan Brecelj/ CORBIS. 318-319: (bkgd) Wolfgang Kaehler.319: (bl) Patrick Aventurier/GAMMA. 320: O. Louis Mazzatenta/ National Geographic Image Collection. 321: (tc) Wolfgang Kaehler. 322: Zhou Kang/ (c) copyright 2001. Imaginechina.com. All rights reserved.323: The Art Archive/British Library.325: Giraudon/ Art Resource, NY. 326: Bonhams, London, UK. 327: Jiang Ren/ Private Collection/ Imaginechina.com. 328-329: The Art Archive/ Genius of China Exhibition. 330: (tcl) Jim O'Connor. 330-331: (b) Wolfgang Kaehler. 332-333: (K.M. Westermann/CORBIS. 334: PhotoDisc/Getty Images, Inc. 335: Pixtal/AGE Fotostock. 336-337: (bkgd) Stephanie Maze/CORBIS. 337: (inset) C Squared Studios/Getty Images, Inc. 354: (tl) Courtesy of Karen English; (cr) Courtesy of Nicole Tadgell. 356-357: (bkgd) Michael Pole/CORBIS; (t) Cydney Conger/CORBIS. 358: (tr) Siede Preis/ Photodisc/Getty Images, Inc.;(bl) Fabio Cardoso/AGE Fotostock. 359: C Squared Studios/ Photodisc/Getty Images, Inc. 362: Morril/Index Stock Imagery.364-365: (bkgd) Bob Daemmrich/CORBIS. 365: (inset) Janis Christie/Getty Images, Inc. 366: Noah Hamilton Photography. 367: AP-Wide World Photos. 368: (t) Duomo/ CORBIS;(bl) Didrick Johnck/CORBIS;(br) © Jamie Bloomquist Photography. 368-369: (bkgd) Photodisc/Getty Images, Inc.; (cr) © Jamie Bloomquist Photography. 370: (br) Royalty-free/ CORBIS. 370-371: (t) Photodisc/Getty Images, Inc.371: (c) © Jamie Bloomquist Photography. 372-373: (t) Photodisc/Getty Images, Inc. 373: (tl) Ed Weihenmayer; (tr) Danny Lehman/CORBIS. 374: (c) © Jamie Bloomquist Photography. 374-375: (t) Getty Images, Inc. 375: (tr) Phoenix Country Day School. 376: (br) C Squared Studios/Getty Images, Inc. 376-377: (t) Photodisc/Getty Images, Inc. 377: (c) © Jamie Bloomquist Photography. 378: (inset) Didrik Johnck/CORBIS; (c) Didrik Johnck/CORBIS. 378-379: (t) Getty Images, Inc. 379: (tr) Duomo/CORBIS.380: (tc) Courtesy of Marty Kaminsky;(cl) Duomo/ CORBIS. 380-381: (bkgd) Photodisc/Getty Images, Inc. 381: (br) C Squared Studios/Getty Images, Inc. 382: Richard T. Nowitz/CORBIS. 383: AP-Wide World Photos. 384: (tr) Lon C. Diehl/Photo Edit Inc.; (bl) AGE Fotostock. 386: Brad Wilson/Photonica. 387: Getty Images, Inc. 388-389: (bkgd) Jeff Rotman/Getty Images, Inc. 389: (inset) James Gritz/Getty Images, Inc. 390-391: Rick Doyle/CORBIS. 394: (cl) Ralph White/AP-Wide World Photos; (bl) NOAA - IFE/URI. 396: (tl) Woods Hole Oceanographic Institution. 397: (tr) NOAA - IFE/URI; (br) CORBIS SYGMA. 400: (bc) Earthship Productions/The Kobal Collection/Picture Desk. 401-402: Woods Hole Oceanographic Institution. 403: Ralph White/ CORBIS. 405-406: Woods Hole Oceanographic Institution. 412: (tcr) Andrew J. Martinez/Photo Researchers, Inc.; (bl) AGE Fotostock. 413: (tr) Getty Images, Inc.; (br) Jack Milchanowski/AGE Fotostock. 414-415: David Young-Wolff/ PhotoEdit Inc. 416: (l) James Keyser/Time-Life Pictures/Getty Images, Inc. 417: (tl) Freddy Lea; (cr) Alex McKnight; (bl) Katherine Lambert. 418: (tr) Ann States; (bl) Oseola McCarty. 419: Timothy Greenfield-Sanders/Corbis Outline. 420: (tr) Terry Ashe/Time-Life Pictures/Getty Images, Inc.; (bl) John Chiasson/Liason Agency. 421: Ann States. 422: Nancy Palmieri. 424: Brand X Pictures. 425: (bcl) Tracy Montana/PhotoLink/Getty Images, Inc.; (br) Dian Lofton for TFK. 426-427: (bkgd) Hulton-Deutsch Collection/CORBIS. 427: (inset) C Squared Studios/Getty Images, Inc. 428: (tc) Hulton Archive/Getty Images, Inc.; (bl) Bettmann/CORBIS. 429: Bettmann/CORBIS. 444: Courtesy of Simon and Schuster. 446: (bkgd) NASA/Handout/ Reuters/CORBIS; (b) © Transtock Inc./Alamy. 447: Mike Brinson Images, Inc. 448: (bl) Joe McBride/Getty Images, Inc. 449: (tr) Ross Horowitz/Getty Images, Inc. 450-451: (bkgd) McPherson Colin/ CORBIS SYGMA. 451: (inset) Steve Cole/Getty Images, Inc. 452: (tc) Scala/Art Resource;(bl) Christie's Images/CORBIS. 452-453: (bkgd) © Royalty-Free/CORBIS. 453: (cr) Réunion des Musées Nationaux/Art Resource. 470: (tr) Courtesy of Houghton Mifflin; (bcl) Courtesy of Julie Kim. 473: (tcl) Craig van der Lande/Getty Images, Inc. (c) Getty Images, Inc. 474: Ingram Publishing/Alamy. 475: Elizabeth A. Whiting/Elizabeth A. Whiting & Associates/CORBIS. 476: Bettmann/ CORBIS. 478: (tl) AP-Wide World Photos. 480-481: (bkgd) Mitch Tobias/Masterfile. 481: (inset) Royalty-free/CORBIS. 484: (tl) Courtesy of Francisco Jimenez. 484-485: (c) Getty Images, Inc. 485: (c) Courtesy of Francisco Jimenez.487-488: Library of Congress.489: (c) Getty Images, Inc. 490-491: Courtesy of Francisco Jimenez. 492: Getty Images, Inc.; (br) Courtesy of Francisco Jimenez. 493: (b) Bettmann/CORBIS. 495: (b) Getty Images, Inc.; (br) Courtesy of Francisco Jimenez. 496: (tr) Photodisc/Getty Images; (inset) Courtesy of Francisco Jimenez. 496-497: (bkgd) Ed Young/CORBIS. 498: David Young-Wolff/Getty Images, Inc. 502: Lisa Pines/Photonica. 503: Jeff Greenberg/Photo Edit Inc. 504-505: (bkgd) Justin Sullivan/Getty Images, Inc. 505: (inset) Royalty-free/CORBIS. 506: (b) Joanna B. Pineo/Aurora. 507: Bill Aron/Photo Edit Inc. 524: Tom Alexander. 528: Barbara Penoyar/ Getty Images, Inc. 530-531: (bkgd) Stuart Franklin/Magnum Photos. 532: Aamir Qureshi/AFP/NewsCom. 533: (cl) Photodisc/Getty Images, Inc.; (bcr) David Arky/Tree Communication. 534: Royalty-Free/Corbis/PictureQuest. 535: Boris Roesslet/AFP/NewsCom. 536: (l) Photodisc/Getty Images, Inc. 536-537: (bkgd) Digital Vision/ Picturequest. 537: (tr) AP-Wide World Photos; (bl) Stepanie Pilick/

AFP/NewsCom. 538: Photodisc/Getty Images, Inc. 540: Rubberball. 541: (bl) Dian Lofton for TFK; (bcl) C Squared Studios/Getty Images, Inc.; (br) Photodisc/Getty Images, Inc. 542-543: (bkgd) Gabe Palmer/ CORBIS. 543: (inset) PhotoLink/Getty Images, Inc. 544-545: (t) Ken Karp for MMH. 560: Courtesy of Dan Gutman. 562: Tom Payne/Alamy. 563: (tl) AP-Wide World Photos; (tr) Royalty-Free/ CORBIS; (br) Max Alexander/DK Images. 564: (tl) J. Kershaw/The British Museum/DK Images; (tcl) Borromeo/Art Resource, NY; (r) The Granger Collection, New York;(b) Herrick Company. 565: India Book House Pvt. Ltd. 566: AGE Fotostock. 567: (tr) Getty Images, Inc. 568-569: (bkgd) CORBIS. 569: (inset) StockTrek/Getty Images, Inc. 570: (tc) AP-Wide World Photos; (b) Walter Hodges/Getty Images, Inc. 572: Bettmann/CORBIS. 573: (bl) Getty Images, Inc.;(inset) Courtesy of the Rosa Parks Foundation. 574: Bettmann/ CORBIS. 575: © CORBIS. 576: (t) Bettmann/CORBIS (bl) Library of Congress. 577: Alabama State University Archives. 578: Bettmann/ CORBIS. 579: Time Life Pictures/Getty Images, Inc. 580: (tc) Courtesy of the Rosa Parks Foundation;(bl) Bettmann/CORBIS. 581-582: Bettmann/CORBIS. 583: (tl) AP-Wide World Photos; (tr) Time Life Pictures/Getty Images, Inc. 584: (t) Time Life Pictures/Getty Images, Inc.; (bl) Bettmann/CORBIS. 585: (bl) Bill Greenblatt/ CORBIS SYGMA; (br) William Philpott/Reuters/CORBIS. 586: (tcl) Dwight Carter 586-587: (b) Time Life Pictures/Getty Images, Inc. 588: (tr) AP-Wide World Photos. 588-589: (bkgd) Kennan Ward/ CORBIS. 589: (tcr) © CORBIS. 590: Rubberball Productions/Getty Images, Inc. 591: NASA. 592: Mark E. Gibson/CORBIS. 593: © Ingram Publishing/Alamy. 594: © imageshop - zefa visual media.uk.ltd/ Alamy. 596-597: (bkgd) Neil Rabinowitz/CORBIS. 597: (inset) Philip Coblentz/Brand X Pictures/Getty Images, Inc. 598: (bl) Nicolo Orsi Battaglini/Art Resource. 598-599: (bkgd) C Squared Studios/Getty Images. 599: (tr) Ted Spiegel/CORBIS. 614: (tl) Courtesy of Houghton Mifflin; (bcr) Courtesy of Hudson Talbott. 616: Gianni Dagli Orti/ CORBIS. 617: Baldwin H. Ward & Kathryn C. Ward/CORBIS. 618: (tc) Scala/Art Resource, NY; (br) Snark/Art Resource, NY. 619: (tr) Snark/ Art Resource, NY. 620: AGE Fotostock. 621: Michael Matisse/ Photodisc/Getty Images, Inc. 622-623: (bkgd) A. Hansen/Getty Images, Inc. 623: (inset) Ryan McVay/Getty Images, Inc. 638: (tl) Courtesy of Lensey Namioka; (tcr) Courtesy of Morgan Gaynin Inc. 640: (bkgd) Roger Harris/Photo Researchers, Inc.; (bl) Jeff Greenberg/The Image Works. 641: (tr) Julian Baum/SPL/Photo Researchers, Inc.; (t) Aaron Horowitz/CORBIS; (l) STScI/NASA/ Ressmeyer/CORBIS; (br) Bettmann/CORBIS. 642: (tr) Rykoff Collection/CORBIS; (t) Aaron Horowitz/CORBIS; (c) STScI/NASA/ Ressmeyer/CORBIS; (bl) Bettmann/CORBIS.643: Erich Schrempp/SPL/ Photo Researchers, Inc. 644: David Schmidt/Masterfile. 646-647: (bkgd) Sissie Brimberg/National Geographic/Getty Images, Inc. 648: Science Magazine/AFP/NewsCom. 649: Bettman/Corbis.650-651: (bkgd) David Coulson.651: Jean-Marie Chauvet/CORBIS SYGMA.652: (b) David Coulson. 652-653: (bkgd) David Coulson; (t) Penny Tweedie/CORBIS. 654: Shelly Katz. 656: Royalty-Free/Corbis. 657: (tcr) Dian Lofton for TFK;(bl) Dian Lofton for TFK; (bcl) Dian Lofton for TFK; (br) Tracy Montana/PhotoLink/Getty Images, Inc. 658-659: (bkgd) Keren Su/CORBIS. 659: (inset) PhotoDisc/Getty Images, Inc. 660: (bl) Archivio Iconografico, S.A./CORBIS. 660-661: (t) Brooklyn Museum of Art/CORBIS. 678: (tcl) (c) Peter Krensky; (bcr) Don Landwehrle for MMH. 680: (t) © CORBIS. 680-681: (bkgd) Jacqui Hurst/CORBIS. 682: (cl) Tom & Dee Ann McCarthy/CORBIS. 682-683: (b) Getty Images, Inc. 684-685: (bkgd) David Trood Pictures/Getty Images, Inc. 685: (inset) Royalty-free/CORBIS. 686: (inset) Mimmo Jodice/CORBIS. 686-687: (bkgd) Sando Vannini/ CORBIS. 689: Erich Lessing/Art Resource, NY. 690: (l) Mimmo Jodice/ CORBIS. 690-691: Archivio Iconografico, S.A./CORBIS. 691: (bl) Scala/ Art Resource, NY.692: (t) SEF/Art Resource, NY. 693: (tr) The Granger Collection, New York; (br) Scala/Art Resource, NY. 694: Araldo de Luca/CORBIS. 695: Erich Lessing/Art Resource, NY. 696: (tl) Scala/Art Resource, NY; (b) The Granger Collection, New York. 697: Scala/Art Resource, NY. 698: Bettmann/CORBIS. 699: Erich Lessing/Art Resource, NY. 700-701: Vanni Archive/CORBIS. 702: (tl) Courtesy of Lawrence Untermeyer; (l) Mimmo Jodice/CORBIS. 702-703: (bkgd) Roger Ressmeyer/CORBIS.704-705: (bkgd) G. Brad Lewis; (t) Casa Productions/CORBIS. 706: (l) G. Brad Lewis. 706-707: (t) Casa Productions/CORBIS. 707: (tr) G. Brad Lewis.708: Rubberball Productions/Getty Images, Inc.709: AGE Fotostock. 710: Randy Faris/Corbis. 712: PhotoDisc/Getty Images, Inc. 716: Peter Turnley/ CORBIS. 717: Jeremy Horner/CORBIS. 718: (cl) Design Pics Inc/Alamy; (cr) Stuart Westmorland/CORBIS. 720: Image 100/Royalty-Free/ CORBIS. 721: Tom Grill/CORBIS. 722: Bill Stormont/CORBIS. 723: Royalty-free/CORBIS. 724: (bl) Jess Alford/Photodisc/Getty Images, Inc.; (br) Royalty-free/CORBIS. 725: (cr) Vittoriano Rastelli/CORBIS. 726: Lawrence M Sawyer/Photodisc/Getty Images, Inc. 727: (tr) Comstock Images/Alamy; (bl) PictureNet/CORBIS. 728: Brand X Pictures/Alamy. 729: Justin Kase/Alamy. 731: Digital Vision/ Punchstock. 732: Photo 24/Brand X Pictures/Getty Images, Inc. 733: Glen Allison/Getty Images, Inc.

Teacher's Notes

Teacher's Notes

Teacher's Notes

Teacher's Notes